SOCIAL PROBLEMS

SOCIAL PROBLEMS

A Canadian Perspective

Lorne Tepperman | Josh Curtis

OXFORD

UNIVERSITY PRESS

OXFORD
UNIVERSITY PRESS

Oxford University Press is a department of the University of Oxford.
It furthers the University's objective of excellence in research, scholarship,
and education by publishing worldwide. Oxford is a registered trade mark of
Oxford University Press in the UK and in certain other countries.

Published in Canada by
Oxford University Press
8 Sampson Mews, Suite 204,
Don Mills, Ontario M3C 0H5 Canada

www.oupcanada.com

First Edition published in 2004
Second Edition published in 2007
Third Edition published in 2011

Library and Archives Canada Cataloguing in Publication
Tepperman, Lorne, 1943–, author
Social problems : a Canadian perspective / Lorne Tepperman,
Josh Curtis.—Fourth edition.

Includes bibliographical references and index.
ISBN 978-0-19-900909-1 (pbk.)

1. Social problems—Textbooks. 2. Canada—Social conditions—
Textbooks. I. Curtis, Josh, author II. Title.

HN103.5.T46 2015   361.1   C2014-908177-4

Cover image: Trina Dalziel/Ikon Images/Getty Images

Oxford University Press is committed to our environment.
Wherever possible, our books are printed on paper which comes from
responsible sources.

Printed and bound in Canada

2 3 4 — 20 19 18

Contents

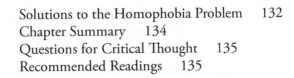

6   Aging and the Life Course   136

Part 3   Outcomes   163

7   Crime and Violence   164

8   Addictions   192

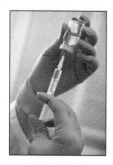

9   Health Issues   218

10   War and Terrorism   247

Part 4   Domains   273

11   Families   274

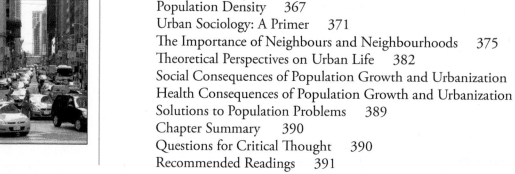

Part 5   The Future   423

Preface

Welcome to the fourth edition of *Social Problems: A Canadian Perspective*. We were very pleased with the reception readers gave the first three editions, and we have tried to make this new edition even better.

In this text we assume that there is such a thing as a "social problem." A social problem is any circumstance that many people experience and that has both social causes and social consequences. The social problems we discuss actually exist. We can verify that fact with our own eyes and with the measurement tools of social science. Yet, each social problem is also socially constructed, in the sense that people think it exists—they define it as a social problem. The condition in question has become a problem for people, and should they stop thinking it is a problem, it would cease being one, at least at the level of consciousness, social definition, and social action.

Because of this socially constructed aspect of social problems, we can trace their rise and fall over time. We can study how people came to share the understanding that a certain circumstance was a problem. To take a simple example, few people in Canada today consider the so-called promiscuity of young women to be a social problem, although this was not the case in the past. Likewise, few Canadians today are troubled by what used to be called "miscegenation"—couples from two different races having sexual relations—although in earlier times many people considered this a serious social problem. On the other hand, many people today consider climate change to be an important social problem, although 50 years ago this issue was barely discussed.

Sociologists study why certain behaviours, and not others, come to occupy our concern and evoke the label of "social problem." This takes us into the areas of changing morality and moral panics—sudden, intense, widespread, and often fleeting concerns about the immorality of one particular group. The rise and fall of social problems also reflects social, intellectual, and scientific changes. At any given time, there are problems in society that can be shown to harm to our quality of life, but only a few people see them as problems and government and other powerful agencies do little to address them.

The social problems that last the longest and evoke the most concern are those that are not merely socially constructed and thus not simply problems "in people's minds." They are serious matters of health and of life and death. Poverty, racial discrimination, poor working conditions, domestic violence—these are all serious social problems because, at the extremes, they hurt or kill people. In less extreme circumstances, they exacerbate illness and reduce people's well-being and quality of life. Increasingly, we live in what Ulrich Beck (1992) has called a "risk society" in which we are all, always, in danger of harm from sources that are often hidden from view and beyond human control. These risks are frequently the result of human activity, especially the applications of science and technology to the natural environment. Often they are the result of what we are taught to regard fondly as "progress."

So, apart from the perceived immorality, injustice, or unfairness of the problems discussed in this book, serious social problems cost our society many human lives and many days lost from work and family life; they also lead to shattered families, workplace conflict, and destroyed hopes. These problems are not merely "in people's minds." In fact, the job of the sociologist, in these cases, is to bring them to people's conscious attention.

To summarize all this, we are particularly interested in issues that are both potential and actual social problems—problems that cause trouble and are seen as causing trouble. We will pay no attention whatsoever to the more pleasant sides of life—making this a somewhat dark-hued book. Moreover, we will pay only passing attention to issues that may briefly be considered problems but, in the end, prove not to be. Actual and potential problems that lurk below the consciousness of most people will make intermittent appearances in this book, especially in the final chapter.

Social science has a poor batting average in solving human problems. It has not done well at bringing about change, as we will see. The problem here is in part the complexity of the roots of social problems and in part the will and ability (or lack thereof) of society's agencies of power to address the problems. Yet we, as authors of this book, believe that the purpose of sociology today, just as in the nineteenth century when it began, is to use knowledge to improve social life. Thus, our goal in a book like this is to aid the understanding of the roots of social problems, their health consequences for individuals and society as a whole, and how these can be addressed. For this task, it is important that we explore facts and theories concerning how problems develop and are maintained and how they are interrelated. We believe that these theories help us organize our facts and work towards solving our problems.

We should say a few final words about the purpose of a book as general as this one. This text duplicates some of what students may have learned in an introduction to sociology course. The duplication is intentional. We want to refresh your memory of the basic principles of sociology before proceeding to a close discussion of social problems. Some instructors may even find that this book can substitute for a book that introduces first-time students to the field of sociology. In addition, this book covers a variety of problems, each briefly. This brevity is also intentional. We want to get students thinking in a particular way so that they can study these same problems, new problems, or changed problems on their own. We do not offer the last word on any social problem presented here—only the beginnings of a discussion informed by sociological principles.

We do not offer sociology as a cure-all. We emphasize how difficult it has been to solve many social problems and how very little has been done about some of them. Like many of our colleagues in sociology, we understand the concerns of postmodernity. The "project" of modernization that engaged thinkers and social practitioners for much of the last three centuries has taken a new turn. The horrors of the twentieth century shook our faith in reason and in the power of humans to build a better world using science and technology, social legislation, mass media, higher education, and secular values. No one who spends a few moments thinking about the Holocaust, the two world wars, the terrorism of September 2001, and the ensuing wars in Afghanistan, Iraq, Pakistan, Sri Lanka, Syria, Palestine, and Israel, not to mention recurring crises in Africa, Asia, and Eastern Europe, environmental degradation in many parts of the world, and continued practices of imperialist domination will readily indulge fantasies about the perfection, or even the perfectibility, of human societies. Part of the reason for this is that the solutions to social problems are often complex and costly. Another reason is that the solutions are political matters requiring strong commitment from society's elites.

In this respect, one of sociology's three founders was particularly prescient. Sociologist Max Weber saw the nightmare of modern society coming. His eyes were open to the "iron cage" of modernity, especially to how bureaucracies and governments can enslave and torment humans more effectively than has ever been known before. Weber believed that bureaucracies would become all-powerful in society and that their elites would end up largely serving their own interests, which would frequently be contrary to the interests of average people. Only those problems and solutions seen as important by powerful interests would be addressed in societies of the future (that is, in our time now).

Another founder of sociology, Karl Marx, believed that communism would solve all problems of the human condition. He appears to have been wrong, although some still argue that his theories have never been put to a proper test in any society. Of the three leading figures in sociology during its developing years, Émile Durkheim was the most optimistic and therefore the most wrong about the twentieth century. He believed that societies change in a progressive direction, solving social problems over time through the differentiation and specialization of tasks, with modest negative side effects of anomie, or alienation, on the part of individuals because of the processes of social change.

Yet, despite having been shaken by the twentieth century and its horrors, we persist in our efforts. As long as we live, most of us strive to build a better world for our children, our community, and ourselves. It is in the hope of continuing this optimistic effort that we, the authors, have written this book. We believe that social problems really do exist and do great harm. Furthermore, we believe that knowledge and purposeful informed action may still improve human life. This, then, is where we begin our study of social problems.

How This Book Is Organized

We will see that sociologists, like other social scientists, have a variety of theories about society and its social problems. Throughout this book, we will return to three sociological theories—structural functionalism, conflict theory, and symbolic interactionism—as well as to two other important perspectives for understanding problems in society—feminism, which varies in its analysis and solutions from liberal to radical points of view, and social constructionism, an outgrowth of symbolic interactionism that posits that groups of people create and recreate their own realities. Each contributes important elements to our understanding of society and social problems. None of them rules out the validity or contribution of any other. Each of the theories approaches social life from a different standpoint, asking different questions and looking at different kinds of evidence. Therefore, each adds to our understanding of social problems, in different ways. These approaches compete for our attention and loyalty. Sociologists tend to prefer and attach themselves to one approach rather than another. At the same time, applied sociologists go about analyzing and solving real-life problems in families, workplaces, organizations, and societies by combining insights from all of these perspectives.

We also employ an additional perspective—the population health perspective—in each chapter. This perspective focuses attention on the physical and psychological harm caused by social problems to individuals and, thereby, on the harm caused to society. This perspective also emphasizes the social sources and consequences of people's illness and health. The population health perspective complements the other perspectives: it not so much contradicts them as it adds to and extends them. This perspective simply focuses more explicitly on the issues of the health of individuals and societies. All of the theoretical approaches will be discussed in further detail in Chapter 1 and the ensuing chapters.

We have organized this book to reflect our assumptions about social problems. We begin each chapter with a brief general introduction to the problem at hand. We then follow with a section containing some facts about the problem, setting the stage for our understanding of it. This section is not meant to replace other information about the problem gained, for example, from academic reports, newspapers, magazines, or television reportage. The facts presented in books such as this one must be somewhat selective, and they tend to age quickly. We therefore urge the reader to seek additional information from other sources about all of the problems discussed in this book.

Next, in each chapter, we review a range of theoretical approaches to the problem under discussion. We show how these approaches ask different questions and come to different conclusions. These theories help us organize our understanding of the problem. Since the theory sections are invariably brief, we urge the reader to explore further the assumptions and implications of the different approaches. Critical thinking questions at the end of each chapter will help the reader do this.

In each chapter, the discussion on theoretical approaches is followed by a section on the social consequences of the social problem in question. As we shall see throughout the book (often by way of mild repetition), most of the social problems we discuss are connected to one another, some more closely than others. For example, there is no adequate way to discuss work and unemployment without discussing poverty; no way to discuss family problems without also considering aging, gender inequality, and sexual orientation; and no way to discuss ageism without discussing stereotypes. A few general principles related to social inequality and social exclusion resurface time and again to inform our discussion.

Many serious social problems share a similar range of consequences. Problems such as exploitation, discrimination, and exclusion tend to impoverish people, isolate them, and weaken their stake in the future of the community. Some social problems are commonly associated with crime, violence, addiction, stress, mental illness (for example, depression), and physical illness. We view these consequences as problems in their own right, and our goal is to help society solve them or at least reduce their prevalence. We therefore need to deal with the root causes of the social problems. These root causes are very much social in nature. As sociologists, we need to explain what occurs and why, and we need to suggest how this situation might be improved. As citizens, we should try to understand the problems and their roots, and we should do what we can to improve the situation—for ourselves and for future generations.

In this new edition, we have updated the examples and references. For example, we have added Canadian Researchers boxes and beefed up the discussions on disabilities and Aboriginal issues. A number of pedagogical features have also been incorporated into the text to make it a more effective learning tool for students. Yet, for all this, the book has remained the same in its fundamental approach.

Each chapter includes the following components:

- learning objectives;
- an introduction that sets the contents of the chapter in a wider context;
- theme boxes that reinforce chapter material:
  — Classic Works boxes cite important research and scholarship of past sociologists.
  — International Comparisons boxes present sociological issues, debates, and practices in various parts of the world.

— Personal Stories boxes highlight the struggles and experiences of individuals as they relate to chapter material.

— Public Issues and Public Policy boxes present differing viewpoints on contentious issues such as poverty, education, and social stratification.

— Canadian Researchers boxes—a new feature—introduce students to recent, significant research on issues relating to social problems.

- a margin glossary in each chapter and a compiled glossary at the back of the book;
- a conclusion that summarizes key points discussed in the chapter;
- questions for critical thought; and
- recommended readings.

The text's well-developed art program is designed to make the book more accessible and engaging. Eighty photographs, 53 figures (including 2 maps), 35 tables, and the numerous boxed inserts covering the full range of subject matter help clarify important concepts and make the subject come alive. Moreover, with the addition of a four-colour design, we have made the book's layout more attractive.

In addition, this text is accompanied by an impressive ancillary package.

- **Test Generator.** This comprehensive bank of test questions contains the following for each chapter: 30 multiple-choice questions, 20 true-or-false questions, and 10 short-answer questions.
- **Instructor's Manual.** Each chapter in this helpful instructor resource contains the following: a chapter overview, 5 to 10 learning objectives, 10 to 15 key concepts and names, 10 to 15 concepts for discussion or debate, and 3 to 5 suggested class activities.
- **PowerPoint Slides.** Multiple slides for each chapter reiterate key points in the text and act as a useful study tool for students and a helpful lecture tool for instructors.
- **New Video-Link Library.** Opening a window to a wider world of investigation, this new ancillary feature includes 8 to 10 video weblinks per chapter, a summary for each video, 3 to 5 discussion questions based on each video, and a correlation guide linking videos with chapters in this textbook.
- **Student Study Guide.** This package of review material is designed to reinforce students' understanding of concepts discussed in the text. Each chapter in this resource contains the following: a chapter summary, 5 to 10 learning objectives, 5 to 10 key terms and concepts, 10 to 15 annotated further readings and websites, 10 multiple-choice questions, 10 true-or-false questions, and 5 short-answer questions.

Instructors should contact their Oxford University Press representative regarding ancillary materials.

Acknowledgements

Our first thank you is to the outstanding University of Toronto undergraduate students who helped us research this book. They are (in alphabetical order) Tarik Ali, Jessica Brown, Sally Chiang, Liana Falzone, Anita Feher, Kate Guan, Caitlin Hamblin, Josephine Lam, Qun Ma, Jessie Macdonald, Caitlin Macleod, Kristina Maitland, Samantha Sarkozi, Ashley Sewrattan, Warren Silver, and Sandra Zhou. It's been a privilege and a pleasure to work with these talented young people—one of the two best parts of working on this book.

The other best part of this project was working with the people at Oxford University Press and their associates. Tanuja Weerasooriya served as developmental editor and oversaw the process of flow and standardization—no small feat in the production of a large book. Thank you, Tanuja, for your ceaseless efforts on our behalf. Judith Turnbull edited the copy, clearly and carefully, forcing us always to improve our thinking and writing.

We also want to thank our anonymous reviewers and undergraduate students who have read and responded to material in the first three editions. They have all given us new ideas about what to discuss and how to discuss it most effectively. We've learned a lot writing this book, and it's been fun, too. So, read the book and let us know what you think. We want this book to make your world clearer and more meaningful. If you have some ideas about how we can do that better in the next edition, send us an e-mail at: <lorne.tepperman@utoronto.ca>.

Finally, we would like to acknowledge the following reviewers, along with those reviewers who chose to remain anonymous, whose thoughtful comments and suggestions have helped to shape this current edition of *Social Problems*.

Darlene Balandin, King's University at Western University
Sarath Chandrasekere, University of Prince Edward Island
Dominique Clément, University of Alberta
Helene Cummins, Brescia College at Western University
Merle Fuller, Lethbridge College
Timothy MacNeill, University of Ontario Institute of Technology
H. Angela Ford-Rosenthal, Concordia University

Lorne Tepperman
Josh Curtis
July 2014

Part 1 Introduction

1

What Are Social Problems?

iStockphoto/Thinkstock

LEARNING OBJECTIVES

- To understand what a social problem is.
- To learn how sociologists think about the sociological imagination.
- To find out how sociologists think about social change.
- To recognize the importance of the historical context of social problems.
- To discover the value of information as a social resource.
- To learn the competing theories that clarify aspects of social problems.

What Is a "Social Problem"?

When you hear the words social problem do you think of juvenile delinquents? Drug addicts? Homeless people? Sex workers? Or do you think about insider trading? Tax fraud? Arms sales? The mass marketing of junk food? How about witchcraft? Devil worship? Interplanetary abduction? Celebrity sex scandals? The secret lives of powerful people? The label "social problem" is applied to each of these topics and to hundreds more.

Today, there is no shortage of social problems in what Staeheli (2008) calls the "terrains of political claims-making." We see struggles everywhere over issues and inequalities (Wilkinson and Pickett, 2007), from rallies against free trade in Canada or in support of Mexican immigrants in the United States, to parades featuring lesbian, gay, bisexual, transgendered, and queer communities in Sweden or Israel. These rallies do not merely represent identities and personal interests; they are efforts to change broader social, political, and economic relationships. Our society is drenched with problems and protests, with claims of importance and demands for consideration and dignity. The political terrain is jammed full—clogged—with political actors and activists trying to influence our views and political lives (Taft, 2009).

Such jostling for attention makes it hard for us to single out the most important problems, those most deserving of our notice. We cannot work for every cause; yet we want to support the right causes. But how can we tell truth from falsehood, fact from exaggeration or deception? At the same time, this competition for attention gives us a sense that our views matter—and they do! We need to understand the social problems and political controversies surrounding problems that are laying claim to our attention. We can have a say in how these problems will be solved.

That's where sociology comes in. As the systematic study of societies, sociology is well-equipped to help us inform ourselves about current problems and their possible solutions. No field does more than sociology to force us to make connections—among problems and among levels of analysis—in seeking answers to the problems that face ordinary Canadians.

Social problem A social condition or pattern of behaviour that is believed to warrant public concern and collective action.

Sociology and the Study of Social Problems

The study of social problems is at least as old as the study of sociology itself (McMullin, 2004). In fact, much of early sociology focused on studying such issues. Marx, Durkheim, and Weber were all concerned with social problems, although they spoke about them in different ways. More precisely, sociology has always been about social change, social conflict, and social cohesion—and all of these are connected to social problems. The rise of sociology itself—like the rise of the study of social problems—coincided with the rise of "modern" societies in the nineteenth century. During this formative period, Western Europe and North America shared a deep confidence in the idea of "progress." Progress during this period included industrialization and urbanization; inventions and scientific discovery; and exposure to new and different ideas and values. Progress also meant the possibility of social improvement or social amelioration.

Most sociologists then, like most social reformers, believed that social life could be improved through the systematic study of social issues—by applying knowledge and expelling ignorance, superstition, prejudice, and blind custom. They believed deeply in the value of social research as the means for diagnosing social problems and for inventing and evaluating solutions. They believed that social change could be directed to good ends, that social conflict could be resolved in just ways, and the social order could be re-established around new principles of organization.

Sociologists today still struggle to see and record the patterns of social life that cause what we will call "social problems." We are not—cannot be—omniscient narrators, as in a novel by Dickens or Hugo. We do not see everything and know everything. Yet, as socially conscious members of our society, we want to take part in a struggle against the social problems we do see—if only by clarifying them. To do so—imperfectly, but as well as possible—we need to learn and to use the knowledge collected by expert researchers. This book is an introductory collection and explanation of the sociological knowledge we have today.

We will examine various social problems using sociological ideas to understand them, sociological tools to measure them, and sociological theories to link them. Certain master themes or accounts will emerge; these reflect different ways of viewing reality.

We will pass over many topics and themes, only because space doesn't allow us to address them. What we discuss will be treated briefly and will point students to further research. For reasons of space, we must ignore non-sociological approaches to the same social problems. For example, genetic, chemical, biological, and psychological factors all influence such social problems as health, addiction, and crime. Nor can there be any doubt that cultural, political, and economic factors influence other social problems we discuss: for example, wars, environmental degradation, populations, and workplaces. Yet, we will have to ignore these factors.

As we cannot delve into every possible topic or examine every possible approach, the reader is urged to seek a "second opinion" on everything we have to say by reading widely in the social sciences.

Objective and Subjective Elements

Social problems have at least two aspects that sometimes seem contradictory: what we will call objective and subjective elements.

Objective elements are the measurable features of a negative social condition. They are also what we might call the "scientific (or empirically verifiable) aspects" of a problem. The condition in question—for example, crime, poverty, or alcohol abuse—can be considered an objective reality in the sense that we can collect precise data that measure the problem. These systematic measurements show that the condition exists and that it harms people. We can study the causes and effects without making a moral judgment and without judging the problem as serious or trivial. Sexual abuse, environmental pollution, and racially motivated hate crimes are examples of such problems. We can count and measure their incidence. We can study the changes in social life that cause the numbers or rates of these events to increase and decrease. And we can make and test theories about their changing rates of occurrence—all in a tone of moral neutrality.

This activity is based on a philosophical premise, sometimes called "positivism," of a material reality we can know with our senses, and what we call "science" is the systematic effort to find and test natural laws through measurements of this reality. (Science is more complex than our definition, but this is the gist of it.)

Subjective elements, on the other hand, are people's *evaluations* of sensed reality and the processes that influence their evaluations. They include the moral labels ("wrong," "immoral," "sick," and so on) people apply to particular acts or situations and the accounts they give for these acts and situations. These moral or aesthetic judgements reflect people's

---

Objective elements The measurable features of a negative social condition. Such a condition might include crime, poverty, or alcohol abuse and can be considered an objective reality.

Subjective elements People's evaluations of objective conditions and the processes that influence their evaluations. They include the moral labels that people apply to particular acts or situations and the accounts they give for these acts and situations.

beliefs and tastes. As sociologists, we know that they can become a social reality in their own right; if people believe, for example, that smoking marijuana is evil, that multiculturalism is good, that homosexuals are sick, or that old people are unfit, then these beliefs become aspects of social reality too. Beliefs set in motion actions that have social impacts (in legislation, for example), as we will see repeatedly throughout the book. In this sense, these subjective elements are what we might also call the "political aspects" of a problem. They are different from the scientific, objective aspects but no less important.

Note that a goal of sociology is also to find and test natural laws about these subjective beliefs and their outcomes. Often, these phenomena are harder to measure and harder to explain than other things we study, and so our theories about them are often less developed. Still, these subjective realities are just as important for understanding the social issues we study.

These subjective aspects of social problems affect and reflect our emotional reactions to information we receive about the world. We do not like to hear about young children dying of malnutrition or suffering the effects of industrial water pollution. Hearing of such things reminds us—at least according to the values and beliefs shared by sociologists and some others in our culture—that global health inequality and corporate environmental negligence are worthy of social concern. Second, our subjective or emotional responses often lead to what we call the "social construction" of social problems, including a search for villains, moral panic, crusades for better behaviour, a demand for improved laws, and so on. A central feature in the social construction of social problems is called "claims-making," a process by which people try to capture attention and mobilize public opinion around particular problems and their solutions.

As we will see, people's understanding of social problems is influenced both by changes in measurable reality and by changes in their *views* of measurable reality. As sociologists, we are well-suited to studying social problems, because we know how to assess changes in measurable reality and we know how to measure changes in people's viewpoints. By bringing together the objective and subjective elements, we can define a *social problem* as both a condition—an empirically observed situation that threatens the well-being of a significant part of society—and a process—the sequence of events by which members of society come to see a situation as a social problem that warrants and needs collective remedial action.

Social Problems and the Sociological Imagination

According to sociologist C. Wright Mills (1959), the sociological imagination is the ability to see connections between one's own life (micro-events), the social world in which one lives (macro-events), and between personal or private troubles and public issues. This macro–micro link between close-to-home aspects of social life and broad social trends is the subject matter of sociology. Further, this core relationship is our key to understanding how social problems affect our lives.

To use Mills's example, unemployed people may view their lack of a job as a private trouble involving only them, their immediate family members, and perhaps their friends. But this view is short-sighted. In fact, widespread unemployment—the source of private troubles for thousands or millions of people—often is caused by such factors as economic recession, corporate downsizing, and advances in technology that replace people with machines. Today's plant closings and the resulting unemployment are part of a centuries-old workplace struggle between workers and the people who own and manage workplaces. Such struggles involve the people who buy the manufactured products

Sociological imagination A term used by sociologist C. Wright Mills in his 1959 book *The Sociological Imagination*, which describes the sociologist's ability to connect seemingly impersonal and remote historical forces to the most basic incidents of an individual's life. The sociological imagination enables people to distinguish between personal troubles and public issues.

and the government they elect that regulates (or fails to regulate) the corporations. Present unemployment results in part from "globalization," a process that sends high-wage Canadian jobs to low-wage countries. Thus, unemployment is not merely a private or personal trouble; it is a public issue. The same is true of other social problems—crime and victimization, family violence, poverty, drug addiction, environmental pollution, racism, and so on. The sociological imagination connects the conditions of our personal lives and the larger social context in which we live.

Sociologists make these connections by closely analyzing reality at two levels, micro and macro. Microsociology, or *micro-level analysis*, focuses on the interactions between people in small groups. This approach studies people's understanding and experience of social problems at the local, personal level (Fine and Fields, 2008). Macrosociology, or *macro-level analysis*, focuses on the societal level. It explores the ways that social trends occurring within major bureaucratic organizations and social institutions, such as the economy or the government, affect the population as a whole (Krejci, 1994).

We need both levels of analysis for a proper understanding of social problems and to see that many private troubles are essentially public issues. Take the case of street youth, or homeless youth, written about in a classic work of sociology by John Hagan and Bill McCarthy (see Box 1.1). Hagan and McCarthy (1998) take a purely objective,

Classic **WORKS**

BOX 1.1   **John Hagan and Bill McCarthy's *Mean Streets: Youth Crime and Homelessness* (1998)**

If anyone has ever approached you asking for money or offering to squeegee your (perfectly clean) car window, you may have wondered why people are begging on Canadian streets. In fact, you may have wondered why many seemingly healthy young Canadians *live* on the streets, in shelters, or in other temporary accommodations.

Sociologists have found that many street youth are "runaways." Most street youth come from families that suffer serious emotional, mental, or substance abuse problems. Unlike street children in developing countries, Canadian youth rarely are on the street for reasons of family poverty, although family financial difficulties increase the likelihood of physical abuse and abuse increases the likelihood of young people running away. Sexual abuse is another frequent element in the stories of homeless youth.

The classic work in this area is *Mean Streets: Youth, Crime and Homelessness* (1998) by sociologists John Hagan and Bill McCarthy. To do their study, they gathered data from 400 high school youth to compare the backgrounds of youth in Toronto and Vancouver, some of whom live at home and some of whom live on the street.

They found that, compared to school youth, the majority of homeless youth come from troubled families. For example, a disproportionate number of street kids come from homes where there is family violence and sexual abuse. Once on the street, youth's lives are dominated by a daily search for food, shelter, income, and companionship. This is the dominant reality of street life and the reason for involvement in crime: namely, lack of the necessities of life (i.e., food, shelter, or source of income). Crime, for street youth, is a practical response to need. However, peers also influence street youth's involvement in crime.

Once they arrive on the street, youth quickly become immersed in networks of other street youth and street adults, many of whom are involved in crime. On the other hand, employment is a turning point in the lives of these street youth. Although involvement in the street network encourages crime, involvement in paid work discourages it. So, employment has an important effect on street youth's involvement in crime and other dangerous activities. That said, it takes awhile for employment to stabilize. Most street youth are in and out of employment, for a period. Those street youth who find stable, long-term employment gradually move away from crime and spend less and less time hanging out on the street.

positivistic approach to the study of homeless youth. They show us that (1) there are identifiable homeless youth they can study; (2) they can find out all the necessary facts about the lives of these homeless youth; and (3) they can devise explanations or theories about the reasons these young people live on the streets. This is sociology in the traditional scientific manner.

An alternative approach might be to ask the youth to give personal accounts of their homelessness, then to analyze and compare their narratives to understand why some youth account for homelessness in one way, while others do so in another way. This is called a "postmodern approach."

Finally, Hagan and McCarthy might have carried out the study a different way: to find out the reason few people consider youth homelessness a major social issue, despite the efforts by some to raise public awareness about this issue. This is called a "subjectivist" or "constructionist approach." As you can see, each approach would involve collecting and analyzing different kinds of information.

Social Problems Research as a Moral Enterprise

As you probably learned in an introductory course, sociology is an engaged, progressive, and optimistic discipline founded on the notion that we can improve society through research and the application of research-based knowledge (Zazar, 2008). Thus, many sociologists—like Hagan and McCarthy—do research aimed directly at reducing poverty, violence, injustice, and inequality.

Paradoxically, however, our human efforts to improve society sometimes backfire. Modernization itself and its associated features, such as a free market and bureaucratic organization, not only leave many problems unresolved, but also create new ones. In general, they fail to ensure most of us a decent quality of life (Morgan et al., 2006). The costs of our efforts to modernize society can include homelessness, discrimination, recurrent warfare, mass deaths, and even genocide—realities throughout the twentieth century and into the twenty-first. As others have remarked, modernization also carries heavy costs for the natural environment. No other century in human history combined as much technological progress with as much organized killing and environmental destruction as the twentieth century (Tippelt, 2009).

Undeterred by this record of destruction and despair, sociologists soldier on. Those who study social problems often think of themselves as engaged in a moral enterprise whose goal is to improve human societies through social change. Therefore, much of the sociological research on social problems is guided by seven value preferences (Alvarez, 2001):

- life over death;
- health over sickness;
- knowledge over ignorance;
- co-operation over conflict;
- freedom of movement over physical restraint;
- self-determination over direction by others; and
- freedom of expression over restraint of communication.

These values, we can agree, are desirable and worth achieving, but most societies fall far short of them. As a result, much of the research on social problems criticizes the existing social order. Much of the literature on social problems aims at changing society to protect the vulnerable and redress the injustices done them.

In this effort, sociologists often find they are competing with common sense and the mass media—both sources of misinformation. Popular myths, ideologies, and stereotypes perpetuate harmful conditions. For example, too often, we find the media turning public issues into private troubles, blaming the victims and stigmatizing them for having these problems. Homeless youth, for example, may be blamed for running away from home, dropping out of school, committing petty crimes, using drugs, and so on. Yet, there are reasons they ran away from home, dropped out of school, and so on—those are the underlying causes we need to address as sociologists.

Consider mental illness, a widespread and growing public health problem today (including on college campuses). Outbreaks of depression, for example, cause people severe suffering and often lead to higher risks of death, disability, and secondary illness. Mental illness of every kind is a growing problem in our society—whether in the form of depression, anxiety, obsessive/compulsive disorder, panic, addiction, or other—and its prevalence points to significant strains and pressures throughout society (Moore et al., 2009). We are mistaken in blaming the sufferers of mental illness for a problem that is claiming ever more victims. How can the problem be personal if it is shared by a huge and growing fraction of the Canadian population?

Sociologists identify the social-structural conditions that make people vulnerable to these so-called personal troubles. For example, many mentally ill people suffer from inadequate social support (Edwards, 2009). Durkheim, over a century ago in his classic study, *Suicide*, pointed out that a lack of social integration and social control are likely to cause great mental distress, even to the extent of leading to suicide. Nowhere is this

Rick Madonik / GetStock.com

Rapper Khari (Conspiracy) Stewart, left, and filmmaker Jonathan Balazs, seen outside Ryerson University, collaborated on the Mars Project, a provocative look at mental illness and the mental health system in Canada.

INTERNATIONAL **COMPARISONS**

BOX 1.2   Discrimination against Old People in the East

One would imagine that collectivistic Eastern cultures that hold elders in higher regard than we do in the West would hold less negative beliefs about aging than we do. However, research examining cross-cultural attitudes towards seniors appears to contradict this notion.

In fact, some studies have even found an opposite trend. McConatha et al. (2004), for example, looked at the anxieties and fears of young and middle-aged adults in Turkey and the United States associated with aging. Contrary to their original hypothesis, they found that Turkish participants had much higher psychological anxieties about aging and also considered a person to be old at a much younger age.

Many studies found, however, that attitudes towards aging, and often ageism, tend to be more similar than different between countries despite cultural differences. Korean and Canadian university students hold similar negative-memory stereotypes about 65-year-old adults with regard to declines in memory capacity, change, and locus of control (Ryan et al., 2009). Israeli participants (more collectivistic) showed a similar structure of ageism as their Western counterparts, with regard to negative stereotypes, avoidance of seniors, and negative views about the contribution of the elderly to general society (Bodner and Lazar, 2008). Older males upheld views about the elderly that associated the avoidance of older adults with negative stereotypes. Older females linked avoidance of the elderly with negative attitudes about the contribution of older adults to society.

Interestingly, despite being an individualistic society, younger and middle-aged Swedish participants report an overall positive attitude towards embodied aging (Öberg and Tornstam, 2003). On scales assessing the attractiveness and sexuality of older adults, the youth image ideal, and elderly appearance status, the younger and middle-aged participants consistently rated the elderly on a much more positive note than older participants; ageist attitudes were found more frequently in the older participants.

more obvious than among homeless people, a vulnerable population with few social supports. Besides their social isolation, they typically also suffer from unemployment, poverty, physical weaknesses, substance abuse, and mental illness (Caan, 2009; Weir-Hughes, 2009).

When doing research, sociologists look for social-structural factors that increase the likelihood of problem behaviours—indeed, sequences of problem behaviours. For example, risky sexual behaviour in adolescence may lead to teenage parenthood, which reduces the likelihood of school completion and increases the likelihood of unemployment and financial dependence (Domenico and Jones, 2007). Dropping out of school early also significantly increases the risk of early parenthood, as do low socio-economic status, low academic achievement, and social isolation (Westcott, 2005). As sociologists, we need to study the links among these problems and find ways of preventing them—controlling them at their source—since efforts to correct them later have proved largely unsuccessful.

As the data in Figure 1.1 show, school dropout rates have been falling over the past 20 years, but they still point to a problem for tens of thousands of potentially unemployed, underemployed, and unemployable Canadians.

Social Construction

All social reality is conditional and temporary. By that we mean that, unlike physical reality, social reality is constantly changing in large and small ways. Every day, there are

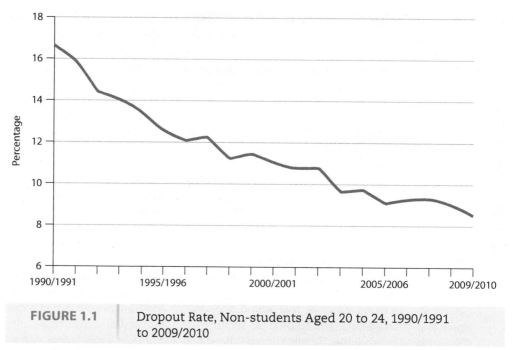

FIGURE 1.1 | Dropout Rate, Non-students Aged 20 to 24, 1990/1991 to 2009/2010

Source: Statistics Canada, *Labour Force Survey*, at: <www.statcan.gc.ca/pub/81-004-x/2010004/article/11339-eng.htm#a>.

new ideas, beliefs, opinions, inventions, and practices. Social "reality" is (almost) infinitely flexible and always open to interpersonal influence (Searle, 2006). This is the central finding of social science research on religion, culture, ideology, mass communication, propaganda, and the like. The widely varying ways people think about reality are amply clear in historical and cross-national research on any topic.

To help them make sense of the world and their lives in it, people invent all kinds of stories about reality. These stories—however imaginary—lead to actions that are real in their effects. This observation is attributed to the early American sociologist W.I. Thomas, who stated the so-called Thomas dictum: when people define a situation as real, the situation will be real in its effects. Stated another way, people's subjective view of reality—not reality itself—shapes their behaviour.

Consider a prominent example: through the mass media, we are familiar with the work of professional "spin doctors"—in politics, advertising, and elsewhere—whose job it is to promote a self-interested concern, belief, or wish, often at the expense of the truth. Lying has become full-time professional work for many of the most financially successful people in our society. Only the most naive believe everything they hear or read.

So, it takes no stretch of the imagination to realize that at least some of the supposed social problems we will discuss are not real problems—they are merely "social constructions." Though some people view them as social problems, other people do not. But bear in mind, these social constructions can have important social effects (Ajdukovic, 2008).

An approach to understanding the subjective aspect of reality is called **social constructionism**, and it rests on a sociological theory of knowledge stated by Peter L. Berger and Thomas Luckmann in their book *The Social Construction of Reality* (1966). Often, the social construction of reality involves the work of **moral entrepreneurs**—elites, interest groups, or

Social constructionism
A sociological research approach that examines the ways people interact to create a shared social reality.

Moral entrepreneurs
Term coined to describe people who "discover" and try to publicize deviant behaviours. Moral entrepreneurs are crusading reformers who are disturbed by particular types of evil they see in the world and who will not rest until something is done to correct the problem.

even community leaders who stereotype and classify some situations as problems. Framing problems also involves **claims-making**, a procedure that describes, explains, and blames people who are involved with the problem, often labelling them as deviants or wrongdoers.

Social constructionists examine the ways people interact to create a shared social reality. Berger and Luckmann, for example, propose that *all* knowledge—including the most taken-for-granted knowledge of everyday life—is created, preserved, and spread by social interaction. According to the social constructionist approach, any idea, however natural or obvious it may seem to the people who accept it, is an invention of a particular culture or society.

But why, among the plethora of ideas, do some become widely accepted as "true" and compelling? The answer to this question grows out of symbolic interactionism and the early twentieth-century work of George Herbert Mead (1934), who wrote that children learn to interact with others by learning a system of **symbols**, including language, which allows them to share and negotiate meanings among those who share the system. Using shared meanings, they can play together, perform complementary **roles**, and relate to the social group as a "generalized other." For Mead, this ability is the basis of all social order. Shared meanings (including shared symbols) make social interaction possible and allow people to co-operate and influence one another. Social life, for Mead, is the sharing of meanings—that is, the co-operative (social) construction of reality.

A generation later, another symbolic interactionist, Erving Goffman (1959), proposed that we can usefully think of society as a theatre in which people compose and perform social scripts together. We come to believe in the truth of the roles we play; often, we become the person we pretend to be. Social life is a set of scripted, directed performances. Inside our social roles we find and express (or hide and protect) our "true" identities.

In the view of social constructionists, human beings react not to physical objects and events themselves, but to the shared meanings of these objects and events. The shared meanings are not essential features of the objects and events, but are socially imposed or constructed. In our society, for example, a red rose is considered "beautiful," while a daisy is considered "simple," and a cabbage, "ugly." Though merely social constructions, such shared meanings are powerful, nonetheless. (If you doubt the social power of this construction, give your loved one a dozen cabbages on Valentine's Day. You might pull it off if you use the French term of endearment "mon petit chou"—"my little cabbage"!) Thus, the meaning of anything, including a social problem, is the product of the dominant cultural and symbolic practices in a group or society.

Nowhere is this so readily obvious—at least to modern eyes—as in the social construction of witchcraft during the Middle Ages. The persecution of midwives and wise women as "witches" shows how a social panic can emerge—that is, can be socially constructed. Today, few of us in economically developed societies accept any of the assumptions that would support a witch craze.

Burr (1995) identifies four basic assumptions of the social constructionist position, all of which we can apply to an understanding of the witch craze:

- *The world does not present itself objectively to the observer* but is known through human experience, which is largely influenced by language. That is, we use language and images to create emotional responses, such as hostile reactions towards suspected witches.
- *Historical and cultural specificity is recognized.* The language categories used to classify things emerge from the social interactions within a group of people at a particular time and in a particular place. So, for example, the witch craze takes place within a

Claims-making The promotion of a particular moral vision of social life and, thus, anything people do to propagate a view of who or what is a problem and what should be done about it.

Symbols Gestures, artifacts, and words that represent something else.

Roles The specific duties and activities expected of those who occupy a specific social status.

social framework in which scientific proof is absent from the rule of law. The notion of witchcraft as a practice that could pose a real threat to the society existed then in a way that does not exist in North American society today. That said, there still exist cultures that believe in the efficacy of witchcraft and similar systems of belief.

- *Knowledge is sustained by social process.* How reality is understood at a given moment is determined by the conventions of communication in force at that time. So, for example, the formal pronouncements of religious leaders about witches, combined with superstition and fear, were sufficient in the late medieval period in Europe to claim legitimacy as "knowledge."

- *Knowledge and social action go together.* Within a **social group** or culture, reality is defined by complex and organized patterns of ongoing actions. We cannot really understand the meaning people attached to witchcraft in the burning times without understanding their politics, religion, and gender relations.

Social group A set of people, defined by formal or informal criteria of membership, who feel unified or are bound together in stable patterns of interaction.

In short, social constructionism looks at the ways people create and institutionalize social reality. And when people act on their shared knowledge of this reality, they reinforce it or lock it in. To think in those terms becomes habitual and seems natural, even unavoidable.

Throughout this book, we will have to repeatedly ask ourselves, with regard to any particular problem, is this a real problem or is it merely (or in large part) a social construction? We will have several reasons for doing this. First, as sociologists, we need to have the clearest possible understanding of reality, even if our own understanding challenges common sense, prevailing wisdom, or the dominant ideology on a given issue. Second, as sociologists, we need to learn as much as we can about the social processes by which imagined social problems receive unwarranted attention and real social problems receive less attention than they deserve. We need to make theories about these developmental processes, since by doing so we learn a great deal about how society works. Most importantly, we need to know which social problems require immediate, concerted action and which ones can be ignored for the time being.

So, we will need to keep asking, is X a real problem or a socially constructed problem? More precisely, we will have to ask, to what degree is problem X real and to what degree is it socially constructed? And, if X is a real problem, in what ways do the usual techniques of social construction help to put the problem on the public agenda for discussion, debate, and legislative action?

A useful variation of this social constructionist approach is *institutional ethnography*, a mode of inquiry devised by feminist sociologist Dorothy Smith and intended to help researchers explore the social organization of everyday knowledge. This approach helps to make the familiar strange and calls into question taken-for-granted assumptions about social organization that, unexplored, serve the interests of the dominant groups in society. In this respect, the method—by challenging relations of domination—helps sociological research to better serve people who are subject to the administration of power.

Sociologists do this by questioning the ways in which knowledge is used to manage institutional life—that is, by defining the categories and conceptual frameworks of administration we all learn to use. Often, these categories and conceptual frameworks are not only inappropriate, they promote ideas about social order that serve the dominant institutions and not ordinary people. Nowhere is this more obvious than in public discourse.

So, for example, when the prime minister of Canada decides to hinder and hide public discussion of public issues, he prorogues Parliament. By using the formal and traditional language of governmental procedure in calling this action "proroguing," he makes it sound more complicated or justifiable than if his action were only called "suppression of dissent" or "crushing the justifiable opposition." Likewise, during the administration of US president George W. Bush, torture of war prisoners was called "enhanced interrogation"—a term intended to legitimate the action and sound "professional." By far the most elegant linguistic confusion was accomplished by "extraordinary rendition" and "irregular rendition," terms used by the US government to describe the illegal kidnapping and transfer of real or imagined US enemies from one state to another, where they might be secretly tortured.

The first job of institutional ethnography, then, is to deconstruct the language used to confuse and obscure public understanding. Second, institutional ethnography aims to shine a light on taken-for-granted relations of power, to demystify the relations of ruling, and to point out ways that ruling relations can be changed to better serve ordinary people in everyday life.

Warnings, Panics, and Claims

One goal of ruling classes is to produce social concern about behaviours they want to control, such as dissent. This means they are likely to use claims-making strategies to provoke intense feelings of fear, anger, and confusion.

To bring a perceived problem onto the public agenda, claims-makers rely on common rhetorical idioms and styles that reflect core cultural values. Often, the rhetoric used urges people to avoid certain types of risk, above all else (Krinsky, 2008). For example, political and other leaders may call on people to act to protect their homeland, their families, and their "way of life." Emotional images may be used to sway public opinion: images of babies crying or houses burning or beautiful young women in attitudes of prayer with the Stars and Stripes fluttering in the background.

The media play a large part in shaping the public view of a problem. In fact, popular opinions today are more often shaped by media depictions than by first-hand experience; how the media present a problem plays a crucial role in how the public will respond. For example, the media can influence public opinion by putting stories about a given "problem" on the agenda for repeated discussion in news reports. As well, they can portray the alleged problem in sensational ways, with clear heroes and villains. Some media manipulation is subtler. In television talk shows, for example, we are taught to infer community standards of behaviour—what is deemed by the talk show host to be "deviant" and "normal," "praiseworthy" and "shocking," as reinforced by the applause of the studio audience. Here, the hosts are moral entrepreneurs and claims-makers, while the audience in the studio becomes the "court of public opinion."

Sometimes, ordinary people begin the claims-making. We all learn how to tell stories that describe or explain problems and how to blame others for these problems; some people learn these skills especially well. For example, high school debaters learn how to take both sides of an argument, express ideas with which they do not necessarily agree, and present powerful if sometimes questionable evidence for those opinions. This teaches them how to engage in social problem debate and trains them for moral entrepreneurship (Bockman, 1991).

Sometimes, organization insiders (for example, in the nuclear power or tobacco industries) take part in the claims-making (Ding, 2009). **Whistle-blowers** are unusual claims-makers who speak out against their own immediate interests and those of their employer. Lacking the organizational power to promote their definitions of the social problem, they gain influence from their seeming inside knowledge and courage. Often

Whistle-blowers
Employees in a bureaucratic organization who bring forward valid information about wrongdoing or illegal conduct by their organization and who are often punished for doing so.

whistle-blowers, blacklisted in their industries, have to turn to social movements for employment. Sometimes, like Wikileaker Edward Snowden, they are viewed as enemies of the state and hunted down by global police organizations.

Framing a social problem in a particular way is especially important for influencing public opinion. Consider, for instance, the attempts of the organization FARM (Farm Animal Reform Movement) to influence public opinion. Its goal was to eliminate the use of cows, pigs, and chickens as human food, a goal it could not achieve. Even its short-term goal, which was to reduce the suffering of farm animals by closing down factories that use modern intensive farming techniques, failed. Claims about the suffering of animals did not persuade a majority of the public, so FARM reframed the problem in the early 1990s, focusing on societal health, longevity, and environmental endangerment instead. These efforts gained wider support for the organization.

Some issues grow slowly and hold the public interest for a long time, such as domestic violence and school violence (Tanner, 2009). Others grow quickly, peak, and rapidly lose the public's interest, as the alleged devil worship and satanic ritual that produced a flurry of concern did in the 1990s. Sociologists refer to such short-lived, intense periods of concern as **moral panics** and to the people responsible for these sensed threats as *folk devils* (Cohen, 1972). Though moral panics, like fads, are short-lived, they sometimes leave a legacy of laws, stereotypes, cultural beliefs, or changed attitudes.

Moral panic The process of arousing social concern over an issue—usually the work of moral entrepreneurs and the mass media.

How to Tell If a Social Problem Is "Real"

A social arrangement can cause problems for people without having been recognized (yet) as a social problem. Some would say problems only become *social* problems when claims-makers and moral entrepreneurs succeed in drawing public attention to them.

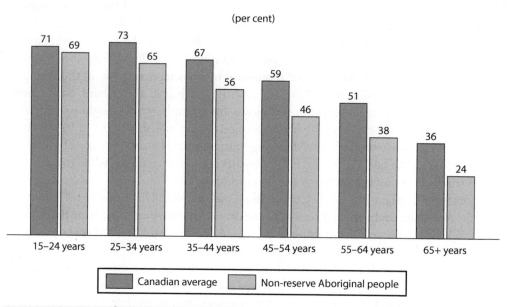

(per cent)

	15–24 years	25–34 years	35–44 years	45–54 years	55–64 years	65+ years
Canadian average	71	73	67	59	51	36
Non-reserve Aboriginal people	69	65	56	46	38	24

FIGURE 1.2   The Self-Rated Health of Canadian Aboriginal and Non-Aboriginal People

Source: Statistics Canada. Aboriginal Peoples Survey 2001—Initial Findings: Well-being of the Non-reserve Aboriginal Population. Ottawa, Statistics Canada, 2003, (Cat. No. 89-589-XIE).

Public Issues *and* Public Policy

BOX 1.3   **The Culture of Poverty and Uneven Distribution of Resources**

Poor families are especially common in certain social groups—for example, among Canadian Aboriginal peoples. Some have suggested that some people are permanently disadvantaged because they have learned "bad values" that limit their ability to improve their lives.

The scientific idea of a "culture of poverty" arose first in the work of anthropologist Oscar Lewis. Lewis described how people become trapped by their culture, as not all cultures espouse values that promote the sobriety, thrift, and planning that a modern capitalist society requires. Lewis proposed that the people he studied—Mexican peasants, among others—were poor because they held values that were not consistent with the need to change their farming practices and adopt more profitable ones. They were not innovative; they valued the family over the individual; they were unwilling to place trust in people outside the family; and they viewed anybody who got ahead economically as taking unfair advantage of others.

Lewis saw these values as cultural rather than as individual. People learned them as children when they were socialized into their culture. The major problems of underdevelopment, Lewis decided, were cultural. This analysis would lead to the conclusion that, to reduce poverty, any government needs to change its people's values.

But what if, instead, we view poverty as the result of an uneven distribution of resources within society? After all,

in a poor neighbourhood, many factors unrelated to culture hinder a person's chances to rise out of poverty. For example, many female-headed households may be poor because of an earnings gap between men and women. Many blue-collar workers may be poor because manufacturing jobs left the country, throwing the workers into long-term unemployment. Some poor people may not be able to work because they are sick, and their illness may be caused by a lack of sanitation, improper nutrition, pests, lack of heating, or lead poisoning (lead paint is common in old low-rental units). They may also lack transportation and easy access to jobs.

As well, children in poor neighbourhoods may have to deal with under-equipped classrooms, crowded home conditions, lack of a place to study, or even hunger during the day, all of which prevent children from giving full attention to their classwork.

Like rich people, some poor people have "bad" values and some don't. Rather than looking to change values, we can look to economic investment, business regulation, and changing the ways poor people are treated by bosses and public officials. Through progressive taxation and social programs that redistribute wealth, some societies (notably the Scandinavian countries) attempt to combat poverty without blaming people for their values. Taking this approach leads us to social policies that will stimulate job creation and provide social supports that enable poor people to complete their education and compete for jobs on a level playing field.

However, as sociologists, we can apply various standards to a stated problem, to decide how serious we think the problem may be. These standards apply especially to the problems of inequality that we will study in the middle portion of this book, but they apply more generally to all social problems.

In connection with all the social problems we discuss in this book—crime, drug abuse, family violence, poverty, and so on—we need to ask similar questions. We need to understand why we think something is a social problem before we study and explain its causes and effects. Consider the lengthy debate about the existence of a "culture of poverty." This debate keeps resurfacing in discussions about welfare recipients, homeless people, and even the chronically unemployed. One's position on this debate will affect the social policies one chooses to support.

Theoretical Perspectives on Social Problems

Social problems are not the exclusive concern of sociologists. For this reason, we will briefly take note of the different approaches that other fields of study have taken. In fact, both the natural and the social sciences have brought their own unique understandings and perspectives to the study of social problems. It is important for students to recognize that, in seeking the truth, disciplines are not competing with one another. We will not find that the contributions made by psychologists are "right" while those made by anthropologists are "wrong." Both disciplines are useful according to their own designs and self-imposed limits. Both approaches can further our understanding of the problems we are considering.

Thus, the study of social problems is best understood as a multi-level co-operative activity. The findings of one field or discipline can be expected to confirm and elaborate on the research of the others. Sociological researchers, for their part, focus on group relations and culture. Some prefer macroanalysis at the societal level, and others concentrate on microanalysis at the small-group level. The two major macroanalytical approaches in

TABLE 1.1	The Main Sociological Approaches
THEORY	**MAIN IDEAS**
Structural Functionalism	• Elements in society are interconnected and interrelated. • Well-functioning societies require value consensus, social cohesion, and social control. • Social change or inequality may create social disorganization and strain and lead to deviance and crime. • Social problems occasionally strengthen social cohesion by renewing commitment to social boundaries.
Conflict Theory	• Conflict and change are basic features of social life. • Social problems are a result of inequality, conflict, and change. • Conflicting groups, classes, and people routinely struggle for domination over others. • The conflict between men and women is a basic feature of all societies.
Symbolic Interactionism	• Society is a product of continuous face-to-face interactions. • Social problems are socially constructed. • Problematic behaviours are socially learned and practised in social settings. • Socialization and labelling shape deviant identities and contribute to the formation of subcultures.
Feminist Theory	• All social life is gendered in important ways. • Women in most societies, and for most of history, have been disadvantaged by men through patriarchy; therefore, victimization is an important element of social experience. • Therefore, social life must be understood from a variety of standpoints, especially a gender standpoint.
Population Health Perspective	• Population health is a sensitive global measure of how well a society is working. • All common social inequalities have significant health consequences. • Social problems are revealed by declines in population health. • The goal in dealing with social problems is always to avoid and reduce harm.

sociology are the structural-functional and conflict perspectives, while the major micro-analytical approach is the symbolic interactionist perspective.

Structural Functionalism

Structural functionalism views society as a set of interconnected elements that work together to preserve the overall stability and efficiency of the whole. Through this view, individual social institutions—families, the economy, government, education, and others—contribute to the survival of the entire society. Families, for instance, work to reproduce and nurture members of society, while the economy regulates the production, distribution, and consumption of goods and services.

Robert Merton (1968), a key figure in developing this perspective, proposed that social institutions perform both manifest and latent functions. **Manifest functions** are intended and easily recognized, while **latent functions** are unintended and often hidden from participants. Formal schooling, for example, is intended to provide students with the knowledge, skills, and cultural values that will help them to work effectively in society. Both the school and its participants formally recognize these roles. At a latent level, however, schools also work as "babysitters" for young children and teenagers, keeping them safe and off the streets during the daytime while their parents are at work. They also work as "matchmakers," giving older high school and university students a place to meet and socialize with potential future lovers or marriage partners.

These latent functions are important to society and are often carried out with great success, even if we are unaware of them doing so. However, they are considered latent because they are not the results imagined by planners of the educational system, nor are they publicly acknowledged by school administrators, students, or parents to have these effects.

According to functionalists, the cause of most social problems is a failure of institutions to fulfill their roles during times of rapid change. This *social disorganization* view of social problems holds that sudden cultural shifts disrupt traditional values and common ways of doing things. French sociologist Émile Durkheim (see, for example, 1964 [1893], 1951 [1897], 1965 [1912]) introduced the term *anomie*, or *normlessness* to reflect the condition in which social **norms** are weak or come into conflict with one another. For example, during the industrialization and urbanization in Western Europe and North America after 1850, crime, poverty, unsanitary living conditions, environmental pollution, and other forms of social disorganization increased sharply.

As traditional norms and relations broke down, social control declined and people felt less tied to one another; as a result they became more likely to engage in nonconforming, deviant types of behaviour (crime, drug use, and so on). The general solution to social problems, according to this perspective, is to strengthen social norms and slow the pace of social change.

Conflict Theory

Conflict theory has its roots in the basic division between "haves" and "have-nots." Conflict theorists criticize the structural-functionalist explanation of social problems, especially its assumption of consensus among members of society and its limited attention to power struggles and competing interests. The conflict perspective instead views society as a collection of varied groups—especially social classes—locked in struggle over a limited supply of assets.

Structural functionalism A theoretical model highlighting the way each part of society works to fulfill the needs of the society as a whole; also called "functionalism"; a macrosociological approach that focuses on the societal, as opposed to the individual, level.

Manifest functions The visible and intended goals or effects of social structures and institutions.

Latent functions Hidden, unstated, and unintended consequences of activities in an organization or institution.

Norms The rules and expectations of the society pertaining to appropriate behaviours under various social circumstances. Norms regulate behaviour in different situations, and large-scale norm violation is often viewed as a social problem; a problem occurs when traditionally normative behaviour is violated.

Conflict theory A theoretical model, drawn from the writings of Marx and Engels, that highlights conflict and change as the regular and permanent features of society; a macrosociological research approach that focuses on processes within the whole society.

Conflict theory originates from the works of German economic-political philosopher Karl Marx (see, for example, Marx and Engels, 1998 [1848]; Marx, 1990 [1862–3]: 89) and others. Marx notes that in an industrialized, capitalist system, two broad groups emerge: the *bourgeoisie*, the owners of the means of production, and the *proletariat*, the working class, who must sell their labour power in exchange for a liveable wage. The capitalists use their great economic power and political influence to ensure that they remain in a position of dominance over the workers.

Conflict theories propose that social problems stem mainly from the economic and power inequalities that exist between competing groups—especially between social classes. For the capitalist class to uphold its wealthy, privileged status, it must ensure that those with less power do not have the opportunity—and if possible, even the desire—to reach for it. For the bourgeoisie to gain wealth from the system, large parts of the population must live in abject poverty. This poverty of the working and unemployed classes produces conflict and despair. It also leads to other social problems, including crime, drug use, homelessness, environmental pollution, domestic violence, and racism, as well as physical and mental health problems.

Conflict theorists also contend that workers in a capitalist system feel alienated from the processes and products of their labour. Because they are unable to control or change the conditions of their work, they are powerless and stuck in jobs that exploit them. In

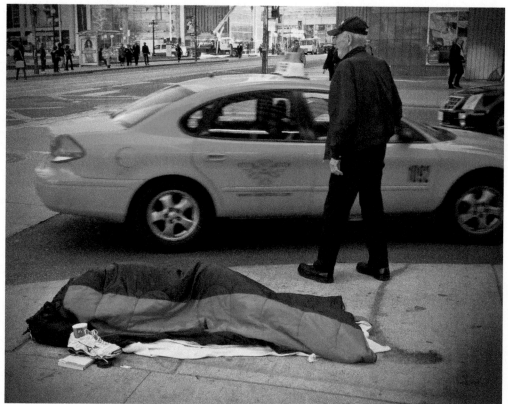

The Canadian Press/Francis Vachon

The image above, of a homeless man in downtown Toronto, illustrates one of the many social problems that arise, according to conflict theory, from economic inequalities between social classes.

CANADIAN researchers

| BOX 1.4 | Daniel Beland, University of Saskatchewan |

Social problems call for policies and programs to remedy those problems, and few Canadian sociologists have been as dedicated as Daniel Beland in studying the policy-making process, in Canada and elsewhere. He has provided us with a strategy for thinking about the ways policy-makers do their job.

In the last 10 years, political sociologist and Canada Research Chair in Public Policy Daniel Beland has studied the convergence of certain key themes in political sociology: notably, power, ideas, language, discourse, and public policy. In a 2009 paper titled "Ideas, Institutions, and Policy Change," Beland draws on the political science literature to discuss three ways in which ideas influence policy change. First, he notes that ideas help to construct the problems and issues that enter the policy agenda. Second, they shape the assumptions that affect the content of reform proposals. Third, they can become ideological weapons that shape reform activities. Yet, institutional constraints also shape the politics of ideas and policy change. National institutions remain central to the politics of policy-making and interact with transnational actors and ideas to bring about change. Consider, for example, the role of ideas about welfare change, as discussed in Beland's 2011 paper "The Politics of Social Policy Language." Here, he notes that key social policy concepts like "welfare state" are both vague and problematic. Focusing on social policy debate in France and the

United States in the last three decades, Beland discusses the meaning and development of the concepts of "social security"/"sécurité sociale" and "welfare state"/"état-providence" in both countries. These concepts have long been controversial, in part because they are enmeshed in the inherently political drawing and redrawing of the contested boundaries of state action.

Likewise, as Beland shows in a 2010 paper titled "The Idea of Power and the Role of Ideas," since the mid-1970s, the sociological debate over the meaning of power has intensified. Beland puts forward an amended definition of political power, then explores the relationship between ideas, interests, and power relations. Doing so suggests that, among other things, ideational processes help actors make sense of their perceived interests. This recognition of the power of ideas sheds new light on the idea of political power, Beland observes. Finally, in a 2009 paper titled "Gender, Ideational Analysis, and Social Policy," he brings gender into this equation. Focusing on social policy, he explains how students of gender have contributed to the contemporary literature on ideational processes. He notes that the gender literature usefully draws our attention to at least three broad issues neglected by many non-feminist scholars: (1) the intersection between categorical inequalities and policy ideas; (2) the role of identities and gendered cultural assumptions; and (3) the relationship between welfare regimes and ideational processes.

every sense, they are alienated—estranged—from their work, their fellow workers, the products of their work, and even from themselves. Also, they are alienated because they are exploited: they are denied a fair and just payment for the value they produce through their labour.

Critics of the Marxian conflict theory approach have noted that, historically, communist societies founded on Marxism have failed either to prosper or to erase inequality. As well, non-Marxist conflict theories propose that many social conflicts are based on non-class-based interests, values, and beliefs—for example, on ethnic or racial or religious differences. They point out the Marxist approach has overemphasized the importance of economic inequality at the expense of other types of inequality and social injustice based on race, gender, age, or other factors linked to inequality. While they recognize the value people place on differences in income and social class, proponents of these perspectives believe that other divergent interests and characteristics can also lead to conflict and oppression.

Symbolic Interactionism

While the structural-functionalist and conflict perspectives focus on social institutions and major demographic groups, symbolic interactionism focuses on small-group interactions. The symbolic interactionist sees society as made up of the shared meanings, definitions, and interpretations held by interacting people. In studying social problems, followers of this perspective analyze how certain behaviours and conditions come to be defined or framed as social problems and how people learn to engage in such activities.

One of the forerunners of the interactionist approach was the German sociologist Georg Simmel (1976), who studied the effects of urbanization on community life. He found the urban lifestyle to be relentless and alienating, with inhabitants limiting their contact with others in order to cope with the excessive stimulation that city life offered. As a result, the fragmentation of urban life leads to a decrease in shared experience. It is within such a framework of distinct, isolated, and isolating experiences that urban people must work out their social lives together.

Labelling theory, a social theory originating in the symbolic interactionist tradition, rests on the premise that a given activity is viewed as a social problem if groups of people define it as such. In this sense, labelling theory is a close cousin of the social constructionist viewpoint discussed earlier. Howard Becker (1963), for example, proposed that moral entrepreneurs are people who can translate their beliefs into social rules and norms. Anyone who violates these rules—for example, by smoking marijuana—is labelled "deviant" and his or her actions are defined as social problems. The act of smoking marijuana thus becomes a social problem only because moral entrepreneurs have made it one.

Consistent with the basic premise of labelling theory, Herbert Blumer (1971) proposed that social problems develop in stages. The first stage is *social recognition*, the point at which a given behaviour—say, recreational amphetamine use—is first identified as a social concern. Second, *social legitimating* takes place when society and its various institutional elements formally recognize the activity as a serious threat to social stability. With drug use, this stage might occur when schoolyard amphetamine use makes news headlines or when public officials discover a connection between amphetamine use and the failure to do homework. The third stage is termed *mobilization for action*, marking the point at which various social organizations begin planning strategies for remedial action. The final stage is the *development and implementation of an official plan*, such as a government-sanctioned "war on drugs."

Critics of the symbolic interactionist perspective propose that social problems may exist even when they are not recognized as problems. Date rape and wife battering, for example, were not considered social problems a few decades ago, but they still hurt their victims, regardless of an absence of public attention and labelling. On the other side, certain kinds of drug use—considered a problem by many parents today—may not be considered a problem when and if such drug use is decriminalized.

Feminist Theory

There are several varieties of feminist thinking—liberal feminism, socialist feminism, radical feminism, eco-feminism, and others. Here, though, it is important to note one important

Symbolic interactionism
A theoretical paradigm that studies the process by which people interpret and respond to the actions of others and that conceives of society as the product of this continuous face-to-face interaction; a microsociological approach that focuses on people and small groups.

© Aurora Photos/Alamy

Homeless teen mom Jaclyn Rivera and her child "shop" in a used donated clothing bank. Socio-economic and ideological factors play an important role in determining whether or not motherhood will have a negative impact on a woman's future.

thing they all have in common: all forms of feminism focus on gender inequality—that is, on relations of dominance and subordination between men and women.

Feminists are especially interested in how gender inequality makes women's lives different from men's. They note that women often act out a role that men have defined, one that shapes their most important social activities at home, at work, and in the public domain. This fact also forces women to acquiesce in their own domination and to risk exclusion and even violence. Thus, acceptance of the female role is far more costly—and even dangerous—to women than is men's acceptance of the male role.

The first wave of the feminist movement occurred between the mid-nineteenth century and the early twentieth, culminating in women's gaining the right to vote in many Western countries. In the last few decades, the focus of feminist scholarship has shifted, coming to stress the diversity of women's experience as members of different nations, classes, and racial and ethnic groups.

A common theme across the many types of feminism is the view the subordination of women is not a result of **biological determinism**—the idea that men's and women's biological differences justify their separate social roles and responsibilities—but of socio-economic and ideological factors. Feminists differ in thinking about how they might achieve change, but they are all committed to erasing women's continued social inequality. As well, they tend to agree that

- all personal life has a political dimension;
- both the public and private spheres of life are *gendered* (i.e., unequal for men and women);

Biological determinism An attempt to interpret all human and social behaviour from a biological perspective; based on the assumption that human behaviour is controlled by a person's genes.

- women's social experience routinely differs from men's;
- **patriarchy**—or male control—structures the way most societies work; and
- because of routinely different experiences and differences in power, women and men view the world differently.

Patriarchy A form of social organization in which fathers—or more generally, the oldest males, or more generally still, men—are the heads and rulers of the household, community, and society. In common sociological use, it means domination of women and children by adult males.

So, for example, men and women typically have different views about divorce, since they each experience divorce differently. For men, divorce means a brief drop in their standard of living, if any decline at all, and quite possibly a huge drop in parenting responsibilities. For women, it means a dramatic, long-term loss in income and a likely increase in parental responsibilities, since mothers generally keep custody of their children.

Three other features tend to characterize all feminist research. First, feminists pay the greatest attention to *the gendering of experiences*—the idea that certain experiences are specifically female or male and cannot be automatically generalized to both sexes. A second common concern is *the problem of victimization,* since women are often made the victims of crime, abuse, and discrimination. Similarly, feminists are often interested in the experiences of other victimized groups, like racial minorities, the poor, and people of alternative sexual orientations. Following from this, feminists are especially interested in *intersectionality*—the interaction of gender with other victimizing social characteristics, such as class and race, to produce particular combinations of disadvantage (e.g., the particular problems of unemployed black men, disabled lesbians, or Muslim immigrant women).

Population Health Perspective

Given the historical variation in views about social problems, it would be useful to find objective criteria that settle what is and what is not a social problem, for social policy purposes.

To this end, some social scientists have focused on the link between social problems and harmful health outcomes. From their research has emerged the *population health perspective*, a broad approach to health with goals of improving the health of the entire population and reducing health inequalities between social groups (Raphael, 2004). According to *The Chief Public Health Officer's Report on the State of Public Health in Canada* (Butler-Jones, 2009), "determinants of health" include income and social factors, social support networks, education, employment, working and living conditions, physical environments, social environments, biology and genes, health practices, stress, coping skills, quality of life, childhood development, health services, gender, and culture, among other factors. Further, these determinants interact and overlap with one another in a complex web that describes overall health.

As we will see in on the chapter on health and health care, some researchers also have suggested changing the notion of "disease" to recognize invariant biological, environmental, and socio-economic factors. If this were done, social gradients in health status would be "independent of diagnostic categories of illness, tending to persist across shifts in disease pattern and in hazardous exposures over time, and across societies" (Frank, 1995: 162). Then, we would know a social problem by the sickness and death it causes, whether people choose to acknowledge this harm or not. This would give us an even more powerful understanding of the most significant social problems and the urgency of their solution.

Solutions to Social Problems

C. Wright Mills, in his classic work *The Sociological Imagination* (1959), claimed "knowledge can be power"—if people choose to act on it. Sometimes, individual solutions are good enough for the problems we face. When we know what is going on in society and then act carefully with an eye to the relevant evidence, we stand a chance of solving these problems in our own interest. Using these individual-level solutions, we can act to "work the system" to our own benefit, even if no one else benefits.

However, throughout this book, we will stress the importance and value of collective solutions. These are solutions sought through the political process—whether by social movements and opinion-makers or by legislators—and that benefit a wide variety of people. Collective solutions are more likely than individual solutions to solve the problem in question and, moreover, to achieve something like consensus and consent among members of society around the nature of the problem and its solution.

In this book, we discuss a wide variety of different social problems, and accordingly, we discuss a wide variety of different solutions. It is never the case that "one size fits all." That said, we can make some general observations about solutions to social problems. A good place to start is by referring to Robert Boguslaw, whose classic work, *The New Utopians*, discusses three main ways of thinking about "new" societies or, more generally, about social reform.

In *The New Utopians*, Robert Boguslaw (1961) notes that Utopian visionaries have tended to imagine three different kinds of social engineering and control.

The first vision details desired goals or *outcomes* of the visionary project: for example, it may specify that, in the ideal society, the means of production will be owned by the state and everyone will have roughly equal wealth and power.

The second vision details particular means or *heuristics* on the assumption that desired outcomes will follow from these. So, for example, the liberal democratic society assumes that certain organizational principles—the rule of law, a market economy, and an open discussion of ideas—will give rise to the best possible society, although the precise features of that ideal society are unknown.

Finally, the third vision of social engineering specifies neither the means nor the ends of the project, but rather the creation of ideal people: a modern man, a good Christian, an ideal communist citizen, and so on. It imagines the features that will characterize this ideal person but not necessarily how that person will behave.

Each of these three strategies has its strengths and weaknesses, and all can be used in combination. Also, note that Boguslaw's analysis focuses on top-down social control and doesn't imagine, with equal force, solutions to problems that start at the bottom and move upwards through, for example, social movements or revolutions. This approach helps us to recognize that people approach social problems and their solutions in different ways.

Many people will focus on a desired outcome and go to extreme lengths to achieve that outcome, whatever the personal and social costs. In the process, they often make society worse and even their own and their families' lives worse. Other people will focus on what they, their community, or their society consider to be the proper way of approaching and solving problems. Typically, they will do this by conforming to the dominant social rules, possibly in conjunction with other, similarly motivated people. Sadly, such efforts often fail to achieve the desired goal thanks to the gap between popular ends and socially acceptable means in the society—a problem we will discuss in a later chapter in connection with Robert Merton's famous theory of "adaptations to anomie."

Other people still will consult self-help books, especially books about how they can transform themselves into the kind of people who are successful, healthy, happy, or otherwise considered admirable in our society. "Solutions" to problems such as these are rarely evaluated, but we do know that attempts to achieve personal perfection often fail dismally; it's well-known, for example, that dietary or smoking-cessation programs fail more often than they succeed. Also, it is by no means obvious that a society of "perfect people" would constitute a "perfect society." Consider the old adage about "too many cooks spoiling the broth."

So, what we should remember in the chapters that follow is that people take a variety of different approaches to solving their own and society's problems. They succeed or fail to different degrees, depending on the society and the moment in history; and likely, all solutions have been tried to varying extents in different societies. What Calabresi (1981) has called "tragic choices" alert us to the fact that no solution works all the time and, in fact, no solution is perfectly workable. All gains entail losses, all choices involve choices foregone. Every solution works imperfectly, and after a while, every solution leads to discontent and to demands for a new solution. On the other hand, the only solutions that are perfect failures are solutions left untried.

People acting together in groups and organizations *make history*. The chapters that follow will show this many times over for different areas, particularly around social policy changes. Consider, for example, the research and political action that have changed our understanding of and control over domestic violence. Political action through groups and organizations can be a long, slow road, and many journeys are unsuccessful. Dominant groups tend to oppose solutions to certain social problems that are not in their short-term interests. However, as citizens and human beings, we owe it to ourselves to make an effort nonetheless.

In short, this book will provide an incomplete overview of social problems in Canada today and, equally, an incomplete overview of solutions that people have considered or tried, here or elsewhere. Students interested in thinking about these issues in greater depth will find satisfaction in other, higher-level courses and more detailed book-length discussions of social problems.

Chapter Summary

The goal of sociology today, just as it was two centuries ago when the discipline began, is to use knowledge to improve social life. Sociologists are concerned about all the social problems that harm people—especially those that do major harm to our health and quality of life. Often, the government and other powerful agencies do too little to address these problems. So, one job of sociology is to issue a wake-up call.

Our goal in this book is to provide an understanding of the roots of social problems, their health outcomes for individuals and society as a whole, and how these can be addressed. For this task, it is important to explore the ways problems develop and are preserved, and how they are interrelated. After all, this bridge between private troubles and public issues is at the heart of sociological study.

As we will see, the individual social institutions—families, the economy, government, education, and others—each contribute to the larger functioning of society. Sometimes, the cause of social problems is a failure of institutions to fulfill their roles during times of rapid change, as functionalists suggest. As well, social inequalities are the key to understanding many social problems. So, we have organized this book around this insight. Its central section is concerned with identifying important social inequalities of class, race, gender, and so on and their social effects, while the section that follows is organized around a variety of social institutions.

The controversial search for explanations and solutions makes the study of social problems fascinating to newcomers and professional sociologists alike. We think the world will look different—and a lot more challenging—after you have read through this book.

Questions for Critical Thought

1. If there are so many different sociological views about any particular social problem—so many approaches, so many theories—and some people may not even view an issue as a "problem," why do we spend so much time and money studying the problem and trying (often unsuccessfully) to fix it?
2. What difficulties do we face trying to measure the true extent of a social problem and its human outcomes? Will we ever be able to overcome these difficulties? In answering, focus on one particular problem of interest: for example, poverty, sexism, or drug addiction.
3. What factors affect the "claims-making process" and its effectiveness? For example, how effective would you be if you tried publicly to promote the idea that Canadian colleges and universities deaden students' minds rather than stimulate them? What strategies might you use to increase the effectiveness of post-secondary education?
4. What social factors influence people's willingness to line up for tickets or buses, and are they the same factors that influence people's civility more generally (e.g., their politeness, etiquette, and table manners)?
5. If the manifest function of this social problems course (and this textbook) is to teach you about social problems, what is its latent function and how can you tell if this latent function is being achieved?
6. Why are so many people unwilling to join groups to protest against inequality or to remedy the social problems discussed in this book?

Recommended Readings

Collins, Randall. 2008. *Violence: A Micro-Sociological Theory*. Princeton, NJ: Princeton University Press.

Kadison, Richard, and Theresa Foy Digeronimo. 2004. *College of the Overwhelmed: The Campus Mental Health Crisis and What to Do about It*. San Francisco: Jossey-Bass.

Laub, John H., and Robert Sampson. 2003. *Shared Beginnings, Divergent Lives: Delinquent Boys to Age 70*. Cambridge, MA: Harvard University Press.

McKnight, David. 2002. *From Hunting to Drinking: The Devastating Effects of Alcohol on an Australian Aboriginal Community*. London and New York: Routledge.

Rapping, Elayne. 2003. *Law and Justice as Seen on TV*. New York: New York University Press.

Seidman, Steven. 2004. *Beyond the Closet: The Transformation of Gay and Lesbian Life*. New York: Routledge.

Part 2

Rubberball/Mike Kemp/Getty Images

2

Class, Poverty, and Economic Inequality

Paul-André © Belle-Isle/Thinkstock

Introduction

Economic inequality refers to income and wealth differences across individuals and groups, as well as the differences in the economic power of nations. The sociological approach on this is that poverty and inequality are important public issues (Morgan et al., 2006) with causes and consequences. Through the use of the "sociological imagination" we can begin to see how poverty and inequality relate to each other and to issues of ideology, governance, and power. Karl Marx provided this sociological imagination in developing the notion of "social class."

In the nineteenth century, Marx first introduced the notion of social class and its relation to poverty and inequality in his social, economic, and philosophical works. Marx stressed that people always organize around their relationship to the means of production. Some own it, and the others do not. Those who do will enjoy the greatest power. In a capitalist industrial society, those who own the capital and productive technology will control the available jobs. The rest—proletarians—will have to sell their time and labour power to capitalists to earn wages that allow them to survive. The capitalists, to maximize their profits, will pay the workers as little as possible and sell the product for as high a price as possible (Marx and Engels, 1955 [1848]).

"Classes," in sociological thinking, are groups of people who share a common economic condition, interest, or, as Marx described it, relationship to the means of production (i.e., to technology and capital). In Marx's logic there are two main classes: stated simply, *owners* and *workers*. This binary—have and have-not—is fundamental to all social relations, since these two classes are forever locked in conflict.

The relationship of people to the means of production is critical to this way of thinking. This dividing line separates those who must sell their work, their time, or their labour power to earn wages so they can survive from those who buy this work and gain profits from the goods and services that workers produce. The profit gained by the second group depends mainly on the price of the manufactured product minus the cost of labour. As a result, profit-making depends on keeping prices high and wages (and other costs of production) low. But high prices, low wages, and poor working conditions are not good for workers; so workers struggle—through unions, co-operatives, legislation, and other means—to improve their wages, working conditions, job security, and the prices they have to pay for food, shelter, and health care.

People with the same relationship to the means of production ought to have an interest in banding together—the workers to protect their wages and working conditions, the employers to protect their profit and control. But for this to happen, people in the same class must develop an awareness of their common interest, commit themselves to working together for common goals, and come to see their individual well-being as connected to the collective well-being of their class. Marx referred to this process as obtaining a "class for itself." Developing class awareness and class-consciousness is difficult. Many factors interfere with it.

This capitalist class system will have a long-range tendency to produce monopolies of wealth and ever-increasing inequality, globalization and imperialism, overproduction and recurrent financial crises. Those at the bottom will be impoverished, desperate, and willing to do almost anything to survive.

In this system, employers may take steps to prevent the formation of unions or to curtail discussions of workers' concerns. Legislators sympathetic to the interests of owners

Economic inequality
Large differences in income and wealth across individuals and groups within a society; differences in the economic power of nations.

may make laws that give employers more power or workers less power in the event of a conflict. The police or military may be used to break strikes. Workers themselves may be reluctant to share a common cause with people of different racial or ethnic groups. Or, the unions and workers' representatives may not agree on how best to promote workers' interests. The workers may suffer from what is sometimes called "false consciousness": an acceptance of the discourse and values of the dominant class and thus a willingness to believe arguments that promote individualistic solutions to problems. Workers may also be so alienated from politics and from one another that they cannot put their trust in the collective enterprise of unionization and class conflict.

Thus, workplaces, where the classes meet, are "contested terrains," in the words of economist Richard Edwards (1979). Here workers and bosses struggle for control, devising first one strategy and then another to overcome opposition. Of course, this sounds mechanical—almost automatic. Yet it is far from automatic. Marx didn't think inequality was inevitable—that's why he tried to promote a revolutionary overthrow of capitalism and the formation of a communist (egalitarian) society. However, he realized, too, that the critical element was a development of class awareness and consciousness. Oppressed classes can bring about change only after they become aware of their position in relation to the ruling class and their historic role. So, in his correspondence with socialist leaders in various countries, Marx often discussed the practicalities of class formation: How should the working classes organize in reaction to exploitation? What kinds of revolutionary strategies will likely work, and what stands in the way of success?

This portrayal is far too simple by today's standards. Class structures across many industrialized nations have become increasingly complex. First, it is no longer necessary to own a business to control the means of production. Second, today the working class is international, a result of global ownership and economic competition. Third, now more than ever, working classes may form their economic and political identities around consumption patterns rather than around the means of production. This introduces an even greater difficulty into the mass mobilization of workers.

Some sociologists have argued that the inequalities in a modern, democratic society are chiefly based on agreement about the value of different jobs and social roles. The "functional theory of stratification" credited to Kingsley Davis and Wilbert Moore (1945) maintains that most people in most industrial societies agree about the relative social value of particular roles. They agree, for example, that a doctor, judge, or scientist is worth more to society than, say, an unskilled labourer, door-to-door salesman, or store clerk. Therefore, people are willing to see the first group receive higher salaries (also more respect and authority) than the second group. As a society, we can replace store clerks more easily than we can replace doctors, so we agree to reward the doctors more to ensure a continuing flow of recruits into medical training.

Some research supports this argument. It has shown that popular ratings of different occupations—their prestige and social value—tend to be stable over time and vary little from one industrial society to another. (That said, non-industrial societies with different value systems that put a high premium, for example, on warfare or religion will rank jobs differently.) This means that inequalities of wealth, authority, and respect are to some degree based on shared values.

However, this functional theory fails to consider several facts. First, it cannot explain why the difference between top-paid and bottom-paid workers is wide or narrow—why, for example, the range of salaries in major American manufacturing companies was roughly tenfold in 1980 but three-hundredfold in 2008. Nor does it explain why the range of salaries is much wider in one capitalist society, the United States, than it is in others, such as Germany, France, or Japan. Nor does such a theory of functional value address why some people get high salaries regardless of whether they confer a social benefit. Consider, for example, movie stars, sports stars, professional criminals, auto executives, and bank executives. In fact, sometimes the public knows little about the amount these people are paid or the reasons for this payment.

All we can say for certain is that not all inequality in Canada or the US is due to exploitation in the form that Marx imagined. Some of it is a result of unregulated market forces, such as inadequate laws governing the financial services industry. Some is a result of the tax structure, which enables more or less wealth to be redistributed from poor to rich or rich to poor. In turn, this redistribution is a result of the connection between the state and the ruling class, and the extent to which rich, powerful people can rely on elected politicians to serve their interests.

Marx recognized that, in general, all classes rest on inequality and that all inequality rests on social differentiation. However, not all differentiation leads to inequality, and inequality doesn't necessarily result in class formation. For revolutionary purposes, class formation requires the growth of class consciousness, which in turn demands four important changes in the thinking of workers: (1) identifying themselves as members of an exploited class; (2) seeing that the owners of the means of production are their enemy; (3) realizing that everything is at stake in the battle for equality; and (4) recognizing that societal change is possible through conflict.

As John Porter showed in *The Vertical Mosaic* (1965), there is some opportunity for people to cross class lines at the highest occupational levels. People from humble backgrounds—having performed well at university and risen through the organizational ranks into positions of ever-increasing authority—may acquire the opportunity to work and socialize with people who have inherited their wealth and power. The professions of engineering, management, accounting, medicine, and law are especially good ladders of upward mobility. And at the elite levels of society, people in the highest union positions, political positions, and civil service positions are sometimes able to work and socialize with people in the highest economic positions of society; again, this can happen regardless of their class of origin.

Social mobility in capitalist societies has its limits. There is little chance of entering the "upper class"—say, the top 1 per cent of income earners or wealth-holders—from below. Similarly, there is little chance of escaping the "poorest class," say the bottom 1 per cent. There is more opportunity to enter the top income decile (i.e., the top 10 per cent) and more opportunity to escape the bottom income decile, though such movements are still rare.

Social mobility The movement of people from one social class to another during the course of their lifetime.

Social mobility also varies significantly by country. A classical thesis by Lipset and Zetterberg (1959) observed that mobility rates were much the same across all industrialized societies. More recent work, however, lends little support for this premise (Breen and Jonsson, 2007).

Social mobility is greatest in societies where the opportunity structure is open and when barriers and advantages associated with people's backgrounds are few. In this regard, research has demonstrated that economic factors affect rates of mobility. While explanations tend to be mixed, they often rest on the notion that there is a positive relationship between mobility and educational expansion, income inequality, and economic success. **Intergenerational income elasticity** refers to the correlation between a parent's and a child's income. In other words, the higher the intergenerational elasticity, the less likely it is for people to become socially mobile within a society. As this figure shows, Canada (0.19), Finland (0.18), Norway (0.17), and Denmark (0.15) had the highest rates of social mobility in 2006. Near identical patterns are also shown today (Corak, 2013). This is concerning when we consider that economic prosperity has been steadily rising in each country. This implies that the benefits of economic growth are seldom distributed equally across the class structure (Andersen and Curtis 2012; Curtis, 2013).

In the middle of the income distribution, among the middle 80 per cent of all income earners, there is plenty of intergenerational mobility, both upward and downward, in income and occupational prestige. What makes this movement possible is higher education. In our society, educational credentials are the key to social mobility.

People who are more socially mobile are more likely to gain opportunities to interact with people of higher social classes. In fact, educated people are also more likely to interact with people of *lower* social classes. Research shows that people with more education have larger, more diverse social networks. They know more people by name and can link indirectly with a larger number of people through networks of friendship and acquaintance. This is partly through their exposure to many people in institutions of higher education and to many people in their professional and managerial work.

Measuring Poverty

Sociologists agree that people who live in poverty have much less than the average standard of living (Defina and Thanawala, 2009). However, we can view poverty in two ways: as absolute and as relative. People who live in **absolute poverty** do not have enough of the basic requirements—food, shelter, and access to essential health care, for example—for physical survival. By contrast, people who live in **relative poverty** can survive, but their living standards are far below the general living standards of the society or social group to which they belong (Sarlo, 2007).

Researchers disagree about how to measure poverty. Although you may think that it is easy to decide whether a lifestyle qualifies as "poor," in practice, deciding what makes up poverty is difficult. Cross-national evidence from the United States, Great Britain, Canada, and Australia shows that the **poverty line** is elastic, responding both to changes in real income and to the success of advocates fighting to increase social welfare by redefining or remeasuring poverty (Fisher, 1998).

Until recently, Statistics Canada, the primary data-gathering agency for all of Canada, has relied on two different measurement strategies when compiling statistical data on poverty: LICOs and LIMs. The first method, **low-income cut-offs (LICOs)**, is based on the percentage of income devoted to daily necessities such as food, shelter, and clothing. Although some consider LICOs to be equivalent to poverty lines, Statistics Canada stresses that they are not. Low-income cut-offs are income thresholds, determined by analyzing family expenditure data, below which families will devote a larger share (approximately 20 per cent more) of income to the necessities of food, shelter, and clothing than the average family would (Statistics Canada, 2012a). To take into account differences in the costs of necessities among different community and family sizes, LICOs are defined for five categories of community size and seven of family size (Sarlo, 2006). These cut-offs

---

Intergenerational income elasticity The correlation between a parent's and a child's income.

THE WOLF OF WALL STREET
This 2013 film tells the true story of Jordan Belfort, whose career as a wealthy stockbroker ends in crime, corruption, and imprisonment.

Absolute poverty Lack of the basic necessities (food, shelter, medicine) for survival. Starvation is an example of absolute poverty.

Relative poverty Survival, but far below the general living standards of the society or social group in which they live; affects people's lives in dramatic ways.

Poverty line It represents a usual standard of living and differs across countries. The definition of poverty varies by society, within societies, and also over time.

Low-income cut-offs (LICOs) A formal definition used by Statistics Canada for measuring relative poverty on the basis of the percentage of income devoted to daily necessities (food, shelter, clothing) and determined both regionally and by population (size of city or rural).

vary with the size of the family and the size of the community of residence because of geographic differences in the cost of living for families of different sizes. Thus, LICOs are higher in a large city than in a rural area and higher for a large family than for a small one. In a community with a population of 500,000 or more, if "the average family" of four spends 35 per cent of its income on food, shelter, and clothing, then any four-person household that spends 55 per cent or more of its income on these necessities is considered "low-income" (Diekmeyer, 2001).

The second method used by Statistics Canada (2012b) is the **low-income measures** **(LIMs)**—a set of figures representing 50 per cent of the median "adjusted family income," which is based on a consideration of the varying needs of families of differing sizes. Each family's actual income is compared with the corresponding LIM for its particular family size; those that fall below are considered "low-income." LIMs are strictly relative measures of low income, set at 50 per cent of adjusted median family income. These measures are categorized according to the number of adults and children present in families, reflecting the economies of scale inherent in family size and composition (Kirkpatrick and Tarasuk, 2003).

A third, alternative measure is the **market-basket measure (MBM)**, developed by the Federal/Provincial/Territorial Working Group on Social Development Research and Information. Its purpose is to define and measure poverty in absolute, non-relative terms. This working group proposed a preliminary MBM of poverty based on an imaginary basket of market-priced goods and services. This measure, then, is based on the income needed to purchase the items in the basket (Watson, 2003).

The MBM measure signals a change in our perceived obligations to the poor because it replaces a relative (or comparative) measure of poverty—the LICO—with an absolute market-basket measure. Human Resources and Development Canada (HRDC) officials were instructed by politicians to create a measure based on the cost of a specific basket of goods and services (Statistics Canada, 2013b). Implicit in the market-basket approach is the idea that our obligations to low-income people consist of a particular basket of essential goods, not a share of Canada's wealth. Critics have pointed out that what goes into the "basket" is not determined by those who must try to survive on it but by bureaucrats or right-leaning think-tanks, and some MBMs exclude such "necessities" as transportation and a minimal amount of expenditure on entertainment (CCSD, 2001).

Measuring Well-Being and Inequality

Poverty as measured by income in these ways is only a pale reflection of people's well-being. Other socio-economic variables also contribute to well-being. The United Nations Development Program (UNDP, 2005), for example, monitors social and economic progress through a broad measure known as the **Human Development Index (HDI)**. The HDI is a combined measure of achievement in three areas: a long and healthy life, as measured by life expectancy at birth; knowledge, as measured by adult and youth literacy; and standard of living, as measured by the natural logarithm of the gross domestic product (GDP) per capita.

However, even the HDI may not accurately reflect the extent of important differences among the world's most developed countries, which all score similarly high in the three dimensions of the index. So, for these nations, population well-being is measured by the second variant of the human poverty index (HPI-2). The HPI-2 assesses relative *deprivation* in these same dimensions: vulnerability to premature death, as measured by the

Low-income measures (LIMs) A set of figures representing 50 per cent of the median "adjusted family income." Actual incomes are compared with LIMs to determine whether or not a family can be considered "low-income."

Market-basket measure (MBM) A way of measuring income and poverty in absolute, non-relative terms that was added in 2003 to Statistics Canada's methods of measuring income and poverty. It is based on an imaginary basket of market-priced goods and services and on the income needed to purchase the items in the basket. The determination of what goes into this imaginary basket, however, is subjective and tends to exclude all but the absolute essentials of bare survival.

Human Development Index (HDI) A combined measure of achievement in three areas of human development—life expectancy at birth; literacy; and GDP per capita—used by the United Nations Development Program to monitor social and economic progress across countries.

likelihood at birth of not surviving to age 60; exclusion from reading and communications, as measured by adult illiteracy; a deprived standard of living, as measured by the percentage of the population living below the income poverty line; and social exclusion, as measured by the rate of long-term unemployment.

When this measure is used, Canada's ranking falls to eleventh in the world (though Canada is still above the OECD [Organisation for Economic Co-operation and Development] average). Although our country provides a high average standard of living, this standard of living is not equally distributed across all levels of society (UNDP, 2013). This suggests that social inequality—and relative poverty—may be at least as important for people's well-being as absolute poverty. We will see later that social inequality has a dramatic effect on people's physical (as well as mental) health, as demonstrated in the classic Whitehall studies, which investigated the social determinants of health among British male civil servants. This research provided early evidence of the relationship between education and mortality 9.

Therefore, we need systematic measures of social inequality as well as of poverty. A widely accepted measure of income inequality is the *Gini coefficient*, or *index*. A perfect score of 0 on this index reflects total income equality across a society, while a score of 1 reflects total income inequality. To illustrate this, imagine distributing $1,000 among 1,000 people. If every person received $1, the Gini index would be 0. If one person received $1,000 and the remaining 999 people received 0, the Gini index would be 1.

Income inequality increased in Canada over the past 20 years. During the 1980s, Canada's Gini index score was about 0.281. In the late 2000s, however, it had risen to about 0.32 (see Figure 2.1 below). This was far lower than the highest scores on record. To put it in context, the Gini index for the US according to the 2011 US census was 0.48. The Gini index for Sweden was only 0.23. In general, the highest Gini index scores—in the range of 0.5 to 0.6—were found in the least-developed nations of Africa and South America, and typically, the greatest poverty was found in continents and countries with

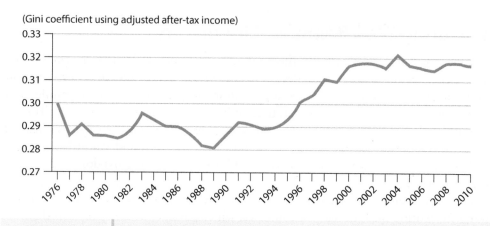

(Gini coefficient using adjusted after-tax income)

FIGURE 2.1   Income Inequality in Canada, 1976 to 2010

Source: <http://www.conferenceboard.ca/hcp/details/society/income-inequality.aspx.>

the greatest inequality. By contrast, the countries of North America, Europe, and the rest of the developed world were more affluent, more equal, and had fewer desperately poor people (Andersen and McIvor, 2013; see also McMullin, 2004).

As mentioned, the exact measurement of poverty is complicated and politically controversial. Errors can make a huge difference to needy people, taxpayers, and program administrators.

Poverty in Canada

The face of poverty and economic inequality in Canada has been described as "racialized, destitute, and young" (Curry-Stevens, 2004). In addition, poverty is on the rise in urban areas, in some cities more than others. Cities in Quebec tend to have the highest rates of poverty, while those in southern Ontario have the lowest.

Poverty is also more common among racial minorities, both non-white visible minority immigrants and Aboriginal communities. Racial minorities earn much less on average than their white counterparts and are also more likely to experience unemployment and underemployment (Reitz, 2007a). Recent immigrants who arrived in Canada within the past five years earn much less than their Canadian-born counterparts, often because they are unable to gain acceptance of their foreign credentials (degrees, diplomas, and training experiences). Over time, this gap between immigrants and native-born Canadians narrows, but not by much; and some groups never reach equity (Reitz, 2007b; Raza et al., 2013).

The disadvantaged social and economic status of Aboriginals in Canada is also well documented. For example, the median income for non-Aboriginals in 2005 was $33,394, while the average income for the total Aboriginal population across all groups was only $22,366. It was even more striking that the average earnings of First Nations Aboriginals were only $19,114 (Statistics Canada, 2006). At 1.5 per cent of Canada's urban population but 3.4 per cent of the urban poor, they are over-represented among the nation's impoverished urban populations. On reserves, the situation is equally bad, if not worse, with the average income of Aboriginals on reserves being approximately $17,000. A lack of employment opportunities combined with a sense of cultural isolation has resulted in economic, social, and health conditions that are in some instances as bad as those found in the least-developed countries of the world.

The immediate cause of Aboriginal poverty is joblessness. Two forms of joblessness are especially important. Unemployment can be understood as out of work but seeking employment. Many other Canadians, however, are out of work but are *not* seeking employment, often because no opportunities exist. In 2013, the unemployment rates among Aboriginals was higher than the national average of 7.0 (Statistics Canada, 2013a). Within some communities, moreover, unemployment rates remain significantly higher. Not surprisingly, rates of unemployment in Aboriginal communities are significantly higher than for the rest of the Canadian population because many of these communities are in remote areas with few job opportunities. This employment and income disparity likely explains the higher incidence of substance abuse, imprisonment, and diseases such as diabetes, as well as early mortality among Aboriginal peoples (Currie et al.,2011).

Poverty is in many ways self-perpetuating. Structural mechanisms ensure that the poorest Canadians remain poor. The poorest of the poor lose proportionally the most

INSIDE JOB

This 2010 Oscar-winning documentary explores the root causes of the 2008 financial crisis, looking at the corruption within the American financial system that led to the crisis, as well as its devastating effects on the global economy.

Robert Bonner hangs a sign on a mock Olympic torch while preparing for a demonstration near the 2010 Winter Olympics countdown clock in Vancouver, BC. Social awareness groups held a Poverty Olympics event and torch relay alongside the Olympic Games in 2010 to bring awareness to poverty and homelessness in Vancouver.

during economic recessions and gain the least during times of prosperity. Curry-Stevens (2004) estimates that upward of 90 per cent of the total income of the poorest tenth of the Canadian population comes from Employment Insurance, welfare, and other government transfers, which are usually among the first social programs to see reductions in benefits during economic slowdowns.

However, chronic, continuing (absolute) poverty is a minority experience in Canada. In fact, large numbers of Canadians move in and out of poverty. Poverty is a widespread, common experience for many, but unrelenting poverty is rare in Canada. This gives us two reasons to view it as a social problem: for the few who are chronically, desperately poor, only a change in social policies can save them. On the other hand, the many who at some point have experienced poverty will readily see the merit in fixing a system that is so patently unjust.

Poverty as an Urban Problem

The incidence of urban poverty in Canada is rising. One of the most serious problems associated with urban poverty is the lack of affordable housing for low-income families and individuals. Economists argue that, as a rule, housing is "affordable" if either the monthly rent or mortgage payments consume no more than one-third of household income.

Currently, affordable housing is scarce in many major Canadian cities. There are several reasons for this scarcity. First, the ownership of rental housing is being concentrated in the hands of a few property owners. Second, developers stand to make larger profits by investing in housing solely for the middle and upper classes. As a result, upscale homes are abundant for people who can afford them, while low-income housing remains scarce (Wratten, 2010).

When affordable housing is available, it is often found in city neighbourhoods that are economically stagnant and physically decayed. In these areas, rates of crime, violence, and drug use are typically higher than anywhere else in the city. People who are unable to afford even the most modest housing increasingly come to rely on urban shelters for places to sleep at night. Although "the poor" are often stereotyped as shiftless and unattached, two-parent families with children are the most rapidly increasing category of shelter-using poor (Reese, 2009). Still, as desperate and humbling as reliance on shelters may be for poor people, the alternative—homelessness—is even worse.

The Homeless

Connected with the shortage of affordable housing in cities is homelessness, one of Canada's most pressing social problems. Most low-income families are renters, not homeowners. Thus, when rent prices increase or owners change rental units into owner-occupied condominiums, many families are forced onto the streets and into shelters, while others must live in crowded conditions with parents, other relatives, or friends (Davis, 2008).

The exact number of homeless people in Canada is unknown, but some have tried to estimate the size of the problem. Trypuc and Robinson (2009) estimate that Canada's homeless population is 157,000 people. A study published in 2007 reports that

> Canada's homeless population is somewhere between 200,000 and 300,000 people, while another 1.7 million residents struggle with "housing affordability issues." . . . In a report . . . from the Calgary-based Sheldon Chumir Foundation for Ethics in Leadership, journalist and author Gordon Laird argues homelessness is now chronic and is quickly becoming one of the country's defining social issues. He makes a case for a national housing strategy and a more robust income security program. Citing statistics from a wide range of organizations, Laird says poverty is the leading cause of homelessness in Canada, not substance abuse or mental illness. "Roughly half of all Canadians live in fear of poverty, and 49 per cent polled believe they might be poverty stricken if they missed one or two paycheques," he writes. (CBC News, 2007)

A 2011 study of homelessness in Toronto, commissioned by the Wellesley Institute (2011), an organization concerned with urban health problems in relation to social vulnerability, noted that "about 1.5 million of Canada's households are in 'core housing need.'"

In response, the Canadian government has strengthened its focus on providing the homeless with shelter beds. As of March 2011, there were 1,086 shelters serving the homeless, with approximately 28,495 available beds. Given the overall homeless

BOYZ N THE HOOD

John Singleton's 1991 debut is a penetrating look at teenagers' lives in the desperately poor and violent South Central region of Los Angeles.

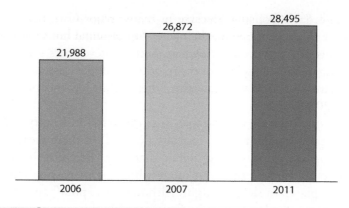

| | FIGURE 2.2 | Regularly Available Shelter Beds, Canada, 2006, 2007, and 2011 (number of beds) |

Source: For 2006 and 2007, Canada, Homeless Partnership Secretariat, *Homeless Individuals and Families Information System (HIFIS) Initiative 2006–07 Annual Report* (Ottawa: Human Resources and Skills Development Canada, 2007). For 2011, Homelessness Partnership Secretariat, *2011 Shelter Capacity Report* (Ottawa: Human Resources and Skills Development Canada, 2012).

population in Canada, these services are only marginally solving our homelessness problem. As Figure 2.2 shows, the number of available shelter beds has steadily increased since 2006.

The homeless are a varied mix of single men and women, young people, families, and individuals with serious health problems (such as HIV/AIDS). Many are able-bodied, free from substance or alcohol abuse, and willing to work. Some even have jobs but lack enough income to pay the rent on the cheapest city apartment. Nonetheless, life on the street can be dangerous and unhealthy, with Canada's homeless population having a life expectancy of only 39 years—about half the national average (Robinson and Trypuc, 2009).

In large cities, many of the homeless are young people who have run away from home. Most street youth are from families suffering serious emotional, mental, or substance abuse problems. These youth are not necessarily on the street because of socioeconomic pressures, though family financial difficulties increase the chance of physical abuse (Aratani, 2009). Research shows that runaways overlap, in experience and background, with a variety of other social types.

Repeatedly, research has shown that families of runaways tend to give their children less support, supervision, and acceptance than other families. Evidence also suggests that the parents of runaways themselves had a history of running away from home when they were children. Runaways run a heightened risk of suicide attempts: in one study (ibid.), 30 per cent of runaways report having tried suicide in the past. Suicide attempts by runaway youth are most commonly a result of trouble at home—arguments, disappointments, and humiliations—trouble at school, assault, and sexual abuse.

Thus, a principal reason that runaways remain on the street, refusing to return home or try foster care, is their stated belief that family conflict is inevitable. Runaways develop their own substitute families on the street, among other street people, rather than risk further rejection or abuse. Many chronic runaways grow up to be homeless adults. As a result, homeless adults with higher than average rates of criminal behaviour, substance abuse, and other forms of deviant behaviour tend to report more abusive and deprived childhoods (*The Nation*, 2009).

The Government's Role in Reducing Poverty

Governments play an important role in reducing levels of income inequality. Countries whose populations are more financially equal typically have strong welfare programs—a social system in which the government undertakes the responsibility of providing social and economic security to its citizens. This is generally done through taxation and certain types of social programs, which include pensions, health care, employment insurance, child care, and various educational programs and subsidies. Canada is considered to be a liberal social welfare regime, one that is characterized by very limited social spending (Esping-Andersen, 1990; Myles, 1998). Both Canada and the United States are liberal regimes, but the two countries have many differences in how their governments redistribute wealth and how their social services are provided—Canada's universal health-care system being the most notable example.

Canada's public spending efforts are much less extensive than those of most European countries. In recent decades, the size and scope of Canada's spending efforts have declined dramatically. This shift in policy helps to explain why income inequality in Canada has been on the rise (Obinger et al., 2005).

The Canadian Press/Sean Kilpatrick

In this photo, Employment Minister Jason Kenney announces that a deal on the Canada Job Grant has been reached with all provinces except Quebec. The Canada Job Grant is designed to provide grants for skilled workers seeking training in order to qualify for an existing or better job. Despite this kind of government-funded education support, Canadian income inequality is still on the rise.

BOX 2.1   **Marx and Engels, *The Communist Manifesto* (1848)**

Karl Marx was born in 1818 to well-off parents in Prussia. He studied at Bonn and in Berlin, where he was involved first with the Young Hegelians and later discovered the writings of Feuerbach. In 1843 he married Jenny von Westphalen and moved to Paris shortly thereafter, where he met Friedrich Engels. They both joined the Communist League and agreed to write the "Manifesto of the Communist Party" after the League decided in 1848 to put its ideas into writing. This sparked a short revolutionary burst across Europe, which was ultimately unsuccessful, and both Marx and Engels moved to London. Marx's views continued to get him both admiration and persecution for the remainder of his life, especially following the Paris Commune in 1870. Though Marx was influential in communist movements, he was rarely a direct leader and stayed away from large gatherings and even debate with other academics.

Friedrich Engels, born in 1820, was the son of a factory owner in Barmen (Prussia). He was well educated and harboured a secret passion for revolutionary thought, kept hidden from the more moderate views of his parents. In 1842 he was converted to communism, mainly through the efforts of Moses Hess. This new ideology led him to live parts of his life with working families so he would be able to understand their conditions. He published his experiences in the 1845 book *The Condition of the Working Class in England*. The unity of their views soon brought Marx and Engels together in a lifelong companionship, and they jointly published *The German Ideology* in 1845 and *The Communist Manifesto* in 1848.

In *The Communist Manifesto*, Marx and Engels proclaim the inevitable collapse of the capitalist system of production and consequently the end to social inequality and social strife.

The *Manifesto* is divided into four parts, the first of which is the most theoretically interesting. In it, they show how the capitalist system of production continually splits society into two opposing classes: the bourgeoisie and the proletariat. "By bourgeoisie is meant the class of modern capitalists, owners of the means of social production and employers of wage labour. By proletariat, the class of modern wage labourers who, having no means of production of their own, are reduced to selling their labour power in order to live" (Marx and Engels, 1955 [1848]: 3). This antagonism will result in the downfall of the bourgeoisie and the end of all class conflict. There are several stages to this argument.

Though the history of the world has always been a struggle between the oppressed and their oppressors, the relationship between bourgeoisie and proletariat is markedly different and is the last of such struggles, for three main reasons. First, whereas previous ruling classes needed to conserve the existing modes of production to stay in power, the bourgeoisie "cannot exist without constantly innovating the instruments of production, and thereby the relations of production, and with them the whole relations of society." The owners of the means of production do this by expanding across the globe and exploiting existing areas more thoroughly. The two tactics either polarize class division in new areas or increasingly polarize the division in already

Theoretical Perspectives on Poverty

Structural Functionalism

The sociological perspective or approach called "structural functionalism" argues that society consists of a connected network of groups, organizations, and institutions that work together to maintain the survival of that society. In the eyes of a structural functionalist, everything in a society has a purpose or function that, when fulfilled, allows society to continue, or "survive," in its present form, largely resisting change.

The structural-functionalist perspective, therefore, argues that poverty and inequality may serve important functions in society. For example, poverty (or the threat of poverty) motivates people to work harder to move up the ladder. Jobs at the top of this ladder need much more investment in education and effort, but they also carry greater industrialized areas, which inevitably is a self-defeating tactic. The rich will exploit the poor to a greater degree, and so, too, will rich nations exploit poor nations. The entire world becomes similar and of a piece, with regard to both material production and intellectual production.

Second, in capitalist production, the worker increasingly becomes mechanised and all individual character of work is lost; thus, the cost of work is restricted only to that which ensures the worker's continued existence. The more monotonous the work, the lower the wage, and everything related to the production process moves in this direction in order to continue the existence of the bourgeoisie. Previous production regimes, such as feudalism, rationalized exploitation with religious or other reasons, but the bourgeoisie have no obvious sources of justification for their quest for individual profit, so their increasing exploitation cannot help but affront the worker. Individual profit and individual property are therefore the key to the proletariat revolution. When the worker owns nothing, when all private property is in the hands of the bourgeoisie, when workers no longer compete, the worker has nothing to lose and can see that private property is just bourgeoisie property.

Third, for these reasons, only abolishing private property will end class conflict. The proletariat have no property to secure. Its abolishment, in and of itself, will end oppression and class divisions. Marx and Engels prominently declare this the end of history.

The second part of the *Manifesto* makes the communist program explicit and addresses many of the critiques raised against it. Ultimately, the Communist Party wishes the defeat of the bourgeois class by the proletariat, which is accomplished through the abolition of private property (Marx and Engels, 1955 [1848]: 14).

The Communist Manifesto is generally critiqued and praised on two major points: its materialist conception of history—whereby history is seen as being driven by material (in this case economic) forces—and its prophetic ability. The materialist conception of history is both revolutionizing and hotly contested. This materialistic interpretation of history and society has been, if not disproved, consistently challenged by historians and sociologists, starting first with Max Weber.

One of the most obvious prophecies is the inevitability of the revolution owing to the polarization of the populace into a working class and a bourgeoisie of dwindling size. This did not happen with any lasting success in the Western world. Although there is currently some evidence of the middle class being "hollowed out," for the most part, beyond the early and dirty years of industrial capitalism, a large middle-income class with more skilled jobs was created to a greater extent than the ever more mechanized work that Marx and Engels foresaw for the proletariat. Marx and Engels, however, were correct in their prediction of globalization and the homogenization it entails, as well as in their prediction of the accompanying exploitation of poor countries by rich countries. They also predicted the cyclical crises of capitalism, but not the Keynesian regulating state that resulted from these.

rewards. This motivates people to stay in school, get more education, and work harder for longer to get the top rewards (Mooney et al., 2001). Thus, inequality promotes economic growth.

Conflict Theory

The conflict theory of poverty and inequality relies heavily on ideas first developed by Karl Marx and Max Weber. As we saw earlier, according to Marxist theory, the bourgeoisie or capitalists own the means of production. As owners of the factories and other business establishments, the bourgeoisie can set the terms of employment for the other, less powerful class of society, the proletariat. This latter group, lacking the means to produce and sell goods on their own, must resort to selling the only commodity they possess: their labour power (Marx and Engels, 1955 [1848]).

TABLE 2.1	Theoretical Perspectives
THEORY	**MAIN POINTS**
Structural Functionalism	• Inequality and poverty serve important functions in society. • Poverty motivates people to work harder to improve their life conditions. • Those who invest the most time and effort receive the best-paying jobs and working conditions (e.g., physicians). • Such a view is most applicable in situations where effort corresponds with rewards.
Conflict Theory	• A structural power imbalance exists between capitalists and employees. • Employees depend on wages for survival and are therefore vulnerable to exploitation. • By exploiting workers through poor working conditions and poor pay, owners amass more wealth for themselves.
Symbolic Interactionism	• This approach focuses on the labels attributed to the "wealthy" and the "poor." • Labels attached to the poor, such as "lazy," are often unjustified stereotypes. • However, widespread subscription to these stereotypes makes them real in their consequences.

The bourgeoisie, recognizing the proletariat's dependence on the wages earned from work, exploit the labour of the working class as a means to gaining wealth for themselves. They keep wages low to ensure that their workers remain dependent on them for economic survival. By manipulating the schools and mass media, they ensure that popular thinking, sometimes called ideology, will continue to support the unequal distribution of wealth and power (Marx and Engels, 1955 [1848]).

This practice continues in the present era, the theory argues. Today, multinational corporations—or, more precisely, the powerful executives who run them—build up huge annual profits that are grossly out of line with the payments offered to their employees. In developed nations, owing to the influence of unions and labour legislation, employers are more likely to pay workers a reasonable wage for work done under safe conditions. In developing nations, however, employers are less constrained (Calvano, 2008). The result of this process is continued and increasing inequality—indeed, class polarization, with an ever-widening gap in wealth between rich and poor. Another result is alienation.

In an early work, Marx identified four types of alienation in labour under capitalism: alienation of the worker from his or her "species essence" as a human being rather than a machine; alienation between workers, since capitalism reduces labour to a commodity to be traded on the market, rather than seeing it as a function of a social relationship; alienation of the worker from the product, since this is appropriated by the capitalist class and so escapes the worker's control; and alienation from the act of production itself, such that work comes to be a meaningless activity, offering little or no intrinsic satisfactions.

Conflict theorists also recognize the biased nature of laws and policies that favour the rich, such as low-interest government loans to bail out failing businesses and tax breaks to corporations. As might be expected, conflict theorists are more likely to discuss the types of social-structural and cultural causes of continued poverty that we discussed in the introductory chapter. Many of the mechanisms of exclusion and suppression that create economic inequality are familiar to conflict theorists.

Symbolic Interactionism

In relation to poverty, symbolic interactionists focus on the ways that people assign the labels "wealthy" and "poor" through social interaction. The typical though unspoken stereotype of a poor person in North American society runs as follows: a lazy, irresponsible, undeserving, freeloading ethnic minority (probably black, Latino, or Aboriginal) who would rely on welfare and social assistance rather than find a steady job to support himself or herself; a person who likely dabbles in petty crime and spends much of his or her money on alcohol and drugs; possibly a violent and dangerous threat; and a nuisance to society.

On the other hand, the stereotypical depiction of a rich person is this: greedy, shallow, snobbish, egotistical, callous, wasteful, and probably white; has no qualms about stepping on others for personal gain; born with a silver spoon in his or her mouth and used to living a life of sheltered privilege; inherited the already sizable wealth of mummy or daddy, and therefore hasn't had to expend any personal effort to build or increase the family fortune; and willing to take advantage of an unjust economic and social system that favours the privileged few at the expense of the disadvantaged many.

Like all stereotypes, these ones are exaggerations. Still, even if such labels are arbitrary and unfounded, their effects are real enough. Being labelled "poor" creates many problems that contribute to further poverty. Employers, mindful of these stereotypes, are less likely to offer poor people well-paying, stable jobs. Poor people are more likely to be the targets of unwarranted police scrutiny and harassment. Members of the public will see any reliance on government assistance by the poor as proving the truth of the applied stereotype.

Social Consequences of Poverty and Economic Inequality

Work and Unemployment

Both poverty and wealth are closely tied to employment, the main source of money for most people. Today in Canada, most families have trouble living comfortably on a single income (Defina and Thanawala, 2009). To avoid poverty, many households, in contrast to previous generations, are becoming increasingly reliant on two or more incomes. Yet even this is no guarantee of prosperity. Often, even the gainfully employed live on the edge of poverty.

Many work lives are characterized by periods of employment followed by stretches of unwanted idleness. This is especially the case for people working in the secondary sector of the dual labour market. Secondary-sector jobs such as unskilled labourer, cab driver, and salesperson generally are characterized by poor pay, low status, low job security, high turnover, and easy entry. At the same time, low wages prevent many people from saving part of their income to provide a safety net during times of unemployment (Breau, 2007). As a result, many must rely on social assistance programs, such as Employment Insurance, welfare, and workfare. These programs, though helpful and well

Naim Alli has seen her wages and working conditions deteriorate along with her health since she arrived in Canada 20 years ago. She is part of a group advocating for a $14-an-hour minimum wage, calculated to provide a decent living just above the poverty level.

intentioned, help the poor survive but rarely help them improve their lives (Poliakova and Reut, 2008). According to Statistics Canada (2012), in December 2012, 517,140 Canadians received Employment Insurance benefits. This number had fallen by 7.1 per cent in 2011, however. Table 2.2 below displays a breakdown by sex of Canada's EI expenditures in 2012.

TABLE 2.2	Employment Insurance Beneficiaries Receiving Regular Benefits by Age and Sex			
	DECEMBER 2011	DECEMBER 2012	DECEMBER 2011 TO DECEMBER 2012	DECEMBER 2011 TO DECEMBER 2012
	Number		Change in Number	% Change
Canada				
Both sexes	556,890	517,140	−39,750	−7.1
Under 25 years	56,020	50,150	−5,870	−10.5
25 to 54 years	376,380	345,880	−30,500	−8.1
55 years and over	124,500	121,110	−3,390	−2.7
Men	342,280	317,170	−25,110	−7.3
Under 25 years	40,450	36,430	−4,020	−9.9
25 to 54 years	224,090	205,330	−18,760	−8.4
55 years and over	77,740	75,410	−2,330	−3.0
Women	214,610	199,970	−14,640	−6.8
Under 25 years	15,560	13,720	−1,840	−11.8
25 to 54 years	152,290	140,550	−11,740	−7.7
55 years and over	46,760	45,700	−1,060	−2.3

Source: Statistics Canada, at: <www.statcan.gc.ca/tables-tableaux/sum-som/l01/cst01/labor02b-eng.htm>.

Crime and Violence

Many believe the poor, desperate to improve their financial state, are more likely than other people to commit opportunistic crimes, such as petty theft, muggings, or burglary. Research has shown that individuals at the lower end of the socio-economic status spectrum are often more likely to commit crimes, especially property crimes (Braun, 1995; Hagan, 1994; Kennedy et al., 1998). After all, the poor have fewer legitimate opportunities to achieve the economic and social goals our culture teaches us to value. Consequently, rises in the crime rate may reflect desperation or even an increase in self-destructive attitudes among those who are poor, or they may reflect a decrease in community social cohesion (Baron, 2006).

Still, this is only half of the story. The poor do not commit all of society's crimes. As a later chapter will point out, violations of the law committed by the wealthy—so-called corporate crimes and white-collar crimes—are equally challenging and may harm many more people's lives. However, such crimes are rarely reported or punished.

Drug and Alcohol Abuse

Another result of poverty and inequality is the excessive use of alcohol and drugs, whether for pleasure or escapism (Gallupe and Baron, 2009). This behaviour, like crime, is found in all social classes and is not limited to the poor. Nor is it caused only by social inequality.

However, the desperately poor, deprived of conventional opportunities to achieve wealth and success, are more likely to use alcohol and drugs. They do so to deal with what Robert Merton (1957: 131–60) and, before him, Émile Durkheim called "anomie," the gap between what they have been taught to want and what they can get. Rhonda Jones-Webb and colleagues (1997), for instance, found that people living in poor neighbourhoods are more likely to suffer from alcoholism. Not only does poverty affect the use of drugs and alcohol, it also increases the influence of drug and alcohol use on people's lives. Studies have shown that individuals in low-poverty neighbourhoods are less likely to abuse alcohol and be exposed to violence and experience health problems (Fauth et al., 2007). One study found that poverty accounts for 69 per cent of the variance in the cocaine and opiate overdose mortality rates in New York City (Marzuk et al., 1997). So, by far the single best predictor of death from a drug is the poverty of the drug user. Drugs do their worst harm when people are already leading lives stressed by low income, poor health, bad nutrition, and inadequate housing. All of these conditions reduce the immunity to disease that helps us survive, and they also reduce a person's will to live.

Children and Poverty

Poverty is also age related in most societies. People without an income (e.g., children) or with a fixed income (e.g., elderly people) are more susceptible to the risks of poverty and inequality than other members of society. They are also regarded as the most blameless victims of poverty in any society (National Advisory Council on Aging, 2005).

Research on children who grow up poor leads to three conclusions about poverty. First, raising the incomes of poor families, even just barely above the poverty line, will improve the learning ability and performance of young children. Second, raising the educational status of poor parents will have a similar effect. Third, raising both the income and the education of poor parents will have the greatest positive effect (Smith et al., 1999).

ENRON: THE SMARTEST GUYS IN THE ROOM

This 2005 documentary explores the rise and then eventual collapse of the Enron corporation, providing an exposé on what many consider to be the worst case of white-collar crime in American history.

However, it may be easier to raise family incomes (e.g., through transfer payments) than to raise parental education levels (Prus, 2007).

Children are especially vulnerable to dire and degrading consequences of poverty. One of the world's most serious threats to healthy child development is the underground trafficking of minors, for cheap labour and especially for the purposes of commercial sexual exploitation. The illegal sex trade is a shadowy business, and reliable statistics about the extent of the problem are hard to find. However, the International Labour Organization (ILO, 2008) has conservatively estimated that human trafficking, defined as the illegal transport of people across national borders, affects at least 1.2 million children per year.

INTERNATIONAL **COMPARISONS**

| BOX 2.2 | **Girls' Education in Afghanistan** |

In North America and other developed regions, the extent to which international education is available to women has, to a certain degree, been much overlooked—if not entirely taken for granted. The women's movement has taken many progressive steps forward during the past two centuries, yet the availability of education for women has not been under as immense scrutiny since the late nineteenth century as other areas of concern, such as voting rights, representation in Parliament, and even labour force participation. Though women all over the world have had to claim their place in the education system at many times throughout history, education has never been as valued as it is at present.

Considering the role of education in the modern world, both for employment and for self-actualization, it has been increasingly important for both men and women to have varying levels of education available to them. Though this has not been a problem for the world's most recent generations of young adults in developed nations, youth of many developing nations are facing a sad reality in which they are being deprived of such an opportunity. This is especially true for females: most educationally deprived youth in developing nations are girls and young women. In 2009 the United Nations Girls' Education Initiative (UNGEI) published a book by researcher Roshan Chitrakar (2009), who investigated the barriers to girls' education and gender inequality in South Asia. One country in which the barriers to girls' education have been under much public attention on a global scale is Afghanistan, the first on the list of countries that Chitrakar examines (other countries discussed in the report are Bangladesh, Bhutan, India, Maldives,

Nepal, Pakistan, and Sri Lanka). In her report, Chitrakar writes:

The long-standing war in Afghanistan prior to and during the Taliban regime stalled not only the education of girls but also the entire process of development for many decades. The consequence of the war history looms large in present-day Afghanistan with the education sector facing massive challenges. Lack of female teachers and infrastructure are among the key obstacles to girls' education. With the advent of democratic government in the country in 2001, promoting girls' education has become a priority development agenda. Afghanistan's constitution recognizes the education of girls as their fundamental right. The first 5-year National Education Strategic Plan has tried to uphold this constitutional provision through priority programs for a speedy promotion of girls' education. The challenges of promoting girls' education are massive, hence concerted efforts will need to be made for many more years to come. Special measures such as incentive packages are essential to bring more girls to school and narrow the gender gap. The incentive for girls to pursue higher education is even more critical to ensure that they are motivated not only to enrol in basic education but also to complete it and acquire further qualifications. . . . Enhanced capacity of stakeholders at macro- and micro-levels to carry out gender audits and meet gender-related targets will be a significant step forward. With a secure and violence-free environment at and on the way to school, the enrolment of rural Afghan girls in school can be multiplied many-fold. However, the state will be required to accept the high cost involved in raising the status and level of educational attainment of girls in the country. (Chitrakar, 2009)

The purpose and extent of underage human trafficking vary from one region to another. In East Asia, for instance, trafficked children, the vast majority of whom are girls, are used largely as child prostitutes. Tourists mainly coming from wealthy neighbouring and Western nations create the demand. In Europe, minors are trafficked from east to west (e.g., from Poland to England) across the open borders of the European Union for similar purposes.

In South Asia and West and Central Africa, too, children are recruited to take part in the exploitative child labour market, though many are still destined for the sex trade. Often, debt bondage—where children are forced to work off money given to their parents—is the route by which children enter the downward spiral of exploitation (UNICEF, 2013). In African nations experiencing civil or tribal conflicts, children may also be abducted and forced to fight in militias.

Many girls and women who live in poverty in the developing world are limited to a few tough choices: domestic subservience, sex work, forced labour, an unwanted marriage, or a handful of other grim options. One way to break the cycle of exploitation and poverty, then, is to empower women rather than marginalize them.

Health Consequences of Poverty and Economic Inequality

Poverty and Health

Poverty directly hinders secure access to high-quality foods—food that contains essential nutrients, vitamins, minerals, and so on—and this lack of access then leads to poorer health (Kirkpatrick and Tarasuk, 2003).

It has been estimated that because of poor nutrition, one-quarter of children under the age of five who live in the developing world—more than 150 million children—are underweight. Chronic hunger leads to serious health problems, including rickets, scurvy, intestinal infections or damage, a depressed immune system, and impaired cognitive development. As well, hungry children are more likely to be hyperactive, have problems concentrating in school, and have other serious behavioural problems (Raphael, 2004).

Poverty is also likely to worsen health problems through the social problems associated with it, such as crime, depression, and substance abuse. These other problems can also lead to poverty and the health problems that poverty entails (Heflin and Iceland, 2009). We discuss the specific health consequences of these other social problems in their respective chapters.

Effects of Inequality

Inequality—like poverty—is bad for our health. Research shows that being at the bottom end of a hierarchy—no matter how affluent that hierarchy may be—leads to health problems (Sanmartin, 2009).

The world's poorest populations—whether they live in Sudan or Canada—experience worse health than people within the same country who are not so poor. In less-developed countries like Sudan, the causes of ill health are obvious: a lack of clean water, famine, infectious disease, and so forth. In more-developed countries like Canada, however, these

ANGELA'S ASHES

This 1999 film, based on the best-selling book, shows the extraordinary health and lifestyle deprivations found within Limerick's poorest classes.

conditions are not significant health threats except in some northern Aboriginal communities (Trovato, 2001). Something else, therefore, is at the root of much of the disparity in health outcomes in Canada, and this "something" appears to be inequality itself. Relative poverty, not absolute poverty, is the problem.

Much research has focused on the relative income hypothesis, which proposes that income inequality alone (as opposed to absolute deprivation) is enough to bring on various health problems, including premature mortality, within a population (Gravelle and Sutton, 2009). This theory argues that the fact of inequality itself has real and measurable health outcomes for people at the lower end of the hierarchy. One influential study (Wilkinson, 1994) found a correlation between life expectancy and the proportion of income received by the poorest 70 per cent of the population. The author showed that the greater the difference in income distribution between the least well-off 70 per cent and the most well-off 30 per cent, the higher the levels of early mortality in an entire society or community.

The best-known investigations of the relationship between inequality and health are the so-called Whitehall studies, which involved 18,000 male British civil servants in the late 1960s and the 1970s. A major finding was that mortality rates, especially from coronary heart disease (CHD), were three times higher among workers in the lowest civil service positions (messengers, doorkeepers, and so on) than among workers in the highest positions (such as top administrators). This difference remained even after taking into account risk factors such as obesity, smoking habits, amount of leisure time and physical activity, other illnesses, baseline blood pressure, and height (Marmot et al., 1984).

One explanation of this variation in CHD mortality is the difference in control and support that workers experience at different levels of the job hierarchy (Marmot et al., 1987). In short, people in low-status jobs have less control over their work; this lack of control produces more stress; and more stress appears to produce higher blood pressure and higher risks of heart disease.

A second Whitehall study was conducted in 1985, involving more than 10,000 male and female British civil servants. It confirmed that low work control—characteristic of low-status occupations such as clerical and office support workers—increases the risk of developing CHD (Bosma et al., 1997). Even those working *near* the top of the civil service hierarchy had poorer health outcomes than people working at the *very top*. Also related, low levels of work control, of workplace autonomy, and in the workplace hierarchy are associated with more negative mental health outcomes (Schieman, 2002).

Further evidence showing the importance of relative—not absolute—deprivation comes from the finding that GNP (gross national product) per capita is correlated with health only up to a boundary of $5,000 GNP per capita per year. Beyond this threshold, increases in standard of living have little effect on a population's health. Thus, in developed countries, people's disadvantage *in relation to others*, not their absolute deprivation, leads to health inequalities. As Daniels, Kennedy, and Kawachi (2000: 9) note, "the health of a population depends not just on the size of the economic pie but on how the pie is shared. . . . Differences in health outcomes among developed nations cannot be explained by the absolute deprivation associated with low economic development."

Thus, social inequality contributes directly to poor health and social problems for two main reasons: first, it increases social inequality and decreases social cohesion, and second, social inequality, in the form of relative disadvantage, increases the experience of stress. For various other reasons, it also reduces access to health information and health-care services.

Relative income hypothesis The proposal that income inequality alone (as opposed to absolute deprivation) is enough to bring on various health problems, including premature mortality, within a population.

BOX 2.3 **Neil Guppy, University of British Columbia**

Neil Guppy is a professor of sociology at the University of British Columbia. For the past several years, Neil has also served as the head of the sociology department. His research focuses on patterns of educational inequality in Canada. In an early piece, "Changing Patterns of Educational Inequality in Canada," Neil explored the relationship between social class and educational attainment and how this relationship changed by birth cohort (Guppy et al., 1984). He found that the relationship between social class and educational attainment had weakened over time. However, children from more affluent backgrounds still had the best chance of becoming university educated themselves.

In recent years, Neil has moved beyond looking at education as just a means of learning the skills required to gain access to higher skills, and thus higher-paying work. He now examines how education teaches the cultural norms that help people become successful in the labour market. One study looked at the effect of cultural knowledge (such as knowledge of the arts), referred to as "talent," on occupational status (Garnett et al., 2008). It concludes that education (i.e., credentials) alone does not account for career and employment success. Cultural knowledge—or cultural capital—is an important tool that facilitates the attainment of skilled, complex jobs.

Beyond the studies described above, Neil has also written and published many other works that explore social inequality and education. One of the most notable, *Social Inequality in Canada*, addresses various dimensions of social inequality and investigates the objective and structural conditions of this issue. It also investigates different forms of inequality, including class, education, gender, and race, many of which deal with the poverty and economic obstacles covered in this chapter.

Social integration plays an important part in dealing with stresses associated with inequality. Robert Putnam (2000), for example, finds in many studies a link between social cohesion and social connectedness, on the one hand, and health and longevity, on the other. People with higher levels of social involvement are healthier and live longer. As well, communities with more social integration have better health and mortality records. Finally, cross-national comparisons find better health experiences and greater longevity in the countries with higher social integration (De Looper, 2009; Putnam, 2000; Wilkinson, 1996).

Solving the Problems of Poverty and Economic Inequality

Solutions to the problems of poverty and inequality have been debated for centuries. They fall into two main categories—individual and collective (Bradley and Cole, 2002). People, in their own interest, undertake individual solutions. Collective solutions require the co-operation of many people for their mutual benefit. Let us begin by considering some of the ways that people deal with their own personal experience of poverty and/or inequality in North American society.

Individual Solutions

As an individual, you may best solve the problem of exclusion by obtaining whatever credentials allow you to enter the group in which you hope to spend your life. Higher education is the single best investment you can make if your goals are material and perhaps even if they are creative. However, racial and ethnic discrimination continue to limit people's educational and economic opportunities (Reitz, 2007a, 2007b). For example, members of groups that suffer discrimination may not do as well in work settings controlled by people from other ethnic groups as they would if they remained within their own ethnic community, even with less education. The decision to be made here—and it is a complex one—depends on several factors: the actual extent of discrimination against your ethnic or racial group, the chance of a significant reduction in that discrimination during their lifetime, the range of attractive occupational opportunities within your own racial or ethnic community, and the chance of a significant increase in these opportunities during your lifetime.

Alone, people can do little to influence any of these factors. As individuals, they can only choose between getting a higher education (and possibly cutting themselves off from the their ethnic community) and getting less education (and building contacts within the ethnic community). The first choice risks discrimination outside the community; the second limits opportunities for selecting a career and advancing within the community. The individual's contribution to a group solution, to be discussed shortly, will be much more important.

It is often the case that people seeking to escape from poverty should change the way they think about themselves—not an easy task, but one that a great many people manage to accomplish. This is partly what the major social movements of our time—for example, feminism, Native rights, and gay rights—are all about. People learn more about the history of their oppression as members of a despised or belittled group, discuss this problem with others, and find mentors and role models within the community who have done what the society of the majority would have them think cannot be done. Most important of all, this consciousness-raising enterprise rejects the victim-blaming ideology that oppressed peoples use against themselves. Those who are oppressed have enough problems without being their own worst enemies.

People trying to escape from poverty can build and make use of social networks—that is how people find good jobs. The size and variety of one's network of acquaintances can be improved by getting to know people who have larger and "better" networks. People who are themselves mobile and well known in the community, who are (typically) higher in status, or who operate within institutions that encourage interpersonal contact are valuable people to know (Bradley and Cole, 2002). As we have seen, this social connectedness seems to be related to later state of health and the ability to deal with illness.

Social institutions that break down traditional gender, class, and ethnic barriers to interpersonal contact include colleges, universities, and government. Thus, higher education and involvement in civic affairs are doubly beneficial: they allow self-improvement and they encourage contact with others. However, both activities leave less time for participation in one's own community. Here, wrong choices are potentially costly. Thus, one should try to become a "cosmopolitan" member of one's community, with feet in both camps (Merton, 1957). This connects the individual and the community with the larger networks of influence and opportunity beyond (Myers, 2005).

Finally, as an individual, one can cope successfully with real scarcity by producing more of what people need, by adjusting one's thinking downward from the imaginary to the possible, and by seeking creative alternatives to scarce goods. It is the human ability to do this that has kept our species alive for a million years.

The danger here lies in confusing scarcity with inequality, considering scarcity beyond remedy, or lowering our heads rather than raising the bridge. French demographer Alfred

Black Press

Chief Ron Sam celebrates the opening of the Songhees Wellness Centre in January 2014. Conceived, funded, and overseen by the Songhees Nation, the centre is home to a health centre, an elders and youth centre, after-school training programs, adult education programs, a gym, and a conference centre. This is an example of a group working collectively to fulfill a need in their community.

Sauvy (1969: 391) has called this approach the "Malthusian Spirit . . . a state of mind characterised by the fear of excess—faced with two quantities that need adjusting, it tends to lower the highest instead of boosting the lowest. It is the opposite of courage and generosity." The Malthusian is the person who, at a dinner party with too little food for all the guests, tries to send guests home rather than find more food in the pantry.

Group remedies are called for when what appears to be scarcity is just a result of inequality or of a temporary shortage that could be remedied through innovation and higher productivity. But group remedies depend on the personal commitment of people who are willing to accept the effects that these remedies will have on their lives along with the solutions that they offer.

Collective Solutions

The chief actors in a large, modern society are groups and organizations, not people. That is why we must look beyond people for adequate solutions to inequality.

Karl Marx and Friedrich Engels (1955 [1848]) contended that a revolution that would eliminate ruling classes forever by eliminating private property—by putting the means of production in the hands of the state—would bring better conditions for all. With the eventual "withering away" of the state, communism would end history as we have known it, for it would end social classes and class conflict.

There are two problems with this formulation. First, a reading of history shows that every society of any size has had a class structure and a ruling class. This would not lead

The 2012 Quebec student protests were an example of collective action aimed at making Canadian society more equitable. The series of protests that came to be known as "Maple Spring" were in reaction to a government proposal to raise university tuition in the province of Quebec by 75 per cent over five years.

sociologists to the confident conclusion that a society with no class structure and no ruling class is truly possible. Rather, it would lead in the opposite direction—in the direction most often associated with the name of Robert Michels (1962 [1916]), who formulated the "iron law of oligarchy." Michels's principle—based on a sympathetic socialist's study of a radically democratic organization, the German socialist party—holds that in every social grouping a dominant group will struggle to perpetuate its power, whatever its original ideology. That is, inequality is inevitable in human groupings, whatever their size or their members' ideology.

Michels's "iron law" has not proven unbreakable. For example, a sociological study of the International Typographical Union, a democratic printers' union in the United States and Canada, found some of the conditions that prevent or minimize oligarchy (Lipset et al., 1963). So, not every organization must be oligarchic. Yet oligarchic organizations in our own society and elsewhere far outnumber the democratic organizations. No evidence exists of there ever having been a society that has broken the hold of oligarchy. At best, there is only a slim chance that Marx was right about the possibility of a fully democratic society.

Second, the premise that history can end with a democratic, class-free society is far from supported by empirical evidence. History does not show that communist revolutions have succeeded in bringing about either equality or democracy. In the century and a half since Marx and Engels wrote the *Communist Manifesto*, many groups in different countries have experimented with communism. Some attempts have been Utopian or anarchistic, based in a small community or region (see Hobsbawm, 1959; Kanter, 1972).

But, except for Cuba, the Israeli kibbutzim, and Hutterite communities, these have all failed, for various reasons. Some have been forcibly overturned; others have lacked a sufficient material base; and still others have suffered from demographic pressures from within and attack from without. Even the successful kibbutzim and Hutterite communities have suffered serious losses of population, as native-born members deserted. For its part, Cuba's revolution has produced neither prosperity nor democracy.

Contrary to Marx's expectation, attempts to bring about communistic equality at the state level have produced new kinds of inequality. In every instance—in Russia, China, Albania, Cuba, Vietnam, Nicaragua, and so on—rule based on ownership of the means of production has merely been replaced by political and bureaucratic control. So inequality has lived on in a new form. In many places, communism has greatly reduced material inequality and the worst effects of this inequality, but a certain form of inequality—rule by a political elite, or "vanguard of the proletariat," as Lenin called it—never disappeared.

Many believe that the excesses of control under communism were due to an over-centralization of planning and political power. That is why throughout Eastern Europe and the former Soviet Union, people have rejected communism as unworkable. Communism has collapsed as a system of organization, and in the end, citizens' behaviour in rejecting it suggests that Marx's remedy does not work as he thought it would.

The communist alternative has proven more attractive in less-developed parts of the world. In fact, the benefits of capitalism and liberalism have meant little to many people in developing countries. They consider European nations unsuitable models to imitate, since they carry the stigma of colonialism. Further, "free enterprise" seems less likely to succeed in the developing world than large-scale economic planning. As Geoffrey Barraclough (1967: 223) wrote many years ago, "one of the outstanding attractions of communism to Asian and African eyes [is] that it [offers] the underdeveloped peoples a blueprint for development."

On the other hand, material inequality within a society can be significantly reduced without the adoption of communism, as demonstrated in the democratic socialist countries of Scandinavia and, to a smaller degree, in certain other countries. Also, many people in the industrial capitalist countries—and not only the rich and powerful—do not want to give up private property in favour of communism. Values justifying acquisitiveness and free enterprise arise whenever personal acquisition becomes possible. People offered the chance to improve their wealth and status seize that opportunity almost without fail. They do not easily give it up.

As we will see throughout this book, liberal democracy does not give people an equal chance to get what they want out of life, and so it would be satisfying to believe that some alternative (such as communism) could do so. However, researchers have been unable to show that Marx's proposed remedies lie within the realm of the possible or that they satisfactorily link the advancement of group and individual interests. That is not to say that more modest socialist remedies would also fail to meet our needs. Indeed, any remedy that equalizes income and power will benefit the majority. So let us turn to some truly feasible remedies and see whether they meet our requirements.

Other Group Remedies

Wherever opportunity is limited, any wholly individual remedies are no more than quick fixes with temporary effects. In the long run, the chance of gaining more opportunity is greater for a group of people working together than for an individual working alone. But if we rule out the revolutionary option, what remains? Again, what follows is merely schematic. It would be impossible to encompass all remaining scenarios within the scope of this book.

Two group remedies to exclusion are truly possible: legislation and group action. To bring the first about requires banding together with others who suffer discrimination, joining forces across ethnic, class, gender, and regional boundaries where necessary. It also means electing sympathetic legislators to push for changes. If successful, the result will be a more assimilated, less discriminatory society (Addison et al., 2009).

The second remedy involves mobilizing within one's own group—whether class, ethnic, religious, or regional—to increase community organization. This has the effect of discriminating in one's own favour to counter the discrimination of the larger society. Many groups use this tactic today, notably class-based political parties, unions, lobbies, and associations (Hills et al., 2009).

Group mobilization carries the risks of increasing inter-group conflict without eliminating the underlying conditions that gave rise to it. By pitting one group against another—women against men, blacks against whites, gays against heterosexuals—this tactic increases the risk of misunderstanding and injustice. A society torn by such disputes is no further ahead than a society marked by smouldering resentment. Events in the Balkans, Somalia, Israel, Northern Ireland, Syria, and Ukraine show that civil war is considerably worse than smouldering resentment (Addison et al., 2009).

The benefits of slow, incremental individual change are much more limited (Kanter, 1977). For example, a lone woman given the opportunity to "model" executive abilities in a large organization is under unusual pressures to succeed on behalf of all women and is judged by criteria unlike those applied to men. Confusion will arise over the unique characteristics of the individual and the "type" she represents. Consequently, we do not learn what excluded groups can do until we see many group members performing in emotionally neutral, common situations. For this to occur requires legislation that ensures the inclusion of as many representatives of a social type as may seek it. Laws against discrimination not only break down traditional patterns of exclusion, they also repudiate a dominant ideology in our society that blames poor and vulnerable people—society's victims—for the problems they suffer. Again, governments will not pass and enforce such laws without group mobilization.

Groups can remedy decoupling by building bridges to other groups—for example, to other racial, ethnic, regional, and occupational groups. Typically, increased communication among the leaders of these groups is the key to success. But everyone can play a part in this process by participating in broadly based activities and organizations.

Finally, material scarcity can be reduced if more of what people want and need is produced. This requires an international commitment to economic growth and redistribution and the breaking up of monopolies that restrict productivity as well as sharing.

These solutions to inequality are group remedies, not individual remedies. All are truly possible. However, they do not systematically address the question of how people might link their own advancement with that of society as a whole. C. Wright Mills (1959) maintained that personal lives are linked with public issues; another way of putting it is that personal troubles are shared and socially structured. This implies that personal and social problems must be solved at the same time.

Chapter Summary

Poverty has many definitions. Typically, governments decide where to draw the poverty line, and so the meaning of poverty varies by society and, within societies, over time.

Some think that poverty is caused by the continuation of economically damaging cultural habits (this is the culture of poverty approach), while others believe it is caused by an unfair distribution of resources (the conflict approach). Functionalists believe that economic rewards are merit-based and inequality and poverty are mostly inevitable. It is not clear, however, from this standpoint, why women and ethnic minorities have the most poverty.

Widespread poverty is evident in Canada and throughout the world. For this country in 2008, Statistics Canada (2009) classified 9.2 per cent of the population (3 million people) as living in a "low-income" situation. Even though this is the lowest low-income rate since Statistics Canada began measuring poverty in 1976, it is not a constant figure. Since the recession of 2009, this rate has increased. As a result of such shifts in the economy, many people move in and out of poverty. Longer durations of poverty produce more harmful outcomes, and children who are continuously poor have higher rates of anti-social behaviour than transiently poor or non-poor children. Sometimes, poor health is a cause of poverty, not vice versa. However, for most people, the reverse is true. Poverty and inequality will be continuing problems that they cannot handle on their own.

As we have seen, both inequality and poverty are thorny issues. They are not merely conditions of economic deprivation, but are also causes of physical and mental health problems. Further, lower income means a higher probability of dying young. These patterns make it especially important—for individuals and for society—that we try to lessen economic inequality and discover ways of unlinking health and death from income level. Much of the research discussed in the remainder of this book is directed to these two ends.

Culture of poverty Theory developed by Oscar Lewis characterizing the urban poor as having a distinct set of values and norms, including short-sightedness, impulsiveness, and a tendency to accept their marginalized status in society, and as remaining poor because they pass on these values to future generations.

Questions for Critical Thought

1. What type of resources do people in poverty have available to them?
2. Do you think it's possible to end poverty in the world?
3. It is often said that the rich are growing richer and the poor are growing poorer. Why?
4. What makes poverty such a pervasive problem?
5. What barriers are there to helping people in poverty?

Recommended Readings

Davies, Matt, and Magnus Ryner, eds. 2006. *Poverty and the Production of World Politics: Unprotected Workers in the Global Political Economy*. London: Palgrave Macmillan.

DiFazio, William. 2006. *Ordinary Poverty: A Little Food and Cold Storage*. Philadelphia: Temple University Press.

Handler, Joel F., and Yeheskel Hasenfeld. 2007. *Blame Welfare, Ignore Poverty and Inequality*. New York: Cambridge University Press.

Kendall, Diana. 2005. *Framing Class: Media Representations of Wealth and Poverty in America*. Lanham, MD: Rowman & Littlefield.

Kilty, Keith M., ed. 2006. *The Promise of Welfare Reform: Political Rhetoric and the Reality of Poverty in the Twenty-first Century*. Binghamton, NY: Haworth Press.

Raphael, Dennis. 2007. *Poverty and Policy in Canada: Implications for Health and Quality of Life*. Toronto: Canadian Scholars Press.

Ross, Robert J.S. 2004. *Slaves to Fashion: Poverty and Abuse in the New Sweatshops*. Ann Arbor: University of Michigan Press.

Sachs, Jeffrey. 2005. *The End of Poverty: Economic Possibilities for Our Time*. New York: Penguin Press.

Wagner, David. 2008. *Ordinary People: In and Out of Poverty in the Gilded Age*. Boulder, CO: Paradigm.

3

Race and Ethnic Relations

ValeStock/Shutterstock

Introduction

This chapter discusses racial and ethnic inequality. The many outcomes of racial and ethnic prejudice—such as discrimination, exclusion, hatred, and distrust—create conflicts in our society. These conflicts—for example, between minorities and the majority—are politically and economically wasteful because they keep us from making the most efficient use of our human resources. No matter how we define the causes and allocate the blame, racial and ethnic inequality is a problem that we must remedy. But first, let's be sure we know what we are talking about.

Race

Is *race* a physical fact or a social construction? People with the most difficulty accepting other races are likely to believe that race is an inescapable physical and biological fact—an essential, permanent feature of any human being. They believe that each race has specific genetic features, with unique physiological markers and even unique cultural or psychological dispositions. In this view, there are at least three categories of human beings—Negroid ("black"), Caucasoid ("white"), and Mongoloid ("yellow")—from which all racial groups are derived (Omi and Winant, 2009).

However, growing genetic evidence shows that these so-called human races are more alike than different. The Human Genome Project has shown that only a tiny fraction of humanity's genetic makeup varies in characteristics historically associated with "race." Studies have shown that 85 per cent of the genetic variability that exists within the entire human species can be found within a single local population—for example, within the "white" population of Moncton, New Brunswick. That is to say, there is far more genetic variation within "races" than among "races."

To elaborate on this, recent studies show that racial variation is extremely small, with genetic diversity between continental populations accounting for only 3 to 7 per cent of the human genome (Elhaik, 2012). There could be more genetic difference between two randomly selected Cambodians than between a Cambodian and a Norwegian, for example. Besides, the physical features commonly associated with race—skin colour, hair texture, and eye colour, for example—are not genetically associated. That is, the pieces of DNA that control a person's skin colour are inherited separately from the pieces that control whether that person's hair is curly or straight.

Yet, many people choose to continue believing that the traditional view of race is useful and biologically meaningful, while rejecting the possibility that they are racist (Blatz and Ross, 2009). In short, race is a mere social construction, but so long as it continues to influence social behaviour, it is a sociologically significant issue.

Ethnicity

The concepts of "ethnicity" and "race" are often viewed to be, if not the same, then closely related. However, they are not the same. To be sure, there are occasional linkages. Cultural differences do exist between groups of people, and when they are sharpened by differences in skin colour, height, and other physical features, these cultural differences seem somehow significant. Yet, the two concepts are different in important ways.

THE HELP

Tate Taylor's 2011 blockbuster is about a young white woman, Eugenia "Skeeter" Phelan, and her relationship with two black maids, Aibileen Clark and Minny Jackson, during civil rights era America (the early 1960s).

The physical features allegedly shared by members of one race are often a result of a collective evolutionary adaptation to specific environmental conditions—for example, the darkening of skin colour in locations with strong sunlight near the equator (Baran, 2008). Even the shape of our noses seems to have a climate determinant: short, wide noses prevent overheating in a warm climate, while long, narrow noses are functional in colder climates, allowing air to warm before entering the lungs (Seren and Seren, 2009). However, race and ethnicity are different and not necessarily connected. People who differ in appearance may share the same cultural values, and people who look the same may not.

Culture is defined by social scientists as the set of values and practices that frame people's lives (Ruffin, 2009). These cultural features are the result of collective experiences in a particular historical and regional setting. Cultures are constantly changing; this is due to a variety of reasons that include globalization, travel, contact with outside groups, and mass media exposure. This means that members of an ethnic group, with a common, shared culture, see the world in similar ways, and these ways are constantly (though sometimes imperceptibly) changing.

Ethnic groups are created through social interaction. People form and maintain ethnic groups through processes of exclusion and inclusion around symbols of real or imagined common descent, such as a common language, common rituals, and common folklore. These social and cultural features are learned; consequently, ethnic boundaries are made and unmade over time (Fleras and Elliott, 2009). This fact opposes the commonly held *primordialist view* of ethnicity, a view that ethnicity is a fixed identity, a feature that an individual is born with and dies with and passes down to future generations.

Just as cultures change, ethnic groups change, and so do ethnic identities. For example, many Sri Lankans who had once identified themselves as "Kandyan" abandoned regional identities to unite under a single "Sinhala" identity (Chandra, 2012). These changes can be politically or economically motivated. A prime example of ethnic change is the effort made by lower-caste people in India to raise their caste by changing public perceptions of it or by blurring their membership in the caste. In effect, ethnic identities and values are always changing.

> **Culture** The way of life of a society that includes dress, language, norms of behaviour, foods, tools, beliefs, and folklore. This framework of values and practices adapts to the changing socio-historical context.

Multiculturalism in Canada

Canada's ethnic groups are mainly made up of immigrants—people who have migrated from other countries for permanent residence—and the children of immigrants. These ethnic groups make up a large fraction of the population of Canada's cities. This is evident in Figure 3.1, which shows the proportion of the total population that is comprised of people born outside of the country. Canada, compared to many other countries, has an especially large percentage of immigrants—20.6 per cent of our population is foreign-born, 6,775,800 people. Since 2000, a staggering 2,155,000 immigrants have come to Canada. The result is an ethnic mosaic. According to the 2011 National Household Survey (NHS), Canadians report more than 200 different ethnic origins (Statistics Canada, 2011a). It is clear that immigration has been important throughout Canadian history, and cultural diversity continues to be a prominent fact of Canadian life.

Canada's famous multicultural policy was initiated in 1971, and many factors—political as well as sociological—influenced its introduction (Fujiwara, 2008). For one thing, the 1960s had been marked by ever more stormy relations between English and

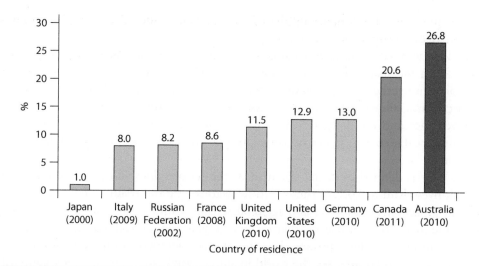

FIGURE 3.1 Foreign-Born Population, as a Proportion of the Total Population, G8 Countries and Australia

Source: Statistics Canada (2011a).

French speakers, especially in Quebec. To address the situation, the Royal Commission on Bilingualism and Biculturalism, established in 1963, conducted original research—some of it by sociologists—and held hearings across Canada. In 1969, following from this research, the Official Languages Act was voted into law (Forgues, 2007).

During the parliamentary proceedings that led to this legislation, spokespersons for many ethnic minority groups voiced their concerns to the commissioners. They said that the old policy of cultural assimilation did not give them the respect and benefits of Canadian citizenship that English and French speakers received. They urged the adoption of a new model of citizen participation—a "cultural mosaic" model—and asserted their right to group survival.

The royal commission agreed, recommending that the government recognize the value of cultural pluralism and encourage Canadian institutions to reflect the value of pluralism in their policies and programs. This view was supported and promoted by the then prime minister Pierre Elliott Trudeau, who was eager to win the political support of immigrant and ethnic minorities and oppose the demands by Quebec nationalists for unique rights within Confederation (Haque, 2007).

When first announced, the policy proposed that multiculturalism operate within a bilingual framework, affirming English and French as the two official languages. However, it also declared ethnic pluralism a worthy goal in its own right. Canada's provinces followed the federal lead by introducing their own multiculturalism policies in their own areas of jurisdiction. In 1971, multiculturalism became official federal policy with the passage of the Multiculturalism Act and the creation of a junior cabinet position for multiculturalism (now subsumed within the Department of Canadian Heritage). In 1982, the intention to preserve and enhance "the multicultural heritage of Canadians" was entrenched in the Constitution (section 27 of the Constitution Act, 1982), and in 1988, a new Canadian Multiculturalism Act became law.

Today, Canada officially prides itself on its multicultural diversity. Yet, as multiculturalism is a complicated notion, Canadians have found it useful to distinguish between traditional, or liberal, multiculturalism and modern multiculturalism. One type is more problematic than the other.

Traditional multiculturalism, or pluralism, is concerned with protecting the rights of people—specifically, the rights of minority people. It does this through provincial human rights codes. By contrast, *modern multiculturalism* is concerned with the survival of diverse cultural groups. In this case, the individual is treated as a member of an ethnic or racial group, and the group—not the individual—is protected by law (Fleras and Elliott, 2009).

Consider the difference between these two approaches, for it is important. With its focus on fostering civil liberties, traditional multiculturalism, in the realm of employment, protects individual job-seekers against employer bias. In contrast, modern multiculturalism supports blanket preferences, such as employment equity, to promote the hiring of underrepresented group members (Reitz and Banerjee, 2007). Other things being equal, employment equity (known in the US as affirmative action) gives *preference* to members of the specifically protected groups (e.g., visible minorities) over otherwise white people. Certain groups are advantaged under such policies, while others are disadvantaged; as a result, people may disagree about whom to include under the label "visible minority" or may ask whether they are truly disadvantaged. For example, they might deny that an able-bodied Asian college graduate is truly disadvantaged in Canada compared to a "white" unemployed person with less than high school education and a physical disability.

Five students jumping for joy at graduation. Traditional and modern multiculturalism perspectives are likely to differ on their assessment of the disadvantages these graduates may face while searching for employment.

PERSONAL *stories*

BOX 3.1 | **Is Sally a Racist?**

Sally says she isn't a racist—she just finds certain kinds of people more attractive, easier to relate to, and more likeable. The people she likes to date are the same colour as she is—white—and of the same ethnic background—English/Scottish/Irish. If she ever looks for dates online, she will be sure to advertise her racial preferences—no point leading people on.

Is it racist to identify racial preferences this way, even in online dating? According to studies of online dating statistics, the vast majority of users discriminate against potential love matches based on race.

While most online racial discrimination manifests itself in the choices people make regarding whom they message and whom they ignore, some users specify specific racial turn-offs in their profile pages. One profile on the gay hook-up site Grindr reads, "No Asian, No Indian, No Latino, No Black, No Fat, under 30 years old." At what point does racial preference in dating become racist? According to Alexander Chee, author and contributor to *Out Magazine*, "it's not racist to not to be attracted to Asian men," but if your profile explicitly states "NO ASIANS" . . . [y]ou're looking for a fellow Asian hater to

date. You're using the disguise of a semi-socially acceptable way to say you're a racist and looking to hook up with other racists."

A psychology professor at the University of Rochester, Harry Reis, also sheds some light on the "Is it racist?" question. He says, "People should be free to have sex or not have sex with anyone they want. But if you categorically rule out an ethnic group, it is by definition racist. One may not be racist in other ways but when it comes to sexual preferences, the person is. And in my estimation, it is fine (although self-limiting) to be racist with regard to sexual preferences." Reis suggests a new category of racism—"racist with regard to sexual preference."

Elena Tepperman, based on: Zosia Bielski, "'No Asian. No Indian': Picky Dater or Racist Dater?," *Theglobeandmail.com*, at: <www.theglobeandmail.com/life/relationships/no-asian-no-indian-picky-dater-or-racist-dater/article548736/>; Alexander Chee, "No Asians!," *Out.com, at:* <www.out.com/news-commentary/2012/01/11/no-asians>; Bonnie Rochman, "Love Isn't Color-Blind: White Online Daters Spurn Blacks," *Time.com*, at: <healthland.time.com/2011/02/22/love-isnt-color-blind-white-online-daters-spurn-blacks/>; Chelsea-Lyn Rudder, "Study Reveals Racial Segregation in Online Dating," *Thegrio.com*, <thegrio.com/2011/11/15/study-reveals-racial-segregation-in-online-dating/>.

The Vertical Mosaic

Despite historically high rates of immigration, Canada has not always been as welcoming towards immigrants as one might imagine. Throughout the nineteenth and early twentieth century, the majority white Anglo-Saxon population excluded and devalued immigrant groups who were culturally or racially different, allowing minority newcomers less-than-average access to better occupations and a higher income. These facts led John Porter (1965) to describe Canadian society as a **vertical mosaic** in which English and French Canadians are at the top of a patchwork hierarchy, with other ethnic minorities positioned below.

Porter traced this stratification pattern to Canada's historical reliance on selective immigration—a strategy that fulfilled specific workforce needs. At different periods, workers of different types were imported from particular countries to do the work Canada needed done. The Chinese were imported to build the railroads, the Ukrainians to farm the Prairies, the Italians to build our cities, and so on. So, gradually, as Canada industrialized, a close relationship developed between ethnicity and social class. The earliest-arriving ethnic groups—English, Scottish, Irish, and French—took and held on to the best available roles in society, leaving the less desirable work roles for other ethnic groups—especially, for more recent immigrants. New immigrants would arrive

Vertical mosaic Coined by John Porter, a socioeconomic hierarchy in which French and English Canadians live at the top and other ethnic groups are positioned below.

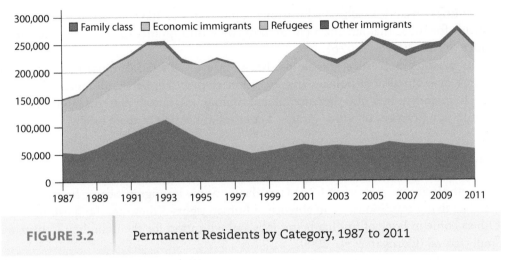

Legend: ■ Family class □ Economic immigrants ▨ Refugees ■ Other immigrants

| FIGURE 3.2 | Permanent Residents by Category, 1987 to 2011 |

Source: Citizenship and Immigration Canada (2011).

to find Canada's best jobs taken, and they had to settle for those typically lower in the social hierarchy (Reitz, 2001). With each decade, fewer of the desired kinds of immigrants—Northern European white Protestants—were available for migration. Canada's new, hard, and dangerous jobs—such as mining in northern Ontario—required new "kinds" of immigrants, first from Europe and then from Asia, the Caribbean, and countries in the southern hemisphere. As the data in Figure 3.2 show, many immigrants who arrived over the past 25 years came as economic immigrants, to fill particular economic roles.

"Ethnic differences," Porter concluded, "have been important in building up the bottom layer of the stratification system in both agricultural and industrial settings" (1965: 73). Also, the descendants of these immigrants were stuck in their low positions. With few exceptions, the children and grandchildren of immigrants were unable to move up the hierarchy because mechanisms for upward mobility—especially, institutions of higher education—were largely inaccessible. So, from generation to generation, particular ethnic groups remained stuck in their **entrance status**: the status attained when their group first arrived in Canada—for example, as prairie farmers from the Ukraine or urban construction workers from Italy (Reitz et al., 2009). Today, this has largely changed. Immigrants no longer retain their entrance status permanently, as they did in 1965 when Porter was writing. Thanks to the continued expansion of educational opportunities, many of Canada's minority groups have moved out of low-status entrance jobs.

However, some problems have persisted. Even today, recent immigrants find that the job they held in their previous country is difficult and costly to obtain in Canada. For example, international medical graduates are required to pass federally administered exams to become certified in Canadian provinces and thereby able to continue their practice; and even passing the exams does not guarantee a job. These are expensive exams, costing up to $6,000, and can take a lot of time because of the limited number of scheduled exam dates in a year. In the meantime, these immigrants are obliged to take lower-level jobs—for example, as cab drivers or factory workers—to earn a living (Teelucksingh and Galabuzi, 2005). As well,

Entrance status The status granted to an individual upon official entry into Canada. Statuses may be temporary (visitor visa, student authorization, live-in caregiver) or permanent (independent, professional, or skilled worker class).

discrimination and a lack of educational opportunities have continued to make it difficult for the Canadian-born children of some immigrants to climb the economic ladder (Reitz, 2007a, 2007b).

At present, the vertical mosaic persists—especially for racial minorities—not only because of multicultural policies and exclusionary practices by the dominant English-French majority, but also because of continuing migration patterns and the self-organization practices of ethnic groups. Let us examine each of these briefly.

Chain Migration into the Mosaic

Most ethnic groups migrate to Canada gradually. Some immigrants come here to escape war, bad living conditions, or an absence of human rights—these are the "push factors." Others come in hope of finding better jobs and education for their children—these are "pull factors" (Costigan et al., 2009).

Typically, immigrants have arrived, generation after generation, as links in a long **chain migration** process. Historically, family members would come, one or two at a time, set up a home, get work, and send for spouses, siblings, and children, gradually creating a chain (or sequence) of linked migrations. Eventually, these chains would extend outward to include relatives and even acquaintances. This pattern was partly due to structured information flow through social networks: people tend to migrate to places they have heard about from people they knew at home.

Historically, many immigrants have spent their first Canadian years in large old houses packed with family members who had just arrived and were looking for a foothold (Bailie et al., 2006). However, differences in sex and age influenced the living arrangements of immigrants. Women and children tended to live with adults who had immigrated previously; working-age men often came first and lived alone or with relatives, then brought their families over when they could afford it (Thomas, 2001).

Even today, many immigrants face barriers after arriving in Canada. Success is not easily attainable and depends on three main factors: (1) the province and city they immigrate to, (2) the generation of immigrants to which they belong, and (3) race. For example, many immigrants are underemployed because their professional certification or years of experience back home are not recognized in Canada or counted as appropriate for purposes of hiring. That said, well-educated immigrants tend to do well in Canada, and on average recent immigrants tend to be better educated than native-born people.

How immigrants do in Canada, indeed, is largely the result of their educational background and length of time in Canada, which means some immigrants do better than others. Consider data provided by Statistics Canada (2013b) that looks at labour force characteristics by immigrant status of people aged 25–54 and by educational attainment. Among people with a university degree, only 2.8 per cent of those born in Canada are unemployed, compared with 5.4 per cent of immigrants who landed 10 or more years earlier, 7.1 per cent of immigrants who landed 5–10 years earlier, and 11.6 per cent of immigrants who landed 5 or fewer years earlier. This "recency" effect is nearly as large as the education effect itself: among people born in Canada, only 2.8 per cent of university graduates are unemployed, compared with 5.0 per cent of those with a post-secondary certificate or diploma, 6.3 per cent of those who graduated high school, and 12.0 per cent of those who earned no degree, certificate, or diploma.

Chain migration The successful migration of one family member creates a chain for the kin and community network. Migration is not random but is increasingly about networks, rational choices, and kinship relations.

Some immigrant groups do better than others in Canada because they come to Canada with higher educational credentials, on average. The educational attainment of Chinese and South Asian immigrants, for example, is typically higher than that of Afro-Caribbean immigrants, whose educational levels resemble those of the native-born population in Canada, Australia, and the United States. As a result, Chinese and South Asian immigrants tend to outperform the native-born population in terms of income and occupational attainment. In short, it is foolhardy to generalize about all immigrants or even all visible minorities—let alone, to try to generalize across Western nations that receive these immigrants. The immigrant experience, though wrenching for all groups, is widely different in other respects, depending on the country of origin, the "human capital" and social contacts of these immigrants, and the countries of destination.

Institutional Completeness

On arriving at their new destination, immigrants look for others like themselves, for people, for example, who speak the same language. Gradually, immigrant groups build up communities of people based on ethnic, linguistic, and cultural similarities. Gradually, these communities become larger and more complex. With each arrival, the immigrant community becomes larger and more differentiated, with a wider variety of communal institutions. As Raymond Breton (1964, 1978; Breton et al., 1980) has shown, many immigrant communities gradually develop **institutional completeness**: they build schools, churches, newspapers, lending societies, shops, and so on. This allows

Institutional completeness A measure of the degree to which an immigrant ethnic group gives its own members the services they need through its own local institutions.

An example of institutional completeness is Toronto's Chinatown, an ethnic enclave in downtown Toronto with a high concentration of ethnic Chinese residents and businesses extending along Dundas Street West and Spadina Avenue.

Songquan Deng/Dreamstime.com

immigrants to carry out most of their daily activities within the ethnic group, preserving ethnic culture and ethnic social ties (Landry et al., 2007).

In part, institutional completeness is a response to real and imagined discrimination. In the face of restricted access to economic opportunities, new immigrants are forced to use their ethnic membership and assert their ethnic pride as a matter of economic and cultural survival. People who do not do so—who try to assimilate socially—may find themselves marginalized, accepted by neither their ethnic community nor the host culture.

This is a particular problem for the children of immigrants, as sociologists W.I. Thomas and Florien Znaniecki (1971 [1919]) pointed out in their classic work *The Polish Peasant in Europe and America*. Often, immigrant families facing problems of survival and assimilation experience intergenerational value conflicts. Immigrants' grandchildren find themselves fully accepted into the society; immigrants' children—their parents—are only partly accepted; and the immigrants themselves, often limited in education, language skills, and social capital, are the least accepted of all. Therefore, members of the same extended family can have different experiences of the same society and different degrees of access into the society.

This process also leads to profound changes in family organization. The most acculturated members of the immigrant family—often the children—assume duties and responsibilities within the family that would have been denied them in their home country.

Diasporas

In our own society, immigrant groups may feel included or excluded. However, from an international standpoint, immigrant groups such as the Arabs of Montreal or the Sikhs of Edmonton are often the members of a much larger community—the global Arab or Sikh community, for example.

Originally, the word "diaspora" described the scattering of the tribes of Israel and, in modern times, Jewish communities outside the state of Israel, especially as they were forced to flee the persecution of Nazi Germany. Today, we use **diaspora** to mean the global spread of migrants of any ethnic group and their culture. The term is used as well to describe the global dispersion of any historically victimized minority, such as the Roma (gypsies) or Armenians, or visible and potentially victimized minorities, such as Arabs in Africa and Chinese people in Indonesia.

The result is a worldwide network of ethnic enclaves—of Chinese communities in Toronto, Sydney, Singapore, Paris, and Buenos Aires, for example. Within any given location, each of these ethnic enclaves seeks and often achieves institutional completeness. The result is a network of worldwide cities, each of which is ethnically segregated, all connected to one another through inter-community linkages.

For example, the municipalities that make up Toronto are now home to specific communities of ethnic groups. In fact, 72.3 per cent of Markham's population is made up of specific and visible minority groups (Statistics Canada, 2011a). Table 3.1 illustrates the prevalence of these specific diasporic groups within the metropolitan cities of Canada. For example, the top three visible minority groups of Montreal—black, Arab, and Latin American—represent members of ethnic communities that belong to larger international groups. While many critics believe these enclaves signify a reluctance to integrate into Canadian society, research has shown that these enclaves are socially and economically, as well as politically, integrated.

Diaspora The dispersal of any group of people throughout the world; originally applied to the tribes of Israel. Any migrant community with some degree of international heritage is referred to as "diasporic."

42
Brian Helgeland's 2013 film is about the life of baseball player Jackie Robinson, who wore jersey number 42. Guided by team executive Branch Rickey, Robinson—signed with the Brooklyn Dodgers—became the first African-American player to break the baseball colour barrier.

TABLE 3.1	Visible Minority Population and Top Three Visible Minority Groups, Selected Census Metropolitan Areas, Canada, 2011			
	TOTAL POPULATION	VISIBLE MINORITY POPULATION (ALL VISIBLE MINORITIES)		TOP 3 VISIBLE MINORITY GROUPS
	Number	Number	Percentage	
Canada	32,852,325	6,264,755	19.1	South Asian, Chinese, black
Toronto	5,521,235	2,596,420	47.0	South Asian, Chinese, black
Montreal	3,752,475	762,325	20.3	black, Arab, Latin American
Vancouver	2,280,695	1,030,335	45.2	Chinese, South Asian, Filipino
Ottawa-Gatineau	1,215,735	234,015	19.2	black, Arab, Chinese
Calgary	1,199,125	337,420	28.1	South Asian, Chinese, Filipino
Edmonton	1,139,585	254,990	22.4	South Asian, Chinese, Filipino
Winnipeg	714,635	140,770	19.7	Filipino, South Asian, black
Hamilton	708,175	101,600	14.3	South Asian, black, Chinese

Source: Statistics Canada (2011b).

Theoretical Perspectives on Race and Ethnicity

TABLE 3.2	Theoretical Perspectives
THEORY	MAIN POINTS
Structural Functionalism	• Ethnic identity provides social connectedness in an individualistic society. • Ethnocultural diversity provides a wide range of opinions, perspectives, and values that enrich society. • Ethnocultural conflict enforces boundaries, which give groups more cohesion and a sense of identity.
Conflict Theory	• Majority groups benefit from excluding and marginalizing minority groups. • Corporate leaders benefit by hiring minorities at low wages to secure shareholder profits. • Racial tension divides workers by setting up competition among them, diverting their anger from the exploitive capitalists.
Symbolic Interactionism	• Ethnic differentiation is constructed by a labelling process. • Racial slurs further undermine the inferior status of minority groups. • Racial labels and slurs can shape the way groups view themselves. • Constant awareness of race (racial socialization) in daily social interaction increases the likelihood of racial conflict.
Feminist Theory	• Focuses on the type of victimization experienced by racialized minorities. • Interested in the intersectionality of race with class, sexual orientation, and gender. • Views race and ethnicity as performances, like gender—not essential qualities.
Structural Theory	• Minorities that are more visible are streamed into the secondary labour market and rarely into the primary market. • Job markets sometimes exclude people on the grounds of race or ethnicity. • A general bias against hiring non-whites has made many visible minority immigrants become "middlemen."

Structural Functionalism

Structural functionalists have sometimes been accused of glossing over the nasty unfairness associated with inequality. According to functionalists, even the inequalities between racial or ethnic groups—the "verticalities" in *The Vertical Mosaic*—have a value for society. Functionalists propose that social inequality encourages people to struggle for social and economic success. As well, ethnoracial diversity, however unequal, benefits society as a whole. It allows for the discussion of a wider range of opinions, perspectives, and values, and for the development of a wider range of skills.

Even social conflict between ethnic and racial groups has a social value (see, for example, Coser, 1965; Pruitt et al., 2003). By drawing and enforcing boundaries, conflict intensifies people's sense of identity, giving groups more cohesion and a heightened sense of purpose. So, functionalists may even see ethnic exclusion, prejudice, and discrimination as benefiting society as a whole, since it stimulates institutional completeness. In short, maintaining distinct ethnic identities helps to socially integrate people into distinct communities. This integration provides them with roots and social connectedness in an otherwise individualistic, fragmented society.

Conflict Theory

Unlike functionalists, conflict theorists focus on how different groups benefit, to different degrees, from diversity and exclusion. They explore, for instance, how economic competition results in the creation and preservation of racial stereotypes and institutionalized racism. Conflict theory proposes that majority groups seek to exploit minorities economically. They also seek to dominate them, especially when feeling threatened by the minority. This was clear historically, as in British Columbia during the early twentieth century when the white majority saw Chinese and South Asian workers as a threat to their jobs and their way of life. Even today, majority native-born Canadians benefit from the depressed job opportunities and wages of new immigrants who are forced to take work that is often below their educational attainment and skill levels.

Feminist Theory

Some feminist theorists, such as Susan Moller Okin (1998), believe that giving ethnic minorities special rights ignores the rights of women and furthers female subordination and oppression (Reitman, 2005). In response to multiculturalism, these feminist theorists propose that oppression occurs when certain minority groups—those who are led by traditional values and come from traditionally oppressive cultures—are granted group rights that are at odds with gender equality. With these rights, the traditional groups have coercive and sometimes sexist authority over their members.

In 2005, for example, Muslims living in Ontario proposed that *sharia* law—typically associated with the subordination of women—be applied to settle certain familial disputes in the Islamic community (Moghissi et al., 2009). This proposal was rejected, despite a government-commissioned report by former provincial attorney general Marion Boyd that spoke favourably about some aspects of the proposal. Had it passed, the law would have given traditional gender values primacy over modern, egalitarian gender values.

Canadian minority groups do not have the legal right to exercise formal power over their members. Canada's form of multiculturalism rejects internal restrictions and provides only certain external protections (Adams, 2007). Through what Spinner-Halev (2001) terms "integrative multiculturalism," ethnic minorities are only granted rights that enable them to maintain their culture (e.g., freedom of religion and the right to claim public funding for cultural festivals). At times, additional rights are granted, such as extra representation in political bodies and exemption from certain laws; multicultural theorists believe these special policies further facilitate integration into mainstream society. Despite this, ethnic minorities are expected to integrate into Canadian society and abide by national laws (Adams, 2007).

Feminist scholars note that certain groups of women experience more discrimination than others. In particular, those who hold several minority statuses, such as Aboriginal women living off the reserve or married to non-Natives (Green, 2001), are likely to be isolated from both their own society and that of the mainstream. Like other traditional cultures, certain Aboriginal cultures discriminate against women and, in so doing, violate the Canadian Constitution. These cultural practices are often justified as an evocation of tradition—and hence as a powerful method of resisting colonialism (ibid.)—but they still pose a danger to women's rights.

Symbolic Interactionism

Symbolic interactionists focus on microsociological aspects of race and discrimination, such as the ways people construct ethnic and racial labels to subordinate minority groups.

Interactionists point to *racial socialization* as a factor that contributes to continuing racial conflict in society (McKown and Strambler, 2009). Racial socialization is a process of social interaction that exposes people to the beliefs, values, cultural history, language, and social and economic realities of their own and other people's racial or ethnic identities (Scottham and Smalls, 2009). In other words, it is the process of learning "what it means" socially and culturally to be a Jew, a Chinese person, a Ukrainian, and so on. Often, this includes the learning of long-term biases and prejudices that have no place in an egalitarian, pluralistic society.

Interactionists stress that "race" is a social construct; we imagine it and then enact it. Likewise, the supposed attributes of race—for example, racial intelligence or virtue or instinct—are socially constructed. Ezeonu (2006) proposes that, in similar ways, even racial violence is socially constructed. He notes that public concern about crime and criminal victimization may be shaped by the operation of what Joel Best (1989) calls the "social problem marketplace." In the competition over how a social problem is defined, people whose definitions win public support or attract the sympathy of policy bureaucrats are most able to influence the making of social policies to control the problem.

Claims-makers may call for new laws, new programs, or particular forms of government intervention in dealing with particular problems, and sometimes policy-makers respond to the typifications used by those making claims about particular policies. In other words, social policies are often the products of the competing interest groups' claims-making about how particular social problems are conceived and how they can be dealt with (Burns, 2002).

Structural Theory

Structural theory, in particular, helps us understand the experiences of racial and ethnic minorities in economic life. Those who are the most similar—racially, culturally, and educationally—to members of the host society will enjoy the easiest, most rapid assimilation into the labour market. They will be the most successful minority groups in competing for the better jobs, especially during times of economic growth. In recessionary times, everyone's assimilation will be slower and more conflictual. People's experiences will reflect the characteristics of the economy more than anything they do or believe (Kashefi, 2004). That said, the least-advantaged groups are the ones hardest hit by a recession.

In Canada, the sorting out of people according to the jobs they will hold begins in schools. Through the deliberate application of subtle and complex procedures like tracking and grade weighting, some students are encouraged while others are discouraged, which reduces the opportunities of the latter group following high school graduation. On entering the workforce, people of "different kinds" are streamed into some types of jobs and away from others. For example, far more women and visible minorities are streamed into the secondary labour market—and far more white men into the primary labour market—than could have occurred by chance. However, even within these markets, there are important differences among jobs. For instance, although teachers and doctors are both in the primary labour market, few teachers feel that they have the sort of benefits and opportunities that doctors do. Therefore, it is of interest to sociologists to know the criteria according to which people become teachers or doctors—or Shakespearean actors.

Some job markets exclude or discourage people because of race, ethnicity, or gender, though this is becoming less common. Throughout Canada, there exist vast differences in immigrant employment across the provinces, with employers in the Prairies hiring the most foreign workers (Figure 3.3). However, immigration tends to level the playing field, whatever the immigrant's credentials, or background experience. Whatever their origins, new immigrants tend to hold the lowest entrance statuses. That said, some immigrants do better from others: for example, immigrants from the Philippines have had the

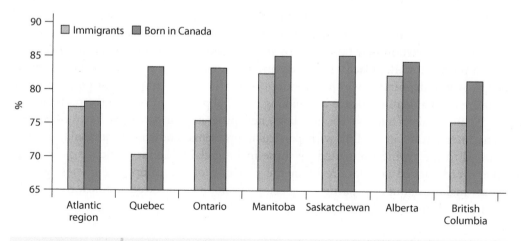

FIGURE 3.3 | Rate of Employment among Immigrants and Canadian Born Aged 25–54, by Province or Region, 2011

Source: Statistics Canada (2012b).

highest employment rate of all groups, while immigrants from Africa have had the lowest rates (Statistics Canada, 2011a).

Immigration carries severe economic costs for many, and we see immigrants with a variety of advanced degrees—such as doctors, engineers, social workers, and nurses—driving taxis or providing low-paid personal services in various parts of the country. Even when they earn good wages, there is a large wage gap between university-educated recent immigrants and university-educated domestic-born Canadians (Statistics Canada, 2011b).

Many immigrants respond by starting their own businesses. Research on middle-man minorities finds the following typical pattern. A culturally or racially distinct group immigrates and suffers discrimination (Godwyn, 2009). Members of the group come to see themselves as "strangers" in the country and, to protect themselves, settle in the larger towns and cities. There, they work to become self-employed as wholesalers, small merchants (e.g., shopkeepers), or even professionals. Their economic and social survival depends on thrift, a high degree of education and organization, and the use of family and community ties in business. By these means, the group eventually achieves a middle-class standard of living (Yamamoto, 2009).

Most Canadians prefer to ignore or deny the evidence of discrimination and segregation in their society, but it is healthier and more realistic to face the matter, head-on.

Public Issues *and* Public Policy

BOX 3.2 | Race May Shorten Housing Wait

With more than 6,000 people on the waiting list for social housing in York Region, two local housing providers have recently asked if they could restrict who is eligible for their subsidized units.

It is an issue that goes to the heart of Canada's multicultural ethos, Richmond Hill regional councillor Brenda Hogg points out. "It would prolong the time other people must wait. . . . It sends the message to the public we are going to allow specific groups to self-impose segregation." The former community services and housing committee chairperson says, "That's not the Canada I'm part of."

The province once encouraged housing providers to serve ethnic and religious communities, but that changed with the passing of the Social Housing Reform Act in 2000. Responsibility was given to municipalities, and while private homes can do what they want, York Region administers a central list of subsidized units, prioritized chronologically.

But Vaughan's Friuli Terrace has a different perspective on the issue. It was built in 1989 for Italian seniors, with Italian as the lingua franca, and everything from meals to entertainment is geared towards that. When slots open at Friuli Terrace, the director of social services—Ms Anthony—has the job of filling them, based on who is next on the region's list. But if the terrace is forced to house someone who is not Italian and has requested to be somewhere else, "[it] can't service the group we were meant to service . . . they also don't want to be here."

A report by the Ontario Human Rights Commission with comments on social housing is expected soon. In the meantime, the Richmond Hill regional councillor would like to see public money continue to go to members of the public most in need, regardless of their ethnicity.

Ms Anthony countered that her tenants are all taxpayers too.

Sources: Adapted from Gail Swainson, "Housing Subsidy Blasted," *Toronto Star*, 19 February 2010, <www.thestar.com/news/gta/2010/02/19/housing_subsidy_blasted.html>.

Racism and Prejudice: Social Problems

Defining and Measuring Racial Prejudice

Prejudice A hostile or aversive attitude towards a person who belongs to a particular group just because of that person's membership in the group.

Racial discrimination "Any distinction, exclusion, restriction, or preference based on race, colour, descent, or national or ethnic origin that has the purpose or effect of nullifying or impairing the recognition, enjoyment of exercise . . . of human rights and fundamental freedoms" (Office of the High Commissioner for Human Rights, 1969).

Institutional (structural) racism Any form of racism that occurs specifically from within an institution, such as public government bodies and private business corporations. This form of racism is "built into" these prominent structures.

Individual racism "Classic" form of prejudice in which a person makes unfounded assumptions about the motives and abilities of another based on a stereotypical understanding of the person's racial or ethnic group characteristics.

Internalized racism When members of an ethnic or racial group accept and sometimes behave according to imposed stereotypes.

Psychologist Gordon Allport (1954: 7) defined **prejudice** as "an aversive or hostile attitude toward a person who belongs to a group, simply because he belongs to that group, and is therefore presumed to have the objectionable qualities ascribed to the group."

Racial discrimination, for its part, has been characterized by the United Nations Office of the High Commissioner for Human Rights as "any distinction, exclusion, restriction, or preference based on race, colour, descent, or national or ethnic origin which has the purpose or effect of nullifying or impairing the recognition, enjoyment or exercise, on an equal footing, of human rights and fundamental freedoms in the political, economic, social, cultural or any other field of public life" (Office of the High Commissioner for Human Rights, 1969).

It is in this context that we can understand the meaning of "racism," a complex and emotion-laden term. Some racism is hidden and some is easily on view, for racism appears in multiple versions. Least visible is **institutional (structural) racism**—any systemic bias embedded in an existing social structure, policy, or process that deprives some groups of equal access to goods, services, and rights because of their ethnic or racial membership (Kent, 2009). Examples of institutional racism include rental-housing markets that try to keep "undesirable" ethnic groups out of certain communities and banks and insurance companies that deny loans to people in certain neighbourhoods based on crude economic (and racially tinged) criteria, a practice known as "redlining" (Morris, 2008).

Such actions result in unequal educational opportunities for some minority groups and an unequal distribution of wealth among ethnic and racial groups. Eventually, this translates into an under-representation of visible minorities in political offices, corporate boardrooms, and other positions of power. Policies such as employment equity seek to offset the effects of institutional racism on vulnerable groups (Thompson, 2008).

Individual racism is the more visible classic form of prejudice in which a person makes groundless assumptions about the motives and abilities of another based on a stereotypical understanding of the person's racial or ethnic group membership. Its epitome is the dangerous and unrepentant bigot—the Ku Klux Klan member, say, or the neo-Nazi. However, it would be wrong (and dangerous) to suppose that the practice of racism is limited to these extremist groups. Research has found subtle expressions of racism among a majority of people. These expressions include evidence of aversive racism in medical interactions with black patients (Penner et al., 2010), subtle bias against Muslim job applicants (Park et al., 2009), and other evidence of discrimination and implicit bias (Banks et al., 2006). In short, unconscious racism still exists (Quillian, 2008).

Perhaps the most destructive form of racism is **internalized racism**, where members of an ethnic or racial group come to believe the stereotypes that others have imposed on them (Cort et al., 2009). This tragic consequence of institutional and individual racism leads some people to devalue their own worth, compromise their life goals, and passively accept the racial barriers that perpetuate a cycle of oppression and inequality (Bryant, 2009).

So far, no academic consensus exists on the best method for measuring people's levels of racial and ethnic bias. Asking people direct questions about the prejudices they hold against a particular ethnic or cultural group is unlikely to yield accurate results (Cea D'Ancona, 2009). Most people have a hard time admitting their biases to themselves, let

The Canadian Press/Jeff McIntosh

An example of individual racism can be found in the actions of an Aryan Guard supporter who salutes at a White Pride rally while yelling at anti-racism supporters in Calgary.

alone to others, and feel obliged to respond in a socially approved (i.e., non-prejudicial) way. Thus, social scientists often use indirect measures instead. One way to do this is to measure the **social distance** between ethnic groups, which E.S. Bogardus does in his classic 1928 study.

Other measures of racial prejudice are based on social psychological principles. The Modern Racism Scale (MRS) was designed as another way of indirectly tapping into respondents' prejudices about various ethnic groups (McConahay, 1981, 1986). The MRS shows that everyone considers adherence to explicitly racist notions (such as support for segregation or slavery) socially unacceptable, but racial ambivalence and prejudice persist in more subtle forms.

For example, so-called **aversive racists** sympathize with the victims of past injustice; support public policies that, in principle, promote racial equality and reduce the harm of racism; identify more with a liberal political agenda; and view themselves as non-prejudiced and non-discriminatory. However, they still harbour negative feelings about the members of other races, such as "discomfort, uneasiness, disgust, and sometimes fear, which motivate avoidance rather than intentionally destructive behaviours" (Gaertner and Dovidio, 2000: 289–90).

Researchers have also developed the Implicit Association Test (IAT) as an indirect cognitive measure of racial bias (Greenwald et al., 2009). In this procedure, two types of test stimuli are displayed in rapid succession on a computer screen—photographs of the faces of blacks and whites, posed with neutral facial expressions, and positive and

Social distance Feelings of aloofness and unapproachability often felt between members of different social strata or of different ethnic or "racial" origins.

Aversive racists Those who sympathize with the victims of past injustice and support public policies that promote racial equality but who nonetheless hold prejudicial views towards other races.

CANADIAN researchers

BOX 3.3   Monica Boyd, University of Toronto

Much of the research on race and ethnic relations in Canada concerns issues of inequality, prejudice, exclusion, discrimination, and social distance. However, in her work, Monica Boyd, Canada research chair in immigration, inequality and public policy, presents a much rosier picture of ethnic and race relations, even in the case of immigrants and visible minorities.

Over her long career as a sociologist, Monica Boyd has studied educational and occupation opportunity in Canada, and in the last two decades, she has focused on the opportunities available to immigrants. This research has included the study of education, housing, professional accreditation, and marital assimilation (or exogamy). In the article "Marrying out: The Marital Blending and Integration of Asians in North America," Professor Boyd and her collaborator Sharon Lee (2008) find more similarities than differences between the two countries. Intermarriage variations by age, gender, education, immigrant generation, Asian ethnic group, and other characteristics are generally similar in Canada and the United States. The main difference is lower overall Asian exogamy in Canada, reflecting differences in the history, composition, and distribution of the Asian populations here. This aside, the authors conclude that exogamy is likely to increase in both Canada and the US.

Other research by Professor Boyd confirms this rosy prospect for immigrants, including visible minorities. For example, in her 2002 paper "Educational Attainments of Immigrant Offspring: Success or Segmented

Assimilation," Boyd notes that the adult visible minorities in Canada achieve higher educational levels than non-visible minorities. What's more, the educational achievement of these visible minorities is even higher among members of generation 1.5 and 2 than it is among members of generation 3 in the same groups, pointing to rapid and unimpeded mobility by minority newcomers and their children. Indeed, subsequent research reported in Boyd's 2009 paper "Social Origins and the Educational and Occupational Achievements of the 1.5 and Second Generations" confirms that visible minorities are doing well in Canada and that the achievements of adult immigrants vary by region of origin, as well as by family background characteristics.

Further, other research points to continued problems facing recent immigrants. In their 2007 paper "Re-accreditation and the Occupations of Immigrant Doctors and Engineers," Boyd and colleague Grant Schellenberg find that foreign-educated physicians and engineers are less likely than physicians and engineers educated in Canada to find employment commensurate with their professional training. Underemployment is particularly common among foreign-trained immigrants coming from Southeast Asia and East Asia. Engineers and physicians who received their training in Western Europe, by contrast, are most likely to find work in the field for which they trained. The obstacles involve Canadian re-accreditation requirements, which favour the latter group over the former.

negative words, such as "peace" and "happy" or "nasty" and "failure." Subjects are asked to quickly group each stimulus object under one of two headings, which are either consistent (e.g., "black faces/negative words" and "white faces/positive words") or inconsistent (e.g., "black faces/positive words" and "white faces/negative words") with popular racial stereotypes.

A fast response is interpreted as a sign of a stronger mental association between the stimulus object and the category heading, and therefore an implicit cognitive bias. That is, according to the test, racial prejudice may be signalled by a faster response time in assigning a photograph of a black person to the "black faces/negative words" category than to the "black faces/positive words" category. Conversely, it may show a faster response time in assigning a negative word to the "black faces/negative words" category than to the "white faces/negative words" category.

Classic WORKS

BOX 3.4 **Emory Bogardus's "Social Distance"**

Social distance is a concept devised by the psychologist Emory S. Bogardus in the early twentieth century to measure the extent of intergroup segregation and, conversely, the willingness of group members to mix with other groups (1933). Bogardus devised a scale that ranked people's willingness to accept members of a certain racial, ethnic, or other group in a range of social relationships, from close to distant. These relationships are listed here from the closest to the most distant:

1. Close relative by marriage
2. Close personal friend
3. Neighbour on same street
4. Co-worker in same occupation
5. Citizen in own country
6. Temporary visitor in own country
7. Someone excluded from own country

In effect, social distance is like a ladder: a group that is accepted at a certain level of closeness is also accepted at all the more distant levels below it. In other words, a group acceptable for close personal friendship would also be acceptable as neighbour or workmate (Zhang and Van Hook, 2009). However, this distance preference is not perfectly symmetrical. For example, people are more likely to accept their daughter marrying a distant "higher status" group member than an equally distant "lower

status" group member, because people—especially, daughters—are supposed to "marry up."

By asking a variety of respondents the same questions, we can calculate an average social distance measure for each "target group"—for Jewish Canadians, black Canadians, Italian Canadians, and so on. In consequence, we can find out which "types" of minorities are most accepted and rejected by the majority. As well, we can determine which "types" of people are most open to minorities and which are most closed or distant.

Through research using this scale, sociologists have learned that people who place other groups at a distance from themselves often hold prejudices about those other groups and sometimes act on these prejudices. This creates hardship for members of minority groups so named, not only because they are few but because they are powerless.

Another unobtrusive way to measure the social distance between groups is to examine rates of intergroup marriage. In a study by Heaton and Jacobson (2008), Canada was found to have increasing intermarriage rates, suggesting that social distance (and racism) is decreasing. This conclusion is supported by data from the 2006 census, which showed a growth rate of mixed unions five times larger than that for other couples (Milan et al., 2010). Those most likely to enter into mixed-race marriages are young people, people born in Canada, and people with a higher-than-average education.

Racialization

Racism is the everyday outcome of a historical process called **racialization**, the tendency in a community to introduce racial distinctions into situations that can be understood and managed without such distinctions (Abu-Laban and Bakan, 2008). In this way, race sometimes becomes the basis for decisions about hiring, buying, renting, befriending, and respecting others. Such practices of racialization can happen easily unless people take pains to avoid them.

In the police and judicial systems, racial profiling—the tendency to look for and interpret people's behaviour differently, based on their race—is all too common. For example, police may pull over cars driven by young black or Aboriginal men, but not by young white men, in the expectation of finding alcohol, drugs, weapons, or other grounds for arrest there (Parmar, 2007).

Racialization The tendency in a community to introduce racial distinctions into situations that can be understood and managed without such distinctions—in other words, the way social institutions impose racial identities on minorities.

Social Consequences of Race and Ethnicity

Gender Relations

The interaction of gender and racism leads to unique problems for women of some minority groups. Women continue to hold a lower status than men within many immigrant groups, with a high degree of oppression found in certain groups. This oppressiveness creates further conflict when new immigrants realize that their notions of proper gender relations clash with those accepted in North America (Hong, 2008).

Subordinated by both their racial identity and their gender, many immigrant women find themselves isolated and devalued in Canadian society, often with few social supports and nowhere to turn. The results often take the form of mental and physical health problems.

Work and Unemployment

As already noted, discrimination in the workplace may be directed along racial and ethnic lines. Aboriginal people, members of visible minority groups, and recent immigrants to Canada all tend to experience lower-than-average employment and pay rates in most regions of Canada. Such discrimination is also frequently a result of differences in human capital, such as education, experience, credentials, and scarce expertise (Rodlandt, 1996; Galabuzi, 2006).

This disparity in employment rates can be seen in Table 3.3. Those born in Canada have a consistently higher percentage of employment as compared to landed immigrants.

TABLE 3.3	Labour Force Characteristics by Immigrant Status, by Detailed Age Group			
	2013			
	15 YEARS AND OVER	15 TO 24 YEARS	25 TO 54 YEARS	55 YEARS AND OVER
Employment rate				
Total population	61.8%	55.1%	81.5%	35.1%
Landed immigrants[1]	57.3	44.5	77.0	33.0
Immigrants, landed 5 or less years earlier	58.9	37.2	67.1	28.3
Immigrants, landed more than 5 to 10 years earlier	66.4	44.0	75.7	38.6
Immigrants, landed more than 10 years earlier	55.3	49.2	80.3	32.9
Born in Canada	63.3	57.3	83.3	35.9
Unemployment rate				
Total population	7.1	13.7	5.9	6.0
Landed immigrants[1]	8.1	16.3	7.7	6.9
Immigrants, landed 5 or less years earlier	12.4	18.5	11.2	19.6
Immigrants, landed more than 5 to 10 years earlier	9.1	17.2	7.7	11.7
Immigrants, landed more than 10 years earlier	7.0	14.8	6.7	6.2
Born in Canada	6.7	13.3	5.3	5.7

[1] Refers to people who are, or have been, landed immigrants in Canada. A landed immigrant is a person who has been granted the right to live in Canada permanently by immigration authorities. Canadian citizens by birth and non-permanent residents (persons from another country who live in Canada and have a work or study permit or are claiming refugee status, as well as family members living here with them) are not landed immigrants.

Source: Statistics Canada (2013a).

However, this table does not reveal the whole story. Immigrants with a university degree are often forced into jobs that are below their credentials.

In brief, highly trained immigrant visible minorities are the last hired and the first fired, and many recent immigrants find that their educational and work credentials are not recognized in the Canadian employment system.

Yet many employers deny that they discriminate against anyone on racial or ethnic grounds. In order to show the discrimination at play in work settings, Frances Henry and Effie Ginzberg (1985; Henry, 1999) conducted a set of field experiments in Toronto. In one study, two equally qualified applicants—one black and the other white—applied for the same advertised jobs. With the results, Henry and Ginzberg created an Index of Discrimination and found that "whites have three job prospects for every one that blacks have" (1985: 308).

Oreopoulos (2009) conducted a similar study to gain more recent results; in this study, resumés with either English-sounding names or "foreign"-sounding (i.e., non-English) names (i.e., Chinese, Indian, or Pakistani) were submitted to employers. The results showed that English-sounding names had a 15.8 per cent call-back rate—much higher than the rate for people with non-English-sounding names and the same amount of experience. The call-back rate fell even lower if the resumé of a foreign-named candidate listed experience outside of Canada (Oreopoulos, 2009).

This study and others like it (e.g., Beck et al., 2002; Austin and Este, 2001; Pager, 2007; Bertrand and Mullainathan, 2004; Rooth, 2010) have shown that racial discrimination is more common than we would think. Moreover, not only do members of

Colin McConnell/Toronto Star via Getty Images

Richard Wang, pictured here in front of his Dixon Road apartment building in Toronto, is an immigrant from China and a former social scientist and university professor. He is now a single father who takes part-time temporary work wherever he can find it, including jobs as a warehouse labourer, toilet cleaner, and coat check attendant.

minority groups face discrimination when seeking a job, they also face it when competing for promotion. Compared to non-visible minorities, members of visible racial groups and Aboriginal people with a university degree are less likely to enter managerial or professional positions. For those who do, more than half are self-employed, compared to only one-third in non-minority groups.

Poverty and Wealth

Although most of the poor people living in Canada and the United States are white, higher *proportions* of minority groups are impoverished. Immigrants, visible minorities, and Aboriginal people are *over*-represented at the bottom of the income scale (Gee and Prus, 2000; Hou and Balakrishnan, 1996; Attewell et al., 2010). Similarly, Aboriginal people and visible minorities are *under*-represented among the top 20 per cent of income earners.

Studies have shown that Aboriginals living off reserve are among the least residentially concentrated groups and thus have less social capital than other Canadians. As a result, they often endure greater economic difficulties compared to residentially concentrated groups, such as the Chinese and Jewish populations in Canada (Adams, 2007: 55). In recent years, however, Native Canadians have made economic progress. According to a 2010 Statistics Canada report, the employment rate of Natives between 25 and 45 years old living off-reserve is now 75 per cent, only 12 per cent lower than that of non-Aboriginals (Zietsma, 2010).

The disparity between Aboriginals and the general population largely stems from historical injustices. One of the most disadvantaging, unjust conditions came in the form of residential schools, which removed young people from their cultural roots and subjected many to physical and sexual abuse. In 2008, Prime Minister Stephen Harper apologized for the forced assimilation instituted in residential schools, saying, "Today, we recognize that this policy of assimilation was wrong, has caused great harm, and has no place in our country" (Fenlon, 2008). With this apology, the government included a $4-billion compensation and healing package.

Discrimination can take the form of residential segregation, and although less advanced than in the US, some race-based residential segregation is evident in Canada. Already, an "isolation index," which measures the extent to which minority group members meet one another within their neighbourhoods, shows that segregation and concentration of ethnic minorities has increased in Canada (Hou and Picot, 2004). However this is nothing new. As early as 2002, Bauder and Sharpe (2002) were remarking on the residential segregation of visible minorities in Canada's gateway cities. Using data from the previous decade, they report finding "fragmentation" and "dispersal" (or ethnic separation) in Toronto, Vancouver, and Montreal, despite "an atmosphere of diversity and multiculturalism."

Crime and Violence

As we will see in a later chapter, blacks and Aboriginal people are over-represented in the criminal justice system, both as perpetrators and as victims. These statistics reflect group differences in unemployment, poverty, and substance abuse. They also suggest discrimination at the bail and sentencing stages (Roberts and Doob, 1997; Demuth, 2003). Further, evidence suggests that law enforcement officers may racialize and stereotype

DJANGO UNCHAINED

Quentin Tarantino's 2012 film follows a freed slave who treks across the United States with a bounty hunter to rescue his wife from a cruel slave-owning plantation owner.

ethnic minorities, especially when dealing with street gangs (Smith, 2007; Pettit and Western, 2004; Dharmapala and Ross, 2004).

In a recent study, Aboriginal youth made up only 6 per cent of the eight jurisdictions from which data was collected, yet they comprised 26 per cent of the youth entering correctional systems in these jurisdictions (Statistics Canada, 2011a, 2012b). Likewise, in the United States, blacks account for only 13 per cent of the population, yet they represent 30 per cent of all the people arrested and half of those imprisoned. In short, disadvantage and poverty increase the likelihood of law-breaking by racial and ethnic minorities, while prejudice and discrimination increase the likelihood of arrest, conviction, and imprisonment (Gabbidon, 2010).

Health Consequences of Race and Ethnicity

Effects of Disadvantage

Disadvantaged ethnic and racialized groups lead different lives from the rest of the population. In Canada, for example, the life expectancy of Aboriginal Canadians is still significantly lower than that of other groups (D'Arcy, 1998; see also Waldram et al., 1996; Rodney and Copeland, 2009). Similarly, in the United States, of all racial groups, American blacks live the fewest years and spend the highest proportion of those years with chronic health problems (Hayward and Heron, 1999; Harper et al., 2012; Williams and Mohammed, 2009).

How do we explain this? Researchers have advanced three different types of explanation: biological explanations based on genetic differences; cultural explanations that link differences in disease prevalence to cultural factors (such as diet); and socio-economic explanations that focus on the association between poor health, minority status, and economic disadvantage (Spencer, 1996; Williams and Jackson, 2005). Whatever the role of genetics and culture, the link between poor health, material disadvantage, and socio-economic status is clear (Adler and Ostrove, 2006; Demakakos et al., 2008). No wonder, then, that racial and ethnic differences in health shrink significantly when we control for education and other factors related to income (Williams et al., 1997).

Effects of Immigration

Institutional racism can lead to economic hardships with bad health outcomes, but Canadian research has found that neither the health status of immigrants nor their use of health services differs much from those of the Canadian-born population (Laroche, 2000).

However, immigration can still have harmful health effects besides those due to poverty and discrimination. In fact, on arrival, new immigrants typically have better health than the host population does, largely owing to strict immigration selection criteria. Yet, for many ethnic minorities, this health advantage disappears within a generation or two; some groups even experience worse health status than the native-born.

As noted earlier, many immigrants find employment in lower-end and lower-paying jobs where they are often exposed to higher-than-average health risks. Added to this, many have difficulty accessing health-care information and services, sometimes hesitating to use health services because of a low level of English- or French-language literacy.

Problems with their personal lives may also have health consequences. For example, 80 per cent of refugees to Quebec from Africa and Latin America had experienced or were experiencing separations (averaging three years) from their partners or children (Moreau et al., 1999). Children and adolescent refugees separated from parents are especially likely to have mental health problems (Derluyn et al., 2009). Such separations, often associated with traumatic events, can cause emotional distress and hinder the process of adapting to a new country.

In addition, immigrants may suffer from loneliness, boredom, and post-migration anxieties about discrimination. People who have been displaced by war are even worse off than people who are impoverished, for their suffering is over and above their material disadvantage. The trauma of displacement often results in fear, disorientation, and distrust—conditions that are not easily relieved (Segura Escobar, 2000).

Access to Health Care

Research shows that, on the whole, visible minority groups in Canada have access to adequate general care to meet their overall health needs (e.g., Quan et al., 2006; Wardman et al., 2005; Wu et al., 2005; Wen et al., 1996).

However, these same studies also find evidence of systemic barriers in accessing specialized health-care services, such as surgery, emergency room visits, and dental care. Obstacles include a lack of knowledge about where to find suitable help, language barriers between medical staff and patients, concerns about encountering institutional racial discrimination, and, for rural Aboriginal communities, a shortage of professionals and facilities. Researchers have called on governments and health-care practitioners to address these issues by ensuring , for example, the availability of language interpreters (Tang, 1999; Gerrish et al, 2004; Ramirez, 2008).

Different cultures have different views about health and illness. As a result, different cultures provide their members different culturally meaningful diagnoses and frameworks for appropriate intervention. Ethnic groups living in a Western culture often find that non-Western health-care alternatives are scarce. So, when forced to seek help from the only available caregiver—the modern hospital—they are hesitant and worry that going to a hospital will worsen the illness.

The Health Effects of Racism

Both racial discrimination and socio-economic discrimination contribute to the poor health of minorities. Some of the effects are obvious. Discrimination, by increasing stress, increases the likelihood of experiencing psychiatric symptoms and unhealthy addictions, such as cigarette smoking (Landrine and Klonoff, 1996; Lavalle and Yale, 2004). Other factors, such as alienation, poverty, inequality at work, and worries about unemployment, contribute to the poor health of minority people. Shelly Harrell (2000: 45–6) has identified six sources of racism-related stress:

- "racism-related life events"—acute, intense, but rare events, such as police harassment or discrimination in the workplace;
- "vicarious racism experiences"—includes the transmission of specific incidents of prejudice and discrimination experienced by family and friends, or through the news media;

- "daily racism micro-stressors"—subtle and frequent reminders of one's subordinate status in society, such as being ignored or overly scrutinized by sales staff;
- "chronic contextual stress"—arises from the need to adapt to the broad racial and ethnic inequalities in social/political/economic structure;
- "collective experiences"—reflect "the idea that cultural-symbolic and socio-political manifestations of racism can be observed and felt by people" and include the "economic conditions of members of one's racial/ethnic group, the lack of political representation, or stereotypic portrayals in the media"; and
- "trans-generational transmission"—or the historical context in which modern racial and ethnic discrimination has been bred and preserved, such as the experiences of current refugees.

The health outcomes of racism-related stress can be severe. Several researchers have found, for instance, that the resentment and distrust bred by racial victimization can raise a person's blood pressure. Stress can also erode one's mental health status and adversely affect a person's sense of self-worth; it can also lead to substance abuse and other chronic physical health problems (Rollock and Gordon, 2000; Malin, 2000; Mays et al., 2007; Gee et al., 2007).

Claims-Making in Studies of Race and Ethnicity

Constructionist views of ethnicity and race go back some time in sociological and political science literature. In particular, political sociology has long had an interest in understanding ethnic identities, sometimes with the goal of learning where and why ethnonationalist conflicts erupt.

In this field, approaches to ethnicity have varied from "primordialist" positions, which hold that ethnicity is an immutable, tangible quality, to "instrumentalist" positions, which acknowledge the important role played by ethnic elites in selectively producing an ethnic history with the goal of uniting the nation. More nuanced constructivist positions hold that ethnopolitics are both real and imagined (Robertson, 1997). The construction of race as tied to class, national origin, culture, and language, some propose, may amount to a type of "ethnoracism" that persists in a climate of "colour-blind" racism (Aranda and Rebollo-Gil, 2004).

Constructionist views on race have had a substantial impact in sociology. Indeed, this chapter has presented evidence on the socially constructed nature of race. However, it is easy to lose sight of this notion and uncritically accept race as an simple idea. This is especially true in the case of survey-based research, but it can also occur in qualitative work (Morris, 2008). Thus, the constructionist viewpoint reminds us of the complexity of race as a concept and cautions researchers against unwittingly reproducing racial inequalities in their research of it.

Governmental and Organizational Solutions to Prejudice and Racism

The Employment Equity Act, passed in 1986, applies to the federal public service, Crown corporations and agencies, and private companies employing 100 employees or more. It is intended to ensure that the proportion of visible minorities and women hired in the workplace reflect the proportion of these groups among those who are applying for work. To ensure that hiring practices are equitable, employers are obliged to file annual reports on their employees to the federal government. Data from these reports are then made public (Lamarche et al., 2006).

As well, employers are obliged to identify and make an effort to remove the barriers facing members of under-represented groups by planning initiatives to increase their representation. Employment equity is intended to tackle what many sociologists believe to be the cause of racial and ethnic inequality—that is, the structural barriers erected by the dominant majority to support their advantage.

The Canadian Multiculturalism Act of 1988 requires all federal institutions and employers to act in accordance with the country's stated multicultural policy when making their economic, social, cultural, and political policies. Although this process is not flawless, UNESCO (the United Nations Educational, Scientific and Cultural Organization) has cited Canada's approach to multiculturalism as the ideal model to be followed by other countries.

Canada's Charter of Rights and Freedoms (s. 15[1]) declares that "[e]very individual is equal before and under the law and has the right to the equal protection and equal benefit of the law without discrimination and, in particular, without discrimination based on race, national or ethnic origin, colour, religion, sex, age or mental or physical disability." In addition, the Criminal Code provides for strict enforcement against racist acts known as "hate crimes." These crimes can be both violent and non-violent, but they are always damaging. Figure 3.4 shows the number of police-reported hate crimes for the year 2010.

However, to be effective, these commitments of the government must be supported by sustained efforts to protect the rights of all ethnic groups.

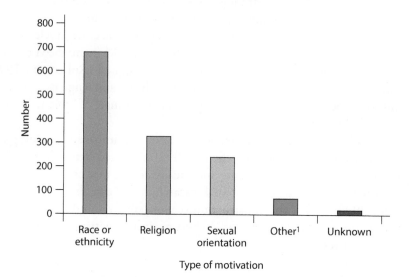

FIGURE 3.4   Police-Reported Hate Crimes, by Type of Motivation, Canada, 2011

[1] Includes mental or physical disability, language, sex, and other similar factors (e.g., occupation or political beliefs).

Note: Information reflects data reported by police services covering 99% of the population of Canada.
Source: Statistics Canada, Canadian Centre for Justice Statistics, Incident-Based Uniform Crime Reporting Survey <http://www.statcan.gc.ca/pub/85-002-x/2013001/article/11822-eng.pdf>.

Chapter Summary

People often try to justify racist beliefs and behaviour by repeating misinformed views about a minority group's physical, psychological, and cultural inferiority. These views often rest on the flawed belief that "racial groups" bear similar genetic or inherent characteristics.

However, research has led to increasing evidence that the physical traits by which people are grouped into racial categories are not at all intrinsic to that "racial group." Furthermore, the common cultural traits by which people distinguish between cultures are now understood to be learned and impermanent. In different ways, both racial and ethnic groups are "imagined communities."

As we have seen, "prejudice" refers to biased beliefs about people based on their presumed membership in a particular racial or ethnic group. Prejudice always starts with stereotyping. Some propose that prejudice is learned through socialization, without harmful intentions. In other situations, it is a strategy practised by a dominant group to preserve its dominance.

We are a long way from achieving the well-integrated society Durkheim imagined a century ago, built on organic solidarity and an enthusiasm for diversity. Today, Canada needs immigrants more than ever—to make up for declining fertility, provide tomorrow's workers and taxpayers, link us to the rest of the world, and provide us with innovations. This means that we are likely to keep grappling with issues of racial and ethnic inequality and with the topic of immigration. It is in Canada's national interest to solve these issues of inequality fairly and effectively.

Questions for Critical Thought

1. Which of the various consequences of racialization—health, social, economic, or other—do you find the most unacceptable or harmful? Why is that type of consequence more harmful than others?

2. Some African Americans have said that US president Barack Obama is "not black enough." What does this say about the social construction of race? What does it mean to be "black enough"? White enough? South Asian enough?

3. Do you believe that racism has increased or decreased over the past century? How should sociologists measure the phenomenon of racism? For example, would increasing numbers of Caribbean Canadians filling corporate executive positions show a decrease in the racism that occurs here?

4. In what ways have rising urban crime rates been racialized? Do you feel that looking at the race of individual criminals provides fruitful understanding of the larger social problem?

5. Compare the treatment of Native peoples by the government of Canada with the treatment of blacks in South Africa during apartheid. What similarities do you see? How did both situations contribute to the social construction of the group that lacked agency and power?

6. Which form of multiculturalism—traditional or modern—do you think contributes more to the functioning of Canadian society? If you were a legislator, how would you approach the issue of multiculturalism within Canadian law?

Recommended Readings

Henry, Frances, and Carol Tator. 2005. *The Colour of Democracy: Racism in Canadian Society*, 3rd ed. Toronto: Thomson Nelson.

Murji, Karim, and John Solomos. 2005. *Racialization: Studies in Theory and Practice*. Oxford: Oxford University Press.

Satzewich, Vic, and Nikolaos Liodakis. 2007. *"Race" and Ethnicity in Canada: A Critical Introduction*. Toronto: Oxford University Press.

Wade, Peter, ed. 2007. *Race, Ethnicity, and Nation: Perspectives from Kinship and Genetics*. New York: Berghahn Books.

4

Gender Relations

© okeyphotos/iStockphoto

Introduction

Sex—the biological distinction between male and female—is a universal and ancient basis of social differentiation. We know of no human society that does not divide work and status along the lines of sex. This social demarcation has some basis in biology and the fact that women alone can bear and nurse offspring. Women, on average, are physically smaller and weaker than men and, therefore, less suited for hunting and combat and certain types of work. Child-bearing makes women vulnerable and more dependent for extended periods. These biological realities have led to the widespread social practices of men's roles as protectors/breadwinners and women's roles as procreators/caregivers.

However, this distinction varies from one society to another. History and anthropology show us that women can be breadwinners and protectors; men, though they cannot be procreators, can be caregivers. What's more, in societies with low fertility, this male–female distinction fades in importance, since in these societies women spend little time in reproduction and much of their lives breadwinning.

Societies differ in the extent and ways they dramatize this sex-based difference—that is, in the ways they "enact" gender roles and gender differences. Some societies enlarge these differences, while others diminish them. In other words, societies vary in the degree to which they make sex differences *seem* large or small, important or unimportant. There is also much variation in how they rationalize their enactment of these differences. Some invoke religious edicts; others draw on secular principles like the moral commitment to equality; and still other societies rely on scientific or pseudo-scientific theories to justify differences in how men and women are treated.

Although half of all people are women and the other half men, the study of gender relations had almost no presence in sociology before the mid-twentieth century. Gender and gender roles were just assumed. It was only in the nineteenth and early twentieth centuries that women became more visible as thinkers about social matters; prior to that, few were university educated and it was not until the mid-twentieth century that many taught in universities. More important than this change, the growing feminist movement continued to press for gender equality and related social concerns (for example, abstinence from alcohol). Feminism, as political activism, has as its goal to free a people from oppression. It's worth noting that the early feminist movement was mainly concerned with women's suffrage—hence its alternative title, the suffrage movement. Though their tactics were cautious and moderate, women's right to vote was eventually achieved in Canada, the United States, and Britain in the early decades of the twentieth century.

Tellingly, until the early 1970s, no sociologist seemed to notice that housework was work of economic value, not just the result of an outpouring of family affection. It was only in 1974 that English sociologist Ann Oakley published her seminal book on the sociology of housework that drew needed attention to domestic inequality and its relation to other forms of gender inequality (see Box 4.1, p. 93). The arrival of a full-fledged sociology of gender relations coincided with, and was promoted by, the large-scale entry of women into higher education throughout the West. It took women's contributions, and the third wave of the women's movement, to bring gender inequality and gender relations to the full attention of sociologists. The third feminist wave arose in response to the "failure" of, or backlash against,

Suffrage movement The central aim of many in the "first wave" of the women's movement in the late nineteenth and early twentieth centuries was the right for women to vote in elections. With women's suffrage (i.e., voting rights), other goals—social reform, legal rights—would then be more readily attainable.

various initiatives established by the second feminist wave. The third feminist wave embraced racial and class diversity and accommodated differences in nationality and cultural background (Mane, 2012), where the second wave largely had been a white, middle-class movement.

With a few exceptions—notably J.S. Mill and Friedrich Engels—the failure by major male sociologists and theorists, from Marx, Weber, and Durkheim onward, to contribute to gender issues tells us something interesting about the connection between social structure (especially the social distribution of power) and the propagation of knowledge: only the powerful get noticed, studied, and discussed. Therefore, to put gender issues on the list of research topics, women needed access to power. Once they became powerful, the next step was to draw attention to topics that concerned them directly and that had been historically neglected.

In fact, then, we can see the subject matter of sociology itself is a measure of a society's equality, openness, self-awareness, and social concern. Changes in sociology reflect changes in the distribution of power. These changes are achieved largely through changes in the intellectual class and the institutionalization of knowledge, peer review, research funding, and journal publication. The "discovery" of gender relations as a field of study was a necessary (though not big enough) step towards addressing some of the problems we will now consider.

The Battle over Gender Today

Since this chapter is about issues associated with gender, we will discuss some of the disadvantages associated with being a *man* in our society. Indeed, as we will see, norms of masculinity are as much an impediment to men as norms of femininity are to women—especially if those men are elderly or disabled. However, the principal focus here is on the disadvantages associated with being a *woman* in our society. Historically, women have suffered more disadvantages than men at school, in the workplace, and in the public realm (Knudson-Martin and Mahoney, 2009). To a large degree, Canadian women have overcome these disadvantages in the past two decades. For example, formally, Canadians support rules that make it illegal for employers to limit or separate their employees by sex. Informally, however, many Canadians still discriminate against women or in favour of men. Gender stereotyping and discrimination hinder women far more than they do men, and often they do so in almost invisible ways (Bloom, 2009).

An example is found in engineering professions. As it is a male-dominated career, some females entering it feel the need to break free of the gender stereotype in order to gain acceptance by their male co-workers. However, in doing so, they take on an "anti-woman" role, encouraging an environment non-conducive to females. In a situation like this, women are set up for failure, which in turn leads to potential unequal opportunities for female employment (Powell et al., 2009).

Women also face significant barriers in politics. In 2008, women held only 22.1 per cent of all possible seats in the House of Commons. Though this number has increased from the early 1980s—9.6 per cent of seats—the past decade has witnessed only marginal, if any, gains (Parliament of Canada, 2010). Table 4.1 outlines women's participation in Canadian Parliament since 1984.

TABLE 4.1	Women in the Canadian House of Commons since 1984		
YEAR	TOTAL NUMBER OF SEATS	SEATS HELD BY WOMEN	PERCENTAGE OF SEATS HELD BY WOMEN
1984	282	27	9.6
1988	295	39	13.34
1993	295	53	18.0
1997	301	62	20.6
2000	301	62	20.6
2004	308	65	21.1
2006	308	64	20.8
2008	308	68	22.1
2011	308	76	24.7

Source: Parliament of Canada. 2011, revised 2013. Women in Parliament. <www.parl.gc.ca/Content/LOP/ResearchPublications/2011-56-e.pdf>.

Sexism Discrimination and derogatory attitudes and beliefs that promote stereotyping of people because of their gender. Sexism and gender stereotyping are problems for both men and women, and they are most often experienced in institutions and social relationships.

Gender inequality The differential success of men and women in gaining access to valued rewards. This tends to stem from structural arrangements, interpersonal discrimination, and cultural beliefs.

Sex A biological concept that differentiates female and male. Most people are (mainly) male or (mainly) female from the moment of conception, with biological differences between the sexes that are anatomic, genetic, and hormonal.

Gender A social division referring to the social and psychosocial attributes by which humans are categorized as "male" or "female." Biology is deemed irrelevant to an understanding of the social distinctions between males and females. Gender encompasses the shared understandings of how women and men, girls and boys, should look and act. It is a label that subsumes a large assortment of traits, beliefs, values, and mannerisms, and defines how we should practise social interactions.

Defining Sexism and Gender Inequality

Sexism includes discrimination, insulting attitudes, and beliefs that stereotype people because of their gender (Lillian, 2007). Sexism and gender stereotyping can be problems for either men or women. However, since males have traditionally occupied the dominant roles in Canadian society, sexism has harmed women more than men. **Gender inequality** is any difference between the experiences of men and women in gaining access to societal rewards. It can grow out of structural arrangements, interpersonal discrimination, or cultural beliefs (Rammohan and Robertson, 2011).

Sex and Gender

Sex is a biological concept. From a purely biological standpoint, the Y chromosome must be present for the embryonic sex glands to develop maleness. Further, a preponderance of particular hormones must be present in both sexes for sexual maturity to be reached. Most people are (mainly) male or (mainly) female from the moment of conception, with biological differences between the sexes that are anatomic, genetic, and hormonal.

However, research has not revealed any simple split between the sexes or any direct link between genetics and the behaviour of each sex. Current thinking is that "male" and "female" are not discrete biological categories, but opposite poles along a continuum of sexual variation. Consider the example of the rare condition known as adrenogenital syndrome: an individual is born with an intersexed appearance; they have normal internal genitalia (ovaries, uterus, inner vagina) and an external phallus that is intermediate in size between a clitoris and a penis. Male or female? For practical purposes, the answer is socially determined through socialization and social interaction (Minto et al., 2003).

Whatever biological differences may exist between men and women, these have few (if any) unavoidable effects on modern-day social life. Men and women have different reproductive functions, but there is no scientific proof of the existence of biologically based psychological differences (such as a "maternal instinct") between human males and females. And as women spend less and less of their lives bearing children, the reproductive difference becomes less socially relevant to a definition of people's roles.

Gender refers to culturally learned notions of masculinity and femininity (Srinath, 2008). From a social standpoint, gender is the social enactment of a biological difference.

Males are treated as men because they play masculine roles, and females are treated as women because they play feminine roles. All known societies have distinguished between male and female roles in some way. However, the precise distinctions made between men and women, and the resulting divisions of labour, have varied through time and across cultures. Gender distinctions are by definition socially constructed (Staudt, 2009). They work within social institutions to determine the roles that men and women can enter and the kinds of experiences they will have within these roles. The use of the term "gender" suggests that biology is largely irrelevant to an understanding of the social distinctions people make between males and females.

Masculinity/Femininity

Not only is the dichotomy "masculinity/femininity" an oversimplification of the real differences between people, but it is also the source of many problems for both men and women.

Gender roles are learned patterns of behaviour that a society expects of men or women, and they are a widespread aspect of social life (Nagoshi et al., 2012). By masculinity, then, we mean that package of qualities that people in our society expect to find in a typical man. By femininity, we mean the various qualities that people expect to find in a typical woman.

People learn their gender-based habits of behaviour through gender socialization (Rodriguez-Dominguez et al., 2009). The socialization process links gender to personal identity—in the form of *gender identity*—and to distinctive activities—in the form of gender roles. The major agents of socialization—family, peer groups, schools, and the mass media—all serve to reinforce cultural definitions of masculinity and femininity.

Men, as well as women, suffer from gender stereotypes. Just as the stereotype of women as sex objects undermines their pursuit of respect and equal opportunity, overly masculine stereotypes of men may lead to the restriction of emotion, creativity, or artistry (Mohr et al., 2013). Besides reducing men's opportunities to live as they wish, this stereotyping can have serious effects for mental health and social relations.

It is possible that this stereotype influences different social behaviours. For example, men are far more likely to commit violent crimes and to be victimized in violent crimes (Lauritsen and Carbone-Lopez, 2011). They are more likely to work in dangerous work settings and more likely to be victims of occupational accidents. In our society, as in many others, male anti-social behaviours are associated with striving for a masculine self-image. Further, social practices that undermine men's health are signifiers of masculinity and are seen as appropriate instruments for them to use to negotiate social power and status (Thien and Del Casino Jr, 2012).

As a result, Canadian men suffer more severe chronic health conditions; are more likely to die from diabetes and arterial diseases; have higher death rates for all leading causes of death in cancer (especially men 65 and over); and die, on average, five years earlier than women (Evans et al., 2011). Even the experience and expression of illness are gendered. Though men and women have similar overall rates of mental disorder, women more often develop symptoms of depression and anxiety, while men more often develop symptoms of alcoholism, drug abuse, and social withdrawal (Olso et al., 2011).

Gender roles The patterns of behaviour that a society expects of males and females and that all members of the society learn, to a greater or lesser extent, as part of the socialization process.

Masculinity A socially constructed idea of how boys and men should act; qualities that people in our society expect to find in a typical man.

Femininity A socially constructed idea of how girls and women should act, or the various qualities that people expect to find in a typical female.

Gender socialization The process by which people learn their gender-based behaviour. This socialization process links gender to personal identity in the form of gender identity and to distinctive activities in the form of gender roles. The major agents of socialization all serve to reinforce cultural definitions of masculinity and femininity.

BOYS DON'T CRY
This 1999 true story of a transgendered teen who adopted male identity.

Steve Russell/GetStock.com

One Canadian family made headlines when they decided to raise their child Storm without revealing his or her gender in order to combat gender socialization. In this photo, four-month-old Storm gets a loving nuzzle from five-year-old brother, Jazz.

Factors that Reinforce Gender Inequality

Sociologically, the most important difference between the sexes is that most women can and do bear children, while men can't and don't. Gender researcher Nancy Chodorow, in the often-cited work *The Reproduction of Mothering* (1978), even explains women's subordination by the fact that women mother. If women and men shared equally in parenting, gender inequality would diminish, she argued. Today, gender inequality remains, as does motherhood.

To some degree, this difference between men and women is played out differently in different societies. In most, however, mothers carry the main burden of child care and housekeeping, which, in turn, has enormous effects on other aspects of their lives. Until recently, this burden has limited women's education, work, income, political representation, and legal rights.

At Home

Reproduction and child-rearing continue to be mainly female activities in Canadian society. Women's genes and hormones make child-bearing possible. However, child-bearing is no longer unavoidable. Effective birth control, by reducing the risk of unwanted pregnancy, has made the outcome of sexual intercourse more predictable and controllable than at any other time in history (Abbasi-Shavazi et al., 2009). As a result, men and women can lead more similar lives than ever before. Even sexual practices and sexual ideas, like the traditional double standard, have changed because of this contraceptive revolution (Gordon, 2012).

However, the family household remains a workplace for women more than for men. Before industrial capitalism, it was the workplace for men, too, but the separation of home and paid work largely brought this to an end (Tilly and Scott, 1987).

Under this system, though each family has its own particular division of labour, what is remarkable is how similar this division is across families and even across nations. Domestic labour, in short, is gendered labour. We still expect adult women to carry out more of this work than men, and daughters to do more of it than sons. This pattern also persists in caregiving. When it comes to child-rearing and the labour associated with it, the interference of labour supply and investment in human capital affects women more than men. Also, mothers are more likely to drop out of the labour force or take on part-time employment (Raley et al., 2012). This example shows that while women are present in the workforce, they experience work/family conflict much differently than men.

Families do vary, however. In some studies, for example, remarried couples report a less complete or weaker version of gendered inequality than first-time married couples (Ishii-Kuntz and Coltrane, 1992). Couples who become parents in their twenties are more traditional in their gendering of domestic work than couples who make this transition in their thirties (Coltrane and Ishii-Kuntz, 1990; Lachance-Grzela and Bouchard, 2010).

Women in common law relationships do much less household work than women who are legally married (Baxter et al., 2010). And dual-career couples often renegotiate their domestic division of labour as outside work duties change (Gregson and Lowe, 1994). Yet, while dual-career couples tend to have more equality in their domestic division of housework, the reality stands that their roles are still mapped out and navigated by gender (Van Hooff, 2011). This is clear in Table 4.2, which shows how men and women in a dual-earning relationship divide up household work and compares the number of hours they spend doing paid work. It also compares the lives of dual-earning couples with children and without children.

TABLE 4.2	Average Daily Time Spent on Paid Work and Housework for Individual in a Dual-Earner Couple at Ages 20 to 29							
	PAID WORK			HOUSEWORK			WIFE'S PROPORTION	
	BOTH SEXES	MEN[†]	WOMEN	BOTH SEXES	MEN[†]	WOMEN	PAID WORK	HOUSEWORK
	Hours						Percentage	
Generation X	**13.3**	**6.9**	**6.4**	**3.2**	**1.3**	**1.9***	**48**	**59**
No children at home	14.0	7.2	6.8	3.3	1.4	1.9	48	57
Has children	11.7	6.4	5.4	3.2	1.2	2.0	46	61
Generation Y	**14.1**	**7.5**	**6.7**	**3.1**	**1.5**	**1.7**	**47**	**53**
No children at home	13.5	6.5	7.0	3.2	1.7	1.5	52	48
Has children	14.1	9.0	5.1*	3.4	1.2	2.1	36	64

[†]Reference group
*Statistically significant difference from the reference group at at p < 0.05.
Note: For the population, time per day is averaged over seven days.
Source: Statistics Canada, General Social Survey, 1998 and 2010, at: <www.statcan.gc.ca/pub/11-008-x/2011002/article/11520-eng.htm>.

The Arrival of Children

With most women in the paid workforce, who looks after their children? Some families rely on daycare provided by professional caregivers. More, however, rely on babysitters who come to the parents' houses, on small-scale child-care operations, or on family members' voluntary care.

Most babysitters are female, and most of the non-household family members who "help" with child care are female. When researchers ask parents how they divide the responsibility of the household, they find women taking much more responsibility for the events or tasks of child care (Baker, 2012). While men might take children to doctor's appointments, most often women will have made the appointments.

Women's lives become much more complicated with the arrival of children. Helena Willen and Henry Montgomery (1996) refer to this fact as the "Catch-22" of marriage: wishing and planning for a child increases marital happiness, but achieving this wish reduces that happiness. The birth of a child and the resulting intense mother–child relationship strain marital relations (Carlson et al., 2011). New parents are less happy with one another and experience more frequent, sometimes violent, conflicts with one another after the baby arrives (Biehle and Mickelson 2012). For some, the conflict may begin even before the baby arrives.

The radical shift from spousal (adult-centred) activities to parenting (child-centred) activities creates an emotional distance the partners find hard to bridge. Mothers, the main providers of child care, change their time use much more than fathers do. Especially after the birth of a first child, marital quality and quantity of time together decline immediately. Mothers report feeling angrier and more depressed than before the child arrived (Monk et al., 1996; Cowan and Cowan, 1995). Husbands experience less marital satisfaction after becoming a parent, while mothers report less marital satisfaction when their husbands are experiencing a higher workload than normal (van Steenbergen et al., 2011).

The transition to parenthood increases gender inequality between partners (Fox, 2001). Wives, as mothers, devote more time to their infants and less time to their husbands. Husbands often resent this change, and wives may adopt a new, subservient way of dealing with husbands to reduce the resentment and conflict. This role change produces resentment on the wife's side.

Typically, marital satisfaction, which decreases with the arrival of children, reaches an all-time low when the children are teenagers. The presence of children in the household, though pleasing in many respects, increases conflict as well as the domestic workload for parents. Once the children leave home, creating what some sociologists have called an "empty nest," many marriages improve to near-newlywed levels of satisfaction (Mitchell, 2010).

In part, this return to marital satisfaction is due to the decline in parental and other work responsibilities, allowing time for couples to become reacquainted (Piercy, 2012). Thus, older couples show much less distress, less desire for change in their marriage, and a more accurate understanding of the needs of their partners than do younger married couples (ibid.).

Problems of Structural Sexism

Problems of *structural sexism*—that is, the ways social institutions outside the home treat men and women differently—and the problems that this different, unequal treatment poses for men and women reinforce one another. It would be hard to get rid of one without getting rid of them all.

Classic WORKS

BOX 4.1   **Ann Oakley's *Sociology of Housework* (1974)**

Ann Oakley was born in London in 1944, the only child of a social worker mother and an influential architect father. Oakley is credited with introducing the term "gender" into academic as well as everyday use, contributing substantially to future women's studies, since this discipline needed a distinction between biological sex and socialized gender. In 1974 Oakley published her most famous work, *The Sociology of Housework*. She argued that the social sciences were ignorant when it came to housework and other issues socially constructed to be solely women's concerns. She also emphasized the importance of considering culture as a backdrop to social phenomena.

Oakley's housework research was based on a small sample of working-class and middle-class homemakers. Social class, in her sample, made little difference: both middle-class and working-class women reported similar negative attitudes about housework and a similar high degree of identification with their role. Both middle-class and working-class women found housework unpleasant. But in spite of this dislike, the role of homemaker was central to their identity. They saw themselves to be the authority figures (only) in the household, while tending to the home and children. Most of these women accepted their dissatisfaction with the monotony, isolation, and low social status of homemaking, especially compared with higher-status occupations.

Oakley concludes that women are both disempowered and imprisoned by their beliefs about the proper role of women, and especially of mothers, in a modern society. Despite their unhappiness, they feel obliged by our culture to play a fundamentally alienating and frustrating role. They are socialized by a patriarchal gender ideology into accepting servitude in marriage and motherhood. Housework is the visible symbol of this submission. Oakley has strong views on this topic. Consider a few of her more pointed observations about marriage as a gendered institution:

- Society has a tremendous stake in insisting on a woman's natural fitness for the career of mother: the alternatives are all too expensive.
- Families are nothing other than the idolatry of duty.
- Housework is work directly opposed to the possibility of human self-actualization.
- If love means that one person absorbs the other, then no real relationship exists any more. Love evaporates; there is nothing left to love. The integrity of self is gone.
- There are always women who will take men on their own terms. If I were a man, I wouldn't bother to change while there are women like that around.

Oakley called our attention to the neglected topic of housework. Thanks to her insight, we are more aware of its relation to gender inequality and of the necessity for sensitive qualitative methods to explore this problem.

Work

Throughout most of the twentieth century, women still were expected to be homemakers (see Box 4.1) and were discouraged from taking on jobs that would prevent them from fulfilling these duties. The range of available jobs in the paid workforce was narrow. During the first half of the twentieth century, women could find work as teachers, nurses, retail salespeople, or domestic servants in higher-class homes. One attractive feature, for employers, was that women could be paid less than men for the same work (Crespo, 2007).

This changed significantly with the onset of World War II. Record numbers of women entered factory jobs to replace men away at war, working harsh and unsafe jobs for up to 60 or more hours per week. With the end of the war, many women returned to the male breadwinner/female homemaker family model. But a precedent had been set, and many women sought to continue working as well (Vallee, 2002).

TABLE 4.3	Employment Trends of Women and Men Aged 15 and Over, 1976 to 2009				
YEAR	WOMEN AGED 15 YEARS AND OVER		MEN AGED 15 YEARS AND OVER		WOMEN AS A PERCENTAGE OF TOTAL EMPLOYMENT
	Thousands	Percentage	Thousands	Percentage	Percentage
1976	3,618.2	41.9	6,129.3	72.7	37.1
1981	4,556.6	47.7	6,748.4	72.8	40.3
1986	5,138.2	50.3	6,870.3	69.6	42.8
1991	5,790.5	52.8	7,066.9	66.9	45.0
1996	6,099.0	52.1	7,322.4	65.0	45.4
2001	6,910.3	55.6	8,035.8	66.8	46.2
2006	7,757.2	58.3	8,727.1	67.7	47.1
2007	7,977.5	59.1	8,888.9	68.0	47.3
2008	8,104.5	59.3	9,021.3	68.1	47.3
2009	8,076.2	58.3	8,772.7	65.2	47.9

Source: Statistics Canada, Labour Force Survey, at: <www.statcan.gc.ca/pub/89-503-x/2010001/article/11387/tbl/tbl001-eng.htm>.

IN THE COMPANY OF MEN

This 1997 art-house hit discusses issues of misogyny in the workplace as two men plot to manipulate the emotions of a female co-worker.

Glass ceiling Women can have considerable success, but can rarely reach and enter the topmost positions.

Feminization of poverty Women are over-represented among the impoverished people of the world. In the West, economic liberalization and the dominance of the market have meant that those with the least earning power—single mothers with children—have suffered most.

Much has changed since then. We now understand that by excluding women from the most important jobs, we significantly limit the country's supply of human capital. Today, in many parts of the industrialized world, discrimination against women is illegal. Both women and men are encouraged to follow their educational and occupational talents to the maximum, in whatever field they have chosen. Statistics Canada shows that women accounted for half of the total national labour force for the year 2009 (Statistics Canada, 2013b). Furthermore, the data in Table 4.3 shows that the percentage of women in total employment has risen by over 10 per cent since 1979.

Unfortunately, women continue to suffer inequalities in the workplace. If we look at the distribution of occupations, we still find fewer women than men in high-paying positions, and on average, full-time working women still earn about 70 cents for every dollar earned by men in similar employment. Some men might say this is because women are seen to be more transient—more likely to quit their job for family reasons, especially during the child-bearing years.

In many workplaces, women do have an equal opportunity, but in many others, they still hit a **glass ceiling** when they strive to advance. This term points to the fact that women face hidden obstacles when it comes to advancing into the highest-status jobs. Women are less often hired into these jobs in part because of an "old boys' club" mentality and a belief (sometimes) that women are inferior (Barreto et al., 2009). The gendering of work opportunities is far narrower and stricter in developing countries, such as Bangladesh, as described in Box 4.2.

Feminization of Poverty

Women are over-represented among the poor people of the world, a fact referred to as the **feminization of poverty**. High rates of female poverty are the result of (1) women's occupational disadvantage in society, (2) women's overall subordinate position to men, and (3) women's economic difficulties following abandonment, divorce, or widowhood (Angeles, 2009).

INTERNATIONAL **COMPARISONS**

| BOX 4.2 | **Women's Advancement up the Economic Ladder in Bangladesh** |

In the best-selling book *The End of Poverty: Economic Possibilities of Our Time* (2005), author Jeffrey Sachs discusses the recent progress made by the working women of Bangladesh, thanks to a burgeoning garment industry and micro-financing initiatives. During his visit to the city of Dhaka, he noted the young female workers dominating Bangladesh's flourishing garment industry. These women often get little to no break time and are constantly under risk of sexual harassment of male bosses and co-workers. Despite these difficulties, Sachs argues that the Bangladeshi women have managed to gain a foothold on the first rung of the modern economic ladder out of poverty—an undeniable improvement.

While in Bangladesh, he encountered a newspaper article of interviews with female garment workers. The Bangladeshi women in the article repeatedly expressed that working was a great opportunity for them, despite the long hours, lack of labour rights, and threats of harassment. Having grown up in a poverty-stricken, male-dominated society, these women were now able to save a small surplus, manage their income, and exert a measure of control over their own lives. Furthermore, women involved in microfinanced small-scale commercial activities were now able to get small loans for financing microbusinesses, something previously unheard of. Overall, the majority of these working women had only one or two children. Sachs argues that reduced fertility has helped fuel the rise in incomes and literacy of Bangladeshi women, since there is more money left over to invest in the health and education of each individual in the household. This, Sachs argues, shows that the Bangladeshi women have made great strides in their quest for personal liberation.

Fully up-to-date statistics on the feminization of poverty are hard to find. Statistics Canada (2013) showed that, overall, more men than women had full-time employment in the labour force. More Canadian women 45 and older were employed part-time than Canadian men. Not only are the women who head poor families affected by their impoverished state, but their children feel the results of poverty as well. Eight per cent of Canada's children, or 546,000 people under 18, live in poverty (Statistics Canada, 2012), which means their parents do too. Gender differences also increase with age. The transition to widowhood has been described as requiring more psychological and social adjustments than any other life event. Furthermore, widowhood has been linked to mortality for both widows and widowers. In that women live longer, they are more likely to experience widowhood and thus are more vulnerable to the effects of it (Piercy, 2012).

Women overall, and single mothers in particular, are more likely to be impoverished than any other demographic group. Various health consequences trouble women who are economically deprived, including increased vulnerability to infectious and other diseases, arthritis, stomach ulcers, migraines, clinical depression, stress, vulnerability to mental illness, self-destructive coping behaviours, and increased risk of heart disease (Smith, 2009).

Gender Stereotypes in the Media

Despite major advances in women's opportunities and rights during the twentieth century, portrayals of girls and women in the mass media, especially in television, keep harmful gender stereotypes alive. In this way, they continue to keep women from achieving full equality with men at home or at work (Das and Das, 2009).

Despite the gender stereotyping associated with Barbie dolls, they remain a popular toy among girls. Angelica Pupo plays with a Barbie doll during the annual Hot Toys for the Holidays from the Canadian Toy Association.

In the mass media, we still see gendered images of women and men, boys and girls. These gendered images are paralleled in media advertisements for consumer items. By showing us what they expect us to want, they produce a self-fulfilling prophecy—our children turn out how society expects them to.

Consider Saturday morning children's television. Advertisers aim the commercials directly at girls or boys, typically matched to the show—Barbie dolls (or the equivalent) for girls, droids or Transformers (or the equivalent) for boys. These programs entertain children, but they also teach them which toys are for them, how we expect them as girls or boys to behave, and what we expect them, as gendered beings, to want in our society.

Some socially conscious agencies are trying to use commercial media (e.g., television advertisements) to promote change. We will occasionally see, for example, male sports stars talking about problems of violence against women and trying to promote models of masculinity that are concerned, caring, and nurturing though strong. However, the idea that rapid, direct, and imitative media images may change the attitudes of viewers, and therefore of society, may be too simplistic. The media may reflect and reinforce culture more than they can easily change culture and society (Royo Vela y Otros, 2005).

The mass media may not be the main cause of gender inequality in Canada, but they help to perpetuate existing inequalities between men and women.

Theoretical Perspectives on Gender Relations and Inequality

TABLE 4.4	Theoretical Perspectives
THEORY	**MAIN POINTS**
Structural Functionalism	• Elements in society are interrelated. • Inequality rewards effectiveness and efficiency. • Inequality is based on value consensus. • Gender inequality stems from what was at one time an effective household arrangement but which has failed to develop with the times.
Conflict Theory	• Gender inequality results from struggle for economic and social power. • Capitalists benefit from gender inequality. • Gender inequality forces women to support the workforce without pay.
Symbolic Interactionism	• Socialization and labelling shape gender identities. • Most variations between men and women are cultural and learned. • A gendered self develops out of a process of gradual socialization at all levels of social life: women learn to do women's jobs and see themselves as suited for these tasks. • Media, religion, and language help maintain gender differences. • Double standards are considered normal.
Feminist Theory	• Gender inequality is almost universal. • This inequality is a result of patriarchal values and institutions. • Gender inequality favours men over women.
Social Constructionism	• The creation of gender equality is a social process. • It requires leadership and organization. • Some social periods are more conducive to equalization than others.

Structural Functionalism

Remember that structural functionalists ask of every social arrangement: *What function* does it perform for society as a whole? In this case, how does gender inequality contribute to the well-being of society as a whole? Functionalist theorists starting with Talcott Parsons (1951) would say that a gendered division of labour is the most effective and efficient way to carry out society's tasks. It may even have evolutionary survival value for the human race. Mothers, by their early attachment to the child (via pregnancy and breastfeeding), are well-suited to raising the family's children. Since they are at home with the children anyway, mothers are also well-suited to caring for the household while the husband is at work outside the home.

Conflict and Feminist Theories

Conflict theorists and feminist theorists, by contrast, always ask the question: *Who benefits* from a particular social arrangement? In this case, who is best served by gender inequality? Marxists would tend to answer this question in the context of class relations: capitalism requires the low-cost social reproduction of a workforce from one generation to the next. Families are the best and cheapest way to raise new workers. Mothers have the job of keeping all the family earners and earners-to-be healthy and well fed, housed, and cared for emotionally. They do this at no cost to capitalists, who will benefit from the surplus value workers produce.

The Marxist approach assumes that working-class men and women are on the same side, both equally victims of the capitalist class. By contrast, the feminist approach assumes that women have a different experience from men and may be exploited by men of their own class, as well as by capitalists. Therefore, they see gender inequality as mainly serving the interests of men, who, by lording it over their girlfriends, wives, and daughters, at least have someone subservient to them just as they are to their own bosses. The theory of patriarchy—that men are the main and universal cause of women's oppression—is compatible with Marxist analyses that view working-class women as being the victims of both class and gender oppression (Knudson-Martin and Mahoney, 2009).

Symbolic Interactionism

Symbolic interactionists, for their part, ask: *How* is an arrangement *symbolized*? For example, how is gender inequality negotiated, symbolized, and communicated in our society? The presumption is that inequalities arise where social differences have been symbolized, communicated, and negotiated—that is, made into something that is "taken for granted" by the population at large. From this standpoint, people are always trying to understand and normalize social interaction through shared meanings. Thus, symbolic interactionists are concerned with the ways that gender differences become gender inequalities—for example, the ways that young women become "objectified" and turned into sex *objects*. They would also want to understand how the double sexual standard, which has allowed men more sexual freedom than women, has been "negotiated" so that many women go along with an agenda that, it would seem to many people, benefits males more than females.

Social Constructionism

Related to this approach, social constructionists always ask the question: *When and how* did the arrangement *emerge*? When, for example, did gender inequality begin to emerge in a particular society, what events preceded this emergence, and what individuals or groups were especially instrumental in this process of "moral entrepreneurship"? This approach is much more historically oriented than the symbolic interactionist approach to which it is related. So, for example, a social constructionist would note that gender equality began to increase (a second time) in the 1960s and 1970s, largely because of the actions of the women's movement.

The women's movement was especially successful because social protest against many things—the rich, imperialists, and racists, for example—was prevalent throughout the Western world. The baby boom had ended and there was less interest in child-bearing. However, there was now a desire for two family incomes and therefore a need for more education for women. This new agenda—getting women out of the home and into the work world—was aided significantly by the development of reliable birth control that made it possible for people to have sex without having babies. Cutting the links between gender, sexuality, and child-bearing was central to the emergence of women as contenders in the working world of men. It also helped gay and lesbian people stake a claim to full social inclusion, for similar reasons.

Notably, all these explanations are compatible with one another. Each focuses on a different aspect of the rise of gender equality. However, by far the most influential approach to studying gender issues has been the feminist approach, and that approach has shaped this chapter.

Social Consequences of Gender Inequality

As one would expect, issues of gender are involved in most aspects of Canadian social life. We have already discussed issues associated with education, work, and income that pose particular problems for women. In this section, we consider crime, violence, and self-esteem.

Crime and Violence

Statistics Canada (2011a) reported that in 2011 women and men tend to be victims of similar offences. However, when it came to sexual offences, women are 11 times more likely to be victims compared to men. This number grows when a woman is between the ages of 15 and 24, where the rate of crime against them rose by 42 per cent more than the rate for women aged 25 to 34 (Statistics Canada, 2011a).

Although men are sometimes the victims of rape and sexual assault, these vicious crimes are mainly directed towards women. Rape is devastating for the victim not only because of acute physical and psychological violations, but also because the victim must come to terms with the fact that she was attacked solely because of her gender. Rape offenders, who are almost always male, typically harbour misogynistic, sadistic attitudes towards their victims.

According to Statistics Canada (2011a), 91.6 per cent of victims of police-reported sexual offences were female, while 8.4 per cent were male. It is important to note, however, that 9 in 10 of all non-spousal sexual assaults are never reported to the police (Statistics Canada, 2011a).

While these numbers do reflect a disproportionate number of victimized women, it is important to note that women as well as men commit violent acts (Weizmann-Henelius et al., 2009). However, while women are more likely to *start* violent episodes—by slapping, kicking, or throwing an object—men are more likely to respond with more force, which comes in the form of beating, choking, or threatening to use (or using) a knife or gun. This is reflected in Statistics Canada's (2009) report stating that females were more than twice as likely as males to report an injury. Of these women, 1 in 10 reported bone fractures, while bruising was the most common form of injury for both males (75 per cent) and females (95 per cent) (Statistics Canada, 2009).

This propensity to engage in violence is reflected in a Statistics Canada report (2011a) for police-reported domestic violence. As reported, 41 per cent of female victims had been injured as a result of violence, which was less than the 46 per cent of males. However, women are more at risk of violence from dating partners than from spouses, with the rates for dating violence sitting at 60 per cent higher than the spousal violence rate (Statistics Canada, 2011a). This general discrepancy between male and female victims in the area of intimate partner violence can be seen in Figure 4.1. This is in sharp contrast to the category of stranger, where men are more likely to be victims of violent crimes (Statistics Canada, 2013a).

THELMA AND LOUISE

Ridley Scott's 1991 film discusses hypocrisies regarding gender and violence and portrays how two women who kill a man in self-defence must subsequently flee the law.

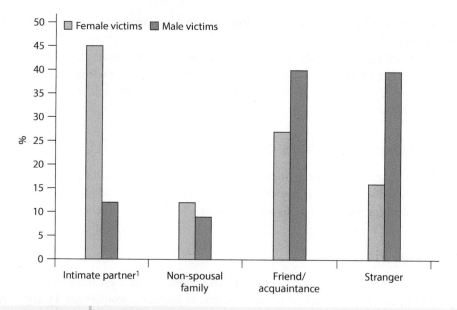

FIGURE 4.1 Victims of Police-Reported Violent Crimes, by Sex of Victim and Accused–Victim Relationship, 2011

[1]Intimate partner includes spousal and dating partners.
Source: Statistics Canada, Canadian Centre for Justice Statistics, Incident-based Uniform Crime Reporting Survey, at: <www.statcan.gc.ca/pub/85-002-x/2013001/article/11766/11766-1-eng.htm>.

In general, however, there has been a significant decline in spousal violence against women since 1999 (Statistics Canada, 2013a). This general decrease in violence can be seen in Figure 4.2, which graphs the 30-year trend of spousal homicide rates since 1979. Figures 4.1 and 4.2 can be considered together to gain a better idea of the differences between gendered experiences of violent crime.

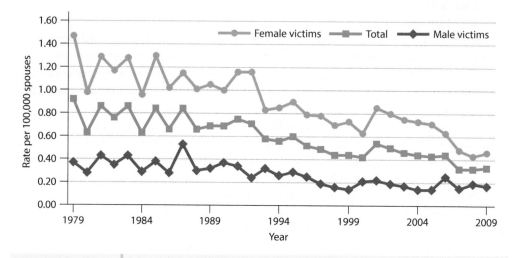

FIGURE 4.2 Spousal Homicide Rates, by Age of the Victim, 1979 to 2009

Source: Statistics Canada, Canadian Centre for Justice Statistics, Homicide Survey, at: <www.statcan.gc.ca/pub/89-503-x/2010001/article/11416/c-g/c-g004-eng.htm>.

One survey of self-reported domestic violence in Canada shows that (1) younger people are more violent to their spouses than older people; (2) unemployed people are more violent than employed people; but (3) people with less education and lower income are no more violent than those who are highly educated and who have higher incomes. There is also a relationship between a belief in patriarchy and wife-battering, where husbands who believe men ought to rule women are more likely to beat their wives. In turn, a belief in patriarchy depends on educational and occupational level (Obeid et al., 2010). Another factor is ethnicity. Some cultures in multicultural Canada and elsewhere are more patriarchal than others. All other things being equal, patriarchal beliefs tend to appeal to lower-status, less-educated men, as they have so little control over other aspects of their lives (Tichy et al., 2009).

The most revealing finding is that high rates of domestic violence are associated with high levels of domestic stress—that is, the more stressful events a person reports experiencing in the previous year, the more violence will have taken place within the household. Still, this does not serve as an excuse. The real problem underlying violence is the fact that some men find it acceptable to channel their frustrations into violence towards family members.

Date Rape and Sexual Inequality

Most instances of forced sex occur between people who are friends, acquaintances, or even relatives (Estrich, 2007). The result, too often, is that women blame themselves for the experience. Because they know the assailant, they may react passively to the sexual assault. Because they react passively, they blame themselves for not reacting more forcefully (Humphreys and Herold, 1996).

Looking at rape through a symbolic interaction approach, the construction of "victim" is important to note. When this word is used to label a person, our cultural discourse depicts that person as helpless or even blameworthy. This can have an effect on the reporting of rape, as well as on the person's search for treatment or even on attempts to determine her or his identity (Leisenring, 2006). Today, it is more appropriate to refer to living people who experienced sexual violence as "survivors."

Historically, women who faced violence from intimate partners could not rely on police protection. Often the community saw domestic violence as a private matter, and police were taught only to defuse the situation or to try to mediate the "dispute," thus reinforcing the view of the victim and assailant as equal parties. Victims were left feeling confused and at fault.

Only recently have we come to understand that domestic violence is uneven. Even if men don't initiate physical violence during an argument, once it is launched, they tend to use more physical force than women do. Further, men and women often have different goals in using force. Men are more likely to use force to prevent a partner from leaving, and women will use violence mainly to protect themselves. Men will also use violence to compel partners to give them sex. Only recently have law enforcement agencies and the public come to accept spousal rape as a criminal offence (Hovmand et al., 2009).

Sexual and Criminal Harassment

Another problem that women sometimes face is **sexual harassment** in the workplace.

It is impossible to know the full extent of gender-based harassment in Canada today, since much of it goes unreported (Antecol and Cobb-Clark, 2006). Sexual harassment

Sexual harassment Any unwanted physical or verbal conduct directed towards a person that is sexually offensive or humiliating.

PERSONAL *stories*

BOX 4.3   Women and Girls in the Canadian Military

It is 2009. R.W. is a 17-year-old First Nations girl enrolled in the cadet program in Ontario. She comes from a long line of soldiers and warriors and is ready to begin a career in the Canadian Armed Forces. On the first day of her enrollment, she is treated to a terrifying and uncomfortable medical examination by the now retired petty officer James Wilks. Her heart is broken, and her spirit crushed. She files a civil lawsuit against petty officer Wilks in the Ontario Superior Court of Justice, where he is found guilty of breach of trust. More women step forward to allege similar accounts of sexual assault; the charges mount, and a disturbing tale of Wilks's career emerges. Found guilty of one count of sexual assault and four counts of breach of trust, Wilks is sentenced to nine months in jail. New charges continue to be put forth.

Women comprise 12 per cent of the Canadian military, a traditional institution of patriarchy and hierarchy. Violence against women is prevalent despite a zero-tolerance policy in place. This problem exists on every level of the armed forces. Young women recruits in the cadet program—as in R.W.'s case—are especially vulnerable to sexual harassment and assault. Intimidated by the powerful male chain of command and holding the least amount

of power, they are under great pressure *not* to report such incidents. Between 2004 and 2008, there were 219 reported incidents of sexual interference and assault, with or without a weapon, and other related situations. Many others go unreported.

Higher up in the ranks, women are faced with similar pressures. Holding only 8 per cent of positions above the rank of lieutenant-colonel, women fear the potential repercussions of speaking out against sexual assault. Not only are they wary of being blamed, they face the problem of being re-victimized and discredited by the system and their subordinates.

Sergeant Cheryl Ross, a former clerk with the military police in Afghanistan, was discharged with post-traumatic stress disorder years after being raped by an allied soldier at knife point. Knowing she would not be able to identify her attacker, she kept quiet at the time for fear of losing the respect of the men she was in charge of leading. The Canadian military continues to be one of the many fields where gender equality seems a distant goal.

Source: Adapted from *The Globe and Mail*, at: <www.theglobeandmail.com/news/national/sex-assault-complaints-against-former-petty-officer-probed/article11448906>.

Quid pro quo sexual harassment The blatant demand by employers for sexual favours in exchange for promotion opportunities, salary increases, and preferential treatment.

comes in at least two forms: (1) as an open demand by employers for sexual favours in exchange for certain advantages—also known as **quid pro quo sexual harassment**, or (2) as subtler sexist remarks, ultimately fostering a hostile and unpleasant work environment. This second type of harassment is least likely to be reported.

Criminal harassment is the legal term for *stalking*, a menacing form of relationship abuse that may evolve into violent physical, psychological, and sexual forms. This is another field in which women are disproportionately targeted; in 2011, women represented 76 per cent of all reported cases of criminal harassment, with numbers increasing each year (Statistics Canada, 2011a). Stalking often follows a relationship breakup or a rejection in a proposed relationship; in effect, most stalkers are former or imagined, rather than current, intimates. Many stalking victims must resort to seeking help from the authorities in the form of restraining orders to protect themselves from the emotional abuse and prevent it from intensifying into violence.

Self-Esteem and Appearance Issues

Gender discrimination also carries social-psychological costs. For women, decreased self-esteem, increased depression, and other psychological problems often result from derogation by men, awareness of their subordinate status in society, or a failure to achieve the stereotypical ideal female body (Foster, 2009).

As we have already noted, one area in which physical limitations occur is in the choice of careers. Women are often reluctant to enter professions that involve dangerous, physically demanding work, such as firefighting or the military. By contrast, men are informally, and sometimes directly, cautioned against entering professions that "undermine their masculinity," such as early childhood education or nursing.

To protect their self-esteem, women sometimes attribute negative criticisms made to them about their work or their abilities to prejudice by male evaluators, whether the men believe in gender stereotypes or not (Crocker and Park, 2003). This defensive strategy may lead some people to see prejudice where none exists. This becomes a problem when it leads a person to imagine that every member of the opposite sex (or of a different "race," ethnic group, age cohort, etc.) is the "enemy." Sometimes, workplace criticism is just criticism.

Furthermore, cultural "appearance norms" that idealize certain features of appearance can prove restricting and even detrimental to the health of both men and women. Our cultural ideals are manifested by the plentiful photos and media images that glorify youth, slender toned bodies, and symmetrical, delicate facial features as the ideal in beauty. There is pressure for all to fit in, as departures from these norms suggest poor genes, poor grooming, or a lack of self-discipline and self-worth (Jung and Peterson, 2007). This media spotlight on body image is far more intense for women than for men. As a result, women tend to experience more insecurity about their bodies than men and are much more likely to strive for perfection by starving their bodies through anorexia or bulimia. After the 1983 death of singer Karen Carpenter from cardiac complications

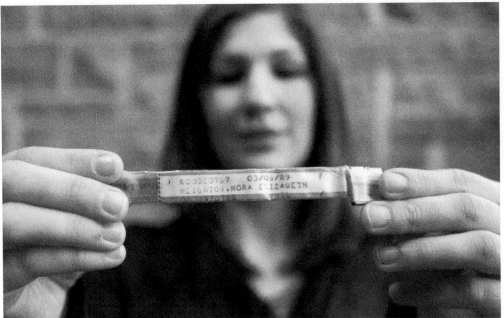

The Canadian Press/The Chronicle-Herald—Christian Laforce

Pictured in the Seaton Academic Centre in Halifax, Nora Heighton holds the hospital bracelet she wore when hospitalized at the age of 10 after being diagnosed with anorexia.

caused by anorexia nervosa, there was an increased focus on the life-threatening results of eating disorders.

Gender scholars continue to note the pronounced gap between male and female hospitalizations for eating disorders such as anorexia and bulimia. It is significant that girls in the age group of 15–19 are at the greatest risk of suffering these disorders—a fact that says something about their susceptibility to the pressure to conform to appearance norms (Public Health Agency, 2006).

Fertility and Abortion Issues

Adolescent fertility is another big problem for women in North America (Benokraitis, 2008). Young women without long-term goals and stable, cordial relationships are more likely to produce children in adolescence. The results are regrettable, for the children as well as for the mother: an end to the mother's education; a limit to the child's economic future; or, all too often, abortion, which effectively has become contraception of last resort. In 2011, for example, 12,502 cases of induced abortion were recorded for young women under 19 (Canadian Institute for Health Information, 2011).

Patriarchy is, by its nature, pro-natal; it views women's primary responsibility as bearing and raising children. Many societies press women to bear as many children as they can, stigmatizing them if they are childless (Tomczak, 2012). Yet, high rates of pregnancy often result in high rates of illness and mortality. Every day, 800 women around the world die due to pregnancy-related complications, worsened by poverty and remoteness (WHO, 2012). Many women, especially in developing countries, die during pregnancy and childbirth (and as result of botched abortions).

For example, in Guinea-Bisseau, the rate for maternal mortality sat at 790 per 100,000 live births in 2010. Compared to the Western Pacific region, where the maternal mortality rate sits at 49 per 100,000 live births, the African region statistic is dismal, sitting at 480 deaths per 100,000 live births (WHO, 2012). When it comes to the children themselves, especially in low-income settings, 20 per cent of all deaths occur among children less than five years old. These deaths, injuries, and disabilities are preventable, and they are symptomatic of women's vulnerability and the violation of their human rights. This fact turns women's health issues into a matter of social justice.

Limitations on women's child-bearing and enforced abortion, as in China, also create serious problems. An experiment in one province in China found that permitting couples two children—rather than the usual one—led to a drastic drop in the abortion rate, equal acceptance of female children, happier parents, and a better-integrated society (Schiller, 2010).

Claims-Making in Gender Relations and Sexism

Of importance to discussions of gender is the backlash against women's rights movements found in conservative counter-movements. These groups have an interest in framing societal trends in certain ways; for example, they may describe divorce as a "problem" associated with moral decline, even as divorce rates have dropped or stabilized (Adams and Coltrane, 2006).

John Leyba/The Denver Post via Getty Images

Raleigh Washington, a leader with Promise Keepers, poses for a portrait at Promise Keepers headquarters.

In thinking about claims-making with regard to gender relations, we should also briefly discuss *men's rights movements* (or men's rights activists, known as MRAs). These groups vary in values and tactics, but men who are anti-feminist in orientation have an interest in making particular claims about gender roles and the state of relations between men and women in society. One example of these anti-feminist groups is the Promise Keepers, a Christian men's movement that has been characterized as patriarchal and male-supremacist (Abott, 2007). Such groups may hold that the "pendulum has swung too far" in the direction of women's rights, and thus claim that they, and not feminists, represent a sensible "middle ground" of equality. Studies suggest, however, that such backlash claims may only reinforce gender inequalities. Melanie Heath (2003), in discussing the Promise Keepers, suggests that social movements on the part of privileged groups are often efforts to reform or rehabilitate that privilege. In other words, anti-feminist MRAs are involved in a process of claims-making with the goal of defending male privilege against feminist claims to gender equality.

Gender relations are not constructed by social movements, but by people in their everyday lives. One study of male university students found that they saw current gender relations as empowering for women and disempowering for men (Gough and Peace, 2000). The idea that women are already in a favourable position seems to rule out change of the status quo. Thus, apart from the actual state of gender inequality as discussed in this chapter, the ways in which gender relations are perceived and constructed by men and women are important in their own right.

Policy and Institutional Solutions to Gender Inequality

Many institutional policies are designed to protect women in their private lives and remove barriers that prevent them (and other marginal groups) from taking part fully in public life. For example, discrimination in the workplace based on sex or gender is no longer tolerated in Canadian society, either by the judicial system or by most public opinion.

However, policies are not yet in place that would will women the same occupational freedom that men enjoy. For example, we know that many women—as employees, wives, and mothers—have been affected by lack of high-quality, inexpensive child care. One study suggests that policies to increase the availability of daycare or to lower its cost could increase the female labour supply substantially, with an even greater rise among women most at risk of poverty and of reliance on public assistance (Mason and Kuhlthau, 1989). A more recent study revealed that the Quebec Family Policy (formalized social programs that target family-related needs, such as daycare and unemployment) affected the labour supply only half as much as it did daycare utilization (Baker et al., 2008).

Finally, employment discrimination remains a problem. More effective workplace sexual harassment policies would likely improve women's work lives by preventing sexism from impeding a woman's career ambitions. Canada's Employment Equity Act protects all workers in federal employment (and all people who work for an employer that employs 100 or more employees on or in connection with federal work) against discriminatory hiring procedures, whatever their gender, race, ethnicity, disability status, or sexual orientation, by ensuring that employee composition reflects the diversity of society.

In relation to gender specifically, this means that the workforces of large companies and the federal public service must have an equal number of men and women in all levels of employment, at least in theory. In practice, the division is not as exact, although the gap is closing.

The process of finding and implementing solutions will continue to be difficult as society overcomes its inertia and undergoes the painful process of unlearning centuries of outmoded gender socialization. The system has been skewed in favour of men for generations. In the attempt to correct this problem, it may be necessary to have some policies that temporarily favour the marginalized group until the playing field has been levelled. Yet, how do we distinguish between what is a fair reaction to violence within patrilineal cultures and what is not? When it comes to issues of domestic violence, Sokoloff and Dupont (2005) suggest a multicultural approach that could support the use of culturally competent services for both victims and perpetrators.

Cross-national research makes clear that women's long-held concerns must be transformed into well-understood social problems before policy proposals are drafted and passed. Around the world, women have worked to place issues such as equal pay, affirmative action, educational equality, child care, abortion, domestic violence, and sexual harassment on the policy agenda. They have done so most directly and effectively in countries such as Norway, Sweden, and Finland, where women play a key role in politics and in the legislative process, largely through a history of effective mobilization in unions, social movements, and political parties (Bacchi, 1999; Tyyska, 1994). Canada has also made impressive progress, yet much more work remains to be done.

CANADIAN researchers

BOX 4.4 **Brenda Beagan, Dalhousie University**

Professor Brenda Beagan has held a Canada Research Chair in Women's Health at Dalhousie University since 2007. Her work focuses on how and why women and families make the decisions about food. More specifically, Beagan's research focuses on how the food choices women and their families make are shaped by expectations, habits, and social identities, and how these expectations are influenced by ascriptive characteristics, such as gender, race, ethnicity, class, and geographic location.

In a co-authored piece titled "Food Practices and Transnational Identities: Case Studies of Two Punjabi-Canadian Families," Beagan explores how food practices were implicated in identity constructions in the context of transnational migration. Along with her co-author, Gwen E. Chapman, Beagan challenges the notions of (1) dietary acculturation, and (2) resistance to acculturation as a form of ethnic identity maintenance. They argue instead that food practices reflect simultaneous, ongoing attachments to multiple national identities. In other words, "taste" is transnational and need not be restricted to any single national identity.

In a 2011 article, "'Food Is Culture, but It's Also Power': The Role of Food in Ethnic and Gender Identity Construction among Goan Canadian Women," Beagan—with co-author Andrea D'Sylva—examine the meaning of "food and foodwork" for Goan women in Toronto and the role of food in creating and maintaining distinctly gendered ethnic identities. They argue that the gendered role of women in foodwork carries with it significant power—or "currency"—within the family and community. Cooking is valued for fostering, and supporting, Goan national identity. Beagan argues that the same foodwork practices that constitute gendered oppression for women—that is, the long-standing claim that domestic work is subservient—may simultaneously confer a form of "culinary capital" within the Goan diasporic community.

Beagan's work shows how social context shapes women's abilities to do things they believe are good for their health—particularly, with respect to food consumption and food practices. By looking at food choices, Beagan explores the everyday health practices of consumers. Her focus on gender demonstrates the role women play in improving family health practices in Canadian society.

Sources: Andrea D'Sylva and Brenda L. Beagan, "'Food Is Culture, but It's Also Power': The Role of Food in Ethnic and Gender Identity Construction among Goan Canadian Women," *Journal of Gender Studies* 20, 3 (2011): 279–89; Gwen E. Chapman and Brenda L. Beagan, "Food Practices and Transnational Identities: Case Studies of Two Punjani-Canadian Families," *Food, Culture, and Society* 16, 3 (2013.): 367–86.

Chapter Summary

Are gender inequality and sexism in Canadian society "real" problems or merely socially constructed problems? On the one hand, there can be little doubt that the "moral entrepreneurship" of the leaders of the women's movement was critical in calling public attention to many of the issues associated with gender inequality—poverty, violence, discrimination, and so on.

However, gender inequality was, and is, not merely a manufactured issue. It did exist prior to the first and second waves of the women's movement. And although there has been considerable improvement in Canada over the past two generations, gender inequality is still a fact of life for many women. We have seen that women suffer the material, psychological, and emotional outcomes of inequality and discrimination. They even suffer significant health problems—our touchstone for measuring the "reality" of a social issue.

As we have seen, gender inequality is a social phenomenon. Gender discrimination and gender inequality are not due to the intrinsic or biological inferiority of one or the other sex. Instead, they are the result of political, economic, and ideological structures. Women have increasingly entered the workforce in both developed and less-developed countries. Despite this, women are still subject to discrimination within the workforce. This discrimination often takes the form of sexual harassment and the "glass ceiling." Women who work for pay are also likely to face the double shift—heavy workloads both at the workplace and at home. Within the home, gender inequality extends across domestic work, child care, and caregiver duties with parents and spouses.

Socialization plays an important role in subordinating women. It causes people to internalize values that, in turn, lead them to enforce and act out gender roles. This socialization occurs not only in the family, but also through the media, language, schools, and religion. Images of, views of, and beliefs about gender are learned both in childhood and through adult socialization.

In Canada, women still do not hold many positions of real power in political or legal spheres. Therefore, women's issues are often ignored or receive less political attention than they deserve. In other societies, where women are more powerful politically, gender issues are dealt with more firmly and thoroughly.

Questions for Critical Thought

1. Have there been any instances in your life where you were disadvantaged because of your gender? Evaluate two competing explanations of your experience.
2. Before you read this chapter, what was your understanding of gender? Compare your previous definition with how you currently define "gender."
3. In your opinion, are males truly dominant in Canadian society? Explain your answer.
4. What future trends do you foresee in regard to gender and the job market?
5. Is there a glass ceiling where you work or where you worked? Try to provide examples.
6. Do males experience any disadvantages in society?

Recommended Readings

Armstrong, Pat, and Hugh Armstrong. 1994. *The Double Ghetto: Canadian Women and Their Segregated Work*, 3rd edn. Toronto: McClelland and Stewart.

Gardiner, Judith Kegan, ed. 2002. *Masculinity Studies and Feminist Theory: New Directions*. New York: Columbia University Press.

Kaufmann, Michael, ed. 1987. *Beyond Patriarchy: Essays by Men on Pleasure, Power, and Change*. Toronto: Oxford University Press.

Kimmel, Michael, ed. 2007. *The Sexual Self: The Construction of Sexual Scripts*. Nashville: Vanderbilt University Press.

Pinnelli, Antonella, Filomena Racioppi, and Rosella Rettaroli, eds. 2007. *Genders in the Life Course: Demographic Issues*. Dordrecht, The Netherlands: Springer.

Siltanen, Janet, and Andrea Doucet. 2008. *Gender Relations in Canada: Intersectionality and Beyond*. Toronto: Oxford University Press.

5

Sexualities

© Andesign101/iStockphoto

Introduction

People with alternative sexual orientations have long faced discrimination, ridicule, exclusion, and even violence. However, recent public discussions of this topic have been strongly influenced by current thinking about human rights. Change is also visible in the ways the queer community and others present the issue today—as constructionists would say, in terms of "victim claiming" and "injustice framing" (Berbrier and Pruett, 2006).

Nonetheless, most Canadians still expect people to be either homosexual or heterosexual, and to act accordingly. In the past, many Canadians considered homosexual behaviour to be problematic. However, over the last generation, Canadian public opinion on this and other sexual topics has changed dramatically. Attitudes towards same-sex intimacy and marriage have become more liberal. Today, few Canadians view homosexuality as immoral or worthy of criminalization, as many did in the past. In particular, people with homosexuals as kin, friends, acquaintances, or workmates are more accepting and knowledgeable of the homosexual community (Osterlund, 2009).

As a result, in Canada today, most people consider *anti*-homosexual behaviour—not homosexuality itself—a social problem and a potential violation of hate laws and the human rights codes. To understand how and why Canadian attitudes to sexual orientation have changed, we need first to define our key terms: sexual orientation, gender binary, homosexuality, and homophobia, among others.

Sexual Orientation

Homosexuality Sexual attraction to people of the same sex.

Sexual orientation One's sexual attraction to people of a specific sex.

Queer An umbrella term for anyone who does not identify as heterosexual.

LGBT Acronym for "lesbian, gay, bisexual, transgendered"—often used to speak of the LGBT community.

Homosexuality is an attraction, physical and emotional, to people of the same sex. It is hard to say whether homosexuality is an act (or set of acts), a preference, or an identity, and if it is something occasional, regular, or permanent. Views vary on this topic.

Sexual orientation is defined here as sexual attraction to people of a particular sex (or sexes). The word **queer**, though once thought offensive by the gay community, has now been embraced by that community as an umbrella term to describe people who identify as anything other than heteronormative (Hammers, 2009; Walcott, 2009). However, the term is still not comfortably accepted in the heterosexual community. So, in this chapter, we will refer to the non-heterosexual community by the acronym **LGBT**, which stands for lesbian, gay, bisexual, transgendered or transsexual.

In early twentieth-century North America, most people held the view that sexuality is fixed and binary. "Normal" people were supposed to be entirely heterosexual or entirely homosexual. However, the American sexologist Dr Alfred Kinsey—writing in the 1940s and 1950s, at the end of a long period of what some called "Victorian prudery"—showed that human sexual orientation lies on a continuum, with heterosexuality at one end and homosexuality at the other. Kinsey also noted that people often do not act on their sexual desires, for fear of attracting censure or stigma (Gebhard and Reece, 2008). For these reasons, some people who think of themselves as heterosexual yet feel attracted to people of the same sex may not respond to this attraction. Similarly, people who identify themselves as homosexual yet feel an attraction to one or more people of the opposite sex may not respond to this attraction, in the belief that they should be sexually consistent. Both behaviours reflect the belief that people are normally *either* heterosexual *or* homosexual.

This blurring of the line between homosexuality and heterosexuality leads some people to enforce the boundary with special rigour (Kim, 2007; Madureira and Amaral,

2007). This may sometimes contribute to homophobic behaviour, which we will discuss later. In general, how we think about sexuality is influenced by how we think about sex and gender. In both cases, we tend to fall into binary classifications that discourage the recognition that, in reality, people are complex and varied in all these respects.

Numbering the Homosexual Population

Today, tolerance for homosexuality is widespread, though the practice itself remains rare. Surveys have established important factual information about the prevalence of homosexuality in Canada. According to Statistics Canada (2010), 1.1 per cent of Canadians aged 18–59 reported being homosexual and 0.9 per cent considered themselves bisexual. This survey defines homosexuality in terms of identity rather than sexual behaviour. Nonetheless, data from other countries show the number of people who identify as homosexuals is much smaller than those who report having same-sex relations. As a result, the number of Canadians having sex with people of the same sex may be higher than the number identifying themselves as homosexual.

Researchers agree on several matters. First, it is likely that homosexuals concentrate in larger numbers in some communities than in others—for example, in cities rather than rural areas. Second, the homosexual population may reach as high as 10 per cent in populations where they are most concentrated, though the overall proportion of homosexuals is far closer to 1–2 per cent of the national population. Third, male homosexuals are invariably found to be more numerous than female homosexuals; the reasons for this are unknown. Finally, debate continues to flourish about how to properly define and measure homosexuality (Ramsey and Santiago, 2004).

One study (McCabe et al., 2009) shows the difficulty associated with numbering the homosexual population. The researchers set out to assess past-year prevalence rates of substance use and dependency among heterosexuals and homosexuals, using a large national sample of adults in the United States, the 2004–5 (wave 2) National Epidemiologic Survey on Alcohol and Related Conditions.

The sample numbered 35,000 adults aged 20 years and older, belonging to every racial, ethnic, and educational group and social class. McCabe et al. found that 2 per cent of the sample self-identified as lesbian, gay, or bisexual. However, 4 per cent reported at least one same-sex sexual partner during their lifetime. Also, 6 per cent reported same-sex sexual attraction. As expected, non-heterosexual orientation was associated with a higher-than-average risk of substance use and substance dependence (Brubaker et al., 2009; Gillespie and Blackwell, 2009). However, the more important finding, for our purpose, is that the risks of substance abuse vary by a factor of three depending on how sexual orientation is defined. We must keep in mind this fact—the lack of clarity of our definitions and measurements (Uzzell and Horne, 2006)—in all the discussion that follows.

Coming Out

From a sociological perspective, the most important step in the sexual "career" of an LGBT person is "coming out"—disclosing his or her (until then secret) **sexual identity** to family, friends, co-workers, and others (Bogaert and Hafer, 2009).

This transition is sociologically important for several reasons. First, until a person comes out, he or she has difficulty fully entering the LGBT community—a major social

Sexual identity How a person self-identifies—whether as straight, gay, lesbian, asexual, or otherwise.

▪▪▪▪▪▪▪▪▪▪▪▪▪▪▪▪

EYES WIDE OPEN 🎞️

In this 2009 film directed by Haim Tabakman, a married Orthodox Jewish father of four falls in love with a 22-year-old male student.

PERSONAL *stories*

| BOX 5.1 | **Being Asexual in America** |

Most people consider sexual attraction and romantic relationships to be a natural part of human life. However this is not the case for Becky, a 33-year-old Chicago resident. Becky identifies as asexual, meaning that she has no inclination to be sexually or romantically intimate. Unlike celibacy, asexuality is not a personal choice to abstain from sex but rather an innate disposition that predisposes people to have no desire to make sex part of their interaction with others. Some have even begun to consider asexuality a sexual orientation.

As with other sexual orientations, Becky went through a confusing coming-out period, and it took her 26 years to understand who she really was; this process was ultimately helped through her interactions online with other asexuals. At the beginning of her coming-out journey, she first assumed that her lack of sexual attraction meant that she was a lesbian, but since she was unable to find a women that she was sexually attracted to, she thought that something must be wrong with her—that she must have repressed some traumatic incident that prevented her from functioning "normally." David Jay, the founder of the Asexuality Visibility and Education Network (AVEN) says that this is a common response for those first discovering their asexuality and many

asexuals will seek medical or psychological help to correct their "condition."

Since our society expects people to be sexual and views the lack of a sexual appetite as a signal of a physical or mental health problem, Becky often has to hide her asexuality and try to pass for a sexual person. Given the need to pass, she feels a strong connection with the LGBT community. Asexuality is not usually associated with this community, yet Becky has found that people in the LGBT community are typically more accepting of her asexuality than the general public. She chalks this up to the fact that people who have gone through the coming-out journey have gone through an intense period of self-reflection and tend to respect those who are going through something similar.

Many asexuals, such as Becky, also declare that the LGBT community supports them and accurately represents them, and so Jay is working to incorporate asexuality into the LGBT education and support agenda. The plan involves reaching out to gay-straight alliances, mental health groups, and those involved in public education to begin a dialogue about asexuality and to teach youth and mental health workers that asexuality is a valid orientation, not a health problem in need of a cure.

Source: Adapted from Chaitman (2013).

transition from the heterosexual world to the homosexual world and, often, from old friends and activities to new ones. Second, and equally important, people's identities are linked to the social roles they play (Corrigan et al., 2009). They cannot fully enter, or support, a new identity for themselves until they fully embrace the new role that it entails. So, coming out is as much a statement that people make to themselves as it is a statement to their partner, friends, family members, and the general community.

Finally, disclosure is important in the organizations where individual lesbians or gay men work. People spend so much of their time and energy at work, it is important they be known for who they really are. However, many fear this may jeopardize their relations with other workers and even harm their job security (DeJordy, 2008; King et al., 2008). So, coming out at work is a big decision—a big declaration to oneself and others, and sometimes disclosure may not be the best policy. Workplaces and families vary in this respect. In some situations, secrecy is not dysfunctional—it is preferable. In a family, for example, secrecy about sexual orientation may minimize family disruption and stigma by association, and it controls the spread of information to other members of the community (Chow and Cheng, 2010).

Some LGBT people delay coming out for years (Frost and Bastone, 2008). Others, as camouflage, even marry and raise children with someone of the opposite sex, while recognizing their own deception. They may come out in middle age after leading a life of secret wishes, desires, and activities all that time. However, coming out in mid-adulthood, after decades of secrecy and lies, disrupts relationships and leads people to fear losing everything they have constructed. Many grieve the loss of a "normal" life. In short, coming out in mid-adulthood requires great courage and strength, but the same courage and strength is also needed to preserve the secrecy of sexuality (Wang et al., 2009).

Coming out is not a process that exists in a vacuum, and it affects others as well. For example, after their child comes out, parents may have to deal with a reality that is new, incomprehensible, and even morally unacceptable to them. On top of that, they must put a good face on it for their friends and relatives (Potoczniak et al., 2009). Not all parents can do this—at least not readily—and so do not immediately accept and support their children's sexual identities. Some parents take years to adjust, others adjust quickly, and some never do (Alpaslan et al., 2009).

Attitudes and Laws

Throughout history, sexuality has been one of the most debated and problematized of human activities. Most of us conduct our sexual activities in private and grant the same privacy to others. And, most of the time, people ignore the sexual inclinations of others unless they are brought forcefully to their attention. Once again, we do not know exactly how many people identify themselves as homosexual, nor (identification aside) are we aware of how many people are having sex with someone of the same sex.

On the other hand, most people are aware of homosexuality and of prominent homosexuals, and this has always been so. For example, a great many people knew and accepted Oscar Wilde (1854–1900)—the celebrated Irish playwright—as being homosexual long before anyone thought to charge and imprison him for this then-criminal offence. It was only through the forceful efforts of John Sholto Douglas, the 9th Marquess of Queensberry and the disapproving father of Lord Alfred Douglas—Wilde's aristocratic lover—to discredit the playwright in court that Wilde's homosexuality became a public issue no one could ignore.

Contrast this sexual hypocrisy with ancient Greece, where people considered sexual relations between two men a regular and "normal" part of life (Harris, 2009). As a citizen, a Greek man who was old enough to vote was free to have sex with whomever he wished; this included having sex with young boys. The rule, however, was that a free man must adopt the "top" position—that is, be the partner who would perform penetration. To "bottom," or passively receive, was socially acceptable only for a non-citizen, a woman, or a young boy. For a citizen to assume this bottom position was considered dishonourable and improper. In short, homosexual activity was not only socially accepted, it had its own etiquette (Turner, 2009).

Also, *behaviour* that we would consider homosexual today, such as anal sex between two males, was not assumed in ancient Greece to reveal a person's sexual *identity* (see, for example, Halperin, 1990). The Greeks felt that one could not readily infer sexual identity from sexual actions. This meant that the line between homosexuality and heterosexuality was even more blurred in ancient Greece than it is today, but then it was not seen as an important social issue.

Many cultural attitudes about homosexuality changed—indeed, homogenized—with the spread of Christianity and the Catholic Church. In Christian Europe during

The Canadian Press/Darryl Dyck

Two men participate in a kiss-in outside the Russian consulate in Vancouver, BC, to protest Russia's anti-gay law. The law, which was enforced during the Sochi Olympic Games, imposed fines on individuals accused of spreading "propaganda of nontraditional sexual relations" to minors and on those who expressed these views online or in the news media.

the early Middle Ages, the Church largely ignored or tolerated homosexual behaviour. Hostility and resentment towards homosexuals surfaced in the thirteenth century, however. The religious writings of Thomas Aquinas (1225–1274) spread the idea that homosexuality was unnatural and undesirable, obliging people who considered themselves Christians to condemn homosexual behaviour. As stigma and shame were attached to homosexuality in Christian countries, homosexual behaviour was forced underground. Yet it didn't stop, but merely became hidden (Richlin, 2005; Findlay, 2006).

Even today, homosexual behaviour remains illegal or, at best, highly regulated in many countries. People in countries with restrictive morality laws (e.g., Singapore and Saudi Arabia) tend to believe that homosexual behaviour is morally wrong and threatening to society. In these jurisdictions, punishments for homosexual relations may include imprisonment, lashes, or even death. In some countries, these laws only apply to homosexual relations between two men (Bahreini, 2008; Whitehead, 2010). Sri Lanka's law, for example, doesn't even mention lesbian relations. Belize, however, outlaws sex between two men but allows lesbianism, that is, unless one of the participants is a foreigner (Ottosson, 2009).

Despite the generally oppositional role of Christianity and Islam, not all religions have opposed homosexuality. Confucian philosophy, which regulated Chinese moral behaviour and societies affected by Chinese culture, did not oppose homosexuality unless the family forbade it (Liu, 2009; Rosker, 2009). So long as sexual activity did not interfere with reproduction—a filial duty—Confucianism did not forbid men from having erotic feelings for other men, nor did it forbid sexual relations between men. Still, this did not prevent the development of restrictions on homosexual behaviour in Chinese communities like Singapore. The state of Israel, by contrast, has plainly showed its support for homosexual citizens, despite the opposition of Orthodox Jews in the country.

Sexuality and Disability

Despite similarities in sexual functioning between able-bodied and physically disabled people, society and the medical community often relate to people with physically disabilities as asexual—neither wanting sex nor able to take part in sexual relations. Esmail et al. (2010), for example, found that because of prevalent heteronormative ideas about sex and what is considered natural, people with visible disabilities are often seen as asexual. These socio-cultural barriers may sometimes be even more socially disabling than the physical impairment itself (Neufeld et al., 2002; Mayers et al., 2003).

Similarly, people with intellectual disabilities have historically been denied their sexual rights and viewed as either asexual or sexual deviants. Many once believed in eugenics—and some still do—the idea that sterilizing people with intellectual disabilities was desirable because they were assumed to make poor parents. Routine forced sterilizations occurred in countries like Japan, Australia, and England, even as late as 1995 (Savell, 2004). Until the 1970s people with intellectual disabilities were subject to mass, involuntary sterilizations in Canada. However, the Supreme Court of Canada now holds that depriving a person of their ability to have a child is an infringement of their human and constitutional rights. Forced sterilization of the mentally ill, however, is still permitted in some US states (Marinos et al., 2008)

Among the greatest hardships people living with disabilities face regarding their sexuality are societal misconceptions. Current misconceptions of disability and sex are driven by modes of sexual education that perpetuate a narrow conception of human sexuality. McCabe et al. (2000), for example, found that 50 per cent of people living with a disability had not received any sexual education. The general population received sex education from parents, friends, and other sources; however, people with disabilities were most likely to only receive sex education from other sources. Family members and others close to the disabled participants were less likely to talk to them about sex and sexuality. In short, the issue of sexuality for disabled people was never broached and thus assumed to be non-existent.

In the past, the issue of disability and sexuality was largely ignored because of its taboo nature and the idea that sex is personal and unimportant to the rehabilitation process. However, over the last 20 years, researchers have adopted the idea that disability is the result of social structures that improperly exclude certain people from access to employment, social resources, and positive self-identities. This model proposes that disability is not an innate or essential feature of a person's identity, but rather an external, socially constructed phenomenon. In other words, the repression and ignorance of the sexuality of disabled people is also socially constructed.

According to feminist disability theory, disabled women face a heightened inequality because of their status as both female and disabled (Garland-Thomson, 2002). Society tends to see women with disabilities as possessing devalued bodies and thus places them outside the norm of what it accepts as the "real" female body. Evidence of this is found in an analysis of Dove's Campaign for Real Beauty, which claims to support "real" women (Heiss, 2011). Despite this claim, among the many images of women portrayed, there were no disabled women. Thus the standard conception of disabled women as "other" and devalued becomes reinforced, and the media has failed in its mission to give a true portrayal of what real women look like.

Women with some form of disability often internalize this devaluation of the disabled female body, and this affects their body image and sexual functioning (Moin et al., 2009). Women with spinal cord or polio-related disabilities have the same sexual needs and desires as non-disabled women, yet their sex life is affected by their negative self-perception. They reported lower body-image satisfaction, lower sexual self-esteem, and lower life satisfaction.

A study that questioned young adults with cerebral palsy about their sexuality produced similar results (Wiegerink et al., 2011). Forty-five per cent of the adults reported having negative emotions (e.g., shame) because their disability hindered them from initiating sexual contact.

Polyamorous Families and Couples

A ruling in British Columbia on 23 November 2011 held that a federal law making polygamous unions a criminal offence was defensible, though such a law would violate the freedom of religion and other provisions in the Canadian Charter of Rights and Freedoms. This ruling has fuelled a debate about *polyamory*, a term that means "several (or many) loves" and refers to simultaneous engagement in multiple loving, consensual, and egalitarian adult relationships.

The BC ruling was intended to prevent coercive unions that are harmful to women and children, but it also bans egalitarian polyamorous relations. According to the ruling, if a person has multiple relationships sanctioned by a marriage ceremony (for example), then she or he is guilty of polygamy and, for that reason, subject to criminal punishment. However, a person having multiple relations that are *not* sanctioned by a marriage ceremony is *not* subject to criminal punishments. The problem here is that some people, like other couples, are polyamorous because of their religious affiliation and may wish to celebrate their unions with friends and family. The Canadian Polyamory Advocacy Association proposes that upholding such a law will risk the rights and freedoms of polyamorous people. Because of their beliefs, they will run the risk of being harassed, charged, and even jailed for their lifestyle.

Elizabeth Sheff (2005) importantly distinguishes polyamory from swinging, which involves brief sexual encounters, and from adultery, noting that polyamory focuses on honesty and the full disclosure of one's sexual network. Unlike polygamous relations, where the focus is on a man having multiple wives, polyamorous relations involve both men and women having access to multiple partners. Polyamorous people come from diverse social, racial, and economic backgrounds and may have any sexual orientation, although research has found a strong link between bisexuality and polyamory (Anderlinin-D'onfrio, 2009; Pallotta-Chiarolli, 2010).

Statistics on the number of polyamorous couples and families in Canada are hard to come by. A recent survey showed that about half of polyamorous people are parents (Anapol, 2012). The exact number of polyamorous people is unknown, for several reasons. First, some parents in polyamorous relationships may choose to keep their relations a secret, as polyamory can be used as grounds to deprive them of child custody or access to their children. For example, in 1999 a US court granted guardianship of a child to her grandparents after the child's mother disclosed herself as polyamorous on MTV. Further, polyamory includes a wide array of practices, such as having one main partner and multiple lovers or having multiple main partners; and polyamorous relations can be either long-term or just an occasional affair. As a result, some people who occasionally practise some form of polyamory may not necessarily self-identify as polyamorous. Thus, as we saw with homosexuality, the number of practising polyamorous people may be higher than the number of self-identified polyamorous people.

One of the main concerns surrounding the issue of polyamory is its effect on children. One study of polyamorous families in Australia found that children's attachment to transient partners could be an issue of concern. Yet, in general, polyamorous families establish family arrangements that benefit both children and parents. One of the main advantages to polyamorous relations is their flexibility in sharing child-care responsibilities (Pallotta-Chiarolli et al., 2013). Few problems, other than moral and religious objections, have been found with egalitarian polyamorous relations. Emens (2004) reports that polyamory is typically censured because people cannot imagine themselves having a relationship with more than one partner. This suggests that there is nothing innately unnatural or wrong with polyamory—it is merely an alternative way of setting up a loving and functional relationship or family, one that does not exist in the consciousness of mainstream society.

Homosexual Culture

In the past several decades, there has been an observable shift in the attitudes of social scientists towards homosexuality. The period 1975–2001 saw a significant increase in the quantity of psychological research on homosexuals (Lee and Crawford, 2007). Sociologists, too, have changed their approach to homosexuality. In the past, they commonly viewed it as a learned social behaviour. Today, most sociologists subscribe to the essentialist school, which grants primacy to biological causes (Engle et al., 2006). That is, sociologists—like many others today—view homosexuality as the result of nature, not nurture. With this in mind, one would no more criticize, suppress, or try to change people's sexual orientation than their age or skin colour.

The dramatic changes of the last few decades owe a lot to the efforts of gay rights activists. In fact, scholars trace the beginning of the modern gay rights movement to a police action in New York City's Greenwich Village in 1969 (Conlon, 2004). Throughout the 1950s and 1960s, underground gay bars and clubs had begun to shape the social experience of gays and lesbians. Mainstream culture, however, still viewed homosexuality as a deviant and dangerous lifestyle. Police regularly raided known homosexual establishments (e.g., clubs and bathhouses) and arrested patrons merely for being present. In June 1969, New York City police raided the Stonewall Inn. Unlike in earlier incidents, the gay patrons fought back. A riot ensued, and for the first time, homosexuals resisted as a group, marking the start of a long battle for the equal rights of LGBTs—a battle that continues today (Gillespie, 2008).

Like the gay and lesbian communities of New York City and San Francisco, Toronto's gay community had been routinely victimized by police raids and harassment. On 5 February 1981, during what came to be known as the "Toronto bathhouse riots," the Toronto city police raided four bathhouses in that city and arrested 300 men as found-ins in bawdy houses. The gay community again fought back. The LGBT rights movement had been building for a decade, but this event marked a turning point in the movement's

Toronto police marching in the annual Toronto Gay Pride Parade.

history in Canada. Protests sparked across the city, including one in which 2,000 people gathered at Queen's Park (Ontario's provincial legislature) to express their outrage. This was the largest gay rights demonstration in Canada up to that time.

After that, many new gay organizations sprang up in Toronto and existing ones grew rapidly, with ever more access to support and resources. Eventually, the City of Toronto commissioned a report to examine and make recommendations to improve the relationship between police and the LGBT community. Everyone recognized that it was necessary to normalize relations between the gay and straight communities to promote a peaceful and harmonious city (Valverde and Cirak, 2003).

It is no accident this protest happened when and how it did. Sexual protest in North America owed a great deal to the civil and women's rights movements in the United States. Women and urban minorities taught gays and lesbians something important about social mobilization: namely, the importance of *institutional completeness*—the creation of communities that are fully self-supporting and self-aware. They showed that through group mobilization and institutional completeness, minority *communities* survive, and through community survival, minority *identities* survive. Activists applied the same principle in building large, diverse homosexual communities in Toronto, Vancouver, and elsewhere.

LGBT and Native Communities

The Canadian Aboriginal approach to homosexuality gives us a different way of thinking about sexuality in our own culture, for it appears to have solved some problems and avoided others. In recent decades, researchers have replaced the earlier anthropological term "berdache" with the term "two-spirit" or "two-spirited" to refer to North American Aboriginal thinking about alternative representations of sexuality and gender (Stimson, 2006)

Often, two-spirited or the related concept of the "third gender" in Native communities is invoked as a myth to allow Western notions of transsexuality. However, some have proposed that this attempted correspondence risks oversimplifying the third gender idea. It also risks taking a non-Western concept for particular (Western) purposes. In this way, the popularization of the third gender concept may contribute to ethnocentric ideas about other cultures (Towle and Morgan, 2002).

The term "two-spirited," devised by Native activists in 1990, has been used to reconnect Aboriginal people with their cultural traditions. It signals a fluid sexual identity, and it moves beyond the binary distinction between gay and straight, male and female, that is common in Western traditions (Walters et al., 2006). However, Aboriginal people who identify as two-spirited not only face heterosexism and sexism, but often also suffer discrimination from both society at large and queer identity movements (ibid.).

Still, the two-spirit concept has been a great resource for Aboriginal gay rights activists and organizers because it involves both sexual and gender identities and helps to unify the Aboriginal queer movement. Removing the need for separate gay, lesbian, bisexual, and transsexual organizations, the two-spirit concept has successfully provided culturally sensitive and empowering support for diverse sexual issues (Meyer-Cook and Labelle, 2004).

People who identify as both Aboriginal and LGBT may face particular problems that result from the intersection of these two minority statuses. One study of two-spirited Aboriginals in Manitoba found that this sub-population was more likely than the general population to experience serious illnesses, live in poverty, experience high levels of emotional distress, and be subject to hostility and violence. This study also found that STIs and HIV were especially prevalent in Aboriginal two-spirited people who were designated male at birth.

Theoretical Perspectives on Sexual Orientation

TABLE 5.1	Theoretical Perspectives
THEORY	**MAIN POINTS**
Structural Functionalism	• Homosexuality threatens traditional institutions like the family, which are established largely for procreation. • Homosexual communities and movements provide social cohesion and social acceptance in the same ways as heterosexual communities.
Conflict Theory	• Heteronormativity establishes heterosexuality as acceptable and homosexuality as unacceptable. • The gender binary forces people to accept only one gender and one sexual orientation.
Symbolic Interactionism	• People's identities reflect the roles they are permitted to play. • Stigmatization is damaging, leading to impression management and non-disclosure.
Feminist Theory	• People vary widely along a continuum of genders and sexualities. • People express their sexualities differently in different societies and cultures.
Social Constructionism	• Without claims-making and moral entrepreneurship, few would care about other people's sexuality. • Changes in the media have helped to influence a positive change in public attitudes about sexual orientation.

Structural Functionalism

The apparent decline of traditional marriage in North America—formerly comprising a dominant male household head and submissive wife—has made some people worry about the death of the family (on this, see, for example, Popenoe, 1993; Nell, 2005). Alongside the LGBT movement, gender politics, sexual politics, and the multiplication of sexual identities have added to a general confusion about intimate relations. From the functionalist perspective, anything that upsets clear role expectations and situational norms is socially disruptive.

Therefore, from the functionalist perspective, the decline of heteronormativity and the blurring of gender lines pose problems for social order. On the other hand, functionalists would likely look with approval at the success homosexuals have had in organizing LGBT communities to satisfy their social needs. They have demonstrated that social pluralism works for sexual minorities, as it does for ethnic minorities.

Conflict Theory

In the past, the pressure for heteronormativity (Geller, 2009) was overt through social preaching and restrictive laws against homosexuality. Today, the main sources of information—the media, schools, and churches, for example—still hold up a heterosexual lifestyle as the norm (DePalma and Atkinson, 2009). Government, politics, and even the arts are still mainly oriented towards heterosexuals (Stacey and Meadow, 2009). It was not until 2005 that a major film, *Brokeback Mountain*, examined the subject of homosexuality as one possible relationship between men rather than as a subcultural aberration (*Cabaret*), source of anguish (*The Dresser*), or "camp" entertainment (*The Rocky Horror Picture Show*; *Priscilla, Queen of the Desert*).

In the late 1990s, a record number of Fortune 500 corporations began to extend equal benefits to all of their employees regardless of sexual orientation. Today, at least one-third of these organizations give their gay and lesbian employees domestic-partner benefits, and it is likely that their actions will influence the actions of smaller organizations. Because of their size and wealth, the largest and most powerful corporations act as leaders for the corporate community.

Many large corporations view the adoption of domestic-partner benefit policies and a commitment to "diversity" as "the right thing to do"—a business policy that would also gain them access to a wider pool of potential employees. This attitude shows an effort by the corporate world to upgrade its reputation by including gay issues as part of its diversity programs and policies (Day and Greene, 2008).

Feminist Theory

Lesbianism has been connected with various forms of feminism, especially in the latter half of the twentieth century to the present. Some theorists (e.g., Denike, 2007) have even identified gender inequality and homophobia as springing from the same "heteronormative sexual ethics." We can see this in the ways that gay men are popularly feminized and lesbians are ascribed masculine qualities (Cohen et al., 2009; Blashill and Powlishta, 2009). Also, practices of discrimination around sexual orientation often have an underlying gender basis. In short, women are more tolerant of homosexuality than men.

Feminists are especially inclined to support same-sex marriage, since doing otherwise reinforces patriarchal ideals and entrenches traditional gender roles in the family (Harding, 2007). However, feminism, too, has sometimes employed rigid, heteronormative thinking in defining certain issues like domestic violence. The feminist inclination to explain intimate partner violence (IPV) solely in terms of patriarchy has been an unpopular theory, since IPV afflicts both same-sex and opposite-sex couples, and women, in some opposite-sex relationships, are physically abusive as well.

It's true that empirical studies have found a connection between "masculinity" (as measured by "masculine behaviours") and IPV perpetration (Próspero, 2008). However, this focus on one factor—masculine assertiveness—among many has encouraged hetero-sexism and limited the delivery of support services to lesbian IPV victims. It has left counsellors, police, and other crisis workers insensitive to the particular dynamics of abusive lesbian relationships (Ristock, 2001; Speziale and Ring, 2006). In turn, the lack of support and protection for women in same-sex unions has made these relationships more risky.

Heterosexism
Discrimination against homosexuals in favour of heterosexuals.

Symbolic Interactionism

Symbolic interactionist theories pay attention to the construction and enactment of sexual orientations. They also look at the outcomes of labelling people as gay, straight, lesbian, bisexual, and so on, and at how these roles are internalized.

Sexual identities, like gender and other social identities, vary with culture and time. Societies differ in the degree to which sexual identities are viewed as essential or fundamental and as immutable and uncontrollable (versus chosen). At the same time, rapid social change in people's attitudes and identities challenges our creativity as a society, as we scurry to invent, learn about, and enact new approaches to sexuality.

The question for symbolic interactionists, then, is how do people negotiate different sexualities in different social milieu—why are some friendly while others are not (Valentine and Waite, 2012; McQueeney, 2003)? Further, how do people see one another as sexual partners, given different cultural traditions affecting how we view sex, seduction, intimacy, masculinity, and femininity? No sociologist has come closer to answering these questions than Stephen O. Murray (Box 5.2).

Homophobia and Heterosexism

Homophobia is the fear or hatred of homosexuals. The word "phobia" means an irrational, uncontrollable fear or hatred. Yet, the tendency we are considering under the label of "homophobia" comes in various forms. They range from social distance (e.g., the unwillingness to form a close friendship), to stereotyping (e.g., the view that all gays are the same), to religious injunctions, to bullying and harassment at school or work, to hate crimes, including murder (Balkin et al., 2009; Harris, 2009; O'Higgins-Norman, 2009).

One feature of homophobia is "essentialism"—the belief that all homosexuals have fundamentally the same characteristics (Haslam and Levy, 2006; Tomsen, 2006). Psychologist Gordon Allport (1979 [1954]) proposed that any belief in group "essences" points to a prejudiced personality; so does a rigid cognitive style that cannot accept ambiguity or changeability.

Essentialist beliefs about sexual orientation vary along two dimensions: the "immutability" of sexual orientation and the "fundamentality" of a classification of people as

Homophobia Fear or hatred of homosexuals, or behaviour that suggests such fear or hatred.

HOMOPHOBIA

In this 2012 film directed by Gregor Schmidinger, an adolescent boy who serves in the military forces experiences homosexual feelings towards one of his comrades—feelings that surface during their last night at the border, isolated and armed with loaded weapons.

Classic WORKS

| BOX 5.2 | Stephen O. Murray's *American Gay* (1996) |

Stephen Murray was born in 1950. A gay sociologist and anthropologist, he works mostly out of San Francisco. He earned a master's degree in sociology at the University of Arizona, and in 1979 he received his Ph.D. in sociology from the University of Toronto. After completing his formal education, Murray did post-doctoral studies at the University of California, Berkeley. There, he studied sociolinguistics as well as the history of sociology and anthropology.

Murray has produced several provocative and controversial books and a great number of research papers and journal articles about homosexuality. His better-known writings include *Latin American Male Homosexualities* (1995), *Homosexualities* (2000), and *American Gay* (1996). As a gay sociologist, Murray was especially interested in the prominently gay issue HIV/AIDS. He worked with several California county health departments on this problem. Professionally, he is on the boards of both the *Journal of Homosexuality* and the *Histories of Anthropology Annual*.

Murray's *American Gay* is especially focused on discussing the formation of gay communities and cultures—on developing what sociologist Raymond Breton, in the context of ethnicity, has called "institutional completeness." For example, Murray discusses the role of gay bars and bathhouses in providing safe meeting places for the expression of homosexuality. He discusses the particular cultural issues that arise in this subculture, for example,

the problems of "gay promiscuity," multiple versions of sexuality (such as bisexuality, transgendering, and sado-masochism), and cross-class or cross-racial relationships within the gay community. Most fundamentally, he is concerned with the problem of establishing stable roles and relationships—for example, couple relationships—among people who have long had to hide their relations and now have to invent norms for them.

American Gay delves deep into the topic of homosexuality from a sociological standpoint. The media often sensationalizes and stereotypes homosexuality and tends to associate it with leading a solitary life and dying alone. Murray, however, affirms that gay men care for each other emotionally just as deeply as heterosexual couples do. He regards gay people's efforts to be included in "straight" institutions (such as marriage and the military) as forms of resistance, not assimilation.

At one time, sociologists who wanted to study homosexuality were doubted or even ostracized. Murray encountered great difficulty during his master's program in Arizona. Faculty as well as students expressed their dislike for his "gay lifestyle." In one instance, Murray's research proposal was rejected by his professor, who ignorantly said, "No one is interested in your lifestyle." Overcoming this adversity, *American Gay* proved that studying homosexuality from a sociological standpoint is not only possible, but interesting and provocative as well.

heterosexuals or homosexuals. *Immutability* refers to the belief that under no circumstances can one change a personal feature—in this case, homosexuality. *Fundamentality* refers to the belief that a certain feature—in this case, homosexuality—is central to a person's entire character. Research finds that hostile attitudes towards lesbians and gay men are correlated positively with fundamentality but negatively with immutability.

To put it another way, studies suggest that people are more likely to hold anti-gay attitudes if they think homosexuals have a choice in their sexual orientation. They are also likely to hold anti-gay attitudes if they think of homosexuality as an essential feature of a person, one that overshadows all other qualities (Waldner et al., 2006).

Most gay rights activists today agree with the idea that one is born gay, and therefore it is not a choice: homosexuality is immutable and not a matter of choice (VanderLaan and Vasey, 2008). The idea that a person is born gay is widely accepted within the gay community, and it is an idea that is gaining acceptance and support from the heterosexual public. At the same time, people are coming to realize that homosexuality is not a master status, that homosexuals vary as widely—socially and psychologically—as heterosexuals. However, they may vary in different ways, largely related to the fact that heterosexual relationships are (still) fundamentally organized around reproduction and child-rearing. This difference is important, but it does not show prejudice and discrimination. How *does* the perception of such a difference lead to prejudice and discrimination?

According to the *attribution-value* theory of prejudice, people develop prejudices against particular groups they feel to be morally responsible for their stigmatized behaviour (Haider-Markel and Joslyn, 2008). According to this theory, there are two causes of the behaviour: biological causes, which people cannot control, and behavioural causes, which are subject to a person's will (Boysen and Vogel, 2007). When faced with stigmas they think are the result of voluntary action, like AIDS or drug abuse, people are less likely to provide help and more likely to react with hostility than when faced with stigmas whose causes are seen to be biological, like Alzheimer's disease. Therefore, on this account, homophobia develops when a person believes that homosexuality is both a choice and socially harmful.

George Weinberg's (1983 [1972]) introduction of the term "homophobia" helped focus society's attention on the problem of anti-gay prejudice and stigma. Weinberg called attention to the irrationality and harmfulness of this prejudice, which is no more acceptable than racism or sexism. However, the term "homophobia" itself has some limitations. Its main flaw is the implication that anti-gay prejudice is a "phobia"—a feeling based mainly on fear and thus an irrational defence mechanism (Dermer et al., 2010: 327). This approach, rooted in psychoanalysis, cannot account for historical changes in the way societies view homosexuality and heterosexuality. If we are to gain a sociological (versus psychiatric) understanding of anti-homosexual prejudice, we need a new vocabulary for discussing such behaviour.

To this end, Gregory Herek (2004) has defined three concepts that together capture the most important aspects of the notion of homophobia: (1) *sexual stigma* (the shared

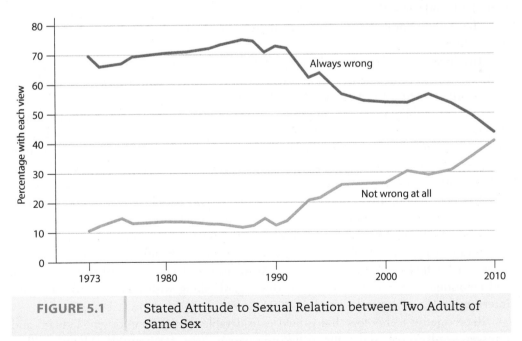

FIGURE 5.1 | Stated Attitude to Sexual Relation between Two Adults of Same Sex

Source: Based on data from Tom W. Smith, "Public Attitudes toward Homosexuality," at: <www.norc.org/PDFs/2011%20 GSS%20Reports/GSS_Public%20Attitudes%20Toward%20Homosexuality_Sept2011.pdf>, pp. 2, 3.

knowledge of society's negative regard for any non-heterosexual behaviour, identity, or community); (2) *heterosexism* (the cultural ideology that perpetuates sexual stigma); and (3) *sexual prejudice* (people's negative attitudes based on sexual orientation). However, it is unclear whether the decline in anti-homosexual attitudes in the last 25 years was caused by change in these ideas.

Media and Technology

People learn a great deal about their normative sexual roles and responsibilities through the mass media. In this sense, then, the media are responsible for teaching us ways to understand sexuality.

Homosexuals, once hidden from movies, television, and other media, are now being actively portrayed in those media. Currently, many popular television shows feature at least one gay character; indeed, the token gay character has become a predictable motif just as the token black character in advertising and television casting was a generation or two ago. Other television shows have dedicated episodes to gay issues. Research suggests that positive portrayals of sexual minorities in the media lead to more favourable attitudes among heterosexuals (Bonds-Raacke et al., 2007). Likewise, the daily news often includes one or more stories dealing with gay issues. These portrayals can have a positive effect on the way youth view their own sexuality. In this way, LGBT youth can now feel that society accepts them as they are.

Many people within the gay community, however, believe that the media fail to represent them accurately. They admit that any representation at all is a step forward, but also note that television shows such as *Glee* promote an unrealistic, "sanitized" image of gay men (Greenlee, 2005). The gay men portrayed on television are asexual, white, feminized, and well-off—qualities that make them acceptable to the heterosexual public. Also, few lesbians or bisexuals are represented in the mainstream media at all (Oakenfull et al., 2008).

The idea of the "good gay" makes heterosexual viewers more comfortable with homosexuality, yet it may not be accurate in its representation of homosexual life. As noted earlier, there are as many kinds of gays and lesbians as there are of heterosexuals.

In short, public understanding of homosexuality is gradually improving, thanks to the media and other opportunities for greater familiarity. Traditional homophobia has declined significantly in the last two decades as a result. Yet, homophobia has far from disappeared; it continues to pose a problem for homosexuals as a form of prejudice that promotes discrimination and even violence.

The growth of online communities has enabled LGBT people to seek support in their day-to-day interactions. Online communities have also proven useful for some transgendered people who can't access information elsewhere. In addition, these virtual communities can provide support and discussion, as one study found for female-to-male transsexuals who face the difficult task of passing the social "test" of manhood. Education and emotional support are also key in this regard, along with medical and biological intervention (Gauthier and Chaudoir, 2004).

Reproductive technology has gained considerable significance for gay, lesbian, and transgendered people who want to become parents (see, for example, Mamo, 2007). Techniques of surrogacy and artificial insemination have been contested politically, with access to these technologies sometimes being denied to anyone other than straight couples who are unable to conceive through intercourse (Bryld, 2001). These technologies and the political contests associated with them have had important results in struggles over parenting and family issues.

Social Consequences of Homophobia

Same-Sex Families

Parents of homosexual or bisexual children may have a hard time accepting their children's sexual orientation. They may be disappointed because they have other expectations for their child or because their child's behaviour embarrasses them and causes them discomfort. Their reactions can lead to harsh words, broken relationships, and depression. Parents often believe they want "what is best" for their children and fear that, if gay, their child will miss valuable opportunities or suffer discrimination. Parents may also take this personally and react with "Why did you do this to me?" when in fact a child's coming out has little to do with his or her parents (Seidman, 2002).

However, this kind of attitude has been changing. Increasingly, same-sex families have disrupted the dominant view of what "normal" families are and what they do. The theoretical tradition, Queer Theory, sets out to deconstruct the dichotomies that shape our lived experiences. Queer Theory views society as "composed of falsely bounded categories that give the impression of fixity and permanence where none 'naturally' exists" (Crawley and Broad, 2008: 551). As we can see from Figure 5.2, attitudes towards homosexuality have been liberalizing all over the Western world, and so are attitudes to same-sex families.

The existence of same-sex partners, especially those with children, "queers the family." That is, their existence forces us to re-examine our preconceived ideas about what makes a family, what families do, and what we want from families. Yet, at the same time, same-sex families "normalize the queer" by showing us that LGBT families behave in much the same way as "normal" heterosexual families.

Lesbian families, in particular, have displayed strengths that would likely benefit straight families as well (Moore, 2009; Röndahl et al., 2009). For example, Savin-Williams and Esterberg (2000) found that these families are more likely than straight families to exhibit an egalitarian decision-making structure. Nonetheless, straight parents and lesbian parents are similar in two important ways: both practise child-centred parenting and both try to parent children according to socially produced scripts.

As more countries legalize gay and lesbian unions, the number of same-sex couples wishing to adopt and raise children will naturally increase. Some have feared that children growing up in homosexual households would also be homosexual, but there has been no evidence to support this concern. Among LGBT families, the parent's sexual orientation neither controls the child's gender development nor increases the likelihood of any psychological problems (Bos and Sandfort, 2010; Volpp and Drescher, 2011; Tasker, 2005). Rather, the quality of family relationships—not the sex of parents—is what influences the child's well-being (Patterson, 2006)

Some observers have wondered if children with same-sex parents would develop as well as children with opposite-sex parents. Many studies support the finding that

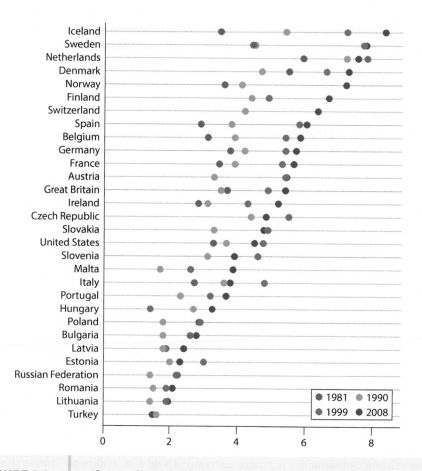

FIGURE 5.2 | Change in Attitudes towards Homosexuality

Note: Respondents were asked to rate on a scale from 1 to 10 whether homosexuality is "justifiable," where 1 means "never" and 10 "always."

Source: Based on a graph created by Erik Voeten (*Washington Monthly* journalist), available at: <http://themonkeycage.org/2012/05/18/changes-in-public-attitudes-towards-homosexuality/>.

gay and lesbian parents are just as capable in child-rearing as heterosexual parents. Children raised by homosexual parents do not have different behavioural and educational outcomes than children of heterosexual unions, nor do they feel any less loved or accepted by their parents (Mattingly and Bozick, 2001). Further, there is no more chance of children growing up gay or lesbian in a same-sex family than in a heterosexual family.

Some critics of homosexual parenting propose that lesbian unions lack a proper father figure, which could affect the growth of the child. Biblarz and Stacey (2010), on the other hand, respond that these criticisms tend to conflate gender with other family structural variables. For example, when discussing the importance of a male role model for children of lesbians, critics tend to cite data comparing heterosexual two-parent families to single-mother families. Biblarz and Stacey note there is no real difference between homosexual and heterosexual two-parent families. Many children of same-sex unions

The Canadian Press/Nathan Denette

Lesbian couple and parents Julia Gonsalves, right, and Andrea Bruner, left, hold their child, Gracie Gonsalves-Bruner, as they take part in an annual Gay Pride Parade in Toronto.

feel they gained important insights into gender relations and broader, more inclusive definitions of family by growing up with same-sex parents (Crowl et al., 2008; Biblarz and Stacey, 2010).

Until recently, most family research ignored same-sex couple families and their parenting practices. This lack of research resulted in an incomplete picture of what same-sex families are and do. More people are now coming to accept homosexuals, but attitudes towards gay parents remain conservative, especially among older and rural people. Only about 20 per cent of Canadians surveyed in Miall and March's (2005) study, for example, were in favour of homosexuals adopting children, compared with the 92 per cent who supported adoption by traditional married couples.

Harassment and Hate Crimes

Schools play an important part in passing on attitudes to homosexuality, and many studies have identified the classroom as a place where gender and sexuality are constructed. In the classroom and the schoolyard, most children first meet the views of their peers about different sexual orientations.

Boys at school often use homophobic terms with one another. But what do they mean when they use these terms? Terms like "faggot" tap a complex array of connotations that have precise meanings in peer cultures. Boys quickly learn to use these homophobic terms against others. Significantly, the evocative use of homophobic terms commonly occurs before puberty, before boys gain an adult sexual identity, and before they know much, if anything, about homosexuality. As a result, early learning provides an entry into understanding adult sexual identities and, significantly, powerful homophobic codes are learned first (Plummer, 2001).

No wonder, then, that hate and fear persist around issues of homosexuality. To combat this, Bill C-250 was passed in 2004, making it a crime in Canada to spread hateful views about other people's sexual orientation. Under this bill, homosexuals are now among the groups protected against hate crimes under the Criminal Code, a list that includes racial, religious, and ethnic minorities.

Unfortunately, such hate crimes continue to be a problem. A study of gay and lesbian victims found that strangers in public places were the most likely to perpetrate hate crimes. However, victimization occurs in other locales, too, and perpetrators can include neighbours, schoolmates, co-workers, and even relatives. As with date rape, not all experiences of victimization are reported. Many people have concerns about police bias and fear that public disclosure of their sexual orientation will influence how officials respond, making them reluctant to report anti-gay crimes; they also fear that perpetrators, if reported, will go unpunished and take revenge. Such concerns are typical among all victims of assault.

Workplace Discrimination

Many companies today claim to seek diversity in their employees. They stress that they are equal-opportunity employers and that all minorities, including gays and lesbians, have an equal chance of being hired, promoted, and treated fairly once employed. These claims sound reasonable, yet many companies do not always follow through on their promises. As a result, many gays and lesbians feel a need to hide their sexual identity while at work for fear of discrimination (O'Ryan and MacFarland, 2010).

Gay men and lesbians who experience discrimination in the workplace are sometimes unwilling to report it. Doing so would often mean revealing their sexual identity to many people. Most people want to keep their personal lives quiet, and reporting discrimination can mean publicizing one's private life to the entire office, receiving unwanted attention. Yet queer rights groups warn that if harassment goes unreported, nothing will ever change. Homosexuals who experience discrimination have a difficult and important decision to make, but the law is on their side. Provincial human rights codes and the Canadian Charter of Rights and Freedoms make it illegal to discriminate against a person based on his or her sexual orientation. It is also illegal, therefore, to discriminate against someone who is in a same-sex relationship.

While employees may be reluctant to invoke the law, bosses can make the workplace environment more (or less) friendly for gays and lesbians. Factors that create a more comfortable environment for homosexual workers include support from top management, policies to prevent discrimination, the presence of LGBT employee networks, and a non-heterosexist organizational climate (Ragins et al., 2003). Conversely, conditions that influence a person to stay "in the closet" at work include a lack of racial balance and work teams that are composed mostly of men. Having a male supervisor also increases the likelihood that homosexual employees will stay in the closet, as people report experiencing more discrimination and homophobia under male supervisors.

WERE THE WORLD MINE

In this 2008 film directed by Tom Gustafson, a bullied gay student at an all-boys school uses a magical flower derived from Shakespeare's *A Midsummer Night's Dream* to turn many in his community gay.

Countries where a majority of those surveyed say that homosexuality . . .

■ Should be accepted   ■ Should NOT be accepted   ■ Mixed views

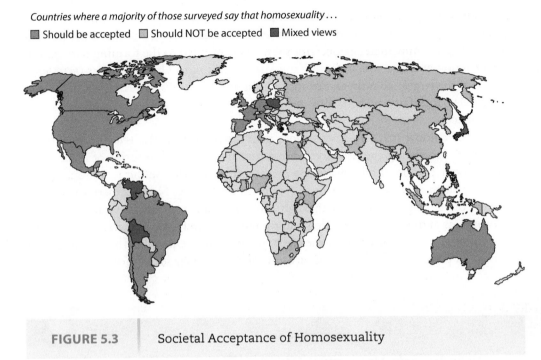

| FIGURE 5.3 | Societal Acceptance of Homosexuality |

Source: Pew Research Centre, at: <www.pewresearch.org/fact-tank/2013/06/04/global-snapshot-sex-marriage>.

The military has been a particularly problematic workplace for LGBT minorities. Only in recent years have Canadian and US military services knowingly permitted the enlistment of homosexual people and protected them against violence and discrimination.

Health Consequences of Homophobia

HIV/AIDS

When the HIV/AIDS epidemic began in the early 1980s, the US government was reluctant to help communities in need (Gross and Bisson, 2009). The virus seemed to affect only injecting drug users and "men who have sex with men"—people who were held responsible for their illness, as they were popularly believed to have complete control over their own risky behaviours. Given the belief that HIV was not affecting heterosexuals and drug abstainers, little was done to stem the growing epidemic. Most doctors at the time were uninformed about how to deal with HIV infection, and they were reluctant to learn about it, treat it, or help people who became HIV-positive.

In the early days, news reports called it a "gay disease." For a long time, people were unsure exactly how HIV/AIDS was passed from one person to another and, therefore, how its transmission could be prevented. Large numbers of gay men in gay communities, in New York City for example, were dying of the disease. AIDS activists tried to raise awareness about the sick and dying communities of gay men infected with the virus by calling attention to the epidemic and pointing out that government inaction was letting more and more people die.

This official indifference and lack of support outraged the gay communities. Many felt certain that if HIV were to affect heterosexual people in large numbers, the government would take immediate action. This sense of outrage led to the forming of organizations for action and support, including the AIDS Coalition to Unleash Power (ACTUP)—now one of the largest AIDS organizations fighting for awareness and research about HIV/AIDS. In New York City, posters with the slogan "silence = death" appeared everywhere around the city.

Today, we know that HIV affects more than just homosexuals. Television commercials, posters promoting the use of condoms, and news and other forms of media have brought about a wide public awareness of the problem. The public is more aware of the AIDS crisis in Africa and of rising HIV rates among young North American women. Members of the gay community, through their activism, were pioneers in promoting this awareness about HIV/AIDS by demanding more research, more access to drugs and treatment, and more protection of the rights of HIV-positive people. These actions have benefited all people infected with the virus, regardless of their sexual orientation.

CANADIAN researcher

BOX 5.3   Eleanor Maticka-Tyndale, University of Windsor

A critical global issue in connection with gender and sexuality has been the problem of unsafe sex. At its worst, unprotected sex has been responsible for a catastrophic epidemic of HIV/AIDS in Africa that continues to the present day. But even in Canada, unprotected sex has led to a rise of STIs among young people and other vulnerable populations. Eleanor Maticka-Tyndale, Canada Research Chair in Social Justice and Sexual Health, has been studying this and related problems for two decades.

In her 2010 paper "Sustainability of Gains Made in a Primary School HIV Prevention Programme in Kenya into the Secondary School Years," Professor Tyndale asks whether the beneficial effects of Primary School Action for Better Health (PSABH), an HIV prevention program delivered in Kenyan primary schools, are temporary or long-lasting. She finds that, indeed, sex education in primary school continues to have a beneficial effect for students who continue on to secondary school.

More generally, in a 2004 paper, "School-Based HIV Prevention Programmes for African Youth," authors Tyndale and Melanie Gallant review 11 published and evaluated school-based HIV/AIDS risk-reduction programs for youth in Africa. Ten of the 11 studies reported significant improvements in sex knowledge. All seven programs that assessed attitudes reported an increase in attitudes favourable to risk reduction. In one of the three

studies that targeted sexual behaviours, sexual debut was delayed and the number of sexual partners decreased. In one of the two that targeted condom use, condom use behaviours improved. The results of this review suggest that it's easiest to change knowledge and attitudes; changing behaviour is much harder.

In her 2001 paper "Twenty Years in the AIDS Pandemic: A Place for Sociology," Tyndale notes that "AIDS has devastated and will continue to devastate local communities, and with them nations and populations, tearing apart social fabric, economies and systems of security and governance. In this it is certainly no less than, and probably will be more than, the dreaded epidemics of the past." She concludes that this is more than a health issue—it is a social justice issue, built on the "inequities within and between nations."

In Canada, the problems are less dire but nonetheless widespread. In a 2008 paper, "Sexuality and Sexual Health of Canadian Adolescents: Yesterday, Today, and Tomorrow," Tyndale reports that Canadian teens today are experiencing better sexual health and taking more precautions to protect their sexual health than in prior generations. However, Canadian teens and young adults continue to face challenges from STIs. This is true especially in rural areas and among Aboriginal youth, who are the least well served by sexual education and sexual health care.

The Canadian Press/Francis Vachon

Lawyer Micheline Montreuil poses in her office in Quebec city. As a transgender person, Micheline Anne Helene Montreuil, born Pierre Montreuil, became known for her legal struggles to defend her rights.

Use of Health Services

The health problems facing gay, lesbian, bisexual, and transgendered people may not be caused by homophobia, but they are often worsened by the homophobia and heterosexism of some doctors and other medical professionals (Diaz et al., 2005; Rutledge et al., 2009). Sometimes, simple ignorance of LGBT issues—not hostility—leads doctors and other health professionals to treat their LGBT patients insensitively or unprofessionally. Such institutionalized homophobia frightens many homosexual people. People who fear they will be judged or misunderstood are likely to visit the doctor less often, leading to poorer health.

Many LGBT people have reported experiencing homophobia or heterosexism from health-care professionals (e.g., Peel, 2008). The extreme cases have to do with transgendered people who are seeking sexual reassignment surgery. Some transsexuals find that doctors refuse to do surgery on them for religious reasons. Many others feel that they were assigned the wrong sex at birth; to correct this, they sometimes seek surgery, as well as hormone treatment. To receive such surgical intervention, they must claim they feel they were born in the wrong body, but not every doctor is willing to go along with this request.

Nor is sexual reassignment surgery the only medical issue facing transgendered people. Some children are born intersexed, with ambiguous genitalia. These may include, but are not limited to, Turner syndrome, 5-alpha reductase hermaphroditism, or androgen insensitivity syndrome. In cases like these, the child may be born with both a vagina and a small penis but no testicles; a difficult decision must then be made. Because our society works on a rigid gender binary, both doctors and parents may feel that they have to choose a single gender for the child and the "appropriate" surgery accordingly. Often, repeat genital surgeries are needed as the child gets older, mainly for cosmetic purposes to make the genitals look more "normal."

The doctors who perform these surgeries believe that a child cannot develop properly with ambiguous sexuality, so the doctor and family must decide whether the child is to "become" male or female. These decisions, and the important actions that follow, are stressful for the doctors, parents, and the children themselves.

Solutions to the Homophobia Problem

One of the greatest changes in recent years has been the establishment of *sexual orientation* as a personal domain legally protected from discrimination.

In *Vriend v. Alberta*, a 1997 Supreme Court of Canada case, Delwin Vriend—a lab instructor at King's University College in Edmonton—claimed that he was unjustly fired from his job because of his sexual orientation. This challenge was necessary because sexual orientation was not included under the Canadian Charter of Rights and Freedoms. Gay and lesbian activists in the early 1980s had sought specific inclusion in the Charter of Rights and Freedoms and in the Alberta Individual Rights Protection Act as a basis for legal protection against discrimination, but they had not succeeded.

Vriend successfully argued that sexual orientation is similar to the other grounds stated in section 15 of the Charter, such as race, religion, and sex, and should be protected as such. As a result of this success, today no one can legally discriminate against homosexuals because of their sexual orientation, any more than they can discriminate against blacks because of their skin colour or against Jews or Muslims because of their religion.

Nonetheless, the important legal precedent achieved in *Vriend* is not as powerful as the explicit constitutional protection that the Charter, as part of the 1982 Constitution Act, provided to women, ethnic groups, visible minorities, the disabled, and the elderly. More remains to be done to achieve equality on this score.

Canadian Research on Homophobia and Social Change

The timing of the 1982 Charter and the associated increase in the powers of the courts coincided with the beginnings of the LGBT movement. The movement was gaining ground just as Canadian courts acquired a new political importance through new constitutional decision-making.

However, legal change alone will not be enough to gain gays and lesbians full social acceptance. As with any social "other," familiarity and visibility will continue to be important in the acceptance of the LGBT community. Personal experience with LGBT people will continue to improve the relations between homosexuals and people who might otherwise disapprove of them.

Education and Policies

As we have seen repeatedly, some acts once considered sexually deviant—for example, homosexual acts—are increasingly accepted in the general population. Today, homosexuals are receiving new recognition and inclusion in society.

Increasingly, government institutions show concern about fair and equal treatment for the LGBT minority. In 1997, the Quebec Ministry of Health and Social Services proposed ways to erase heterosexism from health and social services, highlighting problems to which LGBT people are vulnerable, such as psychological distress, substance abuse, suicide, and HIV/AIDS. The Quebec government conducted a critical examination of the value of public services and organizations, focusing especially on their accessibility to the LGBT community. Most importantly, it established a new set of policies and interventions, created with the LGBT community in mind, and enforced its implementation. Then, in 1999, British Columbia's Ministry of Health and Ministry Responsible for Seniors published a similar document; it focused on lesbian and gay experiences in the health-care system and included a set of tips for health planners, policy-makers, and practitioners.

Another victory came in 2001, when the Canadian census included for the first time a question about same-sex relationships. This represented a step forward in recognizing homosexuals as a part of Canada's diverse population. The census found 34,000 same-sex common-law couples living in Canada. Likely, this number has increased since Canada's subsequent legalization of same-sex marriages.

The numbers are important, because they influence the extent of government funding for this community. Tom Smith (1998) of the National Opinion Research Center at the University of Chicago (NORC) reports that "few debates have been so contentious as the controversy over the sexual orientation of Americans." The gay and lesbian communities have long claimed to make up 10 per cent of the population of the United States, but a series of national studies show that only about 2–3 per cent of sexually active men and 1–2 per cent of sexually active women are currently homosexual. These national American estimates are consistent with figures from local communities in the United States, indirect measurements, and statistics from Great Britain, France, Norway, and Denmark.

Rates of same-gender contact increase as the reference period is extended. Recent US research finds that more people report having a past same-sex partner and having some same-sex attraction than report identifying themselves as homosexual. In fact, 8.2 per cent of Americans report having engaged in same-sex relations, and 11 per cent report having experienced some same-sex attraction at one time or another (Gates, 2011). The 2001 Canadian census also revealed that 15 per cent of lesbian couples and 3 per cent of gay couples are raising children. These data probably underestimate the number of gay and lesbian couples, but they begin—finally—to number homosexual people among Canadian citizens.

Like other minority groups, homosexuals and lesbians have tried to educate the public, change the laws, and form self-protective organizations. Two kinds of organizations created by the gay community have been especially effective. The first includes formal and informal support groups directed towards the LGBT community. The second presses for political and social change by educating people outside the gay community. The latter organizations include Equality for Gays and Lesbians Everywhere (EGALE), Parents, Family, and Friends of Lesbians and Gays (PFLAG), and Gay and Lesbian Alliance against Defamation (GLAAD), among others. Their goal is to change policies and attitudes about people who identify as homosexual (Lax and Phillips, 2009).

In recent years, there has been an increased emphasis on educating students about homosexuality. Groups such as Teens Educating and Confronting Homophobia (TEACH) have tried to teach their peers about being LGBT. Speakers present their "coming out" stories to high school and university classes. Their goal is to get students to understand that LGBT people deserve to be treated equally and to be given the same respect as heterosexuals.

Some high schools include information on homosexuality in their sex education classes, and many urge their teachers to stop assuming that all their students are heterosexual. These changes in education are steps in the right direction, but the discrimination against and harassment of gay students remains an issue (Chesir-Teran and Hughes, 2009). Many high school and elementary school students use the term "that's so *gay*" when referring to something they dislike, or they use the term "faggot" to make fun of other students. Groups like TEACH work towards promoting awareness of the harmful effects of such casual use of homophobic language.

British Columbia has led the way in trying to solve the problem of homophobia in schools. To familiarize themselves with the problem, a Safe Schools Task Force travelled around the province, hearing about the school experiences of gay- and lesbian-identified youth. Their report noted that many LGBT students are afraid to go to school. With prodding from the homosexual community, in April 2005 the BC Ministry of Education established regulations to protect LGBT students in the public school system. It banned not only discrimination against LGBT-identified youth, but also discrimination against youth merely believed to be LGBT.

Chapter Summary

As we have seen, the LGBT community is made up of people who differ in many ways. Yet, often they are viewed and treated as just one deviant group.

Owing largely to the influence of religion, people have long stigmatized homosexuality as a sexual perversion. Some parts of Canadian society continue to do so; however, this is changing. It is hard to say whether the changing attitudes have led to changing laws or vice versa. Religion continues to play a huge role in popular views about homosexuality, especially outside of Canada. Whether in the US or Saudi Arabia, traditional religious beliefs misinform people about homosexuality and promote laws that make homosexual behaviour contemptible and even dangerous.

In Canada, liberal Christian denominations and the liberal segments within other religious faiths, such as Judaism, openly accept LGBT communities into the fold. However, even within liberal denominations, conflict continues. More moderate, secular people are for the most part more accepting of homosexuals, as is the urban population in contrast to the rural population, and this acceptance includes a greater willingness to protect the civil liberties of homosexuals. Urban secularists also are more willing to allow free expression to people with non-conformist political views and to support political activism.

Changes in how the media portray homosexuality have helped the LGBT community to become both less threatened and more open about who they are. As gays and lesbians mobilize, change is slowly taking place. As we have noted, in general people who know homosexuals personally are less homophobic than people who do not. In fact, personal contact with homosexual friends and relatives has more influence on attitudes towards gay men and lesbians than any other social or demographic variable.

Questions for Critical Thought

1. In this chapter, we see how homosexuality came to be "normalized." Can you think of other types of sexual activity that have also been normalized in recent decades? If so, what were the processes behind the normalization of these sexual activities?

2. Think about the double standard concerning the expected sexual behaviours of males and females. Has this double standard affected research on the topic of homosexuality?

3. Identify the reasons why homosexual activity is often limited to distinct parts of cities. What purpose might this geographic segregation serve?

4. In what ways is the LGBT community similar to other stigmatized communities—for example, Aboriginals, visible minorities, homeless people, or the unemployed? In what ways is it different?

5. What are the problems associated with including transgendered and transsexual people in the LGBT community? What are the benefits?

6. Does sexual variation seem to gain more attention and be more "problematized" in our society than many other issues (such as poverty, homelessness, and poor health)? If so, how do you account for this? If not, why might some people think this is so?

Recommended Readings

Butler, Judith. 1990. *Gender Trouble: Feminism and the Subversion of Identity*. New York: Routledge.

Laqueur, Thomas W. 2003. *Solitary Sex: A Cultural History of Masturbation*. New York: Zone Books.

Laumann, Edward O., Stephen Ellingson, Jenna Mahay, Anthony Palk, and Yoosik Youm, eds. 2004. *The Sexual Organization of the City*. Chicago: University of Chicago Press.

Nelson, Claudia, and Michelle H. Martin, eds. 2004. *Sexual Pedagogies: Sex Education in Britain, Australia, and America, 1879–2000*. New York and Basingstoke: Palgrave Macmillan.

Tweedy, Ann. 2011. "Polyamory as a Sexual Orientation," *University of Cincinnati Law Review*. 79, 4: 1461–516.

6

Aging and the Life Course

dmanjoe/Thinkstock

Introduction

In this chapter, we will discuss young people and seniors, youth, aging, retirement, and physical decline. We will also discuss ageism. Although the average age of Canadians is rising with each passing decade, and despite our growing awareness of older people and age variation, many Canadians openly practise **ageism**—direct or indirect discrimination against people based on their age (Dobbs et al., 2008; Jonson and Larsson, 2009). This includes refusing jobs to qualified and willing candidates because of stereotypic attitudes towards people—young or old—who violate the age norms and expectations of our society.

Ageism Prejudice or discrimination, mostly against seniors, but by implication against any member of society, based on their age.

The topic of this chapter is unlike most of the other social problems or issues in Canada today. After all, many people will never experience sexism or racism (for example)—because many people will never be women or members of a racial minority group. However, almost everyone will get to be elderly and almost everyone who gets to be elderly will experience ageism. So, this chapter likely concerns you and what you will likely experience as you move from being young to being older and then to being elderly.

Cross-Cultural Attitudes to Aging

In earlier times, advanced age brought respect, authority, and attention from others. In pre-industrial societies, the old enjoyed a high degree of control over their children and over young people overall (Lasch, 1977). Today, this is no longer the case.

As Western populations industrialized, children could more readily enter the workplace. They no longer had to rely on the help or good opinion of their fathers and mothers to "get ahead." With increased mobility, young people were able to marry, set up their own households, and make themselves less available (or willing) to provide help to aging parents, if they wished (Cullen et al., 2009). This transition, which unfolded throughout the West during the nineteenth and twentieth centuries, eventually began in the East during the second half of the twentieth century (Gottlieb, 1993). Nevertheless, cultural differences in attitudes towards aging remain. Many cultures continue to revere their elderly members as keepers of wisdom and authority (Merz et al., 2007; Gans and Silverstein 2006), while by contrast our culture tends to stereotype and exclude old people. Western culture reveres youth and fears aging, with its concomitant physical decline towards death.

One common belief in our culture is that most seniors are frail and ailing and the majority need full-time care in nursing homes or other institutional settings. The fact is that only 2.6 per cent of men and 3.3 per cent of women aged 65 to 74 live in a special-care institution, while 82.1 per cent of men and women between the ages of 65 and 74 live alone or with family members (Statistics Canada, 2011a, 2011b). Likewise, another common belief is that most elderly people are senile or rapidly headed in that direction. In fact, most seniors keep their cognitive and perceptual functions for many years after middle age. Alzheimer's disease, the most common form of neurological dementia, affects only 1 in 11 Canadians over the age of 65 (Alzheimer's Association, 2014).

We learn our negative attitudes towards aging and older people from the mass media, jokes, and cartoons. By shaping the popular views of older people, the media create a self-fulfilling prophecy in which elderly people begin to think and behave as people expect, thus reinforcing and lending legitimacy to the stereotype (Angus and Reeve,

Seniors dancing outdoors in Rocky Harbour, Newfoundland. The event was part of Parks Canada's 100th anniversary festivities. Unlike the stereotypical representation of seniors, most seniors retain their cognitive and physical functions well past middle age.

2006). Unfortunately, here, as with the other stereotypes we have examined, what people believe to be true can become true as a consequence.

The Idea of a "Life Course"

Our ability to think usefully about aging is helped immeasurably by the sociological idea of a "life course." In sociological thinking, the *life course* is a patterned sequence of individual age-linked experiences over time, entrenched in social institutions and historical influences. There is in each society—indeed, in each social group—an expected life course that fits (more or less) with the generally experienced life course. These life courses, ideal and actual, are not identical; the gap between the life courses we expect and those we experience may cause much distress. Living may sometimes also mean "breaking the rules" or failing to live up to age-related expectations (Ho and Raymo, 2009).

According to sociologist Glen Elder (1999), currently considered the most eminent researcher studying this topic, the life course approach rests on five main assumptions, and each is important to understanding age and aging. First, "human development and aging are lifelong processes" (ibid., 7). They start at birth and stop only with death. As people get older, their lives change. At each stage, some concerns become supreme and others trivial. Certain important life events typically are concentrated in certain periods of a person's life. Social institutions are gatekeepers in this respect. They divide and regulate life course transitions, pushing people in and out of school, in and out of marriage, in and out of jobs, and so on (Bengtson et al., 2012). They set up, teach, and reward the social expectations connected with a life course. We cannot understand the ideas, actions, and beliefs of people at any given age without some understanding of how they got to that age—that is, their developmental pathway. This means that longitudinal studies are the best ways of understanding all people, and especially older people.

Second, Elder (1999: 9) notes that "the developmental antecedents and consequences of life transitions, events, and behaviour patterns vary according to their timing in a person's life." Simply put, it makes a difference at what age you make a key life transition—whether you divorce at 25 or at 55, for example, or graduate from college at 20 or at 40. The age at which people make such transitions affects how they view themselves, not least because self-image is often based on a comparison with others. However, the usual sequence of major changes in our lives has an important impact on the experiences we have and people we meet.

Third, "lives are lived interdependently and socio-historical influences are expressed through this network of shared relationships" (ibid., 10). Since our lives are embedded in social relationships, we may find ourselves entering new statuses because of the actions of others, not through our own choosing. The teenage pregnancy of her daughter may make a woman a grandmother "before her time," just as the early death of her spouse may make her a widow "before her time." Our degree of preparation for new roles and statuses is important in how we experience and perform our key roles and statuses.

Fourth, "the life course of individuals is embedded in and shaped by the historical times and places they experience over their lifetime" (ibid., 13). Coming of college age means something different in wartime (for example, the 1940s) than it does in peacetime (the 1970s), in prosperity (the 1950s) than in financial depression (the 1980s), in a period of gender equality (the 1990s) than in one of male dominance (the 1890s). The historical period affects our opportunities and the choices we are likely to make, and it will affect other opportunities and choices throughout our lives.

Fifth, "individuals construct their own life courses through the choices and actions they take within the opportunities of history and social circumstances" (ibid., 15). In other words, though social forces influence our opportunities and actions, we do have choices in our lives. This means that within any social category or historical period, we will find variations in human lives because people can choose different paths (Wong and DeGraff, 2009). This helps us to understand why all 20-year-olds are not the same, nor all 50- or 80-year-olds. Often, the differences in people can be accounted for by their different choices. On the other hand, most people follow a predictable sequence of life experiences as they move from 20 to 50 to 80, and they feel uncomfortable when they deviate from that sequence.

Not everyone passes through the life course in the same way, so not everyone "ages" socially in the same way. Still, we can observe some similarities related to physical change.

NOBODY'S FOOL

Paul Newman earned an Oscar nomination in 1994 for his portrayal of an immature sixty-year-old construction worker who must learn to finally grow up.

Aspects of the Sociology of Aging

From birth onward, an individual's physical and mental abilities gradually improve, then decline in a biological process known as **senescence**. However, exactly at what age and in what form the decline takes place varies widely from one person to another.

Today, older people can look forward to a longer and healthier old age than in the past. Yet our culture has not fully kept up with these changes in the social

Senescence The biological aging of an organism as it lives beyond its maturity, usually accompanied by chemical and organic changes.

definition of who is elderly and what elderly people are like, largely because with an increased interest in childhood, there has been a decreased interest in later adulthood. Paradoxically, we have lost interest in the elderly just as their numbers have been increasing dramatically.

In 1901, only 5 per cent of the population was aged 65 or older. Over the past century, this fraction has more than doubled to 14.8 per cent (Statistics Canada, 2011b). Though the Canadian population is aging rapidly, it is far from the oldest population. Many Northern and Central European populations have much higher proportions of elderly people than one finds in North America.

We might best describe Canada's **age pyramid** today as a diamond shape, with a small base among the youngest groups, spreading out gradually as age groups increase in size until ages 45–55 before tapering off into a high, thin peak around ages 80–90 (Statistics Canada, 2011c). A diamond shape reflects a population undergoing change— a triangle that is gradually becoming a rectangle as the birth rate slows.

Age pyramid A graphic depiction of the age composition of a population, broken down by age and sex—pyramid-shaped if the birth rate is high but otherwise more rectangular.

Age Stratification

Though not all physical and social change leads to inequality, it does so where aging is concerned. Age stratification theory focuses on the way social structures affect individual aging and the stratification, or vertical segregation, of people by age. It is concerned with the segregation and mistreatment of certain age groups in the same sense that class stratification is concerned with the segregation and mistreatment of certain social classes (Uhlenberg and Gierveld, 2004).

Because of age stratification, aging and ageism pose various problems for society, especially as increasing percentages of the world and Canadian populations are getting older (see pp. 151 and 153). First, ageism, like discrimination based on race or gender, is repellent to a society like ours that is pledged to judging people by what they do rather than who they are. We say we believe in rewards based on achievement, not ascription. However, ageism is a sign that we do not, as a society, live up to our own proclaimed values of justice and equality. Second, ageism poses practical problems for victims of this discrimination (Sev'er, 2009). Like all discrimination, ageism has both material and psychological effects. Materially, it limits people's opportunities to get the jobs and incomes they may need to survive. Psychologically, ageism makes people feel rejected, excluded, and degraded (Clarke and Griffin, 2008). They feel they are less than they want and need to be as human beings.

Stereotyping aside, aging poses challenges for a society. Populations with a high proportion of old or young people—that is, low-fertility populations like our own or high-fertility populations like, say, Iraq's—consume a high proportion of their national economy in the form of supports for dependent populations: health, education, welfare, housing, and so on. Populations with a high proportion in the workforce, aged 25–65, can invest more of their economy in development, savings, or war, without significantly reducing their spending on human capital.

Thus, the increased proportion of elderly people in the population means at least two important things for society: (1) an increasing proportion of people need costly care and support and (2) an increasing proportion of people are considered useless and held in low regard. Figure 6.1 highlights Canada's aging populations by province and territory.

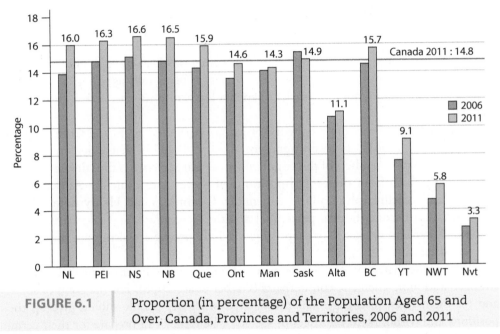

FIGURE 6.1 | Proportion (in percentage) of the Population Aged 65 and Over, Canada, Provinces and Territories, 2006 and 2011

Sources: Statistics Canada, censuses of population, 2006 and 2011, at: <www12.statcan.gc.ca/census-recensement/2011/as-sa/98-311-x/2011001/fig/fig7-eng.cfm>.

Theoretical Perspectives on Aging

TABLE 6.1	Theoretical Perspectives
THEORY	**MAIN POINTS**
Structural Functionalism	• All elements in society are interrelated. • Disengagement theory accounts for the relegation of older people to the sidelines of society. • Retirement serves several functions, especially the reinvigoration of social institutions.
Conflict Theory	• Conflict and change are features of social life. • Age-related discrimination does not benefit society. • Elderly people do not disengage; they are pushed out of the workforce. • The most powerful groups in society command resources and are the decision-makers.
Symbolic Interactionism	• Social life involves continued interaction. • Socially constructed definitions of age and aging affect one's experience of growing old. • People take on new roles as they age (they do not disengage). • Media portrayals reflect and reinforce society's stereotypes about older people.
Feminist Theory	• Aging affects men and women differently. • Women, because they live longer than men on average, are more likely to suffer the hardships associated with aging. • Generally, women provide care in aging while men receive it.
Social Constructionism	• Views of aging are shaped by moral entrepreneurship. • Popular beliefs about aging are propagated by the mass media and do not reflect reality.

Structural Functionalism

As we have noted repeatedly, structural functionalists think society is like a living organism, made up of interconnected parts that together work as an efficient, productive whole. This perspective, therefore, also views society as being only as strong as its weakest members. From this standpoint, society benefits least from its least active, most infirm members.

One structural functionalist theory of aging, attributed to Elaine Cumming and William Henry (1961), is **disengagement theory**. It holds that elderly people are among the weakest members of the population and that society has thus devised a means of displacing them from the central positions of power and influence. As people age, they gradually decline, physically and mentally, Cummings and Henry note. Muscles weaken, bones become fragile, perceptual abilities deteriorate, and cognitive faculties become slower and weaker. Not surprisingly, elderly people are also more prone to illness and disability.

This means that, at work, elderly people are often less efficient than their younger, stronger, and more energetic counterparts (Garber et al., 2008). For the good of society and for themselves, disengagement theory argues, elderly people should give up their positions and withdraw to the edges of society, where they can prepare for their certain death. This theory is not advocating so much as observing that this is how modern societies work: they retire their older workers on the assumption that to do so is just, necessary, and beneficial to all.

According to this theory, age-based retirement from work serves several functions for society: (1) it empties job positions, allowing younger people to move up the occupational and social hierarchy; (2) it gives the retiree a moment of celebratory recognition—for example, a retirement party—to honour his or her contribution; and (3) it ensures that society replaces outdated skills and ideas with more useful ones. Though the theory may sound cold and cynical, especially to elderly people obliged to retire from jobs they may like, structural functionalists stress that this change is both natural and crucial to society's effectiveness. Without such turnover, the economy would be less efficient and less equipped to compete globally. Thus, age-based retirement—even if discriminatory—is socially functional and, therefore, widespread.

Conflict Theory

Many, however, disagree with the assumptions of functionalism, especially with the assumption that excluding older people from financially rewarding and socially important roles is good for society. Age-related discrimination against the young or old is not useful to society. Thus, ageism does not serve society as a whole but is merely a form of inequality exercised by one group over another, to further its own interests.

Many scholars have criticized disengagement theory for being too simplistic. It seems to view humans as robots who make a 40-year contribution to society, then voluntarily jump into the social dustbin—a retirement community, perhaps—where they wait mindlessly for death to erase them (Foner, 2000). This view is wrong. While society may need older people to disappear from the workforce, many seniors remain active, refuse to retire, and fight their obsolescence. Many refuse to withdraw from society voluntarily.

Disengagement theory The theory that as people age, they voluntarily and normally remove themselves from activities and social contacts, to ease their passage into a less active lifestyle.

UP

In this 2009 animated hit, an elderly widower fulfills his dream of seeing the wilds of South America by tying thousands of balloons to his home.

Even after retirement from paid work, many stay active as long as opportunities in the family and the wider community will allow. When elderly people do disengage, it is often due to other people's wishes, not their own.

This is the perspective taken by most conflict theorists. It recognizes that most people seek to satisfy their own goals, not the goals of society as a whole. Members of different age groups hold different interests, and each group competes against the others to enlarge its share of society's resources. In this struggle, typically the young and old are unable to prevail, since, compared to middle-aged people, they lack the organization and power needed to influence public policy. As a result, middle-aged decision-makers may ignore the interests and needs of elderly people and children. However, we should not assume that the old and young willingly consent to such treatment.

Symbolic Interactionism

Symbolic interactionists focus their attention on how we symbolize elderly people and enact aging in our society. They also study how socially constructed definitions of age and aging affect people's experience of growing old. Symbolic interactionists stress that age is a state of mind shaped by the labels society applies. To a large degree, satisfaction with aging means rejecting the definition of old age as inadequate or outdated.

Activity theory (Havighurst and Albrecht, 1953) argues that, contrary to disengagement theory (the idea that people give up roles as they age), people take on new roles and identities as they age. Through such continued activity, they preserve a sense of continuity and self-worth, and gain greater life satisfaction, though by new means. People who keep up a high level of activity—whether in old activities or new ones—age more "successfully" than people who do not (Hardwicke and Sproule, 2010; Bezerra et al. 2012). This might correspond to the age-old notion that, in aging, we commonly trade passion for wisdom; so there is no loss, only change.

Feminist Theory

Feminists note that the experience of aging is different for men and women. For both, aging is associated with retirement from paid work—that is, with socially enforced deprivation of authority and income. For women, however, aging is associated with a culturally defined loss of youth and glamour—a less critical concern for men. Women and men also bring different resources to old age, and they are subject to different expectations throughout the aging process (Ross-Sheriff, 2008). For all these reasons, women in our culture dread getting older in a way that most men do not (Lewis et al., 2011).

Some feminist scholars suggest that this is a natural reaction to what they call the "double jeopardy" of being female and old. According to this perspective, both "stigmatizing" statuses combine to make older women especially disadvantaged. Advocates of this perspective argue that more needs to be done to help older women achieve economic and social equality in later life.

One might think that, today more than ever, women and men lead increasingly similar lives, in the sense that both often aim for careers. However, their careers are likely to be in different sectors of the workforce. While in the workforce, most women earn less pay than men and accrue smaller private pensions, if any at all. Because of this, and because their spouses or partners usually die before them, women are at particular risk of finding themselves living alone on a meagre income in their later years (Matthews, 2011). As well, older women have more domestic duties and social responsibilities than older men. For example, they tend to play a more central role in kin-keeping—maintaining family contacts—through social networks and caregiving.

These social responsibilities over the lifespan have important outcomes in old age. The family caregiving roles that women take on at younger ages often remove them from the labour force, limiting their pension benefits (Young, 2011). As noted earlier, this limits their lifetime earnings and may result in poverty after retirement. At the societal level, this contributes to a "feminization of poverty."

Social Consequences of Aging

Retirement Income

After retiring from paid work, Canada's elderly support themselves in various ways: through government and private pensions, savings, and contributions by other family members. This situation promises to pose huge financial problems for Canada and other developed societies in the future. Already, the baby-boom generation has entered retirement age, and continued population aging will produce large increases in age-related government spending on public pensions and health care. More people of working age will be needed to help pay, through their taxes, for the pensions and benefits received by a growing number of elders.

In turn, efforts will be needed to increase Canadian productivity by fully integrating women, the disabled, new immigrants, and Aboriginal people into the labour market. And, despite the disengagement theory, older Canadians who want to continue working for pay should not be discouraged from doing so, for economic reasons.

Recognizing the need for readiness, more and more Canadians have been saving for old age (O'Rand and Shuey, 2007). As a result, the "feminization of poverty" has shown signs of slowing. Between 1991 and 2001, the gap in the numbers of men and women in registered pension plans narrowed significantly, from 1 million to less than half a million, owing largely to the increase in female registration. This change was due to the growth in women's labour force participation and the drop in membership among male workers, thanks mainly to the recession of the early 1990s that pushed many men out of work (ibid.).

Careers and Mandatory Retirement

Throughout the twentieth century, in all industrial and post-industrial societies, most people have earned an income through paid work. Further, most paid work has been organized into careers in large organizations, such as government, large businesses, law firms, universities and other parts of the education system, hospitals, and so on. People have marked their professional progress through what sociologists call "career mobility" (McGuinness and Wooden, 2009).

Traditionally, career mobility—financial and occupational advancement over the life cycle—has largely been age related. As people get older, they move up the occupational or organizational (or income) ladder. This ascent has depended on two reliable sources of opportunity: continued economic growth and the continued elimination of older workers through death or retirement. Elderly people have been routinely pushed out of their positions to make way for younger people seeking careers.

However, this situation changed in recent years for three main reasons: the lengthening of the average lifespan; a decline in economic growth; and the elimination of compulsory (or mandatory) retirement. These factors have been intensified by tightly organized labour markets that strictly control access from the outside. Consider, as an example, the profession of medicine. Many people want to enter the medical profession, yet entry is limited to a few. As population size increases (through immigration and otherwise), it becomes harder and harder to get into a desirable labour market to have a career there. Meanwhile, the increasing population is consistently underserviced in the health field.

Careers and aging are correlated, because most career mobility is based on seniority or the length of tenure (Brooke, 2009). Other things being equal, the longer a person works in an organization, the higher the salary and degree of authority, autonomy, and prestige that person will enjoy. However, as workplaces have become more specialized, seniority no longer guarantees advancement. Today, in multi-level organizations, people enter at different levels, according to their credentials. Positions requiring only an undergraduate education (or less) may start entrants near the bottom, while positions requiring a graduate degree or significant job experience may start entrants higher up the organizational ladder.

Internal labour markets impose a high degree of control over who enters an organization (or profession, or industry)—at what level, through what stages people will move, and at what rate. The result is that, even today, society sorts people into different types of careers. Within each of these internal labour markets, career progress remains largely predictable and based on seniority. However, "achievement" has become far more important than in the past. Also, seniority alone will not allow a person to jump from a lower internal market into a higher one (e.g., from being a nurse to being a doctor). Thus, career mobility has been altered through industrial growth and differentiation and through the rise of achievement as a basis for ranking (Mendenhall et al., 2008).

Technology has been another force that pushes older people out of their careers, making room for younger workers. Not surprisingly, new technology is usually built by young people for the use of other young people. Often, it doesn't have the needs of seniors in mind (Pew and Van Hemel, 2004). In fact, some technologies may be harder for seniors to learn—due to arthritis and declines in fine motor skills—than for their younger counterparts. So, older people may have trouble keeping up to date, especially in fields that depend on rapid technological advancement (Magnusson et al., 2005; Blit-Cohen and Litwin, 2004). There is evidence, though, that this "digital divide" is shrinking and seniors are more able to keep up with technology than in previous years (McMurtrey, 2011).

The decision to leave a job or career voluntarily depends on career opportunities. People stay where the opportunities are best. Seniority is much more relevant than age for departure decisions. Thus, a 55-year-old low-seniority worker is more likely to leave than a 55-year-old high-seniority worker or even than a 65-year-old high-seniority worker. That said, women are different from men, more often leaving the organization for personal reasons than men do, and less often for career reasons.

Compulsory retirement—the legal right of an employer to forcibly retire an employee and the accompanying eligibility of an employee to receive various private and public pensions—has been a staple arrangement of industrial societies for well over a century. In Canada, where compulsory retirement was in place until 2005, employees of most public and private organizations routinely retired at age 65, if not earlier. For most workers, salaries had peaked a decade or more earlier, in the ages 45–55; so there was little financial incentive to stay on if they were offered a satisfactory retirement package.

Self-employed professionals (e.g., doctors or lawyers) or business-owners (e.g., shopkeepers), however, had much more choice about when to retire. And since they would receive no organizational or union pension benefits when they retired, they had little incentive to retire at age 65 or earlier. Likely, their standard of living and quality of life would be higher if they continued to work. Also, they tended to be more engaged in their work than many wage-earning employees. For many, work was a vocation—a source of personal identity—as well as a source of income and sociability.

Before 2005, professionals working in large organizations—for example, university professors—found themselves forced to quit a job they liked and accept a much reduced income simply because they had reached the age of 65. So, it is not surprising that academics and librarians were the first to challenge the compulsory retirement laws that applied to universities and other public organizations. In 2005, the Supreme Court ruled that compulsory retirement was a form of age discrimination and therefore could no longer be practised (for examples of early retirement, see Kim, 2009). This had enormous financial implications. Immediately, universities and other large organizations scrambled to adjust their operations to this change, and they continue to do so.

The Canadian Press/AP Photo/Nati Harnik

Thanks to a Supreme Court decision on compulsory retirement, academics like Dr Denham Harman are able to continue their scholarly work long after age 65. In 1954, Harman developed the "Free Radical Theory of Aging," which is now the most widely accepted theory on the aging process.

Issues Associated with Inheritance

"Inheritance" is what we call the downward flow of property after death, usually along kinship lines and passing from the older to the younger generation. In all societies, unless other instructions are provided, it is assumed that close kin (spouses, parents, and children) will have first claim on the property of the deceased person (Payling, 2001).

Cultures differ in how they split up the resources released at death. In some societies, the dominant inheritance pattern is primogeniture, where the eldest son receives everything; in others, the property is split among all the surviving children. In some societies, males and females inherit equally, while in others, women are denied a portion of the inheritance except through their husbands (Ugiagbe et al., 2007). Historically, primogeniture has been a conservative strategy for ensuring the survival of the family by keeping the family's property intact. However, unwittingly, inheritance practices have influenced marriage patterns, the relationships between parents and children, and the relationships between siblings. This is because those who control the inheritance (usually parents) exercise influence over those who wish to receive it (usually children), and those siblings who receive it often exercise influence over those siblings who do not. Similar dynamics were evident in Irish rural society, where elderly parents were able to tyrannize their adult children through the control of an inheritance (see Box 6.1).

This influence is evident in the submissive behaviours of children in various cultural forms and social milieus. Take filial responsibility—the moral responsibility of a grown child to look after his or her aging parent (Lundberg, 2009). Notions of filial responsibility, or filial piety, are especially marked in societies influenced by the teachings of the Chinese philosopher Confucius (that is, in China, Korea, and Japan). Recent social changes associated with urbanization and industrialization have weakened the traditional Confucian norms. With the nuclearization of the family, newlyweds in Asia have been setting up their own households, and so daughters-in-law and mothers-in-law no longer share the same home. Thus, mothers-in-law have been deprived of a traditional source of caregiving (Lin and Chin-Chun Yi, 2009).

Primogeniture A system of inheritance in which only one child, the oldest son, inherits all of the family property on the death of his parents.

Filial responsibility The sense of personal obligation or duty that adult children often feel for protecting, caring for, and supporting their aging parents; filial piety.

Health Consequences of Aging

Physical Illness

Physical quality of life declines in old age. One reason for this is senescence, the fact that physical and mental abilities naturally decline during the aging process. Muscles grow weaker, the mind is less sharp, and aches and pains become routine complaints. Exactly at what age and in what form this decline takes place varies from one person to the next, but decline is inevitable (Johnson et al., 2009; Poon and Knight, 2009).

Health problems often arise alongside and because of changes in the life course. Death of a spouse and divorce, for example, are associated with health problems, especially in men (Antonucci et al., 2001). According to some research, health declines accompany both retirement plans and actual retirement for women, though not for men (Pyper, 2006). Equally important, the loss of independence as one ages—for example, the loss of a driver's licence, the need to rely on others for help with activities of daily living, as well as the loss of physical control—can also cause emotional and physical distress (Harkins et al., 2006).

AWAY FROM HER 🎬
Sarah Polley's 2006 feature is the story of an aging couple (Gordon Pinsent, Julie Christie) grappling with the effects of Alzheimer's disease on their relationship.

AMOUR 🎬
This 2012 French-language drama focuses on an elderly couple whose love is tested after Anne, the wife, suffers from a stroke that paralyses her on one side of her body.

Classic **WORKS**

BOX 6.1   Family and Aging in a Traditional Society

A classic analysis of aging and the relationships between family generations in a traditional rural Irish community was provided in an anthropological study by Arensberg and Kimball, *Family and Community in Ireland*. A review of the third edition of this book, by Patricia Lysaght, is abridged below.

Family and Community in Ireland is a famous social anthropological study undertaken in Ireland in the 1930s known as the "Harvard Irish Survey" (1931–6).

In the course of their fieldwork, the authors became aware of the central influence of family structure and kinship on community form and life, and this became the "principal area of investigation" (ibid., xxvi). The emphasis is on what the authors call the "complete family," "consisting of father and mother and sons rather than daughters alone" (ibid., 67), while the term "incomplete" identifies those farms run by bachelors, spinsters, widowers, and widows (ibid., 66). The daily, seasonal, and annual routine of the male and female members of the farm family, centred on the "spatial unit of land and house," is described in detail, and the authors illustrate the importance of common effort during crucial points in the annual agricultural round, when all family members, male and female, including children, contributed to the work in hand, according to their age, sex, and ability. Interfamilial co-operation ("cooring," Ir. *Comhair*) was also expected, and expected to be reciprocated, at tasks such as turf-cutting and at harvest time.

The farm-family children are described as "subordinated" to their parents and remained "boys" and "girls" until marriage. They were trained in farm and household duties by their parents in preparation for marriage and the setting up of farm households of their own. Marriage itself is described by Arensberg and Kimball as a mechanism that transferred farm ownership and economic control by the old couple to the inheriting son or daughter, in this way advancing the marrying couple to adulthood in the eyes of the community.

The services of a matchmaker were employed to negotiate the dowry to be brought in by the bride, or by the groom, if he was marrying into a farm, in order to ensure social and economic parity between the contracting parties. The introduction of the old age pension, which gave a measure of regular financial support to old farm couples, eased the relinquishing of control of the farm and household by the parents. Indeed, it might be added that an old couple in receipt of the old age pension were considered a financial asset in some households. The sibling for whom a dowry was available was in a position to marry, but the other less-fortunate family members had to "travel" and make a new life for themselves without the family farm.

A primary concern of the new family created at marriage was the birth of children, as this was necessary to preserve family unity and family identification with farm and household in the future. Indeed, the harshness of country sentiment against a barren wife, or against a young widow without issue, persisted well beyond the 1930s. Both barren wife and widow were expected, in accordance with social custom, to accept repayment of their dowry and to return to their families. It should also be pointed out, however, that where a husband had married into land (*cliamhain isteach*), he, too, was expected to return to his people on being refunded his dowry, if no children were born of the marriage after a reasonable period of time.

While emigration was seen as contributing to the large proportion of the aged in the community, longevity was also viewed as an important factor. Arensberg and Kimball were of the opinion that the old people "live long because they have much to live for. In their own sphere of life, they are honoured. They have power" (ibid., 162). By comparison, the gatherings of the younger men, concerned mainly with recreation, and those of a third group, characterized as intermediate or transitional, were of less import.

Source: Lysaght (2002).

Home Care Issues

An aging, longer-living adult population leads to increased demands for informal (non-professional) care. Indeed, recent research suggests that the demand is already considerable: 78 per cent of senior primary care receivers continue to live in their homes, and only 22 per cent live in formal care facilities. Compared with 30 years ago, the elderly

AP Photo/Jae C. Hong

Evelyn Volk, left, asks her 13-year-old daughter, Sofia, for help while making treats with her mother, Maria Koenig, who suffers from dementia. These bookend family responsibilities land Volk squarely in the "sandwich generation"—pressed between dual roles of supporting aging parents while rearing children.

today are more likely to live independently (Lau and Kirby, 2009). At the same time, more adult children in their fifties, besides being more likely than in past decades to be divorced (and therefore not having a spouse present to assist with elder care), are more likely to have a surviving parent.

One result is the so-called "sandwich generation," middle-aged adults caring for both elderly parents and their own young children (Rubin and White-Means, 2009). These "women in the middle" have competing roles in addition to their elderly caregiving responsibilities—including being a spouse, a parent, an employee, and/or a volunteer (Wassel, 2006). In 2002, 712,000 Canadians balanced paid employment with caring for both children and seniors in the home (Williams, 2004). Other societal changes include a shift from institutional to community-based (in-home) care, a growing ideological commitment to elder care by the state, and (at the same time) funding cuts by the federal government for such services (Rosenthal, 1997).

This Canadian trend to viewing elder care as a private matter rather than a public responsibility may have negative outcomes in the future. Because of cuts to the health-care system, Canada, as well as other industrial nations with universal medical care, risks sliding back to the "non-system" found in the United States (Hanlon and Halseth, 2005). Yet public surveys repeatedly show that Canadians value public health care, desire health and longevity, and view health as a public good.

Aging and Disability

While old age is inevitably associated with some disability, there is great inequality in the effect that social economic status (SES) has on the extent of the disability. Countless studies have demonstrated that seniors who are lower in SES have significantly greater disability associated impairment than their higher SES counterparts (see, for example, Coppin et al., 2006). Higher social inequality over the life course is associated with greater likelihood of disability during the senior years (Guerra et al., 2008). The life course social inequalities predictive of greater future disability that the Guerra study (ibid.) assessed were status of housewife, insufficient income, illiteracy, employment in a low-skill occupation, and poverty and hunger early in a person's life. Experiences of racial inequality are also predictive of disabilities later in life. Mestizo/Native elders in a Brazilian community have higher incidences of disability than white or black elders (ibid.). Despite experiences of sexism, women tend to be much more resilient to the effects of social inequalities experienced over the life course than men.

SES inequalities affecting people in their senior years have a tremendous influence on the onset and severity of their disabilities. Compared to those in higher socio-economic statuses, elderly British men with lower social status have a greater risk of acquiring disabilities associated with "activities of daily living" (ADL) and "instrumental activities of daily living" (IADL), as well as more functional limitations (Ramsay et al., 2008). ADL disability involves not being able to do simple tasks such as self-feeding or walking from one end of the room to the other; IADL disability involves an inability to perform tasks like managing money or using the telephone. Factors associated with lower SES, such as not owning a house or car, further increase the likelihood that ADL-associated disabilities and functional limitations will develop.

However, one study found that subjective, not objective, SES detriments have the biggest effect on disability (Jaggera and Spiersa, 2005). Residents of Leicestershire, UK, who were over the age of 75 and had the perception that their income was inadequate experienced the onset of an ADL-associated disability, on average, seven years earlier than those who did not consider their income inadequate.

The data in Figure 6.2 show that Canada is far behind various other G8 countries (like Japan and Germany) in the current size of its aged population and, therefore, in the need to provide senior care. However, as we have seen, the situation for this population is changing rapidly.

Elder Abuse

Living longer brings unprecedented opportunities but also presents serious social challenges. One of these is elder abuse. Elder abuse occurs in various settings (McGarry and Simpson, 2008). Typically, the older person is mistreated in their own home by a spouse, sibling, child, friend, or trusted caregiver. Other seniors are mistreated by staff and professional caregivers in facilities for elderly people.

As a Public Health Agency of Canada report (2012) on elder abuse in Canada has shown, elder abuse takes various forms, including physical abuse, sexual abuse, emotional or psychological abuse, neglect, abandonment, and financial or material exploitation. This last category includes improper use of an elderly person's savings, property, or assets without authorization or beyond the terms set out in a caregiver–patient contract. Such offences include stealing money or material possessions, forging signatures, and improperly using guardianship or power of attorney rights. The National Centre on Elder Abuse also notes that self-neglect can be a problem among seniors. Self-neglect shows itself in the older person's refusal or failure to give himself or herself enough food, water, clothing, shelter, hygiene, medication (when responsibly prescribed), and safety precautions.

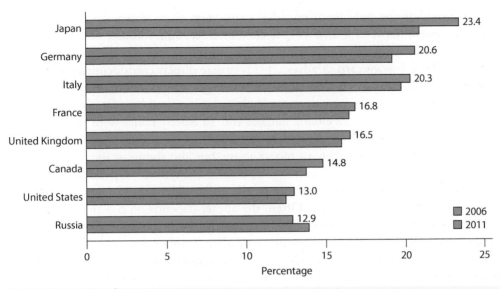

FIGURE 6.2   Proportion (in Percentage) of the Population Aged 65 and Over, G8 countries, 2006 and 2011

Sources: Statistics Canada, censuses of population, 2006 and 2011; US Census Bureau, 2006 and 2010; National Institute of Statistics (Italy), 2006 and 2011; National Institute of Statistics and Economic Studies (France), 2006 and 2011; Statistics Bureau of Japan, 2006 and 2011; Russian Federation Federal State Statistics Service, 2006 and 2010; Human Mortality Database for Germany, 2006 and 2010, and for United Kingdom, 2006 and 2010/20; <www12.statcan.ca/census-recensement/2011/as-sa/98-311-x/2011001/fig/fig3-eng.cfm>.

PERSONAL *stories*

BOX 6.2   Nursing Home Abuse

It would be well over 20 years now that I recognized that an older client was physically abused by a professional care provider, a nurse, working in a long-term mental health facility. I had just completed a full day workshop with a colleague, and we were having a tour of the facility from one of the nursing administrators. I saw a nurse literally shove an older lady into a chair. I saw, too, the "rope burn" that was given to the arm of this same client. I caught my breath and did nothing. I look back and know the experience at that time was simply one that I did not understand. I knew what I saw but I really could not fully comprehend it.

Looking back to this experience, I know now it was aged abuse. I know that I did nothing at the time. However, I also know that it changed both my professional and personal lives in so many ways. My colleague and I talked about what we had seen and we both acknowledged that we should have done something. We wondered if the administrator had seen it too but had simply said nothing. We had been shocked, but we should have done or said

something. We introduced the word "violence" into our conversation.

I made a real and conscious decision to be an advocate and not to stand quietly again. I have spent a large part of my professional nursing career since this episode addressing the real challenge of aged abuse within society in general and within long-term care facilities in particular. I am proud of how I have moved forward to speak out publicly and at professional conferences about this serious issue. I have talked about how we need to promote awareness of aged abuse. I have raised the need for professional associations to provide guidelines to their members so that accurate assessment and appropriate interventions can be initiated.

Story told in the words of Sandra P. Hirst, RN, PHD, GNC(C) Director, Brenda Strafford Centre for Excellence in Gerontological Nursing, University of Calgary

Source: Accessed at: <www.nurseone.ca/Default.aspx?portlet=StaticHtml ViewerPortletandptdi=661>.

Estimates of the prevalence of elder abuse vary, with Statistics Canada showing that somewhere between 4 and 10 per cent of elders suffer abuse, while a survey of CARP (Canadian Association of Retired People) members suggests the number is closer to 10 per cent (<www.carp.ca/advocacy/adv-article-display.cfm?documentID=3923>). One study estimates that five elder-abuse incidents go unreported for every incident that occurs and that elderly women are more likely to be assaulted by a family member than elderly men are. In 2010, 22 elderly females and 10 elderly males were abused by their spouse per 100,000 people (Statistics Canada, 2012).

Relatives are the most likely to report abuse, but also the most likely to perpetrate abuse and neglect (Muehlbauer and Crane, 2006). The typical perpetrator of domestic elder abuse is an adult child or spouse of the child; older family members and non-relatives may also be perpetrators. Often, the abuser depends on the victim for shelter, financial aid, or emotional support. In other words, the perpetrator may be financially dependent, while the victim is physically dependent. Other common correlates of elder abuse are alcohol addiction by the abuser or prior abuse perpetrated years earlier against the present abuser by the now elderly victim. Table 6.2 shows that it is much more likely for a senior to be abused by family and friends than by strangers.

TABLE 6.2	Senior Victims (65 Years and Older) of Family Violence, by Sex and Accused–Victim Relationship					
				SEX OF VICTIM		
ACCUSED–VICTIM RELATIONSHIP	**TOTAL**		FEMALE		MALE	
	Number	Rate [1]	Number	Rate [1]	Number	Rate [1]
Total family	**2,427**	**54**	**1,467**	**59**	**960**	**48**
Grown child [2]	785	18	461	19	324	16
Spouse or ex-spouse [3]	680	15	466	19	214	11
Sibling [4]	270	6	156	6	114	6
Parent [5]	249	6	131	5	118	6
Extended family [6]	443	10	253	10	190	9
Total friends, acquaintances, others	**2,429**	**54**	**908**	**37**	**1,521**	**75**
Friend or acquaintance [7]	2,044	46	799	32	1,245	62
Business relationship	373	8	105	4	268	13
Criminal relationship	12	0	4	0	8	0
Stranger	1,997	45	802	32	1,195	59
Unknown	1,018	23	440	18	578	29
Total violence against seniors	**7,871**	**176**	**3,617**	**147**	**4,254**	**211**

[1]Rates are calculated on the basis of 100,000 seniors (65 years and older). Populations based upon July 1st estimates from Statistics Canada, Demography Division.
[2]Includes biological, step, adoptive, and foster children.
[3]Includes current and former legally married and common-law spouses.
[4]Includes biological, step, adoptive, and foster brothers and sisters.
[5]Includes biological, step, adoptive, and foster parents.
[6]Includes all other family members related by blood, marriage, or adoption. Examples include grandchildren, uncles, aunts, cousins, and in-laws.
[7]Includes friends, current or former boyfriends or girlfriends, neighbours, authority figures, and casual acquaintances.
Note: Excludes incidents where the victim's sex and/or age was unknown. In 2009, data from the Incident-based Uniform Crime Reporting Survey covered 99% of the population of Canada.
Source: Statistics Canada, Canadian Centre for Justice Statistics, Incident-based Uniform Crime Reporting Survey. Statistics Canada, at: <www.statcan.gc.ca/pub/85-224-x/2010000/t016-eng.htm>.

Solutions for Problems of Aging

One finds repeatedly that older people who are married, healthy, and have strong social networks are the most satisfied with their lives (Ayalon et al., 2013). Elderly people put a great deal of weight on social relations and health status when it comes to what they feel makes their life most satisfactory (Wilhelmson et al., 2005). Though more social activities can enhance the well-being of seniors, there is a gendered difference in participation in social activities for those over 65 as evidenced in Figure 6.3.

Informal and Formal Social Supports

Solving the problems of aging will have to include supporting the individuals and institutions that provide social integration: caregivers, families, support networks, and community organizations (Giblin, 2011).

The shift from independent parent to dependent parent represents a shift in power and responsibility from parent to offspring. Depending on the quality of the relationship between parent and child throughout life, this onset of dependence may provide an occasion to repay the parent for past debts or to seek revenge for real or imagined injustices. So, this shift is not without complications.

The need for aging parents to support middle-aged children who have become unemployed or divorced is also on the rise. However, as parents age, the problems associated with supporting children multiply. Consider the older generation's own need for independence or support. Seniors must deal with both the family and planning for the financial difficulties that come along with retirement. In the past decade, there has been an increase in the number of young adults who move back into their parents' home. Few parents will turn out their child. Comparisons of the 1990 and 2000 censuses show that

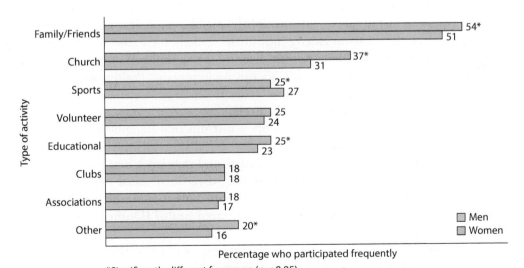

Percentage who participated frequently

*Significantly different from men (p < 0.05)

FIGURE 6.3 | Percentage of Canadians Aged 65 and Older Who Participate in Social Activities

Source: Statistics Canada. Data source: 2008/2009 Canadian Community Health Survey—Healthy Aging, at: <www.statcan.gc.ca/pub/82-003-x/2012004/article/11720/c-g/fig1-eng.htm>.

John Moore/Getty Images

Tamara Lycholaj, 89, receives a hot meal from nutrition worker Al Patalona as he makes "Meals on Wheels" deliveries to elderly rural residents. "Meals on Wheels" is a tangible support program for the elderly that is offered in urban centres across most of Canada.

25 per cent of young adults (aged 18–24) lived with their parents in 1990, but that by 2000 this figure had changed to 56 per cent of young adult males and 47 per cent of young adult females (Wassel, 2006).

Four types of social support—informational, tangible, emotional, and integrating— all help to reduce the stress on elderly individuals. Elderly men tend to rely emotionally on their spouses, while elderly women diversify their emotional supports when possible (Waldron et al., 2005). Close friends can be important. Positive social contacts with friends promote well-being, so more contacts—a larger social network—lead to improved well-being (Helliwell and Wang, 2011).

Some of the support provided to seniors is instrumental (tangible), while some is emotional. Instrumental support and subjective social support protect elderly people against decline. Both types of support are needed, and they work best in an integrated approach (Savard, 2006). More-resourceful and -diversified social networks—those that include friends and neighbours—can contribute more than simply family-focused networks in promoting daily activities and self-rated health (Dosman and Keating, 2009).

Social supports—whether doctors, support groups, social networks, or assistive communication technology—help caregivers and patients. One such example is that they can influence sick people to comply with treatment advice they receive from their doctor. Ensuring compliance with medication is one of the most important—yet the most often neglected—ways of helping elderly or sick people. As shown in Figure 6.4, as Canadians age, the percentage of the population with at least one close friend declines, although the numbers have been rising.

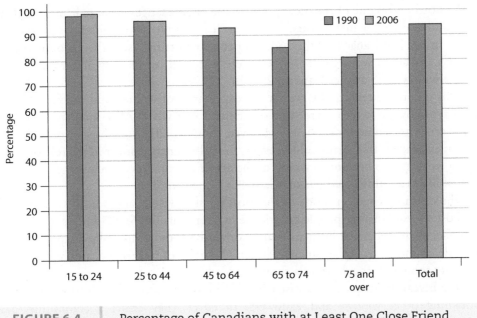

FIGURE 6.4 | Percentage of Canadians with at Least One Close Friend (by age)

Source: Statistics Canada, General Social Survey, 1990 and 2006, at: <www.statcan.gc.ca/pub/89-630-x/2008001/c-g/10652/5201032-eng.htm>.

Personal Efforts to Adapt

Some elderly people have a harder time than others making use of services and supports. Many elderly members of ethnic groups are now retired without a pension and, often, in poor health (e.g., Hicks and Kingston, 2009; Shugrue and Robison, 2009). Whether because of low levels of education or language problems, they may underuse social and health-care services owing to a lack of knowledge about such programs or because they cannot be served in their own language. Further, they may be unwilling to enter long-term care institutions because of differences in language, customs, beliefs surrounding medical practices and death, food preferences, or the desire for privacy (Kaestner et al., 2009).

However, immigrants are not the only ones who face problems. Some role changes, such as marriage and retirement, are common and predictable; anyone can usefully begin to think of how they will adjust to these major life events. Other changes, however, such as widowhood or becoming a father at the age of 55, may occur unexpectedly. Still others, even if expected, can be stressful and lead to loneliness or a decreased quality of life. One example is the empty-nest syndrome, which occurs when children leave home for university or marriage (Xie et al., 2010).

In short, aging *always* involves change—in friendships, health, financial status, role relationships, and more. Changes in daily routines can create stress because they force people to cope with new life situations. Anticipatory socialization can ease the stress associated with later-life role changes, however. Important aids in making these age-related changes include the social support of friends and family. Social support networks have been found to increase life satisfaction for both female and male seniors (Gadalla, 2009).

Widowhood is one of the most problematic of all changes because it can occur suddenly and endure for many years. Moreover, it is mainly a women's issue (Lindström, 2009). In 2011 in Canada, of the 163,115 people reporting losing their spouse to death, 128,565 Canadian women aged 65–69 were widowed, while only about 34,550 men became widowers (Statistics Canada, 2011b).

This difference reflects the greater life expectancy of women and the fact that husbands typically are two to three years older than their wives. Also, men are more likely than women to remarry after being widowed (Dupuis, 2009). Thus, not only do more women experience this sorrowful life event, they also remain longer in the role of widow. Even a woman who becomes a widow at the age of 80 can expect an average of 9.7 more years of life as an unmarried person (Statistics Canada, n.d.).

The death of a spouse is one of the most stressful role changes in the life cycle and the most stressful change people experience in later years of life. Widowers, who are less often faced with financial burdens than widows, have more difficulty adapting to their new role, as shown by higher suicide rates, higher rates of remarriage, and higher rates of mortality soon after the death of a spouse.

The bereavement process is easier if the widow or widower has a friendship group containing other widows and widowers. In effect, they create a community-based "widow-to-widow" program to provide emotional and social support. After a period of acute grief and mourning, the widowed person often begins to rebuild a new identity and lifestyle (Cornwell, 2009). She or he adjusts to being alone, having no spouse to talk to, cooking for one person, losing friends who were more closely tied to the deceased spouse, and managing financial affairs alone (Yang and Victor, 2008). Often, the widow will also learn to live on a reduced income (Bonnet and Hourriez, 2009; Gillen and Kim, 2009).

Government Legislation

There is much debate about the state's duty to support retired individuals. This issue is especially significant because many older adults, especially widows, live in poverty. As well, with the population of seniors growing, the income provided from retirement plans may become inadequate to cover even necessities owing to the sheer number of seniors being paid (Schellenberg and Ostrovsky, 2008).

Income after retirement depends on a person's pattern of lifetime employment (regular or sporadic), place of employment (whether it offers a private pension), income while in the labour force, and pattern of savings, investments, and expenses over the life course. All of these factors will affect a person's quality of life after leaving paid work.

Given the rising number of seniors (Figure 6.5), an elderly-friendly environment is needed, so we have to start planning for it now. Such an environment would include creative social policies and programs; improved private-sector products and services; changing attitudes towards health, nutrition, physical activity, and stress; political involvement and empowerment; new attitudes towards retirement and leisure; and innovative long-range financial planning during the early and middle years of adulthood. Then, with plans in hand, we have to bring about these changes.

Canadians will have to focus on creative management of private and public pension funds (FitzGerald, 2008). This will mean examining choices for both early and late retirement as labour surpluses and shortages occur overall or in specific regions or occupational groups. As John Myles (1984) has pointed out, "The social character of old age

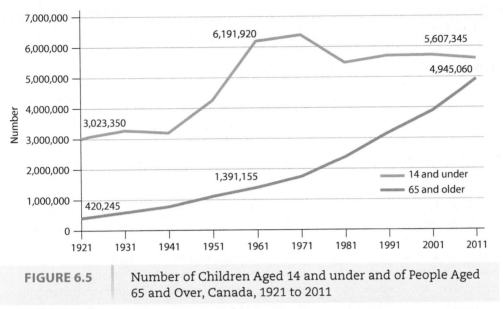

FIGURE 6.5 | Number of Children Aged 14 and under and of People Aged 65 and Over, Canada, 1921 to 2011

Sources: Statistics Canada, censuses of population, 1921 to 2011, at: <www12.statcan.gc.ca/census-recensement/2011/as-sa/98-311-x/2011001/fig/fig1-eng.cfm>

is very much a product of the welfare state . . . old age became retirement." The development of retirement as a mandated social policy, with fiscal and economic implications, is recent, dating back only a little more than a century. Changes in the ability or willingness to pay the costs associated with retirement, therefore, will have implications even for our ideas of aging and old age. Figure 6.5 shows that the number of Canadians aged 65 and older is rising steadily, while the number of those 14 and under has kept pace.

Finally, Canadians will have to address such ethical issues as the right to die, the creation of living wills, guardianship for the dependent elderly, empowerment of the elderly population, and equity across genders, races, ethnic groups, and religions in developing policies and the delivery of services.

Lobbying Efforts by Elderly People

As a varied group, elderly people have experienced widely different lives and have not voted with a common voice. Yet, through organizations like the United Senior Citizens of Ontario, One Voice, CARP, the National Academy of Older Canadians, and the Fédération de l' Âge d'Or du Québec, Canada's seniors have been making their concerns known to politicians, businesses, and younger voters. Such lobby groups play an invaluable role in promoting the interests of elderly people (for a European example, see Kemmerling and Neugart, 2009).

Currently, the largest lobby group for the elderly population in Canada is CARP. This set of initials once stood for the Canadian Association of Retired Persons. However, because of the changing characteristics of its membership, the group's name was changed to Canada's Association for the Fifty-Plus (though CARP remains the preferred acronym). Formed in 1984 by Murray and Lillian Morgenthau, CARP initially consisted of no more than 10 friends who met to share their experiences of being elderly. Today, CARP

| BOX 6.3 | **Pension Reform in the Twenty-first Century** |

Today, pension spending accounts for a tenth of gross domestic product (GDP) in most EU countries. Assuming no change in entitlement rules or benefits, population aging alone will raise this level by 30–50 per cent over the next three to four decades. At the same time, we shall witness a sharp fall in the ratio of contributors to recipients. The real challenge we face is how to ensure that we can meet this additional financial obligation.

The core issue of pension reform is how to find an equitable formula that, at once, minimizes contribution rate growth and allocates the additional costs fairly between retirees and workers. A choice in favour of intergenerational equity must, however, also consider intragenerational fairness. . . . The idea is to fix, once and for all, a relative per capita GDP ratio between the "old" and the "young." . . . Once the ratio is fixed, the tax rate is adjusted periodically to reflect both population and productivity changes. One obstacle is that it would be difficult to apply to private and occupational pension plans that are not under government control.

The intra-generational equity problem is a question of welfare distributions within any given cohort of retirees. The necessary starting point has to do with heterogeneous life courses and "generational luck." . . . The pensioner cohorts of the 1950s were poor mainly because they had poor lives. Born at the close of the nineteenth century, their youth was marred by WWI and their careers straddled the difficult twenties, the Depression of the 1930s, and WWII. In brief, they were unable to accumulate much during their lifetimes, and this was especially the case for the weakest. Moving forward, today's retirees are broadly well-off . . . in large part because they had good lives. Beginning their careers during the booming postwar decades, enjoying job security and rising real wages, they have accumulated substantial savings and resources. Starting poorly (especially in terms of human capital) in the "new economy" is likely to have lasting adverse consequences. Citizens with less than the equivalent of secondary education will face strong probabilities of labour market precariousness and low pay. They will in, say, 2050 look more like the retiree generation in 1950 than those now in retirement. It also is well documented that not only is average longevity increasing (we now live 10 years more than our grandfathers

did) but that longevity is positively correlated with socio-economic status: the resourceful live longer and will, therefore, consume more pension benefits. The ultimate cause of population aging is low fertility. Yet, a return to replacement fertility is now unlikely to solve the sustainability problem over the next decades in any event. Immigration is often cited as an alternative solution. Unfortunately, the most comprehensive simulation models show that realistic levels of immigration can help but will not make a decisive difference. This leaves us with the two most realistic and effective policy options: raising overall employment levels among women and raising the retirement age. . . . The main challenge with the "women's employment" strategy is that it will likely further aggravate the fertility crisis unless accompanied by adequate daycare provision.

The last—and by far most effective—solution is to raise the age of retirement. . . . Delaying retirement is an effective tool because it cuts both ways: reducing pension years while raising contribution years simultaneously. . . . The huge educational gap that exists now between old and younger workers will disappear within the next 10 years or so (when the baby-boom generations arrive at retirement age). Additionally, the health conditions of older workers are improving rapidly. . . .

Still, two principal problems do remain. Firstly, while older workers' productivity declines, seniority-based wage setting implies constantly rising earnings, and this affects employers' incentives to keep older workers. Secondly, given that life expectancy is correlated with socio-economic status, delaying retirement will be unfair to the lower-income workers (for whom a curtailment of "leisure years" will appear more drastic). . . . The welfare inequalities within one generation swamp all differences between generations. The equity and the cost problems associated with any pension reform would be far more manageable if inequalities in earnings, careers, and life-long resource accumulation were minimal. Such inequalities spring from conditions in childhood and youth, including the impact of social origins.

In brief, the best way to think about pension reform is to begin not with the aged, but with the welfare of children. Good pensions begin at birth.

Source: Abridged from Esping-Andersen (2003).

is a non-profit organization with a membership of more than 400,000 Canadians and a mandate to promote the rights and quality of life of seniors.

CARP seeks to make policy-makers and the public aware of elderly people's views about social, financial, and political issues. Among other things, it has organized national forums on scams and frauds against seniors, on home care, and on the environment. It has also addressed health-care issues such as long-term care, hospital closures and mergers, national health strategies, and the funding, availability, cost, and taxation of drugs. CARP has also identified and combatted instances of ageism and elder abuse. Finally, CARP has helped to design strategies to provide safe, affordable living conditions for seniors. Its many reports, publications, and videos address various topics of interest to the elderly population (CARP, 2001).

Protecting Rights and Limiting Risks

As people get older, they often have a harder time making their wishes heard and respected by family or caregivers. Some caregivers will defer to the senior's choice, showing respect to the senior. However, seniors may not always be the best judges of their own best interests; and where their decisions involve risk for others, collective rights must be considered. The risk of harm may be compounded by chronic disease or mental incapacity. For example, with weakening vision and slower reaction times, older drivers may not be the best judges of whether they should continue to drive an automobile (Gagliardi et al., 2010). It may be in the interest of the community and of the senior to have the driver's licence withdrawn, even though this may reduce the senior's mobility and independence.

The problem of respecting individual freedom versus protecting a senior from harm arises in many situations. For example, caregivers need to question whether seniors who want to continue living in their own homes should be allowed to do so at the risk of suffering serious harm. Likewise, they need to consider whether or not to override the right of seniors to refuse treatment that could restore or preserve their health (National Advisory Council on Aging, 2006).

Caregivers need to balance the rights of seniors with the needs and rights of other people. Respecting a senior's right to make choices—even risky choices—does not mean withdrawing care and support. It does mean finding a balance between the wishes of the senior and those of the caregivers. Making a valid assessment of the senior's capabilities may call for expert testing. Competency assessments may consist of mental tests managed by health professionals to determine if an individual can reason well enough to care for himself or herself. People unfit to do so may lose the right to decide for themselves (ibid.).

This is more complicated than it sounds. There is, for example, the matter of selecting the right test for the occasion, in view of possible risks to the senior and his or her caregivers. As well, a person's competency may rise and fall over time. A senior who tests as mentally competent today may not test as competent next week, and vice versa. This suggests the need for ongoing assessment to ensure that the right decision is made at the right time.

Claims-Making and the Social Construction of Aging

While we have discussed aging in this chapter with respect to social consequences such as poverty, the social construction of aging is extremely important as well. We should not lose sight of the fact that as we frame and solve problems, we also are constructing ways—unnecessarily narrow ways—of thinking about these problems.

Consider the matter of male sexual potency and the role of Viagra. Does Viagra (and other drugs like it) solve a problem or create one? As one study points out, the success of this drug has contributed to the medicalization of aging masculinity (Marshall, 2007). Viagra solves a problem only after men have been persuaded that they are unmanly if their sexual performance declines—even if the decline is commonly and normally associated with aging. In effect, this represents a wholesale redefinition of beliefs about aging and sexuality, not hard scientific evidence about men's health in later life (Vares, 2009).

A constructionist perspective takes "old age" as a culturally arbitrary category. After all, the boundaries between middle age and old age are often based on loose, poorly defined criteria (Kehl Wiebel and Fernandez Fernandez, 2001; Degnen, 2007). In a capitalist society, people falling into the category of "old" may be seen as problematic because they are failing to participate in the labour force (Ben-Moshe, 2004; Vincent, 1996). Equally, in a consumerist society, people who are failing to consume their time and money in youthful ways may be viewed as problematic. It is important, then, that we try to get around discourses that treat the "elderly" as an easily distinguished group of people or that view age as necessarily disabling.

Some have even challenged well-established ideas about universal stages of development. One comparative study found that the concept of adolescence (normally associated with ages 12–18) is differently constructed in communities around the world. That is, different social expectations are associated with this particular age category in different societies. At the other end of the age distribution, the "very old" stage (ages >75) does not even exist in some places (Chatterjee et al., 2002). Others are suggesting that the commonly defined thresholds of "elderly" and "very old" should be raised as the population lives longer (Addington, 2013). As well, the idea of a universal progression has been challenged along gender lines, with some authors proposing that such false universals

CANADIAN researcher

BOX 6.4   Susan McDaniel, University of Lethbridge

Susan McDaniel has held a Canada Research Chair in Global Population and Economy at the University of Lethbridge since 2009. She is also a Fellow of the Royal Society of Canada, the highest honour for academic achievement and excellence. Her research on the life course, demographic aging, generational relations, and family change has strongly shaped Canadian sociology.

McDaniel's research connects large demographic and economic changes to the lives of individuals. In her 2013 article titled "Generationing Relations in Challenging Times: Americans and Canadians in Mid-Life in the Great Recession," McDaniel explores how the 2008 economic recession affected the mid-life generation (people aged 45–65) in the United States and Canada, two countries very differently affected by the economic crisis.

The United States witnessed significant home foreclosures, bankruptcies, high unemployment, and widespread poverty. By contrast, Canada had far fewer foreclosures and bankruptcies and considerably less unemployment. Her findings suggest that the shock of the economic crisis has deeply transformed the lives of those in the middle generations and all those whose lives are linked to theirs, particularly in the US. McDaniel emphasizes the notable *indirect* consequences that occurred in the lives of those associated with the mid-life generation, on which this study focused. She concludes by arguing that there are broad implications for families, societal cohesion and social order that extended well beyond the mid-life generation.

Source: McDaniel et al. (2013).

deny women's unique life experiences (Smith, 2001) and others proposing that they focus on women's issues over men's when it comes to aging (Russell, 2007).

The reality of aging, like many other issues, is complicated, and few today would hold to a totally constructionist or totally essentialist view of aging. Biology, culture, and physical and social environments all interact to some degree in determining life experiences—as we acknowledged in an earlier discussion of the life course. This is true even of health in later life, however we define the term "health."

Thus, constructionist perspectives help us to better understand aging—its main features and its many variations. They remind us that the definitions and meanings a society attributes to age are as important from a sociological view as the biological process of aging.

Chapter Summary

Medicine, disease control, and biotechnology have brought about significant increases in human life expectancy in the past century or so. As scientists continue to extend their knowledge of how the human body ages, they will be ever more likely to design treatments and drugs that can compensate for or delay the processes of deterioration.

In the future, people will not only live longer, they will likely also experience a better quality of life in the later stages as medical technology succeeds in reducing the significant differences in physical and mental functioning between young adults, middle-aged people, and the elderly population (McMunn et al., 2009; Saini and Jasal, 2009; Windsor, 2009).

Still, we must not lose sight of the social construction of aging. We are taught "suitable" ways to behave at each age, and these age rules can act like straitjackets. The mass media, in both their programming and advertisements, are the main vehicles of socialization about the meaning of age. In part, the media give back to viewers what they already want and believe. What we see on television, in movies, and in print largely reflects what many already value or deride. However, the media also shape how we view the world, and overall, they promote images of elderly people that are outdated, disrespectful, and ridiculous.

These images support ageism, which in turn supports discrimination in the workplace and elsewhere. As a result, seniors may not receive the opportunities, payments, or legislation they need, because ageism discourages those with political power from developing programs to help the elderly population.

From the functionalist perspective, aging is a social problem because the institutions of modern society fail to meet the needs of the dependent aged. Conflict theorists, on the other hand, view problems of the elderly population as stemming from their lack of power to shape social institutions in ways that meet their needs. Symbolic interactionists show us that elderly people are stigmatized because they do not conform to the images, ideals, and norms of a youth-oriented culture. Feminist theorists note that the most disadvantaged seniors are women and other social minorities.

Governments, voluntary associations, and informal and formal social networks all help to promote successful aging. However, elderly people also need to play a role in securing their own well-being. Research has confirmed that regular social contact with friends and relatives improves well-being among elderly people. We are social beings: we need and value the company of other people. As well, social integration markedly improves quality of life by reducing stress and increasing positive health practices. The media can play a valuable role in promoting health and social integration among elderly people, and in this way will help to solve age-related problems.

Aging is unavoidable and every society takes note of this in its own culturally meaningful way. Increasingly, however, every society has to deal with the public responsibility for increased longevity and reduced family care. This will be one of the leading social problems of the twenty-first century.

Questions for Critical Thought

1. What is the main factor that has contributed to a significant rise in the proportion of older people worldwide?
2. Under conditions of an economic recession, how do you think the large population of old people will impact your life in Canadian society?
3. How are the experiences of aging different for women and men, and how would you explain these differences?
4. A Statistics Canada survey found in 2003 that poorer and less-educated seniors were no more likely to seek health-care services than their wealthier, more-educated counterparts. Do you find this surprising, and if so, how do you explain it?
5. How are the concepts of "childhood" and "adolescence" socially constructed? What is their social role or value?

Recommended Readings

Ariès, Philippe. 1962 [1960]. *Centuries of Childhood: A Social History of Family Life*, trans. Robert Baldick. New York: Knopf.

Bengston, V.L., N.M. Putney, and D. Gans, eds. 2009. *Handbook of Theories of Aging*, 2nd edn. New York: Springer.

Carmel, Sara, Carol A. Morse, and Fernando M. Torres-Gil, eds. 2007. *Lessons on Aging from Three Nations*. Amityville, NY: Baywood.

Chappell, Neema, Lynn McDonald, and Michael Stones. 2008. *Aging in Contemporary Canada*, 2nd edn. Toronto: Pearson Prentice-Hall.

Cole, Jennifer, and Deborah Durham, eds. 2007. *Generations and Globalization: Youth, Age, and Family in the New World Economy*. Bloomington: Indiana University Press.

Connidis, Ingrid Arnet. 2001. *Family Ties and Aging*. Thousand Oaks, CA: Sage.

Part 3

Trevisophotography/Thinkstock

7

Crime and Violence

LEARNING OBJECTIVES

- To know the definitions of "crime," "laws," and "social order."
- To be able to distinguish among different types of crime.
- To appreciate the demography of crime.
- To learn about theories explaining crimes.
- To understand the economic, social, and psychological outcomes of crime.
- To discover the impact of crime on health.
- To know about possible solutions to the crime problem.

Introduction

Crime is a social problem for several reasons. First, as we will see, crime has real effects on people's health, safety, and sense of well-being. Victimization can be traumatic. It can cause people to withdraw from normal social life (Turner et al., 2010). Second, and consequently, victimization on a large scale can reduce people's trust in social institutions and their willingness to take part in community life (Pottinger and Stair, 2009). Thus, the fear of crime can reduce a community's vitality and cohesion. Third, crime and its aftermath can damage the central institutions of civil society—families, workplaces, and schools, for example (Palmer et al., 2005)—and in this way hinder our ability to carry out the social activities of learning, earning, and raising children (Kitchen and Williams, 2010; McKee and Milner, 2000).

As we will also see, crime is a social activity, with social causes and effects (Lovell, 2009). Men are more likely than women to be involved in violent crimes, both as victims and as offenders. Men are more likely than women to commit acts of murder, forcible rape, armed robbery, aggravated assault, and arson, for example. Many researchers believe that differential socialization provides the best explanation for this pattern (Lauritsen and Heimer, 2008).

Researchers from different theoretical backgrounds differ in their views about criminal causation and responsibility. Some propose that criminal behaviour, especially where property crimes are concerned, is a result of rational calculation that takes into account the profitability and risk of a crime. Others think that crime will result whenever groups have unequal amounts of power and influence. As a result, crime will increase whenever social inequality increases (Farrell, 2010). Some believe that strict law enforcement and harsh sentencing would solve the "crime problem." Others assert that prisons cause as many problems as they solve—that, in fact, they teach crime and harden criminals (Chen and Shapiro, 2007).

We will also learn in this chapter that, where crimes are concerned, moral panic tends to run rampant, especially in cases involving sex, violence, or children. Griffin and Miller (2008) have called this phenomenon "crime-control theatre." Consider the intense public interest in child abductions. The mass media, public safety organizations, and the public together have constructed a social mythology and recurrent moral panic about the supposed pervasiveness of this threat to children. The result has often been harsh "memorial" legislation enacted in response to sensational cases.

One outcome in the United States, where such panics have been most common, is America's Missing Broadcast Emergency Response (AMBER) alert system, designed to interrupt serious child kidnappings in progress by soliciting citizen tips to help officials quickly rescue victims. Research suggests that the AMBER alert has not achieved and probably cannot achieve the ambitious goals that inspired its creation (ibid.). It is an imaginary "solution" to a socially constructed problem, one that encourages public officials to symbolically address fear of a threat that will never go away. Such crime-control theatre creates unintended problems, such as public backlash when the theatrical policy fails and a distorted public debate about the nature and extent of crime in our society.

Defining Crime, Laws, and Social Order

All societies have rules about good and bad behaviour, and they all punish bad behaviour. Economically developed societies like Canada's proliferate and codify these rules—that is, make formal rules called "laws"—about what their members can and cannot do; and they use large, specialized agencies—the police and courts—to enforce these rules.

We know these formal rules as laws, and when someone breaks a law, we say that he or she has committed a crime. Such laws are important tools for promoting good behaviour—if people know that the police and courts will enforce these laws. The regularity of enforcement and the certainty and severity of punishment, in turn, reflect how seriously a society takes the offending behaviour.

Social order exists only when people obey rules. Though most of us don't like following rules we didn't make ourselves, social order is better than social disorder, for with social order, life is more predictable and "safe" (Aradau and Van Munster, 2009). The rules in place not only serve to show which behaviours are acceptable, they also allow people to predict the behaviour of others. But social order does not emerge routinely out of kind impulses and spontaneous co-operation; there are too many people and too many competing interests for this to happen. Order must be manufactured and protected. Under the best circumstances, a social order emerges that is fair and widely accepted (Jackson and Bradford, 2009).

Crime in Canada and Elsewhere

A few crimes that are common, easily investigated, and cheaply prosecuted account for most of our criminal statistics at any given time. Chiefly, these are simple assaults and property crimes, what criminologists call "street crimes." So, changes in a society's crime rate likewise reflect changes in the reporting and prosecution of a few particular crimes. Changes in the crime rate also reflect changes in victims' willingness to report crimes and the ability of police to investigate them.

The most important thing to understand about criminal statistics is that the most familiar of them—statistics for conviction and/or imprisonment—offer the palest reflection of the total amount of crime in Canadian society. By contrast, a stronger but—for obvious reasons—not always reliable picture is provided by victimization statistics. The reason is that criminal justice operates like a funnel: of the many criminal incidents, only a few are reported, and of these even fewer result in arrests and convictions, let alone imprisonment. This is nicely depicted in Figure 7.1. Though the data are from over 10 years ago, the process, and resulting funnel shape, has not changed for decades.

For this reason, when criminal statistics change, we often have trouble knowing if this reflects a change in the incidence of crime or a change in the enforcement of laws against crime. As the data in Figure 7.2 show, from 2001 to 2011, the Canadian crime rate fell and so did the severity of the average crimes committed.

Measuring the total rate of crime is difficult because both police reporting and self-reporting typically are incomplete. Victimization surveys may yield a more precise account, because victims have a closer connection to the crimes committed; victims have suffered the effects directly. In victimization surveys, samples of people report how often, within a given period, they have been the victims of particular crimes (Vollaard and Koning, 2009). However, these surveys, too, are subject to distortion. Thus, all the sources on which we rely for our information—including official statistics on arrest, conviction, and imprisonment, self-reports, and victimization statistics—are incomplete and possibly biased.

As the data in Figure 7.2 suggest, it is useful to consider the seriousness of the crimes committed if we are to have a good idea of the seriousness of the crime "problem" in

Laws Rules of conduct that may provide for the punishment of violators—in other words, the formal rules about what a society's members can and cannot do.

Crime Any behaviour that, in a given time and place, is prohibited by applicable statutory law. When a law is violated, a crime is said to have been committed.

Social order The prevalence of harmonious relationships; used synonymously with "social organization." This condition exists when rules are obeyed and social situations are controlled and predictable. Rules serve not only to show which behaviours are acceptable, but also to allow participants to anticipate the behaviour of others.

Social disorder The uncertain and unpredictable condition in which rules are not obeyed. The environment is unsafe, and the boundaries of acceptable behaviour have broken down.

Self-reporting The victim reports to authorities that a crime has occurred. This is the most direct method of measuring crime rates. However, it is not the most accurate, as changes in the crime rate reflect changes in victims' willingness to report.

Victimization surveys Samples of people are asked how many times within a given time period they have been the victim of particular crimes.

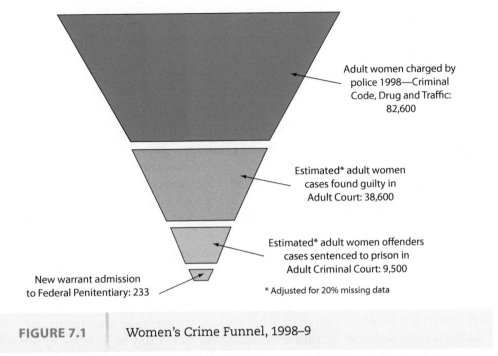

Adult women charged by police 1998—Criminal Code, Drug and Traffic: 82,600

Estimated* adult women cases found guilty in Adult Court: 38,600

Estimated* adult women offenders cases sentenced to prison in Adult Criminal Court: 9,500

New warrant admission to Federal Penitentiary: 233

* Adjusted for 20% missing data

FIGURE 7.1   Women's Crime Funnel, 1998–9

Source: Adapted from Roger Boe, Cindy Lee Olah, and Colette Cousineau, *Federal Imprisonment Trends for Women 1994–95 to 1998–99*. Research Branch, Correctional Service of Canada, December 2000.

Canada. According to a Statistics Canada report in 2008, a decrease in the number of break-ins made a key contribution to the drop in the severity of overall crime in a 10-year period. Over the same period, the seriousness of (less frequent) violent crimes remained stable. The crime index that tracks changes in the severity of police-reported crime assigns each offence a weight, with more serious crimes like break-ins and robberies

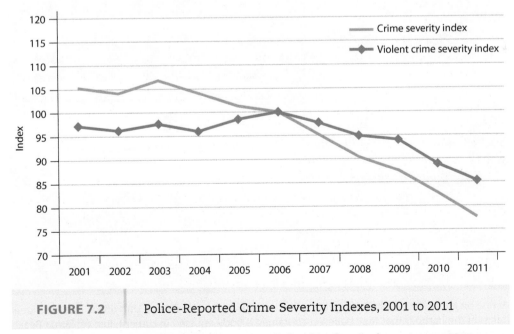

FIGURE 7.2   Police-Reported Crime Severity Indexes, 2001 to 2011

Source: Statistics Canada, Canadian Centre for Justice Statistics, Uniform Crime Reporting Survey, at: <www.statcan.gc.ca/pub/85-002-x/2012001/article/11692-eng.htm>.

assigned higher weights and others, like shoplifting, lower weights. According to the index, overall crime severity fell by 28 per cent from 2001 to 2011, driven by a 40 per cent drop in break-ins.

Crimes of Violence

Conventional crimes The traditionally illegal behaviours that most people think of as "crime." For example, homicide and sexual assault are given the most media coverage but account for only 12 per cent of all crimes.

Homicide The killing of a human being by another, directly or indirectly, by any means, including murder—that is, the unlawful killing of another human being with malicious intent—and manslaughter—the unlawful killing of another person without sufficient intent to constitute murder.

Contrary to the impression presented on the nightly news, violent crimes account for only about one in five crimes (Brennan and Dauvergne, 2011). Yet, criminologists refer to these types of offences as **conventional crimes** because they are the illegal behaviours that most people think of as crime. Also, they are crimes that most people agree are serious and deserve harsh punishment. They are conventional in every sense except their relative rarity (Ruback and Thompson, 2001).

The most headline-grabbing violent crime is **homicide**, the killing of one person by another. Homicide can be subdivided into two categories, murder and manslaughter, depending on whether the homicide involves malicious intent (Cole and Gramajo, 2009). Typically, men are more likely to be involved in homicides than women, both as victims (67 per cent of all victims are men) and as offenders (88 per cent of those charged with homicide are men). Contrary to what the media suggest, we tend to kill and to be killed by people we know. Victims of homicide are more likely to be killed by a family member or acquaintance than by a stranger. Still, homicides are rare in Canada; in 2011, for example, the homicide rate was only 1.8 (OECD, 2011).

By contrast, *assaults* are common, accounting for 60 per cent of all violent crimes reported (Statistics Canada, 2011a). Assaults can be differentiated depending on

The Canadian Press/Toronto Star - David Cooper

Acting on information from Toronto homicide detectives, Toronto Marine Unit divers located a steel barrel in the harbour that they believed contained a body encased in cement, just off Sugar Beach on Queen's Quay.

whether a weapon was involved or if major bodily harm was inflicted. Sexual assault, most seriously rape but also sexual harassment, is another form of violent crime. Most sexual assault victims do not report their experience to the police because they are ashamed or embarrassed and believe they are partially responsible for the occurrence (Jones et al., 2009).

Stalking has emerged as a new social problem. This crime has gained much notice in recent years because it has become common and is associated with gendered harassment, abuse, and violence. In 2004, approximately one in ten men and women reported that they had been victims of stalking (AuCoin, 2005). Most stalkers are former, rather than current, intimates, and they are more likely to be men than women. Typically, stalking includes efforts to re-establish a former relationship. It is a worrisome type of relationship abuse that may evolve into other physical, psychological, and sexual forms, including violence against women. Stalking has various determinants—socio-cultural, interpersonal, dyadic, situational, and intrapersonal (White et al., 2000), often with deep roots in the history of the stalker.

Violence between intimates is common, with men especially likely to carry out the most extreme types of violence, up to intimate-partner homicide (Liem and Roberts, 2009; Straus, 2011). Prior intimacy between the stalker and victim does not predict violence unless the stalker was abusive in their previous relationship (Sheridan and Roberts, 2011). The combination of violence with stalking is frequently lethal. Compared to battered women (who are only occasionally stalked), women who are relentlessly stalked report more severe physical violence, sexual assault, and emotional abuse after separation. They also suffer higher rates of depression and post-traumatic stress disorder (Mechanic et al., 2000).

Non-violent Crimes

Most crimes committed in Canada, as already suggested, are non-violent crimes. The major non-violent crimes include theft, mischief, and property damage; drug production and trafficking; and breaking and entering.

In this category we also find **vice crimes**, including the use of illegal drugs, illegal gambling, communication for prostitution, and the possession, distribution, or sale of child pornography. These crimes provide the greatest opportunities for organized crime, since most societies bar legal access to these goods and services; yet many people are willing to pay for them nevertheless.

White-collar crimes can be defined as crimes "committed by a person of respectability and high social status in the course of his occupation" (Sutherland, 1949). These include fraud, bribery, insider trading, embezzlement, computer crime, and forgery, and they can amount to anywhere from hundreds to millions of dollars. Often, white-collar criminals take advantage of gaps in the social structure—such as loopholes or confusion about new laws or economic conditions—to profit from their crimes (Shichor, 2012). They prosper wherever governments decline to supervise the economic marketplace, as has happened increasingly in capitalist societies over the past 35 years.

Typically, governments give white-collar crime a lower priority than conventional crime, despite evidence that white-collar crime does economic, physical, and psychological harm to a much larger number of people than does street crime (Dutcher, 2005; Friedrichs, 2009).

Vice crimes Deviant behaviour that may be defined as immoral (e.g., gambling, prostitution, drug trafficking). These crimes provide the greatest opportunity for organized crime.

White-collar crimes The crimes committed by white-collar workers and management in the course of their occupations. They are always distinguished from conventional criminal offences such as robbery or murder. White-collar crimes are performed in the course of normal work and usually occur in reputable organizations.

Actor Matt Bomer (left) on the set of *White Collar*, one of many popular television programs to depict fictional stories that glamorize crime.

Organized Crime: A Window on Our Culture?

Organized crime A group or system of professional criminals who practise illegal activities as a way of life and whose criminal activities are co-ordinated and controlled through a hierarchical system of bosses.

North Americans are fascinated by the glamour and excitement of organized crime as depicted in numerous films and television programs. However, organized crime is far from glamorous—it is vicious, harmful big business with transnational networks that reach across the globe.

Organized crime rings that currently exist in Canada include the Sicilian Mafia, Chinese Triads, the Big Circle Boys (Chinese), the Colombian Mafia, the Russian Mafia, and motorcycle gangs like the Hell's Angels and the Outlaws (Cheloukhine, 2008; Dawson, 2009). These groups have been variously involved in vice crimes—drug trafficking, prostitution, extortion, bribery, money laundering, and pornography—as well as in assaults, homicides and contract killing, kidnapping, human trafficking, counterfeiting, insurance fraud, auto theft, truck hijacking, and the illegal arms trade. Worldwide, the gross value of organized crime activities has been estimated at between $600 billion and $1.5 trillion (Knight and Keating, 2010: 277). A more recent study declares that "[t]he annual turnover of transnational organized criminal activities such as drug trafficking, counterfeiting, illegal arms trade and the smuggling of immigrants is estimated at around $870 billion, [according to] the UN Office for Drugs and Crime (UNODC)" (Global Research, 2012).

Early sociologists believed that crime results from poverty and crime in poor neighbourhoods results from social disorganization: the more disorganization, the more crime. After around 1940, however, with the publication of William Whyte's classic *Street Corner Society* (1981 [1943]), sociologists changed their views. They came to recognize that crime—especially crime in poor neighbourhoods—was often highly organized and often connected to "organized crime." It was also closely connected with the social, political, and economic life of the people in the community. Crime, then, was a part of city life—and a part of corporate and political life.

Modern organized crime today operates at the crossroads of legitimate and illegitimate business, family, and formal organizations. It has as strong connections to white-collar crime as it does to vice crimes (such as drug trafficking, pornography, and prostitution). Organized crime draws on the talents of professionals and amateurs, older and younger criminals. What organized crime shows us is that crime is a learned, organized social activity with historical and cultural roots—it does not spring from disorganized irrationality. It is often grounded in traditional notions of kinship and friendship, honour and duty, for example. Organized crime is by nature a social phenomenon, not a departure from normal social life. It is fully a part of our society and plays a crucial role in the world's economic and political activities (Dawson, 2009).

Organized crime in urban North America prospers under four key conditions. First, organized crime flourishes under conditions of scarcity and inequality. It is most common in poor communities with a wide range of economic inequality and, often, with strong family traditions. Second, it is common where poverty and prejudice keep people from moving to find work elsewhere. Third, organized crime provides protection in communities that lack easy access to welfare, health care, good-quality education, and police protection. Finally, organized crime flourishes among people who lack human capital and cultural capital. North American capitalism is one type of economic and social system that produces these conditions, though it is not the only one. In these respects, South American neo-feudalism and Russian neo-capitalism produce these conditions just as well. Also, failing and failed states and societies undergoing rapid change provide a breeding ground for organized crime (e.g., post-Communist Russia, Iraq, Afghanistan, and Albania).

The Demography of Crime

Members of the Canadian population are unequally likely to commit crimes and unequally likely to be victimized by criminals. In some instances, these two go together: young, less-educated men, for example, are more likely to be both perpetrators and victims of crime than the average Canadian adult, especially for crimes like assault.

However, some Canadians are disproportionately likely to be victimized. We will briefly discuss some of the inequalities here and will return to them throughout the chapter, for the relationship between crimes and victims provides an *entrée* into Canadian crime as a whole.

Gender: Offenders

Women commit far fewer crimes than men, and this gender gap in crime—whether organized, professional, or amateur crime—is universal (Davies, 2008). A Statistics Canada study (Brennan, 2012) reports that "[i]n general, males tend to commit crime more frequently than females, a trend which continued in 2011. Of the 413,800 adults (age 18 years and older) charged with a criminal offence in 2011, 79% were male."

Regardless of the type of offence, males were consistently more likely than females to be the accused. Sexual offences showed the highest representation of males: 98 per cent

Differential socialization The processes whereby people learn to behave in accordance with prevailing standards of culture or gender. For example, boys and men learn to be less inhibited in using aggressive and violent actions, and this may account for the disproportionate number of males involved in criminal activity.

of all people charged with sexual assault level 1, child pornography, and sexual violations against children in 2011 were male. The offences with the highest representation of females included abduction (49 per cent), prostitution (47 per cent), and theft under $5,000 (37 per cent) (ibid.).

While the rate of adult males charged with a criminal offence has been declining over the past 20 years (1992–2012), the rate of adult females charged has been increasing over the past decade. This difference in trends is even more pronounced for violent crime, especially over the past 20 years. Since 1991, the rate of males charged with violent crime has declined 32 per cent, while the rate for females has increased 34 per cent. However, males still accounted for more than four in five people accused of violent crime in 2011 (ibid.).

This gender gap is especially pronounced with respect to violent crimes, as we can see in Table 7.1 below. In Canada, the ratio of males to females charged with violent crimes in 2004 was more than 4.5:1. Research shows that men are 7 times more likely than women to commit arson, 9 times more likely to commit murder, 10 times more likely to commit armed robbery, 35 times more likely to discharge a firearm with the intent to harm, 54 times more likely to commit sexual assault, and 78 times more likely to commit forcible rape (ibid.).

Explanations of these gender differences vary. Some researchers say that biology is the answer, that higher levels of testosterone incline men towards aggressive and hostile actions. Others say that **differential socialization** is the cause: the male subculture is

TABLE 7.1	Females and Males Accused of Homicide, by Relationship of the Accused to the Victim, 1997 to 2009			
RELATIONSHIP OF ACCUSED TO VICTIM ACCUSED WAS:	**FEMALE ACCUSED**		**MALE ACCUSED**	
	Number	**Percentage**	**Number**	**Percentage**
Total solved homicides	**677**	**100.0**	**5,195**	**100.0**
Intimate relationship	**226**	**33.4**	**973**	**18.7**
Spouse[1]	172	25.4	553	10.6
(Ex) spouse[1]	21	3.1	211	4.1
Other intimate relationship[2]	33	4.9	209	4.0
Family (non-spousal)	**236**	**34.9**	**880**	**16.9**
Parent	159	23.5	297	5.7
Child	32	4.7	230	4.4
Other family	45	6.6	353	6.8
Acquaintances	**178**	**26.3**	**2,411**	**46.4**
Criminal relationship	21	3.1	563	10.8
Casual acquaintance	102	15.1	1,177	22.7
Other acquaintance	55	8.1	671	12.9
Other	**37**	**5.5**	**931**	**17.9**
Stranger	36	5.3	886	17.1
Unknown	1	0.1	45	0.9

[1]Includes common-law relationships.

[2]Includes current and former dating relationships as well as "Other intimate relationships," such as extramarital lovers.

Source: Statistics Canada, Homicide Survey, 1997 to 2009, at: <www.statcan.gc.ca/pub/89-503-x/2010001/article/11416/tbl/tbl009-eng.htm>.

more violent and young males are encouraged to use aggressive and violent behaviours to solve problems. Of these two, the hormonal theory of gender differences is less able than the socialization theory to account for observed declines in the gender gap in recent decades, so it is probably the weaker theory.

Gender: Victims

Just as criminal offenders are mainly male, so are the victims of crime. This is true for most criminal offence categories, including homicide, robbery, and assault. There are, however, several exceptions. For example, men are disproportionately the perpetrators of domestic and sex-based crimes, and women are disproportionately their victims.

Domestic abuse—violence against women and children—is a serious social problem throughout the world, and it is especially problematic in cultures that subscribe to a patriarchal world view in which wives and daughters are seen as inferior to husbands and sons (Alaggia et al., 2009). Canada, like other nations populated largely by immigrants of scores of ethnicities, is caught in a dilemma. On the one hand, Canada wants to provide its citizens with free religious, cultural, and ethnic expression. On the other hand, it wants to protect the rights and safety of its more vulnerable members, including women and children. This may mean depriving men in some households of the right to use patriarchal (cultural) norms to justify their criminal abuse of women.

Victims of sex-based crimes, including sexual assault and rape, are also mainly female (Doepke and Tertilt, 2009). One social explanation for this is the continued ambivalent attitudes that North American society holds towards sex and, in particular, female sexuality. On the one hand, the female body is endlessly displayed on television, in films, and in marketing campaigns as a sexual object for male consumption. On the other hand, women who take control of their sexuality are often accused of being too aggressive and are characterized as "tramps" or "sluts."

On the whole, women are safer and freer today than they were in the past. Increased gender equality may, in the long run, reduce rates of sexual abuse; Whaley and Messner (2002) have referred to this as the "ameliorative hypothesis." Nevertheless, women often face great risks in the short run: as gender equality increases, so do rates of sexual assault against women. This "backlash hypothesis" is popular among radical feminist theorists. The two hypotheses are compatible, and both are supported by research on this topic conducted by Rosemary Gartner (1997; also, Aizer, 2010).

Age

Young people are more likely to commit crimes than old people. For this reason, as the Canadian population has aged, the crime rate has dropped (Mishra and Lalumière, 2009).

An older society is a more law-abiding society. One explanation is that young people are more likely than people aged 20–60 to be unemployed or to work in low-wage jobs. As sociologist Robert K. Merton (1938) has proposed, they are more likely to use criminal "innovations" to achieve their culturally desired goals (i.e., money and material goods). They have less investment in the old, conventional ways of doing things.

In addition, aggressiveness is a cultural norm for many young men. This means that wherever social occasions bring together large numbers of young men—especially unemployed or underemployed young men—there will be high risks of crime. This is

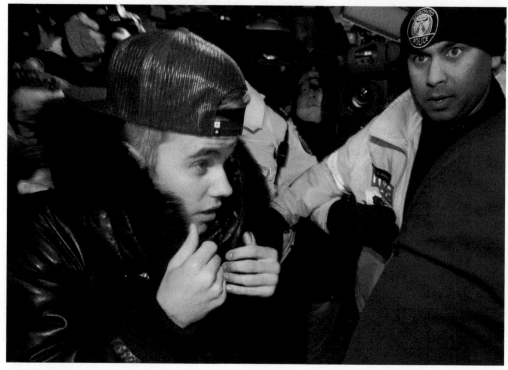

The Canadian Press/Nathan Denette

Justin Bieber is swarmed by media and police officers as he turns himself in to city police in Toronto. The cultural norm of aggression for young men is one potential explanation for the behaviour that led to his arrest.

especially true of cities with high unemployment rates and high rates of recent immigration from less-developed countries.

Sociologists know, however, that crime rates reflect at least three realities and only one of these is the commission of crimes. First, there are the actions of the criminals: they commit the crimes that are measurable and measured. Second, there are the activities of

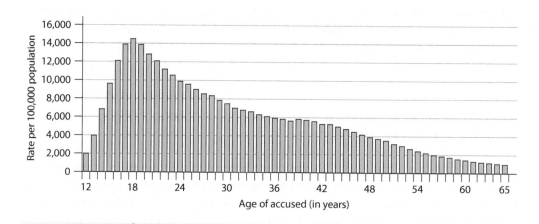

| **FIGURE 7.3** | People Accused of Crime, Age 12 to 65 Years, Canada, 2011 |

Source: Brennan (2012).

victims: they may choose to report or not report information about crimes to which they have been subjected. Third, there are the actions of police: they investigate and document the "facts" of the crime and may or may not lay charges.

Demographic and Community Correlates of Criminal Victimization

Some people are at higher risk of victimization than others. These risk factors include demographic variables, such as being male, young, unmarried, or unemployed (Arnold et al., 2005). Added to these, some neighbourhoods are riskier than others. Many factors determine the safety of a neighbourhood or community: socio-economic vitality, social cohesion and trust, community resources and infrastructure, and mechanisms of informal social control. Typically, crime rates go up when neighbourhoods decline, such as when there are drops in average household income and home ownership. As crime increases, a vicious cycle is established, driving community cohesion down and crime up.

Suitable Targets

Suitable targets are people who are routinely exposed to crime or who, for other reasons, have heightened vulnerability. Taxi drivers, for instance, have a greater than average risk of victimization because of their repeated interaction with strangers at night (Xu, 2010). Gay men and lesbians have a higher than average risk of assault because of hostile public attitudes towards them in some quarters (Tiby, 2001). Tourists are more likely than natives of the same class background to experience victimization while on holiday in a strange place (Holcomb and Pizam, 2006).

Three characteristics put people at particular risk of victimization. These are (1) the target's (i.e., victim's) vulnerability (e.g., a physical weakness or psychological distress), (2) gratifiability (e.g., female gender for the crime of sexual assault), and (3) antagonism (e.g., an ethnic or group identity that may spark hostility or resentment) (Burrow and Apel, 2008). Powerful and rich people are generally less vulnerable than poor people, with one exception: people with more and better property—larger homes, newer cars—are more likely to have their property stolen (Wu and Wu, 2012).

As we have noted several times, women run a higher risk of certain kinds of victimization than men do. For some crimes, such as assault, men are more likely to be victimized by strangers or acquaintances, while women are more likely to be victimized by intimates. For example, 64 per cent of women homicide victims are killed by an intimate partner, while only 10 per cent are killed by strangers (Catalano et. al, 2009).

Elderly people run higher risks of victimization than middle-aged people, especially for crimes of robbery, intimidation, vandalism, and forgery or fraud. Robbery is the most serious offence committed against elderly victims, and men and women are equally likely to experience it (Bourns, 2000). Their risk of theft-related homicide is also high because seniors are more likely than younger people to be seen as suitable targets and as lacking capable guardians. This risk is especially high among seniors who are socially isolated.

At the other end of the age distribution, juveniles aged 12–17 are more likely than adults to be victims of violent crimes and suffer from crime-related injuries. Juvenile victims are more likely to know the people who victimize them (Baum, 2005). A Canadian

TRANCE

In this 2013 film directed by Danny Boyle, an art auctioneer gets mixed up with a group of criminals and partners up with a hypnotherapist in order to recover a lost painting.

Classic WORKS

BOX 7.1   **Richard Ericson's *Reproducing Order: A Study of Police Patrol Work* (1982)**

Richard Ericson (1948–2007) was a leading Canadian sociologist in the field of criminology, especially police research. He received a BA from the University of Guelph, an MA in sociology from the University of Toronto, and a PhD in criminology from Cambridge University. Besides holding a position as principal of Green College at the University of British Columbia, Ericson was a professor of law at that university (1993–2003) and a professor of criminology at the University of Toronto (2004–7).

As the subtitle (above) suggests, Ericson's book *Reproducing Order* examines how the patrol police preserve, reinforce, and restore social order. It approaches this topic by asking: How do the police spend their time? What do they concentrate on and what do they ignore? How do they deal with the public? Whose interests are served by those outcomes? What wider functions of the police can be theorized from this? Ericson proposed that the main police job is not "fighting crime" but merely reproducing— that is, reinforcing—social order.

To do this study, Ericson and a team of five researchers employed a mixture of field observation and qualitative measures to study patrol officers in an "urban area of Eastern Canada." First, using field observation, they studied the police force for five months in 1976. During the 348 shifts observed on ride-alongs, the team recorded a variety of activities, noting general shift activities, how contact in police–citizen encounters was initiated and by whom, which violations were recorded and which were ignored. This structured observation was supplemented by unstructured interviews with police, supervisors, and other officials. Additionally, the team studied the way negotiations were conducted between police and citizens.

Ericson found that patrol officers have little work to fill their time during shifts. Police work is often boring. Officers spend little time directly combatting criminal behaviour, instead dealing with only one or two altercations and two or three minor incidents (e.g., traffic violations) in any eight-hour shift. Ericson noted that "the bulk of the patrol officer's time was spent doing nothing other than consuming the petrochemical energy required to run an automobile and the psychic energy required to deal with the boredom of it all."

When the police did interact with citizens, half the interactions were launched by officers because of real or imagined affronts to the public order, in the view of patrol officers. These incidents did not involve crime, but displayed an offensive demeanour and lifestyle. Specifically, Ericson noted that many interactions were initiated with "pukers"—young men of low socio-economic status—and/or minorities. The police were able to apply wide discretion in choosing when, how, and against whom to apply law and force. They did so in ways that not only preserved social order, but also preserved the status quo. They showed respect to middle-class people but less respect to poor people and minorities. In this way, they reproduced the value system of the existing class structure.

study of high school students in 23 schools found that both boys and girls commonly experienced sexual harassment, with girls describing more sexual jokes and unwanted touching than boys, and boys describing more homosexual slurs or receiving undesired sexual contact than girls. As well, being the victim of sexual harassment in Grade 9 was found to strongly predict victimization later on in high school; two and a half years later, victimized students were more likely than those who had not been victimized to report victimization by peers and even by dates (Chiodo et al., 2009).

Immigrants and ethnic minorities are at higher than average risk of victimization, especially for crimes against persons. In some instances, these may be "hate crimes." The most prevalent hate crime reported to the police is linked to race, followed by religion and sexual orientation (Hayman, 2011). Recent debates about the cultural and legal status of sexual-orientation minorities have increased the awareness of violence against

CANADIAN researchers

BOX 7.2 **Myrna Dawson, University of Guelph**

For Myrna Dawson, Canada Research Chair, Public Policy in Criminal Justice, violent acts between intimates, including femicide, are the subject of repeated analyses. Of particular interest to her is the role of the victim–defendant relationship in criminal justice decision-making and the question of whether those who commit violent acts against intimates receive, and should receive, more lenient treatment. In a 2004 paper, "Rethinking the Boundaries of Intimacy at the End of the Century," for example, Dawson examines court outcomes in more than 1,000 cases and finds that defendants who kill intimates do not always receive the same treatment—nor, for that matter, are defendants who kill non-intimates treated similarly.

In a 2006 paper, "Intimacy and Violence: Exploring the Role of Victim-Defendant Relationship in Criminal Law," Dawson argues that the courts treat—and should treat—intimate violence more leniently than violence between those who share more distant relationships. There are many good reasons for doing so, though Dawson questions the validity of some common assumptions, as well as their impact on court outcomes in cases of violence.

In a 2012 paper, "Intimacy, Homicide, and Punishment: Examining Court Outcomes over Three Decades," Dawson draws on data documenting court outcomes in homicides in one Canadian urban jurisdiction from 1974 to 2002 to find out whether the accused in intimate-partner homicides will be subject to "less law" than those in non-intimate-partner homicides. Results show that differential treatment of intimate- and non-intimate-partner homicide was evident at some stages but not always in the direction hypothesized. Further, while patterns in treatment did change over time, plea resolutions remained more common for intimate-partner killers than for those who killed victims with whom they shared more distant relationships.

In a 2003 paper, "The Cost of 'Lost Intimacy': The Effect of Relationship State on Criminal Justice Decision Making," Dawson examines data from 144 cases of intimate femicide that occurred in Toronto. She finds that offenders who kill estranged partners are treated more severely by the court than those who kill current partners, perhaps because of assumptions about the act and the killer that support such a punishment rationale.

Finally, in a 2005 paper, "Intimate Femicide Followed by Suicide: Examining the Role of Premeditation," Dawson notes that "people who kill others rarely kill themselves afterwards," but this rule is bent if not broken where intimate violence is concerned. Using data from over 700 intimate femicides, Dawson finds that premeditation is more likely to have occurred in cases involving the offender's subsequent suicide, though the link between premeditation and suicide is complex and depends on the "type" of suicidal killer.

gays and lesbians (Mertus, 2007). It is not clear whether anti-gay violence has increased, however. Our information about the extent of hate crimes against these groups is hindered by a reluctance of gays and lesbians to report victimization because of additional concerns about police abuse (Tiby, 2001).

Inmates of "total institutions" also suffer high risks of victimization. Common offences against prisoners include assault, robbery, threats of violence, theft of property from cells, verbal abuse, and exclusion (Chubaty, 2001; Leddy and O'Connell, 2002). The main perpetrators are other prisoners. Though much has been said and written about the abusiveness of guards, such abuse is harder to document.

Secondary Victimization

Being the victim of a crime is painful and stressful. The trauma does not stop with the crime itself. The victim may suffer additionally as she navigates the complex and often frustrating justice system in hopes of seeing justice done.

Secondary victimization
Additional pain and suffering caused to a victim of crime by the negative responses of the justice system (e.g., police) and significant individuals (e.g., family members) following his or her original victimization.

Secondary victimization refers to "the victimization which occurs, not as a direct result of the crime, but through the response of institutions and individuals to the victim" (Canadian Resource Centre for Victims of Crime, 2005). Examples of secondary victimization include the refusal by law enforcement officers to recognize an individual's experience as a victim of crime and intrusive or inappropriate conduct by police or judicial officers. The criminal investigation and the trial, as well as criminal-justice processes and procedures that ignore, marginalize, or discount the role and input of the victim, are other problems victims often face, along with the associated psychological stress. They all serve to discourage victims from seeking official assistance after victimization.

Theoretical Perspectives on Crime

Structural Functionalism

Strain (anomie) theory
Merton holds that strain is produced when social structure prevents people from achieving culturally defined goals through legitimate means, and according to Durkheim, anomie is a condition characterized by a breakdown of norms and personal disorganization, which may lead to crime. Merton outlines various adaptive strategies: conformity, ritualism, retreatism, rebellion, and innovation. Innovation is most commonly associated with criminal activities, which include theft, robbery, tax fraud, embezzlement, and organized crime.

The functionalist approach to deviance includes a variety of theories that unite around a few central views, namely, that crime is normal, universal, and unavoidable—in short, that it is to be expected in any society. Here, we review one theory that focuses on the link between crime and social disorganization—the so-called "social disorganization theory"—and a competing theory that focuses on the "functions" served by crime in a capitalist society—the **strain (anomie) theory**. The former views crime in a negative light, while the latter views it in a positive, or at least value-neutral light. Other structural functionalist approaches—**social bond theory** and **subculture theory**—are outlined in Table 7.2.

Social Disorganization Theory

Durkheim's early work in *Suicide* (1951 [1897]) provides the basis for a theory that crime and other social pathologies (including suicide) result from a breakdown in social norms and social integration.

This breakdown, in turn, typically results from rapid social change and organizational problems associated with rapid change—for example, rapid increases in population, in cultural diversity, and in social (or geographic) mobility associated with the rise of urban industrial society. As the theory would predict, international data show that people in developing and transitional countries have higher victimization rates, express less satisfaction with law enforcement, and support a more punitive approach to controlling crime than people in fully industrialized societies (Sung, 2006; Gibson and Kim, 2006).

Social bond theory A type of control theory. A strong social bond prevents most people from succumbing to the temptation to engage in criminal activities.

Social disorganization leads to the loss of social cohesion—a central concern of functionalist theory. Other things being equal, a loss of social cohesion increases the risk of robbery and assault near home and of robbery and assault by strangers (Lee, 2000). Areas with high crime rates also have higher mortality rates from all causes, suggesting that crime rates mirror the quality of the social environment (Wilkinson and Kennedy, 2008). Also, random violence and exposure to the continual use of guns and knives in the community produce children who are more likely to act violently themselves (Silvestri et al., 2009). In short, according to this theory, we can reduce crime mainly by increasing community cohesion.

Subculture theory This approach to the study of deviance investigates the norms that set a group apart from mainstream society. Specifically, it gives special insight into the subculture of the criminal, looking into the values and belief systems that may be conducive to delinquent and criminal action.

Strain Theory

By contrast, strain theory focuses on inequality: the gap between what people want and what they can get by legitimate means. Implicit in strain theory—pictured schematically

TABLE 7.2	Theoretical Perspectives
THEORY	**MAIN POINTS**

Varieties of Structural Functionalism

Social Disorganization Theory	• Crime results from a breakdown in social norms and social integration following rapid social change.
	• Social disorganization leads to a loss of social cohesion, which in turn increases the likelihood of criminal behaviours such as robbery and assault.
	• Exposure to chronic random violence produces people who are more likely to act violently themselves.
	• Increased cohesion reduces crime.
Social Bond Theory	• Travis Hirschi's social bond theory (1969) proposes that developing a strong social bond, established in childhood, can prevent people from giving in to the temptation to commit criminal acts.
	• Instead of explaining why people commit crime, this theory explains why people abstain from offending.
	• Four elements are involved in a strong social bond: an attachment to other people, a commitment to conventional goals, an involvement in conventional activities, and a belief in the legitimacy of conventional values, norms, and moral standards encouraged by society.
	• Criminal activities increase where bonds are weak and people are exposed to anti-social values and activities.
Anomie Theory	• Merton (1938) theorizes that anomie and strain arise whenever unequal social opportunities prevent some people from achieving the culturally defined goals (such as money) by using legitimate means (such as a job).
	• One way to circumvent the gap between culturally approved ends and the culturally approved means to achieve them is through innovation (e.g., theft, robbery, tax fraud, embezzlement, and organized crime).
	• This theory assumes that criminals hold the same values and goals as everyone else.
Subculture Theory	• Violent subcultures, such as gangs, provide minority youth with an alternative community for achieving social status, friendship, and economic mobility.
	• Using violence to right a wrong or defend one's honour may be considered justifiable under the value and belief system of delinquents and criminals.
Conflict Theory	• Conflict theories of crime and violence point to inequalities in society as the cause of such deviant behaviour.
	• Criminal activity increases as inequality increases.
	• Dominant ideology and formal laws protect the privileged status of the ruling class and mask white-collar crimes that benefit the social elite.

Varieties of Symbolic Interactionism

Social Constructionism	• Constructionists look at how deviant behaviours come to be defined as "deviant."
	• Behaviours are not innately right or wrong; they only become wrong, deviant, or criminal when someone in power ascribes a moral value to them.
Labelling Theory	• Deviance is not a quality of the act a person commits, but rather a result of the application by others of rules and sanctions to an "offender."
	• Being labelled as deviant or criminal may promote further deviancy because the labelled person is unable to escape stigmatization and internalizes the "deviant" identity.

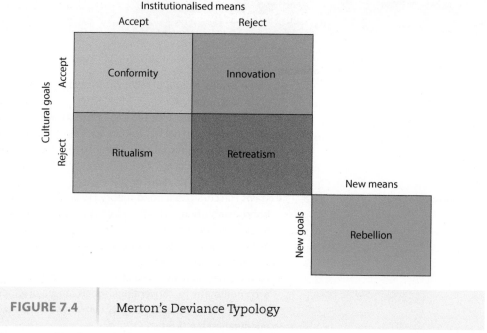

FIGURE 7.4   Merton's Deviance Typology

Source: <en.wikipedia.org/wiki/File:Mertons_social_strain_theory.svg>.

in Figure 7.4—is the idea that criminals hold the same values and goals as everyone else; they just use alternative means to pursue those goals and values. If everyone wants a nice house in the suburbs, a shiny new car, and a comfortable income, people with less education or fewer job opportunities may find crime the best way to get these things.

This approach would predict that people who are economically disadvantaged will react to inequality by getting money through unlawful means, such as robbery or embezzlement. For similar reasons, it would predict that declining wages will lead to increased rates of crime, especially among those who are unemployed or unable to afford proper health care (Stogner and Gibson, 2010; Almén and Nordin, 2011).

This approach, however, does not work as well to explain crimes against persons (such as assault, rape, or murder of an intimate) or crimes against property that yield no gain (such as vandalism). For this, we must turn to conflict theories.

Conflict Theory

Conflict theories of crime and violence point to inequalities in society as the cause of such deviant behaviour. Obviously, they would predict that as inequality increases in a society, crime also will increase and that people most subject to inequality would be the most likely to commit crimes.

For less obvious reasons, people who are disadvantaged are also more likely to embrace subcultures of violence, which leads to higher rates of crimes against other people. These are subcultures preoccupied with amassing and protecting honour and respect, and they typically are found where cults of masculinity (machismo) are present. These tend to be found in less-prosperous, less-educated, and more-traditional (often rural) communities, though they may also be found in urban ghettos marked by a culture of poverty. As a

PERSONAL *stories*

BOX 7.3 | **Stalked for 28 Years**

Here's a story about stalking that happened in the United States. There have been similar occurrences in Canada but perhaps none quite as dramatic or extreme as this one. At its worst, stalking can be a nightmare for the person who is victimized—in this case, a person named Kathy Nebel.

Kathy Nebel enjoyed a pleasant life in California with her two children and her second husband, an officer in the military. After her husband was discharged for defrauding the government, however, her life changed drastically. Kathy told him that she was moving back to Iowa with the children, and his response was to lock himself and their daughter in a bathroom and threaten to kill them both if Kathy left. He had never threatened her or displayed signs of violence prior to this incident. Police had to force him out of the bathroom, but that was just the beginning of Kathy's troubles.

In due course, Kathy left for Iowa with the children, but her husband followed them and continued to stalk Kathy for 28 years. To make his presence felt, he broke her windows, slashed her tires, and hung parts of dead animals on her front door. He even appeared at Kathy's workplace, threatening to kill her and her co-workers; this resulted in Kathy having to quit jobs and seek new employment numerous times.

Also distressing were the over 800 court visits Kathy had to make over minor issues. For example, her ex-husband brought her to court for not informing him which church she and the children attended and not seeking his permission before having their daughter's hair cut. These court appearances gave the ex-husband information about Kathy's whereabouts, increased contact between the two ex-spouses, and drained Kathy's energy. Her ex-husband made his intentions clear during a court appearance when he said, "I will not stop until this woman is destroyed."

Kathy eventually obtained a permanent restraining order against her ex-husband, and she carries it wherever she goes. She has now remarried and has tried to move on with her life. When her ex moved to Florida in 2000, she hoped this would mark the end of his harassment, but he continues to disrupt her life; for example, he faxed her employer a copy of a psychiatric evaluation his ex-wife had received.

Elena Tepperman, based on: Mary Pieper, "Woman: Former Husband Stalked Her for Decades," *Globe Gazette,* 5 Oct. 2012, at: <globegazette. com/news/local/woman-former-husband-stalked-her-for-decades/ article_0965f074-0f70-11e2-8b92-001a4bcf887a.html>; and Department of Justice, Presentation to Justice Systems Appropriations Subcommittee, 2009, at: <www.legis.iowa.gov/DOCS/LSA/SC_ MaterialsDist/2009/SDBAL017.PDF>.

result, homicide rates are the highest in poor communities marked by a high percentage of female-headed families and a high dropout rate from schools (Rosenfeld, 2009).

The conflict perspective notes that people in privileged positions work to preserve their status. Thus, the conflict approach also focuses on white-collar crime and the crimes committed by privileged people. Both the dominant ideology and formal laws—social constructs shaped and upheld by the ruling class—help the powerful to stay on top. They ensure, for example, that most people in society will view street crimes, such as public drug use and vagrancy, which are more common among the disadvantaged, as deviant and undesirable. At the same time, corporate crimes that profit the wealthy but harm far larger numbers of people continue to be hidden from the mass media, the public, and policy-makers.

Conflict theory also focuses on power differences between men and women in male-dominated societies. One example of such inequality is the perpetuation in some cultures and subcultures of "rape myths." These myths depict women as responsible for their own victimization and occasionally help acquit men of wrongdoing. They include the belief that "no" means "yes," that wearing a revealing style of dress is like "asking for" sex, and that "good girls" don't get raped. They illustrate the conflict theorist's contention that people in power benefit from the criminal laws, while people without power do not.

Currently, despite higher rates of female arrests and convictions than in the past, there is little evidence that women are committing higher numbers of crimes today, only that they are more likely today to be treated as criminals. This suggests an equalization of treatment of males and females by the police and courts or even a disproportionate tendency to criminalize women for certain crimes.

Social Constructionism

As we noted in the first chapter, social constructionism looks at how deviant behaviours come to be defined as "deviant." This perspective stresses that no behaviours are inherently right or wrong: they become wrong, deviant, or criminal only when someone in power attaches a moral label to them.

As a result, we can view hate-motivated violence, or hate crime, as a social construct. Some deny that hate crimes are different from, or need different treatment from, equally severe crimes of violence. The specification of "hate crime" was originally developed to combat expressions of racial, ethnic, and religious prejudice. In recent years, gays, lesbians, children, and women have been seen as potential victims of hate crimes, too. The enlargement of this umbrella to protect more types of victims is the result of claims-making by special interest groups as they document such crimes and call for legal remedies (Jenness, 1995; Lyons, 2008).

Constructionist theories illuminate the ways in which the notions of crime, violence, and criminality are built up and sustained. However, there is currently no agreement on how best to depict crime and violence if our goal is to prevent or deter such acts. For example, stories that depict incidents of violence against women as somehow routine or inevitable may lead to a "culture of resignation," which is as dangerous in its own way as a moral panic. In short, few researchers would deny that violent crime—domestic and otherwise—is problematic; yet they might disagree about the extent of a "crime problem" in our society.

Differential Association Theory

This theory can be most easily viewed as a functionalist theory, because it is about the ways people, through simple association, are socialized into their criminal environment and reproduce the prevailing order. There are two distinguishing features of differential association theory. First, it is a sociological rather than psychological theory: it proposes that people are social and imitate one another to gain acceptance and approval. Second, it is a theory that assumes social organization, not social disorganization; crime is a result of too much of the "wrong kind" of organization, not too little of the "right kind" of organization (Kissner and Pyrooz, 2009).

Living in a neighbourhood with a high crime rate and merely seeing others benefit from a criminal lifestyle seems enough to increase the likelihood of someone engaging in similar illegitimate activity. Seeing criminals act illegally, without seeing them condemned or punished, is likely to teach people not only the techniques of crime, but also the motives, rationalizations, and attitudes of such a lifestyle. In this respect, jails are graduate schools for crime. Time spent in jail or prison is time spent fostering friendships, dependencies, and interests that lead to continued anti-social behaviours on release from prison (Church et al., 2009).

Social Consequences of Crime and Violence

Poverty and Inequality

The crimes most often featured in the media are violent street crimes. And of all the people arrested for violent street crimes, most are undereducated, poor, unemployed, or working in low-wage, low-status jobs. Other kinds of crimes and criminals receive less attention, both from the media and the police.

Conflict theories have a lot to say about this tendency of police and courts and politicians to target lower-income criminals and overlook upper-income criminals. These theories suggest that if police explored corporate, occupational, and political crimes as energetically, they would find equally high rates of crime among the wealthy. As a result, "the wealthy might even be convicted and punished more than the poor" (Pepinsky and Jesilow, 1984: 81).

The arrest and conviction of poor people, however, is not merely a result of bias in the police and courts (Bush, 2010). The existing social order treats poor people worse than it treats the rich and well-educated. Braithwaite (1993) provides a useful distinction between what he calls "crimes of poverty" and "crimes of wealth." The former are motivated largely by a need to get goods for personal use, and the latter by a greedy desire to obtain goods for exchange—that is, goods beyond those needed for personal use. Social inequality and economic inequality promote both kinds of crime. A system of wide inequality and extreme competitiveness results in a class of needy poor and a class of greedy rich. A large middle class, meanwhile, strives endlessly to avoid falling into the former category and succeed in rising into the latter.

The Racial Dimension

Class, gender, and age are not the only social characteristics that predict criminality and conviction. Over the last few decades, Canadian researchers have paid more attention to the unduly large number of Aboriginal people arrested and convicted of law violations. Aboriginal adults made up only 3 per cent of the Canadian population in 2007/8, yet they made up 22 per cent of those people sentenced to custody (Perreault, 2009).

This over-representation of Aboriginals in the criminal justice system is especially striking in Manitoba and Saskatchewan. Figure 7.5, which looks at Aboriginal youth admissions to correction services, demonstrates this. As well, compared to non-Aboriginal inmates, Aboriginals are less likely to have a high school diploma, are more likely to be unemployed, and are more likely to have needs in the area of family and marital relationships (Perreault, 2009).

One common explanation is that, like some other ethnic groups, Aboriginal people are mostly poor, and poverty drives them to crime. Other explanations include a racially prejudiced law enforcement and correctional system; a conflict between the values of Aboriginal culture and mainstream Canadian culture; the social and economic effects of colonization and oppression by European settlers; and a breakdown in the traditional social fabric of Aboriginal communities. These explanations are not mutually exclusive. In fact, these factors support and interact with one another.

Any solution to this problem will require more cultural sensitivity on the part of non-Aboriginal policy-makers than in the past. Many of the more promising

THE PLACE BEYOND THE PINES

In this 2012 thriller directed by Derek Cianfrance, a motorcycle stunt rider considers committing a crime in order to provide for his wife and child. This puts him on a collision course with a cop-turned-politician.

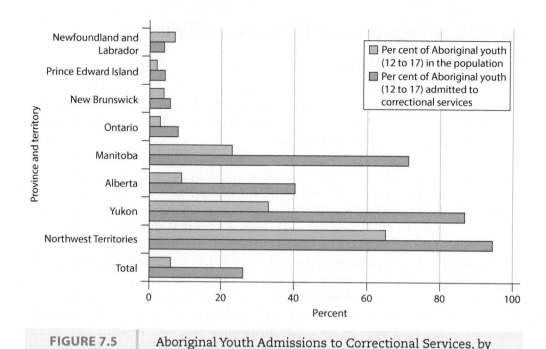

FIGURE 7.5   Aboriginal Youth Admissions to Correctional Services, by Province and Territory, 2010/11

Source: Statistics Canada, Canadian Centre for Justice Statistics, Youth Custody and Community Services Survey, at: <www.statcan.gc.ca/pub/85-002-x/2012001/article/11716-eng.htm#a4>.

initiatives—healing and sentencing circles, First Nation police forces, elders' courts, and so on—are being developed by Aboriginal communities themselves.

However, because Canadian authorities do not tabulate crime statistics by the race of the offender, the connection between race and crime is hard to flesh out quantitatively. Typically, we know little about the racial characteristics of people convicted of committing different crimes, and many people would say that is a good thing. Many police forces oppose collecting statistics based on race. They fear that doing so might encourage the racial profiling of suspects, which is a constant and troubling issue in law enforcement. It might also attract negative attention from the public and the media. Others believe that collecting and publishing race-based crime data would serve to reinforce existing racial stereotypes.

The Issue of Racial Profiling

Racial profiling is usually defined in a law enforcement context. One study (Wortley and Tanner, 2004) published in the *Canadian Review of Policing Research* defined it as "a racial disparity in police stop and search practices, customs searches at airports and border-crossings, in police patrols in minority neighbourhoods and in undercover activities or sting operations which target particular ethnic groups."

The Ontario Human Rights Commission took a broader approach (OHRC, n.d.), defining racial profiling as

any action undertaken for reasons of safety, security or public protection that relies on stereotypes about race, colour, ethnicity, ancestry, religion, or place of origin rather than on reasonable suspicion, to single out an individual for greater scrutiny or different treatment. . . . Accusations of differential treatment arise in areas

Mike Carroccetto/Getty Images News

National Chief of the Assembly of First Nations Phil Fontaine walks into the House of Commons to receive a formal statement of apology for the Indian residential schools system from Prime Minister Stephen Harper on behalf of the federal government and all Canadians. Residential schools were one result of colonization that continues to have social and economic consequences for Aboriginal people.

where authorities can exercise their discretion . . . when that discretion is exercised, members of many minority groups feel that they come out on the short end of the baton—that they somehow always have to prove their innocence.

Police chiefs say their forces try to weed out racists and can often point to disciplinary action or firings related to racist behaviour. But critics say racial profiling tends to be more subtle and, therefore, difficult to monitor. Formal stats are often hard to come by and can be open to alternative interpretations.

Most police forces in North America don't collect race-based data on such things as traffic stops. That's why a series of articles published in 2002 in the *Toronto Star* caused such a sensation. The articles were based on stats collected by the police. Analysis of those figures by *Star* reporters suggested that blacks in Toronto were over-represented in certain offence categories, such as drug possession, and in what were called "out-of-sight" traffic violations, such as driving without a licence. The analysis also suggested that black suspects were more likely to be held in custody for a bail hearing, while white suspects facing similar charges were more likely to be released at the scene.

A study of police statistics in Kingston, Ontario, released in May 2005 found that young black and Aboriginal men were more likely to be stopped than other groups. The data showed that police in the predominantly white city were 3.7 times more likely to stop a black as a Caucasian and 1.4 times more likely to stop an Aboriginal person than a white. Several field studies in Canada have also uncovered evidence that some minority groups, especially black youth, are far more likely to report "involuntary police contact," as one researcher called it, than either whites or Asians.

Some propose that all the debate over whether racial profiling actually exists is missing the point. They say that if a huge portion of an ethnic group believes it exists, then that, by definition, amounts to a serious problem that must be addressed. University of Toronto criminologists Scot Wortley and Julian Tanner (n.d.) write that "being stopped and searched by the police . . . seems to be experienced by black people as evidence that race still matters in Canadian society. That no matter how well you behave, how hard you try, being black means that you will always be considered one of the 'usual suspects.'"

Wortley proposes that police should conduct more research and collect more data, saying that the refusal of police to deal with the issue will "ensure the issue of racial discrimination continues to haunt law enforcement agencies for decades to come."

Some believe that racial profiling is already a conventional practice among Canadian police. A study of possible racial bias by the police of Toronto, using 2007 survey data, shows that within the two years prior to the survey, blacks were much more likely to be stopped and searched by police than white and Asian respondents (Wortley and Owusu-Bempah, 2011). As the researchers note, these results do not conclusively prove the existence of racial profiling, but they do suggest that at least some "routine" police stops are racially motivated.

Economic Consequences of Crime

Crime costs a society a lot of money. The financial costs result from losses of property through identity theft, bank robberies, auto theft, breaking and entering, embezzlement, and copyright violations. Other costs result from criminal violence; they include the loss of productivity by injured workers and the medical costs of treating crime victims. And even "crimes without victims" carry financial costs. Just consider the unrecorded or illegal spending on drugs, prostitution, gambling, and other underground activities; it all diverts cash away from legitimate businesses and goes untaxed.

Increasingly, criminal activity is shifting to cyberspace. And increasingly, new computer-based technologies are being used to commit new types of crimes, or to commit old crimes more effectively and transnationally. A rapidly growing concern is the rise of "identity theft," which comes in a variety of forms.

Besides victims' financial losses, crime also imposes an economic burden on the broader public through government spending on law enforcement, the criminal court system, and correctional services. According to Statistics Canada (2011b), the number of police has risen steadily over the past 10 years, resulting in a total of 69,438 active police officers. This has also meant a steady increase in police expenditures for 11 consecutive years. In 2010, the amount spent on policing in Canada was $12.6 billion. This level of spending was 43 per cent higher than a decade earlier. This has occurred despite a continuing decline in the recorded crime rate: "The 2007 crime rate was at its lowest point in over 30 years. At the same time, the proportion of crime solved by the police reached a 30-year high" (ibid., 5).

On average, it costs taxpayers $357 per day to house one inmate in a federal penitentiary (though only $171 per inmate in a provincial/territorial prison) (Dauvergne, 2012).

SIDE EFFECTS
In this 2013 film directed by Steven Soderbergh, a woman turns to prescription drugs as a way of handling her anxiety over her husband's upcoming release from prison.

With $357 per day—$130,305 a year—two or three readers of this book could pay an entire year's expenses for tuition, room, board, books, clothing, and recreation at a college or university. Some might consider that a better way to spend the money—if only we could find ways to prevent the crimes that jailed offenders are committing.

Health Consequences of Crime and Violence

Not surprisingly, crime carries costs for its victims. Victims of crime report lowered levels of well-being after their victimization, and victims of *violent* crime are especially likely to suffer psychological distress (Green and Pomeroy, 2007). They also report lower levels of health and physical well-being, with younger victims of violent crime reporting the greatest decline in their health.

Victims of property crime also report lowered levels of health and physical well-being, but older victims suffer the most negative effects of these crimes (Britt, 2001). Violent crimes result in physical pain and suffering because of the injuries inflicted. Victims of crime have an overestimation of risk and live in constant fear and anxiety that they will soon be the victim of another crime, and this fear of the future can affect their physical and mental well-being (Dolan and Peasgood, 2006). As a result, the victims of violent crimes report more distress and more stressful life events than non-victims and victims of non-violent crimes (Green and Pomeroy, 2007).

In particular, rape (sexual assault) exacts a heavy psychological and social toll. Victims of rape are often unwilling to report their victimization to the police because of the trauma associated with rape, fear of retaliation by the rapist, and fear of stigmatization. Many victims also have trouble trusting men again and establishing or resuming intimate relations.

The emotional outcomes of criminal victimization can be serious. Victims of crimes are more likely than non-victims to suffer from post-traumatic stress disorder (PTSD), major depressive episodes, and various phobias. A victim's reaction depends largely on the type of crime. Completed rape, for example, is likely to cause deep and long-lasting emotional disturbance, while robbery and burglary are not (McMullin and White, 2006; Shapland and Hall, 2007).

The Health of Criminals

Crime is also hard on criminals, and for most offenders, a life of crime is stressful. Always having to look over one's shoulder, on guard against the authorities, leads to an unhealthy level of stress that eventually harms a person's health.

Prisons are especially harmful to a person's health. Studies show that disease is more prevalent among prisoners than among the non-incarcerated because crowded living spaces, close contact, and shared hygiene facilities serve as breeding grounds for disease transmission (Schnittker and John 2007, Massoglia, 2008). Violent assaults, rapes, and staff brutality also harm the health of prisoners. Prisons, lacking the facilities to do otherwise, often ignore all but the most severe mental illnesses, such as schizophrenia or other psychotic disorders. As a result, in prison, PTSD, often the result of rape and violent assaults, can go undiagnosed or untreated because of inadequate treatment resources, fear of stigmatization, and lack of anonymity and safety (Kupers, 1996).

At the same time, some aspects of prison life are intended to pose health risks to inmates. These mechanisms are part of a strategic ceremonial degradation of prisoners, meant to break their will and increase their submission. Vaughn and Smith (1999) list six forms of intentional ill-treatment in prison facilities: (1) the use of medical care to humiliate prisoners (e.g., invasive procedures that may not be necessary); (2) the withholding of medical care from prisoners with HIV and AIDS; (3) the withholding of medical care from other prisoners; (4) the subjection of inmates to sleep deprivation and extreme temperature changes; (5) the use of dental care as a means of torture; and (6) the falsification of prisoners' medical records.

These health risks are common in all prisons, but they may not be as common in some prisons as in others, and they may not be as consciously intended in all cases. Still, prisons are not designed to ensure the well-being of prisoners; prisons are run with efficiency—not prisoners' health—in mind. And so it seems safe to say that at least some penal health-care providers may violate their professional ethics from time to time.

Psychological Effects

Not all crimes are violent, but violent crimes are most likely to make news and remain in our minds. Violent crimes can shatter people's lives. As well, such crimes may create "(a) diminished faith in a free economy and in business leaders, (b) loss of confidence in political institutions, processes and leaders, and (c) erosion of public morality" (Moore and Mills, 2001: 54).

At the societal level, violent crimes breed fear and wear down neighbourhood cohesion. People grow suspicious of one another; in turn, increased isolation and social distance reinforce prejudicial stereotypes based on race, gender, and age. As the US National Research Council (1994: 5–6) concluded, "If frightened citizens remain locked in their homes instead of enjoying public spaces, there is a loss of public and community life, as well as a loss of 'social capital'—the family and neighbourhood channels that transmit positive social values from one generation to the next."

There are harmful outcomes for the criminal, too, especially the psychological and social issues that must be dealt with after being labelled a "criminal." Sometimes, these harmful outcomes increase the likelihood that a criminal, after labelling, will become a repeat offender. A criminal record often takes away many opportunities. Convicts returning to the community from prison are sometimes greeted with unease and fear. Many cannot find jobs, or the jobs they can find are degrading and menial. At the least, an ex-convict carries the social stigma of having once been a criminal. Labelling leads people to expect further acts of (secondary) deviance, so they close their doors to the ex-convict. The closing of doors, in turn, may lead to the fulfillment of people's expectations of criminals, forcing some of them to return to illegal ways of earning a living.

Solutions to the Crime and Violence Problem

Reducing Crime

Communities are better off focusing on preventing crime rather than on punishing it. Investments in crime prevention include improving education, creating jobs, supplying daycare, upgrading low-income housing, increasing access to health care, and otherwise supporting poor families. All of these front-end strategies to prevent crime are likely to work better, in the long run, than trying to cure crime through imprisonment.

Other useful strategies of crime reduction include more use of probation, better gun control, and expanded treatment for drug addicts (Byrne and Taxman, 2006; Chandler et al., 2009). Reducing crime means addressing the social factors that are directly related to producing crime. This means reducing teenage pregnancies, high school dropout rates, youth unemployment, drug abuse, and the lack of job opportunities.

The Criminal Justice System

Part of the crime problem in many societies is that people feel dissatisfied with and distrustful of public officials and institutions—especially politicians, police, lawyers, and courts. Though people dislike crime and criminals, they also dislike and distrust people in authority.

Even though crime rates have been declining for over a decade, some people remain concerned about crime and victimization in Canada, not always because of media manipulation. Some concern reflects the inadequacy of the justice system to prevent or deter crime. The Canadian criminal justice system is largely based on the principle of **deterrence**. This principle assumes that most crimes are rational acts in which the offender weighs the imagined benefits of committing the crime against the chance of being caught and the severity of the punishment. This assumption may be unwarranted. The implication is that the threat of punishment will keep most people from breaking the law or from breaking it a second time.

However, a criminal justice system based on deterrence assumes that the likelihood of being punished is high—that is, that law enforcement agencies are efficient in catching offenders. This assumption also may be unwarranted. The deterrence approach ignores the subcultural (criminal) socialization that takes place in jails and prisons. And, worst of all, a deterrence-based approach to criminal justice fails to address the societal, economic, and political factors that encourage crime: unemployment, racial inequality, poverty, and the unequal distribution of resources and opportunities.

Deterrence A justice system based on deterrence assumes that crimes are rational acts in which the offender weighs the imagined benefits of committing the crime against the probability of being caught and the severity of the punishment. It assumes that the probability of being punished is high and that law enforcement agencies are competent and efficient in apprehending offenders.

The Victims' Rights Movement

In the past few decades, a victims' rights movement has emerged that seeks to expand the rights of crime victims (Joffee, 2009). This grew out of the feminist movement, in particular, in response to domestic violence and sexual abuse.

All of Canada's 13 provinces and territories have now set up a victims' bill of rights that is similar to statutes enacted by other jurisdictions worldwide. While the precise rights vary from one jurisdiction to another, they all include access to information throughout the trial; the right to file a victim-impact statement at sentencing; compensatory damages for victimization; offender restitution; and notification of applications for release (Department of Justice, 2012).

Though these are not binding "rights," they serve as guidelines for judicial officers to keep in mind as they conduct their cases. Only in Manitoba are victims' rights rigorously enforced in the legislation and is a procedure for filing complaints in place should those rights be violated (Canadian Resource Centre for Victims of Crime, 2006).

Some critics have suggested that by giving the injured party an equal voice in the criminal justice process, the movement has mainly led to demands for harsher and more punitive verdicts. So, while pretending to speak for crime victims, some groups—mainly a subset of the conservative "get tough on crime" proponents—are more concerned about lobbying for more severe penalties than in achieving some form of closure (Sanborn, 2001).

Chapter Summary

Within the Criminal Code, many different kinds of crime are specified. Some are crimes considered harmful by most people, such as murder, armed robbery, extortion, arson, sexual assault, and kidnapping. Generally, there is widespread agreement in Canadian society—and in most other societies—that these behaviours are wrong and should be harshly punished. In contrast, there are also crimes—like the possession of marijuana—over which people disagree to such an extent that the law has, in effect, lost control. Today, in Canada, police do not arrest people for possession of marijuana if they have only a small amount, and the federal government is currently expanding access to medicinal marijuana.

Then there are the more standard or common crimes. Most people consider them wrong but do not wish to debate or increase the severity of punishment. These include offences against property such as breaking and entering, automobile theft, and shoplifting; minor assaults; drunk driving; and white-collar offences such as embezzlement and fraud. All these offences have a victim or (as with drunk driving) run a serious risk of harming someone.

Despite biases and errors in reporting, the data on crime are credible enough to permit several inferences. First, crimes against property have increased over the last 25 years, but the rates of homicide and other "serious" crimes have declined. Contrary to what we might hear in the media, there is no wave of violent crime sweeping through our towns and cities. Second, crimes of violence are rarely committed for gain; they often result from fights between spouses or friends. This is especially true when women are the victims. Men, more than women, are likely to be attacked by mere acquaintances or strangers. Third, crimes committed for gain—for example, drug peddling, solicitation for prostitution, illegal gambling, and extortion—are often tied (however indirectly) to organized crime.

Common, or street, criminals, as we have seen, tend to be young, poor men. The complex connection between these demographic variables and criminal behaviour is the result of the interaction of economic, social, and cultural variables. And, paradoxically, criminals are more likely to be victimized than non-criminals, largely because of the factors discussed in differential association theory.

Questions for Critical Thought

1. Some believe that the public views violent crimes as more conventional, and therefore more inevitable, than property crimes. Discuss this perception and its likely social consequences.
2. What factors increase a person's chances of becoming a criminal? Compare the ways theorists from different theoretical backgrounds might answer this question.
3. How does one's lifestyle affect one's risks of offending and victimization? What changes can be made by the government to reduce these risks?
4. The gender gap in crime is starting to close. Do you think this is due to an actual increase in female offending or to a decrease in leniency towards female offenders?
5. What programs or policies can be instituted to reduce the over-representation of Aboriginals in the criminal justice system?

6. What is the likely effect of social inequality on crimes of different types? How would you explain the effect on street crime? Would the same explanation work for white-collar crime? Domestic violence?

Recommended Readings

Barker, Jane. 2009. *Women and the Criminal Justice System: A Canadian Perspective.* Toronto: Edmond Montgomery Publications.

Finkelhor, David. 2008. *Childhood Victimization: Violence, Crime, and Abuse in the Lives of Young People.* New York: Oxford University Press.

Savage, Joanne. 2009. *The Development of Persistent Criminality.* New York: Oxford University Press.

Walker, Samuel, Cassia Spohn, and Miriam DeLone. 2011. *The Color of Justice: Race, Ethnicity, and Crime in America.* Belmont, CA: Wadsworth Publishing.

8

Addictions

Michael Blann/Thinkstock

Introduction

We are used to hearing, and even using, the word "addiction" to refer to behaviour that is uncontrollable, socially disapproved, and potentially harmful. For example, people tend to think of alcoholics or drug addicts as those who cannot stay away from alcohol or drugs, despite the harm such substances do to their bodies and their social relationships.

More recently, other socially disapproved behaviours, such as excessive sex, shopping, Internet use, or overeating, have emerged as addictions. So far, there has been too little research on any of these topics to justify their discussion here, and it is unclear whether they should even be included in a chapter on addictions.

Perhaps they are not addictions—just habits, hobbies, minor sins, or what people once referred to as "personal weaknesses." The label "addictions" implies they are equally as significant as other behaviours considered addictive, and should thus be dealt with medically. Even if we think these are symptoms that can be treated, we wonder if they should be called "addictions" or "obsessions," terms that imply different sets of symptoms and treatments.

These questions are especially pressing with respect to gambling addiction, or problem gambling, which has come closest to proving itself as a new form of addiction (Griffiths, 2009). We begin this chapter with a brief discussion of addiction, then consider problem gambling (or compulsive gambling, or gambling addiction), alcohol, tobacco, and illicit drug abuse.

Addiction

The medical definition of **addiction**, based on criteria used by the American Psychiatric Association (DSM-IV) and the World Health Organization (ICD-10), has seven criteria. Deciding whether a person has an alcohol or drug addiction, therefore, requires asking and answering questions in only seven categories.

In the DSM-IV definition, the frequency of drug or alcohol use is not taken into consideration, whether once a month or once an hour. The issue is whether you have trouble controlling your use and if negative consequences arise whenever you use the substance.

Why is addiction a social problem? Alternatively, what turns this personal trouble into a public issue? In part, the answer is that the *social effects of addiction*—whether to drugs, alcohol, or (as we will see) gambling—lead to health consequences for addicts and their loved ones, decreased productivity at work, and the cost of treating and "fixing" the addicts. In addition, crime and safety issues are also at stake (Lozgacheva, 2008).

Addiction Socially disapproved behaviour that is uncontrollable, repetitious, and possibly harmful.

Addictive Gambling

Certain factors in our society, our communities, and our families predispose people to having gambling problems or gambling addictions. However, before we look at these factors, let us define and measure problem gambling.

Problem gambling is behaviour on a continuum, ranging from non-gamblers to recreational gamblers to problem gamblers (Hodgins et al., 2008; Derevensky and Gupta, 2004; Williams et al., 2012). In any population, a fraction will progress across this continuum.

OWNING MAHOWNY

This 2003 film portrays the gambling addiction that threatens to destroy the life of Toronto banker Dan Mahowny (Philip Seymour Hoffman).

How widespread is this problem and why should we care? In Canada, 2.4 per cent of Canadian adults are affected by moderate to severe problem gambling (Hodgins et al., 2008). In Canada, problem gambling rates differ based on the time in question and the province, ranging from 6.5 per cent in 1996 in New Brunswick to 0.8 per cent in 2008 in Ontario (ibid.). While Quebec, Nova Scotia, and Prince Edward Island have consistently reported low rates of problem gambling, Alberta, New Brunswick, and British Columbia all fare much worse. In addition, 3.5 per cent of university students are at risk of becoming problem gamblers, and 4 per cent of university students are flagged as probable pathological gamblers (Pascual-Leone et al., 2011). While the estimates vary, they suggest that one Canadian adult in 50 has a serious gambling problem. This means that, in a population of 35 million Canadians, of whom 80 per cent are over age 20, there are roughly 481,000 Canadians with a gambling problem (Statistics Canada, 2012).

Table 8.1 is used to measure problem or addictive gambling. To gain some idea about the nature of the problem created by problem gambling, consider the items that make up this index.

The chief difference between the general measure of addiction (e.g., to drugs, alcohol) and the measure of problem gambling is that physiological effects can be detected in drug or alcohol addiction that can't be detected in gambling addiction. Conceivably, with

TABLE 8.1	Are You a Compulsive Gambler? 20 Questions

Gamblers Anonymous is an organization seeking to help people with a gambling addiction. Those who meet the criteria of having a compulsive gambling problem will answer "yes" to at least seven of the questions below:

1. Did you ever lose time from work or school due to gambling?
2. Has gambling ever made your home life unhappy?
3. Did gambling affect your reputation?
4. Have you ever felt remorse after gambling?
5. Did you ever gamble to get money with which to pay debts or otherwise solve financial difficulties?
6. Did gambling cause a decrease in your ambition or efficiency?
7. After losing did you feel you must return as soon as possible and win back your losses?
8. After a win did you have a strong urge to return and win more?
9. Did you often gamble until your last dollar was gone?
10. Did you ever borrow to finance your gambling?
11. Have you ever sold anything to finance gambling?
12. Were you reluctant to use "gambling money" for normal expenditures?
13. Did gambling make you careless of the welfare of yourself or your family?
14. Did you ever gamble longer than you had planned?
15. Have you ever gambled to escape worry, trouble, boredom or loneliness?
16. Have you ever committed, or considered committing, an illegal act to finance gambling?
17. Did gambling cause you to have difficulty in sleeping?
18. Do arguments, disappointments, or frustrations create within you an urge to gamble?
19. Did you ever have an urge to celebrate any good fortune by a few hours of gambling?
20. Have you ever considered self-destruction or suicide as a result of your gambling?

Source: Gamblers Anonymous, at: <www.gamblersanonymous.org/ga/content/20-questions>.

brain-imaging research, we will eventually find similar effects within the brain's pleasure centres. At present, the problem gambling measure focuses more on financial and social outcomes.

Gambling has become a major global industry in the last 20 years, and it continues to grow rapidly (Moodie and Hastings, 2009). Gambling is advertised everywhere as a source of fun and recreation. What's more, national, provincial, state, and local governments promote gambling to raise their own revenues. They appear to reason that people are going to gamble anyway, so government should take a percentage in taxes. Like alcohol and drugs, gambling has historically been a major source of revenue for organized crime. Thus, in the second half of the twentieth century, many governments legalized and promoted gambling in order to obtain a share of the profits. Some of this money is reinvested in "public goods," which include research on problem gambling.

Gambling has become a *public* health issue in the usual sense: it has social causes and health implications (Afifi et al., 2010). Gambling is not merely the expression of a personal taste, individual psychopathology, or genetic inclination. It is socially learned behaviour—through observation, experimentation, reward, and emulation, or through the modelling and example of social role models. In fact, gambling is often learned in families during childhood (McComb et al., 2009). Research shows that children of problem gamblers are seven times more likely to report their own problem gambling in early adulthood. Adolescents with siblings or extended family members with gambling problems also report a higher prevalence of problem gambling in adulthood (McComb and Sabiston, 2010).

The Canadian Press/Corner Brook Western Star/Gary Kean

It's not the sort of issue most families would want made public, but the Pierceys say that sharing the story behind their 33-year-old daughter Susan's suicide could help others dealing with the scourge of compulsive gambling. They say her 10-year obsession with video lottery terminals—an addiction that cost her and her family more than $100,000—played a significant role in her recent suicide.

Classic WORKS

BOX 8.1   **Howard Becker's *Outsiders* (1963)**

Born, raised, and trained in Chicago, sociologist Howard Becker spent most of his professional life in the Chicago area. There, he learned the characteristic Chicago style of ethnographic sociology from Everett Hughes and other masters of the practice. Also, as a professional jazz musician, Becker gained insights into the "outsiders"—jazz musicians and marijuana smokers—he described in *Outsiders*, the book that made him famous.

In *Outsiders*, Howard Becker set the groundwork for labelling theory, as it is known today. Becker notes, "Social groups create deviance by making rules whose infraction constitutes deviance, and by applying these rules to particular people and labeling them as outsiders" (1963: 9). Deviance is thus the result of a dominant group—insiders—devising and applying moral rules to less powerful groups of "outsiders." These groups often respond by further entrenching themselves in "secondary deviation," including deviant careers and deviant subcultures.

This is not a book about the reasons people smoke marijuana or commit any other deviant act. The causes of deviance may be unknowable or unimportant, compared to their consequences. Also, Becker wants us to focus attention, instead, on the social context that labels people deviant.

A key point in *Outsiders* is that we must pay as much attention to the rule *enforcer* as we do to the rule *violator*. Instead of asking, "Why are they deviant?" we should ask, "Why do we label such behaviour as deviant, and with what consequences?" Doing so removes the assumption of fault, blame, dysfunction, or illness. The pleasures of smoking marijuana or playing jazz or stealing cars may remain unclear to people who forgo these activities. However, sociologists have to assume the actors' motives "make sense," though we cannot necessarily understand them or identify with them.

Labelling The process of defining and treating others as deviant. Labelling theory explores the effects of negative labels on people's self-conceptions and is interested in the development of a "deviant identity." Social reactions of condemnation and criminalization can lead actors to alter their individual characteristics and to adopt the values of their labelled identity.

Tactics commonly used in the general society, as well as in the gambling environment, contribute to gambling problems. Games—such as slot machines or video lottery terminals (VLTs)—are designed to get us to bet more than we planned to, using speed, noise, flashing lights, and slanted information. As well, advertising and other mass media messages shape our views about gambling by normalizing it and making gambling seem cool, fun, and desirable (Valentine, 2009). It's possible to gamble online 24 hours a day, seven days a week. Finally, casino promotions and incentives offer free buses, meals, drinks, and hotel accommodation for high rollers who play (and lose) often.

Most of the work on gambling by social scientists takes a psychological approach: it focuses on the thinking and behaviour of people without considering their social environment. It views addictive gambling as the result of cognitive distortions—bad thinking—about the odds of winning and the value of chasing losses (Kuo et al., 2009). The goal of psychological counselling is to get gamblers to think differently about what they are doing and to act differently, whatever their personal inclinations.

This is not to deny the importance of psychological factors in gambling behaviour. A large body of research has identified links between gambling and mood disorders, including depression, anxiety, and bipolar disorder (Di Nicola et al., 2010). Current estimates show that 60 to 80 percent of problem gamblers experience depression, anxiety disorders, and suicide ideation (Delfabbro, 2012). This suggests that there is a genetic base to problem gambling, just as there is to these mood disorders. Equally, research has found that problem gambling is often linked to people who are drug users, who are impulsive or display anti-social behaviour, who are lonely, who drink excessively, and/or who display excessive or inappropriate anger, which leads us to wonder if gambling promotes or capitalizes on the display of violence. Research also shows that approximately 15–20 per cent of problem gamblers are affected by substance abuse, while 67 per cent are smokers (ibid.).

However, this model places the burden of "responsible gambling" on the shoulders of the gambler, citing personality weaknesses or cognitive distortion as the primary cause of gambling problems (Westphal, 2007). Policy-makers, industry representatives, and the public all share this viewpoint. It is reflected in everything from government gaming policies to gambling treatment and intervention programs.

Are Drugs and Alcohol Social Problems?

We can define a **drug** as any substance that causes a biochemical reaction in the body. However, law prohibits certain drugs that induce biochemical reactions (Moreno and Janda, 2009). What people define as a legal drug or an illegal drug usually depends less on its chemical properties—less on the reactions in your body—and more on surrounding economic, social, and political factors (Hogan, 2009).

In Canada, the use of legal drugs, such as alcohol, tobacco, and prescription medicine, is much more common than the use of illegal drugs, such as heroin, cocaine, and marijuana (Health Canada, 2012). In society, many people treat the use of illegal drugs as a major problem while ignoring the harm done by legal drugs. Society's response to drug use is, therefore, largely irrational. Some substances that harm public health, such as alcohol and tobacco, are welcomed or tolerated everywhere, yet others that may be less dangerous, such as marijuana, are often condemned and banned.

Our attitudes towards specific drugs vary over time and from one society to another. When social and cultural sensibilities shift, people start rejecting what they once accepted. Thus, we cannot understand drug attitudes and laws without a historical account that explains how and why the attitudes have evolved (McBride et al., 1998). The fluctuation in attitudes towards drug use has affected the delivery of care, as it functions on the basis of positive or negative views to the substance. For example, Chan, Stoove, and Reidpath (2008) found that patients with HIV/AIDS in Thailand failed to receive proper treatment owing to the nurses' view of them as "social cheaters," careless and harmful to society. Similarly, Galvani and Hughes (2010) reported that social workers' attitudes towards drug use vary depending on their colleagues' positions.

Examples of such attitudinal changes abound. Consider opium, from which morphine and heroin are derived. Opium was a commonly used painkiller until the early 1900s (Witters et al., 1992). From then on, opium and cocaine were thought to be dangerous and were subject to strict control, if not an outright ban. The reason was sociological, not pharmacological: that is, the chemical properties of the drugs did not change, only the public's opinion.

In this and other instances, a commonly used drug was restricted or criminalized when prevailing attitudes changed. The changes were rarely because of new medical research findings or because the drug was found to cause social problems. Often, as with cocaine and marijuana, the changes were because of new attitudes towards immigrants or racial minorities who were associated with the drug (Herzog et al., 2009). These changes, in turn, often reflected new economic and social concerns. Typically, these changes penalized the least powerful members of society.

Drug Any substance that causes a biochemical reaction in the body.

TABLE 8.2   Selected Addiction Statistics

Prevalence and incidence
- One in 10 Canadians 15 years of age and over reports symptoms consistent with alcohol or illicit drug dependence.
- 3.8 per cent of adults in Ontario are classified as having moderate or severe gambling problems.

Who is affected?
- Young people age 15–24 are more likely to report mental illness and/or substance-use disorders than other age groups.
- Overall, men are 2.6 times more likely than women to meet the criteria for substance dependence; 25 per cent of male drinkers are high-risk drinkers compared to 9 per cent of female drinkers.
- The average age drug use begins is 15.7 years old.

Alcohol Abuse
- Among Ontario grade 11 drinkers, 13 years was the average age of first exposure, and 14 years was the average age of first intoxication experience.
- More than 2,700 children are born each year with fetal alcohol spectrum disorder.
- Motor vehicle crashes, liver cirrhosis, suicides, esophageal cancer, and arrhythmias were the leading causes of alcohol-related deaths.

Drug Abuse
- 67 per cent street-involved youth in British Columbia reported having used crystal meth.
- Only about 3,000 of the estimated 400,000 people who use medical marijuana in Canada are licensed.
- 62 per cent of meth found in Japan is from Canada.

Cost to society of addictions
- Tobacco is responsible for one-quarter of cancer deaths in Ontario.
- $34 billion is the cost of mental illness and addictions to the Ontario economy.

Source: Centre for Addiction and Mental Health, Mental Health and Addiction Statistics, at: <www.camh.ca/en/hospital/about_camh/newsroom/for_reporters/Pages/addictionmentalhealthstatistics.aspx>.

Drug abuse This concept begins with the notion of excessive or inappropriate drug use resulting in social, psychological, and/or physiological impairments. It stems from a chronic physical and psychological compulsion to continue taking a drug in order to avoid unpleasant withdrawal symptoms.

In the same vein, what constitutes **drug abuse** depends largely on what people define as an "acceptable" drug at a particular time and place. Overall, trends in alcohol, cigarette, and cannabis (marijuana) use are similar in the United States and Canada. One study shows that adolescent alcohol use in Ontario and throughout the US—perhaps throughout Canada—has steadily decreased since the late 1970s (Dauvergne, 2009). Cigarette and cannabis use peaked in the late 1970s, decreased throughout the 1980s, and then began to increase dramatically in the early 1990s. The same study shows that cocaine use was consistently higher in the United States and LSD use consistently higher in Ontario over the period 1975–95. Similar trends in the use of alcohol and cigarettes in the US and Ontario suggest similar shifts in attitudes over time. In Canada and the US, marijuana is the most-used illicit drug. In the US, the number of users increased from 5.8 to 6.9 per cent, with a similar trend in Canada (SAMHSA, 2010). Different trends in the use of less common drugs—cocaine and LSD—may reflect deeper cultural differences or national differences in drug policy or availability (Hall and Pacula, 2003).

CANADIAN researchers

BOX 8.2   **Scott Schieman, University of Toronto**

Scott Schieman, Canada Research Chair in the Social Contexts of Health, explores how stress emerges in the intersection between home and work. More specifically, Schieman focuses on the relationships between job status, family roles, stress, and health in an era of rising technology (i.e., Internet, smart phone, and other related technologies). In particular, Schieman explores how different stressors are associated with high-status positions and roles in the workplace. His paradoxical theory, the "stress of higher status," argues that job authority does not benefit health outcomes. In fact, authority often leads to greater stress, interpersonal conflict, and work–family conflict, which he argues reduces the net benefit of holding a higher-status position in the workforce.

In a 2009 piece in the *American Sociological Review* titled, "When Work Interferes with Life: Work-Nonwork Interference and the Influence of Work Related Demands and Resources," Schieman finds that a very high percentage of working men and women report that their jobs interfere with their non-work life. In support of the stress of the higher-status model, Schieman argues that "individuals with a strong commitment and emotional allegiance to work encounter more frequent role blurring that, in turn, increases work-nonwork interference" (Schieman et al., 2009: 986). This pattern, he argues, is very prevalent among high-status workers.

Schieman's piece is an important contribution in sociology because it encourages a discussion about how contemporary job demands shape our lives in today's changing work culture. While he deals with more-*extreme* forms of mental illness, he demonstrates how prevalent stress can be for *all* people in Canadian society—even the very affluent.

Sources: Scott Schieman, Melissa A. Milkie, and Paul Glavin. "When Work Interferes with Life: Work-Nonwork Interference and the Influence of Work-Related Demands and Resources," *American Sociological Review* 74, 6 (2009): 966–88; and CRC profile.

As we have seen, the concepts of alcohol and drug "abuse" begin with a notion of extreme or unsuitable use that results in social, psychological, and physiological harm. There are two aspects to this concept of abuse: objective and subjective. The objective aspect relies on physical, mental, or social evidence that the use of a drug harms the individual and society. For example, drug abuse may lead to **drug dependency**—that is, to the routine need for a drug for physical reasons (e.g., to avoid withdrawal symptoms) or for psychological reasons (e.g., to keep a sense of well-being) (Hathaway et al., 2009).

Related to drug dependency is the notion of "tolerance." **Tolerance** refers to the decreased effectiveness of any given drug because of repeated use. People dependent on drugs and alcohol experience increasing tolerance to the substance over time, meaning they need larger and larger doses of it to get the same effects. Typically, people who do not drink on a regular basis have low levels of tolerance to alcohol and may feel the effect of intoxication after just one or two drinks. Often, occasional drinkers are labelled as being unable to "hold their liquor." However, people who can withstand large amounts of liquor are not immune to its effects. They have simply had more experience drinking heavily.

Medicalization and the Transformation of a Problem

Increasingly, over the past century, we have seen a tendency to "medicalize" addictions to drugs, alcohol, and even gambling. **Medicalization** is the process through which behaviours—especially those formerly defined as deviant, sinful, or immoral—are

Drug dependency The routine need for a drug for physiological and/or psychological reasons.

Tolerance A symptom of repeated and frequent drug use. It refers to the decreased effectiveness of any given drug.

Medicalization The process through which behaviours are reconceived as instances of illness and are deemed no longer sinful, since they are outside personal control.

INTERNATIONAL **COMPARISONS**

BOX 8.3 | Internet Addiction

Societal change brings with it a whole range of contemporary, novel addictions that have important implications for the well-being of people. One recent global phenomenon is Internet addiction, defined as an inability to control the urge to access the Internet, to the extent where it causes personal distress and impairment (Shaw and Black, 2008). Internet users around the world are at risk of developing this addiction, though prevalence rates vary across countries. An analysis of Dutch adolescents revealed that 3.7 per cent are potentially addicted to Internet usage (Kuss et al., 2013).

Another study on Internet addiction in public school, private school, and university students found that 17.6 per cent of students (aged 12–25) in Doha, Qatar, reported problematic Internet usage (Bener and Bhugra, 2013). Of these students in Qatar, problematic Internet usage was positively associated with being male, having Qatari nationality, having a non-working mother, regularly eating fast food, and getting a higher score on the Beck's Depression Inventory. Another study looking at high school students living in rural and urban regions in

Greece found a 3.1 per cent prevalence rate of Internet addiction (Stavropoulos et al., 2013). In this Greek study, students who were male, lived in an urban region of Greece, and were academic-track students had the greatest risk of developing an Internet addiction.

A study looking at Internet usage for middle and high school students in Seoul, South Korea, found a 10.7 per cent prevalence rate of students at high risk of developing an Internet addiction (Park et al., 2008). Family dynamics played a big role in how these students handled their Internet usage and their potential addiction.

A direct comparison between Chinese and US university students found that Chinese students have a much higher prevalence rate of Internet addiction (14 per cent heavily addicted and 64 per cent mildly addicted) compared to US students (4 per cent heavily addicted and 23 per cent mildly addicted) (Zhang et al., 2008). A possible reason for this is that China's rapid industrialization is still recent and the Internet has the appeal of novelty, while in the US people have been exposed to the Internet much longer.

reconceived as instances of illness; that is, they are deemed no longer sinful, since they are outside personal control (Murphy, 2009; Suissa, 2007).

This process of medicalization, which we discuss further in Chapter 9, has become increasingly important in defining social problems, given the triumph of science over religion in the past century and a half. Where alcohol abusers were once thought of as sinners or moral weaklings and subjected to scorn or criticism, with medicalization they became sick people in need of treatment (Warden et al., 2004). This was a new way of controlling the same deviant behaviour, but control was now put in the hands of doctors rather than of clergy. In the end, medicalization is a means by which the medical realm extends its influence in society. Medicalization temporarily excuses the "affliction" and raises the power of doctors in society (Valverde, 1998). Medicalization views illness to be socially constructed, bestowing on doctors, psychologists, and criminal justice lawyers, and the like the power to label people as sick or ill (Schierenbeck, 2010).

The redefinition of alcohol abuse as a disease is not merely a process of medicalization. The temperance and prohibition movements of the last two centuries also reflected deeper cultural themes, such as the importance of purity, hygiene, and health. The specific targets of historical temperance movements have varied over time and have included alcohol, drugs, smoking, prostitution, and homosexuality (Wagner, 1995). The common element was an obsession with cleanliness (also purity, virtue, and hygiene) versus dirt (also sin, wickedness, and filth). Below the surface of this cultural dichotomy raged struggles between clean and dirty classes (middle and upper classes versus the working classes), clean and dirty communities (native-born versus immigrant), clean and dirty subcultures (rural versus urban), clean and dirty sexes (female versus male) (Herd, 1984). These struggles provide excellent examples of the processes of exclusion that we discussed in Chapter 2.

A century later, groups and professions still fight over the right to define drug use and abuse. Currently, those who use alcohol in moderation are considered "clean" but those who use illicit street drugs are considered "dirty" and part of a **drug subculture**. An example can be seen in current views about crack cocaine, spread mainly by the police and religious or moral leaders in their "war on drugs." Three prevailing views are that crack is instantly addictive, that it leads to drug binges, and that it inevitably ruins lives (Reinarman and Levine, 1997). Recent reports have shown that non-users believe that crack users have a weak character, are ignorant and untrustworthy, and are willing to have sex for drugs and/or money (Mateu-Gelabert et al., 2005). Poor people are said to be more likely than others to use crack cocaine, while middle- and upper-class people are more likely to use powder cocaine (Provine, 2011). Because of crack's class connotation, the label "crack head," "junkie," "dope head," or "dope fiend" is intensely stigmatizing (Mateu-Gelabert et al., 2005).

> **Drug subculture** A group of people who share common attitudes, beliefs, and behaviours surrounding drug use. These attitudes and beliefs differ significantly from those of most people in the wider society.

Social and Physical Characteristics of Addictions

Alcohol

Like most other drugs, alcohol is relatively harmless when used moderately and responsibly. However, it is one of the most destructive substances when abused (Murray et al., 2010). People drink alcohol to achieve its chemical effects: to relax, smooth social events, reduce tension, and slow down perceptual, cognitive, and motor functioning (Vaughan at al., 2009). The goal of drinking, then, is to escape from the speed, boredom, stress, or frustration of everyday life and, often, to do so in the company of others, as part of a shared, sociable haze. Impaired judgement often accompanies these chemical changes (Kuntsche et al., 2010). From 2010 to 2011, the rate of heavy drinking among Canadians increased from 17.3 to 19.0 per cent (Statistics Canada, 2012). Although males reported heavier alcohol consumption than females, there has been a general increase in heavy drinking.

Many people drink responsibly, remaining below their tolerance limit, practising restraint around minors, and giving up their driving duties to a designated driver. Other drinkers are not so responsible. As Figure 8.1 shows, men are much more likely than women to drink heavily. Although women drink more responsibly than men (Carey and DeMartini, 2010), they are more likely to use other chemical substances to cope with stress (Statistics Canada, 2012).

Furthermore, higher education exercises a moderating influence on heavy drinking. Canadian men with post-secondary education (33.7 per cent) or a university degree (25.7 per cent) are less likely to drink heavily than those with less than a high school education (36.2 per cent) (Health Canada, 2008). However, paradoxically, 90 per cent of Canadian university students drink alcohol on a regular basis (Tamburri, 2012). This suggests that the positive effect of education on healthy living emerges only later in the life course.

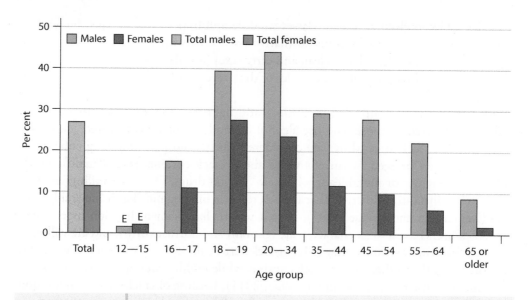

According to data from the recent Canadian Addiction Survey, "past year use" peaks between the ages of 18 and 24, with about 90 per cent of those in this age range consuming alcohol within the past year (Adlaf et al., 2005a). According to the 2011 OSDUHS Drug Use Report, about one-quarter of the students—approximately 250,000—reported binge drinking during the previous school year (OSDUHS, 2011). Students who do not live with their families, who are from the Atlantic region, or who value recreational activities such as parties and athletics are more likely than average to engage in risky levels of consumption (Adlaf et al., 2005b). As well, 10 per cent of the students reported incidents of alcohol-related assault, 9.8 per cent reported alcohol-related sexual harassment, and 14.1 per cent reported having unplanned sexual encounters while under the influence of alcohol (ibid.).

Problem drinking extends well beyond Canadian youth. This is alarming, considering that alcohol consumption in 2010 was associated with around 200 different diseases and injuries, ranging from simple accidents to more serious outcomes, such as assault and even suicide (Shield et al., 2013).

There is also evidence that job loss—and other widespread economic inequalities—can lead to greater alcohol consumption, especially among men and middle-aged groups (Mulia et al., 2008).

Tobacco

Tobacco is Canada's other major legal drug. Like alcohol, nicotine—the psychoactive substance in tobacco—is highly addictive; it is a drug to be blamed for many health problems and a costly habit, both for the individual and for society.

SMOKING IS PROHIBITED WITHIN
6 METRES OF OPENINGS INTO
THIS BUILDING INCLUDING
DOORS AND WINDOWS THAT
OPEN AND ANY AIR INTAKES

CAPILANO
UNIVERSITY

BYLAW 7792

The Canadian Press/Jonathan Hayward

A "no smoking" sign posted outside a Capilano University building in North Vancouver is part of a larger, ongoing concerted public health effort to reduce tobacco use as well as reduce the risk of exposure to second-hand smoke across Canada.

Tobacco remains widely popular, though a concerted public health movement has led to a steady decline in tobacco use in recent years. According to the 2011 Canadian Community Health Survey, roughly 5.8 million Canadians, or 20 per cent of the total population, reported smoking on an occasional basis. This number was down from about 26 per cent in 2001 (Statistics Canada, 2012).

Most adult smokers develop their habit of smoking before the age of 20. As with alcohol, men are more likely than women to use tobacco, although the gender gap has been narrowing for the past quarter-century. According to Figure 8.2, 22.3 per cent of men are regular smokers, compared to 17.5 per cent of women. In other words, it is far less common today for Canadians to smoke on a regular basis. However, rates of casual smoking have increased for both men and women. Between 2001 and 2011, both sexes reported a rise of "light" smoking, though this increase was more prominent for women (from 51.2 per cent to 62.6 per cent) than for men (from 36.7 per cent to 43 per cent) (Statistics Canada, 2012).

And like alcohol, tobacco smoking is influenced by social factors. A study of more than 22,000 Ontario high school students found that teenagers are at increased risk for smoking if they (1) have smoking friends, (2) have smoking family members, and/or (3) attend a school with a high senior-student smoking rate (Leatherdale et al., 2005). European data also suggest that smoking is more common among teenagers in single-parent and blended-family households than among those in intact families. The researchers suggest that these trends may be due to lower levels of attachment, a tendency towards rebellion, and less parental supervision in stepfamily and lone-parent homes (Griesbach et al., 2003).

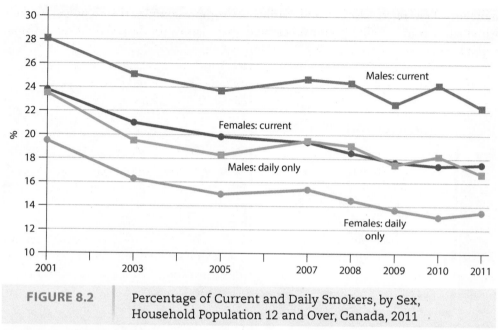

FIGURE 8.2 | Percentage of Current and Daily Smokers, by Sex, Household Population 12 and Over, Canada, 2011

Source: Janz (2012), at: <www.statcan.gc.ca/pub/82-624-x/2012001/article/11676-eng.htm>.

Among adolescents who experiment with smoking, the development of a smoking habit is positively correlated with poor academic performance, parental smoking, and having more than half of one's friends smoking. It is negatively correlated with attending a school with a clear anti-smoking policy and having confidence in one's ability to succeed academically (Karp et al., 2005).

Illicit Drug Abuse

Much of what we have said about alcohol abuse applies equally to drug abuse. In general, factors that reduce the likelihood of drug use and abuse include strong family bonds, which reduce the use of all illegal drugs except marijuana (Ellickson et al., 1999; Livosa, 2010); a strong religious commitment (Yarnold, 1999; Borras et al., 2010); and normative boundaries that separate adolescents who occasionally use drugs socially from those who use them often or in isolation (Warner et al., 1999; Livosa, 2010).

Marriage and parenthood are also important influences (Liu and Kaplan, 1999). Married people and parents who adhere to conventional values may use illegal drugs when they come under stress in order to control that stress so that they can continue to conform to dominant values. The drugs reduce stress in a private and non-disruptive fashion (ibid.). However, in a longitudinal study by Leonard and Homish (2005), spouses were more likely to stop using marijuana (as well as other drugs) once they entered marriage. Other research finds that husbands were more likely to use the substance if their wives did, but there was no significant reversal pattern, which suggests a stronger influence of the wives' behaviour on that of their husbands (Heinz et al., 2009).

Factors that increase the likelihood of drug use include friends who are users, parents who use tobacco or alcohol, and a history of parental abuse (Bensley et al., 1999). Working conditions also make a difference. Workers with low cognitive ability make

DRUGSTORE COWBOY

A group of drug addicts, led by charismatic Bob (Matt Dillon) travel the country, robbing drug stores in hopes of feeding their addictions.

more use of cigarettes, alcohol, and marijuana the more complex their jobs are; workers with high cognitive ability, on the other hand, make less use of these substances the more complex their jobs are (Oldham and Gordon, 1999).

Even more than alcohol use, drug use is a learned behaviour that depends on social opportunities and inclusion in social occasions where drugs are being used. Opportunities to use drugs are more common as youths get older. The likelihood of trying drugs, given the opportunity, also increases with age. Ethnic and gender differences in adolescent drug use correspond to differences in opportunities to try drugs with acquaintances, dating partners, and even parents (Moon et al., 1999).

Males are two to three times more likely to develop a drug abuse disorder than females, but this may be due to opportunity differences rather than vulnerability to using drugs (Becker and Hu, 2008). However, there is a greater addiction rate for women than for men once they are exposed to a substance, particularly nicotine.

In Canada, the overall rates of illicit drug use are low. Nevertheless, drug use is prominent among certain populations, including people who are economically disadvantaged, who are in jail or in communities with other social problems, or who suffer from mental problems.

Substance Abuse among the Aboriginal Population

For thousands of years after arriving in North America, Aboriginal peoples lived in many small communities or bands that varied widely but had certain features in common. Notably, a strong sense of community and communal cohesion, with cultural custodians standing guard over the group's traditions, promoted the sharing and defence of group values.

Selective use of psychoactive substances had long been a part of the customs and rituals of the Aboriginal population in North America (French, 2008). However, contact with the Europeans severely affected Aboriginal culture and its practices. Forced European assimilation contributed to widespread social, health, and economic problems on First Nation reserves and in northern Aboriginal communities, as well as among Aboriginal people living in urban areas (Johnston et al., 2008). This has led to the use of illicit substances as a means of escape rather than as an intricate part of a cultural tradition.

In addition to living a difficult life, many Aboriginal people suffer from trauma related to sexual abuse and family violence; many also have parents who abuse substances. These factors, as well as others, increase the likelihood of substance abuse. Alcoholism and addiction is common among Native Americans (French, 2008). For example, 62.5 per cent of Aboriginals reported using illicit drugs, most commonly cannabis and cocaine, during the past calendar year (Currie et al., 2013). In addition, the age of first alcohol use has dropped in the Native population over the past 50 years (Kunitz, 2008).

The high prevalence of drug use correlates with poor academic performance, stress, and delinquent behaviour in Aboriginal communities. Mehrabadi et al. (2008) found that female Aboriginal survivors of sexual abuse in Canada are especially prone to using illicit drugs. They are also vulnerable to serious emotional and physical health problems (ibid).

One study found that treatment programs benefited Aboriginal people, decreasing their alcohol intake, arrests, and suicide rate (Evans et al., 2006). Still, in order to improve, a patient must want to get better and be willing make the necessary behavioural changes to ensure continued improvement. The method of treatment that has worked best includes addiction counselling by other Native people, sharing Aboriginal experiences, relearning the traditional culture, and practising Aboriginal rituals (Munro and Allan, 2011). Using this approach, the people of the Alkali Lake Reserve saw the percentage of alcoholism in their community drop from 95 per cent to 5 per cent in 10 years (McCormick, 2000).

Theoretical Perspectives on Addiction

TABLE 8.3	Theoretical Perspectives
THEORY	**MAIN POINTS**
Structural Functionalism	• Alcohol and drug abuse results from the social structure's influence on the individual. • Drug and alcohol use is common because it serves social functions.
Social Disorganization Theory	• Institutions that traditionally discourage deviant behaviour are rendered less effective by rapid social change. • Breakdown in community norms and traditions deprives people of a sense of meaning and moral guidance. • Relearning or re-establishing traditional institutions can reduce substance abuse.
Merton's (1957) Strain (Anomie) Theory	• Drug and alcohol abuse is the result of the incongruence between culturally defined goals and the socially approved means for attaining these goals (i.e., anomie). • One adaptation to this gap is to retreat (abandon efforts to achieve goals, escape reality via substance abuse).
Conflict Theory	• Alcohol and drug use affect different socio-economic groups differently. • Powerful capitalist members of society are in a position to define whether a substance is legal or illegal. • The poor tend to suffer harmful outcomes of substance abuse more than the rich due to labelling and the criminalization process.
Symbolic Interactionism	• The social meanings and values associated with drug and alcohol use and with the labels attached to people when they use these substances are the focus for understanding. • The term "alcoholic" is laden with negative characterizations, judgements, and stereotypes in a way that "social drinker" is not.

Structural Functionalism

Structural functionalists hold that alcohol and drug abuse, like all social problems, result from the way social structures influence the individual.

Some argue that recreational drug and alcohol use are common because these substances serve an important social function. For example, heavy alcohol use, for many people, seems compulsory on certain occasions—for example, Mardi Gras in New Orleans or Carnival in Rio de Janeiro or New Year's Eve anywhere—where it breaks down personal inhibitions and fosters conviviality. Structural functionalism also seeks to explain substance abuse. Two of the more influential camps within this perspective are social disorganization theory and anomie theory.

Social Disorganization Theory

Social disorganization theory argues that institutions that have traditionally acted to discourage deviant behaviours become less effective during times of rapid social change. Rapid changes cause norms and values to become unclear. Without traditional sources of moral guidance to restrain behaviour, deviancy—including drug and alcohol use—becomes more common.

We can usefully apply this perspective to Canada's Aboriginal population and its problem with addictive substances, especially alcohol. Forced off their traditional hunting lands and onto reserves by the arrival of whites, Aboriginal community norms and traditions broke down, speeded by the imposition of residential schooling. Alcohol abuse and suicide spread among Aboriginal peoples throughout the nineteenth and twentieth centuries. Few methods worked to stem this problem because most did not address the issue of social disorganization: the loss of traditional controls and values passed on by family, community, and religion. With the reversal of social disorganization through treatment, alcohol abuse has begun to subside.

Merton's Strain Theory

According to Merton (1957), the cause of excessive drinking and other substance abuse lies not in an absence of values and institutions but in the conflict between them. According to this theory, excessive drinking is driven by a conflict or paradox—a gap between culturally defined goals and socially approved means for reaching those goals.

Merton, using American society as his example, argues that one of the primary goals of that society is success, especially in getting money, material goods, and "the good life." Most people have been taught to value success. Yet social inequality ensures that most people will not succeed because they will not have access to the socially approved (that is, legal) means and resources that allow them to attain success—for example, higher education and good jobs. Merton calls this gap between goals and means "anomie." This state of anomie allows for various solutions, which Merton calls possible adaptations. They include what he calls ritualism, retreatism, rebellion, and innovation. Substance abuse results from adopting one such adaptation—retreatism.

However, the use of drugs and alcohol is not merely an individual adaptation; it is socially organized. Groups of people with higher levels of social capital, especially social network connections that offer them access to valued jobs, have less need for the numbing escapism that drugs and alcohol offer. Those exposed to adverse community-level conditions—poverty, unemployment, and other measures of social breakdown—are more likely to retreat from their harsh realities.

Conflict Theory

Conflict theorists focus largely on the labelling and criminalization processes. They note that, in a capitalist economy, the powerful members of society can define whether a substance is legal or illegal. The powerful are also able to criminalize drug use by the powerless through their control of the law and police activities.

Besides, they can benefit from widespread drug use even while they publicly reject it. Alcohol and tobacco, for example, are produced and sold by the powerful. Both of these billion-dollar industries are regulated but not considered illegal. Both also heavily brand and market their addictive products, reaping huge profits for wealthy stockholders while harming the heavy users, who tend to be poor. Conflict theories also note that banned substances are often forbidden not only because of their harmful pharmacological properties, but also for social and political reasons.

Symbolic Interactionism

Symbolic interactionists focus on the social meanings and values associated with alcohol and drug use and on the labels people attach to others when they use drugs.

What do you think of when you hear the term "alcoholic"? Does it bring to mind a person who cannot control the harmful effects of alcohol use? A person who is less educated, unemployed, and trapped in the lower socio-economic strata of society? Contrast that image with the "social drinker." Friendly "social drinking" is the drinking code of middle-class people in a modern, capitalist society. Some people not only drink in their free time, but often do so to have a good time (Carruthers, 1993). Social drinking is also seen in universities and on college campuses among large bodies of students. Drinking in social contexts depends on the environment and on the drinkers' age, gender, work, and other traits that create group cohesion. It is reported that drinking in social contexts decreases depression, makes people more sociable, and promotes greater acceptance in a social group (Baer, 2005). Yet only "alcoholics" and heavy drinkers are stigmatized and stereotyped in our society.

Social Consequences of Addictions

Crime and Violence

According to Criminal Intelligence Service Canada (2006: 8), "the illicit drug trade . . . is the most prominent criminal market for organized crime groups." For example, Vietnamese criminal organizations and the Hell's Angels motorcycle gang play major roles in the Canadian domestic marijuana trade, while Southwest Asian crime groups are especially active in heroin trafficking.

Drug use is strongly linked to other forms of deviant and even criminal activity, though the chain of cause and effect is often unclear. Prison inmates are 10 times more likely to be lifetime heroin users than the general population. Most inmates face difficulties with multiple drug addictions and overdoses. It is reported that 60 per cent of injecting drug users have a history of imprisonment (Kanato, 2008). This suggests a strong correlation between drug use and crime—a cycle that, for some, is difficult to break.

As alcohol is one of the most abused substances, its effects consistently show a positive correlation with physical assault. Livingston (2008) shows this correlation in a police-reported cross-sectional study. Markowitz (2005) estimates that raising beer taxes will decrease the probability of assault incidences but will have no effect on rape or robbery rates, as there is a lower correlation between these crimes and alcohol use.

Poverty and Income

Although alcohol use rates are higher among well-educated, high-income people than among poorly educated, low-income people, alcohol abuse and problem drinking are reported more often among the latter group (Spillane, 2008; Health Canada, 2008). It is difficult to distinguish whether poverty causes drug abuse or vice versa. This may reflect a vicious circle, with poverty leading to substance abuse and abuse, in turn, reinforcing joblessness and poverty (Mulia et al., 2008). Grinman et al. (2010) studied the prevalence of drug problems among homeless people in Toronto. They found a link between people with drug problems and irregular mental health statuses, but there was no correlation in physical health statuses. In addition, they found that 40 per cent of the studied population had used marijuana and 27 per cent had used cocaine within the past two years.

Racism

The "war on drugs," especially in the US but to a degree in Canada as well, has served to increase racial and class injustice by targeting the poor and racial minorities unduly. It has focused on drug users and street traffickers, not on others (such as money launderers) in the drug economy, and has credited their targets' drug abuse and criminality to moral weakness rather than to a loss of manufacturing jobs (Duster, 1997).

In the US, an inflated number of black Americans were arrested for criminal activity—59 per cent of all arrests for murders, 51 per cent for violent crimes, and 30 per cent for drug use (Martin et al., 2011). As these figure suggest, black Americans are disproportionately targeted for these crimes compared to other ethnic groups.

In short, the enforcement of laws against substance abuse reflects an undue bias against racial minorities that, in turn, reflects a biased focus on poor and working-class people or racism, or both (Coker, 2003).

Health Consequences of Addictions

Alcohol and Drug Abuse

By definition, substance *abuse* is bad for health, though the implications vary depending on the substance. Its impact will depend on various characteristics of the individuals, such as their size, sex, age, and physical fitness.

Health effects are not limited to the alcohol user, however. Pregnant women who drink may be placing their unborn children at risk. Fetal alcohol syndrome (FAS) is caused by prenatal exposure to alcohol and can result in facial abnormalities and stunted growth after birth. Fetal alcohol effects (FAE) have an incidence rate 5–10 times greater than FAS, but both are greater than Down's syndrome or spina bifida (Health Canada, 2012b). Roughly 1,000 babies per 370,000 babies are born with FAE each year in Canada, while 123–740 babies are born with FAS.

Health outcomes faced by users of illegal drugs include shortened lifespans, dietary irregularities, severe weight loss, vomiting, mucous membrane damage, and brain lesions. Among injection drug users, the risk of contracting HIV/AIDS from shared contaminated

LEAVING LAS VEGAS

Nicholas Cage won an Oscar for his turn as Ben, an alcoholic Hollywood screenwriter, in this 1995 film.

needles is especially high. With an 11.4 per cent increase in people with HIV and AIDS from 2008 to 2011, intravenous drug use (IDU) is the second most common cause of HIV/AIDS, as the prevalence of IDU is 16.9 per cent (Public Health Agency of Canada, 2012).

These practices are particularly common in prisons. Even women drug offenders are found to engage in many high-risk drug and sexual behaviours while in prison; on release, they are a major public health risk. Criminal justice policies, grounded in deterrence and based on imprisonment, may be contributing to the spread of HIV infection in the wider society.

Drug abuse can also lead to mental health problems. White and Labouvie (1994) have shown that drug users are more likely to develop anxiety disorders, phobias, depression, and anti-social personalities. It is speculated, for example, that continual consumption of cannabis impairs oculomotor control, especially tasks requiring our saccade system, such as reading (Johnston et al., 2011). In 2010, it was reported that heavy cannabis users (use cannabis every day or more than once a day) had a 19.1 per cent likelihood of developing anxiety and mood disorders as opposed to the 8.7 per cent in abstainers (do not use cannabis) (Cheung et al., 2010). Suicide is also more common among drug users, especially adolescents. Marijuana, the illicit drug of choice among teenagers, has been associated with short-term memory loss, impaired learning, loss of motivation, and emotional deficits.

Tobacco

Tobacco smoking, despite decades of public health warnings, remains the primary cause of lung cancer, which is the leading cause of cancer death. In 2006, over 19,000 Canadians were expected to die from lung cancer and 23,000 were expected to develop the disease.

Another 12,000 were expected to die of cancer of the mouth, larynx, esophagus, stomach, bladder, kidney, and pancreas, all of which have been linked to cigarette and cigar smoking (Statistics Canada, 2006). Further, smoking can lead to elevated risk of asthma, pulmonary disease, emphysema, heart disease, stroke and other cardiovascular diseases, spontaneous abortions, and premature births. (For detailed information on these and other smoking-related health problems, see the Action on Smoking and Health website at ash.org/.)

Smoking near infants and children can also increase the child's susceptibility to sudden infant death syndrome (SIDS), asthma, respiratory infection, and mental retardation. Every year, smoking kills more people than alcohol, AIDS, car collisions, illegal drugs, murders, and suicides combined. In the United States, the yearly number of tobacco-related deaths is equivalent to three 747 jumbo jets crashing every day for an entire year, with no survivors. Not surprisingly, then, smoking is the leading cause of preventable disease and death in Canada and elsewhere.

Claims-Making and Construction of Addiction

Few would challenge the notion that many drugs have harmful effects and that high doses of many drugs can be fatal. However, some have challenged the idea that "drugs kill," arguing that such a logic is based on unfalsifiable theorizing about an imaginary world without drugs. Thus, the construction of "drug deaths" is not a neutral statistic, but one that is shaped by political ideas designed to justify the war on drugs.

PERSONAL *stories*

| BOX 8.4 | Addiction among Canada's Innu Population |

In recent years, an uncontrollable addiction has raged among the Innu population of Canada (Bailey, 2013). People as young as six years of age within the Sheshatshiu population have become addicted to gas-sniffing. During the transition from a traditional to modern society, the Sheshatshiu people have fallen into dangerous patterns of alcoholism and drug addiction that have led to a high prevalence of poverty, illness, and death within the population (Clancy, 2004).

Many have adopted gas-sniffing to cope with their unhappiness and difficult conditions. Philip, a teenager, experiences euphoria when sniffing gas. Sometimes he leaves home for days, drugging himself in unfamiliar locations to escape from reality. Many other Innu children are found in the woods or in cars sniffing gas. Many gas-sniffing teens consume gas during the evening and spend the remainder of the day sleeping (Clancy, 2004).

An overwhelming number of the children addicted to gas-sniffing come from broken homes and experience feelings of loneliness and unhappiness. In July 2012, a reported 12 out of 36 children in provincial care and 13 of 76 of the youth living with their parents had abused gas (The Canadian Press, 2012).

Those with this gas-sniffing addiction are labelled "inhalants." This addiction is widespread due to its easy access, inexpensiveness, and rapid effects. Other solvents with similar effects include glue. Addictions to gas-sniffing can cause "sudden sniffing death," where the heart, experiencing extreme stress, goes into cardiac arrest. Other consequences are lead poisoning, hallucinations, slurred speech, lethargy, physical infections, or internal organ damage (Clancy, 2004).

The RCMP and Sheshatshiu community leaders are hoping to receive aid from the government that will help this Innu population rebuild family and community relationships and create a secure and safe environment for their children (The Canadian Press, 2012).

Mariana Valverde's study (1998) on the historical construction of alcoholism found that alcoholics and their families have resisted the medicalization of drinking and the associated treatment. We can see this resistance to labelling in other populations as well. However, drug users may be relatively powerless compared to those voices calling for punitive or medical responses to "drug problems." Social construction analyses draw our attention to the battles fought for the right to define drug use and abuse as individual failing, uncontrollable disease, or social problem.

As well, constructionists cast doubt on the veracity of the disease model of addiction, which they claim did not arise out of scientific discoveries but from a widening of the addiction concept to include more and more activities. In calling the disease model into question, the sociologist's intent is not to diminish the weight that addictions carry for those afflicted, but rather to remind us of the ways in which the view of addiction as disease justifies both humane health services and repressive drug policies (Reinarman, 2005).

Solutions to Addiction

Legalizing Drugs

By framing substance abuse as an enforcement issue rather than a health issue, countries that take this punitive approach continue to rely on fines and imprisonment to discourage addictive behaviours. Other governments, including Canada's, have recognized the flaws of this strategy and have experimented with progressive, practical policies that focus

The Canadian Press/Jonathan Hayward

Locked containers for used needles can be seen hung on the walls of the injection booths at Insite in Vancouver. Insite, located in Vancouver's Downtown Eastside, is the first legal supervised injection site in North America.

on minimizing harm rather than punishing offenders. The Insite safe-injection experiment in Vancouver is one such experiment in harm reduction (DeBeck et al., 2009).

The alternative is much worse: just like alcohol prohibition in the 1920s, drug prohibition in North America has produced a large, profitable criminal industry. Research shows that decriminalization of the possession of marijuana elsewhere since the early 1970s has resulted in decreased costs of enforcement and prosecution of marijuana-related offences (for a detailed account of this, see Haans, n.d.). Although not there yet, Canada has taken steps towards reducing the legal penalties for marijuana possession. Police typically don't arrest for marijuana possession of very small amounts for recreational use, and legislation with respect to the medicinal use of marijuana is changing quite dramatically in Canada. By 2014, the Canadian government will launch a "billion-dollar" medical marijuana industry. Large indoor RCMP-certified marijuana farms will soon produce, package, and distribute medicinal marijuana to qualified patients. While Canada may never see complete legalization, this shift in ideology stands in stark contrast to the social and political perspectives that have prevailed until now (Beeby, 2013).

However, so long as drug use is illegal, we can do little to oversee the quality of drugs available to users or the conditions under which people use these drugs. A study by Hughes and Stevens (2010) has shown, however, that the decriminalization of drugs had positive consequences in Spain and Italy. Following the decriminalization of the use and possession of illicit drugs in 2001, there were fewer problematic uses, harms, and clusters of drug-related crimes in 2007 and 2009. Contrary to belief, there was no increase in the rate of drug use (ibid.).

Why not regulate all drugs? Where alcohol, caffeine, and prescription medicines are concerned, food and drug laws seek to ensure that we do not consume dangerous or poor-quality substances. (The same cannot be said of cigarettes, which contain known carcinogens as well as nicotine.) Similarly, health protection rules would apply to recreational drugs if they were legalized.

One reason for the repeal Prohibition in the US was the realization that when quality-controlled alcoholic drinks are not available, people will drink just about anything. In the 1920s and 1930s, people experienced complications such as blindness and death from drinking beverages that contained dangerous impurities or different forms of alcohol (e.g., methanol instead of ethanol). Moreover, alcohol abuse can result in severe brain damage leading to blackouts, Korsakoff's syndrome, memory loss, and nerve damage (National Institute on Alcohol Abuse and Alcoholism, 2004). Similarly, some drug users have died of drug overdoses because they had no way of knowing the strength of the drug. Legalization could prevent this by regulating strength and quality so the user would be always aware of how much is a safe amount to use.

When drugs are illegal, users take fewer health precautions. Needle-sharing among intravenous drug users, for example, is a primary factor in the spread of HIV/AIDS in many developing nations (DeBeck et al., 2009). By driving the drug culture underground, punitive drug laws work against safety, good hygiene, and disease prevention. Programs in other countries—such as Switzerland—have reduced the sharing of contaminated equipment without increasing drug use (Arnaud, 2011).

Media and Technology on Addiction

People around the world are spending more and more time in front of the television, listening to music, playing video games, and using the Internet. Some researchers suggest that this increase in technological involvement has contributed to the various unhealthy behaviours that are prevalent today (Escobar-Chaves and Anderson, 2008).

Ad agencies and television corporations are aware that youth, owing to their inexperience, are especially vulnerable and receptive to media messages. For instance, studies have shown that youth are likely to view smoking favourably and become smokers themselves "as a result of exposure to smoking in the media" (ibid, 157).

Similarly, the advertising of alcohol on television, at sporting events, and in popular movies contributes to adolescent drinking (ibid.; McClure et al., 2006). Alcohol use and brand appearances are widespread in Hollywood movies (which are distributed internationally). So, youth "are exposed to hours of alcohol use depictions . . . and most of this exposure is from movies rated for this segment of the population" (McClure et al., 2006).

Today, many youth—especially as college students—conclude from the media (e.g., beer ads) that heavy drinking is a social norm. They are inclined to drink heavily because it is seen as a normative and socially attractive behaviour. However, many are unaware of the long-term health consequences of this behaviour.

It will be hard to control the mass media advertising that promotes such views, but we can find examples of successful efforts. For instance, in a 2005 project in Montana, drug users were depicted in an unfavourable light on television. Drugs were associated with people who were unhygienic, dangerous, and bad-tempered. This promoted a negative attitude towards substance abuse among those who watched the specified programs (Erceg-Hurn, 2008). This project demonstrates the efficiency of using a popular and effective media outlet to promote and spread a health-conscious message. Currently, it is being tested in various parts of the United States.

Canada would benefit from such a project, given that many of the channels broadcasted in the country are American. However, for now, Canada has different policies for handling substance abuse issues.

Canada's Drug Strategy

Surveys show that many Canadians still oppose the use and sale of illegal drugs and some oppose their legalization. However, many others are indifferent to the legalization of recreational drugs: they just do not care. They oppose efforts to mount a "war on drugs," which they consider unnecessary. Some strongly favour legalization, for the reasons noted above.

Canada's current federal drug strategy was first conceived in 1987 and was most recently renewed in 2007 as "Canada's National Anti-Drug Strategy." In its present form, the strategy is built on the following pillars: prevention, treatment, and harm reduction.

This strategy recognizes that drug abuse is a public, medical, and social health concern that should be averted and discouraged where possible and treated where necessary. The plan also recognizes that the supply of illicit drugs must be controlled and limited. In May 2003, the government of Canada announced an investment of $245 million over five years to support various programs implemented under this federal initiative.

The Canadian effort towards prevention, treatment, and reduction of harm has undergone important changes in recent years. It builds on public health lessons learned

Don MacKinnon/Getty Images

Marc Emery addresses a crowd of 400 that attended an anti-extradition rally held for him in front of the US Consulate in Vancouver, BC. Emery, leader of the British Columbia Marijuana Party, was extradited to the United States in 2010 to serve a five-year sentence for selling marijuana seeds on the Internet.

from various infectious diseases and pushes for an integrated approach towards both legal and illegal drugs (Erickson, 1998). Research has looked at how the implementing of certain drug policies might decrease the number of drug-related deaths. The first step, instead of abolishing drugs completely, should be to gradually decrease the amount of drugs consumed to prevent overdosing (Svetlana et al., 2006).

Together, prevention, treatment, and enforcement, with minimal reliance on criminal law, may be the most effective public health policy on drugs. By licensing the production and sale of soft drugs, the Canadian government can regulate the quality of drugs, explore the various potential access mechanisms for drugs (free market versus government monopoly versus medical control), tax the profits on legalized drug sales, and then use the taxes for drug education. Equally, governments can reduce the penalties for using hard drugs, treat unlicensed drug-selling as a regulatory or tax offence punishable by huge fines, develop a public health approach to addressing drug problems, and educate the public against drug overuse and the use of harmful drugs.

The federal government has heard renewed calls from influential groups, including the Canadian Medical Association and the Senate Special Committee on Illegal Drugs (2002), to amend the Controlled Substances and Drugs Act to decriminalize the possession of small amounts (roughly 15 grams) of marijuana (Hathaway et al., 2003). Decriminalization is not the same as full legalization. While it would still be illegal to possess the drug for personal use, this would be considered a non-criminal offence similar to a parking violation and also punishable by a ticketed fine (ibid.).

In other words, marijuana's legal status would not change, only the manner of the law's enforcement. However, decriminalization is opposed by some groups, including many municipal police, who worry about increased drug trafficking, and by the US government, which is concerned that easier access to drugs in Canada will trickle drugs south across the border.

Chapter Summary

To some extent, we all have addictions—to television shows, video games, or favourite pastimes. However, these so-called addictions are unlike those some have to harmful substances such as drugs and alcohol. Such substances alter the mind and behaviour, and therefore interfere with every aspect of the abuser's life.

Substances we consider "drugs" are not always defined as good and bad by any absolute criteria. Instead, their definition depends on politics and culture. In this sense, drugs—our perceptions of them and responses to their use—are social constructions. Likewise, laws that deem certain drugs legal and illegal are socially constructed and influenced largely by politics. Laws are not consistently based on a drug's potential for harm. As we have noted, many legal drugs, including nicotine and alcohol, may be more harmful to health than illegal drugs such as marijuana or even heroin.

In fact, criminalizing drugs may be causing more harm than good. Criminalization creates a black market, encourages organized crime, prevents quality control, and places injection drug users at higher risk of HIV/AIDS. People of high socio-economic status are most likely to be heavy drinkers, yet they are safe from the law. How we view a drug, use it, and regulate it can have a large impact on the experiences of drug users. Our peers and social milieu influence these views.

Substance abuse, as we have seen, has many negative outcomes for users and for those around them. These outcomes involve other social problems and, often, severe health problems for users and their associates. For these reasons, we must view, and handle, substance abuse as a social problem.

Questions for Critical Thought

1. Evaluate the view that since human beings are chemistry sets with an obvious desire to perform experiments on themselves, we spend far too much time and money trying to control a few of these experiments.
2. Given the long, historical connection between drug use and sacred ritual, how do we account for the continued popularity of drug use in increasingly secular societies?
3. Discuss why some drugs are legal and others are illegal. In connection with this, explain what factors play a role in defining some drug use as a "drug problem."
4. Howard Becker explains that one must learn how to use marijuana. Is there any evidence that people also need to learn to use and enjoy other drugs—for example, alcohol, nicotine, ecstasy, or cocaine?
5. Do you support the decriminalization of marijuana? Use sociological theories you have learned in this chapter to support your views on the issue.
6. "Widespread drug use—of whatever kind—is symptomatic of a society in crisis." Evaluate this statement with respect to several different societies, communities, or groups for which you have information.
7. What are the advantages and disadvantages in supervised drug injections? Do you believe this is an effective solution to drug abuse? Why?
8. The initial exposure to alcohol varies in different parts of the world. For example, some European countries encourage alcohol drinking among adolescents during celebratory occasions, whereas North America maintains a strict drinking age. Do you believe early exposure to alcohol is more beneficial than delaying exposure to an older age? Is it the same if children receive early substance exposure through media? What are the disadvantages?
9. What recurring factors may occur for an individual to develop an addiction?
10. If drugs were legalized and alcohol could be drunk legally at any age, what would the potential consequences to society be (e.g., crimes, family relationships)?
11. Do you believe that the medicalization label reinforces addictive behaviours? Discuss.

Recommended Readings

Barton, LeRon. 2013. *Straight Dope: A 360 Degree Look into American Drug Culture.* Fremont, CA: Mainline Publishing.

Ferentzy, Peter, and Nigel Turner. 2013. *The History of Problem Gambling: Temperance, Substance Abuse, Medicine, and Metaphors.* New York: Springer.

Fletcher, Anna. 2013. *Inside Rehab: The Surprising Truth about Addiction Treatment— and How to Get Help That Works.* New York: Penguin Group.

Hames, Gina. 2012. *Alcohol in World History.* New York: Routledge.

Kuhar, Michael, and Sylvia Wrobel. 2011. *The Addicted Brain: Why We Abuse Drugs, Alcohol, and Nicotine.* Upper Saddle River, NJ: Pearson Education.

Lewry, Christine. 2012. *Thin Wire: A Mother's Journey through Her Daughter's Heroin Addiction.* Cornwall, UK: TJ International.

McKnight, David. 2012. *From Hunting to Drinking: The Devastating Effects of Alcohol on an Australian Aboriginal Community.* New York: Routledge.

Nutt, David. 2012. *Drugs without the Hot Air: Minimising the Harms of Legal and Illegal Drugs.* Cambridge: UIT Cambridge.

Raab, Diana, and James Brown, eds. 2012. *Writers on the Edge: 22 Writers Speak about Addiction and Dependency (Reflections of America).* London: Loving Healing Press.

Raikhel, Eugene, and William Garriott. 2013. *Addiction Trajectories (Experimental Failures).* Durham and London: Duke University Press.

9

Health Issues

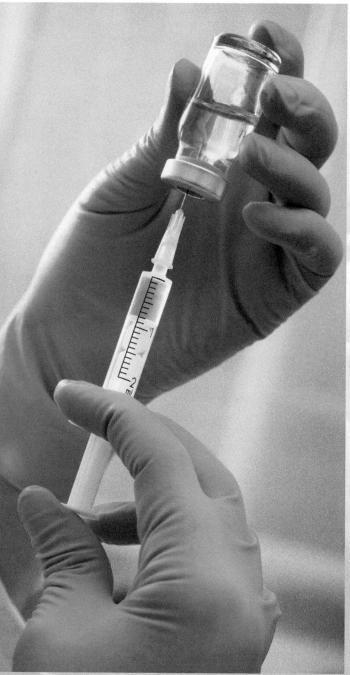

LEARNING OBJECTIVES

- To know the biomedical and biopsychosocial definitions of health.
- To understand different ways to measure population health.
- To recognize the basic facts of Canadian and global health threats.
- To know how globalization and air travel affect the nature of disease.
- To identify the social determinants of health and illness.
- To understand how public health interventions improve population health.
- To discover the problems in Canada's health-care system.

Introduction

We like to think of health and disease as "objective" facts about us or other people. However, this chapter will propose that much social construction and labelling also go into how we perceive and deal with illness and disease. Robert Aronowitz (2008), for example, calls our attention to the process of "framing disease," which he considers "an underappreciated mechanism for the social patterning of health." Epidemiologists have focused on material and psychosocial causes of illness, especially the ways income inequality causes health disparities. Aronowitz, however, encourages us to recognize, define, name, and classify disease states and assign them to a cause or set of causes.

These framing effects influence beliefs about health and illness; patterns of consumption and other behaviours; perceptions of what interventions and policies work; class, ethnic, and other social dynamics; and clinical and public health practices. Important characteristics of such framing phenomena are their capacity to perpetuate themselves and affect people's behaviours. As always in social life, the "Thomas Dictum" proves correct about sick as well as healthy behaviour: what we believe to be true is true in its consequences.

In one sense, illnesses are *personal problems* that we face. As sufferers, we alone feel the physical and neurological pains of an illness. Family and friends may sympathize, but in the end we bear the experience of sickness and internalize the identity of being "sick" as people.

However, health and illness are also *social problems* for several reasons. First, many illnesses are common, affecting millions of people. Second, as we will see, health and health-care resources are unequally divided throughout society. One of the main areas of research in **medical sociology** involves the social factors that promote illness and contribute to health inequalities. Other areas focus on the practice of medicine and explore the social construction of "illness" and "health," the economics and politics of health-care delivery, and the features of physician–patient interaction. Finally, inequalities in health and health care are social problems because, as we see at the end of this chapter, improving the health of whole populations will need the efforts of governments and other large institutions (Mikkonen and Raphael, 2010).

Medical sociology The field of sociology that examines the social context of health, illness, and health care.

Defining and Measuring Health

Definitions of Health and Illness

According to the **biomedical view of medicine**, which has dominated industrial societies since early in the twentieth century, health is the absence of illness. By this standard, health is a "passive" default state of normalcy, whereas illness is an "active" problem in need of treatment (Engel, 1977).

This emphasis on illness is partly due to the Western medical profession's focus on curing the sick rather than on preventing sickness from occurring. In the biomedical model, the doctor is like a mechanic and the human body is like a machine that occasionally needs repair. Only when something goes wrong—a broken spark plug, a failing kidney—are the professionals called in to mend or replace the faulty part and get "the machine" working again.

Biomedical view of medicine A medical perspective that emphasizes Western scientific principles, defines health as the absence of illness, views the human body as a machine that sometimes requires repair, and promotes the use of therapeutic intervention to "cure" disease and injury.

Defining health in strictly somatic terms is inadequate in several ways. There is a growing recognition that the symptoms of biologically identical illnesses vary with differences in personal history, socio-economic condition, and cultural background (Ritsatakis, 2009), leading doctors to "treat the patient rather than simply the disease."

More ideas about health have therefore moved away from a solely physiological model towards a more holistic understanding. Here, health is viewed synonymously with **well-being**—that is, as a state of existence characterized by happiness, prosperity, and the satisfaction of basic human needs. The World Health Organization (WHO, 1970: 29), for example, defines health as "a state of complete physical, mental, and social well-being," a definition that has gone unchanged since the organization's formation after World War II. Health Canada takes an equally broad stand on the meaning of "health," viewing it as a state of social, mental, emotional, and physical well-being that is influenced by a broad range of factors, including biology and genetics, personal health practices and coping skills, the social and physical environments, gender, socio-economic factors such as income and education, and cultural practices and norms (Joint Working Group on the Voluntary Sector, 1999).

These various definitions represent the **biopsychosocial view of health and illness** (White, 2005). As the name implies, this perspective recognizes that health and disease are products of the interaction of body, mind, and environment, and not just of biology alone. As well, it reminds us that health is not an all-or-nothing condition. The relative contributions of each factor—mind, body, and social environment—vary from condition to condition and from case to case. The challenge is to find out the role of each factor and tailor interventions—medical as well as social—accordingly.

Well-being A positive state of existence characterized by happiness, prosperity, and the satisfaction of basic human needs, and not simply by the absence of negative conditions, such as illness or injury.

Biopsychosocial view of health and illness A medical perspective that considers health and disease as products of the interaction between body, mind, and environment.

Measuring Health and Illness

Epidemiology is an applied science that examines the causes, distribution, and control of disease in a population. Epidemiologists use various techniques to study the patterns of health and illness in society, drawing on the knowledge of many disciplines, including medicine, public health, sociology, psychology, and economics, among others (Rothman, 2012).

Rather than trying to assess seemingly vague ideas like "well-being" directly, most epidemiologists measure health with standard quantitative indicators. One of the most common is **life expectancy**.

Global life expectancy has increased dramatically because of advances in medicine, public health, and technology. Fifty years ago, worldwide life expectancy was 47 years; by 2011, it had increased to 62 years (WHO, 2012). However, significant disparities in life expectancy still exist between rich and poor nations. Monaco, for instance, continues to lead, with an average life expectancy in 2012 of just over 89 years, while Chad has the lowest, at just 49 years (CIA, 2012). Canadian life expectancies increased dramatically from 60 years in 1920 to 81 years in 2010—with women's expectancy several years higher than men's in every instance (World Bank, 2010). As the data in Figure 9.1 and Table 9.1 show, the gap in life expectancy between the rich and the poor is also apparent in Canada, since the northern parts of the country are less affluent than the southern parts. In particular, this reflects the greater poverty of Aboriginal people who live in northern remote communities.

Epidemiology An applied science that examines the causes, distribution, and control of disease in a population.

Life expectancy The average number of years remaining to a person at a particular age, given current age-specific mortality rates.

Life expectancy at birth (years)
☐ <75   ☐ 75–78   ■ >78
— North–South boundary

| FIGURE 9.1 | Canadian Life Expectancy at Birth, by Region |

Source: Conference Board of Canada's Centre for the North, at: <www.centreforthenorth.ca/blogs/herethenorth/lifeisshort>.

TABLE 9.1	Life Expectancies in Northern and Southern Canada

SHORTEST LIFE EXPECTANCY AT BIRTH	YEARS
Nunavik (Northern Quebec)	66.7
Nunavut	68.7
Burntwood/Churchill (Northern Manitoba)	72.3
Mamawetan Keewatin Athabasca (Northern Saskatchewan)	74.1
Norman (Northern Manitoba)	74.7

LONGEST LIFE EXPECTANCY AT BIRTH	YEARS
Richmond (Southern British Columbia)	83.4
Peel (Southern Ontario)	81.4
North Shore/Coast Garibaldi (Southern British Columbia)	81.4
Halton (Southern Ontario)	81.2
Fraser South (Southern British Columbia)	80.9

☐ Northern Canada   ☐ Southern Canada

Source: Conference Board of Canada's Centre for the North, in "Northern Canada lags in life expectancy: Nunavik, Nunavut trail much of the developing world," NUNATSIAQ NEWS, Around the Arctic May 19, 2011, at: <www.nunatsiaqonline.ca/stories/article/190511_northern_canada_lags_in_life_expectancy>.

Mortality rate The death rate associated with a given disease or population, typically measured as deaths per year per 1,000 people.

Maternal mortality rate The number of deaths of women due to complications during pregnancy, childbirth, or abortion, typically measured as deaths per year per 1,000 live births.

Infant mortality rate Number of deaths of children under one year of age per 1,000 live births.

Under-five mortality rate (U5MR) Number of deaths of children under five years of age per 1,000 live births.

As well as life expectancy, epidemiologists examine **mortality rates** and **maternal mortality rates**.

In Canada, abortions are mainly carried out under safe medical conditions. As a result of the wide availability of contraceptive technology, the number of abortions continues to fall. They are often a last resort for preventing unwanted births. However, the same cannot be said for many countries of the world, where uncontrolled pregnancy often leads to unwanted births and dangerous abortions. As might be expected, a large majority of induced abortions in Canada are for women under 30 years of age (Figure 9.2).

The maternal mortality rate is a problem linked to global poverty, with 99 per cent of all pregnancy- and childbirth-related deaths worldwide occurring in developing countries (WHO, 2014). Thus, in the developing world, maternal mortality is the leading cause of death and disability among women of reproductive age (15–49 years), with an estimated 533,000 women dying yearly.

The **infant mortality rate** and the **under-five mortality rate (U5MR)** are two other statistical indicators of population health, focusing on society's youngest and most vulnerable members. Globally, the infant mortality rate was estimated at 39.5 deaths per 1,000 live births in 2012, while the U5MR was 24 deaths per 1,000 live births in 2011 (WHO, 2012); again, both indicators are highest in the developing world. At the national level, war-ravaged Afghanistan had the world's highest infant mortality rate in 2012, at 122 deaths per 1,000 live births. By contrast, Canada's infant mortality rate during the same year was 5 deaths per 1,000 live births (CIA, 2012).

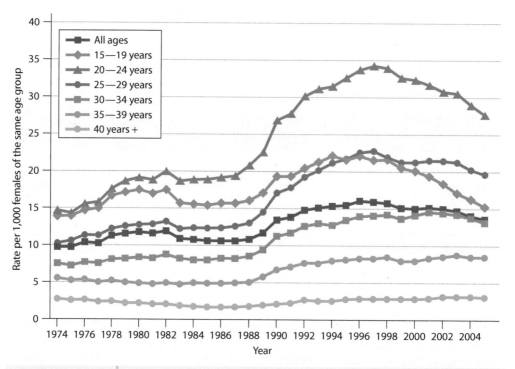

| **FIGURE 9.2** | Age-Specific Rate for All Induced Abortions in Canada from 1974–2005 |

Source: W.V. Norman, "Induced Abortion in Canada 1974–2005: Trends over the First Generation with Legal Access," *Contraception* 85, 2 (2012): 185–91.

The **morbidity rate** shows the extent of disease in a population. Morbidity can be reported according to its *incidence*, the number of new cases in a given population during a given period of time, or its *prevalence*, the total number of cases of a disease in the population at a particular time. Diseases also can be classified as *endemic*, or constantly present within a population; *epidemic*, being a local or national outbreak; or *pandemic*, an epidemic of international or global proportions. Like mortality rates, morbidity rates vary according to social variables such as sex/gender, racial grouping, and social class.

Morbidity rate The extent of disease in a population, reported by incidence (the number of new cases in a given population during a given period) and/or its prevalence (the total number of cases of a disease in the population at a particular time).

Threats to Canadian and Global Health

The AIDS Pandemic

"Rare cancer seen in 41 homosexuals"—so read the headline from the 3 July 1981 edition of *The New York Times*, among the first mainstream media reports about what would become known as "acquired immune deficiency syndrome" (AIDS).

Despite exponentially rising infection rates throughout the 1980s, AIDS was too often labelled and dismissed in those early days as a disease for "them" rather than "us," an affliction limited to three socially marginalized populations: homosexuals, injection drug users, and Haitians. According to a US Centers for Disease Control (CDC) spokesperson interviewed in *The New York Times* article, "the best evidence against contagion is that no cases have been reported to date outside the homosexual community or in women" (Altman, 1981).

Today, we know better. By the end of 2011, an estimated 34 million people worldwide, including 17 million women and 3.4 million children under 15 years old, were living with the human immunodeficiency virus (HIV), the pathogen commonly viewed as the cause of AIDS. Nearly 2.5 million people were infected in 2011 alone, 330,000 of whom were children under the age of 15. The number of global AIDS-related deaths is equally staggering—25 million since 1981, with 1.7 million in 2011 alone (UNAIDS, 2012). Globally, AIDS is the leading cause of death among adults ages 15–59 and the fourth leading cause of death overall (WHO, 2012).

HIV is transmitted via the exchange of bodily fluids. Infection occurs mainly through unprotected sexual intercourse, sharing of intravenous needles, perinatal transmission (from an infected mother to a fetus or newborn), infusion of tainted blood products, and, rarely, through the breast milk of an infected mother. Worldwide, heterosexual intercourse is the primary mode of HIV transmission, while in Canada, homosexual intercourse between two men carries the highest risk (Public Health Agency of Canada, 2010).

SARS, Pandemic Influenza, and the "Globalization" of Infectious Disease

Like the movie *Contagion*, the global AIDS pandemic is a stark reminder that infectious disease remains a major health problem throughout the world. Another disease, malaria, which is exclusive to the world's poorest nations, claims over one million lives each year and is estimated to have slowed annual economic growth in Africa by 1.3 per cent.

A striking example of how present-day globalization has increased the risks posed by emergent communicable viruses is the 2003 outbreak of severe acute respiratory syndrome (SARS). The epidemic has been called "a product of globalization" because its rapid spread

AND THE BAND PLAYED ON

Based on Randy Shilts's book, this 1993 film traces the research and discussion of the AIDS pandemic, beginning with its 1981 discovery.

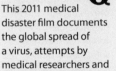

CONTAGION

This 2011 medical disaster film documents the global spread of a virus, attempts by medical researchers and public health officials to contain the disease, the loss of social order in a pandemic, and finally the introduction of a vaccine to halt its spread.

A billboard in Freetown, Sierra Leone, encourages people suffering symptoms of the Ebola virus to visit a health facility for treatment. The 2014 outbreak of Ebola caused health and government officials worldwide to implement travel bans, airport screening, and other measures designed to contain the virus and prevent its spread across national borders.

from Guangzhou, China, to Singapore, Hanoi, Toronto, and elsewhere was promoted by the movement of people along international air travel and trade routes (So and Pun, 2004: 5).

By the end of the outbreak in July 2003, 8,422 cases of SARS and 916 SARS-related deaths had been officially reported in 30 countries, including places as far from southern China as Canada and Brazil (WHO, 2004). Global economic costs owing to lost trade and declining tourism were estimated in the tens of billions of dollars, including a $1.5-billion loss for Canadian businesses (Conference Board of Canada, 2003). The volume and speed of global commerce and international air travel—as many as 1.1 billion tourist arrivals per year, according to one estimate (World Tourism Organization, 2013)—have increased the risk of major infectious pandemics, at least as was feared with the appearance of the H1N1 (swine flu) virus in Mexico in 2009.

Scientists have since expressed concerns that SARS was merely the forerunner to an even larger global pandemic, one that is likely to involve a new strain of virulent influenza. Major influenza outbreaks occur in human populations about three or four times per century, the most recent being the 1918 Spanish flu, the 1957 Asian flu, and the 1968 Hong Kong flu. The deadliest of these, the 1918 Spanish flu outbreak, killed an estimated 30,000 to 50,000 people in Canada and 20–50 million people worldwide, more than the number of combined military and civilian deaths during World War I.

Mental Health and Mental Illness

Mental health refers to the ability of people to feel, think, and act in ways that improve the quality of daily functioning, the range and depth of social relations, and the ability to adapt to life changes.

SILVER LININGS PLAYBOOK

Bradley Cooper stars in this 2012 film about a man with bipolar disorder who, after release from a psychiatric hospital, moves back in with his parents, determined to win back his estranged wife, then promptly gets involved with a recently widowed sex addict.

Mental health The capacity for people to feel, think, and act in ways that enhance the quality of daily functioning, the range and depth of social relationships, and the ability to adapt to both positive and negative life changes.

Conversely, a **mental disorder**, according to one definition by Health Canada, is a condition "characterized by alterations in thinking, mood, or behaviour . . . associated with significant distress and impaired functioning over an extended period of time" (Health Canada, 2006). The terms *mental disorder* and *mental illness* are often used interchangeably, but some reserve the term **mental illness** for clinical diagnoses requiring medical and psychotherapeutic treatment. Mental illnesses and disorders should not be confused with the momentary feelings of loneliness, sadness, or emotional agitation that we all experience.

Mental disorders and illnesses are social problems because they often interrupt the normal functioning of families, groups, and other social institutions (Pescosolido et al., 2013). At the same time, their causes are still poorly understood, which contributes to a general sense of unease and stigmatization by the public (Szasz, 2011).

The most widely accepted classification of mental illness is found in the American Psychiatric Association's (APA) *Diagnostic and Statistical Manual of Mental Disorders* (*DSM-IV*) (American Psychiatric Association, 1994). The most common categories of mental illnesses are anxiety disorders, mood disorders, schizophrenia and other forms of psychosis, dementias, eating disorders, and personality disorders.

Most experts now agree that most mental illnesses arise from a complex interaction of genetic/biological, psychological, and social/environmental factors (Plakun, 2009). Major social disruptions, such as wars or natural disasters, can also promote the development of mental illness through stress and the breakdown of social order. Other experts contend that the individualistic nature and speeded-up pace of life in modern industrialized societies erodes traditional sources of social stability, such as family and religion.

Occurrence and Impact of Mental Illnesses in Canada and Worldwide

In industrialized nations, major depression, bipolar disorder, schizophrenia, and obsessive compulsive disorder (OCD) account for 4 of the 10 leading causes of mental illness.

Globally, mental illness, together with alcohol and drug addiction, comprises the leading cause of disability, accounting for one-third of total years lived with a disability among adults 15 years and older. Unipolar depressive disorders make up the single largest category of non-fatal disabling conditions and are the third-leading cause of lost years of productivity (WHO, 2011). Depression alone is expected to become the world's second-leading cause of disability by 2020 (WHO, 2004).

As the data in Figure 9.3 show, suicide rates vary widely from country to country. On this scale, Canada falls near the middle. These variations suggest different socio-cultural settings—or as Durkheim proposed a century ago, different degrees of social integration and regulation.

However, mental illnesses are far from unknown in Canada. Here, mental disorders have a combined lifetime prevalence rate of 20 per cent, meaning one person in five—or 6 million Canadians. Among young adults aged 15–24, the age group at which most mental illnesses first appear, the risk is about one in four.

Often, the presence of one mental illness predisposes an individual to other mental health problems, such as depression and anxiety. This condition is known as **co-morbidity**. According to a major US study of mental illness involving 10,000 adults, 45 per cent of those who experienced mental illness within the past 12 months had suffered from more than one disorder during that time (Kessler et al., 2005). Stephens and

Mental disorder A condition "characterized by alterations in thinking, mood, or behaviour (or some combination thereof) associated with significant distress and impaired functioning over an extended period of time" (Health Canada, 2006).

Mental illness Clinical diagnosis of mental disorder requiring medical and/or psychotherapeutic treatment.

Co-morbidity The susceptibility of an individual with an illness to additional health problems.

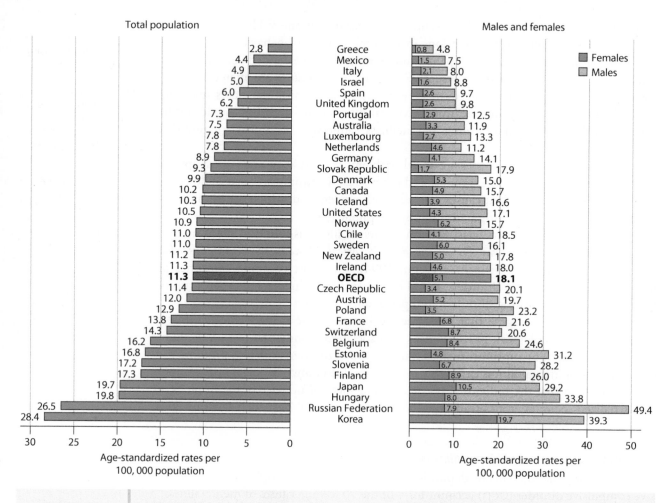

Total population

Country	Total	Females	Males
Greece	2.8	0.8	4.8
Mexico	4.4	1.5	7.5
Italy	4.9	2.1	8.0
Israel	5.0	1.6	8.8
Spain	6.0	2.6	9.7
United Kingdom	6.2	2.6	9.8
Portugal	7.3	2.9	12.5
Australia	7.5	3.3	11.9
Luxembourg	7.8	2.7	13.3
Netherlands	7.8	4.6	11.2
Germany	8.9	4.1	14.1
Slovak Republic	9.3	1.7	17.9
Denmark	9.9	5.3	15.0
Canada	10.2	4.9	15.7
Iceland	10.3	3.9	16.6
United States	10.5	4.3	17.1
Norway	10.9	6.2	15.7
Chile	11.0	4.1	18.5
Sweden	11.0	6.0	16.1
New Zealand	11.2	5.0	17.8
Ireland	11.3	4.6	18.0
OECD	**11.3**	5.1	**18.1**
Czech Republic	11.4	3.4	20.1
Austria	12.0	5.2	19.7
Poland	12.9	3.5	23.2
France	13.8	6.8	21.6
Switzerland	14.3	8.7	20.6
Belgium	16.2	8.4	24.6
Estonia	16.8	4.8	31.2
Slovenia	17.2	6.7	28.2
Finland	17.3	8.9	26.0
Japan	19.7	10.5	29.2
Hungary	19.8	8.0	33.8
Russian Federation	26.5	7.9	49.4
Korea	28.4	19.7	39.3

Males and females

■ Females
□ Males

Age-standardized rates per
100, 000 population

Age-standardized rates per
100, 000 population

FIGURE 9.3 | Suicide Mortality Rates, 2009

Source: OECD, *Health at a Glance 2011: OECD Indicators*, at: <www.oecd.org/health/health-systems/49105858.pdf>.

Joubert (2001) estimate the economic costs of mental health problems in Canada—the direct costs of treatment (including psychological and social work services not covered by public health care) and the indirect costs due to lost productivity—at $14.4 billion. Using data from *The Life and Economic Impact of Major Mental Illnesses in Canada: 2011 to 2041*, a 2011 study conducted by RiskAnalytica for the Mental Health Commission of Canada (Lopez-Pacheco, 2013) notes that 21.4 per cent of Canada's working population are currently experiencing mental health problems. These analyses do not include the great psychic and social costs to family members who care for sick relatives.

Overall rates of most mental illness are higher among women than among men, while substance dependence is higher among men (Mathers et al., 2003; Canadian Centre on Substance Abuse, 2009). When one-year prevalence rates for both mental health disorder and alcohol and drug addiction are pooled, an approximately equal number of men and women are affected—1.2 million or 10 per cent of the male population versus 1.4 million or 11 per cent of the female population (Langlois et al., 2011).

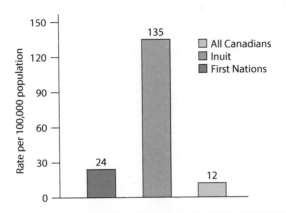

FIGURE 9.4	Suicide Rates for First Nations, Inuit, and All Canadians

Source: S. Khan, "Aboriginal Mental Health: The Statistical Reality," *Aboriginal People* 5, 1 (2008): 6–7.

Mental health is also poorer among marginalized ethnic and cultural groups, especially among Canada's Aboriginal population. Kirmayer et al. (2007) report that the suicide rate among Aboriginals is twice as high as that among the general public and continues to grow (Cutcliffe, 2003: 96; Health Canada, 2006; Tracey, 2009). Suicide in turn is highly correlated with depression and mood disorders. Figure 9.4 shows that the suicide rate of the Inuit population is 6 to 11 times higher than the Canadian average.

Some think that the link between mental disorders and social class can be explained by social selection and various "downward drift" hypotheses. They propose that mental illnesses prevent some people from functioning effectively, resulting in poorer educational outcomes, higher rates of unemployment, increased downward social mobility, and consequent over-representation among the poor. Others have proposed social causation theories. They propose that stresses associated with life in the lower social classes—featuring poverty, unemployment, discrimination, family fragmentation, and the absence of social supports—promote frustration and despair while eroding coping abilities. Such stresses also contribute to the onset of mental health problems among vulnerable individuals and groups (Hudson, 2005; Clarke, 2001).

Obesity

Throughout the world, obesity is increasing at an alarming rate (WHO, 2013). The primary causes are energy-dense, nutrient-poor diets high in saturated fats and sugars, and sedentary lifestyles with little physical activity or exercise. Also to blame are larger portion sizes, increased television viewing, technological advancement that makes everyday tasks less labour intensive, increased use of prescription drugs (which have been linked to obesity), and an urban environment that encourages driving over walking (Wright and Aronne, 2012; Frank et al., 2004; Cameron et al., 2003; Caballero, 2001).

The most common measure of "obesity" is the body mass index (BMI), defined as weight in kilograms divided by the square of height in metres (kg/m²). "Overweight" is defined as a BMI measurement over 25 kg/m², while "obesity" is defined as a BMI

Social selection A correlation suggesting but not proving causation, because a third, unmeasured factor is involved; also known as "adverse selectivity."

Social causation Common social factors that produce widespread health problems. Prime examples might include the effects of epidemics and other infectious diseases and the effects of poverty, access to health care, and work-related health problems; related to social determinants of health.

SUPER SIZE ME
Directed by and starring Morgan Spurlock, this 2004 film follows Spurlock over a 30-day period during which he ate only McDonald's food, and documents the drastic effect on his physical and psychological well-being.

Body mass index (BMI) Weight in kilograms divided by the square of height in metres (kg/m²); "overweight" is defined as 25 kg/m² and "obesity" as 30 kg/m².

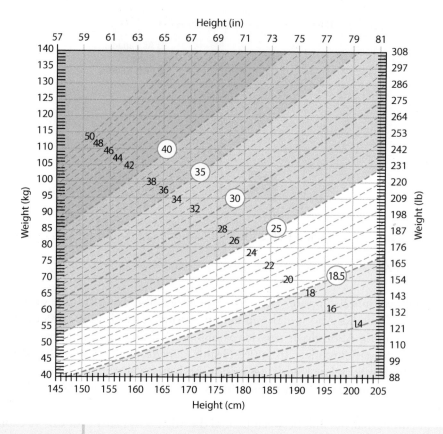

FIGURE 9.5 | Body Mass Index Calculator

measurement over 30 kg/m². Using these definitions, researchers estimate that, globally, at least 1.4 billion adults are overweight, including 40 million children under the age of five; and at least 300 million more are clinically obese (WHO, 2013; see also Rennie and Jebb, 2005; CIHI, 2011; Matsushita et al., 2004; Cameron et al., 2003; Flegel, 1999). Figure 9.5 shows how the BMI works, and how you can calculate BMI, overweight, and obesity. To estimate BMI, locate the point on the chart where height and weight intersect. Read the number on the dashed line closest to this point. For example, if you weigh 69 kg and are 173 cm tall, you have a BMI of 23, which is in Zone B. You can also calculate your BMI using this formula: BMI = weight(kg)/height(m²).

Obesity is a Canada-wide problem, with rates increasing especially in Atlantic Canada and the Prairie provinces (CIHI, 2011). However, province and region per se have not been identified as a separate risk factor for obesity once we control for factors like education and socio-economic status (Le Petit and Berthelot, 2005). The direct costs (related to health-care expenditures) and indirect costs (associated with economic output lost because of illness, injury-related work disability, and premature death) of obesity to the Canadian economy are estimated to total $4.6 to $7.1 billion per year (CIHI and PHAC, 2011).

Theoretical Perspectives on Health, Illness, and Health Care

TABLE 9.2	Theoretical Perspectives
THEORY	**MAIN POINTS**
Structural Functionalism	• Health is normative and is maintained by social institutions and structural relationships. • Health care is a social institution responsible for maintaining the well-being of all members of society. • Illness is a form of deviance that threatens the ability of society to function. • Ill people typically adopt a "sick role," which allows them to temporarily *withdraw from society while they recuperate.*
Conflict Theory	• Problems in the delivery of health care result from the capitalist economy, which sees medicine as a commodity that can be produced and sold. • People struggle over scarce resources (such as medical treatments). • Health, health care, and research are affected by wealth, status, and power or the lack thereof.
Symbolic Interactionism	• Unique meanings and experiences are associated with specific diseases and with being labelled as "sick." • What constitutes "health" or "sickness" varies from culture to culture. • Crises in health care are socially constructed notions and can be used to promote certain political objectives.
Feminist Theory	• Gender is an important social determinant of health. • Women's health has often been defined and understood on the basis of a male model and male norms.

Structural Functionalism

For structural functionalists, good health is considered the normal, desirable state of an individual; it allows a person to be active and productive, which benefits society. Sickness, on the other hand, is a deviant state of being that threatens society's ability to work effectively. Widespread illness—during an epidemic, for instance—can undermine a society and damage its social, economic, and political infrastructure. Structural functionalists therefore stress the roles of social institutions and relationships in preserving the health of society's members.

The earliest contribution to the sociology of health was, undoubtedly, Émile Durkheim's book *Suicide* (1951 [1897]), which showed that we can explain personal health issues like suicide in social-structural terms. This insight is not only the basis of all sociological research; it is the basis of all public health research.

The social institution mainly responsible for a population's health is the health-care industry, which includes doctors, nurses, pharmacists, allied health professionals, and health administrators, as well as material structures such as hospitals, clinics, laboratories, and dispensaries (Raphael, 2009). In addition, societies devise procedures for isolating the ill and reintegrating them into society when they are "well." Talcott Parsons's idea of the "sick role" is the classic statement of this perspective. In Parsons's view (1951), people who are sick take on a specific role and must fulfill this role to be accorded sympathy, assistance, and exemption from their normal daily roles. The assumptions of this role are that the sick person is without blame or fault for her or his condition, that she or he will try to get well, and that, in trying to get well, the sick person should seek competent medical help and co-operate with medical practitioners.

Conflict Theory

Conflict theorists see health and medical services as "goods" that are unequally distributed among different social groups. According to this view, health inequalities are largely the result of income, economic, and social inequalities that expose vulnerable populations to harm and hinder access to medical services and health-affirming lifestyles.

In *The Condition of the Working Class in England* (1887 [1844]), political philosopher Friedrich Engels showed how the deplorable conditions of disadvantage in Manchester—substandard housing, lack of sanitation, inadequate diet and clothing, and harsh work environments—affected the city's death rate. Four years later, the German physician Rudolf Virchow, often credited as the "father of modern pathology," completed a state-commissioned investigation of a typhus epidemic in the Prussian province of Upper Silesia, finding that the root causes of the outbreak were regional poverty, poor education, and inept government policy-making. He famously remarked that "medicine is a social science and politics is nothing else but medicine on a large scale" and asked, "Do we not always find the diseases of the populace traceable to defects in society?" (Rather, 1985).

There is now ample evidence confirming Virchow's statement that people who are socially, economically, and politically disadvantaged—including women, the elderly, visible and ethnic minorities, the homeless, and others—experience poor health relative to their counterparts who are better off (Melchiorre et al., 2013; Marmot, 2005; Mackenbach and Bakker, 2003).

Symbolic Interactionism

Researchers who adopt the symbolic interactionist perspective remind us that ideas of "health" and "illness" vary from one society to another and are constructed by groups that reflect their own needs, values, and beliefs.

Mainly, symbolic interactionists examine microsociological issues connected with health. For example, they might look at the ways medical and nursing schools teach students their new "professional" identities or the ways doctors and patients talk during medical visits, following a predictable script that reflects the power difference within these relationships.

Feminist Theory

Perhaps the single most important social factor affecting health, aside from social inequality (or poverty), is gender. Gender and its social construction are important social determinants of health. However, because gender interacts with each of the other determinants in complex ways, its connections to health are often addressed within these other discussions.

PERSONAL *stories*

| BOX 9.1 | **Emotional Mistreatment Hurts as Much as Physical Abuse** |

"Psychological or emotional maltreatment of children and adolescents may be the most challenging and prevalent form of child abuse and neglect, but until recently, it has received relatively little attention," Hibbard et al. (2012) report. You don't have to tell that to Wendy Cho, who still has nightmares and feelings of guilt remembering how she had to raise her siblings when she was six years old. Her parents worked long hours and left Wendy in charge of her three younger siblings, which is against the law. Being tasked with such a heavy responsibility left a lot of room for feelings of anxiety and a failure to develop.

Researchers today recognize that pediatricians need to pay closer attentions to signs of psychological abuse among patients. However, the signs of psychological maltreatment can be difficult to identify and have long gone unreported. There are no definitive statistics on the prevalence of psychological abuse, but in a study of adults in the US and UK, 9 per cent of women and 4 per cent of men reported that they had experienced some form of psychological maltreatment during their childhood. "There's not enough understanding about it," says Dr Harriet MacMillan, a professor of psychiatry and pediatrics at McMaster University and co-author of the AAP position paper. "Pediatricians need to be alert to the signs and symptoms. It can be a hidden problem."

The long-term effects of psychological abuse during childhood can be devastating, especially when the abuse occurs within the first three years of life. Children who are abused often have lower academic achievement, display angry non-compliant behaviour, and have difficulty forming attachments and healthy relationships. Later in life, these people have an increased likelihood of suicide and mental illness.

Experts assure parents that only a consistent pattern of severe maltreatment constitutes abuse. "We are talking about extremes and the likelihood of harm, or risk of harm, resulting from the kinds of behaviour that make a child feel worthless, unloved or unwanted," says MacMillan, giving the example of a parent who leaves an infant alone in a crib all day or who repeatedly says he regrets bringing the child into the world. Parents who repeatedly belittle, humiliate, or ignore their children may significantly hinder their healthy psychological development. However, emotional abuse can take even more subtle forms, and the parents may not even realize the harm they are doing.

Elena Tepperman, based on: Frketich, Joanna. "Psychological Child Abuse Needs More Attention, Doctors Say." *TheSpec.com*. Metroland Media Group Ltd, 30 July 2012, at: <www.thespec.com/news/local/article/770245-psychological-child-abuse-needs-more-attention-doctors-say>; "Child Mental Abuse as Harmful as Physical Assaults." *cbc.ca*. CBC/Radio Canada, 30 July 2012, at: <www.cbc.ca/news/health/story/2012/07/27/child-psychological-abuse.html?cmp=rss>; Ubelacker, Sheryl. "Mental Abuse Can Be as Harmful to Kids as Physical Abuse: Report." *Vancouversun.com*. Postmedia Network Inc., 30 July 2012, at: <www.vancouversun.com/health/Mental abuse harmful kids physical abuse report/7011209/story.html>.

Historically, men have controlled women's bodies—as fathers, husbands, and even employers. They have also controlled women's bodies as physicians by defining how women's symptoms and experiences might be interpreted medically. It is easy to find, in such assumptions, "scientific" legitimacy for the sexual objectification of women, for women's secondary social status, and for the tendency to dismiss women's health complaints as unfounded. Depression, for instance, was viewed as a women's mental health disability and a form of "gendered incompetence" (Eckes and Trautner, 2000).

Even today, "women's" illnesses and health conditions are often considered more trivial or shameful than men's. Consider menopause. Women going through menopause often view their physical symptoms as shameful or disruptive. They struggle to hide and control the changes, to keep up appearances (Nosek and Kennedy, 2010).

The Social Determinants of Health

As the story in the box above suggests, we are all formed by our social conditions, and anything that abuses our minds or bodies is likely to leave a scar. This is true of family conditions and it is no less true of abusive social conditions more generally—conditions that include poverty, inequality, and lack of access to food, housing, and good health care.

Research shows that major improvements in population health over the past century have mainly been the result of improved socio-economic conditions rather than improved individual behaviours (Raphael, 2002, 2009). Others, pointing to flaws in the health-care system, propose that poor health is the result of not enough access or funding (Raphael, 2008). However, health inequalities still exist where universal, publicly funded health care is provided, so access alone is not the problem.

Social scientists have turned towards examining the effects of various social, economic, and political factors—together commonly referred to as the social determinants of health—on population health outcomes (Raphael, 2009). Some researchers have adopted a *materialist* approach, proposing that disadvantaged populations suffer from higher levels of total exposure to negative conditions over their lifetimes, resulting in poorer health outcomes than more advantaged groups (Fox and Meier, 2009). *Neo-materialists* agree that material conditions are important, but they also point to important social structural contributors (including income inequalities, systemic racial and gender discrimination, and cuts to government social spending) as playing key roles in health disparities.

Finally, *social comparison* theories have been developed to explain the noted health inequalities that exist even among well-off people. The best example of this is found in the Whitehall studies of British civil servants. The groups in question were all white-collar and at least middle-class, so differences in health status could not be attributed to material deprivation. These workers did, however, experience subtly different opportunities and varying degrees of control over their life decisions—differences that affected their health through accumulated psychological stress.

A mountain of research has followed the Whitehall studies (e.g., Marmot, 2005; Wilkinson and Marmot, 2003). Europe in general and the United Kingdom especially have been open to the notion that health status is closely and subtly related to the social environment and that health policies must harmonize with social policies. Canada, too, has been active in theorizing about the social determinants of health but has been less successful in translating academic research into government policies.

A York University conference of experts in 2002 identified key social determinants of health in Canadian society, and the following list captures the most important elements recurring in the public health literature.

1. *Early life*. The benefits of healthy development begin at the earliest stages of life. Programs that provide parenting education and enough nutrition for young mothers and their infants help to ensure the best start to life (Mikkonen and Raphael, 2010: 23).
2. *Education*. Educational attainment in adolescence and early adulthood is also linked to health outcomes later in life. A solid education helps build the skills, resourcefulness, and sense of mastery that prove useful when dealing with problems later in life (Mikkonen and Raphael, 2010: 15).
3. *Food security*. Nationwide, food bank use has increased by 2.4 per cent and the use of meal programs has increased by 23 per cent in 2012. To put these figures in

Social determinants of health The complex causal relationships between various social, economic, and political factors and population health outcomes.

perspective, each month Canadian food banks provide five days worth of food for a population equivalent to that of the province of New Brunswick (Food Banks Canada, 2012).

4. *Housing.* Renters have lower average incomes than homeowners, yet face a national shortage of affordable rental housing. This shortage means a difficult choice for the poor: either live in substandard housing conditions or rent costly apartments that leave little after-rent income for necessities.

5. *Employment security and work conditions.* Unlike bad jobs, good jobs include job security; high control and low demand in work responsibilities; opportunities for growth and personal challenge; work–life balance; safe conditions; and suitable managerial acknowledgement of workers' efforts.

6. *Income inequality.* Income and economic inequality, discussed in Chapter 2, are key determinants of health disparity. Research has consistently shown that as one moves up the income hierarchy, health status improves.

7. *Social exclusion.* "Social exclusion" refers to the marginalization of some groups in society from the economic, social, cultural, and political resources that affect quality of life. Research finds a clear link between exclusion and health. Exclusion reduces access to education and work opportunities, health-care services, and technological and social innovations.

8. *Aboriginal status.* Aboriginal communities have higher-than-average rates of mortality, infant mortality, suicide, potential years of life lost, infectious disease, and many chronic illnesses (Mikkonen and Raphael, 2010: 41).

9. *Social safety net.* The social safety net includes unemployment insurance benefits, welfare payments, publicly managed pension plans, universal health-care access, job training, and other community programs and services provided by the state as elements of a system of supports for those who for various reasons are unable to cope on their own.

10. *Health-care services.* Health-care services are obviously related to health outcomes. Limited access to health care, which is especially prevalent among poor and marginalized people, contributes to society's health disparities.

Claims-Making and the Social Construction of Health Issues

Our approach throughout this book has been to focus on population health, showing in many cases the demonstrable health effects of a particular social problem. In our view, the negative health effects of a particular social condition lend credibility to calling the condition a social problem. Health and health care have been researched from a social construction perspective to reveal the ways in which health messages are delivered to us (McPherson and Armstrong, 2009; Bern-Klug, 2009).

One Canadian study found that such messages were selectively delivered and that they stressed individual blame for health, discounting the impact of social determinants of health (Gasher et al., 2007). As we have seen, social determinants are important, so any messages playing down their influence should raise flags.

The construction of medical issues in the public mind is of great interest to researchers. Studies have looked at the successful and unsuccessful claims made by many actors about the risks posed by particular phenomena, such as sleep disorders (Kroll-Smith, 2000), adolescent aggressive behaviour (Potter, 2003), and physical inactivity (Bercovitz, 2000). As we noted earlier, some authors see the medical and pharmaceutical industries as being complicit in these processes of **medicalization**. After all, they stand to profit from the "discovery" of new diseases to research, combat, and treat.

However, the medical industries are not alone in their claims-making activity. The media, too, play a large role in the construction of health problems. According to a study that examined media reports on second-hand smoke, the reports focused less on the actual science involved than on moral narratives concerning the battle between individual liberty and public health (Malone et al., 2000).

So, many actors can be involved in constructing health problems. Social constructionist ideas about health point to the need to trace back claims to the actors making them. Many claims-makers and lobbyists are trying to gain public support or at least public awareness of truly destructive illnesses or conditions. However, we should be aware that many supposed health problems—such as the construction of "fat" or obesity as a health issue—have more to do with social and cultural issues than with actual health risks (Pieterman, 2007).

Solutions to Problems in Health Outcomes and Health-Care Delivery

Public Health Promotion

Most of the improvements in global population health and well-being over the past century and a half are due not to advances in medicine, pharmaceutical agents, or lifestyle changes, but to socio-economic development and public health programs that focused on preventive medicine rather than on treatment or cure (Marmot, 2004). The **population health perspective**, a framework for understanding health and illness in society, highlights the importance and benefits of preventive health care. It recognizes that preventive actions are not only the most effective way to improve societal health indicators, but also the most economically cost-effective.

Primary prevention refers to steps people take to prevent a disease from occurring. Louria (2000) identifies four aspects to the primary prevention of infectious diseases: (1) immunization; (2) a well-functioning public health infrastructure; (3) prudent use of antimicrobial medicines; and (4) "the amelioration of the societal variables that provide the milieu in which emerging and re-emerging infections arise and flourish"—that is, improving the social determinants of health.

The need for better health promotion is especially urgent in the developing world. Spreading information about causes, effects, and prevention is vital to controlling outbreaks of communicable diseases. Finally, research points to the importance of information sharing between governments and international bodies. For example, China has been criticized for trying to cover up the extent of the SARS epidemic in its southernmost regions during the early stages of the 2002–3 outbreak. Most epidemiologists would agree that early detection and response are crucial to the effective control of communicable diseases, so it is likely that this delay cost lives.

Medicalization The process whereby the medical profession comes to be viewed as being relevant to an ever-widening range of traditionally non-medical aspects of life.

Population health perspective An approach to health that focuses on social determinants of health and, therefore, on preventive societal strategies and societal responses to health problems.

Primary prevention Proactive steps taken to prevent a disease from occurring.

SICKO
Michael Moore's 2007 investigation of public health in America seeks to bring international attitudes towards health-care access to American audiences.

Improving Health in the Developing World: Honouring Global Commitments

Improving global health will require co-ordinated reforms that address the underlying social inequalities that complicate efforts to deliver health prevention, screening, and treatment programs (Hecht et al., 2009).

In 2000, the United Nations adopted the Millennium Development Goals, an unprecedented agreement between all 191 member nations and participating international agencies to co-ordinate efforts to wipe out poverty and improve global health by 2015. Three of the eight goals plainly address population health needs; the others address issues like poverty, development, and vulnerability to disease that affect population health. Together, they form the central objectives of the UN development agenda, for the first time addressing jointly the related issues of peace, security, fundamental freedoms, and human rights.

In the years since the adoption of the Millennium Development Goals, some targets have been met while others have been delayed. Achievements in some areas—better access to safe drinking water, lower child mortality rates, and global increases in girls' primary school enrolment—have been tempered by such setbacks as the continuing HIV/AIDS pandemic and higher rates of hunger in Southeast Asia and Sub-Saharan Africa. More must be done to meet these goals. For example, five diseases—pneumonia, diarrhea, malaria, measles, and AIDS—account for over half of all deaths globally among children under five years old.

Many of these deaths can be prevented through inexpensive interventions, such as encouraging the breastfeeding of infants and increasing the availability of antibiotics, vaccines, and oral rehydration salts (UN, 2005). According to UNICEF's *State of the World's Children 2006* report, at the current rate of progress, meeting the target of reducing child mortality by two-thirds will not happen until 2045, 30 years beyond the agreed-upon date for this goal's achievement (UNICEF, 2005).

Meeting the Millennium Development Goals is slowed by a lack of funds. In 1970, the developed nations of the UN agreed to give 0.7 per cent of their respective gross domestic products (GDP) to development aid, a target set up by an international commission led by former Canadian prime minister Lester B. Pearson. Commitment to achieving this target was reaffirmed at UN summits in 1992 and 2002. By 2005, total development aid in dollars had reached an all-time high, but remained at a historic low as a percentage of the donor countries' combined GDP.

Only five nations—Denmark, Luxembourg, the Netherlands, Norway, and Sweden—have met or exceeded the 0.7 per cent mark; however, at least eight others have committed to doing so by 2015 (UN, 2005). The Canadian government currently gives about 0.31 per cent of its GDP to foreign aid (*The Canadian Encyclopedia*, 2013). So far, however, it has yet to commit to the goal of 0.7 per cent by 2015, saying that to do so would be fiscally irresponsible.

Health research funding must also overcome biases. This is especially true of the so-called 90/10 research gap, which refers to the estimate that 90 per cent of global spending on medical and pharmaceutical research is aimed at finding treatments for diseases that affect only 10 per cent of the world's (wealthiest) population. As a result, much of the research on diseases in developing nations—malaria, tuberculosis, typhoid fever, etc.—is severely underfunded. Various humanitarian aid programs, many supported by private donors and corporations, have tried to correct this imbalance (ibid.).

Health-Care Reform in Canada

The debate over health-care reform in Canada is complex and often divisive. Its main focus is on access and the role that for-profit health services can or should play in Canada's supposedly universal system (Contandriopoulos and Bilodeau, 2009).

Health-care access in underserviced areas, especially in northern Canada, is one critical area in need of improvement. Among the 47 recommendations in the final report of the 2002 Royal Commission on the Future of Health Care in Canada was a call for targeted funding to improve care for Canadians living in smaller communities in rural and remote areas (Romanow, 2002).

International medical graduates, who traditionally have provided health-care services in areas that have had trouble recruiting domestically trained medical school graduates, are one potential source of well-trained doctors. Efforts are underway to reduce the bureaucratic hurdles that immigrants face in getting a licence to practise medicine in Canada. One obstacle to immigrant doctors securing training and medical licences in Canada is that, historically, provincial governments and regulatory bodies have actively discriminated against immigrant doctors (and still do in many ways.) Medical school

Keith Beaty/GetStock.com

Naseem Ahmed Pasha, 44, from India, finished medical school at Mysore University and practised medicine first in India and then in Saudi Arabia for 15 years. He has passed the Canadian exams but can't obtain a residency position, which is required to practise medicine in Canada.

initiatives, such as British Columbia's Northern Medical Program (a partnership between the University of British Columbia and the University of Northern British Columbia) and the Northern Ontario School of Medicine, are another possible source.

Programs such as these are designed specifically to produce young doctors who are trained to deliver health-care services in northern, remote, and Aboriginal communities and in francophone communities in English-speaking Canada. High rates of pregnancy and childbirth are found in many remote, poor communities of the North, and such high rates, as we learned earlier in this chapter, are often associated with maternal injury and death in the developing world. It is difficult to say whether the same holds true of Canada. According to experts Sharon Bartholomew and Rob Liston (2006), "in Canada this information is not well captured. This leads to under-ascertainment of maternal deaths due to unintentional injury, violence and mental illness."

Telehealth (the use of computer and communication technologies to aid health-care delivery) is a growing industry that may revolutionize the medical profession's ability to service its patients. Specialists hundreds of kilometres away now routinely send out diagnostic images, such as X-rays, MRI scans, and pathology images, electronically from rural or remote locations for review. Similarly, video-conferencing technology now allows medical consultations, mental health assessments, and observation of surgical procedures for educational purposes to take place over vast geographic distances (Sevean et al., 2009).

Further, automated voice response systems, electronic health records, emergency response monitoring devices, the Internet, telemedicine, and telehomecare make it more convenient and efficient to do anything from booking an appointment to researching a drug or illness. They have the potential to reduce doctor and hospital visits and to ensure that emergencies are dealt with quickly and accurately.

Telehealth The use of computer and communication technologies to facilitate health-care delivery across geographic space.

Disability and the Canadian Health-Care System

Statistics Canada (2008, 2010) found that 17 per cent of Canadians polled did not have a family doctor and 18 per cent reported problems such as long wait times and difficulty contacting their doctor. Research has repeatedly shown that for any problem of access experienced by the general public, socially disadvantaged groups experience it most strongly.

Now, factor in physical disability as an added impediment. Sanmartin and Ross (2006) have found that the presence of a physical disability increases the odds of failing to receive necessary routine care by more than 50 per cent. Access for people with physical disabilities encompasses a broader variety of issues than it does for able-bodied people, issues such as the physical configuration of the doctor's office (e.g., stairs and examining tables), the attitudes of health-care providers towards people with disabilities, and systematic factors that act as disincentives or obstacles to accessing health care.

The health-care system responds to physical disabilities paradoxically. Veltman et al. (2001) report that one-fifth of doctors do not take adequate account of their patients' disability, but another fifth tend to attribute *everything* to the disability. Moreover, the latter tend to look at a patient's disability as an illness, whereas the patient is more likely to view his or her disability as a condition of life (Jorgensen, 2005). A patient's disability and current medical complaint may be related, but they are not *necessarily* related and may call for different responses. In other words, an illness requires a curative response, but the same approach may not be needed to address a patient's life-long condition. Clinicians who view the patient's physical disability as an illness are likely to thrust the disabled person into the sick role. This adds further stigma to the already challenging disability. It has consequences for the disabled person and for his or her family.

Learning that a child has an intellectual or physical disability disrupts the functioning of the whole family. A common result for parents is psychological and emotional turmoil. In one study (Begum and Desai, 2010), it was found that compared to mothers with able-bodied children, mothers whose children have cerebral palsy report higher rates of depression, anxiety, and stress. The degree to which the child is disabled does not relate to the rate of these negative emotional states. In another study, parents with physically disabled kids were assessed for their mental health (Hung et al., 2010). Forty-four percent of these parents had poor mental health. Mental health was adversely affected if children were of a younger age, depended on assistance for activities of daily living, and had problems walking. If the parents had a low income, no religious beliefs, dysfunctional interactions with their children, difficult children, or high distress, their mental health would be further complicated.

Nevertheless, despite seemingly unfortunate circumstances, not all families experience a child's disability in a negative emotional light (Trute et al., 2010). The burden of care for mothers with a disabled child often involved socio-structural issues (e.g., financial issues) rather than emotional distress, and most mothers were able to discern the benefits associated with having a disabled child (Green, 2007). Other studies similarly found that having a child with a disability does not necessarily have a detrimental influence on emotions. Mothers in an Alberta study were quite adept at meeting the special caregiving needs of a disabled child, to the extent that the disability didn't significantly overwhelm the family (Trute et al., 2010). Mothers who were able to give positive appraisals of the situation (e.g., family values improved as a result of the disability) and higher positive emotions had a much better adjusted family (ibid.). Despite having a disabled child, these mothers experienced increasing maternal satisfaction over the many years of parenting, as demonstrated in a longitudinal study of mothers with Down's syndrome children (Gilmore and Cuskelly, 2012).

Like those with physical disabilities, people with intellectual disabilities have poorer health status than the general public (Emerson and Baines, 2010), largely because of the problems they have accessing health care in Canada. Many factors, including difficulty recognizing signs of ill health and communicating health problems to others, act as barriers to accessing health care (Alborz et al., 2005; Krahn et al., 2006). Many must rely on a third party to recognize their health problems and take the appropriate action.

People with intellectual disabilities experience many of the same barriers faced by people with physical disabilities—for example, the physical configuration of offices, the attribution of health concerns to the disability, and the negative attitudes of health-care providers. However, they also experience unique organizational barriers, including caregivers' failure to make reasonable adjustments (e.g., providing easy-read material or extending appointments) (Emerson and Baines, 2010) and the legal requirements relating to consent (Goldsmith et al., 2008). Health-care providers cannot assume that people with intellectual disabilities will find health-care information as easily as those without the disabilities or that it will be as accessible to them.

Thus, health-care providers must make appropriate adjustments to ensure that their patients are fully aware of their options and of the risks associated with treatment so

Classic WORKS

BOX 9.2 **Howard Becker et al.'s *Boys in White: Student Culture in Medical School***

Boys in White was the first sociological investigation to look at the training medical students received in medical school. The purpose of this study was to determine what medical school did to its students above providing a technical education.

This ethnographic study of young men enrolled in the medical school at the University of Kansas describes their schedules, efforts to succeed, and the latent culture of medical school in great detail. Becker holds a dramaturgy perspective that takes symbolic interactionism as its starting point and believes that social roles are learnt and performed like roles in a play. According to this perspective, the way a social actor presents herself is determined by the cultural values, norms, and expectations of her audience.

According to Becker, medical school is a "rite of passage" where current doctors initiate neophytes into their realm through a series of tests, instructions, and ceremonies. This teaches students not only how to diagnose and treat patients, but also how to *act* like doctors. That is, to be accepted as a doctor, the student must learn how to "play the part of the physician in the drama of medicine" (Becker, 1961: 4). As in theatre, one must *perform* his role

and learn how others will interpret and react to his words and actions.

The process of learning and taking on the role of doctor is a slow process in which the student gradually assimilates the values of the medical community through peer pressure and example. However, there is no dramatic moment when the student, as an understudy to an ill actor, is suddenly thrust onto the stage and required to play his part. A great deal of the student's time in medical school is spent learning how to act the part of the doctor; he must learn how to negotiate with faculty members and how to manage his time and energy.

In short, *Boys in White* shows that becoming a doctor is more than merely learning a set of technical skills. The medical student must learn to perform the role of the doctor for an audience who expects him to act in a particular way. This classic study is also useful in describing the training received by other medical professionals and how this training influences their interactions with patients. For example, think of the role of the nurse or midwife. How are these professionals expected to act? What type of training would be required to teach students these roles?

that they can properly give their consent to a treatment plan; this will require that more accessible health-care literature is made available and that health-care workers, as well as those caring for people with intellectual disabilities, be better educated in how to communicate complicated health information to people with intellectual disabilities. The Supreme Court ruled in 1997 that hospitals must provide sign-language services, and while this may seem like a small advance aimed at a very particular type of disability, it was, symbolically, a major victory for the disability rights movement.

Trans Health Issues

Recent research has shown that transphobia—discrimination based on a person having a gender identity or expression that varies from that assigned at birth—constitutes a barrier to accessing medical care in Canada. Transphobia in the health-care system encompasses a wide range of phenomena, including frank discrimination (i.e., verbal abuse) or subtle processes that make the environment hostile to the needs of trans patients (i.e., gendered washrooms). Both subtle and overt expressions of transphobia act as barriers to general primary care (Bockting et al., 2006; Rachlin et al., 2008) and specialized health care, including mental health care (Avery et al., 2001), substance and abuse treatment (Lombardi, 2007), and HIV treatment (De Santis, 2009; Kenagy, 2005).

Much sociological work on trans experience with the health-care system centres around the concept of *erasure*. "Erasure" is a concept that refers to the systematic failure to acknowledge and validate trans identities (Snelgrove et al., 2012). This includes the failure to make space for a trans person at an institution that has separate male and female wards and the refusal to give a hysterectomy to a male transgendered patient. Erasure is often propagated by a lack of education on the needs of trans people and by the failure to make trans programs available. Even health-care programs directed at the LGBTQ community often fail to properly accommodate the needs of their trans patients (Bauer et al., 2009). Take the Gender Identity Clinic at Toronto's Centre for Addiction and Mental Health (CAMH), for example. Despite its commitment to providing services to those with gender identity disorder, to trans people, and to those with general concerns about their gender, this clinic has been criticized for falling back on dichotomous ideas about sex and gender and promoting heteronormativity (NARTH, 2007).

Transphobia and erasure combine to create ill health outcomes for trans people. Because of a lack of understanding of transsexuality, trans people (regardless of their sexual orientation) have a high rate of STIs (sexually transmitted infections) and HIV. One study of male-to-female trans women in the United States found that 27.7 per cent of participants tested positive for HIV (Center for Disease Control, 2012). As with other socially disadvantaged groups, mental health issues are prevalent in the trans population; one study found that trans people have a 30 per cent chance of attempting suicide (Kenagy, 2005).

Waiting Times: How Long Is Too Long?

A major concern among health-care providers is "waiting time"—especially since a federal court has determined that it is the state's responsibility to pay for treatment in another jurisdiction if doctors cannot provide timely treatment in the home province. This judgement, some say, may start the historic movement towards two-tiered health care in Canada (Siciliani and Verzulli, 2009).

The fact is, our society cannot afford to provide immediate, high-quality care to everyone who needs it. This fact of economic life, in a society preoccupied with efficiency and speed, irritates many of us.

The waiting issue has at least two parts worth exploring. First, what causes long waiting times? And second, what causes people to be upset about long waiting times? To answer the first question, long waiting times are caused by too many customers and too few servers, too slow service, or too slow the allocation of customers to servers. This we would call the "demography of waiting." Viewed from another angle, we could call this the "economics of waiting," and if we consider the issue of power and social inequality—the possibility that some people push to the front of the line—it becomes the "politics of waiting."

If we start with the assumption that there will never be enough money to erase waiting, we need to consider why people react to waiting as negatively as they do and we need to devise ways to make the inevitable waiting more tolerable. Here, social science offers various suggestions. Research shows that people waiting for significant medical care are upset because of pain, risk, fear of death, interrupted daily life, a sense of unfair treatment, and so on. As well, many things shape people's willingness and capacity to "be patient." There is also a psychology of waiting. Some people, given their personality,

JOHN Q

In this 2002 picture, Denzel Washington plays a hysterical father who holds a hospital hostage in hopes of moving up his son's heart transplant.

cannot endure waiting. Others are calmer, more docile, and more patient. As well, social comparison makes a difference: people feel better about waiting when they compare themselves to others who are worse off.

Typically, sick people become frightened if their condition worsens or their pains increase while they are waiting for treatment (Fitzsimons et al., 2003). The longer the time patients remain on a waiting list compared to the time they expected to wait, the more anxiety and depression they experience (Vermeulen et al., 2005; Conner-Spady et al., 2005). That said, men and women react to waiting differently (Parry, 2004). Among patients waiting for coronary bypass surgery, for example, despite similar heart rates and blood pressure levels, men suffer much less anxiety during the wait than women do. One interesting and counterintuitive finding is that waiting patients who are accompanied by someone else find the wait to be much *longer* than patients who come (and wait) on their own (Barlow, 2002).

Research has repeatedly found that the *perceived* waiting time has more impact than the actual waiting time on views of the wait and the assessed service quality. Patients who receive information about the reasons for delay are significantly more satisfied with their wait because they feel better served. Research has shown that patients' perceptions of wait time are influenced by the design of the environment (lighting, temperature, distractions) and early interaction with staff (Soremekun et al., 2011).

The importance of perceived waiting time suggests that health-care providers need to work on improving people's expectations as much as on speeding up the treatment. This may mean developing a better social organization of waiting. Here, sociologists need to study ways to organize the process of waiting more effectively—for example, by providing supportive "waiting communities." Waiting is easier when people are aware of their position in the queue, know how fast the queue is moving, and understand the reasons for delays.

Case management of waiting might solve the problem by giving every person in a queue a case manager who would sympathetically answer questions, provide information, and connect with the relevant medical personnel. Court systems increasingly use such case managers to ensure that cases move smoothly from one stage to the next. These caseworkers may not supply personal counselling, but they do provide an ongoing review of the client.

Such a social arrangement might solve the waiting problem for people with prolonged or chronic medical problems. This would not speed up the illness or the cure, but for many it would speed up the perception of a cure. It would provide a sense of forward movement and a feeling that there are people who are working to remove the barriers to health recovery. Humans would be there to rationalize, explain, and excuse the unavoidable obstacles, delays, and waiting periods. For most health conditions, such waiting would have no adverse effect on the patient's health.

Managing Costs: Is For-Profit Health Care the Answer?

Cutting across the various challenges facing Canada's health-care system is the debate over privatization. The typically heated and divisive nature of the debate is not surprising, since in survey after survey most Canadians cite universal health care as our most cherished social program and a source of national pride.

Note, however, that much of Canada's health-care system is already "privatized." Thirty per cent of health-care spending in Canada comes from private sources, through

CANADIAN researchers

| BOX 9.3 | Neena Chappell, University of Victoria |

Many of the health problems still to be solved in Canadian society involve elderly people, since Canadian society is aging rapidly. Some of the problems are particular to elderly people. However, in her paper, "Aging and Mental Health" (2008), Professor Neena Chappell, Canada Research Chair in Social Gerontology, notes that normal aging does *not* include significant changes in mental health. Mental illnesses such as depression are *not* more prevalent in old age than in the younger years; in fact, evidence has shown that the mental health of seniors is often as good as that of younger people, if not better. What's more, seniors' self-perceptions of their health are overwhelmingly positive.

In her 2014 paper "Change and Predictors of Change in Social Skills of Nursing Home Residents with Dementia," Chappell and her colleagues Helena Kadlec and Colin Reid note that social skills are extremely important for people with dementia—a condition most prevalent in older Canadians. Yet a study of residents in 18 nursing homes found that three-quarters of those studied maintained or improved their basic social skills during the year following admission. To maintain the cognitive health of residents, staff-to-resident communication is crucial, Chappell says, and good social skills will increase the likelihood that the resident will maintain such interaction.

Yet professional interaction is not the only key to the good health of older Canadians. In her 2011 report

titled "Population Aging and the Evolving Care Needs of Older Canadians: An Overview of the Policy Challenges," Chappell emphasizes that when health fails, support by unpaid family and friends is the main source of care. Women are more likely than men to be caregivers, and the caregivers may themselves be seniors. However, caregivers commonly experience stress and feel overburdened, especially when caring for people with dementia. We need to develop policies that support informal caregivers. In addition, we need to establish a complete home-care system that links community organizations with the overall health-care system to form a support network for informal caregivers and care recipients.

Of course, there will still be variations in informal (family) caregiving from one ethnic group to another. In a 2011 paper, "Filial Caregivers: Diasporic Chinese Compared with Homeland and Hostland Caregivers," Chappell and collaborator Laura Funk compare the caregiving involvement of Chinese and Caucasian Canadians. They find that the diasporic or immigrant Chinese are more similar to homeland (Hong Kong) than hostland (in this instance Caucasian) Canadian caregivers. In general, filial caregiving norms are very strong in the Chinese culture. By contrast, Western culture does not have explicit norms of filial responsibility to the same extent as Chinese culture does. This poses an additional health-care problem to Canadian society.

either out-of-pocket expenses or health insurance (CIHI, 2010). Already, most physicians practising in Canada operate as private entrepreneurs, billing their provincial governments for services provided to the public. In addition, most hospitals in Canada are private institutions, although they are managed on a not-for-profit basis. In essence, the universal public health system is a health insurance program that uses public money to pay for privately delivered care (Currie and Stabile, 2003).

The Canada Health Act does not plainly ban private health insurance; it limits private health-care insurance to services not covered by the public insurance plan. By stating that all "medically necessary" treatments by doctors and in hospitals must be delivered through the public system, Canadian health policy exercises a monopoly over health care in the country.

The debate over privatization is therefore a debate over whether health care is a private commodity or a public good. The champions of privatization propose that ending the state monopoly on health care in Canada can ease the various "crises" of cost

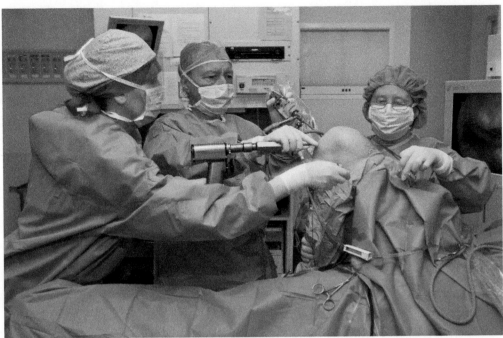

The Canadian Press/Bayne Stanley

A surgical team led by Dr Brian Day (centre) performing arthroscopic knee surgery at the Cambie Surgery Centre in Vancouver, BC. The Cambie Surgery Centre is a for-profit, private hospital that has often been discussed in the debate over privatization of health care in Canada.

and access plaguing the system. A for-profit health-care system governed by free-market principles, it is claimed, will inspire more-efficient delivery models, provide more access and choices for treatment, and produce economic benefits through job creation. Supporters also propose that people who can afford more care choices should have the right to exercise them. Finally, proponents note that many industrialized countries, including Australia, France, and the Netherlands, run publicly funded health-care systems while allowing their citizens to upgrade their services through a privatized health insurance scheme.

Another current debate, and one that is far from resolution, is the right to life debate, which might be more aptly called the "right to die" debate. In 2012, Gloria Taylor died of natural causes following an operation, but she had earlier sought and won the right to die with dignity through assisted suicide, in view of her serious degenerative disease (so-called Lou Gehrig's disease). In a landmark decision in 1993, the Supreme Court of Canada had narrowly ruled against terminally ill Sue Rodriguez, in this way upholding the categorization of physician-assisted death as a criminal offence. Two decades later, the BC Civil Liberties Association argued that the world had changed since the Rodriguez case. Some jurisdictions (e.g., Oregon, the Netherlands, and Belgium) had already enacted laws that allowed physician-assisted death while ensuring safeguards to protect the vulnerable.

After a 22-day trial in December 2011, the BC Supreme Court ruled that the section of the Criminal Code that prohibits physician-assisted death was unconstitutional, a ruling that made it possible for Canadian doctors, without penalty, to help people who wanted to die. However, as the Hassan Rassouli case established in 2013, doctors would

The Canadian Press/Darryl Dyck

Gloria Taylor, who suffered from Lou Gehrig's disease, smiles during a news conference in Vancouver, BC, in 2012. The BC Supreme Court, in ruling that Canada's assisted-suicide ban violated the charter rights of gravely ill Canadians, granted Taylor the right to a doctor-assisted suicide.

need family consent to end even a life that was being extended merely by technological means, a stipulation that safeguarded patients against unregulated use of this new right.

On the other side, opponents of privatization argue that allowing for-profit medicine into the health-care regime would result in a two-tiered system. The for-profit tier would provide better-quality services to the rich and the not-for-profit tier would suffer from decreased funding, burned-out health-care professionals, and poorer service overall. The quality of public health care in Canada would suffer from the gradual loss of health professionals and funding dollars to the private for-profit tier.

Chapter Summary

Throughout this text, we have stressed a population health approach to the study of social problems. One recurring theme has been: "Does a given social condition negatively affect population health, and if so, does that make the social condition a *social problem*?"

The current chapter has adopted a population health perspective that focuses on how social structural variables influence the physical, psychological, and social well-being of large groups of people.

We have learned, first, that different groups view the ideas of health and illness differently and that we must begin any evaluation of population health issues with a consideration of cultural values and beliefs; and second, that some groups are more vulnerable to health threats than others and that these different levels of risk are stratified by economic and social inequalities.

At the same time, the health-care system, the purpose of which is to improve societal well-being, is troubled by serious defects that further threaten population health. Again, not all social groups feel the effects of these health-care inadequacies. Some problems—for example, the nationwide shortage of specialist doctors and nurses—will likely affect everyone; other structural inequalities—such as increasing opportunities to bypass hospital waiting lists or the ability to travel to the US or elsewhere for immediate treatment—ensure that the impact will be least disturbing for the social elite. The health-care system is also a social institution, and so it contains socializing processes, such as medicalization and professionalization. Finally, we have explored some possible solutions to current health problems, both globally and locally.

Professionalization The process by which an occupation raises its standing by limiting the number of entrants and regulating their behaviour. When used to refer to the medical industry, it is the gradual process whereby physicians establish autonomous control over the institution of health care and elevate their collective status in society to become authoritative judges of disease definitions and gatekeepers of medical services.

Questions for Critical Thought

1. Should the Canadian health-care system incorporate varying cultural beliefs and traditional practices? Discuss this issue in relation to the diagnoses and treatment processes of different socio-cultural groups and in relation to the incorporation of international health-care workers into the Canadian system.
2. What are some of the factors that cause mental illness? Describe the individualistic view of mental illness. What is the link between social class and mental illness? Describe the two theory types that have been used to describe this link.
3. According to Parsons, what are the rights and obligations of the sick role? What would be the consequences of treating life-long physical disabilities as illnesses?
4. Being obese has been found to have the same ill health effects as being drastically underweight. Why do you think obesity has received more attention than being underweight? Which social actors have contributed to creating the problem of obesity?
5. How and why is health related to social inequality? Do all kinds of social inequality—such as class inequality, racial inequality, and gender inequality—have equally important effects on health? If not, why not?
6. In ethical terms, who is responsible for making sure Canadians live long, healthy lives? The Canadian individuals themselves, or society? If both, what percentage of the responsibility belongs to society? Explain your answer.

Recommended Readings

Allerton, L., V. Welch, and E. Emerson. 2011. "Health Inequalities Experienced by Children and Young People with Intellectual Disabilities," *Journal of Intellectual Disabilities* 15, 4: 269–78.

Becker, Howard, et al. 1961. *Boys in White: Student Culture in Medical School.* Chicago: University of Chicago Press.

Bourgeault, Ivy L. 2007. "Brain Drain, Brain Gain and Brain Waste: Programs Aimed at Integrating and Retaining the Best and Brightest in Health Care," *Canadian Issues* (Spring): 96–9.

Durkheim, Émile. 1951 [1897]. *Suicide: A Study in Sociology.* New York: Free Press.

Gillett, James. 2004. "Gender Differences in Health: A Canadian Study of the Psychosocial, Structural and Behavioural Determinants of Health," *Social Sciences and Medicine* 58: 2585–600.

Greco, Veronica, and Derek Roger. 2003. "Uncertainty, Stress, and Health," *Personality and Individual Differences* 34, 6: 1057–68.

McClean, Stuart. 2005. "The Illness Is Part of the Person: Discourses of Blame, Individual Responsibility and Individuation at a Center of Spiritual Healing in the North of England," *Sociology of Health and Illness* 27, 5: 628–48.

Mirowsky, John, and Catherine E. Ross. 2003. *Social Causes of Psychological Distress.* New York: Aldine de Gruyter.

10

War and Terrorism

© Bart Sadowski/iStockphoto

LEARNING OBJECTIVES

- To define war.
- To be able to identify and understand various causes of war.
- To describe the potential social, economic, and health consequences of war.
- To briefly describe the evolution of warfare throughout history.
- To describe the nature of war and terrorism in the twenty-first century.
- To describe how gender roles have shifted during times of war.
- To identify common war crimes.
- To compare different sociological approaches to war and terrorism.
- To discuss ways of reducing the frequency of war in the future.

Introduction

This chapter is about war and terrorism, conflict and combat, soldiers and civilians. At no point in recorded history has there been a complete absence of conflict between human groups. When societies form, conflict inevitably arises. Thus, warfare and violent conflict appear to be universal, though outbreaks of violence vary over time and place.

Canada is less prone to warfare than most other nations. According to Global Firepower (2013), which ranks military strength for countries across the world, the Canadian Forces have fewer troops, are considerably less well funded, and are equipped with less-sophisticated aircrafts, ships, and weapons than their American counterparts. As most Canadians seem to lack the desire for war, it follows that the above assumption—the claim that the wish to wage war is a human universal—is fundamentally unreasonable. Canadians go to war only when they are pushed into it, usually by loyalty to a close ally like Britain, as occurred during both world wars.

We cannot understand warfare without understanding politics and statecraft. As the early nineteenth-century Prussian military thinker Karl von Clausewitz (1993 [1833]) wrote, "War is not merely a political act, but also a real political instrument, a continuation of political commerce, a carrying out the same by other means." Just as some groups are more prone to violence than others, some periods of history have been more prone to war than others. It is likely that sociological variables can be used to explain this variation. While we may never find ways to eradicate war from society, we can hope to use sociological analyses to find ways to reduce the occurrence of warfare.

In this chapter, we will see that wars are largely the result of social construction. They often begin with the social construction of a sense of threat, of dangers waiting to overwhelm us. Depictions of the enemy follow, frequently with the intention to confuse us and dehumanize the enemy, making it easier for us to hate those in question (Meyer, 2009).

Changes in warfare have been examined from various sociological viewpoints, and different conclusions have been reached. War continues to have important social and health outcomes (Miller and Rasmussen, 2010). Though often good for the economy, war is bad for living things; and with the pursuit of nuclear, chemical, and bacterial weapons, it is likely to get worse (Moore and Moore, 2009). Warfare may appear to solve social problems in the short run, but in the long run everyone suffers. To understand its resurgence, we need to understand war's roots in politics, ideology, and religion. Only then will we be able to understand why people are compelled to go off by the hundreds of thousands to be killed in battle.

Politics, the State, and Warfare

The Role of the State

The state is a set of public organizations that makes and enforces decisions binding each member of society (Weber, 1946). It includes an elected government, civil service, courts, police, and military. At the extreme of political control is the authoritarian state—one that tries to fully dominate civil society and penetrate everyday life.

In Canada, the military has rarely played a major role in state decision-making. A society like Canada's, in which power is shared among competing political, bureaucratic, and economic elites, is likely to have difficulty mobilizing the desire and the assets to wage war. We can see, then, that decentralized leadership is less likely to engage in warfare than centralized or, especially, dictatorial leadership. This political organization helps to explain why a country with a highly developed military-industrial complex, such as the US, is more likely to enter war.

Ideology and Religion

Another factor influencing politics and war is ideology. An ideology is a system of beliefs about how society is or should be organized. Ideologies are important for social change because they motivate and control people.

In recent decades, organized religions and religious leaders have gained more power than they had in much of the twentieth century. This rebirth of religion as a political force testifies largely to the downfall of communism, an ideology and political system that had tried to destroy organized religion, which Karl Marx had viewed as "the opiate of the masses" (see Tucker, 1978). In many parts of the world today, fundamentalist religions are gaining power: Christian fundamentalism is politically important in the United States, Jewish fundamentalism in Israel, and Islamic fundamentalism in Pakistan, Iran, and other Islamic states.

Here, too, Canada remains distinct in having no state religion and no official dedication to preserving religion or religiosity. Canada's formal commitment to multiculturalism makes a strong, unified religious belief across the country impossible. However, some observers today see the federal Conservative government as leaning towards a narrow Christian ideology (McDonald, 2010).

World System Theory

Politics takes place both between and within states. One theory that is concerned with the relations between states in a global system is world system theory (see Wallerstein, 1976, 2004). We cannot understand Canada's role in the world's "war system" unless we understand Canada's role in the world economic system.

In this world system, industrial core states like the United States and the United Kingdom—and, increasingly, China and India—take much of the raw materials and cheap labour they need from less-developed peripheral states. Because they are financially and politically dominant, core states have the power to extract an economic surplus from the periphery. Investors from the core states control the economies of peripheral states. As a result, profits made in the periphery drain out of the local economy and flow back into the core.

Core states are often accused of engaging in imperialism, the exercise of political and economic control by one state over another (Moore, 2009). Historically, imperialism has been carried out most often through military means. However, domination does not always require military conquest and colonization. In fact, under the right conditions, economic imperialism is far safer, less costly, and more stable than military or political imperialism (Petrosian and Fatkina, 2009).

With the increased imbalance in political affairs since 1989, military imperialism has again resurfaced in Iraq and elsewhere. Chalmers Johnson (2006), in his book *Nemesis: The Last Days of the American Republic*, notes that the United States had over 700 military

Ideology A system of beliefs that explains how society is, or should be; any system of ideas underlying and informing political action. In a Marxist sense, ideological ideas justify and legitimize subordination of one group to another.

World system theory Provides an account of the transnational development of capitalism and a theory of the global structure of inequality among nations. Along with dependency theory, it challenged the prevailing modernization theories of the 1960s.

Imperialism The exercise of political and economic control by one state over another, often by military means. Developing countries are often the focus of imperialistic and exploitative activities that stifle their own development and concentrate their resources and labour for the profit of advanced capitalist countries.

bases on foreign land, 38 of which can be classified as sizeable bases. He goes on to point out that the British and Roman empires had 36 and 37 sizeable bases, respectively, and implies that the US is quietly building a military empire.

Globalization Processes

Globalization The integration on a world scale of economic activities and peoples by units of private capital and improved communications, technology, and transportation. In other words, globalization is the trend of increasing interdependence among the economies and societies of the world.

Economic **globalization** as it exists today is a form of world social organization with six defining features. To understand the current state of global politics and war, we must understand the following characteristics:

1. There is *global economic interdependence*. This means that most societies trade goods and services with one another. All people are buyers and sellers in a single world market.
2. A driving force for change is *scientific and technological innovation*. New methods for producing goods and services are continuously being developed.
3. The key actors in a global economy are *"built" or corporate entities*, especially multinational corporations (like General Motors, IBM, Toyota, and Exxon). Individuals, small local firms, and even nationwide businesses lose in the competition for international markets.
4. *Cultures and polities are polycentric*—that is, they are found in and influenced by activities in many nations. More cultures today are dispersed, with centres of activity throughout the world.
5. A changing "world culture" *homogenizes human ambitions*, narrowing the variety of aspirations and lifestyles. More people everywhere act like Americans; meanwhile, Europeans think and act more like the French, English, and Germans—the dominant actors in the European Union. Homogenization results from large numbers of people of different cultures being influenced by the world's most dominant cultures.
6. Most relevant to this discussion, *economic globalization forces nation-states to change*. With less influence over the culture and economy, governments have less influence over the people they rule. With these changes come political stresses and upheavals and the formation of new **social movements** and ideologies.

Social movements Broad social alliances of people who seek to affect or block an aspect of social change within a society. They may be informally organized at first, but in time they often turn into formal organizations such as political parties and labour unions. Examples of social movements include political movements, labour movements, the women's movement, environmental movements, and peace movements.

The Nature of War and Terrorism

Definitions of War

War A state of armed conflict between different nations or states or different groups within a nation or state.

The concept of **war** can be difficult to define, as numerous factors distinguish war from other forms of violence. According to Dinstein (2011, 202), a classic, well-accepted definition of war is "A contention between two or more States through their armed forces, for the purpose of overpowering each other and imposing such conditions of peace as the victor pleases."

Collective violence Often organized by a group of individuals or a social movement, this type of violence is used to promote an agenda or to resist an oppressive other.

War is an institution of **collective violence**—organized group violence used to promote an agenda or to resist another violent group. Unlike **interpersonal violence**, which is episodic, unorganized, and impulsive, modern warfare relies on impersonal killing and advanced technology. As a result of advances in military technology, modern weaponry used in combat has never been more lethal. A single precision-guided missile released by a B-52 bomber thousands of metres above a war zone can kill hundreds of enemy

Interpersonal violence Violent interactions occurring between individuals, such as murder, rape, and domestic and child abuse.

soldiers. The nuclear bombs dropped on Hiroshima and Nagasaki in the final days of World War II are estimated to have killed close to 200,000 people instantly. Total deaths for World War II exceeded 62 million, of which an estimated 50 per cent were civilians. No wonder, then, that the twentieth century was the bloodiest hundred years in the history of humanity.

Terrorism: The Common Man's War

Terrorism can be defined as:

> the calculated use of unexpected, shocking, and unlawful violence against non-combatants (including, besides civilians, off-duty military and security personnel in peaceful situations) and other symbolic targets perpetrated by a clandestine member(s) of a subnational group or a clandestine agent(s) for the psychological purpose of publicizing a political or religious cause and/or intimidating or coercing a government(s) or civilian population into accepting demands on behalf of the cause. (Loza, 2007)

A dispassionate formal definition of the term is difficult because terrorism is an ideological and value-laden term, as well as a description of events. An even broader, simpler definition characterizes terrorism as any act by an individual or by a group that is intended to undermine the lawful authority of a government or state.

The roots of terrorism can be found in the religious, ethnic, nationalist, political, economic, and social differences that prevent people from living together in peace. There is no evidence to suggest a single motive behind the use of terrorism, but the most accepted theory is that participants feel that, all things considered, violence is the best course of action. A rational cost-benefit analysis—rather than reckless impulse—leads them to this conclusion, often because of various frustrating or limiting social, political, and economic conditions.

Many of the suicide bombers in the Middle East have come from both oppressed and impoverished circumstances, and one factor in accepting suicide is the promise of large cash "compensations" to their families by states, wealthy sympathizers, and various organizations. According to Navarro (2009), the combination of people subscribing to a violent ideology and being isolated can heavily contribute to the actualization of terrorist ideals.

State-sponsored terrorism is the state-sanctioned use of terrorist groups to achieve foreign policy objectives. The current US government has four countries on its "terrorism list": Cuba, Iran, Sudan, and Syria (US Department of State, 2010). Notably, three of these are Middle Eastern or North African countries with mainly Muslim populations. Such lists will differ across countries. For example, some nations may view the United States as a state that sponsors terrorism with the aim of destabilizing foreign governments and undermining particular political movements.

The irony of state-sponsored terrorism is that it can be a powerful form of clandestine warfare, yet it can also be vulnerable to shifts in the international political arena. On various occasions, developing world rebel groups, including various governments, have found themselves suddenly deprived of support from the foreign sponsors they had once relied on. For example, Iraq's Saddam Hussein was under the impression that the US was

ZERO DARK THIRTY
A chronicle of the decade-long hunt for al-Qaeda terrorist leader Osama Bin Laden after the September 2001 attacks, ending with his death at the hands of the Navy SEAL Team 6 in May 2011.

Classic WORKS

BOX 10.1   **Franz Fanon's *The Wretched of the Earth* (1968)**

The book's title comes from the first line of "The Internationale," the official anthem of the international Communist movement. In his introduction to the book, philosopher Jean-Paul Sartre asserts that the book is a call to revolutionary violence. It is also a social-psychological analysis of the pathologies caused by colonial suffering. Fanon theorizes that by internalizing the views of the colonizers, the colonized develop a lack of self-respect and a sense of perpetual inferiority, ensuring their continued economic and political subordination. Promoting self-respect and creating a sense of identity, Fanon believes, are crucial steps towards freeing colonized people. Violence is a key ingredient in achieving this freedom.

To overcome the injustices of the past and to equalize all races, a revolution is considered necessary to redress the colonial damage. Only by expelling colonial rulers and addressing the harm they did will the colonized be able to break free of their pathological ties to the colonizer. Violence is important because it proves the oppressed are just as able to take action as the oppressors. Peaceful solutions fail to bring the self-respect necessary to "cure" the natives and convince them of their own power and sovereignty. Violence binds together the oppressed and engraves in them a national identity—a sense of common cause and collective history.

his ally during the Iran–Iraq War, until it was revealed that America had also been selling arms to Iran (Brands, 2011). Religious fundamentalists such as the Taliban, ISIS, and even Osama bin Laden received support from the US and its allies after the Soviet Union invaded Afghanistan at the end of 1979. This support withered away as relations between these groups and the US became increasingly strained.

Violent Political Protest

As societies industrialize and become democratic, movements of political protest tend to become less violent. Still, political protest continues in many forms, varying in terms of duration, reasons for initiation, scope of activities, degree of engagement in collective violence, motivations of the participants, and means for mobilizing for action.

In stable democracies, political protest is normally peaceful. Some protests become violent, but in countries like Canada, violent political protests are less common than in the past. The violence of the Front de libération du Québec (FLQ)—most widely remembered in connection with the October Crisis of 1970—stands as an exception.

The FLQ was a national terrorist group that wanted to see Quebec separate completely from Canada and establish itself as an independent nation. The group's actions first became violent during the 1960s, when they began bombing national symbols, such as mailboxes, resulting in injuries to police officers. Throughout the decade, as the frustration of radical Québécois nationalists seemed to grow, the bombings became more violent and sophisticated. In October 1970, members of the FLQ kidnapped visiting British trade official James Cross and provincial labour minister Pierre Laporte. Those responsible for the kidnappings threatened to murder both Cross and Laporte unless their demands were met by the federal government, then under the leadership of Prime Minister Pierre Trudeau. These demands included a public broadcasting of an FLQ communiqué expressing their political belief that English-Canadian culture and

The Canadian Press/Peter Bregg/1970

A newsboy holds up a newspaper with a banner headline reporting the invoking of the War Measures Act on 16 October 1970, the first time Canada had invoked the act in peacetime. The act was put into effect following the kidnapping of British diplomat James Cross and Quebec labour minister Pierre Laporte by the terrorist FLQ.

American imperialism were overtaking Quebec culture. Trudeau and the federal government responded by imposing the War Measures Act, which allowed for the indefinite suspension of civil liberties. Laporte's body was eventually found in the trunk of a car, and shortly thereafter the crisis was resolved through having Cross safely released in exchange for allowing a safe exile to Cuba for his kidnappers. Those implicated in the killing of Laporte were tried and convicted for their crimes (Haig et al., 2009).

Where protests arise, many worry that lines between criminal activity and political protest will be blurred by the state's efforts to maintain order. In industrialized societies, non-violent tactics have been used to reduce the likelihood of protests. Urban planning plays a part in this process; for example, public spaces (such as a sidewalk or a public square) may be replaced with "carceral" spaces—architecture that is more secure and easier to defend against attack.

Though some movements of protest are spontaneous, brief, and disorganized, most are planned, continuing, and rooted in both formal and informal networks of social contact. The most developed form of social protest is exemplified by a revolution.

Revolution

Revolutions are defined as any attempt to overthrow a government with the use of violence (Ross, 2011). They are events of immense political and moral contradiction and occasions for celebrating the heroic and the idealistic, but revolutions rarely achieve their original goals. Whatever their goals and ideals, revolutions substitute one form of restrictive power for another. They rarely replace despotism with a secure democracy.

Yet even if they fail to achieve their intended goals, revolutions affect other countries and the world as a whole, as evidenced by the French Revolution, the Russian Revolution, the Chinese Revolution, the Cuban Revolution, and many smaller-scale revolutions such as the recent Arab Spring movement.

In analyzing the revolutions in France, Russia, and China, Skocpol (1979) notes that revolutionary crises developed in those countries when the old aristocratic regimes failed to meet emerging challenges. Skocpol describes pre-revolutionary France, Russia, and China as "fully established imperial states." Because these states were not fully bureaucratic or parliamentary, they could not offer representatives from the dominant class an opportunity to take part in political decision-making.

As a result, the landed class developed a capacity for "self-conscious collective organization." Its members were in a position to "obstruct monarchical undertakings that ran counter to their economic interests" (ibid.). Their obstructions had the unintended consequence of destroying the military and administrative integrity of the imperial state. In effect, the landed aristocracy undermined its own traditional position in the society.

Research by Barrington Moore (1967) shows that the outcome of a revolution depends on class relations—specifically, which social class attacks the ruling class. When the attackers are mainly peasants, as was the case in China, Vietnam, and Cuba, the result is a communist regime that introduces land reform and social equality. When the revolutionaries are independent farmers, craftsmen, and other middle-class people, the result is likely to be parliamentary democracy, as was the case in England, France, and the United States. However, when the attackers are mainly military—supported by a coalition of the landed aristocracy, the Church, and large business interests—the result is fascism, as occurred in Germany, Italy, and Spain.

Rebellion

Rebellion is armed opposition by a portion of the citizenry to an established government or other authority. The difference between a rebellion and a revolution lies in the outcome. If a rebellion succeeds in overthrowing the government and making significant social and political changes, it is classified as a revolution.

The Rebellions of 1837 in Upper and Lower Canada did not overthrow the government and few changes were the result. Everyone who engages in rebellion against a government is liable to the criminal penalties of treason established by that government. If a rebellion becomes widespread, involving a considerable proportion of the country, and the rebels receive the recognition of foreign nations, the government in charge treats captured rebels merely as belligerents. If the rebellion succeeds and the rebels form a new government, the rebels are no longer criminals: they are considered heroes and rulers (Coates, 1997).

Revolutions and rebellions are crimes against the government of the day, and whether history views the rebels as heroes or villains depends on whether they succeed. Winners typically rewrite the history books to show themselves as heroes conforming to a higher standard of moral conduct. Where rebellion is attached to a group that persists in the society, as was the case with the 1869–70 and 1885 Métis rebellions in western Canada led by Louis Riel, opinion may be divided. Riel was condemned and executed as a traitor by Canada following the 1885 rebellion and today is little known by most Canadians, yet the first rebellion was instrumental in the creation of the province of Manitoba and he continues to be celebrated by Native people and by francophones as a hero and martyr. William Lyon Mackenzie, leader of the unsuccessful 1837 rebellion in Upper Canada, is not forgotten because his rebellion paved the way for responsible government in Canada and, eventually, independence.

War Crimes

It may seem strange to define atrocities committed during war as war crimes, since the fundamental goal of combat is to kill your enemies. However, many governments believe that slaughtering soldiers is an acceptable cost of war, while the intentional slaughter of civilians is indefensible. These distinctions are socially and politically meaningful, though some would question whether they are morally meaningful.

Acts of political violence—including war crimes—differ from other kinds of violence in that representatives of a political or national group inflict such violence in order to gain political power (Besley and Persson, 2011). Rationalizations are commonly devised to "explain away" the extent of violence, its effects, or its lack of fairness.

These rationalizations begin with distinctions made between "us" and "them." A group seen to consist of outsiders or strangers is more easily defamed and attacked—more easily viewed as a means to an end or as fully expendable. The most horrific manifestation of this is **genocide**, the systematic execution of an entire national, ethnic, racial, or political group. The most notorious case of genocide was the extermination of the Jews and Roma (gypsies) by Nazi Germany during World War II. Many others—including Slavs, homosexuals, and mentally impaired people—were also murdered. In all, six million Jews were killed, many in concentration camps like Auschwitz, where an estimated one million died.

Though many vowed after 1945 that such an atrocity should never be allowed to happen again, genocides continue to occur, such as in the former Yugoslavia, Rwanda, and Cambodia to name the most notorious recent cases. However, the world now has procedures for dealing with genocidal war criminals.

Issues involving the prosecution of war crimes fall into at least four categories: (1) assigning responsibility for criminal acts; (2) trying and punishing the criminals; (3) bringing about national reconciliation; and (4) ensuring that a nation remembers its criminal past and learns from it. The International Criminal Court (ICC), which Canada was instrumental in establishing and which opened on 1 July 2002, set up a permanent international court to prosecute war crimes and crimes against humanity. However, some countries, most notably the United States, have refused to be participants in this international forum for justice because they do not want to cede any of their own jurisdictional control. They also claim that their own soldiers (or leaders) might be apprehended and tried unfairly.

On the whole, international war crime tribunals are established on an ad hoc basis, in contrast to the permanency of the ICC, and calls for them are sporadic because of the tension between selfishness and idealism within liberal states. Also, war crimes tribunals are physically unable to process thousands of trials. Nevertheless, these tribunals represent a superior alternative to acts of vengeance by aggrieved parties. Right actions following

Genocide The deliberate, systematic, and planned killing of an entire national, ethnic, racial, or political group.

HOTEL RWANDA

The true story of Paul Rusesabagina, a hotel manager who housed over a thousand Tutsi refugees during their struggle against the Hutu militia in Rwanda.

wrongdoing, such as changing institutions, making reparations, or giving apologies, may help to bring about healing and peace (Bass, 2002).

Reparations and apologies are grand principles, but on the ground, it may be more difficult to reorganize people's lives after a genocidal episode. Dragutin Babic (2002) studied 180 war migrants, including returnee Croats, returnee Serbs, and refugee immigrants in Croatia. His findings revealed that the coexistence of the hostile Croats and Serbs remained a problem, both for groups of war migrants in local communities and for the state of Croatia. The returnees are burdened with memories of the conflict, human and material losses, and issues of forgiveness and compromise. Ironically, each of the three groups claims that before the war they valued peaceful coexistence. Today, however, the groups are in disagreement over who holds responsibility for the war.

Rape as a Weapon of War

Despite prohibitions outlined in the Geneva Conventions, rape, assault, and enforced prostitution of women have all continued during armed conflicts. For example, in the years of World War II, the Japanese military forced up to 200,000 young women into prostitution as "comfort women" for military personnel, with many eventually dying of sexually transmitted diseases and from torture. Such atrocities were also common during the conflicts in Bosnia-Herzegovina and Rwanda, as soldiers raped and assaulted women (Engle, 2005).

Dahl (2010) specifically notes the problem of "gendercide"—genocidal acts committed against women as women and men as men—as human rights violations. Gendercide against women typically involves rape, which has come to be recognized as a war crime. Against men, such crimes involve the selective separation of young civilian men "of military age" (i.e., 18–45 years) from old men, children, and women of all ages for punishment, torture, and execution.

Formerly, many believed that rape was an unintended consequence of invasion by foreign soldiers—as occurred in Berlin in 1945, when Soviet soldiers overran the defeated city. For centuries, warriors have considered captive women to be part of the booty of warfare. However, today many believe that a systematic campaign of rape against civilian women is designed to humiliate and break the resolve of an enemy nation. In some African conflicts, rape has been used intentionally to spread HIV. Rape also destroys families by turning husbands, fathers, and brothers against the wives and daughters who have been victimized.

Finally, when rape results in pregnancy, it changes the ethnic composition of a conquered society—a further source of humiliation and conflict that will continue for at least a generation. In some countries, such as Korea, which over the years has been occupied by Mongolian, Chinese, Japanese, and American troops, mixed-ethnic children have been shunned and socially isolated (Greenfeld, 2006).

International feminist activists and women's organizations have played an important role in prosecutions of war crimes committed against women, especially rapes and sexual enslavement (Cooper, 2002). Feminists successfully pressured the UN to label crimes against women as prosecutable human rights abuses and to include female prosecutors and judges in tribunals. Louise Arbour, who became a Supreme Court of Canada justice and later served as the UN high commissioner for human rights, was chief prosecutor of war crimes at the International Criminal Tribunal for Rwanda and the former Yugoslavia in

The Canadian Press/Sean Kilpatrick

Honorine Kabuo, left, bids farewell to Governor General Michaelle Jean following her visit to Goma, Democratic Republic of the Congo, Africa. Kabuo was raped by a gang of militant rebels, was slashed in the neck, and had her pregnant stomach cut open, but she lived to raise her now eight-year-old daughter, whom she named "Victory" for her survival. She and her daughter live with HIV contracted from the rebels.

The Hague from 1996 to 1999 and indicted Slobodan Milosevic, the former Yugoslavian president, among others, for war crimes. In 2001, the ICTY (International Criminal Trial for the former Yugoslavia) convicted three Bosnian Serb men for their role in the mass rape of Muslim women in the city of Focal during the conflict in Bosnia-Herzegovina.

Environmental Destruction

The wilful destruction of the environment as a strategy of war, as practice for war, or as punishment for the defeated occurred at least as early as Roman times and persists in modern-day society. Roman armies routinely destroyed crops and salted the earth to ruin the land's fertility. A millennium later, the Russians burned their own crops and homes not once but twice, to prevent the invading armies of Napoleon and, later, Hitler from making use of them. In a different but no less destructive behaviour, Allied navies during World War II routinely used the whales of the North Atlantic for target practice (Mowat, 1984).

When the coalition forces pushed the Iraqi forces out of Kuwait in 1991, the Iraqis set fire to 732 of the country's roughly 900 oil wells, producing one of the worst environmental disasters in history. Black smoke from the fires blocked out the sun and produced record low temperatures along a 950-kilometre tract of land. Rescue efforts recovered over 22 million barrels of oil, but more is thought to have leaked from the destroyed oil fields into the local environment, contaminating soil and water supplies. Saddam

Hussein also ordered the release of an estimated 11 million barrels of oil into the Arabian Gulf, damaging local marine life.

Military operations also harm the environment during peacetime. The US military is the largest producer of dangerous materials in the country, and "decades of improper and unsafe handling, storage and disposal of hazardous materials while building and maintaining the world's most powerful fighting force have severely polluted America's air, water and soil" (Calhoun, 1996: 60). Disposal is a major problem, and the drafters of disarmament treaties often have trouble suggesting a safe place for the disposal of missiles, mines, bombs, and nuclear warheads.

Modern warfare and the innovative war technologies of the twenty-first century have given rise to nanopollution. The impact and health risks of nanopollutants—such as dust at the nanoscale—have become a concern for researchers. These microscopic particles can enter the bloodstream of humans and spread throughout the body, causing new diseases with unusual symptoms and other yet-to-be-studied health problems (Gatti and Montanari, 2008).

Theoretical Perspectives on War and Terrorism

Table 10.1 describes the various sociological viewpoints and perspectives on war and terrorism. It is important to remember that one perspective is not more correct than another.

TABLE 10.1	Theoretical Perspectives
THEORY	MAIN POINTS
Structural Functionalism	• All elements in society are interrelated. • War and terrorism reinforce group identity and increase social cohesion as well as conformity. • Increased employment and production of weapons lead to economic benefit.
Conflict Theory	• Conflict and change are features of social life everywhere. • War and terrorism reflect struggles between opposite groups over power, limited resources, or ideological domination. • Only some groups benefit, namely, corporations, politicians, intermediaries, and black marketeers.
Symbolic Interactionism	• Socialization and labelling shape attitudes and the roles people adopt towards war efforts and conflicts. • In times of war, leaders use propaganda and euphemistic language to legitimize combat and to reduce the rational and emotional impact of death.
Feminist Theory	• In Western culture, mainly men have fought in wars. • War is seen as misguided protective chivalry or paternalistic sexism towards the "lesser" sex. • Consequences of war: women are raped, forced into prostitution.
Social Constructionism	• Propaganda legitimizes war and reduces the rational and emotional impact of death. • Political parties deflect criticism by focusing national attention on real or imagined enemies, on the valour of the nation's fighting forces, and on the "good" they are doing the country that has been invaded. • People mobilize to form social movements and to influence public policy.

Structural Functionalism

Structural functionalists believe that most elements in society exist to serve some purpose. Conflict and violence are the results of a system malfunctioning—for example, some of the system's needs for integration and consensus not being met. From this standpoint, wars occur because groups or societies do not know how to resolve their conflicts peacefully. They lack shared values or institutions for lawfully resolving disagreement. They lack the leadership and assets to bring peace. By this reckoning, war results from the breakdown of peace. Wars may even arise because military institutions and activities hold great importance within the society and culture.

A large-scale conflict strengthens social cohesion and group identity. Internal squabbles between political parties, ethnic communities, special interest groups, and so on are put aside, at least temporarily, as the entire nation bands together in a show of patriotism to defeat a common enemy (Thomas et al., 2009). Only when this common enemy is no longer a threat to national well-being do the internal conflicts resume. Sometimes the solidarity between allies created through the defence of shared interests persists even after the war is over.

Conflict Theory

Conflict theorists state that wars are struggles between opposing groups over power, limited assets, or ideological domination taken to their logical, violent conclusions. Just as social classes may battle one another for economic positions within a society, so nation-states and interest groups within the society may go to war with one another. The difference is that they routinely use weapons and kill one another.

Conflict theory stresses the ways in which war benefits some groups—most notably, corporations, politicians, and the military—but not others. The "military-industrial complex," a term first introduced in warning by US president Dwight D. Eisenhower in 1961 as he left office, refers to the close relationship between the military and the private defence industry and their combined control of the political agenda. Sociologist C. Wright Mills first analyzed the sociological and structural underpinnings of this power structure in his classic work *The Power Elite* (1956). In Canada, for example, Conservative minister of national defence Gordon O'Connor had been a career officer in the Canadian military, retiring as brigadier general, and had then worked as a defence industry lobbyist for several major military suppliers until he entered politics in 2004.

In the US, several leading figures in the Bush administration, notably Vice-President Dick Cheney and Defence Secretary Donald Rumsfeld, had previously been involved with companies that profit from war. Corporations contracted by the Pentagon to design, develop, and make weapons are guaranteed profits even if they overrun their budgets. It is sensible, therefore, for these companies to ensure that global conflicts and threats to national security continue so that they can run a profitable war machine. Industrialists, politicians, brokers, and black marketeers, among others, make enormous fortunes from war and weapons of war. This has an important effect on the class structure of society.

According to the Stockholm International Peace Research Institute (SIPRI, 2013), world military expenditure is estimated to have reached $1.63 trillion. This represents a 50 per cent increase since 2001 and corresponds to approximately $236 for each person in the world. These costs include the salaries of military personnel, research

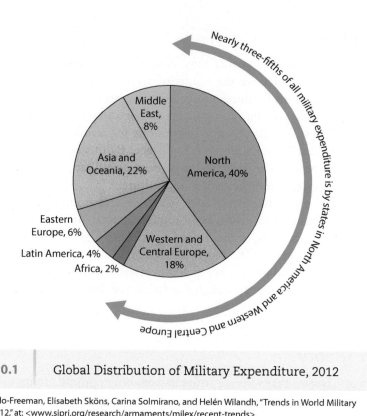

FIGURE 10.1   Global Distribution of Military Expenditure, 2012

Source: Sam Perlo-Freeman, Elisabeth Sköns, Carina Solmirano, and Helén Wilandh, "Trends in World Military Expenditure, 2012," at: <www.sipri.org/research/armaments/milex/recent-trends>.

into and development of weapons and combat technology, the purchase and manufacture of artillery and wartime machinery, and veterans' benefits. This also means that $1.63 trillion was not being spent globally on health care, education, infrastructure, or social services.

Figure 10.1 maps the global distribution of spending on military troops and technologies. Nearly half of the total spending is by the US government, distantly followed by Western and Central Europe, Asia, and the Middle East.

One might expect indicators of peacemaking to vary inversely with indicators of warmaking, such that countries that spent a lot of money on the military would rank low on a peace index. However, this is only partly true. African countries, for example, rank low on military spending in comparison with other countries (though they may rank much higher in their per capita spending as a fraction of GNP); they also rank low on the Global Peace Index. And, at the other end, the US ranks high on military spending but also ranks high on the Global Peace Index (Figure 10.2). The Global Peace Index—developed by the Institute for Economics and Peace—measures the relative position of a nation's "peacefulness." The Peace Index is composed of 23 separate indicators, including perceived criminality in society, jailed population, political instability, and weapons exports, to name a few. Countries are given a score based on these indicators, which range from 1, being the most peaceful, to 5, being the least peaceful (Vision of Humanity, 2009). As this figure shows, the majority of the western hemisphere, Europe, and Australia rank well on the Global Peace Index. On the other hand, the majority of Africa and Asia rank lower on the scale.

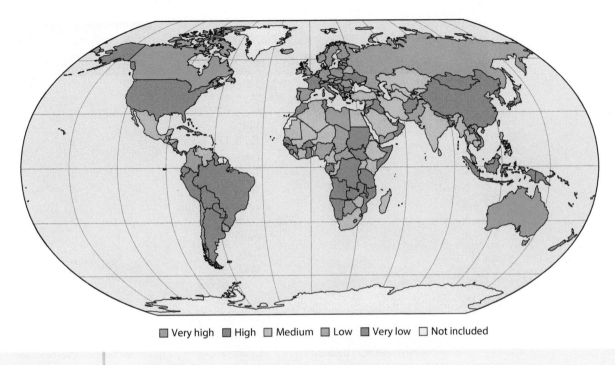

□ Very high ■ High □ Medium ■ Low ■ Very low □ Not included

FIGURE 10.2 | The Global Peace Index, 2012

The Global Peace Index ranks nations on various indicators of peace. The top-ranking nations on the Global Peace Index in 2012 were Iceland, New Zealand, Japan, and Canada.
Source: The Global Peace Index, 2012. Courtesy ChartsBin <chartsbin.com>.

Note also that the countries that rank highest on the Peace Index—among them, New Zealand, Denmark, Norway, Iceland, Austria, Sweden, Japan, Canada, and Finland—spend little (per capita) on the military. They also score high on measures of social development and quality of life.

Table 10.2 reports the military expenditures by the countries under NATO, a military alliance, in 2012. According to the data, Canada spent only 1.3 per cent of its GDP on military expenditures in 2012, compared to the US at 4.4 per cent, China at 2.0 per cent, and the UK at 2.5 per cent.

Symbolic Interactionism

Symbolic interactionists examine the ways in which cultures socialize people to adopt certain attitudes towards war and conflict. Society encourages aggression and the resolution of conflicts through physical force as early as childhood, mostly in boys.

Symbolic interactionists also study the language and labels of war. Propaganda techniques are employed by the government, businesses (e.g., munitions manufacturers), the military, and "patriotic organizations" (such as veterans' groups). Propaganda may include describing the current global "war on terror" as a "justified war" against "evil forces."

In particular, the media play an important role in the spin-doctoring of this message. In times of war, leaders use a special language to legitimize combat and reduce the rational and emotional impact of the deaths that will follow. In this language, soldiers are

TABLE 10.2	Defence Expenditures of Selected NATO Countries, 2012, Based on Current Prices and Exchange Rates (US$ millions)	
RANKING	NATO MEMBER COUNTRY	% GDP
1.	United States	4.4
2.	China	2.0
3.	United Kingdom	2.5
4.	France	2.3
5.	Russia	4.4
6.	Japan	1.0
7.	Saudi Arabia	8.9
8.	Germany	1.4
9.	India	2.5
10.	Italy	1.7
11.	Brazil	1.5
12.	South Korea	2.7
13.	Australia	1.7
14.	Canada	1.3
15.	Turkey	2.3

Source: SIPRI Military Expenditure Database, 2012, NATO-Russia Compendium of Financial and Economic Data Relating to Defence (2005), at: <milexdata.sipri.org/>.

not "murder victims," they are "casualties." A missile does not blow up an enemy barrack, it "services the target." The unplanned but "unavoidable" killing of innocent civilians is reported as "collateral damage." And nuclear missiles are not weapons of mass destruction, they are "peacekeepers."

Feminist Theory

Masculinity and militarism have had a close relationship over time and across cultures, and the "meanings attached to masculinity are so firmly linked to compliance with military roles that it is often impossible to disentangle the two" (Enloe, 1987: 531). The association between masculinity and militarism begins in childhood socialization. In Western culture, boys wage make-believe wars with GI Joe figurines, while girls are much more likely to play with dolls and act out domestic routines such as baking and having tea parties. Children whose parents deliberately raise them in pacifist traditions may have difficulty enacting those values among their schoolmates.

With only a few exceptions through the history of Western culture, it has been mainly men who have fought wars. This is due in part to women's smaller physical stature, to the nature of warfare (which traditionally has involved much face-to-face, close range, physical combat), and to men's greater tendency towards aggression and violence. Some say that a protective chivalry or paternalistic sexism towards the "lesser sex" is involved in men's largely exclusive role in warfare; men try to protect women, they argue.

Some authors propose that the perception of the role of women in war is limited, extending only to women's strategies of survival, resistance, and efforts to protest war and counter its effects. Feminist studies contest the claim for a natural link between women and peace (Blanchard, 2003). They propose that the participation and support of women in war-making, as well as their involvement in shaping the agenda of war, have been neglected. Understanding the gender dynamics of war requires a focus on women's contributions in reshaping the discourse of the war and using it for political gain.

Major wars have allowed women greater entry into the workforce to replace the men recruited for war. During World War II, this meant new job opportunities for women, who until then had been limited to a narrow range of traditionally female jobs. They later found opportunities working in "essential" industries such as engineering, metals, chemicals, vehicles, transport, energy, and shipbuilding (Summerfield, 2000). Even today, however, women—a large fraction of the paid workforce—are only a small minority of all military personnel in today's standing armies.

Social Constructionism

The social constructionist approach stresses the role of moral entrepreneurs in mobilizing support for social causes, such as for waging wars.

To illustrate, false propaganda and misinformation produced by the US administration were used to gain American citizens' support for the 2003 invasion of Iraq. The so-called facts used to justify this unilateral pre-emptive war—such as the presence of weapons of mass destruction and the claimed co-operation between Osama bin Laden and Saddam Hussein—have since been exposed as deceptions and red herrings. Remarkably, once such a war has begun, public awareness of politically motivated lies—to the extent the public is even aware of the deception or believes it to be true—changes nothing when the propaganda machine continues to proclaim the necessity of war to secure the "homeland" against "evildoers."

Propaganda also supports the vilification of certain groups during wartime. Consider the effects of Canada's War Measures Act on Canadian race relations (and vice versa). The War Measures Act was originally legislated in 1914 as a response to anxieties connected with World War I. This legislation was used during both world wars and, in particular, was further used to justify the unjust treatment of Japanese Canadians during and after World War II. Using this Act, the Canadian government uprooted Japanese Canadians from their homes, placed them in internment camps, and had their properties confiscated; some were even deported (Kage, 2002). The war and the War Measures Act helped to justify derogatory and racially hostile views that already existed. In short, it made racism acceptable in Canada (Dhamoon and Abu-Laban, 2009). As well, it held the Japanese Canadians responsible for racially hostile sentiments that they had played no part in creating (Clement, 2008).

The social constructionist paradigm also considers the role of the media in the vilifying and victimizing of war participants. Take, for instance, the coverage of the Israeli–Palestinian conflict by the Israeli press. Despite human losses on both sides—indeed, much greater losses of both life and the means of living for Palestinians—claims-making in the media has resulted in one-sided victimization of the Israelis in the Israeli press. Reporters engage in the dramatization of injury by stressing the severity of the Palestinian terrorist attacks and in the dramatization of innocence by focusing on the undeserved fate of the Israeli victims (Cromer, 2005).

THE FOG OF WAR
Documentarian Errol Morris's 2003 film explores the use of rhetoric and propaganda in America's military forays into Communist Vietnam.

Social Consequences of War

The two most socially consequential facts about war are (1) it kills many people, and (2) it is expensive. It is not only soldiers who are killed during warfare. The cost to society imposed by warfare is massive. The rise in both casualty rates and military expenditures in modern warfare is partly due to the larger scale of conflict and partly due to the advanced technology used in waging war. Additionally, warfare shatters morale and the fabric of civic society and has lasting negative impacts on the health of populations.

Effects on the Economy

Wars sometimes bring economic benefits. For example, Canadian participation in World War II led to increased employment and production that helped to end the financial downturn of the Great Depression. After the war, North America, which did not experience the degree of devastation of many European and some Asian countries, rode the financial momentum throughout the next several decades, experiencing prosperity and growth in all parts of society.

Canadians, the strongest trading partner of the United States, also enjoyed a financial boom during and after the war: the GNP doubled, industry developed exponentially, and consumer spending rose with the baby boom generation (Girvan, 2000). The defeated, including Germany and Japan, suffered significant setbacks to their economies for many years after the conflict ended.

Wars lead to scientific and technological innovations that may benefit society in peacetime. Military research on laser-based defence made it easier to develop laser surgery; experimentation with nuclear weaponry allowed for the widespread development of nuclear power stations; the airline industry's technological innovations were made possible largely through the work of military defence departments; and the Internet grew out of research sponsored by the US military as a possible emergency communications network in case of nuclear war.

In this sense, innovations in weaponry are social innovations as well as engineering feats. At the same time, many technological advances have what may be called a "dual-use status"—that is, there are both benefits and risks associated with them. Though the Internet emerged from research sponsored by the US military, it has become a threat with the rise of cyberterrorism.

According to Weimann (2004), the rise in anxiety about cyberterrorism in American society is due to the combination of two modern fears: the fear of arbitrary, violent targeting and the fear that computer technology itself could lead to catastrophic attacks against computer networks. Further examples relate to new advances in applications meant for hazard detection, prevention, and response to terrorist attacks.

On top of their intended benefits, these same advances can have unintended consequences and contribute to terrorist motives. Differential access to these technologies, for instance, could work to increase stresses in already-divisive societies by widening a digital divide (LePoire and Glenn, 2007).

Effects on Children

Increasingly, wars are being waged with the help of child soldiers. Though the United Nations Convention on the Rights of the Child states that children under the age of

PERSONAL *stories*

| **BOX 10.2** | **Memoirs of a Child Soldier** |

At 10 years old, Michel Chikwanine was struggling with his math homework at home one day when he heard gunshots outside. Terrified, he dove under his bed as rebel soldiers entered his home. He then remembered a promise he'd made to his dad—to protect the family while he was away. He crawled out, and as he took his first steps down the stairs, he heard a click.

"I looked back and it's a rebel soldier with a gun pointed straight toward my face," he says. "He kept pushing me to go down the stairs. They forced me to watch my family be raped in front of me."

Chikwanine, now 23 years old and living in Toronto, also remembered being forced to kill his best friend. He was just five years old when rebel soldiers blindfolded him in his native Democratic Republic of Congo, placed a heavy gun in his hand, and demanded he shoot. Minutes before, they slashed his left wrist and rubbed a substance that included cocaine and gunpowder into the wound. He felt woozy and his head was pounding as he heard the soldiers repeat their demands to "shoot, shoot, shoot."

He remembers his hand vibrating violently as he pulled the trigger.

A rebel soldier removed the blindfold and Chikwanine looked down at the white Superman T-shirt he was wearing. It was covered in blood. That's when he saw his best friend, Kevin, 12, lying on the ground. He ran over to him, screaming and begging the rebel soldiers for help. But they only laughed.

"All of the sudden [Kevin] just looks at me and a tear falls down [out] of his eye." Then a rebel soldier walked over and said something Chikwanine will never forget.

"You've killed your best friend. Your family will never take you back. We are your only family."

His experience as a child soldier in the Congo and later as a refugee trying to flee Uganda with his family brings back terrifying and painful memories, but Chikwanine is determined to retell his story as many times as needed to bring awareness of the conflict in Africa, of the poverty and disease. A motivational speaker for Me to We, an arm of charity, Chikwanine speaks to tens of thousands of Canadian schoolchildren at We Day events across the country. These events are designed to educate schoolchildren on social issues such as poverty, climate change, and hunger, and to motivate them to make an effort on a local or global level.

Source: Adapted from *New Hamburg Independent*, at: <www.newhamburgindependent.ca/news/students-learn-of-horrors-faced-by-child-soldier>.

15 are not to be used as soldiers, children are still being used as soldiers. The *Child Soldiers Global Report* (Coalition to Stop the Use of Child Soldiers, 2009: 389) estimates that 300,000 child soldiers are currently fighting in more than 40 countries around the world. This is not counting the large numbers of children who have enlisted themselves in civil wars as part of liberation armies in Ireland, Palestine, and elsewhere.

This use of children in warfare has been promoted, unwittingly, by technological innovation—specifically, by the development and manufacture of lightweight automatic weapons. These weapons are light enough for a young child to carry and are easy to use (Human Rights Watch, n.d.: 91). The story in Box 10.2 illustrates the harrowing experiences of one child soldier in Africa. No doubt, there are hundreds of thousands of such stories; we have yet to learn the long-term physical and psychological effects of such military service by children.

Health Consequences of War

According to some estimates, military conflicts in the twentieth century led to the deaths of over 100 million soldiers and civilians—more than the total number of casualties in all previous wars in human history combined (Porter, 1994).

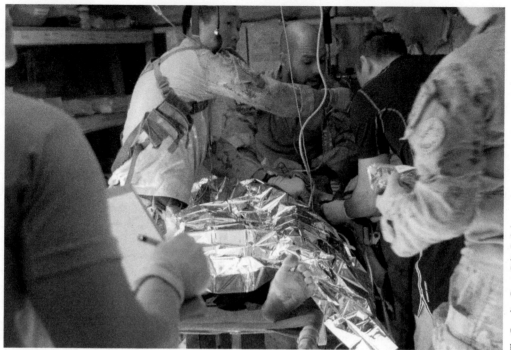

The Canadian Press, Colin Perkel

Corporal Elton Lee, left, Corporal Yann Gauthier, middle, and Warrant Officer Yves Martin, in black T-shirt, tend to a badly wounded Afghan man at the Canadian medical station at Forward Operating Base Ma'sum Ghar. The man and a colleague were injured when their minivan hit a roadside bomb near the base.

BROTHERS

In this 2009 film, Sam (Tobey Maguire) returns from serving in the military in Afghanistan, only to find himself experiencing severe post-combat mental distress.

Post-traumatic stress disorder (PTSD) A form of psychological distress produced by a traumatic experience such as crime victimization, sexual assault, or military combat. Symptoms include nervousness, sleep disturbances, disruption of concentration, anxiety, depression, irrational fear, and flashbacks triggered by loud noises such as thunder or a car's backfiring.

If these numbers seem appalling, they pale in comparison to the possible death tolls humanity would achieve were a full-scale nuclear war to break out. Currently, the nuclear weapons in major military arsenals are more than 4,000 times as powerful as the atomic bombs dropped on Japan. Friedman and Friedman (1998) estimate that a nuclear war today would kill 160 million people instantly. Another billion would perish in the first few hours because of radiation poisoning, environmental devastation, and massive social chaos, while hundreds of millions more would die slowly over the following years.

Just as death is an unavoidable outcome of war, so, too, are physical and psychological injuries. The number of military personnel and civilians who are injured or maimed during a war usually exceeds the number of deaths. One common military strategy is to maim rather than kill the enemy, since it takes more resources to care for the wounded than to discard their bodies. Anti-personnel landmines are used to carry out this task, since they are largely undetectable by civilians or enemy troops without proper equipment.

Surviving a war physically unscathed does not guarantee complete well-being. Many veterans of war suffer the slow torture of psychological disorders. One of the most studied of these disorders is **post-traumatic stress disorder** (PTSD), which occurs after experiencing major trauma. Currently, researchers are focusing on pharmacotherapy as a potential treatment for PTSD (Holbrook et al., 2010).

Solutions to War and Global Conflict

Arms Reduction

As we have already noted, with the coming of the twentieth century the scope of battle increased; more potent weapons killed more combatants and more civilians than ever. Thus, a chief concern has been to find ways to reduce the number and types of weapons in people's hands and especially to find ways of protecting civilians against weapons and their misuse.

A prime example of this effort has been the landmines convention that Canada and its foreign minister, Lloyd Axworthy, were instrumental in achieving. Landmines have been widely and indiscriminately used around the world as a means of killing foot soldiers and spreading fear among enemy combatants and civilian populations. Many of them have remained in place after wars have ended—or have been moved by flooding and slope processes to new locations—and have maimed and killed many unsuspecting civilians, including children. The Convention on the Prohibition of the Use, Stockpiling, Production and Transfer of Anti-Personnel Mines and on Their Destruction, known as the Ottawa Convention, opened for signature on 3 December 1997. By the end of 1998, fully 133 countries had signed the convention, and 55 of those had ratified it a year later. The convention came into legal force in March 1999.

Many countries contributed funds towards making this convention work; Canada alone contributed $2.8 million for mine-action projects in seven countries in Central Europe, Africa, and the Middle East. An example of the work done with this money includes de-mining activities in Cambodia, where over 32,000 mines were removed and 10,000 people, as a result, were able to return to their fields where they could then safely grow rice.

Other efforts have been made to limit the production and sale of small arms. As the United Nations has noted, "small arms and light weapons destabilize regions; spark, fuel, and prolong conflicts; obstruct relief programs; undermine peace initiatives; worsen human rights abuses; hamper development; and foster a 'culture of violence'" (disarmament.un.org/cab/salw.html).

International co-operation on this matter took a giant step forward when the United Nations held the Conference on the Illicit Trade in Small Arms and Light Weapons in All Its Aspects in July 2001. On that occasion, the participating states agreed to adopt the Program of Action to Prevent, Combat, and Eradicate the Illicit Trade in Small Arms and Light Weapons, in All Its Aspects. This agreed-upon program includes a number of measures: it legislates the sale of weapons, provides for the destruction of those that were illegally obtained, and requires co-operation in tracing illicit arms. In the 2005 World Summit Outcome Document (A/60/L.1) the General Assembly reiterated its support for the implementation of this program.

Arms are big business. According to the Stockholm International Peace Research Institute (SIPRI, 2008), in 2012 the top five arms exporters in the world were, in descending order, the United States, Russia, China, Ukraine, and Germany. That year the US exported $8.7 billion worth of weapons, down from $18.5 billion in 2004—then four times as much as its nearest competitors, Russia and France (at $4.5 billion each) and 20 times as much as sixth-place Canada in 2008 (which shipped a "mere" $900 million worth). Though the total value of exports has decreased dramatically, arms exports in the US still amounted to close to 31 times as much as that in Canada (Canada ranked as the sixteenth-largest arms exporter in 2013).

CANADIAN researchers

| BOX 10.3 | David Murakami Wood, Queen's University |

Dr David Murakami Wood holds a Tier II Canada Research Chair in Surveillance Studies at Queen's University in Kingston, Ontario. His research explores the post-9/11 turn towards heightened security and global surveillance. Today, closed-circuit television cameras on street corners, DNA databases, and ever-tighter border controls have become commonplace. No matter where we are geographically, our privacy is quickly disappearing. Murakami Wood asks, "What's really going on, and is it the same everywhere in the world?"

Along with collaborators in North America, Japan, Brazil, and the United Kingdom, Murakami Wood examines *how* and *why* surveillance is being implemented across the globe. In a fascinating 2013 piece, "What Is Global Surveillance? Towards a Relational Political Economy of the Global Surveillant Assemblage," Murakami Wood dissects the complex relationship between surveillance and "the global," arguing that in the contemporary control society, surveillance is employed to facilitate the functioning of neoliberalism and the naturalization of the global as its proper scale of operation. He argues that surveillance has not become "multilevel in a simple scalar sense," but rather in a collective effort from different agencies, bureaus, and private companies that are networked through formal and informal platforms.

Although a global issue, security and surveillance also affect people at a local level. A 2006 paper by Murakami Wood and Jon Coaffee argues just that. They declare that "security is coming home"—in other words, "that the discourses, procedures and in some cases material examples of national and international security are influencing or are directly employed at smaller scales" (2006: 514). This, they argue, is occurring at the expense of the liberty, freedom, and mobility of the common citizen.

Murakami Wood's research moves beyond simply accepting increased surveillance. He seeks to understand how we might thoughtfully respond to it now, and in the future. As this chapter shows, war and terrorism are as old as human society and there is little reason to believe that widespread conflict between groups will ever end. Murakami Wood's work on surveillance shows us how technology and globalization have adapted to reduce the consequences—and potential outbreaks—of war and terror, no matter how limited their efforts may be.

Sources: Jon Coaffee and David Murakami Wood, "Security Is Coming Home: Rethinking Scale and Constructing Resilience in the Global Urban Response to Terrorist Risk," *International Relations* 20, 4 (2006): 503–17; David Murakami Wood, 2013, "What Is Global Surveillance? Towards a Relational Political Economy of the Global Surveillant Assemblage," *Geoforum* 49 (2013): 317–26; and CRC profile.

An illegal trade in small arms is common in many countries and regions of the world—especially those affected by political instability. Often, the legal arms trade feeds an illegal arms trade, with legally purchased weaponry being resold for illegal purposes. In this way, the arms industry poses global problems thanks to its (often secret) business practices.

The Control Arms Campaign, founded by Amnesty International, Oxfam, and the International Network on Small Arms, estimates that over 600 million small arms are in circulation in the world, with over 1,135 companies based in more than 98 different countries occupied in manufacturing them. The result is an average of over 500,000 deaths every year, roughly one death per minute. Many people see the supplying of weapons for conflict as immoral and dangerous behaviour that carries little personal, national, or corporate risk. In this way, the global arms industry enables a few to profit from war and death by prolonging wars that might otherwise dwindle to an end if the arms supply dried up (<oxfam.ca/our-work/campaigns/control-arms>).

Redistributing Economic Assets

Some believe that terrorism and warfare could be reduced, and peace ensured, only by redistributing economic assets more equally among nations and among people within nations. We know that disparities in wealth and assets have been and are causes of many wars, past and present. Thus, we could probably reduce conflict through a more equal distribution of assets. However, it is unlikely that prosperous nations would readily agree to lower their standards of living at home to benefit less wealthy societies.

Redistributing economic wealth from core nations to peripheral nations does not guarantee that poorer nations would have a better standard of living. There must be proper rules to ensure that citizens would benefit from aid funds. Otherwise, politicians and state elites might appropriate the funds to further their own interests at the expense of their citizens.

In addition, aid funds must be targeted for social development, not for military spending. Much of US foreign aid, for example, has been targeted for arms to client states such as Saudi Arabia and Israel, just as it was in the past to Saddam Hussein in Iraq, to Osama bin Laden and freedom fighters in Afghanistan, to the Shah of Iran, and to numerous dictatorial regimes in Latin America. The extreme spending on the war on terror in Afghanistan and Iraq is depicted in Figure 10.3. Note the disparity in spending between Afghanistan and Iraq in recent years.

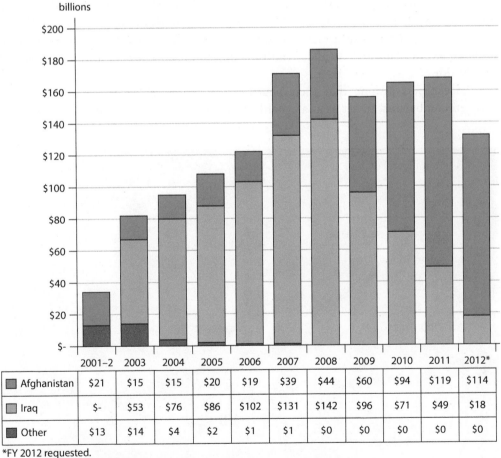

billions

	2001–2	2003	2004	2005	2006	2007	2008	2009	2010	2011	2012*
Afghanistan	$21	$15	$15	$20	$19	$39	$44	$60	$94	$119	$114
Iraq	$-	$53	$76	$86	$102	$131	$142	$96	$71	$49	$18
Other	$13	$14	$4	$2	$1	$1	$0	$0	$0	$0	$0

*FY 2012 requested.

FIGURE 10.3   War on Terror Spending, 2001–2 to 2012

Source: Medill National Security Journalism Initaitive, March 2011, at: <nationalsecurityzone.org/site/a-helpful-new-guide-to-much-has-been-spent-on-the-war-on-terror-since-911/>.

The Role of International Peacekeeping Bodies

Another harm-reduction and risk-reduction strategy has been to form an international body dedicated to peacekeeping and preventing global conflict. The most prominent organization trying to carry out this task has been the United Nations. UN peacekeepers have been patrolling war-torn regions since 1948, when the UN Truce Supervision Organization was set up to oversee the ceasefire agreed to by Israel and its Middle East neighbours.

Canadians have been active peacekeepers in the world since 1956, when then secretary of state for external affairs (and eventual prime minister) Lester B. Pearson sent Canadian forces to Egypt. Seeing a chance to ease tensions around the Suez Canal conflict, Pearson suggested creating a worldwide peacekeeping force to oversee the withdrawal of armed forces from the area and serve as a long-term barrier between Egypt and Israel. This was the first UN peacekeeping mission to be lightly armed and to have more than simple observer status (Knight and Keating, 2010: 176). The UN mission, led by Canadians, was a success and resulted in Pearson's winning the Nobel Peace Prize in 1957.

Since the use of peacekeeping troops in Suez began, there have been 60 UN peace operations involving more than 750,000 military, police, and civilian personnel. Missions have served all over the world, creating buffer zones in Cyprus and the former Yugoslavia, bringing aid to Haiti and Rwanda, and providing observers to conflicts in Angola and El Salvador.

Peacekeepers assume that their neutrality will allow them to insert themselves between combatants, to act as a safeguard. In theory, their presence provides a physical

A delegation of veterans is recognized in the House of Commons on Parliament Hill in Ottawa on the occasion of the fiftieth anniversary of the United Nations' peacekeeping mission in Cyprus.

The Canadian Press/Sean Kilpatrick

and psychological barrier against shots being fired. In practice—for example, in Rwanda during the mid-1990s—the peacekeeping force had no such effect and could not prevent bloodshed. Peacekeeping also assumes that fighters on all sides are sincere in their wish for peace. When this is not the case, violence can break out, as occurred in the former Yugoslavia, where broken ceasefires led to general fighting in 1995 and the first withdrawal of UN troops.

Interventions by UN peacekeeping forces have undoubtedly prevented wars and saved lives. However, UN actions have not been enough to eliminate war, as many outbreaks of war have occurred under "the watch" of the United Nations. To this list we can add the 2001 and 2003 invasions of Afghanistan and Iraq by the United States, Britain, and others, which were launched in spite of extensive efforts by the UN to preserve diplomacy and peace.

Chapter Summary

Some have thought of war as the natural outcome of innate aggression. The opposing view is that people are not born to be violent or aggressive, but that we learn to act so. According to this latter explanation, war is a result of social organization and cultural tradition and a response to cultural symbols.

We could think of the arms race as a symbolic show of power and as a means of securing peace through mutual deterrence. However, the negative outcomes include the obvious potential for mass destruction and the enormous monetary cost. The assets spent to produce and preserve armaments could instead be assigned to relieving other social problems, both at home among the big military spenders and abroad in countries of the developing and less-developed world, where the need for these assets and for foreign aid is most prominent.

Terrorism can exist for different reasons. Common forms are revolutionary terrorism, in which rebels wage war on the state, and repressive terrorism, in which the state wages war in an effort to repress its citizens. Other forms include transnational terrorism or terrorism by autonomous agents.

Massive economic inequalities exist between nations. **Relative deprivation** breeds resentment, and resentment can foment aggression. War will pose a problem for humanity as long as widespread inequalities in wealth and power between nations and extensive differences in beliefs and interests persist along with prevailing weaknesses in those bodies—such as the United Nations—that are charged with keeping the world's peace.

Relative deprivation The feelings and judgements of an individual or members of a group when they compare themselves to others who are better-off materially. People make judgements relative to standards or frames of reference. The feelings generated contribute to the formation of social movements.

Questions for Critical Thought

1. Consider the true cost of war—the many lives lost and the many more scarred. Is war justifiable? If not, what can people justifiably do to fight injustice and break free of oppression?
2. Should nations be responsible for the consequences of war? If so, how?
3. Will concerns about the spread of nuclear weapons blind us to the value of older, more conventional strategies of war?

4. Is it justifiable to kill non-combatants in war?
5. When and how should we intervene on humanitarian grounds in conflicts in other parts of the world—for example, against the abuses of women and children in many parts of Africa and the Middle East?

Recommended Readings

Bashevkin, Sylvia. 2009. *Women, Power, Politics: The Hidden Story of Canada's Unfinished Democracy*. Oxford and New York: Oxford University Press.

Beah, Ishmael. 2007. *A Long Way Gone: Memoirs of a Boy Soldier*. Vancouver: Douglas & McIntyre.

Bertell, Rosalie. 2000. *Planet Earth: The Latest Weapon of War*. London: Women's Press.

Chappell, Louise, and Lisa Hill, eds. *The Politics of Women's Interests: New Comparative Perspectives*. London and New York: Routledge, 2006.

della Porta, Donatella, Massimiliano Andretta, Lorenzo Mosca, and Herbert Reiter. *Globalization from Below: Transnational Activists and Protest Networks*. Minneapolis: University of Minnesota Press, 2006.

Einholf, Christopher J. 2007. "The Fall and Rise of Torture," *Sociological Theory* 25, 2: 101–21.

Fry, Douglas P. 2009. *Beyond War: The Human Potential for Peace*. New York and Oxford: Oxford University Press.

Jones, David H. 2005. "On the Prevention of Genocide: The Gap between Research and Education," *War Crimes, Genocide, and Crimes against Humanity* 1, 1: 5–46.

Pearse, Meic. 2007. *The Gods of War: Is Religion the Primary Cause of Violent Conflict?* Nottingham, UK: Inter-Varsity Press.

Part 4　Domains

© Volodymyr Kyrylyuk/iStockphoto

11

Families

Thinglass/Thinkstock

LEARNING OBJECTIVES

- To understand the historical evolution of the family and its structure.
- To distinguish between the myths and the realities of the family.
- To be familiar with the various definitions of "family."
- To learn about the disparities between Aboriginal and non-Aboriginal families.
- To understand the current patterns of marital unions and parenthood.
- To be alert to the effects of marital disharmony on children.
- To appreciate the different feminist theories on family life.
- To recognize the stressful elements of family life and their health impacts.
- To explore possible solutions for various family issues.

Introduction

For most Canadians, family life is about three main things: the relationships between spouses (or partners), between parents and children, and between siblings. Family life, from this standpoint, is about the everyday face-to-face interactions between people who know one another well.

Sociologists think about family life in other ways as well, seeing families, for example, as part of a large institutional structure of society that includes economic, political, legal, religious, and other activities. Family life, from this standpoint, is something that influences and is influenced by every other element of our society.

Finally, sociologists are interested in the myths and traditions we weave around family life—the beliefs we hold and behaviours we construct around these beliefs. From this standpoint, family life—the image and the reality—is a result of social construction (King, 2007; Brabant, 2006). To illustrate this, we should start this chapter by noting that recent census data show us that the traditional heterosexual married family with children is no longer in the majority in Canada.

From each of these standpoints, families are a crucial institution in any society. In this chapter, we will touch on some of the things families do and some of the problems families encounter. And because families are so important, problems in family living become important social problems for society as a whole.

Different Kinds of Families

Families vary from one society to another, just as they vary within our own society. In most societies, families exist within larger social networks—within kinship groups and clans. The members of a household—the husband and wife, parent and child, brother and sister—are often integrated into a larger web of kin, and their lives cannot be understood without reference to this larger web of relations. Let's start with a few concepts and definitions.

A *kinship group* is a group of people who share a relationship through blood or marriage and have positions in a hierarchy of rights over the property (Skoda, 2007). Kin relationships sometimes control where family members must live, whom they can marry, and even their life opportunities. The definition of a kin relationship varies from one society to another, but kin relationships are important everywhere (Dixon, 2007).

Some societies trace kin relationships through the male line, so any individual's relationships are determined by his or her father's relationships; we call these kinship systems *patrilineal*. Others trace relationships through the female line; these are *matrilineal* systems (Rao, 2005). Still others count relationships through both lines; they are *bilateral* kinship systems (Read, 2010). If the kinship system is patrilineal, a person gains a position in the community just by being the child of his or her father. In a matrilineal kinship system, a person has certain property rights as the child of his or her mother.

Our society is neither matrilineal nor patrilineal—it is bilateral. This means that relatives of both of our parents are thought of as kin. We have maternal and paternal aunts, uncles, grandparents, cousins, and so on. Bilateral descent fits well with an egalitarian authority structure where father and mother have an equal say in family matters.

In many societies, including our own, a household often consists of parents and their unmarried children. In others, what we consider the **family** is embedded in a much

Family A group of people related by kinship or similar close ties in which the adults assume responsibility for the care and upbringing of their natural or adopted children. Members of a family support one another financially, materially, and emotionally.

broader web of kinship relations, and a household will include many kin. These two main forms of family household are referred to, respectively, as the nuclear family and the extended family. The **nuclear family** is the most common family household in our society. It consists of one or two generations living together—typically, one or two parents and their children (Phillips, 2009). The nuclear family is a *conjugal* family, in which priority is given to marital ties over blood ties. Western families are *neolocal*; that is, marriage brings with it the expectation that each of the partners will leave their parental home and set up a new residence together, forming another independent nuclear family (Loveless and Holman, 2007).

An **extended family**, by contrast, contains two or more generations of relatives living together. These may include grandparents or grandchildren, and uncles, aunts, and cousins. The extended family is a *consanguine* family, since preference is given to blood ties over marital ties. Consanguine families stress relationships between parents and their children, and with other "blood-related" members of the kin group.

The types and frequencies of family forms have been changing for centuries, and they are continuing to change, as we see from recent census data. Figure 11.1 shows the changes in household types in Canada from 2001 to 2011. Today, households of couples without children are the most common type of family, but other types of family households are increasing; these include one-person households, lone-parent families, and multiple and other family types. Canadian households are now more diverse, and the traditional two-parents-with-children household is ever less common.

Nuclear family A family unit comprising one or two parents and any dependent children who live together in one household separate from relatives.

Extended family More than two generations of relatives living together in a household. The arrangement often includes grandparents, aunts, uncles, and dependent nephews and nieces.

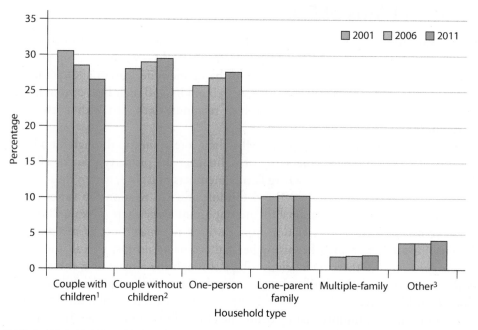

FIGURE 11.1   Distribution of Private Households by Household Type, Canada, 2001 to 2011

Notes: "Couple" households and "lone-parent family" households refer to one-family households.
[1]Refers to one-family households with children aged 24 and under.
[2]Refers to one-family households without children aged 24 and under.
[3]Refers to two or more people who share a private dwelling, but who do not constitute a census family.
Source: "Distribution (in percentage) of Private Households by Household Type, 2001 to 2011," at: <www12.statcan. gc.ca/census-recensement/2011/as-sa/98-312-x/2011003/fig/fig3_2-1-eng.cfm> (Sept. 2012).

Accordingly, sociologists have had to adopt new approaches to studying family life in our diverse and fluid society. For example, those with a life course approach examine how our close relations change throughout our lifetimes. They note how families change to meet new needs, such as those created by the arrival, care, or departure of children and aged parents (Petts, 2009).

Another approach is to study family relations from the perspective of different family members. This recognizes that different family members have different experiences as members of any given family. A son has a different experience from a daughter, and a mother has a different experience from a father. Because different family members have different experiences, and different interests, it is often inappropriate to speak of "the family" as though it had a single interest and acted in a unified way.

Studying families in a context of change and diversity reminds us to stay away from simple definitions and theories about family life that assume all families are the same, and stay the same, regardless of historical context. Consider, for example, how family members are differently affected by changes in the economy. Today, young adult children may stay in school longer, or may return home after having struck off on their own earlier, because they cannot find jobs, or cannot find jobs that pay enough for them to live independently. Similarly, children may be differently parented because of changing policies on parental leave. For example, younger children may have had full-time parents for a period in their early lives, while older siblings may have missed out on this, because their parents returned to work soon after giving birth (Nguyen et al., 2009).

Myths of the Family

One would think that, with so much change and diversity, it would be impossible to hold any simple or universal beliefs about family life, and yet people hold such beliefs nonetheless. In fact, these beliefs almost amount to "myths"—beliefs that resist evidence and personal experience.

As a result, in North American culture today, many people still think the "ideal" family is based on a formal marriage between two people of different sexes who have come together freely to build a monogamous and enduring relationship that includes reproduction and the rearing of children (Grutzmacher, 2007). Many members of the public still view alternatives to this as "departures from the ideal," if not as unusual as they were in the past. Single parenting, stepfamilies, common-law relationships, and same-sex couples may be becoming more familiar as patterns of families (and therefore becoming more acceptable), but they remain departures from the traditional cultural ideal.

Patriarchy and Family Values

Another holdover from "the good old days" of family life is patriarchal tradition. By patriarchy, we mean male dominance that is justified in a society's values and is thus tied to the ideology of gender inequality.

In Canada today, most people believe in a woman's right to choose contraception, to divorce, and to have a legal abortion; in the right of women to work outside the home in equal jobs for equal pay; and in the normality of gay relationships and marriage. However, the patriarchal family remains a powerful model for many in our society and influences the ways parents socialize their children into gender and sexual

Patriarchy Male dominance that is justified in a society's system of values. This dominance is tied to the ideology of gender and can be found in practically every society.

The Canadian Press/Aaron Harris

Single mother Lianne Thompson and daughter Bryanna, three, make dinner at home in Toronto. "Traditional" no longer describes the universal ideal for family in Canada, as census numbers from Statistics Canada suggest.

orientation (Chambers, 2000). This mythology about family life has drawn much of its power from fundamentalist Christians, religious Roman Catholics, Jews, and Muslims, and social conservatives. Immigration has served to reinvigorate these traditional, patriarchal values, since many of Canada's immigrants come to us from highly patriarchal societies.

Basic Aspects of Canadian Families

For practical purposes, we often define families as though they are merely households. The Canadian government, for example, defines the economic family as "a group of two or more people who live in the same dwelling and are related to each other by blood, marriage, common-law or adoption. A couple may be of opposite or same sex. Foster children are included" (Statistics Canada, 2012b).

A broader sociological definition of the family, one that most sociologists support, is "a group of individuals, related by blood, marriage, or adoption, who support one another financially, materially, and emotionally" (Murdock, 1949). This definition excludes people not related by blood, legal marriage, or legal adoption, such as same-sex partnerships.

Most Canadian families—67 per cent in 2011—are classifiable as a "married-couple union." However, this group has declined in size since 1961, when about 92 per cent of all families were based in legal marriage (Statistics Canada, 2012c). Alongside the decreased rate of marriage, we see a matching increase in common-law unions. Statistics

Canada defines common-law status as "two people living together as a couple but not legally married to each other" (Statistics Canada, 2011b). The common-law union is the fastest-growing family category today; the proportion of common-law families increased from 5.6 per cent to 16.7 per cent between 1981 and 2011. Additionally, in 2011, the number of common-law families surpassed the number of lone-parent families for the first time (Statistics Canada, 2012c).

However, we may prefer to define families not in terms of structural similarity, but in terms of similar processes—that is, as units that work in similar ways, however they are constituted. Indeed, the social groups we think of as families typically share many features. These commonalities can help us begin to understand the nature of families. Because families are extraordinarily diverse, it is difficult to generalize about them, though it is possible to focus our attention on their common processes. From this standpoint, "family" is a social relationship that provides daily care and ensures that one's financial and emotional needs are met (Luxton and Fox, 2009). Consider now the ideal "typical" aspects of family life.

First, families are expected to bind their members together in common attachment and some kind of dependency or interdependency. Compared to other types of intimate relations (at work or school), family relations are special in that they tend to include long-term commitments, both to one another and to the family per se.

Second, adult partners—or spouses—within families are expected to have a long-term, exclusive sexual relationship. In families, sexual relations are permitted and expected between spouses but prohibited between other members (e.g., between parents and children, or between siblings).

Third, parents and relatives are expected to keep children safe from accidents and household dangers, and away from drugs, alcohol, predators, and other forms of harm. As well, spouses are supposed to protect one another, and adult children are supposed to protect and help their parents.

Fourth, families are expected to maintain order by establishing rules and regulations that members must abide by, and one or both parents control the family. In much of family law and policy as practised in the past, the father or oldest male was in charge, and such patriarchal domination was seen as a right. In recent years, family decision-making has become much more egalitarian (between spouses) and many households are controlled by women.

If we think about families in ways that are defined by process rather than by structure, one comes to several conclusions. First, from a process standpoint, it is easier to see their differences as being similarities but with different forms and easier to understand the problems families have faced in adapting to modern economic life. Second, some families that seem ideal in terms of form are far from ideal in terms of process, and vice versa. Third and finally, our laws are written with ideal forms in mind, so they do not well serve families that deviate from these forms, no matter how good their processes may be. That said, bear in mind that the description above is an ideal type, and real families tend to fall short of the ideal in various ways. Some families are far less cohesive than others and fail to bind their members together. Some violate the sexual expectations by having no sexual relations, non-exclusive sexual relations, or incestuous sexual relations. Some fail to provide their most vulnerable members with care and protection and may even be abusive. Finally, some families are disorderly and chaotic, with no one in charge.

Families in Aboriginal Communities

Aboriginal families display some of the non-normative features of family life we have described above. Many Aboriginal people have had a hard time adapting to modern economic life, and their family lives have suffered as a result. However, their families have suffered for other reasons as well. Aboriginal communities were once the victims of a systematic campaign to assimilate them forcibly into mainstream Canadian society. This was done, in part, by isolating Aboriginal youth from their families and placing them in residential schools (Petten, 2007). The effects were disastrous.

Years of marginalization, failed assimilation, and abuse have made Aboriginal people sensitive to outside threats to their culture and community. Aboriginal cultures in Canada are diverse in terms of language, norms, practices, and beliefs; yet there have been historical commonalities among these groups regarding child-rearing processes. Aboriginal mothers and families traditionally placed great importance on the maintenance of Aboriginal cultural, religious traditions, and socio-cultural values within the family (Cheah and Chirkov, 2008). Historically, Aboriginal societies were largely egalitarian. Every member of the family was viewed as important, sharing responsibility for collective wellness. Further, the role of the extended family was traditionally important in Aboriginal communities. For example, grandparents and other kin were expected to play a part in the daily activities of family life, such as parenting and teaching cultural and moral values to children (ibid.).

However, harsh conditions had a harmful effect on the nurturing and parental skills within Aboriginal families. Aboriginal child-rearing patterns—including the transmission of cultural and parental knowledge—were weakened among many Aboriginal groups. These cultural and social losses were a consequence of residential schooling, forced assimilation, and the resulting breakdown of traditional cultural values; they were also a result of high rates of alcohol abuse, drug dependency, and suicide (ibid.).

Same-Sex Couples

By contrast, families built around same-sex couples have been maligned in many societies, yet they appear to fulfill their family responsibilities consistently well. In most industrialized countries, gays and lesbians are still unable to marry legally, since marriage continues to be defined as a union between a man and a woman. However, in some countries, like Canada, this has changed. In fact, the legal treatment of lesbian and gay families in Canada has been changing since the late 1970s, as is obvious in child custody, access, and adoption cases in which sexual orientation was a factor (Shkedi, 2005; Maxwell and Donner, 2006).

Lesbian parents have repeatedly challenged the definition of "spouse" and applied to the courts to formalize their relationships with their children by adoption; in doing so, they have challenged the normative content of spousal relations, changing the law itself as a gendering strategy (Brower, 2009). One such challenge was instrumental in the federal government's (then Liberal) passing of Bill C-38, the Civil Marriages Act, on 20 July 2005. This Act validates the legality of marriage between same-sex couples.

TABLE 11.1	Distribution and Percentage Change of Couple Families by Opposite-Sex or Same-Sex Status, Canada, 2001 to 2011						
COUPLE FAMILY	2001		2006		2011		PERCENTAGE CHANGE
	Number	Percentage	Number	Percentage	Number	Percentage	2006 to 2011
All couples	7,059,830	100.0	7,482,775	100.0	7,861,860	100.0	5.1
Opposite-sex couples	7,025,630	99.5	7,437,430	99.4	7,797,280	99.2	4.8
Married	5,901,425	83.6	6,098,445	81.5	6,272,935	79.8	2.9
Common-law	1,124,200	15.9	1,338,980	17.9	1,524,345	19.4	13.8
Same-sex couples	34,200	0.5	45,345	0.6	64,575	0.8	42.4
Married*	...	...	7,465	0.1	21,015	0.3	181.5
Common-law	34,200	0.5	37,885	0.5	43,560	0.6	15.0

*Not applicable in 2001. Same-sex marriage became legal across Canada in 2005.
Source: Statistics Canada censuses of population, 2001 to 2011, at: <www12.statcan.ca/census-recensement/2011/as-sa/98-312-x/2011001/tbl/tbl3-eng.cfm>.

Table 11.1 shows the distribution of family types in Canada. Heterosexual couples are the most prevalent family type, but same-sex couples has been slowly increasing in numbers over time. In 2011, same-sex couples reached a record-breaking 0.8 per cent of the population, higher than in the United States, Australia, and the United Kingdom (<www12 .statcan.gc.ca/census-recensement/2011/as-sa/98-312-x/98-312-x2011001-eng.cfm>).

INTERNATIONAL **COMPARISONS**

BOX 11.1 | Polygamy versus Monogamy

While marriage in most Western countries is conceptualized as a union binding two people together, polygamous marriages (existent in certain Western and Eastern communities) defy the traditional definition by extending the boundaries of marriage to include more than two people. In Canada, Section 293 of the Criminal Code strictly outlaws polygamous marriage.

However, Barber (2008) explains why social and ecological conditions in some countries might facilitate the need for polygamous marriage. Countries with high income inequality, tropical climates, and extensive arable land tend to have higher rates of polygamy because it allows for wealth to be monopolized in terms of land territory. Large family units can control an area of valuable arable land better. Countries where males are scarcer also tend to have more marriages where one man has many wives (ibid.). Healthy males with higher immune resistance may also be married to more than one woman in countries with high rates of infectious disease. Cultural measures like female oppression are not related to

polygamous marriage rates. Developed countries in the West, however, do not have a need for polygamous marriages (ibid.). Public health ensures that there is no shortage of males; cold winters mean that women need more direct help from their husband to raise children; and the costs needed to support a polygamous family would be high in urban cities (ibid.).

Studies comparing polygamous to monogamous marriages also find that women in polygamous marriages tend to experience more hardships than their monogamous counterparts. One study conducted in Jordan that compared women in polygamous marriages with those in monogamous ones found that women in polygamous marriages tend to be less satisfied with life, have greater family and marital issues, and have higher rates of depression, anxiety, and hostility (Al-Krenawi et al., 2011). A similar study, which looked at Bedouin-Arab women in Israel, found that women in polygamous marriages tend to suffer more domestic abuse and to feel less personal potency (ibid.).

Fertility Trends

The World Pattern

The most interesting and revealing fact about families today, in Canada and around the world, is that they have fewer children than ever in history. A classic study on this topic, by sociologist William J. Goode (1963), has revealed that this decline in child-bearing has been part of a larger change in the size, structure, and functioning of modern families around the world. We discuss this further in Chapter 14, on population trends.

For the time being, note the declines in fertility rates shown for all the regions of the world in Figure 11.2. Declines are obvious everywhere, but they are most marked in regions of the world that only began to see fertility rate reductions in the mid-twentieth century—for example, in Asia. They are least marked where fertility rates began to decline much earlier (in Europe and North America) or have yet to begin significantly (in West Africa).

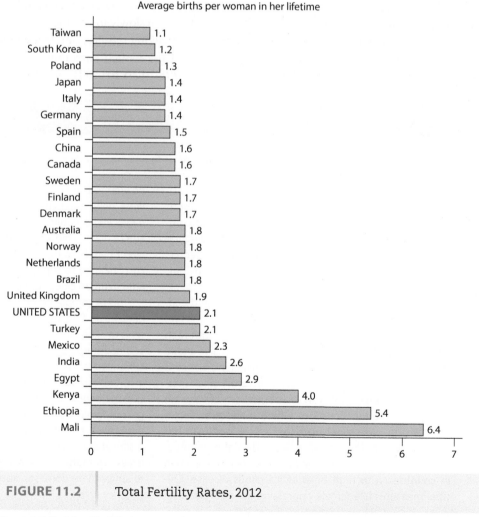

FIGURE 11.2   Total Fertility Rates, 2012

Source: © Philip Cohen, *The Atlantic*, at: <www.theatlantic.com/sexes/archive/2013/02/declining-fertility-is-not-the-root-of-americas-problems/272820>.

The Canadian Pattern

Canadian historical records show a strong decline in the average number of births from the mid-nineteenth to the mid-twentieth centuries, for this worldwide fertility decline began early in Canada (Statistics Canada, 2012c). Canadian women born between 1817 and 1831, for example, had about 6.6 children, compared with 1.7 children for women born between 1947 and 1961.

Today, Canadian women spend less of their lives occupied with parenting, as they are entering parenthood at a later age than ever before. By using effective contraception to avoid pregnancy, most Canadian women are choosing to delay childbirth because of growing opportunities to pursue higher education, careers, and financial independence (Martin, 2000).

This century-long downward trend in child-bearing has continued, with only a brief interruption during the so-called baby boom between 1947 and 1967. Today, Canadian women bear few children and bear them at later average ages. Statistics Canada (2008) reports that "[t]he average age of Canadian women who gave birth in 1991 was 27.7 years. In subsequent years it increased to reach 29.3 years in 2006 where it has since remained stable." Ontario and British Columbia had the highest average age—at 30—of women who gave birth in 2008.

As seen in Figure 11.3, there has been a decline in fertility rates for Canadian women in their twenties and a steady increase in women giving birth in their thirties. Not surprisingly, in 2006, the fertility rate of women aged 30 to 34 surpassed that of women aged 25 to 29. Studies repeatedly show that it has become more socially acceptable for women to wait until a later age to have a child; by contrast, young mothers face a social disapproval for rushing into motherhood without first completing their education and establishing a career (Benzies et al., 2006).

In these respects, Canadian fertility is similar to what one finds in Northern and Central Europe, Russia, China, and Australia; in these countries, stable, below-replacement

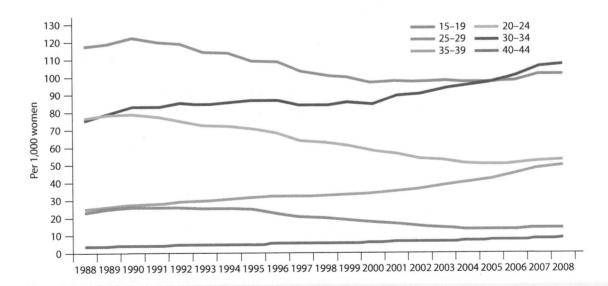

| **FIGURE 11.3** | Age-Specific Fertility Rates, Canada, 1988 to 2008 |

Source: Statistics Canada, CANSIM table 102-4505 and Births, Catalogue no. 84F0210X, at: <www.statcan.gc.ca/pub/84f0210x/2008000/ct002-eng.htm> (April 2011).

child-bearing will erase the national population in foreseeable centuries unless immigrants and their children continue to arrive.

China's One-Child Policy

Most countries have allowed this fertility decline to occur naturally, but this has not been the case in China, where fertility was desperately high and posed a problem to national modernization. As a result, until a decade ago or so, strict policies on fertility control were exercised in the People's Republic of China, where a one-child policy was in effect. China thus applied what we might call a "coercive (or involuntary) model" of fertility decline.

Before the People's Revolution in the 1940s, China had had a huge population with a high fertility rate. When the Communist government formed in 1948, it deemed population growth as a threat to the economic and political stability of China and saw a need to modernize and industrialize China as quickly as possible. Doing so meant enacting laws to ensure the equal rights of women as well as fair conditions of work and marriage for them.

As part of this policy, the Chinese government addressed child-bearing directly with compulsory permits for marriage and pregnancy. Then, in 1980, it legislated the one-child-per-couple policy. The one-child policy was only a contributing factor in the fertility decline, as fertility had been dropping before the policy was enacted. Therese Hesketh, Li Lu, and Zhu Wei Xing (2005) credit this reduction to China's "wan, xi, shao" (or "later, longer, fewer") campaign in 1971, which asked people to marry later, leave a longer space between births, and bear fewer children in total. Likely, even without the one-child policy, this voluntary campaign would have reduced fertility rates significantly.

Taken altogether, these policies achieved a rapid and dramatic success. In 1965, the average Chinese woman had been bearing an estimated 6.1 children in her lifetime—the same rate we see in Central Africa today. By 2005, 40 years later, total fertility was down to 1.7 children—less than the population-replacement (or zero-growth) level (CIA, 2005).

Therefore, within only two generations, Chinese marriage and fertility patterns had changed from those of a developing country to those of a Western industrial country. Combined with other policies, this coercive fertility policy changed Chinese women's lives. Women born in the 1920s, for example, had received little or no education, had married young, had produced many children, and had worked in the fields when not bearing children. Two generations later, many Chinese women had more freedom to marry, gain higher education, and pursue a career, thanks in large part to the reduction in fertility.

Women also enjoyed better health as a consequence. The decline in the fertility rate meant a decline in the health risks and costs associated with pregnancy and childbirth. Moreover, with fewer children born, there was a reduction in the number of parenthood experiences (or years spent in parenthood). As well, the one-child program recognized the need for abstinence or birth control and, in so doing, tacitly repudiated the century-old Marxist position on population control.

At the same time, China's coercive one-child policy carried obvious costs. First, it encouraged sex-selection practices and selective abortion, even infanticide. China has historically been a patrilocal society that favours sons over daughters. By limiting a couple to one child, the Chinese government increased the likelihood that parents would use sex-selection practices such as abortion to ensure their only child was a son, not a daughter. The resulting shortage of women left many men unable find a wife, and this too contributed to a decrease in the birth rate. However, lower fertility rates also led to a rapid aging of the population and growing labour shortages (Wang et al., 2013).

Now, consider an alternative strategy. A voluntary program of family limitation, as implemented in Brazil and India (for example, the sterilization program started by Indira Gandhi), works more slowly but is more humane and leads to fewer unwanted outcomes (like selective abortion). This strategy lowers the infant mortality rate, reduces the economic value of children, and provides an improved lifestyle to people who use less of their income raising children.

Theoretical Perspectives on the Family

TABLE 11.2	Theoretical Perspectives
THEORY	**MAIN POINTS**
Structural Functionalism	• Elements in society are all interrelated. • Families provide nurture and socialization. • A gendered division of domestic labour is functional. • The family is a central institution in society. • The family is a microcosm of society—individual family members come together in a unified and productive whole (Lehmann, 1994). • The familial division of labour is the key to a family's success (Parsons and Bales, 1955). • The regulation of sexual behaviour and reproduction, the provision of physical and psychological needs of members, and the socialization of children are important family functions. • Modern functionalism proposes that certain family forms are natural or inevitable.
Conflict Theory	• Social reproduction in families supports capitalism. • Families maintain the workforce without pay. • We should not assume that families operate as units, perform functions, or accomplish tasks for the good of society. • Families must be understood historically and placed in the context of political and economic changes. • Families are no longer self-sustaining economic units, but are consumption units dependent on outside sources of income for survival. • Under capitalism, household work by women is unpaid, so exploitation of women benefits their husbands' employers. • Thus, gender inequality is perpetuated by economic exploitation under capitalism, not by the needs of "society" or even of a given family for task differentiation based on gender.
Feminist Theory	• The domestic division of labour is arbitrary. • Just as factory workers depend on capitalists for a living wage, wives depend on their husbands; the dependence is easily turned into subordination. • Women have historically endured not only economic reliance on men in the household, but also political and social inferiority. • The capitalist economy affirmed old patriarchal tendencies by providing men differential access to the labour market.
Symbolic Interactionism	• Families involve continued interaction. • They are maintained by shared myths and beliefs. • Their main role is to socialize the next generation. • A married couple builds a shared definition of their family—its goals, identity, and values.
Social Constructionism	• Family life is shaped by moral entrepreneurship. • Popular beliefs about families are media myths. • Moral entrepreneurs channel popular anxieties into hostility against minority groups—single mothers, gays and lesbians, and divorced people, to name a few.

Structural Functionalism

Functionalists view the family as a central institution in society. In fact, they see the family as a microcosm of society, with individual family members coming together to form a unified and productive whole—a model of a successful mini-society.

In Talcott Parsons and Robert Bales's functionalist analysis (1955), the family's division of labour is the key to its success. In a traditional family, the husband of the household performs an instrumental role as the breadwinner, decision-maker, and source of authority and leadership, while the wife fulfills an expressive role as homemaker, nurturer, and emotional centre of the family. Though these roles of the husband and wife have changed since the 1950s, functionalists still view the family institution as accomplishing several important functions, including the regulation of sexual behaviour and reproduction, the provision of the physical (food, shelter) and psychological (nurturance, learning) needs of its members, and the socialization of children.

Functionalism today appears in arguments about the inevitability of certain family forms. For example, psychiatrists Ronald Immerman and Wade Mackey (1999) note that most marriage systems across the world support monogamy. In communities where people have multiple partners, sexually transmitted diseases increase. So do various societal dysfunctions, such as out-of-wedlock births, infant morbidity, violent crime, and lower educational attainment. These outcomes reduce the ability of the community to compete with societies that have maintained pair bonding. This, in turn, reduces the survival capacity of the community.

Other researchers make structural arguments to show that cohabitation is inferior to traditional (legal) marriage. Linda Waite (2000), for example, proposes that cohabiting relationships are often less permanent, fail to provide the many benefits that marriage offers to both participants, are less likely to engage extended families, and provide less support for the cohabiting partners during a crisis.

Conflict and Feminist Theories

Unlike functionalists, conflict theorists do not assume that families operate as units. Instead, they take a historical approach and focus on political and economic changes.

They note that, with industrialization, families move from being self-sustaining economic units (e.g., a farming household) to being consumption units (e.g., a dual-income household that purchases shelter, food, clothing, services, and luxuries). In doing this, they become dependent on outside sources of income to meet their survival needs. Historically, this meant that working-class men had to sell their labour power to the bourgeoisie in exchange for an income. In this process, women gained exclusive control over (or, more accurately, were relegated to) the home, taking the main responsibility for child-rearing, food preparation, and the provision of emotional support.

However, as both conflict and feminist theorists emphasize, women did this work without financial remuneration. In short, gender inequality arises out of economic exploitation, not the need of "society" or even of a given family for task differentiation based on gender.

There are historical reasons for this development and for its association with the rise of industrial capitalism. Feminist theorists propose that, just as factory workers depend on capitalists for a living wage, wives depend on their husbands. This dependence easily turns into subordination. Women have historically endured not only economic reliance on men in the household, but also political and social inferiority. Though these patriarchal tendencies are old, the capitalist economy affirmed them by giving men preferential access and treatment within the labour market.

Feminists propose that these patriarchal tendencies are most common in traditionalist religions. An Orthodox Jewish religious community, for example, demands that women get married and start a family "while young," as their dictated role in life is solely that of a house worker. This traditional mentality prevents girls from pursuing higher education and, subsequently, meaningful employment (Longman, 2008). At the same time, feminists are alarmed by the seeming trend in liberal societies where educated, highly paid women are voluntarily leaving their careers to focus on motherhood (Aune, 2008). However, evangelical Christian (i.e., faith-centred) feminists claim that evangelicalism is "a strategic form of women's collective action," empowering them while also calling men to take responsibility for their families. Yet, in their call to unite women through a religious definition of family, they exclude other women, such as single mothers, working mothers, and lesbian couples (ibid).

Symbolic Interactionism

As we have seen, interactionists focus on the micro level of sociological analysis. Symbolic interactionists study the ways family members interact with one another and resolve conflicts in the family. An important part of this process is the creation and revision of myths about family.

Social constructionists focus on the development and use of family ideologies such as the "family values" promoted by right-wing religious leaders and social conservatives in

Classic WORKS

BOX 11.2   **Friedrich Engels, *The Origin of the Family, Private Property and the State* (1884)**

In *The Origin of the Family, Private Property and the State* (1884), Engels outlines the evolution of the family form and the changing relations between men and women. He identifies three stages in human history, as identified in Morgan's *Ancient Society* (1877): (1) savagery, (2) barbarism, and (3) civilization.

The earliest (the savage) societies were characterized by group marriage. Women and men lived together in groups and had unregulated sex. They produced children but were not concerned with who the biological parents were. In barbarian societies, equality existed between the sexes; a sexual division of labour made women responsible for reproduction and domestic work and men responsible for agriculture and hunting. Living in a matrilineal society where descent passed through the female

bloodline gave women a superior role in the home and therefore a form of power.

As hunter-gatherer societies developed into those based on animal production, however, this power began to shift. With the domestication of animals and the development of farming came agricultural surpluses, and these surpluses resulted in the creation of private property. Men then needed to know who their children were in order to pass on their wealth to the right people. They achieved this by demanding monogamy from women. Women's faithfulness in marriage thus became a central part of an economic system. Men's newfound ability to own private property stripped women of their supremacy in the home in what Engels refers to as "the world historical defeat of the female sex" (Bryson, 2003: 59).

THE DESCENDANTS

In this 2011 film directed by Alexander Payne, the hero (George Clooney)—a widowed husband and father of two girls—is forced to re-examine his past and improve his relationship with two young daughters while deciding whether to sell the family's land, which was inherited from Hawaiian royalty

the US and Canada. By appealing to people's interest in and concern about their family lives, these moral and political entrepreneurs channel popular anxieties into hostility against such groups as single mothers, gays and lesbians, and divorced people.

These antipathies produce support for political initiatives that reduce social welfare spending and coerce the behaviour of other minorities—for example, urban blacks in the US or Aboriginals in Canada. By implication, these groups become a focus for the complaint against those accused of failing to lead moral family lives or to instill family values in their children (McMullin, 2004).

Social Consequences of Family Life

Whatever the approach sociologists take, they all recognize that family life is stressful and consequential. Stressful elements in family life, such as abuse, employment and unemployment, and divorce, all have serious social and health outcomes that can affect the individual, his or her family, and society as a whole (Raphael, 2009). Every family has problems to deal with, and some do a better job of it than others.

In recent decades, the cost of living has substantially increased. As a result, most families have a hard time surviving comfortably on a single income. This development has long historical roots, dating back over 60 years. The desire of families after World War II for more and more of the products of industrialization and technology, coupled with the wartime acceptance of women working outside the home, established a cycle of demand and affluence that encouraged suppliers to keep raising prices higher and higher. Eventually, the second income no longer provided luxuries but became vital to providing the revised norm of minimal comfort. In brief, over the course of a generation or two, luxuries became necessities.

Consequently, today, both parents often have to work to make enough money to cover the necessities, pay for the occasional luxury, and perhaps save enough for their children's post-secondary education and their own retirement (Marshall, 2009). As well, the demands of work life are often in direct conflict with the demands of family life.

Managing a career is difficult for women, especially if they are mothers of young children. Thus, many educated women delay marriage, preferring to go to school, to work, and to achieve financial independence before bearing children. Others avoid marriage altogether, opting instead to have a career and aim for only those personal relationships that do not hinder their professional lives. The higher we look in the occupational hierarchy, in professional or corporate jobs, the more likely we are to find women who did not marry or have children in their early twenties (Mason and Goulden, 2004). Many of these women never married, married and divorced, married early but did not have children, or married late and had few if any children (Houseknecht et al., 1987; Heathcote et al., 1997).

Women today remain unmarried longer than they did in the past. Alessandro Balestrino and Cinzia Ciardi (2008) propose that this is due to a change in the costs and benefits of marriage. With the rise of the welfare state, young men and women are less dependent on marriage for social and economic care and thus are freer to choose when and whom they marry. Other changes, such as women's greater participation in the labour force, have made women less dependent on marriage for income.

Likewise, in the past, having children was seen as necessary for survival in old age. However, with the introduction of adult-care institutions, older adults are less dependent on their children for survival during later stages of life. This means that intangible

Jeff Randall/Digital Vision

One of the consequences of women entering the labour force was the resulting double shift: women facing the responsibilities of both breadwinner and homemaker. In heterosexual married households, men are now increasing the amount of time they spend on household duties and child care, but the distribution of responsibilities is still uneven.

qualities, such as love and companionship, are emerging as primary incentives in deciding to get married.

Whatever their education and career goals, women who marry and bear children often face a **double shift**: responsibilities as both breadwinners and homemakers (Medeiros et al., 2007). Several factors put a lot of additional pressure on the boundary between work and home life: they include (1) a spouse who often works overtime, (2) a bad work schedule, (3) a heavy workload, and (4) a troubled relationship with the boss. These work–home conflicts produce emotional exhaustion, psychosomatic health complaints, and sleep deprivation (Demerouti and Geurts, 2004).

While more and more women have been joining the workforce, women still bear an unequal share of the domestic work at home. Men have increased their share in household duties, it is true, but women are still more responsible for household tasks and child care. Recent data show they still do two-thirds of household tasks such as cooking and cleaning and spend more than twice as much time on child care as men do (Statistics Canada, 2012d).

Access to good-quality, affordable child care is still problematic for many families, but the statistics on this vary from one province to another. Quebec offers, by far, the easiest access to regulated, affordable child care. Other provinces do much worse in this respect. Consider some recent facts on Alberta, for example. In 2013, Public Interest Alberta released a fact sheet using data from a new national study on child care, showing that

> Alberta's per capita funding, for children 0–12 years old, is the sixth lowest of all provinces. The increase in the number of childcare spaces over the past 6 years

Double shift Modern women's dual roles as breadwinner and homemaker.

has not kept pace with the increase in the number of children under the age of 6. The number of preschool children with a mother in the work force who did not have access to licensed childcare went from 69,368 in 2004 to 87,281 in 2010 (62% of all preschool children with working mothers). The subsidy rate for low-income families is not keeping pace with the increased costs of childcare so many low-income families cannot afford to put their children in licensed care. [Finally,] 50% of all childcare spaces in Alberta are for-profit as there is no government support for expanding not-for-profit and public childcare. (<earlychildhood.alberta.ca/Content/New_Statistics_Shows_Childcare_Crisis_Worsening>)

Women—whether employed full-time or part-time or unemployed—take a larger share of household duties than their male counterparts (see Table 11.3 below). This creates a dilemma in work–family relations, because the changes in women's labour force participation have not been accompanied by a change in men's caregiving patterns. Thus, women have to manage work-related responsibilities while shouldering most of the child-rearing and household duties at home. Given this reality, it isn't surprising that many women choose to delay marriage; yet, ironically, single women are often viewed with suspicion or worse.

Divorce

At the beginning of the twentieth century, divorce was rare in Canada. In 1901, out of a national population of five million, only 399 men and 322 women reported being divorced (Morton, 2000). At that time, people widely disapproved of divorce, expressing this disapproval through their religion, popular discourse, and the law that restricted it.

THE SQUID AND THE WHALE

Noah Baumbach wrote and directed this 2005 film based on his own childhood experiences. Two boys watch their parents' marriage fall apart as their novelist-father, whose career has gone into a slow decline, spends less time writing and more time brooding.

TABLE 11.3	Time Spent on Household Domestic Arrangements, 2010	
	WOMEN	MEN
WORKING ARRANGEMENT	AVERAGE NUMBER OF HOURS PER WEEK	
All women and men	**13.8**	**8.3***
Working arrangement		
Respondent was working		
Dual earner couples; respondent working full-time	13.9	8.6*
Dual earner couples; respondent working part-time	21.0	11.8*
Single earner couples; respondent working	15.2	8.8*
Singles; respondent working	7.7	6.1*
Respondent was not working		
Single earner couples; respondent not working	23.4	14.6*
Couples; neither partner working	17.3	10.6*
Singles; respondent not working	10.0	6.3*

* statistically significant difference between women and men at $p < 0.05$
Source: Anne Milan, Leslie-Anne Keown, and Robles Urquijo Covadonga, "Family, Living Arrangements and Unpaid Work," *Statistics Canada,* General Social Survey, 2010, at: <www.statcan.gc.ca/pub/89-503-x/2010001/article/11546-eng.pdf> (Dec. 2011).

CANADIAN researcher

BOX 11.3   Andrea Doucet, Brock University

In studying families, it is around the topic of child care that we encounter most dramatically the rise of gender differences and inequalities, even in modern egalitarian couples, and Andrea Doucet, Canada Research Chair in Gender, Work and Care, wants to understand why. In her 2009 paper "Dad and Baby in the First Year: Gendered Responsibilities and Embodiment," Doucet argues that understanding continuing gender divisions of domestic responsibility, particularly in the first year of parenting, requires attending to issues of identity, commitment, deeply rooted socialization, and community assumptions around gender, breadwinning, and caring. Her findings are drawn from three qualitative research studies conducted over eight years with more than 200 Canadian fathers and 40 mothers. The author concludes that short-term differences in domestic responsibilities in parenting do not necessarily lead to long-term chronic inequities between women and men.

Following up on this theme in a 2013 paper, "A 'Choreography of Becoming': Fathering, Embodied Care, and New Materialisms," Doucet points to the recurring invisibility of physicality and bodies in studies of parental caregiving and argues that one missing link in our understanding of gender differences in care work is that of male embodiment. She ends this article informed by new materialist lenses and argues for the inseparability of body-social linkages and caregiving relations between carers and the cared-for.

In a 2014 paper, "'It's almost like I have a job, but I don't get paid': Fathers at Home Reconfiguring Work, Care, and Masculinity," Doucet remarks that fathers typically note personal and "generative" changes as they make the shift from worker to carer. Similarly, many fathers find that their time at home gives them the opportunity to reflect on what they actually want to do when they return to the workforce. Most fathers mention how parenting is the hardest job they have ever done and come to appreciate how vitally important caring work is, though also how socially devalued. Living and working for sustained periods as primary carers, stay-at-home fathers are in a unique position to create new forms of masculinity. They also provide abundant evidence that masculinities do change.

As Doucet points out in her 2008 Porter Lecture, "Gender Equality and Gender Differences: Parenting, Habitus, and Embodiment," sociologists need to refine their understanding of family and domestic tasks in relation to community-based responsibilities. They also need to develop a more refined and fluid understanding of gender equalities and differences in family settings. Nonetheless, parental responsibilities remain gendered because they are rooted in a mesh of current and historical arrangements, learned through socialization over a long period of time.

Until 1968, adultery was the only legal ground for divorce. The Divorce Act of 1968, however, brought about a massive change in family behaviour. This law allowed judges to grant divorces on the grounds of "marriage breakdown" after a couple had been separated for at least three years. Between 1968 and 1985, the number of divorces in Canada increased fivefold (Ambert, 2005). An amendment to the Divorce Act in 1985 reduced the minimum period of separation to one year.

Before 1968, there was a double standard that forced women to prove that their husbands had committed more than adultery—for example, they had been abusive or generally absent—while men only had to prove adultery. The emphasis, with respect to women, was on showing "fault" and not on establishing that a relationship had "broken down." With divorce being made dramatically easier in 1968, these inequalities were eliminated. Before the reforms, marriages that finally ended in divorce lasted an average of 15 years. The liberalization of divorce laws shortened this process, with these marriages lasting a shorter time, on average. At the beginning of the twenty-first century, the average was 12.7 years. In 2011, 50.8 per cent of lone parents were divorced or

PERSONAL *stories*

| BOX 11.4 | **Is it Okay If Nancy Is Single?** |

Nancy is 31. She holds a well-paying job in a major Canadian city, has her own "very comfortable apartment" downtown, and takes two vacations a year to "interesting, out of the way" places. She has a cat but no husband, children, or other people who might keep her from doing exactly what she feels like doing, whenever she feels like doing it. Yet, for some reason, her friends keep trying to get her married off. They keep fixing her up with dates and talk in what seems like a pitying way to her about her "so-called independence." What's going on here?

Since the 1950s, the percentage of single Canadian households has quadrupled, reports Statscan, and more people are choosing to be single than ever before. Why, then, does pop culture still insist that being in a couple is superior to staying single? In his recently released book *Single: Arguments for the Uncoupled*, University of Toronto English professor Michael Cobb argues that singles have been overlooked in popular culture, pointing out that more people are single than are married and yet there is no cultural narrative for uncoupled people—or even positive media representations of happy singles.

In an interview with *Maclean's* magazine, Cobb explains: "There's always an assumption that you need to be coupled off to complete yourself. Even though we all know that people are not all saved and made happy in their coupledom. There are lots of distressed couples, lots of divorces, lots of frustrating, sad marriages." He also dislikes the negative assumptions made about people who choose to be single. In the lead-up to writing his book, he says, "I got tired of people saying, 'Single? Oh, single!'" that is, swinging singles, relieved of the hard work of relating, off being selfish and enjoying your own physical pleasures." His book looks at how and why society ranks couples above singles, ultimately asserting that the pressure to couple is not about finding happiness but the result of cultural "coercion and control" handed out by the coupled majority.

While plenty of movies and television shows depict unhappy couples, they rarely show singles living great lives without any romantic ties. Cobb says that depictions of singles ignore the positive possibilities of being uncoupled. A single person himself for most of his life, Cobb says he has experienced the "joy of being by myself and being able to cultivate all sorts of relationships and not have one person completely be the centre and focus of the world." In contrast, "couples," he argues, "shrink the world," limiting people's range of human interaction just by being with one person so much and being "exclusive." In being single, a person can form many bonds of varying depths and explore the potential of relationships more thoroughly through this quantity and variety, says Cobb.

Though uncoupled fulfillment is always possible, Cobb emphasizes the difficulty of being single within a couple-centric world because of the myriad media representations of coupled happiness and singled misery. To demonstrate his observation, he points to the coupling mentality behind supposedly pro-single anthems like Beyoncé Knowles's "All the Single Ladies," a song that celebrates marriage as it chides a man for not putting "a ring on it" when he had the chance. Cobb calls this "the couple narrative," the understanding that people are either in or between relationships, never just single and not looking. As part of the couple narrative, pop culture tells consumers that coupling is the key to happiness. But, as Cobb points out, "the problem is it doesn't always work. It seems to be a narrative loop we can't escape and as a result we don't know much about the experience of the single in pop culture except as a miserable person trying to escape their fate." His book volleys a new perspective into the single-coupled discourse, hoping to inspire deeper thinking about and more realistic representations of single life—the life many people are living.

Sources: Adapted from: John Ackermann and Dean Recksiedler, "In Defense of Singledom: Going Solo Doesn't Mean Loneliness!," *News1130.com*, Rogers Communications, 20 June 2012, at: <www.news1130.com/news/local/article/375257--in-defense-of-singledom-going-solo-doesn-t-mean-loneliness>; Brian Bethune, "Two against One: About Coupledom and the Stigma of Being Single," *Macleans.ca*, Rogers Communications, 20 June 2012, at: <www2.macleans.ca/2012/06/20/the-stigma-of-being-single-the-lack-of-role-models-and-how-coupledom-shrinks-the-world/>; and Leah McLaren, "Why Do We Insist That Coupling Up Is Better Than Staying Single?," *Theglobeandmail.com*, The Globe and Mail, 29 June 2012, at: <www.theglobeandmail.com/life/relationships/why-do-we-insist-that-coupling-up-is-better-than-staying-single/article4380875/>.

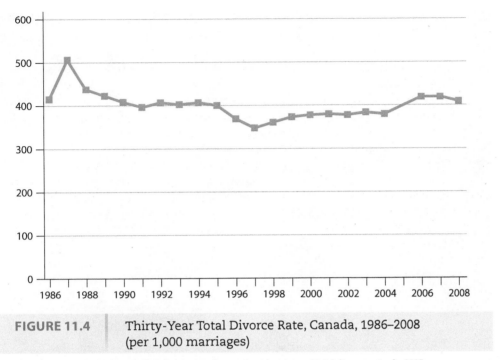

FIGURE 11.4   Thirty-Year Total Divorce Rate, Canada, 1986–2008 (per 1,000 marriages)

Note: Statistics Canada didn't calculate divorce rates by marriage duration and total divorces rates for 2005.
Sources: For 1986 to 1996, Statistics Canada, *Vital Statistics Compendium, 1996* (Ottawa: Statistics Canada, Heath Statistics Division, 1999) (Catalogue no. 84-214-XPE); for 1997 to 2003, Statistics Canada, Divorces: Shelf tables (Ottawa: Statistics Canada, 1999–2005); for 2004: "30 and 50 Year Total Divorce Rates per 1,000 Marriages, Canada, Provinces and Territories, Annual (rate per 1,000 marriages)," CANSIM Table 101-6511 (Ottawa: Statistics Canada, 2008); and for 2006 to 2008: Statistics Canada, Health Statistics Division, "Canadian Vital Statistics, Divorce Database and Marriage Database" (Ottawa: Statistics Canada, 2011).

separated, making this the most common marital status for that population (Statistics Canada, 2012a).

Today, Canadian divorce rates are higher than one finds in many other Western nations. Sociologist Anne-Marie Ambert notes that "[t]he latest estimates by Statistics Canada (2008) put the risk of divorce by the thirtieth wedding anniversary for recently married couples at 38 per cent for the country as a whole—ranging from 21.6 per cent in Newfoundland and Labrador to 48.4 per cent in Quebec." By comparison, the divorce rate for the US is estimated at 44 per cent (Baklinski, 2009). Figure 11.4 shows Canadian divorce trends for the period 1986–2008. As is evident from this diagram, the divorce rate has more or less stabilized now, with only small changes from year to year.

Consequences of Divorce

Though divorce has become much more common, it remains consequential for family members and society as a whole. Yet, divorce affects men and women differently because of gender inequalities in the wider society.

Economically, divorce affects women much more negatively than men (Bould et al., 2008). For example, a study by Bianchi et al. (1999) found that custodial mothers experienced a 36 per cent decrease in standard of living after their separation, while non-custodial fathers experienced a 28 per cent increase. Mothers' post-separation standard

Maria Franks, executive director of the Legal Info Society of Nova Scotia, stands near the Property Guys booth at the Divorce Fair she helped organize at the Lord Nelson Hotel in Halifax. The fair helps those going through a divorce connect with the services they might need.

of living overall was approximately only half that of fathers. Custody of children is often granted to mothers, compounding the economic burden on women, who are already saddled by salaries that are lower than men's, on average. So, for women, not only is their income reduced after the divorce, but that smaller income often must go towards caring for one or more dependants as well.

Taking on the role of primary caregiver also consumes a lot of time. Many lone working mothers report severe time stress and a feeling of being overwhelmed by responsibilities. The combination of work, child-rearing, and household maintenance leaves them little time to develop a social life (Trias, 2000).

As noted, after a separation or divorce, ex-husbands are often better off financially than ex-wives, because they were the dominant income earner during the marriage and they continue to have larger salaries or wages after the divorce. As well, men experience more freedom following a divorce, since children of a marriage often live with the mother. Thus, men have more opportunities to work, travel, return to school, and explore other relationships (McManus and DiPrete, 2001).

Much of the effect of divorce on children can be predicted by conditions that existed before the separation (Grych, 2005). Family and personal distress caused by conflict, poverty, or unemployment leads to less-effective parenting. This is because divorced parents often have too little time and too few resources for fun and too few resources to make plans for the future. The common consequences include difficulty with providing adequate supervision, loss of control over the child's behaviour, inconsistent parenting, and recurrent displays of aggression by both parents and children. In short, divorce increases stress, and stress does not typically bring out the best in people.

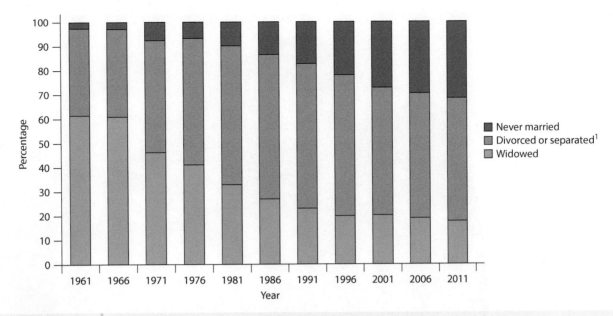

FIGURE 11.5 | Distribution (in percentage) of the Legal Marital Status of Lone Parents, Canada, 1961 to 2011

¹*Divorced* or separated category includes 'married, spouse absent.'
Source: Statistics Canada, censuses of population, 1961 to 2011, at: <www12.statcan.gc.ca/census-recensement/2011/as-sa/98-312-x/2011003/fig/fig3_1-2-eng.cfm>.

In many cases, divorce also has an effect on children's development. In a study by Hyun Sik Kim (2011), children whose parents were in various stages of divorce—pre-, in-, and post-divorce—were surveyed when they were between the ages of 7 and 9 and then surveyed again when they were between the ages of 9 and 11. The results showed that children of divorce experienced setbacks in math scores during and after divorce and a negative effect on interpersonal skills while their parents were in-divorce (ibid.).

It is still unclear to what degree the setbacks recorded after a divorce are the result of divorce per se, the result of associated consequences (e.g., less household income, more stress), or the result of conditions that preceded the divorce (e.g., family conflict, family poverty, unemployment). In any event, lone parenting is often a difficult and stressful activity. Figure 11.5 shows the distribution of lone parents in Canada, illustrating that lone parents status is increasingly due to separation or divorce, not widowhood or never marrying.

Caring for the Elderly

Another problem families increasingly face is providing care for the growing number of elderly family members. Canada's population is aging as the result of lowered fertility and general increases in life expectancy for both men and women. The number of seniors (65 years and over) in Canada has grown steadily to a record-breaking 14.8 per cent of the population, almost catching up to the percentage of children in the population (Statistics Canada, 2012a). With continued declines in fertility, the percentage of old people will continue to rise.

Elder care, like child care, can drastically affect people's time for work, leisure, and other relationships. The 2007 General Social Survey showed that among caregivers aged 45 and older, 34.7 per cent reported having to cut back on social activities and

Caring for an elder can be demanding in terms of the caregiver's emotions, finances, and time. However, elderly parents, while healthy, give more help to their children than they receive. The boomerang effect has opened up new opportunities for some families to share the responsibility of caring for elderly family members intergenerationally.

15.5 per cent reported having to cut back on work hours to fulfill their caregiving duties (Vanier Institute of the Family, 2010). Of course, all of the caring does not flow one way, towards the elderly. In fact, the flow of support favours children: elderly parents give more help to their children than they receive, as long as they remain in good health (Schwarz et al., 2005).

Though care for elders is often hard work, most Canadian seniors continue to live on their own well into advanced age. They can do so, in large part, because of the care they receive from health-care workers and from their children, spouse, or friends. Family members are often the primary source of care for the elderly, and this puts physical and emotional stress on these members, sometimes to the extent of causing caregiver burnout (Schulz and Sherwood, 2008).

The Boomerang Effect

Increasingly, parents are also being called on to provide care or assistance for their grown-up children. In her book *The Boomerang Age* (2005), Canadian sociologist Barbara Mitchell notes that important domestic changes are taking place in the lives of young adults in Western industrialized societies. These changes also translate into changes for the lives of parents.

"Boomerang kids" are young adults returning to the parental home after their first entrance into the adult world. According to the 2011 Census Population, 42 per cent of young adults aged 20 to 29 moved back into their parents' homes at least once before moving away for good. The percentage of young adults returning home has risen steadily over time, as witnessed by the fact that this percentage was only 32 per cent in 1991. Statistics Canada analysts offer several explanations for this trend: high cost of housing, failed marriages, delayed marriages, the cost of higher education, and the difficulty of finding a stable job, among others (Statistics Canada, 2011). In some communities, children are expected to live at home until they marry, and to rely on the family in the face of financial setbacks—so such returns are welcomed. In other communities, they are more disruptive.

Setbacks aside, young adults are taking longer to make the typical transitions into adulthood: from school to work, from singlehood to marriage, and from the parental home to their own home. This rise of boomeranging is strongly gendered. Women are making the transitions to adulthood about as quickly as they did in past years, "although they are more likely to include full-year full-time work and less likely to include marriage and childbearing." Men, on the other hand, are more likely to return home than women and "at age 34 have made fewer transitions than 30 years ago" and "are less likely to have full-year full-time work than their fathers did 30 years earlier" (Clark, 2007).

This comes as a surprise to many parents. Many couples who had thought that their children had grown up and moved away are now having the family home refilled with young, well-educated but unemployed adult children. Adult children without incomes are moving back home in large numbers as a way of meeting or reducing their expenses. The return of grown children to their parental home, often for financial reasons, is an especially vivid example of the generational transfer of wealth from older to younger adults. A significant shift in occupational opportunities or marital status may be enough of a jolt to the young person's finances to send him or her back into the family nest (Mitchell et al., 2000).

For some families, the result is disruptive and disturbing, while for others it is less so. Parental satisfaction with the arrangement is greatest when children pitch in, do their share of the family work, put few additional demands on the parents, and behave like adults (Mitchell, 1998).

This trend is new for some communities, but not others. Some families already live in refilled nests, mainly out of need. They do not see themselves as creating anything new, merely as pooling housing and resources to survive. Others, however, may see huge creative possibilities in refilled nests, such as new opportunities for child care, supplied by grandparents while parents work; new ways of sharing housework among family members; new ways of reducing environmental problems by having fewer separate households; and new ways of intergenerational caring for elders.

Domestic Violence

No discussion of family life is complete without a discussion of family violence, which (though often hidden) is far more common than one might imagine. Family or domestic violence includes domestic and intimate-partner abuse, child and adolescent physical and sexual abuse, and elder abuse (discussed in Chapter 6). Such violence is responsible for a significant portion of all the intentional injuries recorded in Canada. As such, family violence is a major social and health problem (Kaplan, 2000).

Child abuse can take the form of physical or mental harm, neglect, or maltreatment (Ungar et al., 2009). Of these, neglect is the most common form of reported child abuse.

PRECIOUS

Lee Daniels directed this 2009 film about an overweight, illiterate African-American teen who finds a new path in life after she begins to attend a new school. Though only a teenager, Clareece "Precious" Jones is about to give birth to her second child and has long suffered sexual and other abuse at the hands of her mother's boyfriend.

Children also run the risk of sexual abuse, more commonly by a stepfather or a boyfriend of the mother than by their biological father.

The long-term consequences are significant. Abused children often display anti-social behaviour, aggression, low self-esteem, depression, and poor school performance. In adulthood, self-destructive behaviours often continue, including depression, low self-esteem, anxiety, and an increased risk of alcohol or drug abuse and suicide. Children who witnessed or were victims of physical abuse have an increased risk of becoming abusers themselves when they enter adulthood (Nofziger and Kurtz, 2005).

The causes of child abuse are many and complex. Poverty, substance abuse, and (young) maternal age are all strong predictors of confirmed reports of child maltreatment. Young mothers and impoverished mothers are especially likely to harm their children (Malo et al., 2004). This suggests that we need a comprehensive approach to the problem of child abuse, one that lessens the economic stress on young mothers while improving their parenting skills (Sanders et al., 2003).

Likewise, the causes of spouse battering are many and complex. Men who are characterized by alcohol and drug abuse, low education, and low levels of self-control are especially likely to abuse their partners. Abusing husbands typically also have a (childhood) background of family violence and marital arguments (Pollak, 2004). Despite recurrent violence, many women have trouble leaving an abusive relationship or even seeking help. If they divorce, they are often left with the care of children but without financial child support from the children's father. More than that, they are often emotionally dependent on the abusive husband, largely as a result of long-term, repeated assaults on their self-esteem. Sometimes, they also fear for their lives and safety. Table 11.4 shows the reported statistics on family violence in Canada, by province. British Columbia has the

TABLE 11.4	Victims of Police-Reported Family Violence, by Province and Territory, 2010	
	VICTIMS OF FAMILY VIOLENCE	
	NUMBER	RATE PER 100,000 POPULATION
Canada	**98,957**	**294**
Newfoundland and Labrador	1,604	316
Prince Edward Island	330	234
Nova Scotia	2,472	264
New Brunswick	2,384	319
Quebec	26,037	333
Ontario	25,413	196
Manitoba	5,104	430
Saskatchewan	6,534	644
Alberta	13,010	351
British Columbia	13,574	302
Yukon	290	842
Northwest Territories	1,073	2,455
Nunavut	1,132	3,409

Note: Excludes incidents where the sex or age of the victim was unknown and where the relationship between the victim and the accused was unknown.

Source: Statistics Canada, Victims of police-reported family violence, by province and territory, 2010, at: <www.statcan.gc.ca/daily-quotidien/120522/t120522a001-eng.htm>.

highest number of reported family violence incidents, but Nunavut has the highest rate per 100,000 people.

Spouse abuse is not restricted to heterosexual couples, as same-sex relationships are also subject to partner abuse (Blosnich and Bossarte, 2009). Worse, gay, lesbian, and transsexual people often feel uncomfortable or endangered in shelters designed to house abuse victims. There, lesbians may experience homophobic violence from heterosexual women. Likewise, gay men have no shelters they can use other than homeless shelters, which offer little security from abusive partners and no long-term housing.

Health Consequences of Family Life

Despite the prevalence of stress, conflict, and violence, research shows that marriage often adds to people's health and happiness, especially when contrasted with divorce and separation. Yet, what matters is the stability and quality of the relationship, not its legal status.

One study found that married people are better off financially than unmarried people. However, the quality of marriage is important. Only people in a good marriage gain the health benefits of being married, such as lower stress levels, less depression, higher life satisfaction, and lower blood pressure. In fact, people who are unhappily married show higher blood pressure levels than single people. The researchers conclude that "one is better off single than unhappily married" (Holt-Lunstad et al., 2008).

A Canadian study (Strohschein et al., 2005) confirmed the mental health advantages of marriage; what's more, moving into and out of marriage has similar effects on psychological distress for both men and women. Again, the quality of the marriage matters a great deal. There is also some evidence that staying unhappily married is more harmful than divorcing. Unhappily married couples have lower levels of life satisfaction, self-esteem, and overall health than people who divorce and remain unmarried (Hawkins and Booth, 2005).

Divorce and Remarriage

For many people, divorce is an emotionally draining and stressful experience. This is not surprising, because divorce results in the loss of a sexual partner and companion, a potential decrease in contact with children, diminished household income, and so on. The impacts on children can also be significant, and they have been widely studied, with similar results. Typically, children of divorced parents go through a period of disruption and distress. In some studies, they are shown to have more substance-abusing friends and anti-social behaviours and fewer coping and social skills than children whose parents remain married (Ledoux et al., 2002).

Is it in the child's best interest for parents to separate rather than stay together in a fractious marriage? Dronkers (1996) investigated whether being exposed to serious parental conflicts has a more harmful effect on the well-being of children than living in a single-parent family after divorce. Dronkers' findings illustrate the general state of knowledge in this area. First, children living in single-mother families reported a higher level of well-being than children living in two-parent families marked by a lot of parental conflict. Second, however, children living in single-mother families who maintained a high degree of contact with the non-residential father reported a lower level of well-being than children in two-parent families with an equally low level of parent-child conflict. Said another way, other things being equal, two parents are better than one, so long as the level of household conflict is low. Third and finally, the amount of parental conflict after divorce was a more important factor in the well-being of the children than was contact with the departed father. Too much conflict hurt the child more than the absence of a parent. In short, family conflict is bad for children—worse than divorce and worse than losing contact with the non-residential parent, it seems.

Solutions to Family Problems

Work–Family Solutions

Many families suffer from a conflict between work life and family life, and many workplaces have failed to take this into consideration. Yet, even within family-friendly companies that offer their workers various programs designed to increase the time they have to spend with family, few employees take advantage of the programs. Many workers express a wish to cut back on their work and spend more time with spouses and children, yet "policies offering shorter hours that allowed workers more free or family time languished. . . . Only flextime, which rearranged but did not cut back on hours of work, had any significant impact on the workplace" (Hochschild, 1997).

Three explanations have been offered to account for this behaviour. One is that many workers cannot afford to cut back on their work hours, despite their wishes to do so. This is most obviously true among poorly paid workers whose salaries, combined with those of their partners, are so low as to bar either partner from scaling back on hours worked. However, this would not explain why top-level executives, whose salaries are large enough to allow the adoption of a shorter workweek, tend not to take advantage of such policies as job-sharing and part-time work.

A second reason many workers choose not to use family-friendly programs is that they are afraid of being laid off. Company policies may encourage employees to spend more time with their families, but workers often doubt the sincerity of these offers. This argument implies that family-friendly programs are often mere ornaments designed to soothe external critics but not to solve workers' problems.

A third explanation is that despite what workers say about wanting to spend more time with their families, they find the time spent at work is often more pleasant and rewarding than the time spent at home. In her classic three-year study of a top US company, Hochschild (1997) found the duties of home life—caring for the children, sharing household duties, trying to preserve an intimate and loving relationship with one's spouse, and so on—were often stressful, especially to working mothers. For many women, family life was more arduous, stressful, and unfulfilling than paid work—it was, in fact, the "second shift."

Caregiving Solutions

Caregiving is a fundamentally social activity, and it has always been a family activity. Social support networks remain important for caregivers and care recipients alike. Clear and continuing communication between informal and formal caregivers, on the one

Public Issues *and* Public Policy

BOX 11.5 | How Disabilities Affect Family Life

Learning that a child has an intellectual or physical disability disrupts the functioning of the whole family. A common reaction for parents is psychological and emotional turmoil. Compared to mothers with able-bodied children, mothers whose children have cerebral palsy report higher rates of depression, anxiety, and stress (Begum and Desai, 2010). The degree to which the child is disabled does not relate to the rate of these negative emotional states (ibid.).

Other parents with physically disabled kids were assessed for their mental health (Hung et al., 2010). Forty-four percent of parents had poor mental health. Mental health was adversely affected if children were of younger age, depended on assistance for activities of daily living, and had problems walking (ibid.). If parents had a low income, no religious beliefs, dysfunctional interactions with their children, difficult children, or high distress, their mental health would be further complicated (ibid.).

However, despite seemingly unfortunate circumstances, not all families experience child disability in a negative emotional light (Trute et al., 2010). The burden of care for mothers with a disabled child is often socio-structural (e.g., financial) rather than emotional distress, and most mothers were able to discern the benefits associated with having a disabled child (Green, 2007).

Other studies similarly found that having a child with a disability doesn't necessarily have a detrimental influence on the parents' emotions. Many of the mothers in an Alberta study were adept at meeting the special caregiving needs that a disabled child requires, to the extent that the disability didn't significantly overwhelm the family (Trute et al., 2010). Mothers who gave positive appraisals of the situation (e.g., family values were strengthened as a result of the disability) and reported higher positive emotions had a much better adjusted family (ibid.). Maternal satisfaction tends to increase over the many years of parenting a disabled child, as demonstrated in a longitudinal study of mothers with Down's syndrome children (Gilmore and Cuskelly, 2012).

hand, and health-care and social service providers, on the other, remain a necessity. Family and community organization is central to good caregiving.

Naylor (2005) and her colleagues studied the experiences of caregivers of older people with cognitive impairment. The researchers conducted interviews with patients and their primary caregivers, tracking the needs of patients and the demands that providing care placed on the caregivers. They observed that even though primary caregivers found caring for a loved one a significant burden, the caregivers maintained a strong sense of commitment and loyalty. Families reorganized their lives to meet the new demands made of them.

Solutions to Family Violence

We can learn a great deal from research about the best ways to intervene in order to solve problems of family stress and violence.

First, violence is a major reason women leave their marriages and children leave their parents' home. Second, programs that try to address abuse directly—such as civil restraining orders, treatment programs for batterers, and policies requiring mandatory arrest and no dropped charges—are rarely effective in solving the problem of domestic violence (Maytal, 2008; Han, 2003), but they are a necessary first step in protecting the woman and any children in the family. By contrast, treatments aimed at reducing alcohol and drug abuse may make a long-term difference to the likelihood of future violence (Lutze and van Wormer, 2007). Third, problems like stress and violence require active problem-solving. If we want to reduce family stresses, we must create a society that is family-friendly, with increased social support and practical assistance to working parents with small children. Fourth, people tend to view domestic violence as a personal problem that is unlikely to be solved by the intervention of social institutions such as the police and social services. Fifth, research shows us that personal lives, and families, are increasingly diverse. Recently arrived immigrant and refugee women, for example, have needs involving language, cultural, and immigration issues that differ markedly from the needs of battered women in the general population (Balram, 2005).

In the end, however, we must recognize that there will be no major decline in violence against family members until societies reduce stresses on family members, place greater personal value on all people, and treat all people with respect and dignity—especially children, women, elderly people, and sexual and visible minorities. Societies must also reject the cultural justifications for domestic violence and deprive violent people of opportunities to hide or to repeat their behaviour. Ending domestic violence is a societal project no less complex than dealing with unemployment, illiteracy, AIDS, or any other recognized social problem.

Chapter Summary

There can be little doubt that many people have turned their backs on the traditional, idealized family of 50 years ago. Today, people are getting married later in life and having fewer children. Closely related to this trend has been an increase in the number of couples who cohabit. The divorce rate has increased dramatically in the last few decades. Yet, many if not most young people continue to come together in long-term relationships and make them survive.

Although more women have been entering the workforce, women still do more housework than men in dual-income households. This so-called double shift has harmful health outcomes and places stress on the relationships between spouses and between parents and children.

As we have seen, families often have to deal with serious problems. The negative consequences of divorce, both emotional and financial, tend to be greatest for women and children. One-seventh of all Canadian families are single-parent households. Women head about 90 per cent of these single-parent families, which are more prone than two-parent families to financial and emotional strain. However, most families, single-parent or not, are experiencing financial and emotional strain these days. Family violence is more common than many people recognize. Although women and men are just as likely to take part in violence, women are the ones most often hurt.

Questions for Critical Thought

1. Functionalists see the family as a microcosm of society, with individual family members joining and contributing to a whole that is functional for society. Are nuclear families any more functional than other family forms? Why or why not?
2. Identify the various efforts to solve problems of work–family balance. In your opinion, which is most effective and favourable to the different family types today?

3. While some children who are abused by their parents grow up to be abusers themselves, others do not. Why might this be the case?
4. In what ways does elder care by adult parents with families of their own strengthen family cohesion? How might it weaken family cohesion?
5. What kinds of policies can the government implement to improve young adults' transition into adulthood and reduce the number of "boomerang kids" in Canada?
6. How has technology changed family life in Canada in the last 20 years? Has this been a change for the better or for the worse?

Recommended Readings

Albanese, Patrizia. 2007. *Children in Canada Today*. Toronto: Oxford University Press.

Bibby, Reginald W. 2001. *Canada's Teens: Today, Yesterday, and Tomorrow*. Toronto: Stoddart.

Fox, Bonnie. 2009. *When Couples Become Parents: The Creation of Gender in the Transition to Parenthood*. Toronto: University of Toronto Press.

Johnson, Holly, and Myrna Dawson. 2011. *Violence against Women in Canada: Research and Policy Perspectives*. Toronto: Oxford University Press.

Marcus-Newhall, Amy, Diane F. Halpern, and Sherylle J. Tan. 2008. *Changing Realities of Work and Family*. United Kingdom: Wiley-Blackwell.

McDaniel, Susan A., and Lorne Tepperman. 2010. *Close Relations: An Introduction to the Sociology of Families*, 3nd edn. Scarborough, ON: Pearson Educational.

Rayside, David. 2008. *Queer Inclusions, Continental Divisions: Public Recognition of Sexual Diversity in Canada and the United States*. Toronto: University of Toronto Press.

12

Workplaces

Ingram Publishing/Thinkstock

Introduction

This chapter is about employment and unemployment, workers and workplaces, productivity, labour, industry, profits, manufacturing, and health. In particular, it is about work in Canada. But what constitutes "work" and what are the boundaries of this definition? For example, does it include "sex work"?

Larissa Sandy (2009) applies this question to her study of sex workers in Cambodia. She notes that, in global discourses about sex work, the image of the "sex slave" has been influential in constructing the perception that women working in the sex industry in developing countries are "victims." Such discourses have been perpetuated through powerful lobby groups and socially conservative governments. Such an approach may be inadequate. Based on ethnographic research and interviews with sex workers in the port city of Sihanoukville, Cambodia, Sandy's paper questions prevailing stereotypes of "trafficking victims" and the image of "defiled" or "duped" women and girls central to such frameworks. Sandy finds that, in the transition to a market economy, women's choices are constrained by hierarchical structures such as gender, class, socio-cultural obligations, and poor employment opportunities. This is the case whether women take up sex work or not—in all instances, they are both victims and agents.

Compare this with Yasemin Besen-Cassino's (2008) analysis of teenagers in precarious and undesirable jobs in North America. She notes that some scholars characterize typical teenage jobs as "exploitive," highly routinized service-sector jobs with low pay, no benefits, minimum skill requirements, and little time off. To understand the lived experience associated with these jobs, Besen-Cassino focuses on the lived work experience of affluent suburban teenagers who work in these jobs, and explores the meaning these young people create during their everyday work experience.

On the basis of a large ethnographic study conducted with the teenage workers at a national coffee franchise, Besen-Cassino found that outsider views of these "bad jobs" differ from the everyday experience of the actors. From the perspective of the teenagers, these "exploitive jobs" are often seen as fun, social, and empowering; they provide free spaces where the teens can express their creativity and individuality. This finding shows the importance of using a constructionist view to understand teenage employment and inequality. It also suggests that the nature and quality of work—whether experienced as opportunity or victimization—is subjective, largely in the eyes of the beholder.

The point of view might differ with subjects who are not affluent suburbanite teenagers but lone-parent young women, immigrant children whose work at McJobs help to support their families, or school dropouts for whom such jobs can represent a dead end.

In short, our perceptions of work are shaped by our understanding of opportunity and inequality, as well as by claims made about choice and constraint. In this respect, work has not changed much since the days when Marx wrote about the "alienation" of labour under capitalism. He, too, was concerned about the deprivation of choice and its effects on one's identity, social position, and social perception.

Comparative Economic Systems

Capitalism and Socialism

Capitalism refers to the economic system in which private individuals or corporate groups own the means of production and distribution and invest private capital to produce goods and services to be sold for profit in a competitive market. **Socialism** is an alternative economic and political ideology that flourished in the nineteenth and twentieth centuries. It favours public ownership of the means of production and distribution and the investment of public capital in the production of goods and services (Cullen, 2009).

For those who defend socialism—generally Marxists—the capitalist system is just one step in humanity's historical development. They argue that from the early days of human civilization social inequalities were established based on an individual's relationship to material wealth (Dorling, 2011). As societies became more industrialized and capitalistic, imbalances in the relations of production between social classes—that is, between those who had the wealth to purchase and control the engines of production and those who did not—became entrenched in social structures, institutions, and economic organizations. As well, according to this viewpoint, capitalism itself contains certain internal contradictions based on the market structure and the way in which the bourgeoisie exploits the labour of the working class while keeping economic surpluses for itself (Korpi, 1983).

Marxists believe in the eventual inevitability that the proletariat will seize the means of production and redistribute wealth according to a more equitable scheme, for the well-being of the society as a whole.

Those who oppose socialism, on the other hand, consider capitalism to be "the end of history." In his book *The End of History and the Last Man*, Francis Fukuyama (1992) incorporates ideas from Marx and the German philosophers Hegel and Nietzsche. Both Hegel and Marx believed that history was moved forward by conflict; in each era, there are at least two opposing wills or perspectives and these antagonistic viewpoints, and the conflict emerging from them, characterize the *spirit* of the times, referred to as the *zeitgeist*. History is moved forward through a process of *sublimation*: the two opposing forces are combined to form the dominant viewpoint of the next generation.

The end of history means the end of this ideological evolution. Here, the end of history does not entail that events will stop occurring; rather, it signifies a point where humanity no longer tries to overcome itself. Hegel believed that the subjection of domination to reason would bring about the end of history. While he believed that the antagonistic forces were general worldviews, Marx held that they were specifically the opposing wills of different social classes and saw the whole of human history as the socio-cultural evolution of the means of production. Marx believed the universalization of socialism would bring about the end of history.

Fukuyama, however, believes that the universalization of Western capitalism and liberal democracy, *not* socialism, will bring about the end of history. This follows Hegel's conception of the end of history as the goal of liberal democracy and capitalism, which was to make reason the basis of the economic system and public sphere. Those sharing Fukuyama's view argue that socialist societies are inefficient because the common will never drives people to work as hard as their own individual interests and benefits. In

---

Capitalism The economic system in which private individuals or corporate groups own the means of production and distribution. Capitalists invest capital to produce goods and services, which they sell for profit in a competitive free market.

Socialism An alternative economic and political ideology that flourished in the nineteenth and twentieth centuries. It favours the public ownership of the means of production and distribution and the investment of public capital in producing goods and services.

the view of capitalists, the market system ensures maximum efficiency because it maximizes the competition between firms, corporations, and individuals, reducing the prices of goods in the process. This competition also guarantees that resources are assigned in the best way, because production for profit always follows the consumers' demand. Most importantly, supporters of capitalism state that the contradictions pointed out by Marxists will be resolved as the system develops.

Marxists and others have challenged this optimistic view. After all, what drives capitalism is the need for ever-more resources, the need for ever-increasing profits, and the assumption of endless economic growth—and therefore consumption—with some ups and downs along the way. Forty years ago the Club of Rome (a global think tank) noted the limits to such growth (Meadows et al., 1972), pointing out that economic growth depends on the availability of natural resources, many of which are finite in quantity. Since that time, many others have also pointed out the limits to economic growth.

Industrialism and the Industrial Revolution

Since the late eighteenth century, industrialism has transformed the way we work. In pre-industrial societies, people worked collectively in mainly agricultural settings. Because of the small, localized scale of rural communities and the interconnectedness of people's experiences, work was largely inseparable from family and personal life. People led similar lives and held similar moral, religious, and political beliefs (Crisman, 2009).

Two major economic developments changed this: an agricultural revolution and the Industrial Revolution. By the early eighteenth century, an agricultural revolution that had begun thousands of years earlier with plant and animal domestication had reached a point where farmers could produce a large surplus of food, thus enabling many people to work at enterprises outside of food production (Aiken, 2009).

This great number of non-farm workers along with an assortment of technological developments, such as the steam engine, drove the Industrial Revolution. The new system of production introduced innovations in agricultural practices, further increasing efficiency. The new factory system created a large surplus in the manufacturing areas, beginning with the textile and steel industries. Similar surpluses in most economic activities, together with the influx from the countryside of large numbers of workers paid with wages, dramatically increased the complexity of the market and laid the foundations for the emerging capitalist system (Abrams et al., 2009) and the modern city.

During the Industrial Revolution, machines replaced human hands and tools in the production of particular products, while steam (and later, electrical) power replaced much human exertion as the source of energy. As the manufacturing process became more complex, jobs became more specialized (Rosenberg and Trajtenberg, 2004). Early in the twentieth century, Henry Ford invented the assembly line (Schildt, 2006). Cities grew rapidly as people came together in factory towns to seek work in return for wages.

Prior to industrialization, as we've already noted, family life and work life had been carried out in the same place—often on a farm. Now, the two realms of activity became distinct and exclusive, the one still located at home, the other in a factory or office. This marked a new separation of men and women, men's work and women's work, adult work and children's work; it also marked formal education.

The Global Economy and Post-industrialism

In the late twentieth century, industrialism evolved into post-industrialism. Post-industrialism is characterized by the shift from a manufacturing-intensive economy to an economy based on services and information (Chen et al., 2003).

With post-industrialism, geography, distance, and national borders have lost much of their meaning as barriers in communication. Technology and other factors have increased the flow of information, products, and people (Yoon, 2001). They include multinational trade agreements, such as the North American Free Trade Agreement (NAFTA), the European Union, MERCOSUR, which includes several countries in South America, and the proposed Free Trade Area of the Americas (FTAA), and international economic organizations, such as the World Trade Organization (WTO), the World Bank, and the International Monetary Fund (IMF). These agreements and organizations, while benefiting relations between countries, have been laced with political agendas.

Trade agreements are aimed at removing tariffs for import and export. International organizations pressure less-developed countries to open their borders to global trade, dangling the promise of foreign investments and economic prosperity. When they succeed, corporate multinationals find it easier to gain access to raw materials in foreign countries, to employ cheap labour overseas, and in many cases to avoid government controls over workers' rights and environmental pollution. Many believe this process benefits rich nations at the expense of poor ones, and large multinational organizations at the expense of smaller organizations and nation-states.

Global capitalism has supported the growth of huge multinational corporations with revenues larger than the GDPs of most nation-states. They are the dominant political and economic force in the post-industrial world. Sometimes they produce jobs and new wealth (Langman, 2008); sometimes they destroy jobs—which leads to unemployment—and put more wealth in the pockets of the already wealthy (Heinrich, 2008).

Some people leave their birth countries to seek employment, to find better work conditions, or to gain international experience and some adventure along the way. Many Canadians have also gone abroad to live and work, most of them in the prime of their working lives.

Technological Dualism

The explosion of telecommunications and computer technology has resulted in unemployment for many and in the growth of jobs that demand skilled workers. Yet fast-paced development has meant that skills have become outdated faster than ever. Constant upgrading is needed now for workers (and economies) to remain competitive in a continuously changing job market (James, 2003).

Not everyone can achieve this. Such spirited self-improvement is largely limited to those with the financial and educational means to "keep up with the times" and to those who work in a sector of the economy that wants and promotes such changes. For workers mired in low-wage positions—in the retail industry, for example—the market may not force rapid adaptation to technical change, but neither does it offer many opportunities for greater self-improvement and wealth (James, 2002).

Workers in the manufacturing industry increasingly are being threatened with job cuts made possible by the automation of production. Computer-controlled machinery benefits corporate managers for several reasons. First, it removes human error in jobs that are boring and repetitive. Second, high-tech machines can manufacture products with greater uniformity and precision than can human workers. Third, computerization replaces humans with machines that can run continuously, resulting in significant cost-effectiveness. Fourth, computerization and mechanization reduce human conflict between workers and bosses by reducing the number of humans involved. Computing devices do not demand an income, never go on strike (although they do break down), never become tired or bored by their work, and can work around the clock.

As technology continues to transform the workplace, more efficient and less costly machines take over tasks once done by human labour. Only a few well-trained employees are needed to program, supervise, and maintain the otherwise robotic manufacturing process (Carlopio, 2010).

Technology has also affected social interaction and social bonds. The benefit of telephones, texting, fax machines, e-mail, and social media websites such as Facebook is the convenience of allowing people separated by great physical distances to remain in real-time contact with one another, either over a wire or in cyberspace. On the downside, these and other technological inventions have reduced the need for face-to-face contact (Torney et al., 2009). We have replaced activities that once involved human interaction with a machine. Because of the expectations that technology has created, everything must now be accessible and instant. Among many other things, this has changed the way we work.

An increasingly prevalent effect of modern technology in the workplace is the emergence of virtual work—that is, the completion and performance of work duties away from the traditional office through the use of computer technology (Golden and Veiga, 2005). Modern technology enables work to transcend its traditionally designated setting. Virtual work has become commonplace throughout North America. In 2008, 11.2 per cent of Canadian workers and one in five university-educated workers worked from their homes, while about 60 per cent of self-employed Canadians worked from home (Turcotte, 2010).

The Bureaucratization of Work

Besides factories and cities, bureaucracies are a defining feature of modern work life. Bureaucracies are large, complex organizations employing specialized workers who work within the context of what Max Weber (1947) called a *legal-rational authority structure*. This form of authority is distinguished by precisely written rules governing how people are to perform their jobs.

An important aspect of modern **bureaucracy** is the legal idea of "limited liability." This means that a corporation can manage investment and profits impersonally and a given employee is responsible for completing certain tasks and nothing more. In principle, bureaucracies distinguish between the rights and duties attached to a position and the characteristics of the person who (temporarily) holds a position of authority. The impersonal connection between office-holders and the organization makes bureaucracy different from patronage and other personalized systems, such as organized crime.

Industrialization and capitalism favoured the rise of bureaucracies. Bureaucracies are good at controlling large workforces—even highly educated and differentiated workforces. As organizations grow, their differentiation increases. Problems of co-ordination and control—formalization, decentralization, and supervision—are bound to arise.

Bureaucracy A large, complex organization employing highly specialized workers who work within the context of what Max Weber called a legal-rational authority structure.

Frequently, reorganization is needed, especially if the number of personnel is large and growing rapidly. As industrial enterprises grow with the mechanization of work, control structures (that is, for management and administration) grow as well.

Structurally, every member of a bureaucratic organization is enmeshed in a network of **reporting relationships** (Brumback, 2007). The ideal bureaucracy is a spruce tree–shaped structure that branches out, with the hierarchy narrowing towards the top (Ferguson, 2006). At the bottom of the hierarchy, many people have to (1) carry out orders from above, (2) report work-related information to their superiors, and (3) uphold linkages between the organization and its client or customer base. At the top of the hierarchy, only a few people get to (1) issue orders to their subordinates, (2) process information received from below, and (3) preserve linkages between the organization and other organizations—political, economic, and social. In addition, those at the top of this organization are to share information between the heads of planning, manufacturing, shipping, public relations, and other sectors of the organization.

Below the surface of the ideal or formal structure, which prescribes how a bureaucracy ought to work, there inevitably exists an informal structure (Taylor, 2000). This informal organization is developed through communication based on trust. Trust is formed through friendship, acquaintance, and gossip about third parties, which strengthen existing ties. People have stronger attachments to other workers than they do to "the organization," an abstract entity.

Theoretical Perspectives on Work and Unemployment

Structural Functionalism

The structural-functionalist perspective asks, as always, what *function* does work perform? This perspective stresses that, along with the family, work is the most basic of social institutions. Functionalists believe that everyone needs love, work, and hope. Work is especially important because it lets people acquire the material necessities of life—food, water, shelter, and clothing—for themselves and their families.

Not only does paid work give workers an opportunity to satisfy their physical needs, it also allows them to satisfy their emotional needs. These include the wishes to be a productive and valued member of society, to gain recognition and praise, and to interact and cooperate with others. Thus, work has social purposes. It provides a basis for social interaction, social solidarity and cohesion, and the sharing of lifestyles and meanings. The workplace, ideally, lets people exercise all of their social and creative impulses while earning a living.

Conflict and Feminist Theories

Conflict theorists, by contrast, ask, *who gains the advantage* from the current system of work? The competing interests of different classes lead inevitably to conflict. Karl Marx (e.g., 1936 [1887]) claimed that class relations under capitalism cause all the conflict within and between societies.

To his mind, the members of a capitalist society can be divided into two factions. The ruling class, or bourgeoisie, comprises the wealthy owners of the means of production,

---

Reporting relationships Official hierarchical relationships established within a bureaucracy. These relationships are characterized by a power dynamic in which subordinate members adhere to a set of predetermined roles, processes, and functions.

TABLE 12.1	Theoretical Perspectives
THEORY	**MAIN POINTS**
Structural Functionalism	• Work is a basic human need. • Everyone profits when everyone works. • Work is the most basic of social institutions. • Everyone needs love, work, and hope. • Work provides a basis for social interaction, social solidarity, and cohesion.
Conflict Theory	• Capitalists benefit from the current organization of work. • Globalization produces jobs. • Work promotes social inequality. • Work is a place of repression and mistreatment. • Power elites, to boost profits, use unemployment. • Unemployed people depress wages and provide a reserve army of labour.
Symbolic Interactionism	• Work can be organized in a variety of ways. • Socialization and labelling shape the content and perception of different jobs. • Meanings are found in work and unemployment. • Work provides a major part of our identity. • People treat work as a status symbol, and jobs are used as a method of making judgements. • Chronic unemployment is a learned trait—a culture of poverty that perpetuates a sense of learned helplessness.
Feminist Theory	• Women continue to be disadvantaged at work. • Patriarchy operates in the workforce. • Women are paid less than men for the same jobs and work in lower-paying sectors. • Capitalists benefit from the hard unpaid work of women.
Social Constructionism	• The organization of work is an evolving social process. • It reflects changes in technology and worker–management conflict. • The structure of work evolves based on relations between workers and employers. • Technology is a new force in the evolution of work organization.

and the working class, or proletariat, comprises the labourers who work for the bourgeoisie. One group wants to hire labour for the lowest possible price; the other wants to sell its labour for the highest possible price.

Given their opposed interests, the two classes are locked in a conflict that plays out largely in the workplace. In this "contested terrain" (to use economist Richard Edwards's term), there can never be peace and co-operation, or a universally accepted definition of efficiency, because the interests of workers and capitalists are opposed. From this point of view, the workplace is not a place for sociability and creativity; it is a place for repression and mistreatment in which some groups of workers fare better than others. In this system, low-end workers—the most vulnerable workers, those most in need of a stable income—are often the first to lose their jobs when the economy goes into a slump.

Feminist theorists ask, *why don't women benefit* from the capitalist organization of work? They note that Canadian women still are disproportionately engaged in work that has little or no pay—that is, in social reproduction. As a result, capitalists profit from the hard work of women even more than they profit from the hard work of working men; and men, who occupy higher-paid jobs than women, often profit at the expense of women.

Classic WORKS

BOX 12.1   **Rosabeth Kanter's *Men and Women of the Corporation* (1977)**

Rosabeth Kanter's classic work *Men and Women of the Corporation* (1977) challenges assumptions about the traditional system of merit and reward within organizations. Contrary to the common belief that women's opportunities are limited because women act differently from men (for example, that they are too "feminine"), Kanter's study shows that women have less opportunity for promotion and thus they are compelled to act "like women": subservient, devious, yet seemingly unambitious. When men and women have the same opportunities, both act in the same way. People—male or female—who suffer from blocked opportunity, powerlessness, and tokenism display less ambition and low productivity, a result of holding unimportant positions.

All women connected with large organizations—whether executives, secretaries, or even wives—are in a similar bind. Secretaries, however ambitious and talented, are tied to the fortunes of their male bosses. Their earnings rise and fall directly with those of the boss, regardless of the women's own efforts. Similarly, the wives of organizational executives, also often ambitious and talented, are tied to their spouses' fortunes. Both secretaries and wives are powerless, yet heavily dependent on men; their fates rise and fall with those of the men to whom they are linked. Moreover, because of this powerlessness, they behave in "typical" female fashion. These seemingly typical female performances support the male view that women, by nature, are not good executive material.

Kanter hypothesizes that people who are in a numerical minority will feel restricted in what they can do. The more outnumbered they are, the more stress they will experience. As their numbers increase, however, social distance between the minority and majority groups will lessen and interaction and communication across group boundaries will increase. However, adding a few "token women" to an organization will not result in a significant increase in choices for women, nor will it allow women to flourish. Kanter's tokenism theory can be applied to any organizational setting that contains different "kinds" of people, whether men and women, racialized workers and whites, anglophones and francophones, immigrants and native-born, and so on. We can apply the general principle—that tokenism prevents us from seeing how people could potentially adapt and grow into their roles—in a wide variety of situations. This makes Kanter's work fertile and valuable, even beyond the study of gender.

It is in an organization's interest to make the best possible use of its human capital—for example, its talented women. However, external relations with clients and other firms in the industry may hinder an organization's ability to change. More often than not, organizations copy one another and remain locked into patterns set up elsewhere. As well, large organizations have an internal environment that resists change, despite the best wishes of one or more bosses. They contain islands of vested interest—small domains with their own culture and power structure. Those in control will resist change.

The result is job dissatisfaction, a lack of job control, and a rising prevalence of depression and other psychosomatic illnesses among women (Renzetti and Curran, 2003).

Symbolic Interactionism

Symbolic interactionists, as always, ask the question, *how* are jobs and job differences *symbolized*, negotiated, and communicated? They focus on the meanings of work and unemployment for the individual.

Work, especially in a modern, individualistic culture, provides a major part of our identity. Because a person's line of work is so central to his or her identity, others often use it as a source of information. "So what do you do for a living?" is the second most popular question asked whenever two strangers strike up a conversation.

Whether true or not, it is commonly believed that knowing someone's occupation can provide clues to that person's character, personality, and interests. Many people also treat occupational titles as status symbols, basing their assessments of an individual largely on the prestige and income associated with the work that he or she does.

Social Constructionism

Finally, related to this approach, social constructionists always ask, *how* did the arrangement *emerge*?

An example of this would be the work by Richard Edwards (1979) on the historical evolution of management practices—from simple (or direct) control to technological control to what he calls "bureaucratic control." This evolution of management strategies and ideologies reflected changes in the work done and technology used in the workplace. Even more, it reflected changing worker strategies to thwart managerial practices of control. As one means of control no longer worked, another would be invented and taught to new generations of managers.

In addition, social constructionists would be interested in the evolution of popular thinking about work. In the 1950s and 1960s, the dominant concern was with alienating work—how work in large organizations makes people robotic. In the 1970s and 1980s, the dominant concerns were with the exploitation of workers here and abroad, with the possibility of computers replacing humans in the workplace, and with workers securing more leisure. Since then, alongside issues related to the rise of globalism, the principal concern has been job insecurity, job loss (that is, the export of jobs to low-wage countries), and the spillover effects of bad work lives into people's health and family lives.

Social Consequences of Work

Gender Discrimination

Despite the fact that new opportunities, like access to higher-education, have opened up for women in the last few decades, the gender wage gap in Canada has remained stuck since the mid-1990s at one of the highest levels in the industrialized world. The "glass ceiling" that results in this gender-based earning difference, together with other gender-related workplace concerns, such as harassment, was discussed at length in Chapter 4 (Eze, 2009). The problem of gender inequality in the workplace is important because the income earned at work affects a person's access to the necessities of life, education of children, and leisure. Women are over-represented in the lower end of the occupational marketplace, where dead-end and/or part-time work dominates. Low wages and job instability often mean that even full-time workers must live in poverty (Yap and Konrad, 2009).

Stereotypes persist of women as nurturing and emotional and of men as more dominant and rational. As a result, not only are women, even those working full-time, expected to be the primary caregivers within the home, this expectation has also spilled over into the workplace. This has resulted in women being recruited for careers that place them in a caring role—like nursing or teaching—and excusing women from occupations requiring skilled labour or abstract reasoning skills—like engineering. Consider

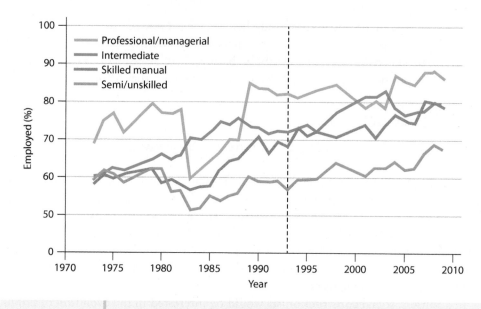

FIGURE 12.1   Employment Rate of Women of Working Age

Source: J.W. Minton, K.E. Pickett, and D. Dorling, "Health, Employment, and Economic Change, 1973–2009: Repeated Cross Sectional Study," *BMJ* 344 (2012): e2316.

advancements within the information technology industry in Canada. While this has led to mass employment opportunities, women seem to be largely under-represented within this sector of work in Canada (Kelan, 2007; Heilbronner, 2013).

For these and other reasons, women are still under-represented in leadership positions, though the share of women in management (see Figure 12.1) has been increasing in recent decades. Yet, the debate continues over whether this increase is attributable to a greater acceptance of femininity in the workplace or whether it merely reflects the increasing success of women at showing more "masculine" traits (Ross-Smith and Hipputz, 2010).

Women's unpaid household labour may account for as much as one-third of the world's economic production. One calculation for South and Southeast Asia found that between 43 and 48 per cent of their GDP is due to unpaid work, most of it performed by women (Hoskyns and Rai, 2007). When unpaid agricultural work and housework are considered with wage labour in developing countries, women's work hours are estimated to exceed men's by 30 per cent (UN Population Fund, 2000: 38).

Those with alternative gender identities or expressions also face discrimination in the workplace. Transsexual people, whether male or female, are more likely to experience discrimination and harassment in the workplace; a recent poll in the US showed that a staggering 90 per cent of transsexual people reported facing some form of harassment at work and 26 per cent had been fired for being transgendered (National Gay and Lesbian Task Force, 2011). Transsexual people are also more likely than those with a normative gender identity and expression to have a lower income. The problems transsexual people face in the workplace typically result from misconceptions, from a lack of official company policies for hiring and working with transsexual people, and, occasionally, from transphobia.

Racial and Ethnic Discrimination

Workers who belong to ethnic and racial minorities are especially disadvantaged in their search for jobs, in the incomes they receive once hired, and in opportunities to advance based on merit (Li, 2003).

In part, these problems reside in stereotypes—employers are unwilling or unable to imagine that certain types of people can do good work. Equally important, these problems are due to weak social networks. People with more social capital are in a better position to hear about good jobs, and employers are more likely to hear about them (Ooka and Wellman, 2006; Lindsay, 2009).

Many organizations have made a conscious effort to overcome these barriers by reaching out to minority communities and welcoming the minority people who come to work in their midst. Nonetheless, visible minority immigrants continue to experience lower average pay and higher levels of job dissatisfaction than native-born Canadians (Magee and Umamaheswar, 2011). It has also been found that certain ethnic minority groups (such as blacks and Latinos in the US) tend to be over-represented in low-skill occupations characterized by low wages (Liu, 2011; Hirsch and Macpherson, 2004).

Social capital Sociologists call having larger, more varied, and more powerful interpersonal networks "having greater social capital."

Worker Dissatisfaction and Alienation

In an ideal world, work is invigorating, satisfying, and socially useful. It fulfills the individual's need for meaningful labour and society's need to get work done. In reality, however, many jobs are not stimulating and challenging. They are repetitious, boring, and often not even socially useful.

As mentioned earlier, at least as far back as Marx, social analysts have noted that industrialization and the resulting division of labour have separated the workers from the work process, from the object they produce, and from their co-workers. This experience of alienation involves feelings of powerlessness, meaninglessness, normlessness (anomie), estrangement, and social isolation in the workplace. Specialized work roles mean that each individual worker is given few responsibilities, performing narrowly defined tasks lacking in variety and challenge, often below his or her full intellectual, physical, and emotional potential, as demanded by the employer. Sociologists have disagreed about the origins of these problems: Marx attributed them to capitalism, Durkheim (1964 [1893]) to specialization, and Weber to rationalization.

Alienation This experience involves feelings of powerlessness, meaninglessness, normlessness, estrangement, and social isolation in the workplace.

Whatever the cause of alienation, the end result is employees becoming just another cog in the wheel, mindlessly churning out the products wanted by their employers as part of a factory line, clerical office, filing department, or retail shop. In extreme cases, this narrow range of tasks is repeated daily for years, even decades. The result is a decline in worker loyalty and productivity, since employees are no longer dedicated to doing an especially good job. Many studies have shown that low levels of work satisfaction result from these work circumstances (Langfred and Moye, 2004; Stanton et al., 2002; Sikora, 2002; Vieira, 2005; Farooq and Ahmed, 2007).

Surveys show that several factors are related to job satisfaction consistently. The list includes safe working conditions, job security, challenging and stimulating work content, pleasant and like-minded colleagues, respect and consideration from superiors, and opportunities for creativity, initiative, and advancement. In addition, it is important that the workers' expectations of the job match their work experience. When the two

Many jobs in today's society are unsatisfying. The decline in job satisfaction results in a decline of worker loyalty and productivity, as well as resentment on the part of the worker.

diverge, resentment, job dissatisfaction, and alienation arise. Most importantly, people crave some measure of autonomy and control over their work (Lambert et al., 2009).

Vulnerable Populations

Sex Workers

Whatever the power of personal experiences that incline a person towards sex work, such work is possible only under specific cultural conditions. Sex work is built on a sexual double standard, widespread poverty, and a gendered labour market. Poor women and children, especially in societies without a social welfare net, are most likely to be engaged in sex work.

In India, for example, women suffer from the double standard of morality that governs a profitable sex trade. Despite the financial vulnerability that leads them to enter sex work and the health hazards they suffer, Indian sex workers endure stigmatization because they must sell their bodies to live. In particular, "floating" sex workers who return to their families after work suffer from the sense of leading a discreditable double life.

In Canada, buying and selling sex is legal, but most activities surrounding prostitution, including public communication for the purpose of prostitution, running a bawdy house, or procuring (pimping), are considered criminal offences. In practice, this makes it nearly impossible to work in the sex trade legally. Recently, however, the laws surrounding sex work in Canada have been challenged. Specifically, in 2010, three sex workers challenged and changed some of the Ontario laws surrounding the sex trade (*Bedford v. Canada*). The basis of this case was that certain parts of the Canadian Criminal Code, such as making it illegal for prostitutes to work indoors or to hire bodyguards, are

The Canadian Press/Darren Calabrese

Dominatrix Terri-Jean Bedford, right, carries a riding crop while walking with sex workers advocate Valerie Scott after leaving the Ontario Superior Court in Toronto. The Supreme Court of Canada struck down prostitution laws in a unanimous 9–0 ruling in December 2013.

unconstitutional, as they can result in significant harm to sex workers, since the workers are forced to operate secretly in extremely dangerous conditions.

Sex trafficking has become an growing problem internationally. It is estimated that over four million people are bought and sold for the purpose of sexual exploitation each year. However, the illegal nature of trafficking makes it difficult to gather accurate statistics on the actual number of people—mostly women—who are involved. Given that participation in the global sex trade is often involuntary, women are often subjected to cruelty, violence, and abuse from their traffickers (Twitty, 2003).

A poll shortly after the verdict was delivered showed that about half of Canadians agree with the verdict (Angus Reid Public Opinion, 2010). In 2012, the Ontario Court of Appeal upheld the lower court's ruling. In June 2013, the case was heard by the Supreme Court of Canada. Even in jurisdictions where sex work continues to be illegal, places to find sex are well known. There, sex workers gather in "red-light districts." These districts may come and go. The unstable location of sex work in a city is a consequence of the interplay between police strategies and community protestors and the resistance movement mounted by sex workers. These strategies depend on whether the society believes in the legalization or criminalization of sex work.

With decriminalized sex work, distinctive red light or brothel districts are created to isolate sex work from more socially approved activities and people and to keep women from walking the streets, propositioning potential clients (Hubbard and Sanders, 2003).

Sex work entails relations between a sex worker, a client, and possibly a pimp. Street-level sex work includes both pimp-controlled and independent entrepreneurial sex work.

PERSONAL *stories*

BOX 12.2 | **Susan Austin: Sex Industry Hit Hard by Recession**

Luxury industries took a major hit during the recession, particularly the business of sin. Gambling revenues on the Las Vegas Strip plummeted 14 percent, and casino construction ground to a halt. And although the recession has technically ended, sex is still not selling so well.

The legal brothel industry in Nevada is ailing, the *New York Daily News* reports. With fewer customers, legal prostitutes are no longer so willing to hand over 50 percent of their pay to brothel owners, and many are striking out on their own. The rise in illegal prostitution has cut even further into the customer base of legal brothels, according to the director of the Nevada Brothel Association. "When I started as the lobbyist for the industry in 1985, we had 37 brothels in the state," George Flint told the *Daily News*. "Now we have just 18, and 12 to 14 of them are not doing very well."

It's the old supply-and-demand story. During the recession, fewer pleasure-seekers came to town, and more women entered the business. "Instead of paying $400 for a room at a brothel, these guys can now go out and get the same service for a third of the money," said Flint.

Vegas's recovery has proven painfully slow; unemployment in the Nevada capital was 9.8 percent in March, the latest month for which data is available, 30 percent higher than the national average.

"When the hotels fired a lot of their low-end workers, and they disappeared, well, then a lot of my low-end clients were gone, my $100 parties were gone," Susan Austin, who runs Mustang Ranch, the state's first legal brothel, told CNBC last year. "And then when a lot of my high rollers all of a sudden discovered they didn't have as much discretionary income . . . that definitely dug into their wallets, which definitely affected us."

Nevada's black market has taken a battering too. Mid-price prostitutes (who charge between $600 and $700) were the main victims of the supply–demand crunch, the *Las Vegas Sun* reported back in 2008, as many of their customers turned to cheaper offerings.

Sex-for-hire, it turns out, is pretty vulnerable to swings in the economy. The only sin that actually appears recession-proof is drinking.

Source: <jobs.aol.com/articles/2013/05/14/nevada-brothels-prostitutes-hit-by-recession>.

Violence towards women involved in pimp-controlled sex work is common (Williamson and Cluse-Tolar, 2002). Even so, the social bonds between pimps and sex workers follow certain rules. As with other forms of crime, public violence is bad for business, so efforts are made to control sex-work activities without much violence, or at least to reserve violent methods of control for when they can be delivered in private.

In many countries, female sex workers must switch daily between the roles of mother and sex worker. As a result, they are constantly subjected to society's double standard for women (Johnston and Swanson, 2007). Sex workers divide their lives between the mother/saint and traitor/sex-worker roles.

The rationalizations of those who wish to legalize sex work include justifying it as a better-paying employment opportunity for women and as a type of social service. These practical considerations, however, are often drowned out by moral outcries, and so sex workers have had difficulty mobilizing for their own protection and advancement. Some sex workers have tried to improve their health and social standing through the formation of social movements. For the first time, sex workers are organizing politically and expressing their claims and grievances in the public debate about sex work—a debate from which they are excluded (Mathieu, 2003).

Usually, people enter the sex trade because they can see no other choice. To confirm this, Nixon and colleagues (2002) studied data from three western Canadian provinces and found that young women tend to enter sex work out of financial necessity. Once there, many experienced violence with such consistency that it seemed "normal." Many sex workers, here and elsewhere, grew up in harsh and even abusive families. Often, they have limited educational backgrounds or have not completed high school, thus making their exit from sex work into other types of work even more difficult.

Survey results (Abramovich, 2005) show that both male and female sex workers experienced high rates of physical and sexual abuse in childhood, as well as parental substance abuse. The result is a spread of sex work—with its attendant problems—among adolescents (Bamgbose, 2002). In Canada, 10–15 per cent of street sex workers are under the age of 18; the average age of entry into the sex trade is between 14 and 15; and the average age of entry for Aboriginals is between 13 and 14 (Hecht, 2001). As is the case throughout the industry, adolescent sex workers vary in their way of working: some work in brothels, while others are streetwalkers, call girls, and casual, part-time, or floating sex workers. Among sex workers in many countries, parental substance abuse, neglect, and emotional, physical, and sexual abuse are common in the girls' lives. They run away from turbulent home lives and are trapped by the illegal world of underground sex work.

While it may be easy in some places and circumstances to drift into sex work, it tends to be far more difficult to leave. Manopaiboon et al. (2003) studied Thai women's ability to leave sex work and the factors influencing their lives after leaving. All but one of the 42 current and former female sex workers surveyed had quit sex work at least once before. Women's decision and ability to leave sex work are determined mainly by four factors: financial situation, link with a steady partner, attitudes towards sex work, and HIV/AIDS experience. Most women assume that their risk of HIV infection will be lower after leaving sex work, yet 3 of the 17 HIV-infected women were infected after having left, presumably by their steady partners.

Everywhere in the prosperous West, sex workers are being imported from Eastern European, Asian, and Latin American countries. The rapid expansion and diversification of the international sex trade can be credited to several factors. These include the simultaneous rise in service occupations, temporary work, and corporate-fuelled consumption; an increase in labour migration, tourism, and business travel; and new forms of gender, sexuality, and kinship (Bernstein, 2002).

Young women suffer the assaults of war as well as the intensifying levels of sexual and domestic violence, poverty, and social dislocation that war brings. They may also be preyed upon by international criminal rackets that exploit the invisibility of poor young women in war zones in order to benefit from their illegal sexual labour as well as from their domestic and industrial labour—part of the tragic underbelly of worldwide economic development that yields billions of dollars annually. In fact, a large portion of prostitution is the result of human trafficking. In India, for instance, it is estimated that as much as 50 per cent of the victims of human trafficking become female sex workers (Decker, 2013).

Child Labour

Child labour is especially common in rural areas where the capacity to enforce minimum-age rules for schooling and work is lacking. Most children in rural areas work in agriculture or as domestics, while urban children tend to work in trade and services, with fewer in manufacturing and construction. Though children are poorly paid in these jobs, they still serve as major contributors to family income in developing countries. The lack of good schools also encourages parents to send their children to work rather than to school. Rigid cultural and social views about children and childhood may also limit educational goals and increase child labour.

Working children are the objects of extreme exploitation, toiling for long hours at low pay. Furthermore, three-quarters (171 million) work under risky conditions in mines, with chemicals, or with dangerous machinery. Not surprisingly, this exposure leads to lasting physical and psychological harm. Working at rug looms, for example, may leave children disabled with eye damage, lung disease, stunted growth, and a vulnerability to arthritis as they grow older. Many children work in order to attend school, so abolishing all child labour may only hinder their education.

However, in general, an improvement in the financial condition of struggling families would free children from full-time labour. Sometimes, a child's work can be helpful to him or her and to the family. Working and earning can be a positive experience in a child's growing up, not least by teaching important lessons in responsibility, independence, and the value of a dollar. The benefits of work depend largely on the child's age, the conditions in which the child works, and whether work prevents the child from going to school. Invariably, exploitative child labour hampers the child's development and preparation for adult life in a post-industrial world.

Without an education and a normal childhood, some children are reduced to slavery. Some are kidnapped and forced to work. Many are beaten or subjected to other severe physical abuse. An extreme form of child labour, bonded labour, takes place when a family receives a small advance payment (sometimes as little as $20) to give a boy or girl over to an employer. The child cannot work off the debt, nor can the family raise enough money to buy the child back. Bonded child labour is widespread in countries around the world (see Figure 12.2).

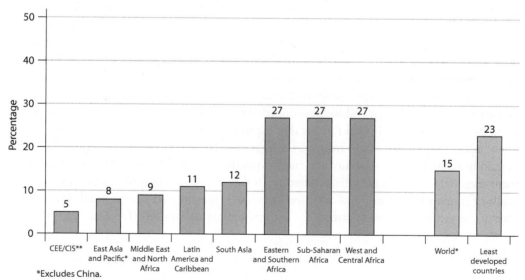

*Excludes China.
**Central and Eastern Europe and the Commonwealth of Independent States.
Notes: Estimates based on a subset of 90 countries covering 71 per cent of the population of children aged 5 to 14 in the world (excluding China, for which comparable data are not available in UNICEF global databases). Regional estimates represent data from countries covering at least 50 per cent of the regional population.

FIGURE 12.2   Children Aged 5–14 in the Labour Market, 2011

Source: UNICEF global databases, 2014. Based on DHS, MICS, and other nationally represented surveys, 2005–12.

Currently, there is no international agreement defining child labour, making it hard to isolate cases of abuse, let alone abolish them. However, eliminating child labour is one of the four fundamental principles of the ILO's Declaration on Fundamental Principles and Rights at Work. ILO Convention 182 calls for the prohibition of and immediate action to expel the "worst forms of child labour."

Convention 182 defines a child as a person under 18 years old, and identifies the "worst forms of child labour" as all forms of slavery or practices similar to slavery such as the sale and trafficking of children, debt bondage and serfdom, forced or compulsory labour, including forced or compulsory recruitment of children for use in armed conflict; the use, procuring, or sale of a child for prostitution, pornographic performances, or illicit activities—especially, for the production and trafficking of drugs. In short, Convention 182 calls for an end to all work that is likely to harm the health, safety, or morals of children (International Labour Organization, at: <www.ilo.org/public/english/standards/ipec/about/factsheet/faq.htm>).

By contrast, work by children in Canada is regulated and the worst forms of child labour are banned. Free primary and secondary schooling are universally available, and school attendance is compulsory until at least age 16. In addition, the federal, provincial, and territorial governments have adopted many laws banning or restricting the employment of children to ensure that their participation in work does not affect their health and development or interfere with their schooling.

At the national level, the Federal Committee against the Commercial Sexual Exploitation of Children was created specifically to examine programs underway across Canada to fight the exploitation of children and youth in the sex trade (for more on this,

The Canadian Press/Jonathan Hayward

Archbishop Desmond Tutu, right, gives performer Angelique Kidjo a high five during We Day in Vancouver. We Day is an annual event organized by the international charity Free the Children, founded by brothers Craig and Marc Kielburger to urge governments to do more to improve life for young people around the world.

Discriminatory unemployment
Unemployment resulting from discrimination against particular groups, such as ethnic minorities and women.

Structural unemployment
Unemployment caused by social and economic factors that affect workers equally across all groups, such as corporate downsizing, capital flight (caused by corporate mergers and the move of operations to another geographic region—"runaway plants"), and the automation of work processes.

Discouraged workers
People who are not actively seeking employment. Specifically, they are thought to have turned their backs on the traditional work system and to have abandoned any desire to be gainfully employed.

see Canadian Strategy against Commercial Sexual Exploitation of Children and Youth, at: sen.parl.gc.ca/lpearson/htmfiles/hill/17_htm_files/Committee-e/Exploit_EN.htm).

Unemployment and Its Effects

Types of Unemployment and Their Measurement

Researchers distinguish between discriminatory and structural unemployment. **Discriminatory unemployment** is unemployment resulting from discrimination against particular groups, such as ethnic minorities and women (Reitz and Breton, 1998). **Structural unemployment** is the result of social and economic factors that affect workers equally across all groups (Heaton and Oslington, 2010). These factors include corporate layoffs, capital flight (caused by corporate mergers and the move of operations to another geographic region—the so-called runaway plants), and automation (replacing human labour with machinery). Yet, the unemployment rate does not affect the entire economy equally (see Figure 12.3). This is because macroeconomic conditions affect the relative demand for workers' services.

Researchers base their measures of unemployment on the percentage of the workforce currently without jobs, actively seeking employment, and available to work. This definition excludes women who work as homemakers without pay and **discouraged workers**, that is, those who have turned their backs on the traditional work system and abandoned efforts to work for pay (Maich, 2008). These discouraged workers consist

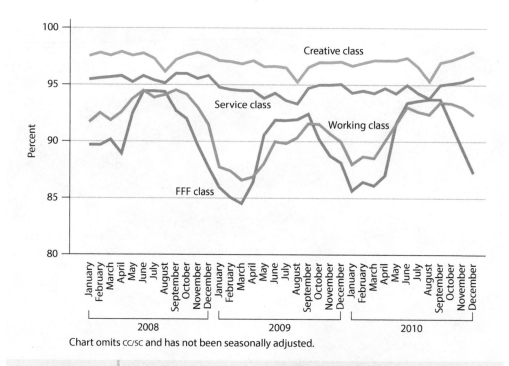

Chart omits cc/sc and has not been seasonally adjusted.

FIGURE 12.3 | Employment in Canada by Occupational Class, 2008–2010

Source: Martin Prosperity Institute. Used with permission.

| TABLE 12.2 | Employment by Age, Sex, Type of Work, Class of Worker, and Province (Monthly) (Canada) |

	MAY 2012	APRIL 2013	MAY 2013	APRIL 2013 TO MAY 2013	MAY 2012 TO MAY 2012
				SEASONALLY ADJUSTED	
	Employment in thousands			% change	
Canada—all ages	17,499.20	17,654.40	17,749.40	0.5	1.4
15 to 24 years	2,434.30	2,428.10	2,482.50	2.2	2
25 years and over	15,064.90	15,226.30	15,266.80	0.3	1.3
Men	9,198.30	9,246.00	9,317.00	0.8	1.3
Women	8,300.90	8,408.40	8,432.40	0.3	1.6
Full-time	14,172.90	14,355.00	14,431.70	0.5	1.8
Part-time	3,326.30	3,299.40	3,317.60	0.6	−0.3
Employees	14,816.30	14,929.90	15,031.10	0.7	1.4
Public sector[1]	3,572.30	3,657.40	3,664.00	0.2	2.6
Private sector[2]	11,243.90	11,272.50	11,367.10	0.8	1.1
Self-employed	2,682.90	2,724.50	2,718.30	−0.2	1.3

[1]Those who work for a local, provincial or federal government, for a government service or agency, a crown corporation, or a government funded establishment such as a school (including universities) or hospital.
[2]Those who work as employees of a private firm or business.
Source: Statistics Canada, tables 282-0087 and 282-0089, at: <www.40.statcan.gc.ca/l01/cst01/labr66a-eng.ht> (May 2013).

disproportionately of women and racial minorities. Other people do not take part in the labour force because they are in school, retired, injured, sick, or otherwise unable to work.

Rates of employment vary widely from one part of Canada to another, and also from one age group to another. Young workers and private-sector workers have been affected the most by the recent recession. According to Table 12.2, there has been some improvement in labour force participation, though participation is still lower than what it was before the economic crises of 2008–9.

Because of these exclusions, most official unemployment rates understate the true percentage of the unemployed (Blendon and Benson, 2009). This in turn underestimates the size of the unemployment problem. Official employment rates also do not distinguish between full-time and part-time work, nor do they recognize odd jobs, temporary work, and other forms of underemployment as different from full-time work. A person who reports working as little as one hour per week is formally considered "gainfully employed." This definition lessens the visible problem of unemployment. So, in the end, our estimates of unemployment provide too rosy a picture of the actual reality in the work world.

Predictors of Unemployment

Some explanations of unemployment focus on the social and financial environment in which jobs are lost; others focus on the people who lose their jobs. In the former category, research has been done on the causes and effects of downsizing. For example, researchers found that downsizing cut out about 60 per cent of the workforce and one-quarter of the job titles in the British Columbia sawmill industry, largely in response to an economic recession in the early 1980s. Job loss tends to affect the youngest workers most severely (Ostry et al., 2000).

CANADIAN researchers

| **BOX 12.3** | **Elizabeth Hirsh, University of British Columbia** |

Elizabeth Hirsh, an associate professor at the University of British Columbia, holds a Tier II Canada Research Chair in Social Inequality and Law. Elizabeth studies how laws and policies minimize employment discrimination based on ascriptive qualities, such as gender, race, ethnicity. She is particularly interested in how people identify, and take legal action against, workplace discrimination. Most affluent societies place legal sanctions on employers for discriminating against their workers. As Elizabeth argues, these laws do not eliminate discrimination in Canada, as thousands of workers are forced to file legal claims based on sex, race, and ethnic background each year.

In a 2008 article in the *American Journal of Sociology* titled "The Context of Discrimination: Workplace Conditions, Institutional Environments, and Sex and Race Discrimination Charges," Elizabeth explores the workplace conditions under which discrimination charges occur. Along with co-author Sabino Kornrich, Elizabeth argues that structural conditions within the workplace influence whether or not workers will "mobilize their legal rights" when discriminated against at work. For example, business size, composition, and having a minority management affect how many charges are put forward by

workers. She also finds that affirmative action and subsidiary statuses play a role in whether or not charges become verified claims. This research suggests that that internal workplace conditions affect how discriminatory experiences are interpreted by both workers and regulatory agents.

Building on this work, Elizabeth's 2009 article "The Strength of Weak Enforcement: The Impact of Discrimination Charges, Legal Environments, and Organizational Conditions on Workplace Segregation" explores whether workplace conditions for women and racial minorities have improved when their employers have been formally charged with employment discrimination. Elizabeth finds that employers are somewhat unresponsive to Equal Employment Opportunity Commission charges and that legal claims are most effective when accompanied by political and economic pressure.

Sources: Elizabeth C. Hirsch, "The Strength of Weak Enforcement: The Impact of Discrimination Charges, Legal Environments, and Organizational Conditions on Workplace Segregation," *American Sociological Review* 74, 2 2009: 245–71; Elizabeth C. Hirsh and Sabino Kornich, "The Context of Discrimination: Workplace Conditions, Institutional Environments, and Sex and Race Discrimination Charges," *American Journal of Sociology* 113, 5 (2008): 256–73; and CRC profile.

Other researchers focus on the characteristics of people who lose their jobs or who are at particular risk of losing their jobs in a recession. They often focus on human capital characteristics, such as educational attainment or particular job-related skills. Age is a predictor of unemployment, with youth more likely to face unemployment than adults at any given time (Jacobs, 2008). Older workers (over age 40) who have been laid off find it harder than younger workers to get a job, especially in work, like construction, that demands physical strength. Family characteristics play a part, too. For example, single marital status predicts unemployment after a layoff among construction and forest workers (Liira and Leino, 1999). Parental divorce, low parental emotional involvement, and parental unemployment (for males only) predict the unemployment of youth (de Goede et al., 2000).

A study of unemployed youth across different countries found that in all cases, unemployed youth scored lower on an assessment of basic skills than their employed counterparts. The extent of the gap did vary, however, with the largest gaps being in the US and Canada and the lowest being in Norway and Italy (Lundetræ et al., 2010). The study attributed this discrepancy to the increased availability of vocational training at the high school level for the latter two countries.

Some have argued that health problems frequently predate and cause unemployment. To some degree, the effects of illness on working life depend on the duration of a disability. In one study, over half of the workers who became limited in activities of daily living as adults had unemployment spells lasting less than two years. Few disabled people who had remained outside the workforce for four years re-entered it (Burchardt, 2000). More than half of the non-working disabled reported that economic, social, and job-based barriers contributed to their inability to work, and one-fourth of working-disabled people reported having been discriminated against in the last five years (Druss et al., 2000). Mental as well as physical health is linked to transitions to early retirement or other unemployment (Wray, 2000). Above-average mental health plays a protective role in keeping workers in the workforce rather than being laid off, on sick leave, or unemployed.

However, health problems do not always lead to long-term unemployment. Specific health conditions, such as asthma or visual impairment, may be associated with work limitation, yet they are not among the main determinants of continuous unemployment (McCarty et al., 1999; Yelin et al., 1999). The risk of unemployment for chronically ill people largely depends on active labour market policies—specific efforts made by government to stimulate employment, job training, and worker mobility. Employment protections also play a role, as shown by lower rates of unemployment and inactivity in Sweden than in Britain (Burstrom et al., 2000).

UP IN THE AIR

George Clooney stars in the 2009 comedy-drama about a man whose profession is to execute company layoffs.

Social Consequences of Unemployment

As unpleasant as work can be, the alternative can be even worse. Unemployment does not only deprive most people of the basis for material survival, it also takes a toll on society. At the individual level, one study found that being unemployed is the largest determinant of life satisfaction, even controlling for income (Ochsen, 2011). This effect increases as the duration of unemployment increases. At a societal level, with people out of the workforce, the economy cannot reach its utmost potential for production. Another reason unemployment affects the overall economy is the cost of preserving a social and financial support network to help those who are between jobs (Slebarska et al., 2009).

From a social-psychological perspective, unemployed people are often marked with the stigma of being lazy and unwilling to work. Some think that employment insurance and welfare undermine the work ethic that has motivated so many others to succeed in life. People who see themselves as masters of their own fate hold unemployed people responsible for their own condition and don't think that they deserve public aid. On the other hand, people who have experienced forces beyond their control can believe that some people are unemployed because of ill health, discrimination, recession, or corporate downsizing and that they deserve help.

Health Consequences of Work

Workplace Safety Issues

Health and safety hazards in the workplace are an obvious social problem. As seen in Table 12.3, for example, 798 Canadian workers died from workplace-related accidents in 1998, and that number rose to 919 in 2011 (Association of Workers' Compensation Boards of Canada, 2011).

TABLE 12.3	Number of Workplace Fatalities, by Province 1998–2011												
	1998	1999	2000	2001	2002	2003	2004	2005	2006	2007	2008	2009	2010	2011
NL	32	27	38	26	23	23	23	25	18	23	23	42	32	33
PEI	3	3	0	5	1	0	1	2	1	3	2	2	0	0
NS	13	17	16	8	14	18	41	27	12	14	23	15	23	20
NB	17	20	7	15	17	7	12	12	15	9	14	17	12	9
QC	208	164	180	180	188	175	176	223	206	206	195	185	213	204
ON	243	283	301	328	383	378	365	412	373	439	396	384	385	306
MB	22	23	19	25	19	24	14	26	26	27	24	28	16	22
SK	28	34	31	35	23	35	30	27	30	29	26	30	45	37
AB	105	114	118	118	101	127	124	143	124	154	166	110	136	123
BC	125	147	157	168	158	170	136	189	160	140	160	121	144	145
NT/NU	2	2	13	11	6	5	5	10	8	9	5	3	5	18
YT	0	1	2	0	1	1	1	2	3	2	1	2	3	2
Total	**798**	**835**	**882**	**919**	**934**	**963**	**928**	**1098**	**976**	**1055**	**1035**	**939**	**1014**	**919**

Source: Association of Workers' Compensation Boards of Canada, at <www.awcbc.org/en/statistics.asp>.

Canada's rate of workplace fatalities—6.1 deaths per 100,000 workers—is among the worst in the OECD (Organisation for Economic Co-operation and Development) countries, with only Korea (29 deaths), Turkey (20.6 deaths), Mexico (12.0 deaths), and Portugal (8.7 deaths) being higher, all countries with significantly lower levels of development than Canada (Dean, 2012). Canada's record for reducing workplace fatalities over the previous 20 years stood alone as the worst (CBC News, 2007), with nearly 10,000 deaths occurring in the past decade alone (UFCW, 2013). This dismal record is explainable, in part at least, by the extent to which Canada, relative to other wealthy countries, is still reliant on the dangerous work of resource extraction—logging, fishing, oil drilling, mining—and on heavy manufacturing.

Employment and Skills Development Canada showed that, in 2010, 14.7 per 1,000 employed Canadians suffered occupational injuries in Canada (HRDC, 2013). Though many of these injuries were minor, one-third were classed as disabling, resulting in significant losses in hours worked.

Some industries are more dangerous than others. The transportation and material-moving sector, in particular, is a dangerous place to work. In 2011, there were 1,213 fatal work injuries in this sector in the US, accounting for about one-quarter of all occupational fatalities (Bureau of Labor Statistics, 2012). Incidence rates are highest among the logging and forestry, construction, and manufacturing industries, and lowest within the finance and insurance sector.

In general, the occupations with the highest risk of occupational injury or death are those that involve semi-skilled manual labour, such as equipment operator and installer, manufacturer, and machine assembler. The occupations with the lowest risk of work-related injury or death are senior management executive, business, and finance professions (HRDC, 2000).

Work Stress

Another health-related feature of employment that is increasingly being studied is work-related stress. This can lead to the neurological condition called "burnout" as well as other significant physical and mental health outcomes. When the demands of the job exceed the abilities, resources, or needs of the worker, job stress occurs (Ariganello, 2009).

Statistics on hours spent at work cannot capture either the full amount of time spent working or the stress associated with work. It is possible to be "at work" without working. One could be at home, yet preoccupied with job issues. It is possible to work 10 hours a day in a leisurely fashion yet do less work and feel less stressed than someone who works seven intense hours a day. Increasingly, for example, professional and managerial workers are expected to take their work home with them and to be on call as needed. Overwork is a big problem in Canada today, as illustrated by the continuing conflict between work life and family home life.

Substance Abuse

Unemployment increases the risks associated with the consumption of alcohol, tobacco, and other drugs, especially in young men (Popovici and French, 2013; MacDonald and Pudney, 2000). Alcohol abuse, associated with unemployment, is correlated with a heightened risk of death by suicide, violence, and driving accidents. Increased alcohol consumption is one of the mechanisms connecting unemployment and suicide (Walsh and Walsh, 2011). Unemployment increases the risk of alcohol abuse, and re-employment reduces the prevalence of alcohol abuse (Patrick and Schulenberg, 2011).

In turn, alcohol abuse increases the risk of violence, especially family violence (Zaleski et al., 2010). Unemployment in men has also been linked to intimate partner violence (Caetano et al., 2001). One study found that the financial crises of 2008–9 resulted in sharp increases in malnutrition and hunger, domestic violence, and child abuse (Chowdhury et al., 2013). Alcohol abuse also increases the likelihood of fatal car crashes at night; insofar as unemployment reduces the frequency of car accidents, it is because those without jobs no longer spend time on the road commuting to and from work (Gonzalez and Rodriguez, 2000).

Psychological Consequences: Depression and Anxiety

More than anything else, unemployment affects health by increasing anxiety and depression (Comino et al., 2000; Flint et al., 2013).

Job loss typically arouses defensive feelings, lowers self-esteem, and creates doubt about the future. It often causes people to become passive and to withdraw from social life, further harming their mental health. Unemployed people report more stress, boredom, doubt, and dissatisfaction with themselves and their lives than do the gainfully employed (Gien, 2000). Typically, unemployment causes people's resources to dwindle, and this has a negative impact on their views of themselves, their aging, and the possibility of their leading a productive life (Schmitt, 2001).

Researchers disagree about whether the effects of unemployment are the same for women and men. Some researchers find that men feel more threatened by job loss than women, which would explain the higher frequency of depression among unemployed men (Ytterdahl and Fugelli, 2000). Women, it is argued, have less of their self-identity defined by paid work and can invest themselves in housework, if necessary, though unemployment for women also involves a loss of personal identity (Desmarais, 1991). However, women often suffer great distress from unemployment, even after giving birth when they are much involved in their maternal role (Saurel Cubizolles et al., 2000). Thus, some argue that men and women experience unemployment in much the same way (Virtanen et al., 2011), though they may show their distress in different ways. Job loss results in anxiety disorders in women, while unemployed men tend to fall victim to substance abuse, depression, and anxiety. Spikes in unemployment also commonly lead to higher rates of suicide (Kondilis et al., 2013).

Unemployment produces distress, fatalistic attitudes, feelings of a lack of control over one's life, and feelings of personal inefficacy. Poor mental health, in turn, reduces the likelihood of finding a job. Depression caused by unemployment may lead to continued unemployment. Conversely, success in finding a job is predicted by a positive attitude and an active way of dealing with unemployment (Schuring et al. 2011).

Solutions to Unemployment

Unemployment Interventions

Interventions for the problem of unemployment might take the form of reducing the number of people who experience unemployment, reducing the stresses of unemployment, strengthening people's life skills and psychosocial resources, and providing counselling and clinical interventions (Avison, 2001).

Job-creation programs can reduce some unemployment. Here, it is important that job creation occurs mainly in full-time, stable, and skill-intensive fields. Such "good" positions are less likely to result in a return to unemployment further down the road. Jobs that are temporary and fail to build new skills and contacts are a waste of effort (Rose, 2009).

As well, since education is the best weapon against unemployment, governments should ensure that schooling is made available to as many people as possible. Schooling opportunities are especially needed by people whose financial condition might otherwise prevent them from getting higher education. This category includes poor people, rural people, disabled people, and Aboriginal people. This initiative should include adult education programs, as they can be another effective tool for increasing the chance of re-employment and career advancement.

Labour unions, which historically have been effective tools in pressuring employers to provide better wages and working conditions for employees (Blanchflower and Bryson, 2010), have experienced a decline in recent decades (Godard, 2009). Initiatives that support unions and political parties that promote working-class interests, such as the New Democratic Party in Canada and equivalent parties abroad (for example, the traditional Labour Party in Britain), are key to ensuring that wages and working conditions remain on the legislative agenda.

Workplace Health and Safety

To reduce the number of annual occupational injuries and deaths, governments will have to obligate employers to respond to the health and safety concerns of their workers more

OFFICE SPACE (1998)

A workplace satire of company workers who hate their jobs and decide to rebel against their greedy boss.

The leaders of the Group of 7 (G7) wealthiest economies—Canada, the US, France, Italy, Japan, Germany, and Britain, along with representation from the EU—recognize that government job-creation programs can be beneficial to reducing unemployment. The G7 met in June 2014 to discuss how to spur job creation in an attempt to reinforce a rebound from the global financial crisis.

effectively. It will likely cost more to do business this way, which is why the government will have to take the initiative and impose penalties for non-compliance (Tombs and Whyte, 2010).

Already, there is strong evidence of support for such changes. Closer public and media scrutiny, combined with constant pestering by anti-corporate and human rights groups, have forced some companies to improve their workplace conditions, especially in the overseas factories of transnational organizations. More of the same pressure, with resulting changes to the workplace, is needed at home as well as abroad (Bello et al., 2009).

Increasingly, workers and lobby groups want more than a minimally hazard-free workspace. They want a higher standard of quality of life at work. In response, progressive employers, aware of the link between employee well-being and corporate profitability, are offering workers on-site health education and medical care. Some have begun to outfit their workplaces with gyms, swimming pools, and other recreational facilities, as well as provide their workers with lunchtime yoga classes and healthy food options in the cafeteria. These efforts to improve employee health and fitness, whether sincere or self-serving, can help ensure that work itself does not become a health risk. It must be said, though, that this phenomenon is occurring more for high-end jobs than for low-end ones.

Job Satisfaction

If we accept the view that a happy worker is a productive worker, then it is in the employer's best interest to ensure that job satisfaction levels remain high. This means designing jobs, careers, and workplaces that provide meaning and stimulation, and opportunities that allow workers to apply the full scope of their abilities (Burke and Fiksenbaum, 2009).

The most satisfying work allows workers to take part in consequential decision-making. It also allows room for workers' needs and commitments outside the workplace. Communication among workers should also be encouraged, as should harmonious employee–employer relations. Regardless of the particular strategy or incentive chosen by the employer, any attempt to improve job satisfaction will necessarily involve an awareness of what people wish to gain from working (Turcotte and Schellenberg, 2005).

Extrinsic rewards are important, and thus income, recognition, promotions, and benefit packages all need to be shared in a way that mirrors both personal performance and company prosperity. Equally or more important are the **intrinsic rewards** or benefits of work, which vary from job to job and from worker to worker. Job satisfaction is an intricate, subjective, and inseparable mix of intrinsic and extrinsic rewards. Some people, for instance, crave a high degree of independence and lack of structure (e.g., freelance writers or entrepreneurs), while others find themselves most comfortable and happiest in a job that is rule-bound and rigidly defined (e.g., chartered accountants) (Wallace and Kay, 2009).

Extrinsic rewards When work rewards the worker with money, prestige, respect, and social recognition.

Intrinsic rewards When work rewards the worker with the feeling of a "job well done."

Chapter Summary

As we have seen, workplace problems include racial and gender discrimination, difficulties juggling work and family, technological advances, and worker exploitation. Some lines of work, such as sex work, can be extremely taxing and dangerous and attach stigma to the workers. Workplaces can also be hazardous and extremely stressful. Such problems can lead to worker dissatisfaction, stress, and health problems. Even so, the alternatives associated with unemployment can be worse.

Unemployment can cause health problems, depressive disorders, and consequently a higher mortality rate. Solutions to unemployment can come from either the community or the individual. Accessible education, financial support for the unemployed, and a positive attitude towards re-employment possibilities are paramount. Companies also need to be more sensitive to workers' needs to ensure their health and job satisfaction.

Questions for Critical Thought

1. The benefits of a unionized workplace outweigh the costs. Do you agree?
2. Proving one's worth at work has taken on a new meaning, especially in the current economy. Is it still realistic to dream of career advancement or is it merely a matter of surviving the next layoff? Relate this to Marx's concept of alienation.
3. Compare the types of barriers faced by Aboriginal people and immigrants in terms of job application. To what extent are both groups similar and how do they differ? Draw up possible policy recommendations to help these vulnerable populations.
4. There has been a growth in ethnic businesses—how do you think this will transform the Canadian labour market?

5. Why are women less likely to work in certain sectors? Discuss from the viewpoint of each theoretical perspective.
6. Why do some groups perform better in the labour market than others? Discuss the different factors that contribute to this problem.

Recommended Readings

Asanin Dean, Jennifer, and Kathi Wilson. 2009. "'Education? It is irrelevant to my job now. It makes me very depressed . . .': Exploring the Health Impacts of Under/ Unemployment among Highly Skilled Immigrants in Canada," *Ethnicity & Health* 14: 185–204.

Chaulk, Kimberly, and Trevor C. Brown. 2008. "An Assessment of Worker Reaction to Their Union and Employer Post-Strike: A Canadian Experience," *Relations industrielles/Industrial Relations* 63: 223–45.

Eliason, Michele J., Jeanne DeJoseph, Suzanne Dibble, Sharon Deevey, and Peggy Chinn. 2011. "Lesbian, Gay, Bisexual Transgender, and Queer/Questioning Nurses' Experiences in the Workplace," *Journal of Professional Nursing* 27, 4: 237–44.

Johnson, Laura C., Jean Andrey, and Susan M. Shaw. 2007. "Mr. Dithers Comes to Dinner: Telework and the Merging of Women's Work and Home Domains in Canada," *Gender, Place and Culture* 14: 141–61.

Livingstone, D.W., and P.H. Sawchuk. 2004. *Hidden Knowledge: Organized Labour in the Information Age.* Toronto: University of Toronto Press.

McKay, R., D.H. Arnold, J. Fratzl, and R. Thomas. 2008. "Workplace Bullying in Academia: A Canadian Study, *Employee Responsibilities and Rights Journal* 20, 2: 77–100.

Mills, S.M., L. Clarke. 2009. "'We will go side-by-side with you': Labour Union Engagement with Aboriginal Peoples in Canada," *Geoforum* 40, 6: 991–1001.

Roscigno, Vincent J. 2007. *The Face of Discrimination: How Race and Gender Impact Work and Home Lives.* Lanham, MD: Rowman & Littlefield.

Saunders, P., A. Huynh, and J. Goodman-Dalahunty. 2007. "Defining Workplace Bullying Behaviour Professional Law Definitions of Workplace Bullying," *International Journal of Law and Psychiatry* 30, 4: 340–54.

13

Schools

Connel_Design/Thinkstock

Introduction

This chapter is about students, teachers, school organization, and school curriculum. It is also about the successes and failures of schooling in Canadian society. Social inequality pervades the schooling experience. In this chapter, we consider issues of educational opportunity, as well as the various social and cultural factors that influence educational outcomes.

A person's education influences his or her life in a great many ways: socially, culturally, economically, and perhaps even spiritually. This chapter examines the impact of educational credentials and socio-economic conditions, as well as the background factors that shape educational success or failure. And, as we will note, people have been getting more and more education over the years.

Defining Education and Its Social Problems

Ascribed Statuses, Stratification, and Inequality

Before we can discuss the social and economic effects of education, we need to develop and define a few concepts associated with education—in particular, concepts associated with social factors that influence education.

Ascribed statuses are social statuses assigned to people or groups because of certain traits beyond their control and without regard for achieved merit (Sasaki, 2000). Examples of ascribed statuses include family structure, socio-economic status, sex, and race or ethnic background. Achieved statuses, as the name suggests, are social statuses achieved or accomplished by the individual. Our educational attainment—how much education we get, and of what kind—is an achieved status. It is influenced by a variety of factors, including ascribed social statuses like native intelligence, class of origin, and ethnic background. But mainly, educational attainment is influenced by effort, ambition, and dedication. As a result, we tend to think of educational attainment as an achieved status. In turn, educational attainment, along with other factors, influences future economic status—also considered an achieved status.

What is of interest to sociologists is the relative weight of achieved and ascribed statuses in educational outcomes. Most people believe, and sociologists agree, that in a modern, liberal society, educational attainment should be an achieved, not an ascribed, status, mainly influenced by social and other factors (like diligence) that are under their own control. That is far more desirable, in modern thinking, than educational, occupational, and economic outcomes that are determined mainly by ascribed statuses unrelated to the effort of the person concerned.

Education in every modern society is a means of gaining upward social mobility—a process by which individuals and families move up an economic or status hierarchy. Traditionally, educational achievements have been viewed as means by which talented and motivated people advance socially or economically. As McMullin (2004) says, "Canadians would prefer not to believe the educational system is also a place where societal inequalities are reproduced and where privileged groups solidify and maintain their advantages." They would rather believe that, at least in the educational realm, people get what they truly deserve.

CHEATERS 🎞

In this 2000 film, a teacher (Jeff Daniels), angered by educational inequities, encourages his inner-city students to cheat at the citywide academic decathlon.

Ascribed statuses Statuses assigned to people because of certain traits beyond their control.

Achieved statuses Social statuses (or positions) that are not inborn but are the result of effort and accomplishment, such as educational or occupational attainment.

Social mobility The movement—usually of individuals but sometimes of whole groups—between different positions within the system of social stratification in any society. Most sociological attention has focused on intergenerational mobility by comparing parents and their children.

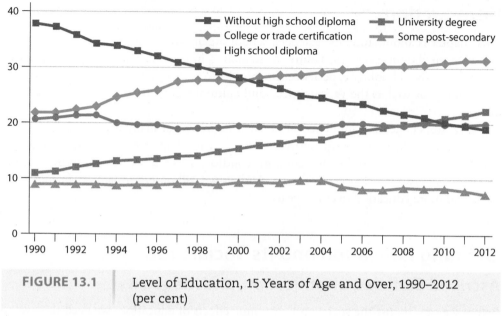

FIGURE 13.1 | Level of Education, 15 Years of Age and Over, 1990–2012 (per cent)

Source: Employment and Social Development Canada, at: <www4.hrsdc.gc.ca/.3ndic.1t.4r@-eng.jsp?iid=29>.

Careers: Linking School and Work

Why is schooling important in our society, and what factors interfere with the "ideal" functioning of education? We can begin to answer these questions most effectively if we take a step back and focus on the linkage between schools, work, and social class. First, consider the idea of "career"—a traditionally valued version of work in our society, but one that plunges us immediately into debates about education, work, and class.

The word "career" originates in words that mean "racecourse" and "road for cars." To say that a person has a career implies that he or she is rapidly and steadily moving towards a goal alongside, or in competition with, others. Every career, like every horse or auto race, has a starting point. Starting from there, competitors move forward past road markers. People enter a given career—for example, teaching, or medicine, or engineering—at roughly the same age and advance at similar (though not identical) rates. Over the ages 18–30, employers tend to rank workers mainly by their credentials, skills, and ambitions.

Ideally, no one starts ahead of anyone else, and no one fails to pass a marker. Some competitors progress faster than others; at least one competitor wins the race, while others "place" or "show." Over an extended period, many competitors get to the finish line or, in our metaphor, complete their careers before leaving the track. Some veer off the track, and we do not consider them winners.

Although simplified, this depiction captures the essence of many careers, traditional and modern. However, as the world of work grows larger, more complex, and less certain, people with different educational credentials enter the workforce at different job and income levels (McMullin, 2004). Typically, post-secondary graduates—people with MBAs and MDs and PhDs, for example—enter above less-educated candidates. Some move ahead, or are moved ahead, faster than others; in addition, some may not pass all the usual road markers in the same order. Some competitors even move horizontally rather than vertically in this great competition.

In an occupation or organization, those "high achievers" who are more highly motivated may move about more than others, gaining wider experience and exposure. And, with the development of widely accepted credentials (such as valued post-secondary educational degrees), high achievers can often move from one organization to another, gaining more exposure within an industry while continually increasing their status and rewards (Halperin, 1990).

We can all agree on what the best end points look like—what constitutes success in a particular occupation or career—and we may also be able to agree about what constitutes the best starting points. People do best if they start life from an advantaged social class position, with highly educated, high-earning parents. It also helps if the parents are supportive and ambitious for their children. So, the career pathway starts the day a person is born and, in a sense, doesn't end until he or she dies.

Education is especially important for career mobility, and thus career mobility increases both through industrial differentiation and through higher educational achievement as a basis for ranking. Professions (such as medicine and law), with their remarkable ability to control career entries, reward systems, and conditions of work, are especially noted for the importance placed on educational credentials (Donnelly, 2009). People with the most education have the best chance of achieving the highest occupations and incomes—also, the best chance of avoiding unemployment.

Ambition and education are not everything, as we have already noted. Ascribed characteristics—characteristics people are unable to change, like the class they were born into—have never lost their importance as ordering and selection principles in our society. Many employers continue to prefer candidates from particular ethnic or racial groups or from certain elite backgrounds (Reitz, 2001). As well, many careers remain gendered today, with many ambitious women facing "glass ceilings" or choosing not to compete for success in a particular field (Harkness, 2001). However, personality factors also play a part in every career. For example, Adams and Funk (2011) report that most women who report hitting a glass ceiling are averse to risk-taking. Women who attain leadership positions tend to be more risk-loving and less tradition-oriented than male leaders, which allows them to surpass what was previously seen as an impenetrable barrier.

Racial barriers are far more limiting today than gender barriers. Despite the presidency of Barack Obama beginning in 2008, African Americans in the US continued to be under-represented in political office. Fully 12.2 per cent of the American population is African American, but only 10 per cent of office-holders identify themselves as African American. It is true that racism (and sexism) has been less commonly voiced in the past few decades, but an invisible barrier still prevents racial minorities and women from gaining enough force to break into political and management careers historically restricted to men (Bouie, 2012).

Still, formal education has played an important part in the career-making process, helping previously excluded groups enter new social and economic roles. The process of movement through the world of work, in nearly every career, starts with movement through the world of schooling.

Four major theories help us to understand the young adult's transition from school into the labour force. *Segmented labour market theory* notes that the labour market is stratified and that entry and upward mobility are difficult for people with only a high school education (Meerkerk, 2006). It proposes that people with different educational attainments are shunted into certain segments of the workforce and excluded from others. *Human capital theory* proposes that there is a linear relationship between education and job attainment: more education gets people better jobs. By this reckoning, the problems people encounter are due to defects in their training that lessen their value to the hiring organization (Reitz, 2001). *Signalling theory* refers to symbolic meanings attached to different attainments on a person's resumé; it also refers to the employer's decoding of signals in assessing the potential worth and trainability of a young employee (Greening and Turban, 2000). Finally, *network theory* notes the importance of social networks and social capital in gaining employment—especially, the importance of friends and acquaintances who vouch for the quality of the potential employee (Rosenbaum, 2001).

In college and university, the sorting of students into different programs with different curricula influences future opportunities by sending prospective employers different messages about the abilities of job candidates. For instance, a BA in philosophy sends a different message from a BA in physics or political science. Employers hiring for a particular career path may feel that a certain degree is best suited for the occupation and may therefore prefer a candidate with that particular degree on his or her resumé.

Graduation from an elite university is important for several reasons: it shows that the person has received a good education, suggests that the person is probably intelligent, signifies ambition and a higher-than-average class background, and hints that the person has valuable social contacts. For these and other reasons, graduates of elite universities tend to receive the best job offers and ever-increasing salaries, at least for a time. As the time since graduation increases, the effect of the university from which a worker graduated diminishes.

Some colleges and universities make special efforts to link their students and graduates up with prospective employers through a variety of work-study, fieldwork, and internship programs. Under the best circumstances, schools come to understand what employers are looking for in job candidates and they make sure their suggested candidates have it, or at least they screen out and divert inappropriate candidates. Some of this screening and streaming even happens in secondary schools. There, high school counsellors play a role as gatekeepers, encouraging talented students while discouraging students whose college plans are inappropriate—in effect, helping the latter address unpleasant realities. When schools do this effectively, employers come to trust available school information (e.g., grades) when hiring graduates. This is a good practice, because it relies more on achieved statuses and less on ascribed statuses (such as class, ethnicity, race, or gender) that carry stereotypical meanings. It also relies less on sometimes irrelevant social networks and random impressions gained during interviews.

Obviously, a great deal more could be said about careers and the process of entry into a career. In effect, careers are work lives—job-related pathways over the course of a lifetime. On the individual level, careers reflect differences (and similarities) in opportunity and human capital. On the corporate level, they reflect linkages between schools and workplaces and linkages at workplaces, within firms, across firms, and across institutions. Just as careers tie together life events, they also link institutional activities.

Another useful concept in this context is the notion of "market." Careers take place within economic sub-markets or sectors in which a segmentation of jobs and careers has occurred. The **primary labour market** consists of jobs that offer good wages, chances to get ahead, and job security; these include careers in law, plumbing, and teaching (Furlong, 2008). The less desirable **secondary (marginal) labour market** consists of jobs that pay low wages, offer little chance to get ahead, and promise little job security: jobs like taxi driver, secretary, or bank teller (Jaarsveld et al., 2009). Primary and secondary labour markets exist within every region, province, and community.

Of interest to sociologists is the fact that people with different social traits, backgrounds, and skills tend to end up in different markets. For example, a disproportionate number of women and visible minorities are found in the secondary labour market, and a disproportionate number of white men are found in the primary labour market—far more than could have occurred by chance alone. Of course, markets and sub-markets also contain different kinds of jobs and different kinds of people. Consider the fact that though both teachers and doctors are in the primary labour market, few teachers have the sort of benefits and opportunities that doctors do. In the same way, though both bank tellers and taxi drivers are in the secondary labour market, few bank tellers consider their work to be similar to that of taxi drivers. That said, jobs in the primary labour market are universally more attractive, remunerative, and secure than jobs in the secondary labour market.

Class: Social Mobility and Educational Inequality

Researchers have found that people are likely to inherit the social class of their parents, and this tendency is much higher in some countries than in others. Conversely, in some countries, children are much more socially mobile and attain social positions higher or lower than those held by their parents. There is more social mobility in Canada than in the United Kingdom or the United States, where intergenerational "elasticities" are much higher. *Elasticity*, an economic term, is the degree to which changing one variable changes another. A low intergenerational income elasticity (as in Denmark) means that social class is less persistent and more amenable to change from one generation to the next.

A large part of social mobility is due to educational attainment. As noted earlier, the social class people are born into will likely affect their educational ambitions and educational pursuits. People born into higher-income, more-educated households tend to get more education than people born into lower-income, less-educated households. This is why family origin and socio-economic status tend to be reproduced across generations. As a result, the effect of class on educational attainment is an especially enduring feature of inequality, reproduced from one generation to the next even in a merit-based society like Canada (Guppy and Davies, 1998).

This link between social class and educational attainment is found, to a greater or lesser degree, in every society, including modern industrial societies. Consider the situation in Greece, a less economically developed society than Canada, but nonetheless a modern society. There, one study found that children from higher socio-economic classes are likely to perform better than other children because of the access to more expensive resources provided by their parents to aid their performance (Sianou-Kyrgiou, 2008). This aid helps the students achieve higher-than-average grades, making it more difficult

Primary labour market
High-paying jobs that provide good chances to "get ahead" and that offer job security.

Secondary (marginal) labour market High-turnover, lower-paying, and unstable or insecure employment. These jobs offer little chance to get ahead and little job security.

WAITING FOR SUPERMAN

This 2010 film examines different aspects of the American public education system and is highly critical of teachers, teacher unions, and school administrators. It shows how teaching standards often suffer because of conflicting expectations at the school, state, and federal level.

for those in lower socio-economic classes to compete against them for entrance into institutions of higher education.

So, paradoxically, while the admissions policies of colleges and universities tend to be unbiased and fair towards people with different social-class backgrounds, children from higher-income, more-educated families tend to be over-represented for the reasons we have mentioned. Still, everyone has benefited from the expansion of higher education in the last 50 years. More and more young people have stayed in school for longer periods. As a result, the educational attainment of average citizens has risen significantly. Yet, the class structure—the shape or extent of social inequality—has not changed significantly; in fact, income inequality is much greater today than it was 50 years ago, despite the expansion of higher education.

Canada is one of the countries in which educational opportunities have expanded. All citizens, regardless of race/ethnicity or class, have the same right to seek a higher degree. However, for people lower down the economic ladder, higher education may still seem more like a privilege than a right. As a result, in Canada and other industrial societies, "class differentials in educational attainment have changed little . . . from those in early decades of the [twentieth] century onwards" (Goldthorpe, 1985). Children in less-advantaged class positions are still less likely than children of more prosperous origins to pursue and earn higher educational degrees.

Added to this, high and rising tuition fees limit the enrolment of lower-income students. Tuition fees have steadily increased over the past decade. Today, the federal government calculates that the average cost of a four-year undergraduate degree (including accommodation, food, travel, and other expenses) is about $60,000. However, an external survey calculates the cost closer to $80,000. Not surprisingly, other research finds students bearing an average of $28,000 of debt upon graduation (Shaker, 2012). Only 81 per cent of students who graduate with a school-related debt have full-time employment for a full year after graduation (Luong, 2010), limiting their ability to start repaying the debt immediately.

Is all this expense and suffering worth it? Well, from a purely monetary standpoint, it is. People with more education make more money. Just as important for women, the hourly wage gap between men and women closes as people get more education, as we see in Figure 13.2. On this, Statistics Canada reports:

> Higher levels of education are associated with higher wages. The supply of workers with very high levels of education is limited, driving up their earnings. Sometimes education is also used as a screening criterion that shows a capacity to learn new abilities or to apply critical thinking in new ways. In 2007, employees with master's and doctoral degrees earned an average of $30.44 per hour, 75 per cent more than employees with just a high school diploma ($17.37 an hour).
>
> The higher the level of education, the narrower the wage gap between the sexes as a proportion of earnings, except for people with some postsecondary education. However, women's hourly wages remain below men's for all levels of education. For example, in 2007, women with a bachelor's degree earned 85 cents for every dollar earned by men, while women with an educational level of Grade 8 or less earned 72 cents for every dollar earned by men. (<www.statcan.gc.ca/pub/71-222-x/2008001/sectionj/j-gap-ecart-eng.htm>)

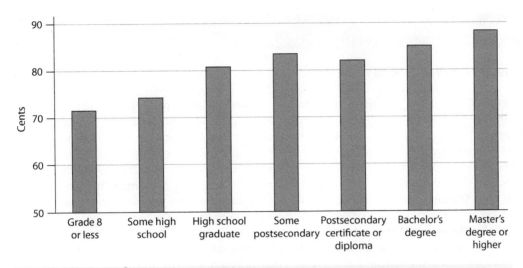

FIGURE 13.2 Wage Gap by Educational Attainment, 2007: Cents Earned by Women for Each Dollar Earned by Men

Source: Statistics Canada, Labour Force Survey, at <www.statcan.gc.ca/pub/71-222-x/2008001/sectionj/j-gap-ecart-eng.htm>.

PERSONAL *stories*

BOX 13.1 | **Max Goes to College: The Tuition Crisis**

Max is going to college this year. For a long time, he didn't think he would be able to afford it. Of course, he will end up with some student debts; he hears that everyone does. He even has some friends who joined a protest against the government, demanding that tuition be lowered, or should even be free. Is that realistic, he wonders, and is it possible? Isn't the government already doing the best it can to make sure students can attend college, even if their families are poor?

Max heard, for example, that the Ontario Ministry of Training, Colleges, and Universities had made it possible for students whose families earned less than $160,000 per year to trim 30 per cent of their tuition off their debt. By June 2012, 200,000 students had received this tuition rebate. Those in a degree program received $800 and those in diploma or certificate programs received $365. It is estimated that this program has helped 93,000 more high school students graduate since 2004. In addition, university and college enrolment increased by 26 per cent and 18.5 per cent, respectively.

However, debates have developed about whether this tuition cut should apply for all families, not just those with an income less than $160,000. In 2012, Ontario universities charged the highest average university tuition fees of any province, at $6,640. To prevent continuous rises in tuition, students are fighting harder than ever to minimize costs so that everyone would have the opportunity to receive the post-secondary education they deserve.

The reason is that children from less-affluent families are less able to handle the financial debts incurred in completing a post-secondary education, and these debts can be burdensome upon completion of a degree. Further, for reasons not fully understood, the extent of people's indebtedness varies from one province to another—likely reflecting differences in the cost of living, the cost of education, and the availability of loans and bursaries in different provinces.

Sources: Crowell (2012); Lagerquist (2012); and Luong (2010).

Classic WORKS

BOX 13.2   *Crestwood Heights* (1956)

It's easy to understand the difficulties facing students at the lower end of the income scale and harder, but still necessary, to understand the difficulties facing more affluent and economically secure students. The problems they face are different but no less important.

The classic Canadian study *Crestwood Heights*, by John Seeley, Alexander Sim, and Elizabeth Loosley, initially set out to learn about the mental health of Canadian children in the affluent Forest Hill area in Toronto, which the researchers called "Crestwood Heights." The specific goal of the study was to learn about "the culture of the child under pressures for conformity." Today, we might describe this as a study of the mental health consequences of parental pressure on ambitious students.

Seeley and his colleagues focused on the strains and conflicts in the family, the school, and the community. Parents in this community saw their children as problems to be solved, just like other employee and organizational problems they faced in the managerial world. The parents themselves were a mixture of "new money" and "old money"—successful and upwardly mobile people in business or the professions. Many were the children of immigrants, with high hopes for themselves and their children. For them, careers were their top priority and career success was critically important.

With this in mind, they trained their children to be "perfect"—competitive and successful in all their pursuits. They taught their children to seek success even at a young age, in Scout groups, music lessons, hockey teams, and summer camps. School, rather than religion, was the most important institution in this community. The school was viewed as the authority on child-raising and the main place where children could prove (and document) their perfection. Concern with school achievement also made the Parent-Teacher Association the most significant voluntary association in this community. It schooled parents in the "newer" ideas and techniques of child-rearing, for example. In parents' eyes, teachers and administrators were important sources of authority and expertise on the topic of children, childhood, and achievement.

However, this drive for excellence was not without problems, including stresses within the school itself. Some of these stresses highlighted the conflicting goals of education. For example, it wasn't entirely clear what children should be taught: individual excellence or teamwork. With the rise of bureaucracies in modern society, people came to place a greater emphasis on co-operation, other-direction, and submergence of the individual in the group. Therefore, school had to train middle-class suburban children for "bureaucratic crawl." However, a modern capitalist society still required—and parents expected—a continued emphasis on individual achievement, independence, and competition. Parents also pressed teachers for higher grades (more successes for their children), and this led to the beginnings of the grade inflation we see today.

Some might say that a lot has remained the same in the more than half-century since the *Crestwood Heights* study was done. Today, many parents still push their children to unparalleled heights of accomplishment at school, music, ballet, sports, and other pursuits. Though much has changed since the publication of *Crestwood Heights* 60 years ago, much has stayed the same.

Education and Gender

As noted earlier, women continue to earn less than men at every educational level, though the wage gap shrinks at the highest levels of educational attainment.

According to Gomme (2004), even though women seem to be making gains, they still suffer disadvantages. Women continue, far more than men, to take degrees in fine arts, the humanities, and the social sciences, but these fields are less directly marketable than others, such as engineering and the applied sciences, where men outnumber women. Further, education in these areas (e.g., engineering and computer science) leads to jobs with higher levels of pay.

However, it is not merely that women seek out lower-paying careers. Research shows that careers tend to lose both prestige and pay as larger numbers of women enter them. In effect, these formerly male-dominant jobs become proletarianized as they become feminized, for example, in pharmacy and law. It remains to be seen whether other feminizing professions such as medicine and dentistry will follow suit. In part, this reflects the increased supply of job candidates. Increased competition in any job domain depresses wages. However, the connections to female participation are hard to miss. No satisfactory explanation of this phenomenon has yet been provided.

Still, just consider how far women have come. Before Confederation, young girls typically went to elementary school with the boys. However, family duties often kept many of them from receiving much primary education, let alone secondary education. Also, until 1862, young women had little chance of gaining post-secondary education in Canada. In that year, Mount Allison University in New Brunswick enrolled its first female students. Shortly thereafter, other Canadian universities and colleges followed suit, opening their doors to female students. And yet, it wasn't until the middle of the twentieth century that large numbers of female students began attending post-secondary institutions.

The benefits of education are dramatic for both men and women, but especially for women. In 2008–9, women accounted for 58 per cent of the enrolment for undergraduate studies and 55.7 per cent for graduate studies. The proportion of women enrolled

Public Issues *and* Public Policy

BOX 13.3 Africentric School Makes History

Drummed into school to a standing ovation and a rocking West African beat, 115 children made Canadian history yesterday in vivid vests of African cloth. Less than two years after fierce public debate over the idea of a school focused on African culture, one of the most controversial educational experiments in the country began with a surprise 30 per cent surge in enrolment.

From the opening assembly, the Africentric Alternative School began weaving African culture into Ontario school culture. Students sang "O Canada," followed by a black national anthem written a century ago by a Florida poet, then recited a pledge titled "The Best Possible Me"—which is popular in Africentric schools in the US. It includes a vow to treat education as a serious matter.

"Let me hear you say 'best'!" called principal Thando Hyman-Aman, a part-time jazz singer and the parent of a student at the school. She will lead a bid to lower the 40 per cent drop-out rate among black students by stretching the curriculum beyond its European roots.

"You will always be the . . . what?" she called, holding the microphone out to the children,

"Best!" they responded.

According to school trustee James Pasternak, if enrolment continues to grow towards the capacity of 150 students, the school may add another teacher, likely a male who would join the currently all-female staff. Jahbril said last night he enjoyed the first day at school: "We learned the seven principles of Kwanza, which is an African holiday." The nine-year-old, who went out last Halloween as Barack Obama and this year as Michael Jackson, said he can't wait to learn about "[his] heritage—Jamaica, but also Africa, where [his] ancestors came from." . . .

Long-time supporters of the project were emotional when seeing the school finally open its doors. "Victory is won!" said Angela Wilson, one of two mothers who pushed for the school during the project's initial stages, when the idea was originally proposed in 1994 by Ontario's Royal Commission on Learning as a way to make education more relevant for black students. Mother Hazel Bridgeman said, "The issue affecting most young black kids is self-esteem, and this school is going to try to address that."

Source: Brown (2009).

in doctoral programs has risen to 46.8 per cent—equal with men (Statistics Canada, 2010b). In 2008–9, the number of women enrolled in university for law, business management, and life science outnumbered the number of male candidates for the same programs (ibid.).

This shift is important in every sphere of life because, in Canada and other industrial countries, the women who gain the highest levels of education are the ones to come closest to job and income equality with men. In other words, formal education closes the traditional gender gap; it brings about actual, and not merely formal, equality between men and women. While it does not solve all the problems women face, higher education is an important path towards social equality.

This is why more educational opportunity is so important for the rest of the world. A large part of the continuing problem of gender inequality in less-developed parts of the world has to do with education or its lack. In many parts of the world, families, governments, and economies do not give young women an equal opportunity for education, jobs, and income independence. Women are especially likely to be illiterate in Sub-Saharan Africa, the Arab states, and South Asia (including India and Pakistan). Increasing educational opportunity for women in these societies would both signal the transition to cultural modernity and help to bring it about.

Education and Race

Yet, even within Canada, certain groups have less opportunity for education than others. Many of the educational disadvantages facing minority groups in Canada stem from long-standing economic exploitation and disadvantage. In this section, we will examine the influence of class, race, and ethnicity on education. The most prominent Canadian example of historical disparities in educational opportunity is provided by Aboriginal Canadians.

Aboriginal Issues and Education

In 1867, through the terms of the British North America Act, the federal government of Canada declared its responsibility for managing "Indians and lands reserved for Indians" (Stonefish, 2007). Today, we are still witnessing the consequences of this inadequate, wrong-headed management.

In 2011, only 48 per cent of the Canadian Aboriginal population held a "post-secondary qualification," which includes trades certificates, university degrees, college diplomas, and university certificates below the bachelor level (Statistics Canada, 2013a). Their under-representation in higher education was especially marked for children from families with an income less than $50,000. Only 31.4 per cent of children in these families entered university and only 34.8 per cent entered colleges (McMullen, 2011).

The under-representation of Aboriginal children in higher education started a long time ago, for originally the Aboriginal people were a rural population living off the land. In the nineteenth century, the Canadian government tried to assimilate the Aboriginal population by developing a residential schools system—a system in which Aboriginal children were transported hundreds or even thousands of kilometres from their home to live in an institution based on white European values. In hindsight, we can see this as a blatant example of Canadian *racialization*—an imposition of unwanted racial identities on minorities. The residential school system showed how "educational programs" built on racist and class-based ideologies can have terrible consequences for students (Nicholas, 2001).

Here's how the program worked: the Canadian government assigned educational responsibility to the Roman Catholic, Anglican, Methodist, United, and Presbyterian churches. They were responsible for running the residential schools, and in doing so, they tried to turn Aboriginal children into proper, European-cultured Christians. They did this by separating Aboriginal youth from their families and communities. Residential schooling was compulsory for most of the Aboriginal youth population.

The intent was to produce a young generation of "modern Indians" (Davies and Guppy, 2006) by forcing Aboriginal children to abandon their cultural heritage and replace their "nomadic hunting and fishing lifestyle" with the ways of the "civilized" Europeans (Furniss, 1992: 13). Many of the subjects of this social experiment were left hanging between two worlds: a white society that rejected their heritage and a Native culture that they were kept from fully understanding.

By 1894, 45 residential schools were filled and funded. They were all modelled to some degree on the first two "successful" schools in southern Ontario: the Mohawk Institute founded in 1829 and the Mount Elgin Industrial School, which began operating in 1848. Officially, residential schools operated in Canada between 1892 and 1969. After 1969, the Canadian government was no longer officially involved in running residential schools. Several schools, however, continued to run until the mid-1990s. Akaitcho Hall in Yellowknife, the last residential school in Canada, closed in 1996.

Aboriginal people across Canada are still feeling the abusive, humiliating effects of residential schooling. Native children—the parents, grandparents, and great-grandparents of present-day Native people—were taught that their heritage was brutish, unacceptable, and shameful. They were stripped of their culture, language, and distinctive world view. The goal was to create new identities for the Canadian Natives; supposedly, the "Indian problem" would no longer exist if the Native population assimilated into the dominant culture. Assimilation meant wearing European clothing, speaking one of the official languages (i.e., English or French), and working as paid labourers within the Canadian economy.

In essence, the goal was to produce a subordinate working class that would not disrupt or disturb the Euro-Canadian majority (Ng, 1993).

To be sure, the experiences of Aboriginal people varied across the country and changed significantly over the course of Canadian history; some would even say relations have improved dramatically in the past 50 years or so. Yet, evidence today suggests that Aboriginal people continue to bear the scars of forced assimilation. This is evident in their high rates of crime, imprisonment, addiction, violence, and victimization. It is also evident in their low rates of educational attainment.

Aboriginal Educational Attainment Today

Today, the schooling of Aboriginal youth is still the responsibility of the federal government, and Aboriginal youth are still far behind the Canadian average in their education. The most recent statistics, contained in the 2011 Census, continues to show an educational inequality between the Aboriginal and the general population.

For example, within the Aboriginal population, there continues to be a large proportion of people without a high school degree (Ministry of Aboriginal Affairs, 2012).

National Aboriginal Achievement Award recipients are honoured following Question Period in the House of Commons on Parliament Hill in Ottawa.

Likewise, only 48 per cent of Aboriginal people have a post-secondary qualification, compared to 64.1 per cent of the non-Aboriginal population. Among those who pursue a post-secondary degree, Aboriginal people are more likely to seek a college diploma or trade apprenticeship than a university degree. Aboriginal women continue to increase their education attainment at a faster rate than Aboriginal men, however. In 2001, 63 per cent of the Aboriginals who completed a university degree were female. As well, Aboriginal women have been pursuing a trade certificate or college diploma at higher rates than Aboriginal men. Geography poses a major obstacle to Aboriginal education. Those who live in cities are more likely to complete a college diploma, while those who live in smaller communities and rural areas are more likely to obtain an apprenticeship or trade certificate.

That said, the Native population is starting to catch up, educationally. For example, Aboriginal people aged 35–44 are more likely to have attained a high school diploma (or more) than those aged 65 and over. This shows the gradual increase in educational attainments by the Aboriginal population (Statistics Canada, 2013a).

The Education of Immigrants and Visible Minorities

Historically, Canada has maintained one of the highest rates of immigration of all nations worldwide, and this fact is especially evident in Canada's largest cities. Based on current trends, researchers project that visible minority groups will constitute 63 per cent of Toronto's population by 2031 (Hiebert, 2012).

From an educational standpoint, this is good news. In Canada today, visible minorities and recent immigrants are more educated than the general Canadian population.

CANADIAN researchers

BOX 13.4 **Terry Wotherspoon, University of Saskatchewan**

Canadian education continues to improve and diversify throughout the country, but problems—educational, as well as social and economic—remain in many provinces, especially in rural areas and First Nations communities. In a 2012 paper, "Education and Class Relations: Canada's Indigenous People and the Knowledge Society," Terry Wotherspoon, professor and head of sociology at the University of Saskatchewan, notes that Indigenous people represent one of the least-advantaged segments of Canada's population, though they are also one of the fastest-growing groups. Governments and Aboriginal organizations have undertaken initiatives to address this disadvantage by trying to raise education attainment rates in regions where the rates are significantly lower than average. However, we must understand these initiatives in the context of a wider political economy. In this context, the analysis suggests that Aboriginal populations will experience increasing in-group inequality, as well as continuing gaps between Aboriginal and non-Aboriginal populations.

Why can't Aboriginal education be improved? In a 2008 paper, "Teachers' Work Intensification and Educational Contradictions in Aboriginal Communities," Wotherspoon examines survey data from Saskatchewan and Manitoba, noting the emergence of what he calls "fragmented professionalism" among teachers. He concludes that Aboriginal students will continue to lack the education they need so long as government fails to commit to educational equity—especially, better funding—and a continued gap continues between teachers' professional needs and Aboriginal community interests.

Wotherspoon expands on these ideas in a 2006 paper, "Teachers' Work in Canadian Aboriginal Communities." There, he notes that teachers are trapped between conflicting pressures—to be catalysts for educational and economic change but also to be protectors against socially disruptive effects. In communities that have been poorly served by schooling, teachers also face competing claims about the nature and forms of the education required to achieve meaningful social and economic participation. So, despite policies and programs committed to meeting present-day objectives, current hopes for educational improvement live side by side with constraint and frustration.

In part, the problem may simply come down to workload. As Wotherspoon notes in a 2007 paper, "Teaching for Equity? What Teachers Say about Their Work in Aboriginal Communities," schools and especially teachers are expected to play a key role in helping Aboriginal people and their communities survive in a difficult social and economic environment. Despite failures in the past, Aboriginal schools and teachers try to help Aboriginal people participate meaningfully in all spheres of social and economic life. But to do this successfully, teachers must be supported and empowered as transformative workers who can balance the educational needs and capacities within Aboriginal communities. Regrettably, current funding and legislation make such educational success unlikely and teachers' overload a daily experience.

This is largely a result of Canada's immigration policy. The federal government has been trying to attract and recruit highly educated immigrants from every part of the world, rather than just manual and skilled labourers from Europe (Davies and Guppy, 2006: 42).

These immigration policies have yielded a highly educated group of immigrant workers. However, many immigrants haven't achieved the success they hoped for, one that would be in accordance with their educational credentials. Access to higher social status and economic positions in Canada is unequal, as we noted earlier. Further, some research suggests that racial discrimination is still prevalent in Canadian hiring, despite the importance accorded educational attainment and other "achieved statuses."

Some immigrant groups fail to do as well as others in adapting to the Canadian education system, as shown by high drop-out rates and low rates of post-secondary education.

The question arises, how might schools be improved to provide the best possible education for Canada's many diverse communities? One approach recently taken in Toronto has been the creation of an Africentric school, in the belief that African Canadians might be better served by schools focused heavily on their culture and history, rather than on conventional topics of Canadian schooling. The evidence on this experiment is not yet in, so we don't know whether it will achieve the intended effects.

Work Discrimination and Unemployment

As mentioned, foreign-born visible minorities experience larger gaps between their educational attainment and their occupation (and income) than do other groups. For example, fewer than half of foreign-born visible minorities with a university degree go directly into jobs requiring a high skill level. This is especially true during hard economic times.

Many recent immigrants report that their educational and work credentials are not recognized in the Canadian job market. As a result, they are forced into jobs below their training and expertise. A longitudinal survey of this problem by Statistics Canada found that six out of ten immigrants to Canada were not currently working in the field they had identified as theirs on their arrival.

Problems of unemployment and underemployment are common among immigrants, especially among those educated in less-developed societies. For example, Xue and Xue (2010) found that immigrants who had earned their highest degree in the US, the UK, Hong Kong, or Poland had just as high employment rates as people earning the same degree in Canada. On the other hand, immigrants with degrees from Pakistan, Iran, and China (for example) had higher-than-average unemployment rates. Immigrants who had lived in Canada for a while or had earned a degree in Canada were more likely to get a job in their field of study than recently arrived immigrants with an outside degree. This was true regardless of the field in which the degree was earned—whether biological and biomedical sciences, physical sciences or engineering, for example. In general, degrees in science were more likely to lead rapidly to employment than other kinds of degree.

The Effectiveness of Schooling

Today, students and parents alike want accountability from their schools and universities; they want to know that these institutions are working as well as possible and educating students in the most cost-effective manner.

This is nothing new. Contemporary efforts to reform schools and to measure school effectiveness have gone on for decades. The (US) Coleman Report was the first empirical study to evaluate educational programs in a highly systematic way, nationwide, addressing issues of unequal academic opportunities and outcomes. Published in 1966, largely in response to concerns about the racial segregation of black and white students in the US, this study concluded that, overall, schools contributed little to reducing inequalities. Specifically, variables such as spending per pupil, teacher experience, and the number of books in libraries contributed little to student achievement compared to students' socio-economic status (measured by parental education, job status, and income). Since that time, educational researchers have continued to challenge this view, arguing that, contrary to Coleman's views, school organization, class size, and teaching methods significantly affect education quality and student achievement.

Today, we realize that both perspectives are valid. It is true that poverty has a large influence on achievement, yet economic factors are not solely responsible for student success and failure. Non-economic factors are also important. Parental education, income, and occupational prestige are all relevant to children's school success, but they are not the whole story either.

David Johnson's (2009) study of Ontario schools suggests that economic inequality may not be as decisive for schools and students as previously thought. In association with the C.D. Howe Institute, Johnson showed how non-economic factors account for students' school performance on standardized Grade 3 and Grade 6 tests. Using census data as well as information about students' socio-economic background, Johnson predicted how various schools across Ontario would be expected to do on Grade 3 and Grade 6 standardized tests, based solely on socio-demographic factors. He found the fit was far from perfect, showing that organizational factors also make a difference.

Stated simply, Johnson's results show that attending a "good school" makes a big difference to people's educational attainment. As the data show, "good schools" in Ontario have "principals, teachers and other staff who are making a positive difference in student performance regardless of their students' socio-economic backgrounds" (Johnson, 2009). In these "good schools," students perform better than similar students in less-"good" schools. However, identifying the "good schools" is only the first part of the story; what comes next is finding out what makes a school "good."

Consider the example of Cornell Junior Public School, a "good school" located in Scarborough, Ontario. The average annual household income in the school neighbourhood is under $50,000, and only 21.5 per cent of the adult residents have earned a university degree. Yet, 80 per cent of the Grade 3 students at this school passed the standardized tests in reading, writing, and mathematics. Based solely on the socio-economic makeup of Cornell Junior Public School, students were predicted to have a pass rate 7.9 per cent below the provincial average. Instead, their pass rate was 15.1 per cent above the average, pointing to the effects of "good school" organization.

These findings show that "good schools" are not only to be found in "good" neighbourhoods, and vice versa. No matter where the students live, the schools they attend have the potential to provide a quality education. This means that student success should not be taken for granted if the students live in rich neighbourhoods or come from rich families; nor should their failure be taken for granted if they come from poorer families and live in poorer neighbourhoods.

According to these results, good teachers can make a difference, and so can bad teachers. Good teachers are fundamental to school improvement efforts. Substandard teachers may not have the skills needed to help students succeed, and they may fail to give students a sense that they can learn. This means that it is necessary to ensure that competent and talented people are chosen to teach, that their teaching quality is high, and that all students have access to high-quality teachers during their school career. However, successful teaching is impossible unless the school atmosphere is organized, peaceful, and controlled. Clear rules for student behaviour must be consistently enforced and regulated by school officials.

These kinds of conclusions about the effectiveness of different teaching or organizational strategies can only be reached where schools use standardized tests and results can be compared. Critics often oppose standardized testing on the grounds that they force teachers to "teach to the test"—that is, to teach only material that will show up on a test. Moreover, they claim that poor test results are often used, without proper socio-economic context, to attack teachers, teachers' unions, or school funding.

On the other hand, standardized testing allows for the kinds of regional and national comparisons made in 2013 by the OECD (Organisation for Economic Co-operation and Development), which showed Canada falling behind many European and East Asian jurisdictions on desired educational outcomes—especially, in mathematics. For example, Canadian 15-year-olds are much more likely to fail the standardized mathematics test than 15-year-old students from countries where mathematics is taught in traditional ways (i.e., by rote) by highly trained and/or highly paid and respected teachers. Within Canada, Quebec students do best on these standardized tests, and the other provinces would do well to study how they achieved their educational success.

Theoretical Perspectives on Education

Structural Functionalism

Socialization The process by which people internalize and learn their culture, much of which occurs during childhood.

From the functionalist perspective, the school as a social institution performs the necessary function of socialization—the internalization and learning of one's culture, most of which occurs during childhood. In this way schools "help prepare new adults for generational succession—they are the major means by which one generation prepares its own replacement" (Davies and Guppy, 2006: 23). Accordingly, then, the education system is one of society's most important institutions. It contributes to the maintenance of social order and provides opportunities for people to become socially mobile.

TABLE 13.1	Theoretical Perspectives
THEORY	**MAIN POINTS**
Structural Functionalism	• The function of schooling is to give people the human capital society needs for economic growth. • Schools socialize people for the work world and for citizenship.
Conflict Theory	• Schooling is a means by which people are trained to endure the boredom and subordination of alienating work. • The myth of upward mobility through merit at school is used by the ruling class to justify social inequality.
Symbolic Interactionism	• Schools help people develop identities that are appropriate to the social roles they will play as adults. • Schools are as important for discouraging disadvantaged people as they are for encouraging advantaged people. • This was especially true of residential schooling for Aboriginal students.
Feminist Theory	• Schools have historically treated boys and girls differently, subtly reinforcing sexism. • Today, girls are doing better at every level of schooling and boys are more likely to drop out prematurely.
Social Constructionism	• Public issues around schooling are connected to a variety of concerns about class, race, and income inequality. • Claims about school quality—quality of education—are back in the news and are hard to verify.

Functionalists see schools as "great equalizers," as neutral social organizations that are designed to both socialize and educate. Under these circumstances, success, then, can be largely attributed to a student's merit or ability. Success in school is "earned." Failure to succeed is due to a personal flaw or weakness—perhaps laziness or an absence of ambition. Schools, if they are fair, create equal opportunity, social mobility, and even meritocracy—the holding of power or authority by certain people based on their ability. However, what happens when a society becomes over-educated in relation to the occupational positions available to its citizens? If this occurs, some people will be forced to take jobs below their acquired educational credentials. Functionalism today emerges in arguments over the notions of *over-education* and *credentialism*.

Meritocracy The holding of power or authority by people selected because of their ability.

From the functionalist perspective, social problems related to education occur when schools fail to perform their *manifest functions*—the visible and intended goals, consequences, or effects of social structures and institutions. Examples of the intended functions of schools include *socialization, assimilation, transmission of knowledge*, and *social control*, as well as *change* and *innovation*. With this in mind, many of the social problems discussed in this book, such as poverty and unemployment (Chapter 2) or crime and delinquency (Chapter 7), can be linked to the failure of education systems to accomplish their basic functions. As we have stressed throughout this text, many social problems are interconnected or intertwined with one another. Often, social and economic disadvantages permeate many aspects of people's lives, and educational attainment (or the lack thereof) is one mechanism by which disadvantage leads to problems.

Conflict Theory

Conflict theory exposes disequilibrium in the education system, arguing that certain groups are favoured over others, while inequalities are perpetuated based on class, race, and gender. While it might seem as though the official goal of education is to provide a universal and equal mechanism for success, educational opportunity and the quality of education available are far from equally distributed across Canadian society.

Consider the issue of student dropouts as an illustration of the conflict perspective. Students who drop out of high school "were much less likely to have a parent with a university degree (11 per cent) than students who graduated from high school (30.6 per cent)" (Bowlby and McMullen, 2002: 143). Thus, our social-class position directs our educational pursuits. Further, in terms of obtaining a post-secondary education, children of disadvantaged class origins are more likely to experience lower educational outcomes. Education systems, thus, have the tendency to support and perpetuate prevailing schemes of stratification in society.

Symbolic Interactionism

The symbolic interactionist is concerned with individuals and the ways they interact in small groups. From this perspective, social interaction is usefully viewed as a "dramaturgical performance where one infers meanings and impressions from the verbal and non-verbal expressions given off by others" (Murphy, 1979). If we apply this perspective to micro-level processes in the education system, we learn things about classrooms and peer group relations that we might otherwise miss.

In particular, we are led to examine the interactions between teachers, the students they love (i.e., teachers' pets), and the students they hate. We also look at the role of cliques in school life, and how they contribute to creating a school environment that is conflictual and stressful—not the best condition for successful learning.

Feminist Theory

From a historical perspective, the experience of education has been vastly different for men and women. These differences have been manifested not only in educational outcomes, but also in terms of what society has expected of girls and boys at various times in history.

Influenced by the seventeenth-century Enlightenment, Mary Wollstonecraft contested popular attitudes towards women and education in her book *The Vindication of the Rights of Women* (1997 [1792]). Wollstonecraft proposed that women deserve social equality and should be given the necessary education to obtain it. Accordingly, she asserted that "the virtue of *knowledge* of the two sexes should be the same in nature, if not in degree, and that women, considered not only as moral but rational creatures, ought to endeavour to acquire human virtues (or perfections) by the *same* means as men, instead of being educated like a fanciful kind of half *being*" (ibid.). Overall, she expressed that men and women, by sharing the same virtues, should be treated the same and be given the same opportunities.

Feminist theorists and researchers who study education today focus on the extent to which disparities within the school system continue to produce and perpetuate disadvantages for girls and women. Historically, in terms of educational opportunity and outcome, young boys have gained greater long- and short-run advantages from education than young girls. According to Dillabough and Arnot (2002: 34), "the long-term goal of feminism here was to empower women to take up their rightful place throughout the development of female autonomy." A central issue for the freedom of choice and greater autonomy was the removal of barriers to occupational choice, subject preference, and decisions surrounding sex roles. Equal opportunities were seen as crucial to producing an adaptive, flexible, and undifferentiated workforce.

Today, as we have seen, Canadian girls and women are doing as well as, and in many fields better than, men. Wollstonecraft would feel pleased with and fulfilled by this discovery.

Social Consequences of Education

Over-education and Credentialism

Throughout this chapter, we have emphasized the importance of a formal education in modern society—especially, a post-secondary education. But what, exactly, does an educational certificate represent? Does it truly represent a certain level of intellectual preparedness or even preparation for the workforce? Or, does it merely give the young graduate a piece of paper that allows him or her to claim a job in a particular area of employment? If the latter, critics say that we have entered the realm of credentialism.

In his book *The Credential Society* (1979), Randall Collins proposes that contemporary schools are over-educating students—educating them unnecessarily and beyond

Credentialism A process of social selection that gives class advantage and social status to people who possess academic advantage.

AP Photo/Elaine Thompson/Canadian Press

In this photo, barista Michael Bledsoe prepares a two-shot coffee drink in a coffee shop. A weak labour market already has left a large number of young graduates either jobless or underemployed in positions that don't fully use their skills and knowledge.

the needs of society. Collins states that the economy cannot support the number of educationally qualified people who are graduating from high school, college, and university today. Accordingly, the contemporary school system is contributing to **credential inflation**—the process by which increased labour-market competition results in more workers acquiring more credentials and in employers raising required credential levels in an effort to balance the increase in credentials obtained by the workforce. Essentially, modern education devalues educational credentials in the same way that monetary inflation devalues money.

> **Credential inflation** The tendency of schools to provide and employers to demand ever-more schooling and ever-higher credentials for work that has not become more demanding or complex.

If this allegation is true, what use do employers make of educational credentials—do they see them as the supposed proof that job candidates have particular skills and aptitudes? Collins proposes that most employers rarely look at student grades when hiring. This is because, according to Collins, the school curriculum develops on its own terms, not necessarily with the goal of meeting the needs of employers or the demands for particular skills in the labour force. If credentials were, in fact, closely tied to the specific needs of employers, then employers would hire on the basis of school grades. Yet, in many cases, only a college diploma is required. Specific grades (and specific skills) are irrelevant.

This is true in many lines of work. For example, an employer who wants to hire someone to sell condos may want the employee to have a post-secondary degree to ensure they have cultural capital, but it is a matter of indifference whether they have a bachelor's degree in history, philosophy, sociology, English, or physics. On the other hand, certain jobs require certain specialized degrees. This is true of the skilled trades: a graduate of a plumbing program will not be hired as an electrician, and vice versa. Moreover, entry into select professional or managerial jobs is limited and closely guarded. In particular, "professionals" such as doctors and lawyers strictly control entry into their profession by limiting the numbers that are permitted to get the desired credentials. They argue that their professional expertise is such that only they have the knowledge to evaluate and adjudicate issues involving the profession. In this way, they justify their high-paying positions.

Thus, the demand for more credentials, and more particular credentials, creates occupations that seek to limit the number of entrants. In effect, what we mean by **professionalization** is the process by which an occupation raises its standing by specifying narrow entry criteria and limiting the number of entrants (Roach Anleu and Mack, 2008). In this way, occupations that were considered trades in the nineteenth century are now seen as modern-day professions. This was accomplished by creating multiple layers of specialization and professional training—even though, as Collins has stated, much of the schooling required is highly theoretical and has little to do with on-the-job experience or training.

Professionalization The process by which an occupation raises its standing by limiting the number of entrants and regulating their behaviour.

While Canada has one of the highest rates of post-secondary education attendance in the world, the skills of the Canadian workforce are not being used to their full potential. **Over-education** means having more education than is needed to carry out a particular job or fulfill a particular role. Immigrants arriving in Canada, for example, often discover that the education they have acquired is underutilized in the Canadian labour market (Chiswick and Miller, 2008). Along these lines, a survey of Ontario residents (Livingstone et al., 2003) showed that rates of over-qualification have risen from 16 per cent to 21 per cent from 1994 to 2002. In 2008, 42 per cent of immigrant workers were reportedly overqualified for their jobs, compared to only 28 per cent of Canadian-born workers (Statistics Canada, 2009a).

Over-education Having more education than is actually needed to perform employment roles and functions successfully.

The growing underutilization of educational credentials has led researchers and policy-makers to consider the social consequences. Over-education may lead to increases in job dissatisfaction, worker discontent, and greater political alienation, as well as weakened loyalty to the dominant achievement ideology. More research needs to be done before conclusions can be drawn on the social effects of over-qualification.

School Dropouts

Earning at least a high school diploma is exceedingly important in a credential society like ours. In part, this is because more education gives people more skills and resources for work-related tasks; also, higher credentials open doors to better job opportunities. So we are right to worry about the large numbers of young people who drop out of formal education before attaining a degree that can help them get a job.

Dorn, Bowen, and Blau (2006) divide student dropouts into three main categories: *dropout*, *pullout*, and *pushout*. By this reckoning, *dropout theories* focus on students who find themselves unable to cope intellectually (or cognitively) with school materials. *Pullout theories* are class-based and focus on students who withdraw from schooling because of financial troubles. Finally, *pushout theories* focus on the school and community as contextual factors that influence high school drop-out rates. An example of a pushout scenario would be a community in which schools offer little encouragement to their students, perhaps telling many them to aim low in order to avoid disappointment. At the very least, a high school diploma signals prospective employers that a person can stick to a task to its completion, an indication of some self-discipline. It also gives people the opportunity to enter post-secondary education, whether college or university.

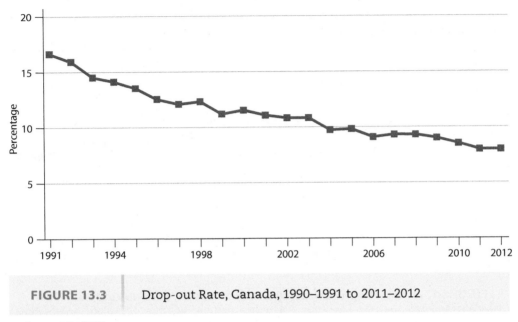

FIGURE 13.3 Drop-out Rate, Canada, 1990–1991 to 2011–2012

Source: HRSDC (2013).

Happily, there is some evidence that drop-out rates in Canada are falling. Figure 13.3 graphically shows the decrease in drop-out rates in Canada over the past two decades. In 1990–1, dropout rates reached 16.6 per cent. By 2011–12, however, the proportion of the population that had not received a diploma decreased to 7.8 per cent. This trend is evident in all Canadian provinces, with British Columbia standing at 5.9 per cent, the lowest provincial drop-out rate in Canada (Statistics Canada, 2013b).

But if dropping out is becoming less common in all parts of Canada, why are social scientists so concerned? The answer is that although this decline is evident across Canada, the decline is much less evident in some regions, and in some groups, than in others. Consider, in particular, the troubling evidence that boys continue to drop out in much higher numbers than girls.

The Increasing Prevalence of Male Dropouts—Reversals in Attainment

As mentioned earlier, today girls and women are doing much better at school than boys and men. The previous gender imbalance—which favoured males—began to reverse during the 1950s. Today, females surpass males on most measures of attainment. In fact, females are less likely to drop out of high school and more likely to enter and complete university/college (Statistics Canada, 2012).

Overall drop-out rates have decreased for both females and males over the past 20 years. The drop-out rate for males decreased by 9.5 per cent over the period between 1990 and 2012, while the female drop-out rate fell as well, but only by 8.1 per cent (hrsdc, 2013). However, over the same period, the *relative* drop-out rates of males compared to females have climbed, leading to an increase in educational gender inequality. As Figure 13.4 shows, males drop out of school disproportionately more often than females—specifically, around 4.2 per cent more often than females (ibid.).

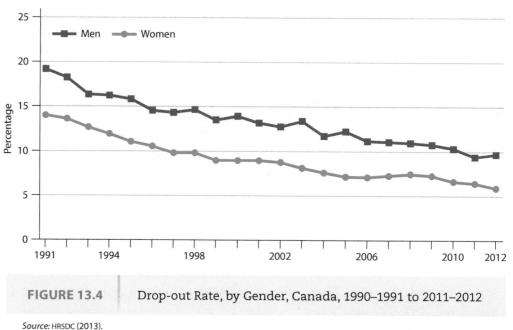

FIGURE 13.4   Drop-out Rate, by Gender, Canada, 1990–1991 to 2011–2012

Source: HRSDC (2013).

What accounts for this trend? The Youth in Transition Survey showed several reasons behind the decision to drop out of high school, which vary by gender. Young men are reportedly less likely to have an intellectual, social, or emotional investment in school endeavours. They are anxious to work and earn money, and this is why they drop out of high school. By contrast, teenage pregnancy plays a more crucial role in a girl's decision to drop out of school. The Youth in Transition Survey showed that 15.9 per cent of female dropouts occurred due to a pregnancy or the need to take care of a child. Forty per cent of female dropouts either had children or were the primary caretakers of a household.

The implications of this are that if we want to further reduce the rate of female dropouts, we should focus on improved sex education and contraceptive availability for young women. Reducing the rate of male dropouts would be more difficult: we would have to find ways to get young men interested in learning, starting with making sure that they develop the reading skills they will need in all further education.

Health Consequences of Education

Education is valuable in all sorts of ways, and it even helps people lead healthier lives. People with higher levels of education tend to adopt better health habits and lifestyles than people with lower levels of education and lower socio-economic statuses. Education helps to build useful life skills and the sense of mastery that are needed when dealing with problems later in life.

For instance, engaging in positive health behaviours—such as exercising, drinking in moderation, avoiding obesity, refraining from smoking, and regularly visiting the doctor—greatly prolong one's life. Middle-class people with a higher education see greater life expectancy and reduced infant mortality (Zhunio et al., 2012). Missing out on education comes at a high price. Those who cannot afford to attend post-secondary school and who will presumably face harsher socio-economic conditions later in life are less likely to be able to send their children to college or university. For this reason, families tend to maintain the same socio-economic standing through multiple generations.

Barbara Ronson and Irving Rootman (2004) provide an additional perspective regarding the effects of education on health. In *Literacy: One of the Most Important Determinants of Health Today*, they propose that literacy predicts health status more accurately than education level, income, or ethnic background. Various research studies suggest that literacy is directly related to people's overall health status, mental health status, co-morbidity burden, and life expectancy (ibid.; Guerra et al., 2005).

Tobacco use is seen more among illiterate people than among those with a college education. Moreover, a study in Mumbai showed that school dropouts were more likely to use tobacco than those in school; the latter received education on the health hazards of tobacco and so were less inclined to consume it (Gupta and Ray, 2007). With a high correlation between illiteracy and poor health, the US launched the Healthy People 2010 project, which strove to help people gain "the capacity to obtain, process, and understand basic health information and services needed to make appropriate health decisions" (Ishikawa and Kiuchi, 2010).

To summarize, higher education enables people to engage in healthy lifestyles and to learn healthy habits. Even a basic education can provide people with the means to understand public health information.

Bullying

Bullying can be defined as repetitive, deliberate, hurtful behaviour that takes place in the presence of an imbalance of power between aggressor and victim (Aalsma and Brown, 2008). We think of bullying, however, as a childhood terror tactic. Two important elements of bullying capture its complexity. First, bullying is characterized as aggressive or assertive behaviour that is imposed from a position of dominance or power. This power can either be physical—using strength or size—or social/hierarchical—belonging to a higher social status peer group. Second, acts of bullying must be repetitive to be influential.

As Shariff (2005) suggests, bullying is typically expressed in either of two forms— *overt bullying* and *covert bullying*. The former involves "physical aggression, such as beating, kicking, shoving, and sexual touching." The latter is typified by the exclusionary practices of peer groups. These include being the victim of gossip, verbally threatened, or harassed. Interestingly, while boys in secondary school are more likely than girls to become victims of bullying, studies show that girls are more likely to fear being bullied at school (Pitts and Smith, 1995; Arnot et al., 1999).

The great changes a girl experiences during adolescence places them at higher risk for bullying. A 2008 study showed that, as a result of these changes, more teenage girls start drinking alcohol and smoking cigarettes than boys. Girls also have a higher risk of abusing prescription drugs (Our Kids, 2012). In bullying situations, boys are more likely to be engaged in physical assaults whereas girls are more likely to be involved in relational bullying (Brank et al., 2012).

Today, bullying has become a source of increasing concern—especially the use or threat of violence against children at or near school. Perhaps the contradictory institutional priorities and cultures of schools might facilitate or perpetuate the existence of

Bullying Any form of repeated aggression marked by an observable power differential between individuals.

bullying: the unending conflict, confusion, and competition we spoke about earlier. And with the evolution of the Internet, much bullying has become a psychological, rather than a physical, form of abuse. Like everything else, bullying has become "virtual" with the Internet, but it is no less real in its consequences. Even adults are being bullied on the Internet these days.

Bullies terrorize their victims, dominating them physically, emotionally, or socially. In face-to-face bullying, they may be bigger and stronger than the victim or they may have a higher status within the school's social hierarchy. Often, they exploit the victim's weaknesses and may operate in groups. This kind of face-to-face bullying can be physical or verbal, but bullies can also opt for indirect means such as gossip or exclusion. Repeated bullying establishes dominance over the victim, who becomes increasingly distressed and fearful. The goal of bullying is to humiliate—to humble—another person, whether through threats, blackmail, gossip, or otherwise.

Research shows that childhood bullies are also likely to display anti-social behaviours in adulthood; 30 to 40 per cent of children who are overly aggressive will have violent tendencies as adults. The motives for bullying originate at home, where children's behavioural patterns are first established. Bullies tend to have parents who are hostile, neglectful, or in conflict, or who punish their children severely. Sometimes, bullies are merely imitating their parents' social behaviour; that is, they have parents who are bullies. Sometimes, they come to believe that bullying is acceptable because their parents tolerate fighting in the household among siblings. These children seek out and enjoy aggressive situations, show little empathy for the people they hurt, and feel no remorse for their actions. Many have quick tempers and are hyperactive, disruptive, and impulsive. Male bullies, in particular, tend to be physically strong and to use their strength to threaten and coerce others.

Like bullies, victims also have certain definable characteristics. Many display anxiety, expressed as tension, fears, and worry; low self-esteem; and depression, including sadness and withdrawal. These traits are commonly reported among both boys and girls who are victimized. As they get older, children are less likely to be bullied, but they will likely continue to be victimized, though perhaps to a reduced extent in adulthood.

Rooted in group culture, bullying focuses on certain culturally supported stereotypes and prejudices. The bully singles out people who are handicapped (e.g., deaf, blind, obese, or given to stuttering and therefore socially isolated), unpopular, or homosexual, for example. Bullying often employs homophobic verbal taunts related to gender non-conformity—words like "gay," for example. This tendency is supported by aggressive, sexist, and heteronormative subcultures.

All forms of bullying—direct, indirect, and even cyberbullying—can have harmful effects on a victim's health and well-being that persist into adulthood. Many children do not tell anyone about their bullying experience or seek help and support. They need to be encouraged to speak up, since peer support programs have already been identified as an important way to tackle and prevent bullying. These programs help by building resilience, promoting friendship, and challenging negative peer group roles.

Even though schools can be the site of physically and emotionally damaging bullying, the school setting allows many children to form and broaden their base of close friendships. These friendships frequently turn into long-term relationships and some even lead to marriage. School integrates people and teaches them how to live with one another.

Andrew Francis Wallace/GetStock.com

Sahar Zairab hugs Nova Browning Rutherford during a vigil at Yonge-Dundas Square to mark the passing of bullying victim Rehtaeh Parsons. Parsons committed suicide in her Dartmouth home following constant online harassment, prompting Nova Scotia to enact a law allowing victims to seek protection from cyberbullying and to sue the perpetrator.

How common is bullying in Canada? Children in this country are far more likely to be bullied and become bullies themselves than children in many other countries. According to the Health Behaviours in School-Aged Children Survey conducted by the World Health Organization, Canada's bullying problem is a key contributor to its ranking seventeenth out of twenty-nine countries on measures of child well-being (Canadian Press, 2013). This suggests that bullying in Canada has become a pervasive and prevalent social problem.

Cyberbullying: Media and Technology

In 2010, 98 per cent of Canadian households had access to broadband technology (CRTC, 2011). In recent years, Internet usage has steadily increased among people 18 years and older, alongside a decrease in low-intensity users (i.e., those who are online less than five hours a week or not everyday) (Statistics Canada, 2010a). Studies on Internet usage show that experience online begins at a younger age, with an ever-increasing number of people with five or more years of Internet experience, year after year.

An overwhelming majority of Canadians, especially young Canadians, have access to and make use of the Internet. Recent data show that Canadians rank number one in the world in terms of Internet usage (Canadian Internet Registration Authority, 2013). The growing use of the Internet, coupled with other forms of technology, has changed the nature of social interaction, especially among young people.

One example of the effects of technology on Canadian youth is **cyberbullying**, a technological extension of physical bullying. Cyberbullying occurs when a person uses information technology (IT) to embarrass, harass, intimidate, or threaten others.

Cyberbullying A technological extension of physical bullying occurring when an individual uses information technology (IT) to embarrass, harass, intimidate, or threaten others.

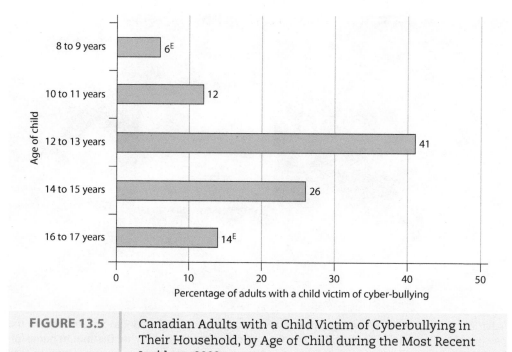

FIGURE 13.5 | Canadian Adults with a Child Victim of Cyberbullying in Their Household, by Age of Child during the Most Recent Incident, 2009

Note: Data are based upon answers from respondents living with at least one child aged 8 to 17 years. Excludes data for Yukon, the Northwest Territories, and Nunavut.

E Use with caution.

Source: Statistics Canada, General Social Survey, "Self-reported Internet Victimization in Canada, 2009," at: <www.statcan.gc.ca/pub/85-002-x/2011001/article/11530-eng.htm#a2>.

Sometimes called "Internet aggression," "digital harassment," or "Internet bullying," cyberbullying is becoming increasingly prevalent as the use of new technologies increases. This emerging form of bullying involves using computers or other IT devices, such as personal digital assistants (PDAs), cellphones, and portable gaming consoles to cause harm to targeted individuals. Colt, Meyer, and McQuade (2009) further caution that cyberbullying seems to have become so prominent or "technologically insidious" that classical "physical" forms of bullying may be increasing as a result.

Cyberbullying has become the most common bullying method. It involves sending harassing messages via text or email, posting derogatory comments on a website or social networking site, or physically threatening someone in online settings (Hinduja and Patchin, 2010). In 2011, 56 per cent of teenagers and people in their early twenties reported being cyberbullied (Statistics Canada, 2011). Roughly one in ten adults reports having a child in their household who has been a victim of cyberbullying (ibid.). Unfortunately, far too few of these cases are being reported to authorities. For instance, in 2009, only 14 per cent of cyberbullying cases directed to children were reported to the police (Statistics Canada, 2009b).

The anonymity of cyberbullying, as Shariff (2005) proposes, "distracts all students (victims, bystanders, and perpetrators) from schoolwork. It creates a hostile physical environment where students feel unwelcome and unsafe." Ultimately, in this type of atmosphere, it becomes difficult for students to contribute to class discussion and learn successfully (Harmon, 2004; Shariff, 2005).

Solutions to Educational Social Problems

Improving Student Learning and Performance

Student achievement and school performance are widely variable—even among schools and students with similar socio-economic backgrounds. As we have noted, student learning is influenced by many factors, including family resources, school organization, effective school curriculum, as well as teachers' skills, attitudes, and practices.

In the short run, factors such as family and community background are difficult for policy-makers to influence. What can be improved, however, are teacher quality and teaching practices. In fact, many commentators agree that improving *teacher quality* is the most influential factor in terms of student achievement (Santiago, 2004; Schacter and Thum, 2004). If instruction and teacher quality are improved, student learning and achievement will also improve.

Improving teaching—especially in low-performing schools—is challenging. Schools must be diligent to ensure that students get on track, stay on track, and receive quality instruction (Quint et al., 2008). The OECD (2005: 26) claims that "moving from being taught by an average teacher to one at the 85th percentile of teacher quality would lead to students improving by more than 4 percentiles." Sanders and Rivers (1996) have estimated that the effects of teacher quality are substantial and cumulative over time. Unequal access to high-quality teachers puts students of low socio-economic status at a great disadvantage, affecting their ability to receive a proper education.

In this photo, Grade 4 students Tray Haye (left) and Dominik Novakovic, both aged nine, work at their desks at Hunter's Glen Junior PS in Toronto, where standardized test scores improved by 31 per cent owing largely to teacher-collaboration efforts.

Akiba, LeTendre, and Scribner (2007) conducted an analysis that showed that students with high-quality teachers achieved higher mathematical scores than those with lower-quality instructors. Interestingly, there was no significant difference in achievement between students with low and high socio-economic status. A string of successful teachers narrows the average attainment gap between students with low socio-economic status and those with higher socio-economic status. One can therefore conclude that low-performing students benefit more from having more-effective teachers than other students do.

Chapter Summary

Historically, people have proposed that schooling outcomes reflect differences in personal abilities. This perspective has fuelled the view that students who are low achievers will ultimately underperform in multiple aspects of life. Underperforming schools have often been labelled as a "lost cause." However, the evidence we have presented suggests differently.

Teachers, for example, can make a difference. While social and economic disadvantages greatly affect student performance, schools, too, can make a measurable impact on the life chances of all students. David Johnson's evaluation of schools in Ontario shows how exceptional schools, in disadvantaged areas, can succeed against unequal odds. Schools such as Cornell Junior Public School in Scarborough should not be treated as outliers or out of the ordinary. When schools and teaching practices become successful, it is important for us to understand how and why this has occurred. If we do so, educational success can be felt throughout society, not just among dominant and affluent groups.

Questions for Critical Thought

1. If you were a paid consultant, how would you suggest schools should reorganize themselves to become more successful at their main line of work—that is, education?
2. Given the correlation between students failing a grade and dropping out, do you think schools should fail students in school? Why might it be a good or bad thing in elementary school?
3. Should bullying in the workplace be acknowledged as a legitimate social problem? If so, how should workplace bullying be defined?
4. How may cyberbullying increase the rates of bullying in Canada? What measures can parents or police take to keep this from occurring?
5. Higher rates of unemployment are emerging. From an employer's perspective, what are the benefits and consequences of relying on academic achievements?
6. Education may still seem to be more a privilege than a right for lower socio-economic people. Do you believe that post-secondary education should be made compulsory?
7. With more women now enrolling in university than men, do you believe that women will increasingly take on managerial and leadership roles?

Recommended Readings

Creasey, Gary, and Patricia A. Jarvis. 2012. *Adolescent Development and School Achievement in Urban Communities: Resilience in the Neighborhood*. Florence, KY: Routledge.

Davies, Scott, and Neil Guppy. 2006. *The Schooled Society: An Introduction to the Sociology of Education*. Toronto: Oxford University Press.

Kincheloe, Joe L., and Shirley R. Steinberg. 2007. *Cutting Class: Socioeconomic Status and Education*. Lanham: MD: Rowman and Littlefield Publishers.

Lampert, Ken. 2003. *Compassionate Education: A Prolegomena for Radical Schooling*. Lanham: MD: University Press of America.

14

Populations, Cities, and Neighbourhoods

ValeStock/Shutterstock

Introduction

This chapter is about population, cities, and neighbourhoods. It examines the interactions between human society and the built environment and the problems that emerge from these interactions. In doing so, it brings together two central topics of modern sociology—population studies and urban sociology.

Two common threads run through these fields of study. The first is that each topic directly addresses the physical and material backdrops of social life; the second is that human ingenuity (or more concretely, technology) is both at the root of various social problems and the source of potential solutions to these problems.

Some worry that we face insuperable population problems. Others are not given to worry at all. Economic theorist Julian Simon (1996), for example, believed that human beings are "the ultimate resource." Simon's work—a direct rebuff to the Malthusian perspective—remains controversial. Some of his theories about the infinite productiveness of the planet have been disproved as too simplistic. Still, one element of Simon's central thesis is hard to refute: namely, the human species, throughout its short history, has proven hugely creative when confronting difficulty.

Simon would argue that to solve the problems associated with population growth, we may not need *fewer* people but, instead, better-equipped and better-educated people; and not a *suspicion* of technology, but instead a commitment to using technology for the good of humanity. The problems we discuss in this chapter are not population and cities per se, but the human failure to manage these facets of human design more creatively and effectively. Humanity is the problem we are discussing, and a better-organized humanity is likely the solution.

Still, we must recognize that humanity faces important population-related problems. One central problem relates to the imperfections in how societies are organized; in the twenty-first century, this mainly means how cities are organized. The continued growth of the world's population only worsens our urban problems by making them larger and more complex. Another problem is the rapidity of population growth and urbanization—processes that sped up dramatically in the last few centuries (Xu and Zhu, 2009; Gajdos, 2009).

World Population in Context

The history of the world's population unfolded in two general stages: an extended period of slow growth from the time when the first humans appeared to around the mid-eighteenth century; and a brief period of explosive growth after 1750.

According to one estimate, human population growth before the modern era was barely a hundredth of a per cent per year. Since then, the world's population has increased rapidly—sometimes exponentially—with especially rapid growth since the beginning of the Industrial Revolution in the late 1700s.

Consider this in terms of the earth's population doubling. Between the year 1 AD and 1750, it is estimated that population size doubled only once, from 300 million to 750 million. In the last 250 years, the world's population has doubled three times, surpassing 6 billion before 2000. As estimated by the United Nations, the world's population reached 6.9 billion in 2010.

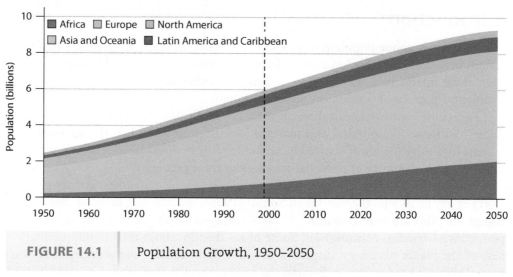

FIGURE 14.1   Population Growth, 1950–2050

Source: United World Environmental Library, at: <http://esa.un.org/unpd/wpp/index.htm>.

Even though the global population continues to increase today, worldwide growth rates peaked in the 1970s and have been in decline for several years now. Currently, the growth is around 1.3 per cent per year and is expected to decline to 0.5 per cent by 2050 (Attane, 2006). Population growth occurs unevenly around the world, with most developed nations, including Canada, experiencing zero or even negative growth. Developing countries accounted for approximately 97 per cent of the world population's growth from 2010 to 2012 (when it reached 7.06 billion), owing to high birth rates and young populations. In contrast, the number of births barely exceeds the number of deaths in developed countries because of low birth rates and older populations. This will result in a decline in developed countries' population growth. For example, the population of Europe is projected to decrease from 740 million to 732 million by 2050 (Haub, 2012). Figure 14.1 expands on this idea by showing the projected population growth of developed and undeveloped countries: population growth is projected to plateau in industrialized nations but to expand rapidly in less-developed ones.

It seems that excessive population growth will soon become a social problem of the past. However, other population-related problems will replace it: problems having to do with location, immigration, internal migration, crowding, and depopulation. But first, how has this problem of population growth (nearly) resolved itself? As we will see, it was partly through population planning—through the application of official coercion and incentives—but mainly through the so-called *demographic transition*.

The Demographic Transition

Demographic transition
Shift in a population or society through a series of stages from high birth and death rates to low birth and death rates.

The **demographic transition** refers to a shift in demographic patterns from high birth and death rates to low birth and death rates (Johnson-Hanks, 2008; Lehr, 2009). Typically, this demographic transition occurs in parallel with a society's socio-economic development. Figure 14.2 illustrates the process.

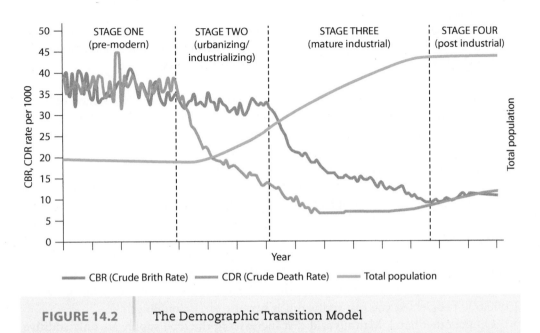

FIGURE 14.2 | The Demographic Transition Model

Source: Keith Montgomery, *The Demographic Transition*, at: <pages.uwc.edu/keith.montgomery/Demotrans/demtran.htm>. Used with the permission of Keith Montgomery.

During the first stage of a demographic transition, when a society is still in its pre-modern phase, the number of births and deaths are both high but equal, resulting in a steady population size with only minimal growth. Stage 2 usually arrives as the population enters the early stages of urbanization and industrialization, when socio-economic advances result in declining death rates. During this period, birth rates remain high, resulting in explosive population growth and a young population profile.

However, in stage 3, the pattern changes dramatically. Birth rates begin to fall, slowly reaching levels comparable to the death rate. As a result, the population continues to grow but the rate of increase slows down. By stage 4, when a society has reached a post-industrial phase of development, population is once again stable, with rates of births and deaths equal again and at historical lows. At this point, with low birth rates, the overall population begins to age. Most important, there is no population growth due to excess births over deaths. Canada is currently at this stage—or more accurately, past this stage, since Canada has a declining natural growth rate. Were it not for immigration, Canada's population would shrink each year.

Numerous thinkers have attempted to explain this remarkable, worldwide decline in birth rates over the past century.

Contrasting Perspectives on Population Change

The Malthusian Position

This natural decline in population growth was not foreseen. In fact, the opposite—a continued population explosion—was feared throughout much of the nineteenth and twentieth centuries (Clark and Cummins, 2009; Weil and Wilde, 2009).

Modern scientific theories about population growth and its effect on societies began with the ideas of Thomas Malthus (1959 [1798]). Malthus is famously remembered for his theory of population, which can be stated briefly as follows:

> Population when unchecked increases in a geometrical ratio. Subsistence only increases in an arithmetical ratio. . . . [Therefore] the power of population is indefinitely greater than the power in the earth to produce subsistence for man.

Malthus reasoned that a population growing exponentially (that is, through a series such as 1, 2, 4, 8, 16, etc.) at a constant rate adds more people every year than the year before. Consider, for example, a population of 1,000 women and 1,000 men. Each woman marries and has four children. If all survive, in the next generation there are roughly 2,000 women and 2,000 men. If all of those women have four children each, then in the next generation there are roughly 4,000 women and 4,000 men. With a constant pattern of four births per woman, the population doubles every generation (roughly 30 years). In only 300 years, the original population of 2,000 has grown to 1,000,000 people! (As you can verify, this is because of 10 doublings.)

On the other hand, Malthus said that increases in the food supply are only additive, or arithmetic (that is, in a series such as 1, 2, 3, 4, 5, etc.). Limits on available land, soil quality, and technology all constrain the growth in the food supply. Malthus believed there is a real risk of populations outgrowing the food supply—that the chance of running out of food poses a real threat to humanity. Thus, checks (or limits) are needed to keep population growth in line with growth in the food supply. Welfare schemes to help the poor by redistributing wealth are futile, said Malthus. If we feed the hungry, they will reproduce until they run out of food and are hungry again (Crafts and Mills, 2009).

The only sure solutions are positive checks and preventive checks. **Positive checks** prevent overpopulation by increasing the death rate. They include war, famine, pestilence, and disease. **Preventive checks** prevent overpopulation by limiting the number or survival of live births. They include abortion, infanticide, sexual abstinence, delayed marriage, and contraceptive use. Among these preventive options, the Reverend Malthus approved only of delayed marriage and sexual abstinence (Simkins, 2001; Nicolini, 2007).

Today, people who believe there is still a "population problem" make some of the same arguments as Malthus did two centuries ago. Neo-Malthusians believe the world is becoming overpopulated, that population growth will outstrip agricultural growth, and that this population burden will permanently harm the environment (Shandra et al., 2003; Hoffmann, 2004). World population is still growing. Even allowing for slower growth, experts predict that in 30 years the world's population, currently 7.06 billion people, will have grown by nearly three billion.

With population growth come new challenges, including increased competition for non-renewable resources; the need to feed, nurture, and educate a larger proportion of young people; increased pressures on the health and welfare systems; and the need for governments to prevent or deal with economic and natural disasters.

Positive checks Part of Malthusian theory, these prevent overpopulation by increasing the death rate. They include war, famine, pestilence, and disease.

Preventive checks In Malthusian theory, these prevent overpopulation by limiting the number or survivals of live births. They include abortion, infanticide, sexual abstinence, delayed marriage, and contraceptive technologies.

Criticisms of the Malthusian Perspective

It is far from certain that the planet's carrying capacity will be fatally strained by population increases; for that matter, it is not clear that population pressures will cause wars. Others blame the recurring conflicts over space and resources on capitalism, imperialism, fascism, tribalism, or a variety of other political motivations. And, evidently, some governments are less inclined to go to war over the population issue and more inclined to handle it in a peaceful, progressive way. Therefore, Malthus and the Malthusians who followed were wrong in some of their fears and predictions (Clark and Cummins, 2009).

Some note that Malthus was wrong in supposing that food supplies can increase only arithmetically. Long-term food production trends reveal that in technologically advanced societies, food production has increased at a faster rate than the human population owing to better seeds, fertilizers, and growth techniques. Past warnings of an impending global food shortage by the end of the twentieth century have been proven unwarranted.

Writing in 1949, the eminent demographer Alfred Sauvy described potential overpopulation as a "false problem" and argued against efforts to control global population (Sauvy and Demeny, 1990). He suggested examining countries case by case to see whether they have the raw materials and natural resources that could support a larger population. Otherwise, we run the risk of under-populating a country (such as Canada) that could support a much larger population. A larger population is not necessarily good, but if unavoidable, we need to find its benefits. And this we can do only if we confront the issues of social and political organization.

Demographer Joel Cohen (1995) notes that a fundamental problem may lie in the notion of a single "carrying capacity" for the planet. This concept, he argues, does not translate well from the plant or animal models on which it was based to human societies. Most animals and plants are stuck with the environment they inhabit. However, humanity—because of its ingenuity, resourcefulness, inventiveness, ability to adapt, awareness of the future, and stubborn free will—can modify its environment through technology.

Therefore, humanity is constantly defying standard ecological models of population behaviour. As well, population sustainability is tied not only to reproductive trends, but also to countless economic, political, and social processes.

Population Density

Some believe that the biggest problems facing humanity result from high **population density**. Population density is the number of people who live within a geographic area, usually expressed as people per square mile or square kilometre (Millward, 2008). It is a measure of the concentration of people in space or, as some might say, a measure of crowding—of how many people have crowded into a house, neighbourhood, community, city, or country (Millward and Bunting, 2008).

All of human history—but especially in the past 300 years—has tended towards increased population density. Since the earth's surface is finite and fixed in size, the growth of human population has inevitably meant an increased population density on the earth's surface.

A potent factor in this growth has been the urbanization of the world—the movement of people from sparse rural settings to concentrated urban settings, as Table 14.1 illustrates. In cities, population is denser than in rural villages, for example. This density is sometimes accomplished by packing more people into households. More often, the

Population density The number of people who live within a geographic area, usually expressed as people per square mile or square kilometre.

A crowded street market in Manila, the Philippines. The city of Manila has one of the highest population densities on the planet.

TABLE 14.1	Population, Urban and Rural, by Province and Territory (Canada)				
	POPULATION	URBAN	RURAL	URBAN	RURAL
		Number		% of total population	
Canada					
1851	2,436,297	318,079	2,118,218	13	87
1861	3,229,633	527,220	2,702,413	16	84
1871	3,737,257	722,343	3,014,914	19	81
1881	4,381,256	1,109,507	3,271,749	25	75
1891	4,932,206	1,537,098	3,395,108	31	69
1901	5,418,663	2,023,364	3,395,299	37	63
1911	7,221,662	3,276,812	3,944,850	45	55
1921	8,800,249	4,353,428	4,446,821	49	51
1931	10,376,379	5,572,058	4,804,321	54	46
1941	11,506,655	6,252,416	5,254,239	54	46
1951	14,009,429	8,628,253	5,381,176	62	38
1956	16,080,791	10,714,855	5,365,936	67	33
1961	18,238,247	12,700,390	5,537,857	70	30
1966	20,014,880	14,726,759	5,288,121	74	26
1971	21,568,305	16,410,785	5,157,520	76	24
1976	22,992,595	17,366,970	5,625,625	76	24
1981	24,343,177	18,435,923	5,907,254	76	24
1986	25,309,330	19,352,080	5,957,250	76	24
1991	27,296,856	20,906,872	6,389,984	77	23
1996	28,846,758	22,461,207	6,385,551	78	22
2001	30,007,094	23,908,211	6,098,883	80	20
2006	31,612,897	25,350,743	6,262,154	80	20
2011	33,476,688	27,147,274	6,329,414	81	19

Source: Statistics Canada, 2011 Census of Population, at: <www.statcan.gc.ca/tables-tableaux/sum-som/l01/cst01/demo62a-eng.htm>.

distance between houses is reduced, so each household has less property. Often it is accomplished by stacking people vertically in high-rise, high-density apartment buildings, tenements, or condominiums.

However, the historical transitions from hunting to agriculture and from nomadism to settlement meant a once-and-for-all movement towards higher population density on earth. Population density arises in two main ways: through high fertility combined with low mortality, and through a migration of people to places of perceived greater opportunity. Moreover, these two elements are linked: reproduction has been shown to be density-dependent for a wide variety of species, including humans. Indeed, population density has also been linked to the historical transition from high fertility rates to low ones. Lutz, Sanderson, and Scherbov (2006) find a consistently negative connection between human fertility and population density in a variety of societies. Even individual fertility preferences decline with population density. In short, as density increases, fertility (eventually) declines.

At the same time, with growing population density the impetus to develop technology increases: there is a pressure towards innovation. Even today in horticultural villages, population density promotes innovation. Researchers found that there were two different effects of population pressure on rural economies in south-central Ethiopia from 1950 to 2004. One was a pressure on existing households to feed and house a growing number of children. The other was an increased demand on the economy for more jobs. When both demand levels were low, people extended agricultural production, taking advantage of the availability of land. When both demand levels were increasing, people intensified and diversified their agricultural practices, which often led to innovation (Malmberg and Tegenu, 2007). No wonder, then, that in rural communities, major agricultural growth and rural development occur in districts with high population density, less-constrained environments, and better access to markets, irrigation canals, and capital loans (Ali, 2007).

These changes in response to population density—for example, reduced fertility and increased innovation—are largely a result of the changed *perception* of available resources and the sense that something can be done. A perceived lack of resources tends to reduce family size and brings about changes in all demographic variables. As Bandy (2005) points out, the historical transition from hunting and gathering to agricultural village life was associated with a two-stage demographic transition—first, to high population growth rates when nomads first settled the land, and second, to much lower growth rates when they started to experience population pressures.

In general, the growth of population density is associated historically with economic growth, the growth of cities, the development of urban lifestyles, and the buildup of creativity. Most people—including sociologists and historians—view this as an advance in human civilization. Cities—owing in large part to their density and large numbers—make possible certain social and cultural experiences that are not possible in smaller, sparser settlements.

In short, the population density in cities allows for what economists call "economies of scale." These are efficiencies—low per-unit costs—made possible by a large volume of production (and consumption) (Huiban, 2009; Kasman and Turgutlu, 2009). Certain activities are only profitable if they are large enough and only large enough if they can draw on a large enough market or demand. Cities are large markets, so they make possible human experiences—such as going to the opera, dining in fine restaurants,

Classic WORKS

BOX 14.1   **William Goode's *World Revolution and Family Patterns* (1963)**

In *World Revolution and Family Patterns*, William Goode reviews changes to family organization around the world in the first half of the twentieth century. Notably, Goode examines the relationship between changing family patterns and industrialization. He draws attention to several major cross-cultural trends. First, family patterns are moving towards the conjugal (nuclear) model. The family unit is smaller today, a self-sustaining unit of production and consumption, separate from the kinship group. In addition, with an increase in the use of contraceptives and decrease in birth rate, family size has begun to shrink. Role relations within the family have also changed. Individual members have more freedom; for example, parental authority over children has declined. With an increase in women's rights, husbands' patriarchal control over wives has also dwindled. Gradually, dowries and payment for brides have disappeared. A final example of the transformation is an increasing acceptance of changes in social "morals" and virtues, including the increased acceptance of divorce, the use of contraception, abortion, cohabitation, and premarital sexual relations.

The family does not change directly because of a modern industrial system; rather, this family model better fits industrial demands. Smaller family units have more freedom and flexibility to meet the changes in industry, for example. The influences of industry on family life are not one-sided, however; family demands, such as housework and child care, act as "barriers" to a complete industrial takeover of family life. Moreover, according to Goode, the family was subject to economic progress and political developments even before industrialization.

Therefore, Goode notes, family systems often resist change, but changes do occur in family life over time. While the global trend is towards the nuclear family, this change has not occurred uniformly (at the same rate) throughout the industrial world. The change towards a conjugal family is not a direct result of industrialization, as it is mediated by cultural influences that predate the Industrial Revolution. And, finally, changing social conditions of various kinds shape the development of ideas about what makes up the "ideal" family.

and browsing in mystery bookstores—that are economically impossible in smaller, less dense places.

Cities make it easier for humans to interact, and one of the great benefits of dense urban areas is that they promote social interactions. Likely, the resurgence of big cities in the 1990s was due, in part, to the increased demand for these interactions and to the reduction in big-city crime, which had made it difficult for many urban residents to enjoy these social amenities (Glaeser and Gottlieb, 2006).

However, not everyone benefits from urban density, because different urban opportunities are spatially segregated. MacIntyre, MacDonald, and Ellaway (2008), who examined the location of urban resources in Glasgow (Scotland), found that poorer, more-deprived neighbourhoods are "rich" in certain kinds of resources—public nurseries, public primary schools, police stations, pharmacies, credit unions, post offices, bus stops, bingo halls, public sports centres, and outdoor play areas—but also in vacant and derelict land and buildings. More prosperous areas are rich in other kinds of resources: private schools, banks, museums, art galleries, subway stations, tennis courts, bowling greens, private health clubs, private swimming pools, colleges, hospitals, parks, and tourist attractions. On the face of it, both benefit from density; however, the more prosperous areas contain more desirable, private, or elite locales.

The rising population density associated with urbanization has brought many benefits to humanity, and we are still enjoying these benefits today. The human race advanced socially and culturally when it "came together" in dense settlements. It is because of these benefits that most Canadians live in or near a large metropolitan area, or at least in a city.

Urban Sociology: A Primer

Cities, as Max Weber (1958 [1921], 1981 [1924]) pointed out, are among humanity's great social inventions. Most important, cities make possible a range of experiences that are unavailable in smaller rural areas or small towns. The sheer size and diversity of city populations allow for specialization and diversity in the goods and services on offer.

Yet, for all that, city life has been surrounded by controversy since the beginning. Some have hailed cities as affording liberty, especially the freedom to think and act as one wishes. Others have viewed cities as lacking in neighbourliness and community spirit. They have depicted city-dwellers as lonely atoms, deprived of purpose and control. Much of twentieth-century American sociology examined these competing views of cities. At first, research on cities was skewed by the dominance of research on the city of Chicago owing to the overwhelming presence of the Department of Sociology at the University of Chicago. When this department was at its peak, roughly between 1900 and 1940, Chicago was a living laboratory for the study of city populations, especially for study of the poor, the marginalized, and the stigmatized. In the last half of the twentieth century, the main goals of urban sociologists broadened to encompass a wider variety of cities, and especially suburbanization, urban renewal, and the development of enormous cities in the Third World.

According to an international survey of mayors undertaken by the United Nations Development Program, the number-one urban problem in the world today is unemployment. The second-most serious problem is insufficient solid waste disposal; the third—which may be related to unemployment—is poverty. Many of the high-profile social problems people associate with urban centres—crime, poverty, and racial segregation, for instance—are found in rural areas as well, though these problems are especially pronounced in cities.

Contrasting Images of Urban Life

The earliest sociological theories about cities and city life—by Ferdinand Tönnies, Louis Wirth, Georg Simmel, and others—were first developed more than a century ago. Tönnies (1957 [1887]) asked, "What social bonds tie together people in small, stable communities, compared with large, fluid communities?" For Tönnies, the movement from rural to city life meant a loss of *Gemeinschaft*—the characteristics typical of rural and small-town life, including a stable, homogeneous group of residents with a strong attachment to one particular place (Brint, 2001). Socially, *Gemeinschaft* is characterized by dense networks, centralized and controlling elites, multiple social ties, intimacy, and emotional meaning. With everyone constantly viewing each other's behaviour, someone deviating from the prevailing social norms would feel social pressures to conform.

In contrast, Tönnies notes, the ties among people in a city take the form of *Gesellschaft*. In urban settings, residents have different personal histories and impersonal, brief relationships. They interact around similar interests, not similar characteristics, moralities,

MY WINNIPEG

In this acclaimed 2007 documentary, director Guy Maddin explores the peculiarities of the history, development, and character of his hometown of Winnipeg.

Gemeinschaft Social situations in which those involved treat one another as ends rather than as means; primary relationships based on sentiment, found most often in rural life.

Gesellschaft Social situations in which those involved treat one another as means rather than as ends; secondary relations based primarily on calculation and individual interest, found most often in city life.

or histories. Social networks in cities are less connected, less centralized, less cliquish, and less redundant.

Following Tönnies's lead, early American sociology considered cities to be anonymous and stressful. In his article "Urbanism as a Way of Life," Louis Wirth (1996 [1938]) explained that cities unavoidably foster less social integration or cohesion than smaller communities because of their huge population size, variety, and fluidity (Vortkamp, 1998; Otte and Baur, 2008). A large population ensures that most people will not know one another; nor will they feel tied to one another in ways that control deviance and support co-operation. A high degree of variety—in values, norms, and interests—can create confusion if not outright conflict when irresolvable differences collide. *Fluidity* means people are forced into many interactions with strangers.

To partially offset the confusion of these interactions, people develop means of control—informally, by social norms of behaviour, such as distancing and civil inattention, and formally, through such institutions as the police—to deal with socially unacceptable behaviour or to tame strangers in public places.

The German sociologist Georg Simmel (1950 [1917]) was among the first to sense how life in a large city affects people psychologically and emotionally. City life is too stimulating, Simmel wrote. Strangers surround us on all sides. We experience countless strange noises, smells, sights, dangers, and opportunities. Walking a city street, we must pay constant attention to our environment. In the end, sensation overload takes its toll on our nervous systems (Haussermann, 2005; Miller and Phillips, 2005).

Research supports at least some of these suppositions. City life is more costly, arousing, and engaging than in a small town, and the tempo of life is faster in a large city. People walk faster, talk faster, and even eat faster, mostly because more people must crowd into the same spaces every hour. City people also make more noise: the larger the city, the more car horns there are for irritated people to honk and the more ambulance and police sirens are heard day and night. In these various ways—through isolation and stresses on mental health—the city enslaves people who may have expected to gain freedom through city life.

The History of Urbanization

Contrary to what some people might first imagine, cities existed thousands of years ago. Babylon, Jerusalem, Byzantium, Alexandria, Athens, and Rome were large and important cities in the pre-modern era. The Maya and Inca, in Central and South America, developed large city-states, and nearly 1,000 years ago, Cahokia, in present-day Illinois, "had a population estimated at 30,000 to 40,000" and "was bigger [in extent] than contemporaneous London, England" (Dickason, 2002: 29). Paris, London, Venice, and Florence were established as world cities long before massive economic developments in the late eighteenth century kick-started rapid urbanization, the process by which a large portion of the human population came to shift from rural to urban homes.

Urbanization The growth in the proportion of the population living in urbanized areas. There is also an increasing appearance in rural and small-town areas of behaviour patterns and cultural values associated with big-city life.

However, modern cities are new in human history, only a few centuries old. With the rise of the urban mode of life came a focus on efficiency, high standards of living, liberty, diversity, and innovative ideas and lifestyles. Modern cities are a prime example of a social organizational strategy, an organic solution to the problem of how to co-ordinate a growing human population. Simply, modern cities are creative efforts by humans to deal with large numbers of varied, mobile people concentrated in a small space. So far, however, a great many of the organizational strategies devised by city governments have been flawed. These flaws have resulted in problems such as overcrowding, epidemics, sanitation issues, inner-city poverty, housing shortages and homelessness, traffic and noise problems, and a tension-filled pace of life.

Statistics Canada defines an "urban area" as one with a population of at least 1,000 and no fewer than 400 persons per square kilometre. All territory outside an urban area is considered rural. The term used for "cities" in Canada is "census metropolitan area (CMA)," defined as a region with an urban core population of at least 100,000.

While these definitions suffice for Canada, they do not apply as well to other nations. In heavily populated countries such as India, for example, virtually all areas have a density of more than 400 persons per square kilometre, yet many do not display any other characteristics associated with "urban" life. For these countries, the criteria for "urban" versus "rural" may require a higher density or may include other factors, such as economic (agricultural or non-agricultural) output. When comparing across countries or reporting on regional or global trends, the United Nations simply allows "urban" to carry whatever meaning each nation gives it. In Japan, for example, an urban area has at least 50,000 people, but in Norway a centre with 200 inhabitants is considered urban (Norton, 2010: 439).

One of the central concerns voiced about urbanization is its association with population growth rates—with how quickly the population is increasing from one year to the next. This issue is troubling because large, rapid growth rates demand flexibility and ingenuity on the part of our political leaders, who need to respond creatively with new housing, jobs, schools, and services. As the data in Figure 14.3 show, of all the large, major industrial nations, Canada currently faces the biggest problem of this kind.

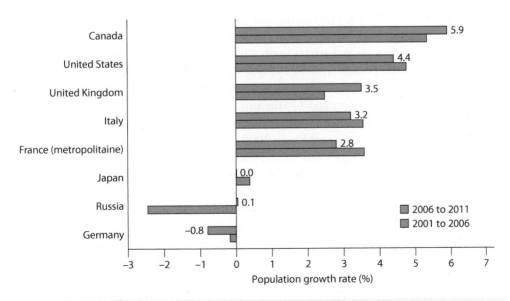

| **FIGURE 14.3** | Population Growth Rate (in percentage) of the G8 Countries, 2001–2006 and 2006–2011 |

Source: Statistics Canada, The Canadian Population in 2011: Population Counts and Growth, at: <www12.statcan.gc.ca/census-recensement/2011/as-sa/98-310-x/98-310-x2011001-eng.pdf>.

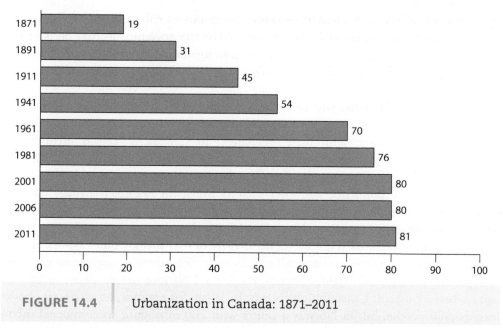

FIGURE 14.4   Urbanization in Canada: 1871–2011

Source: Human Resources and Skills Development Canada, Canadians in Context—Geographic Distribution, at: <www4.hrsdc.gc.ca/.3ndic.1t.4r@-eng.jsp?iid=34>.

What is most remarkable is how very quickly the world's population has urbanized. Canada, for example, has gone from only 19 per cent urban-dwellers in 1871 to just over 80 per cent today (Figure 14.4).

Many consider the twenty-first century humanity's first "urban century," a consequence mainly of the pace of urbanization in the developing world (United Nations Population Division, 2006). Historically, the emergence of cities has reflected an increasing complexity in regional development. Cities, as we have learned, are economic engines. They foster new businesses and attract foreign investments and tourists. The development of cities in the world's poorer regions, then, is a promising sign of economic growth.

The pace of urban growth in the developing world is outstripping the ability of many local and state governments to provide the infrastructure (e.g., the roads and communication networks) needed to house, employ, and support the influx of people into their cities (Jung et al., 2009; Sahoo and Dash, 2009). Many cities are experiencing the serious social and health hazards associated with overcrowding, poor sanitation, slum developments, and a lack of clean water—the same urban problems that plagued Western industrial nations in the eighteenth and nineteenth centuries. In addition, many megacities are expanding chaotically, without any co-ordinated urban planning or management.

A lack of overall vision will likely increase urban problems in the future. Already, seven of the ten largest cities in the world are located in developing countries. By 2050, it is estimated that Tokyo will be the only urban centre on that list from the developed world; India alone will have three cities in the top 10.

Suburbanization

In North America, the period of prosperity following World War II changed the urban landscape dramatically. During the post-war economic boom, spending and birth rates were high, unemployment was low, and families prospered. The affordability of the auto-mobile led to the purchase of homes outside the urban core in the 1940s and 1950s, causing land developers to extend residential housing into outlying regions. In this way, the modern suburb was born.

Suburbanization is the process by which lower-density housing spreads into once-rural regions surrounding the city core. This process greatly expanded the geographic size of cities. For instance, Chicago's population has increased only 4 per cent in the past 20 years, yet its spatial geography increased by 46 per cent between 1980 and 2000.

The first people to move to the suburbs were mainly wealthy middle- to upper-class whites (Fortin et al., 2008; Poulton, 2007). This movement intensified the racial and ethnic segregation of minorities in urban centres. Further, as wealthier residents migrated to the outskirts of the city, their property taxes went with them, leaving the city's centre with less revenue for schools, roads, and other services. Then, as now, suburbanites who work in the city use the city's services, such as road, water, and sewer systems, but do not pay for them. As a result, while the suburbs flourished amid a surplus of property tax income, downtown areas stagnated and dried up.

> **Suburbanization** The process by which housing spreads almost unhindered into once-rural regions surrounding the city core. This greatly expands the geographic size of cities and takes out of production valuable agricultural land, and there is a noticeable shift of the affluent out of the urban centre and into these surrounding areas.

The Importance of Neighbours and Neighbourhoods

Tönnies was wrong to suppose that cities lack communities or community sentiments, or that city-dwellers would not care about such sentiments. As sociologist Claude Fischer showed, cities are collections of communities, each with its own subculture.

People want to live alongside others whom they consider to be similar to themselves. Largely as a result of that tendency, residential segregation by race, ethnicity, and social class is a common feature of life in North American cities (Emerson et al., 2001; Westaway, 2007) and has an enormous impact on people's social relations and social identities. This voluntary sorting of people into urban communities based on culture, language, ethnicity, and income, and on the resulting distinct identities, is a major source of Canada's continuing multiculturalism. It is also an antidote to the randomizing, anonymizing effects of large cities.

Despite the tendencies of mass education and the mass media to make everyone similar, neighbours and neighbourhoods are still important today as sources of personal identity and difference. The importance that people attach to their neighbourhoods can be seen in reactions of NIMBYism ("not in my backyard") under certain circumstances—for example, to the placement in their neighbourhood of economic refugees, homeless persons with co-morbid disorders, halfway houses, or treatment facilities for recovering drug addicts (Young, 2012; van Alphen et al., 2011). Largely, it is because cities are *not* agglomerations of undifferentiated strangers, and because people feel so strongly about keeping strangers and people unlike themselves at a distance that cities have trouble solving typical problems such as homelessness and fear of victimization.

In many cities of the world, and certainly in Canada's largest cities, homelessness is a big and growing problem. It is, often, a problem we prefer to ignore, but it is hard to ignore when—as in Box 14.2—we put faces and names to the people who experience homelessness.

For people who live in houses, neighbours and neighbourhoods continue to be important. Some of the problems associated with neighbours and neighbourhoods—such as traffic, crowding, and turnover—we discuss later in this chapter. They are charac-teristic of all cities—large and small, whether in the West or in less-developed countries.

> **IN AMERICA**
>
> Jim Sheridan's powerful 2002 story depicts the trying lives of an aspiring actor and his family in a depressed neighbourhood in New York City.

BOX 14.2   Homeless in the City: Bruce Lived Here

When the police and bylaw officers arrive, Bruce has some of his goods spread out and a jar of peanut butter open beneath the canopy of a cherry tree at Old Riverside Park. His cart nearby is precariously loaded with an assortment of black plastic bags containing his collectables. When approached by Abbotsford Police officers Sgt Doug Sage and Const. Shaun Nagel, his reaction is muted. He's gone through the process before. He has been living in the green space adjacent to Chief Dan George Middle School and a nearby church for some time.

The city has received complaints, and Const. Nagel has already had a conversation with him a week or so ago about moving his camp to a less conspicuous location.

Bruce is given 48 hours to move all his goods or city workers will. The bylaw officer staples a red removal warning poster to the tree trunk. The police officers offer to contact the Salvation Army, and they ask Bruce if he has somewhere he can stay. He had a room last summer but he had to leave because he had too much stuff. This time he's going to take his belongings to a storage locker. He does not take the offer of shelter.

As they leave the park, both officers say they have dealt with Bruce before. The 62-year-old former civil servant has been living rough for close to a decade.

He poses the obvious question: just what neighbourhood should [homeless people] be moved to? "It's not against the law to be a drug addict." The city has a standard protocol when it comes to camp removal. Homeless camps are usually reported to bylaw officers by the parks department or citizens. If they are inhabited, the Salvation Army is contacted and its outreach workers connect with the individuals before any enforcement action. If the camp is still not evacuated, the bylaw officers post a warning. When the camp is cleaned up, workers are accompanied by police and outreach workers who advocate for the occupants.

Nicole Giguere, with the Salvation Army, says if someone doesn't opt to take shelter, they are encouraged to at least come back for a shower and a meal.

There are a variety of reasons people don't want to move into the shelter, says Giguere. They don't want to leave their belongings, they don't feel safe in a room of strangers, or they have mental health or addictions issues. People often stay in camp because they can't use drugs while at a shelter. Giguere would like to see more mental health workers, especially those who do outreach work on the streets, funding to allow single-room shelter beds, and more low-barrier housing.

In trying to deal with homelessness and establish affordable housing, the city is tackling problems it doesn't necessarily have the resources for.

"Property taxes were never intended to deliver social services. Homelessness is really a problem of the provincial or federal governments. The city is doing what it can by donating valuable land to support housing projects, but the demand is so high it's really difficult to meet the needs. We're stretched . . . but it doesn't mean we'll quit trying."

Source: Baker (2009).

What does require discussion now is the connection between neighbourhood and social inequality, as well as the geography of what sociologists call "social capital." Put simply, most people lead most of their lives within neighbourhoods. This is particularly true of schoolchildren, homemakers, retired people, unemployed people, and chronically ill people (or shut-ins). This means that their life experience will be shaped dramatically by the quality of the neighbourhood in which they live—by whether it has good schools, good shopping facilities, well-kept homes and parks, safe roads, good sewage facilities, easy proximity to transportation, hospitals, and social services, and so on.

People whose neighbourhoods lack these advantages are effectively disadvantaged; their lives are diminished in quality. This is made even worse if their neighbourhood is dangerous, with high rates of criminal victimization and poor policing (Platt, 2009). People who live in such neighbourhoods are less likely to feel safe in, or make use of, public space. This diminishes their social life and their range of social contacts. It diminishes

Children playing hockey on an outdoor rink in Fairmont Park, Ottawa. The presence of a safe park with a skating rink in this neighbourhood is indicative of its social capital. The children in this photo are advantaged because of where they live.

their confidence in government and trust in neighbours. People who live in socially and economically unequal neighbourhoods will have different life experiences, regardless of their own social and economic characteristics. This fact is amply clear among racial minorities who live together in segregated neighbourhoods, regardless of education or social class.

Neighbourhood Effects

Do neighbourhood features affect people's lives and, if so, how? This question is the subject of heated international debate among sociologists, geographers, and policy-makers.

The first problem, of course, is to define what we mean by a "neighbourhood." French sociologist Jean-Yves Authier (2008) asserts that the contemporary city neighbourhood is "neither dying, nor the only place of living, nor a 'village within the city' unifying its inhabitants in multiple social networks, nor the place of all disadvantages." A neighbourhood is, however, the "geographic unit that produces socially and spatially differentiated experiences of city living." Therefore, it is very important in people's lives.

Four broad questions relate to the "neighbourhood effect" issue: (1) Is there a strong relation between housing mix and social mix? (2) How does the social composition of neighbourhoods affect residents' social interaction and behaviour? (3) Do neighbourhoods structure the social opportunities of individual residents? And if so, (4) to what extent is this produced through neighbourhood social interaction?

Most researchers hypothesize that neighbourhood effects are less pronounced in countries like Sweden, for example, where planning practices, social-class differences, segregation patterns, and welfare state regulations differ significantly from those in countries like the US. However, empirical studies confirm the existence of neighbourhood effects even in Sweden (Andersson, 2008; Urban, 2009).

Measurement problems hinder research on this topic, however. Six major challenges confront statistical researchers seeking to measure the independent effect of neighbourhood context on individuals: they must (1) define the scale of "neighbourhood"; (2) identify mechanisms of neighbourhood effect; (3) measure appropriate neighbourhood characteristics; (4) measure exposure to neighbourhood; (5) measure appropriate individual characteristics; and (6) deal with endogeneity (the entanglement of causal variables). To surmount these challenges, sociologists are increasingly turning to datasets with multi-domain measures of neighbourhood characteristics and statistical models for testing neighbourhood effects that consider residential group, density of local social interactions, and duration of residency (Galster, 2008).

Geographers, too, are discussing these problems of measurement. There has been considerable discussion in health geography of the effects of neighbourhood on health: the idea that people's health in one geographical area may be influenced not only by the composition of that area's population, but also by the area's geographical context. For example, Burdette and Hill (2008) claim that as neighbourhood disorder and disorganization increase, so do rates of obesity within the community. This claim supports past research suggesting that residents of neighbourhoods characterized by socio-economic disadvantage, social disorganization, and disorder tend to exhibit increased rates of obesity, relative to the wider population (ibid.).

However, although neighbourhoods and their boundaries are sometimes obvious to local residents, researchers often disagree on the size and contents of a neighbourhood. As well, findings may differ substantially according to how the data are combined. For this reason, some believe that we should look at the effect of neighbourhood conditions by using several different ways to define neighbourhoods, for the size and composition of these neighbourhoods may be different in different parts of a study area (Flowerdew et al., 2008).

Individual Effects versus Neighbourhood Effects

Some supposed "neighbourhood effects" might be due to the kinds of people who collect in certain neighbourhoods. If so, "neighbourhood problems" are due to the characteristics of the inhabitants, not the neighbourhood per se (Schieman, 2009). This may be especially important if, through migration, some neighbourhoods attract disadvantaged people and lose advantaged ones. Therefore, we must examine the role of individual- versus neighbourhood-level variables and the role of migration in shaping neighbourhood characteristics.

Consider childhood accidents: are they a result of neighbourhood influences, family influences, or the characteristics of individual children? Reading et al. (2008), using data from the Avon (UK) Longitudinal Study of Parents and Children, examined information about accidents as well as extensive social, health, and developmental data throughout the first five years of life. This information was combined with census and geographical data to identify neighbourhood influences on accident risks. The data analysis found a small but statistically significant amount of between-neighbourhood variance in accident risk, especially for accidents resulting in injury that needed medical attention. However, this variation between neighbourhoods was accounted for by various individual, parental, and household factors. Conclusion: apparent differences in accident risk between neighbourhoods are explained by the geographical clustering of similar types of (accident-prone) children, families, and households.

Alternatively, consider health behaviours: are they a result of neighbourhood influences, family influences, or individual characteristics? Duke-Williams and Shelton (2008), using data from the London (UK) boroughs of Camden and Islington, studied obesity, alcohol intake, smoking, walking, and self-rated health. Irrespective of the boundary definition, between-area inequalities were small compared with inequalities between individuals. Further, alternative definitions of the neighbourhood boundaries had little effect on the estimates of these neighbourhood inequalities.

Neighbourhood composition is mainly shaped by migration, and different people are more or less likely to migrate. People who can move when and where they wish tend to seek out others like themselves. As a result, they are usually happy with where they live. Such moves are often—perhaps usually—the result of hopes and plans. On the other hand, people who are unable to move usually adapt themselves to where they must live; they take satisfaction where they find it.

Evidence of Neighbourhood Effects

Despite the dangers of overestimating them, researchers continue to find evidence of **neighbourhood effects**. This should not surprise us: many people develop important relationships with their neighbours, and these relationships can be fulfilling. Considerable evidence in the psychology and sociology literature shows that social relationships promote happiness for the individual. But how big and important are these effects?

To measure them, Powdthavee (2008) used "shadow pricing" to estimate the monetary value of the life satisfaction gained by an increase in the frequency of interaction with friends, relatives, and neighbours. Using the British Household Panel Survey, he estimated that an increase in social involvements could be worth as much as £85,000 a year in greater life satisfaction. Actual rises in income, by contrast, buy very little satisfaction.

If neighbours make a difference, then, the quality of neighbourhood should make a difference. Take a simple case of neighbourhood effect: that of freshmen students in colleges. Ehrmann and Massey (2008), using data from the National Longitudinal Survey of Freshmen, found that male students residing on campus are exposed to higher levels of violence and disorder than females during their first year of college. Even though the harmful neighbourhood effects on academic performance appear to be stronger for females than males, male grades are more influenced by this campus neighbourhood effect because relatively few female students experience high exposure to violence and social disorder at college.

Other aspects of health and well-being are also reportedly affected by neighbourhood. Wright and Muhajarine (2008), noting that respiratory illness is a significant cause of infant mortality, examined the relationship between neighbourhood-level variables and rates of respiratory illness for children less than two years old born in Saskatoon between 1992 and 1994. They found that rates of respiratory illness, as measured by proportion of children hospitalized and frequency of hospitalization and ambulatory visits to doctors, are higher among infants who live in socially disadvantaged neighbourhoods.

Neighbourhood effects Influences on people's lives that result from living in one type of neighbourhood (e.g., rich versus poor, or dangerous versus safe) rather than another.

Is life in a largely same-race neighbourhood good for emotional well-being? Yuan (2008) explored this question using a random sample of Illinois residents. He found that living in a largely same-race neighbourhood does indeed improve the emotional well-being of blacks and Hispanics. Mainly, this is because of greater social support provided by others of the same race (especially among blacks). Thus, neighbourhoods confer not only economic resources to their residents, but social and emotional resources as well. These benefits or resources are sometimes called "social capital."

Consider how neighbourhood social capital affects the health of adult female caregivers. Carpiano (2008), using data from the Los Angeles Family and Neighborhood Survey, showed that specific types of social capital are directly associated with positive and negative health outcomes. For example, a female caregiver's social network can promote good health or damage it, depending on whether social contacts provide support or, by demanding support, deplete personal resources.

Alternatively, consider how neighbourhood disadvantage—as measured by levels of concentrated poverty, residential instability, and immigrant concentration—affects the likelihood of early adolescent sexual activity. Using a sample of youth, ages 11–16, from the Project on Human Development in Chicago, Browning et al. (2008) found evidence that neighbourhood disadvantage increases the likelihood of adolescent higher-risk sexual activity—for example, having two or more sexual partners versus one sexual partner (risky because it increases the chance of sexually transmitted diseases).

Neighbourhood influences are not only strong, they are also persistent. Because of persistent neighbourhood stratification, the racial inequality in America's neighbourhoods that existed a generation ago has been transmitted, almost unchanged, to the present day.

Combinations of Individual, Familial, and Neighbourhood Effects

In social science, most outcomes are a result of multiple influences—individual, familial, and institutional—and this is just as true of neighbourhood influences. They combine or interact with social variables working at different micro- and macrosociological levels.

So, for example, Button (2008) reports that approval of family violence is both an individual-level and neighbourhood-level phenomenon. Neighbourhood features such as social disorganization, crime, and collective efficacy, in addition to the individual factors of gender, race, and a history of child maltreatment, all influence the acceptability of using violence within the family.

Not only do neighbourhood influences combine with other factors to produce victimization and misbehaviour, they also combine to produce arrests. The different neighbourhood contexts in which diverse racial and ethnic groups live lead to variations in criminal outcomes. To show this, Kirk (2008) combined individual-level data with contextual data from the Project on Human Development in Chicago Neighborhoods (PHDCN). Findings reveal that black youths face multiple layers of disadvantage relative to other racial and ethnic groups, and these layers work to create differences in arrests.

At the family level, unstable families explain much of the disparity in arrests across race and ethnicity. At the neighbourhood level, significantly higher levels of concentrated poverty and lower levels of collective efficacy disadvantage black youth compared to white youth. That said, even after accounting for relevant demographic, family, and neighbourhood-level predictors, large residual arrest differences remain between black youths and youths of other racial and ethnic groups, perhaps pointing to discrimination.

Neighbourhood influences also combine with other factors to produce poor health. Drawing on four waves of the Changing Lives Study conducted in the US, Yao and Robert (2008) examined the contributions of individual and neighbourhood socio-economic status to explain racial disparities in self-rated health trajectories among black and white older adults. The results show that black older adults have greater declines in self-rated health over time than white older adults, and these disparities are explained by individual and neighbourhood socio-economic status (SES). Yet, there is another cost to blackness not captured otherwise: black disadvantage in mortality exists at older ages and persists regardless of social class or income. These results suggest that racial and socio-economic disparities in self-rated health and mortality persist throughout old age and that individual and neighbourhood socio-economic context—as well as race—contribute to perpetuating these disparities.

As always, perceptions are important—as important as "objective reality" in their effects on people's well-being. Individuals' views of where they live may provide some clues to help us better understand the influence of place on outcomes. Muhajarine et al. (2008) presented findings from an analysis that incorporates the subjective responses to their local environment of individuals living in three socially contrasting neighbourhoods. The researchers found that both perceived neighbourhood characteristics and individual socio-demographic factors are significant correlates of self-rated health and quality of life. Besides, the type of perceived neighbourhood characteristics and the extent of their influence on self-rated health and quality of life vary depending on whether the respondents live in high- or low-SES neighbourhoods.

Findings on the effects of neighbourhoods in Canada are different in some respects from those in the United States. In Saskatoon, household exposure to concentrated poverty is substantially less than in the US (Oreopoulos, 2008). However, the available evidence suggests that, within nations, neighbourhood effects may work the same way as discussed above.

Policy Implications

What, then, are the policy implications of this research on the effects of neighbourhood on well-being? Ambitious work is being done on this issue in Saskatoon by a multi-disciplinary group of social scientists funded by the Social Sciences and Humanities Research Council of Canada.

The University of Saskatchewan's Community-University Institute for Social Research (CUISR) has taken a multi-stakeholder approach to the ongoing sustainability of Saskatoon as a healthy city with an improving and a more equitably distributed quality of life (Williams et al., 2008). Using quantitative and qualitative analysis, researchers have examined the quality of life in three Saskatoon neighbourhoods, representing low, middle, and high socio-economic status in both 2001 and 2004. The project is committed to publishing its findings far beyond the usual academic channels: (1) by engaging local media on a consistent basis; (2) by holding community forums to ensure community co-operation; (3) by helping the work of a steering committee; and (4) by employing an action researcher as a policy entrepreneur.

A part of this process has been the City of Saskatoon's Local Area Planning (LAP) Program, a community-based approach to developing comprehensive neighbourhood plans (Kellett et al., 2008). So far, 11 LAPs have been adopted by City Council and over 200 recommendations have been approved. Resources have been earmarked to co-ordinate implementation, to facilitate work with communities, and to help carry out the various recommendations. In addition, over 1,000 people representing various interests have engaged in one or more LAP committee or implementation meeting. In these ways, partnerships have been formed, program and service delivery has been improved, and, most importantly, communities have taken ownership of their plans.

The LAP communities, City Council, and city planners have committed themselves to measuring changes and progress in the LAP communities. In recognition of this, Saskatoon's City Planning Branch has been working with LAP communities, the CUISR, and other stakeholders to develop a framework for statistically measuring changes in LAP communities and to monitor "Neighbourhood Success Factors." The Neighbourhood Success Factors have worked to detect negative socio-economic conditions before they reach a point of crisis.

Theoretical Perspectives on Urban Life

Structural Functionalism

Some structural functionalists would view social problems in the city as resulting natur-ally from growth and specialization. For example, more wealth in cities typically means more theft and robbery; higher density equals more intense competition for resources; and more privacy translates into more private vice, such as drug use.

Other structural functionalists focus on those tendencies of the city—its size, variety, and fluidity in particular—that promote social disorganization, weak social controls, and consequent deviance and distress. From this perspective, social problems such as crime,

TABLE 14.2	Theoretical Perspectives
THEORY	**MAIN POINTS**
Structural Functionalism	• Malthus argued that excess population would lead to human disasters (e.g., war, plague, and starvation) that would reduce the excess. • Demographic transition theory argues that high fertility rates decline to establish a new level of population equilibrium. • Too rapid urban growth produces disorganization, crowding, and stress.
Conflict Theory	• "Overpopulation" is a myth, and the problem is an unequal distribution of wealth. • High rates of population growth produce conflicts over scarce territory and resources. • Cities contain neighbourhoods of greater and lesser comfort, as well as homeless people.
Symbolic Interactionism	• Cities are not undifferentiated masses of people but neighbourhoods containing distinctive subcultures. • We all have to learn how to live effectively in cities, using urban etiquette (e.g., civil inattention).
Social Constructionism	• The manufacture of concerns about crowding and population pressure reflect antagonism to poor and racial minorities.

addiction, and mental illness are foreseeable consequences of urbanization. They are functional in the sense that they are the normal price to be paid for the positive aspects of city life; they contribute to the survival of the city by promoting integrative reactions.

Pre-industrial societies were mainly small, rural settlements in which members shared the same experiences and developed similar values, norms, and identities. Émile Durkheim (1964 [1893]) called this *common (or collective) conscience*. Besides, the lives of these people were often interconnected in a tight, homogeneous social order, which Durkheim called **mechanical solidarity**. The new social order was based on interdependent, though not necessarily intimate, relationships. Under this **organic solidarity**, no member of society was self-sufficient; all people were dependent on others for survival and prosperity.

Mechanical solidarity
Durkheim's term for the kind of tight, homogeneous social order typical of a pre-industrial, primarily rural society.

Organic solidarity
Durkheim's term for the new social order of industrial society, which was based on interdependent, though not necessarily intimate, relationships.

Conflict Theory

Unlike functionalists, conflict theorists always ask whose interests are served by the actions of dominant groups in society and by their ideology. These theorists attribute urban problems such as homelessness and poverty not to the effects of size, variety, and fluidity, but to the workings of capitalism. By their reckoning, cities suffer problems because it is in no powerful group's interest to prevent this from happening.

Unlike functionalists, conflict theorists also believe that solving urban problems will require more than simply addressing economic stagnation. Unequal power, competing class interests, capital investment decisions, and government subsidy programs mediate the growth of cities. The distribution of urban wealth—not merely its creation—determines whether the majority of city-dwellers will live or die, stay or leave. The flight of well-off residents from the inner city to distant suburbs suggests a lack of interest in solving these problems among those who have the power to do so.

Symbolic Interactionism

Symbolic interactionists study the ways people experience city life on an everyday basis. One of the earliest writers to take this approach was Georg Simmel (1950 [1917]). Others, such as Herbert Gans (1982), have focused on how the meaning of city life varies among groups and subcultures.

A subculture is a group of people who share some cultural traits of the larger society but who, as a group, also have their own distinctive values, beliefs, norms, style of dress, and behaviour. Subculture membership allows individuals who are otherwise isolated within an impersonal city to form connections with their neighbours. An ethnic community is an example of a subculture, as are skinheads and youth gangs. The corporate elites, who have determined the future of urban areas, are also, by this view, a subculture.

SLACKER
Richard Linklater's 1991 Generation-X drama explores a hip, sophisticated subculture of unemployed "slackers" in Austin, Texas.

Social Constructionism

Social constructionists, as we have seen, study the ways social issues are brought to public attention or are kept from public view. Issues are brought to attention or hidden through the various techniques we have discussed throughout the book, most notably, agenda-setting, creating moral panics, and using scientific "evidence" selectively to highlight certain parts of a story.

These techniques of social construction are evident in at least two of the topics we discuss in this chapter. First, they have been widely used to excite or tranquilize public opinion over issues around population growth and overpopulation. In the 1950s and 1960s, concerns about overpopulation were widespread, culminating in the famous Club of Rome study *Limits to Growth* (discussed later in this book). Today, concerns about overpopulation have largely dropped out of sight, only partly because birth rates have continued to fall throughout the world. The public has wearied of this topic and focuses on others, such as issues around environmental pollution and the economy.

Second, these techniques have been used in relation to issues of power in urban settings. We see continued jockeying for power between the major core cities, their suburban peripheries, and the provincial and federal governments. These issues concern taxation, planning, and responsibility for delivering services to urban residents. They are expressed in battles over transportation (e.g., who should pay for the road system that allows commuters to come downtown to work every day) and education (e.g., who should fund inner-city schools that bear the greatest costs of large-scale immigration). On all of these issues, certain themes are highlighted where others are ignored or distorted, to gain political advantage.

Social Consequences of Population Growth and Urbanization

Sprawl

Gentrification The restoration and upgrading of deteriorated urban property by middle-class or affluent people, often resulting in displacement of lower-income people.

Some social scientists have attacked urban sprawl as an inefficient and ineffective urban form that contributes to many of the social problems we discuss in this book; **gentrification**—the revitalization of inner-city neighbourhoods—has been touted as one solution to the outward spreading of cities (see Box 14.3). Others have accepted sprawl as a new paradigm in today's urban life.

Public Issues *and* Public Policy

BOX 14.3 | The Two Sides of Neighbourhood Gentrification

Gentrification is the process whereby established working-class neighbourhoods, usually in the inner city, are converted into middle- and upper-class neighbourhoods. This is typically accomplished through the renovation of existing buildings and landscapes and the introduction of businesses and services catering to higher-income residents. The process results in higher property values and taxes and the gradual displacement of the poor.

For some, gentrification is an essentially positive force, an economic, social, and aesthetic "rehabilitation" of a once run-down, stagnant neighbourhood. Although the dislocation of the relatively poor is usually acknowledged by the defenders of gentrification, this social cost is justified by the salvation of valuable real estate,

the injection of private investments, and resuscitation of the local tax base. For others, the process is tinged with class discrimination, a type of economic genocide in which the vibrant and diverse working-class collectives of artists, labourers, and ethnic minorities are pushed out of their communities, replaced by banal middle-class interests (Atkinson, 2003). Often, the poor are forced to relocate in less desirable neighbourhoods, resulting in the further segregation and concentration of poverty (Fong and Shibuya, 2000). Ironically, as the urban boom continues to reverse the residential trends of the past half-century, the suburban pockets surrounding the revitalized central core are becoming the new "undesirable" neighbourhoods.

The Canadian Press/Jeff McIntosh

Urban sprawl on the outer limits of Calgary.

Urban sprawl is most often characterized as haphazard or unplanned growth, resulting in undesirable land-use patterns. It includes such patterns as scattered development, "leapfrog" development, strip or ribbon development, and continuous low-density development. In Canadian cities, large low-density, low-rise bedroom suburbs dotted by strip malls, shopping centres, and industrial parks epitomize suburban sprawl, and much of the nation's best agricultural land has been and continues to be lost under urban sprawl (Alasia et al., 2009; Ghitter and Smart, 2009).

More than any other single factor, the automobile allowed suburbanization to take place by making it possible for residents to commute long distances every day between where they lived and where they worked. The vast highway programs of the 1950s and 1960s fostered massive migration to the suburbs and a corresponding deterioration of urban centres, though more so in the United States than in Canada (Wassmer, 2008; Johnson and Schmidt, 2009).

The prevalence of auto-centred transport systems largely determines a nation's pattern of transportation and urban sprawl (Squires, 2008). Today, many developing nations are adopting Western standards of "automobility" but face unique problems such as unequal access, inadequate roads, and the cost of importing oil. These nations represent an emerging market for automobiles as well as an environmental threat. China, for example, faces a shortage of arable land—a situation that will be further compromised by auto-centred transport systems. Similar problems beset South Africa, Mexico, India, and other countries.

Los Angeles is a particularly vivid and well-known example of the sprawl problem. The history of California has been characterized by spectacular growth in all aspects: population, economic output, housing construction, and the global impact of its cultural values (Wrobel, 2008). Yet, this growth has come at the price of sprawl and traffic congestion, distressed older neighbourhoods, air pollution, inadequate urban services, water shortages, and a decline in quality of life (Pastor et al., 2004).

Not everyone criticizes this outcome or sees it as a failure to achieve another kind of order. Some view the evolution of economics, politics, and culture in

Los Angeles—historically depicted as outside the mainstream of US urban culture—as having successfully created a new style of urban life. In contrast to the Chicago School, this emerging Los Angeles School of urban sociology regards LA as a model for many of the emerging urban centres in North America and around the world, all of them characterized by dispersed patterns of low-density growth, multicultural and ethnic enclaves, and an array of urban centres in a single region (Dear, 2003; Gilbert and Wehr, 2003).

Traffic

Another major problem mainly affecting urban centres in both the developed and developing world is vehicular traffic (Fazal, 2006). At present, many car users choose the car over alternative modes of transport because it is more convenient and saves time, and because public transport, even when it is a feasible alternative, is deemed bothersome. In most North American cities, cars are given priority over pedestrians or bicycles, as reflected, for instance, in the parking space devoted to cars.

In Paris and Amsterdam, two cities famous for their metropolitan charm and pedestrian-friendly streetscapes, there is only one parking space for every three people living in the central area. By contrast, Houston, with its sprawling web of highways slicing through the urban core, allots 30 spaces per resident. This reflects consumption patterns as well: consider that the parking lots of major suburban shopping centres are now larger than the malls themselves.

The problems related to traffic are many. Hundreds of thousands of people worldwide suffer death or injury in traffic-related accidents each year. Generally, traffic accidents are caused by our increased dependence on automobiles and the supremacy of the automobile over social space. When auto traffic is dense, as in cities, accidents are bound to occur. However, human behaviour is also to blame.

For instance, the use of cellphones by drivers unnecessarily increases the risk of a collision 4 to16 times (Kalkhoff et al., 2009). An analysis of 699 drivers who were involved in motor vehicle collisions that caused substantial property damage but no personal injury found that 24 per cent had used a cellular telephone during the 10-minute period before the collision.

Congestion is another problem caused by traffic. Canadians are travelling farther and farther to get to their workplaces; in 2011, for example, workers in census metropolitan areas travelled on average 25.4 minutes to work. In more densely populated regions, travel times were much longer: Toronto (32.8), Oshawa (31.8), and Montreal (29.7). Not surprisingly, as commuting distances increase, more workers choose to drive rather than to take public transit or other modes of transportation (e.g., bicycles, walking). However, even when the distance to work is less than five kilometres, the car remains favoured over any other single mode of transportation. Moreover, as the rate of growth of new work opportunities in suburban areas outpaces the growth in downtown business districts, more and more workers are travelling across town to get to work, a journey they usually make by car. In most large metropolitan areas, as many as 90 per cent of workers commute by car, either as a driver or passenger, when their job is located 20 or more kilometres outside of the city centre.

Traffic also interferes with people's enjoyment of their neighbourhoods. The high-speed, multi-lane roads that cut through residential areas are often too dangerous for children to cross alone, resulting in their dependence on parents to drive them

CANADIAN researcher

BOX 14.4 | **Susan Machum, St Thomas University**

Professor Susan Machum is a Canada Research Chair Rural Social Justice from St Thomas University. Her work focuses on how rural communities respond to the opportunities and challenges farmers face as they adapt to meet local needs rather than export markets. Her work also examines the effect of policy on farm household income and livelihood. In a 2005 article titled "The Persistence of Family Farming in the Wake of Agribusiness: A New Brunswick, Canada Case Study," Susan conducted a series of semi-structured interviews of dairy and potato farmers in order to explore how and why small farms have persevered in a global competitive market. She argues that small rural farms employ several competitive strategies, including off-farm employment, mixed farming, and inter-/intragenerational family farming. Despite vast pressure to expand and modernize, small-scale New Brunswick farms have carved their own niche in order to maintain economic success in a modern era.

In earlier work, Susan explored how the structural transformation of agriculture had affected farm women and the internal relations of production in household enterprises. In her doctoral dissertation, "The Impact of Agribusiness on Women's Work in the Household, on-the-Farm and off-the-Farm: A New Brunswick Case Study," she argues that women's contributions to the farm enterprise have regularly been taken for granted. As she shows, women's changing role on the farm has been paramount for the continued success of small-scale farming in rural New Brunswick.

Susan's work shows how rural communities are revitalizing their livelihoods and creating new opportunities for themselves in the face of global social and economic change. Her research will improve the relationship between rural and urban communities on food security—an issue of growing importance for the future economic and social well-being of Canadians. What is more, this work underscores how resilient people, communities, and businesses have become in the face of urbanization.

Sources: Machum (1992); Machum (2005); and CRC Web profile.

everywhere: to and from school, to sporting and recreational events, to visit friends' homes, and more. A New York study (Weir et al., 2006) compared the concerns of parents of 5-to-10-year-old children on neighbourhood safety. It found that parents living in low-SES inner-city areas had greater concerns about neighbourhood safety than parents living in medium-SES suburbs, with 60 per cent of inner-city parents considering traffic to be too heavy for their children to play outdoors, in comparison to 27 per cent of suburban parents who felt this way.

In short, traffic has a negative effect on neighbourhood cohesion and community integration.

Health Consequences of Population Growth and Urbanization

Health problems are most concentrated in urban areas. In part, this is a result of large numbers of people gathering in small, densely populated areas. Under conditions of poor housing, poor sanitation, and crowding, rates of illness and disease inevitably rise with increases in population size (McKenzie, 2008; Ng et al., 2009).

At the same time, city life is stressful, and this, too, poses health problems. The rush of traffic, the pace of change, the cost of living, jostling with strangers, the fear of victimization, economic competition, the noise—all of these characteristics are common in the city, and all are stress-inducing. Though people can manage the occasional experience of acute stress, chronic exposure to high stress levels can lead to serious health problems, including heart disease and a weakened immune system.

The homeless and the mentally ill (Yu, 2008), two populations who suffer especially high levels of poor health, are concentrated in urban inner cities. For instance, in a 2002 Toronto Daily Bread Food Bank survey of its clients' self-reported health, over 40 per cent rated their health as fair or poor compared with others of their age. By comparison, when middle-income earners were asked the same question, only 12 per cent rated their health as fair or poor (Daily Bread Food Bank, 2002).

Another urban health concern is the massive amount of sewage, litter, and solid waste produced by the millions of people crowded into a small area. For example, a study of environmental inequality in California found that of the state's population living in areas with above-median risks of air toxins and cancer (approximately half the state's total population), 58 per cent were minorities, compared to 39 per cent of Anglo populations. Furthermore, a disproportionate number of Latinos were found in areas with high pollution, while fewer non-Latino whites lived in areas with low pollution than in areas with high pollution (Pastor et al., 2005).

Some researchers have labelled this correlation between social class, neighbourhood racial composition, and pollution level, replicated in surveys of cities around the world, as a form of "environmental racism." **Environmental racism** is the result of several factors,

Environmental racism A type of discrimination that results in the concentration of poor racial minorities in densely packed, poorly served urban neighbourhoods, often with higher levels of pollution and located near waste dumps and heavy industry.

The Canadian Press/Andrew Vaughan

Warning signs are posted on the fence surrounding the tar ponds in Sydney, Nova Scotia. Approximately 400 people have undertaken a class action lawsuit against the federal and provincial governments and are seeking compensation and the establishment of a medical monitoring fund for contamination resulting from the running of the Sydney steel plant.

including fewer public services—sanitation workers, garbage disposal units, road maintenance crews, and so on—being devoted by local governments to the undesirable areas; it is also the result of a perception among corporate polluters that the local residents lack the political clout to prevent the dumping of industrial trash in their communities. Another contributor is the economically deprived residents' shared sense of general demoralization, which reduces the likelihood of their making any concerted effort to preserve and improve the neighbourhood.

Solutions to Population Problems

Perhaps in no other area have so many efforts been mounted, and so many ideas floated, to solve the problems discussed here.

In respect to population issues, countries have continued with varying success to promote contraception and family planning. Generally, these measures have been successful almost everywhere, although fertility has declined at varying rates. The solution to this population problem, then, would seem to be a continued effort to educate people about the value of family planning and to make contraceptive devices available to them. However, as we have seen, a new problem—population aging—has arisen as a result of this fertility decline. Much more effort will be needed to solve this problem, which previously was seen as a matter of private (family) concern but has now, increasingly, become a matter of public (state) concern.

Alongside the continued declines in mortality and rises in life expectancy throughout most of the world, other new problems have arisen: specifically, how we can improve the quality of life for hundreds of millions who would, in past years, have died at a younger age. This means increasing the access to, and quality of, education and health care; equally important, it means providing employment for those who are employable, and long-term care, as well as income, for those who are not. As with fertility decline, mortality decline calls for more effort to solve the new problems. The goal will be not merely to increase the duration of life, but to improve the quality of longer living.

Cities continue to grapple with a wide variety of problems, as we have seen; and different cities, in Canada and around the world, have looked for solutions in various ways. They have attempted to deal with increased inner-city density by creating and maintaining green space and by regulating traffic. Cities have devised mixed-income housing projects to reduce some of the toxic social problems associated with the geographic and social segregation of poor and minority populations. They have devised new social housing strategies and policies to help with troubled populations, such as the homeless. They have improved public transit to move people more quickly and safely, and have reduced traffic congestion on the roads and auto-related pollution. Some have applied, or considered applying, a surcharge or luxury tax on motor vehicle use in inner cities, to discourage automobile use and promote walking, bicycling, and public transit. And other jurisdictions, such as British Columbia, have devised legislation to limit urban sprawl by seeking to protect agricultural land around the perimeter of urban areas.

None of these solutions has been fully tested. Ideally, in coming years, sociologists and planners will explore the outcomes of these varied solutions and promote the best of them for widespread use in Canada and abroad.

Chapter Summary

As mentioned at the beginning of this chapter, issues surrounding population growth and urbanization are complex, and each could justify its own textbook, let alone chapters within a book. In addition, both of these issues impinge on the problem of environmental degradation, the subject of the next chapter. These topics are related in several important ways.

First, issues of population size feed naturally into discussions of urban problems, since the latter are fuelled in part by the former. Second, we have shown that human ingenuity (and its manifestation, technology) has been both the cause and often the solution to the urban troubles facing the world today. Third, each issue represents a separate component of the material backdrop of social life. To borrow Shakespeare's metaphor of human life as a play, the human population represents the world's actors; our cities, the set; and the natural environment, the stage upon which everything plays out.

Finally, the topics discussed in this chapter are unique in that they will outlive any one individual and thus serve as legacies to later generations in a way that other social problems (e.g., drugs or crime) do not. Eventually, our collective choices will control the outcome of these population-related problems—that is, whether the urban centres of the future are energizing and beautiful or stagnant and bland. Just as we must take collective responsibility for these present problems, so, too, must we draw upon collective efforts to find their solutions.

Questions for Critical Thought

1. China is famous for its so-called "one-child policy," aimed at reducing the birth rate of one of the most populous countries in the world. Research this policy and its effects, noting the drawbacks to such a policy and whether you believe the advantages outweigh the possible disadvantages.

2. It seems as though in a big city there is something for everyone. Pick a certain subculture, such as the gay and lesbian community or ethnic enclaves, and explore its presence in your city. Are certain services, facilities, restaurants, bars, and shops concentrated in a certain area? Do they share similar characteristics? Where are they found, and why there?

3. Everything around us, from banking to movie-ticket sales, is becoming automated. Machines are replacing people's jobs, and human interaction seems to be a nostalgic idea of the past. What might sociologists have to say about this apparent shift away from personalized and intimate relationships?

4. There is no doubt that suburbanization is a major force permeating the modern urban landscape. What effect has this had on your own life? Does living near the city centre offer a different lifestyle than suburban living? Discuss, using specific examples and figures.

5. Do you agree that while population density is considered (by some) a social problem, it may also be a solution to other social problems? Is there a way to reap the benefits of population size and density while addressing the problems it has been linked to?

Recommended Readings

Beall, Jo, Basudeb Guha-Khasnobis, and Ravi Kanbur. 2010. *Urbanization and Development: Multidisciplinary Perspectives*. New York: Oxford University Press.

Dobkowski, Michael N., and Isidor Wallmann, eds. 2002. *On the Edge of Scarcity: Environment, Resources, Population, Sustainability, and Conflict*. Syracuse, NY: Syracuse University Press.

Dunlap, Riley, Frederick Buttel, Peter Dickens, and August Gijswijt, eds. 2002. *Sociological Theory and the Environment: Classical Foundations, Contemporary Insights*. Lanham, MD: Rowman & Littlefield.

Kwesi Darkoh, M.B., and Apollo Rowmire. 2003. *Human Impact on Environment and Sustainable Development in Africa*. Farnham, UK: Ashgate Publishing.

Lefebvre, Henri. 2003. *The Urban Revolution*. Minneapolis: University of Minnesota Press.

Liotta, P.H., and James F. Miskel. 2012. *The Real Population Bomb: Megacities, Global Security and the Map of the Future*. Sterling, VA: Potomac Books.

Polèse, Mario, and Richard Stren, eds. 2000. *The Social Sustainability of Cities: Diversity and the Management of Change*. Toronto: University of Toronto Press.

Simpson, R. David, Michael A. Toman, and Robert U. Ayres. 2005. *Scarcity and Growth Revisited: Natural Resources and the Environment in the New Millennium*. Washington: Resources for the Future.

15

The Natural Environment

© ideeone/iStockphoto

LEARNING OBJECTIVES

- To appreciate the impact of technology on the environment.
- To understand the history of environmentalism.
- To find out about the environmental issues of metropolitan areas.
- To understand issues such as climate change, desertification, and ozone depletion.
- To distinguish sociological perspectives on urban life and environmental issues.
- To understand the social and health effects of continued environmental degradation.
- To learn of possible solutions to urban and environmental problems.
- To know the history of environmental social movements.

Introduction

Today, we are more aware of the natural environment and its effects on our society than we ever were in the past (Crawford, 2009). This is largely due to the work of environmental and climate scientists such as Rachel Carson in the 1960s and David Suzuki, Al Gore, and Ulrich Beck more recently. As well, environmental consciousness-raising organizations like Greenpeace have called our attention to problematic environmental issues, ranging from Alberta's oil sands extraction to the accumulation of plastic waste in our oceans.

"Natural environment" is defined here as the natural processes that affect us as animals. This includes processes that affect the fertility of the land; the availability of soil nutrients, water, sun, and other fundamentals are part of the natural environment that provides for our survival. All humans need food and water, so concerns about the food supply and clean water are obvious, and these concerns have resurfaced throughout history. This is why Thomas Malthus was concerned about the relation of the food supply to population growth (Bandarage, 2008) and why Karl Marx was concerned about the plight of wage slaves, who needed to sell their labour to purchase food and shelter. And this is why sociologists today study agribusinesses—giant corporations that control our access to reliable, good-quality food.

Humans compete with other species for survival. We have developed tools and strategies that gave us advantages over these other species. For example, we invented weapons to hunt some animals for food and keep predators at bay, and we also learned how to domesticate and harvest animals that provide food—chickens, cows, and pigs—and are constantly improving our efficiency at doing so.

However, dealing with the rapid mutation of sometimes-fatal viruses and bacteria is proving to be more of a challenge than dealing with larger life forms. We understand and control many biochemical interactions, creating pesticides, herbicides, fungicides, antibiotics, and other medicines. We are increasingly able to manage our relationships with problematic species—from bacteria to protozoa, mosquitoes to cockroaches, invasive plants to cereal rusts. We keep them under control; yet epidemics like SARS, swine or avian flu, or HIV/AIDS remind us that we still have much to learn (Lamal, 2009).

Water continues to be an especially valuable resource, and its rapid depletion by (mainly) developed nations is bringing this issue to the global forefront. Humans are dependent on water not only for daily use, but also for economic survival. Water is used in manufacturing, mining, agriculture, and energy production, as well as other purposes (PRB, 2008). According to a 2008 report by the Population Reference Bureau, "modern society's demands on water grew rapidly during the last century [and] . . . global water consumption grew six-fold—twice the rate of population growth in the same period" (ibid.).

This prodigious water consumption has been made possible by the building of dams and reservoirs, which affect over 50 per cent of the river basins in the world. However, the water available to humanity is unequally distributed. Currently, 2.3 billion people live in areas that lack adequate water supply, and by 2050, 3.5 billion people will be in this condition (ibid.).

Like water, most of the natural resources that humans need are non-renewable; there is only so much petroleum, aluminum, and iron to be had on earth. Once we have used it all . . . well, no one knows how to finish this sentence yet. One preventive strategy is recycling. Another is inventing alternatives (e.g., nuclear energy) or tapping previously underused natural resources (e.g., wind or solar power). Other strategies include finding new planets to inhabit and looking for new resources in currently inaccessible places (for instance, under the sea or deep in the earth). But the best short-term solution to our much more long-term problem is to reduce the rate at which we use these resources; doing that would delay the inevitable disappearance of these resources.

The Environment and Social Construction

There is no denying that social construction plays a large role in our understanding and response to the environment problems we are facing (Hannigan, 2008). Environmental sociology has been divided by a debate between realists and constructionists centring on the knowledge claims of ecological science—for example, claims about climate change and global warming (Martell, 2008).

Some believe that the environmental problem results, in large part, from the persistent failure of social scientists to bring socially constructed environmental concerns into environmental impact assessments. Others see the problem as a failure and even a refusal of citizens to learn about environmental dangers in the hope they will be able to avoid taking costly and uncertain precautions. Sociologist Raymond Murphy (2004) notes that there is much theoretical debate on this issue, including claims that nature itself is being socially constructed.

What we do is largely a function of how we think about a problem—even, how we name it. The term "environment" originates from the French word *viron*—meaning a circle, a round, or the country around. Human societies are embedded in the natural environment, which consists of the physical and material bases of all life on earth—including land, air, water, and mineral resources (Humphrey et al., 2002). Human life has always been part of the natural environment, but a few centuries ago we began to try to separate ourselves from it and to dominate it.

Thus, severe damage to the environment began only about two centuries ago, with industrialization in Europe. New social practices and behaviours developed out of industrial organization and shaped much of today's society. For a long time, governments ignored environmentally harmful practices because the industries responsible for pollution powered (and dominated) the economy.

Today, harmful environmental practices affect the daily lives of people everywhere—especially vulnerable and disadvantaged populations in less-developed nations. For example, many studies have suggested that there is a relationship between environmental degradation and economic development. Popularly known as the environmental Kuznets curve (EKC), an inverse-U-shaped relationship exists between a country's per capita income and its environmental quality. In other words, increased incomes are associated with an increase of pollution in poor countries but with a decline in pollution in rich countries (Copeland and Taylor, 2004). What that means is that the process of development is associated with a surge in environmental pollution, something we have witnessed in newly emerging economies in Brazil, Russia, India, and China (the so-called BRIC countries).

As for environmental harms within our own nation, we have many environmental problems to overcome. For example, traffic congestion—with its associated lost time, wasted fuel, and higher insurance rates—is considerable and mounting fast

(Greenberg, 2009). Related to the growth of congestion is an increase in air pollution, noise, and lack of green space in and around cities. Automobile and truck exhausts release a huge amount of carbon monoxide into the air, all helping to create the thick, dirty cloud of smog that hangs over many car-heavy cities (Scheelhaase et al., 2010).

Many environmental problems are the result of human inefficiency and waste. For example, industrial pollution—the by-product created when the raw materials used in production are not fully converted into usable products—tends to reflect cost-saving inefficiencies in manufacturing. The consequences of these problems involve not only metropolitan people, they also involve our entire national population, indeed, the world's population. Therefore, we turn now to problems arising from humanity's impact on the natural world.

Theoretical Perspectives on Environmental Problems

TABLE 15.1	Theoretical Perspectives
THEORY	**MAIN POINTS**
Structural Functionalism	• Environmental problems result naturally from population growth, density, and specialization. • Cultural ideologies support ecologically harmful practices (e.g., materialism and the growth ethic emphasize the triumph of progress and ingenuity and encourage the discarding of the old in favour of innovations).
Conflict Theory	• Environmental problems negatively affect the poor more often and more severely than the rich. • The solution to environmental problems is through redistribution of wealth. • Collective action by the underclass is needed to gain political attention to their needs.
Symbolic Interactionism	• How are environmental issues imbued with meaning? • The focus is on the lived experience of humans. • How are environmental issues constructed as "problems"? • Environmental polluters manipulate symbols to protect themselves from criticism.
Feminist Theory	• Ecofeminism links destruction of the environment and the male-centric political and corporate worlds. • The domination over women and nature ultimately leads to gender inequality and environmental degradation. • Humans' relationship with nature should be more nurturing and co-operative.

Structural Functionalism

Functionalists hold the view that modern values and activities contribute to the pollution of our natural surroundings and overharvesting of resources. Consider the following cultural ideologies that support ecologically harmful practices.

Cornucopian view of nature Nature is seen as an endless storehouse of resources that exist only for use by humans, especially by those currently living.

Growth ethic A cultural or subcultural commitment to the idea that economic growth is good in itself, whatever its social effects.

Individualism Belief in the primary importance of the individual and the need to protect individual liberty and choice against collective social or governmental restriction.

Tragedy of the commons A market system based on the capitalist belief that economies work best when left alone. With each self-interested actor seeking what is personally best, it may work against the common good by polluting, destroying, and exhausting common goods that are not owned by a single individual but are shared by all of us—goods such as bodies of water, the air, the land, ecosystems, and, especially, renewable resources such as fish and forests.

One example is the **cornucopian view of nature**. This way of thinking views nature as a storehouse of resources that exist only for the use of humans—especially, currently living humans. Another environmentally unfriendly belief is the **growth ethic**, especially popular in North America. This view, linked closely with *materialism*, celebrates the (imagined) ability of technology to solve all the world's problems easily, including those that technology itself has caused. This, in turn, promotes the belief that the world will *always* improve so long as we indulge in the invention, production, and consumption of new items.

Finally, a third notion, **individualism**, forefronts personal goals and desires over collective interests. This way of thinking is the cause of the so-called **tragedy of the commons**, a reference to what happened when English lords in the sixteenth century allowed commoners to freely graze their livestock on uncultivated pastures. Opening these fields, known as the commons, created a dilemma. Any particular commoner could seek short-term personal gain by increasing his herd, thus putting more pressure on the common land. Alternatively, he could forgo immediate personal gain on the assumption that others would do likewise, and they could all benefit for a longer period of time. However, many people failed to look beyond immediate short-term gain to consider the sustainability of the resource. Soon cattle and sheep were so numerous that the commons became exhausted and could no longer feed any of them.

Then and now, long-term sustainability could only be achieved through co-operation, at the expense of short-term, individualistic (and selfish) thinking. Only value change and regulation could bring about the needed protection.

Conflict Theory

Conflict theorists do not think that environmental problems arise from faulty values, but rather from social inequality. They note that when environmental problems arise, they hurt the poor more often and more severely than the rich. Over 90 per cent of disaster-related deaths, for instance, occur among the poor populations of developing countries, while developed nations experience 75 per cent of disaster-related economic damage, since there is more money invested in these countries.

Thus, an agricultural drought in Canada's prairie region may result in reduced crops but not necessarily any deaths. In Pakistan or Ethiopia, by contrast, a drought can lead to catastrophic famine and many deaths. And, of the 25 per cent of the world's population currently living in regions prone to natural disaster, most live in less-developed countries (Smith, 2001).

Research shows that disasters result more often from "the spread of capitalism and the marginalization of the poor than from the effects of geophysical events." Accordingly, solutions will necessarily involve "the redistribution of wealth and power in society to provide access to resources, rather than . . . the application of science and technology to control nature" (ibid.).

Rich people typically possess the means to protect themselves from the consequences of locally occurring disasters, something that is not possible for most people in developing countries where most of the disasters, whether natural or man-made, occur. And when well-off people are victimized by disaster—as happened in the 2013 Calgary floods, which destroyed many homes in prosperous river-front areas—they are, more likely than not, able to secure government funds to pay the costs of rebuilding.

Symbolic Interactionism

The symbolic interactionist perspective studies how the meanings and labels learned through social interaction affect environmental problems, with a particular focus on how they alter people's perception of these problems.

Here, the social constructionist framework is especially relevant. Sociologists who approach environmental problems from this perspective ask why and how certain environmental problems enter the public consciousness; in different situations, which kind of issue is the most "attractive" to the general public. Davis (2012) reports that people from low socio-economic backgrounds are less likely to view the conservation of environment as a priority. Instead of taking moral responsibility, people in financial distress believe it is appropriate to prioritize things other than the environment.

The symbolic interactionist perspective also offers insights into how environmental polluters manipulate symbols to protect themselves from criticism. Many companies and businesses, increasingly sensitive to greater public awareness over their impact on the environment, try to boost their image and profits by using an advertising strategy known as **greenwashing**. This technique involves redesigning and repackaging their products as "environmentally friendly" or "green," playing to (some) consumers' wish to help the environmental cause. Greenwashing can backfire if words are not backed by actions, as British Petroleum (BP) discovered when its Deepwater Horizon oil drilling rig exploded in the Gulf of Mexico in April 2010, causing an uncontainable blowout from the wellhead at the ocean floor. This unprecedented human-caused environmental disaster was preceded by BP's ad campaign rebranding the company as "Beyond Petroleum," which trumpeted the firm's research and technological innovations in eco-friendly energy sources.

Greenwashing The process of promoting false ideas about the environmental friendliness of certain commercial products.

Mario Tama/Getty Images News

A Rio + 20 sand sculpture is seen on Copacabana Beach on the final day of the Rio + 20 conference in Rio de Janiero, Brazil. The sculpture reads "Rio + 20 Welcome to Copacabana."

INTERNATIONAL **COMPARISONS**

| BOX 15.1 | **Rio+20: We'll Save the Planet with No Specific Plan** |

Marking 20 years since the first Earth Summit, the 2012 Rio+20 summit brought together 130 countries in Rio de Janeiro to create a global plan to protect the environment. The summit took place amidst a flurry of demonstrations, celebrity appearances, cultural celebrations, and riot police. Though outwardly the summit exploded with attention-grabbing activity, media reports expressed dissatisfaction with the world leaders' lack of action. The summit agreement, a 53-page statement signed by those present, promises that governments will eventually define long-term objectives for sustainable development and the eradication of poverty, but makes few new commitments and does not specify particular goals or timelines.

The Rio+20 summit differed vastly in attitude and outcome from the 1992 Earth Summit. In 1992, international media came out *en masse* to cover the event. At the time, many newspapers included sections for environmental reports that contained updates on the event. Major world leaders, including Canadian prime minister Brian Mulroney and conservative US president George H. Bush, came in person to discuss global warming, biodiversity, and strategies for fighting poverty. The summit resulted in detailed treaties aimed at combatting global warming and preventing the extermination of endangered animal and plant species. The treaties laid out dozens of specific goals.

In contrast, the 2012 Rio+20 summit saw a decrease in media attention from the 1992 summit. Several important world figures were absent from the event, including Canadian prime minister Stephen Harper, US president Barak Obama, and German chancellor Angela Merkel. Harper reportedly claimed he was too busy dealing with economic problems to address environmental issues. Obama, caught in the midst of a re-election campaign, sent Secretary of State Hillary Clinton in his stead. His absence from the summit seems to have done nothing to affect his popularity or campaign. Rio+20's new agreement states no definite timelines or financial commitments for improving on sustainable development.

Reporters suggested several possible reasons for the less ambitious goals and reduced popularity of the 2012 summit, pointing especially to disillusionment with the summits themselves. Enthusiasm infused the first summit, pressuring politicians to make bold commitments. However, the pledges went mostly unfulfilled. The first summit's global action plan, known as Agenda 21, provided blueprints for comprehensive environmental protection, but years later, little progress has been made toward achieving these goals. A recent United Nations follow-up study of Agenda 21 found that only four goals (out of the 90 that the UN tracked) had seen some improvement. The areas of improvement were in reducing ozone depletion, removing lead from gasoline, improving water access, and boosting research for marine pollution. Other target areas had actually gotten worse, such as the destruction of coral reefs. The ineffectiveness of previous summits has likely affected public interest in the event.

At Rio+20, leaders may have been more aware of the difficulty of keeping commitments to the environment and thus hoped to avoid broken pledges by not setting any definite goals.

Sources: Adapted from Scoffield (2012); Waldie (2012); and Walkom (2012).

Feminist Theory

The feminist perspective questions the prevailing capitalist celebration of increasing growth, unlimited resources, and unregulated commerce. Ecofeminism emerged as a social movement that linked the exploitation of marginalized groups within society and the degradation of nature in Western cultural values.

Ecofeminists unite in a central belief in the convergence between women and nature. Françoise d'Eaubonne coined the term "ecofeminism" "to identify theoretical work on the potential for women to bring about an ecological revolution and to ensure the survival of the planet" in a way that is more nurturing, co-operative, and communal (Humphrey et al., 2002). Ecofeminism encourages political analysis that explores the links between androcentrism and environmental destruction (Rynbrandt and Deegan, 2002).

Ecofeminists contend that the mutual domination of women is co-dependent with the destruction of nature, in a cyclic relationship. Some ecofeminists identify a link between the exploitation of women and the "rape of the wild" (Plant, 1990; Rynbrandt and Deegan, 2002). According to Greta Gaard, the environment as a social problem "is a feminist issue." As Gaard (1993: 5) proposes:

> The way in which women and nature have been conceptualized historically in the Western intellectual tradition has resulted in devaluing whatever is associated with women, emotion, animals, nature, and the body, while simultaneously elevating in value those things associated with men, reason, humans, culture, and the mind. One task of ecofeminists has been to expose these dualisms and the ways in which feminizing nature and naturalizing or animalizing women has served as justification for the domination of women, animals and the earth.

These arguments seem reasonable when we consider the connection between women, politics, and the environment. Comparing nations around the world, we find a positive correlation between women's involvement in political activities and progressive environmental legislation. Likewise, nations with a higher proportion of women in government are more likely than others to ratify environmental treaties.

Social Consequences of Environmental Problems

Canadian and Global Environmental Problems

Unlike most other social problems, environmental issues are global in their effects. Still, as with other social problems, there are important connections between these issues and the economic organization of society. Often, people with the most economic and political power cause the greatest environmental damage through harmful industrial practices and wasteful personal lifestyles. Meanwhile, people who lack this power pay an unequal toll in their personal health and social well-being (Comim et al., 2009). Again, the problem is not our consumption of natural resources, but the reckless exploitation of these resources for short-term gains—our failure to moderate our use and replenish what we use as we go along.

Air Pollution

In large cities around the world—whether Los Angeles, Paris, Budapest, or Beijing—smog has become a major problem. Emissions from cars and trucks, mixed with chemicals released by manufacturing and other forms of fuel combustion, create high levels of carbon monoxide, sulphur dioxide, and other air pollutants. In Taipei, Tokyo, and other large Asian cities, one often sees people walking on the street—or, ironically, driving motor scooters—with their faces covered by masks to strain out the pollutants. This daily exposure to air pollution has become part of the normal metropolitan experience. No wonder that, in the United States, air quality decreased by 11 per cent between 2000 and 2010.

In principle, nature can repair itself. Through the process of photosynthesis, trees and other vegetation cleanse the air of the carbon dioxide that humans and other organisms produce, replacing it with breathable oxygen. However, the limited amount of trees and bushes can remove only so much pollution per day. When the pollutants exceed what trees can remove, they build up in the atmosphere, making the air potentially dangerous to breathe.

Ozone Depletion

The ozone layer is a thin veil in the stratosphere that shields the earth against the sun's harmful ultraviolet (UV) radiation. Without this protective layer, UV rays would seriously damage most of the life on the earth's surface. Unfortunately, certain industrial chemicals—including chlorine, halons, and the chlorofluorocarbons (CFCs) used in most refrigerators, aerosol cans, and solvents—have weakened the ozone layer, allowing UV rays to go through it. This is the ozone depletion problem.

Ozone declines of varying severity have been detected at several middle-latitude locations and over the Arctic Circle. The damage has been most severe, however, in the Antarctic region. There, by 2003, an area of extreme thinning within the ozone layer (the ozone "hole") had grown to a record size of 29 million square kilometres (larger than the land mass of Canada, the United States, and Mexico combined) and had begun to stretch into densely populated areas of South America.

Some researchers, however, propose that the combined global effort to reduce industrial chemical pollutants over the past decade may be having an effect. The National Institute of Water and Atmospheric Research in New Zealand reported in late 2004 that the Antarctic ozone hole had shrunk 20 per cent since the previous year. This in turn prompted some experts to predict guardedly that the ozone layer, at least in that region of the world, is beginning to recover.

Others are less optimistic. According to the United Nations Environment Program (UNEP, 2011), the size of the ozone hole has fluctuated over time and is thus unpredictable; for example, the hole grew alarmingly in 2006. This suggests that while there may be some hope for recovery, ozone depletion remains an important environmental problem with potentially fatal effects on future generations.

However, some ozone is harmful, and Environment Canada (2012) notes that high levels of ozone at ground level are particularly harmful:

> Ground-level ozone damages vegetation, including crops, flowers, shrubs and forests, by interfering with plants' ability to produce and store food. This damage makes them more susceptible to disease, pests and environmental stresses. . . . The health effects from $PM_{2.5}$ and ground-level ozone can reduce work attendance and overall participation in the labour force. In terms of increased health care costs, missed days of work, and reduced worker productivity, air pollution costs Canadians and the Canadian economy billions of dollars per year. . . . Increased ozone levels also reduce the growth of crops, plants and trees, leading to economic losses in agriculture and forestry. For example, the impacts of ozone on agriculture are known to cost Canadian farmers millions of dollars in lost production each year.

Global Warming

Global warming is caused by a process known as the *greenhouse effect*, where greenhouse gases, such as CFCs, carbon dioxide, and methane, accumulate in the atmosphere, trapping the heat reflected off the earth's surface.

Global Climate Change, published regularly by the National Aeronautics and Space Administration (NASA), in 2014 reports these troubling facts about climate change: "The year 2013 is tied with 2009 and 2006 for the seventh warmest year since 1880." As a result of continued climatic warming, "the September Arctic sea ice is now declining at a rate of 11.5 per cent per decade." At the same time, "ice sheets in both Antarctica and Greenland are losing mass. The continent of Antarctica has been losing more than 100 cubic kilometers of ice per year since 2002." As a result of all this, the world's oceans have been steadily rising since 1870, and since 1995, have been rising at over twice the rate in the early twentieth century.

These patterns of **climate change** have been attributed to the greenhouse effect (WMO, 2000). Even a small increase in global temperatures can lead to elevated sea levels and devastating changes in precipitation rates. Such climate changes, in turn, harm the natural vegetation and wildlife of local ecosystems, alter the crop yields of agricultural regions, and allow deserts to take over fertile regions. Greenpeace (2001) provided a striking example of the effects of global warming, reporting that small islands in Kiribati in the Pacific Ocean have entirely disappeared because of rising sea levels. Rising sea levels, like many natural disasters, come with enormous costs in both lives and money.

International action to solve these problems has occasionally been dramatic and encouraging. Consider the Kyoto Protocol, adopted in 1997: by July 2006, 164 of 168

Climate change A departure from expected patterns of temperature and other climatic properties resulting mainly from an accumulation of greenhouse gases in the atmosphere, trapping the heat reflected off the earth's surface.

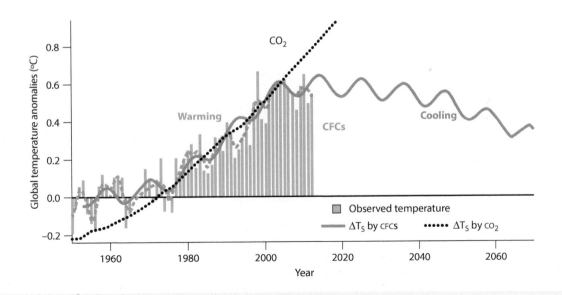

FIGURE 15.1 | Annual Global Temperature over Land and Ocean

Source: Waterloo News, University of Waterloo, at <uwaterloo.ca/news/news/global-warming-caused-cfcs-not-carbon-dioxide-study-says>. Used with permission.

countries had signed and ratified the protocol in an effort to reduce global emissions of greenhouse gases. Canada did not ratify the accord until December 2002, but then it withdrew in December 2011, despite heavy opposition from environmentalists, having failed to meet its target: a reduction in greenhouse gas emissions to 6 per cent below 1990 levels by 2012. The Canadian government claimed it withdrew for economic reasons, saying the decision would save Canada an estimated $14 billion in penalties. "Kyoto for Canada is in the past. As such, we are invoking our legal right to formally withdraw," said Environment Minister Peter Kent.

The United States, for its part, called the Kyoto Protocol irresponsible because the reduced use of fossil fuels required by the accord would hinder the American oil industry and US economic growth. Today, few signatory countries are on track to meet the emissions reduction targets set out within the accord.

In late 2005, the US, Australia, China, India, Japan, and South Korea—which together account for approximately half of the world's greenhouse gas emissions—agreed to sign an alternative international agreement known as the Asia-Pacific Partnership on Clean Development and Climate (AP6). This agreement allowed member nations to set targets for reducing emissions individually, without a mandatory enforcement scheme. Canada became the AP6's seventh member in 2007.

At the international talks on climate change in Copenhagen in 2009, Canada—like the US—refused to make significant changes. Many throughout the world declared the Copenhagen talks a dismal failure for environmentalism, though some believed that US president Barack Obama had signalled a willingness to begin dealing with important environmental issues. In the end, the following goals were stated:

- to hold the increase in global temperature to below 2°C (over 100 nations had wanted a lower maximum of 1.5°C);
- to co-operate in achieving a turnaround of global and national emissions as soon as possible, recognizing that developing countries will take longer to do this;
- to start work immediately on achieving national emissions reductions pledged in 2005 for 2020;
- to commit funds to prevent deforestation and to further technology development and capacity-building; and
- to provide new and additional resources amounting to $30 billion for 2010–12, with developed countries together aiming to mobilize $100 billion a year by 2020 to address the needs of developing countries.

Water Pollution and Scarcity

Water pollution is another environmental problem caused largely by environmentally damaging industrial practices. Fertilizers, waste from industrial plants, oil spills, and acid rain have all polluted much of the world's drinking water, with disastrous consequences for many of the world's poorest people.

The Great Lakes, a major source of fresh water in North America, have experienced much pollution (Gilbertson and Watterson, 2007). Pollutants from the surrounding regions—heavily farmed rural areas and densely populated urban areas—have found their way into the lakes, poisoning the water, promoting the extreme growth of algae, and killing the aquatic life (Phillips, 2006). Today, most of the beaches along the shores

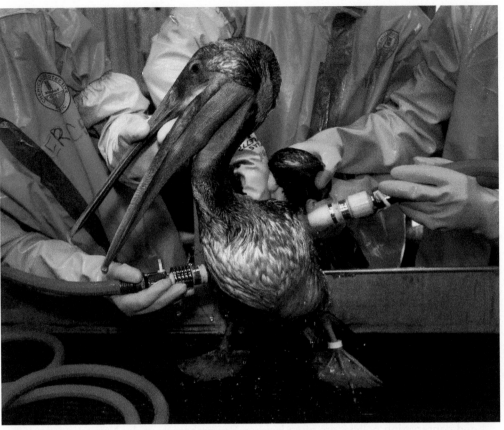

The Canadian Press/AP Photo/Charlie Riedel

A brown pelican is cleaned at the Fort Jackson Wildlife Rehabilitation Center at Buras, Louisiana. The bird was rescued after being exposed in an oil spill in the Gulf of Mexico, now known as the worst oil spill in US history.

of the Great Lakes are too polluted for authorities to allow swimming. Similar conditions have been reported at points all along the North American seacoast.

Global water use has increased greatly in the past 50 years, especially for agricultural purposes and to support population growth in arid regions such as the US Southwest. Such use further strains the supply of clean, drinkable water, and Canada has been among the worst of water abusers. Among the 29 members of the Organisation for Economic Co-operation and Development (OECD), the most-developed industrial nations, "only Americans use more water than Canadians." As Boyd (2001) notes, "Canada uses 1,600 cubic metres of water per person per year. This is more than twice as much water as the average person from France [uses], three times as much as the average German, four times as much as the average Swede, and more than eight times as much as the average Dane. Canada's per capita water consumption is 65 per cent above the OECD average."

More and more countries are experiencing "water stress," a level of supply that only allows each person an average of 1,000 to 2,000 cubic metres of water per year. Many other countries are at the level of "water scarcity," defined as a level of supply that is less than 1,000 cubic metres of water per person per year. By contrast, in 2004, Canada's daily household use of water per capita was 329 litres, the second-highest rate in the world, while our municipal prices lie at \$0.31, the lowest price for water (Environment Canada, 2011).

Abuse of Canadian water supplies through the construction of "megaprojects"—dams, diversions, canals, and resource extraction, from the Klondike gold rush at the end of the nineteenth century to Alberta's oil sands today—are common. Too often, there is little concern for environmental degradation—the downstream consequences of alterations in water-flow regimes—or for social and community disruptions (Windsor and McVey, 2004).

There has been debate about whether to follow in the footsteps of the US and commercialize water within Canada. Although Canada claims to have one-quarter of the world's freshwater supply, corporate ideologists are nonetheless trying to get Canada to sell its water. This would bring immense hardship to those of the lower socio-economic classes, making it difficult for them to gain access to resources fundamental to survival and exacerbating economic stratification even further (Canadian Press, 2010).

However, water scarcity issues in Canada pale by comparison with the problems many nations face in Africa, where massive deforestation and desertification have marked a chronic lack of water. Increasingly, the global flows of water mirror the global flows of other trade, where people can pay for the commodity. According to a recently published report,

> More than one-fifth of the world's water supplies go towards crops and commodities produced for export. . . . As developed nations import water-intensive goods from overseas, they place pressure on finite resources in areas where water governance and conservation policies are often lacking. Researchers from the Netherlands have quantified and mapped the global water footprint, highlighting how patterns in international commerce create disparities in water use. (Nature.com, 2012)

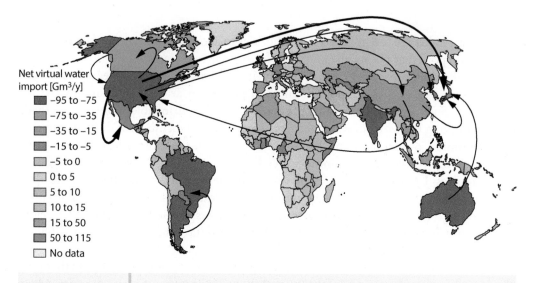

FIGURE 15.2 | World's Water Footprint Linked to Free Trade

Source: A.Y. Hoekstra and M.M. Mekonnen (2012). "The water footprint of humanity," *Proceedings of the National Academy of Sciences*, 109(9): 3232–7.

Deforestation

In principle, nature is a self-cleaning system. Through photosynthesis, trees remove carbon dioxide from the air and convert it to oxygen. Forests are also vital to the health of a region because they help to protect the thin layer of fertile topsoil from wind erosion. Widespread clear-cutting—whether for harvesting or to make room for expanding farmland and ranching—eliminates the protection for the topsoil and causes the expansion of deserts (Anonymous, 2008). Deforestation of the world's rainforests also results in the dislocation of indigenous peoples and the loss of many animal and plant species.

Sometimes, we can more easily imagine the future if we look back at history. At one time, the barren Sahara Desert in Africa was woodland. All of the parched and sandy beach land around the Mediterranean Sea was covered with trees. Today, there are few trees and the land cannot be farmed; it can be used only for grazing, fishing, or tourism. Similar transitions will likely take place eventually on BC's Vancouver Island, in the vast wooded interior of New Brunswick, and in northern Ontario, although different environmental and climatological regions, with widely differing population densities, respond to long-term stresses and change in various ways. Nonetheless, damage done to the environment is not necessarily irreparable and permanent.

Natural Resources Canada (2012b), in its "State of Canada's Forests, Annual Report, 2012," notes that

> Canada is making significant progress toward sustainable forest management. . . . Less than 0.2% of all forest and other wooded land in Canada is harvested each year—well below the level needed to maintain sustainable stands. The rate of deforestation (meaning the permanent conversion of forest land) is declining. And the forest sector's overall greenhouse gas emissions have decreased by 51% over the past two decades, through decreased reliance on fossil fuels, increased energy efficiency and reduced energy use. (ibid.: 6, 7)

That said, the combination of climate change and deforestation leads to an increase in so-called hydrological disasters—"events caused by deviations in the normal water cycle and/or overflow of bodies of water caused by wind set-up. Such events are further classified as Flood (river flood, flash flood, storm surge/coastal flood) and Wet Mass Movement (rock fall)" (United Nations Statistics Division, 2010).

Waste Disposal and Pollution

The mass production process creates useless by-products that need disposal. People also produce a great deal of leftover paper, clothing, food, metals, plastics, and other synthetics. Canadian governments and businesses alone generate millions of tonnes of garbage each year.

Two disposal methods are used to deal with this garbage: landfills and incinerators. In a landfill, organic materials decompose naturally in a short period. By contrast, plastics can survive in one piece indefinitely when left in a landfill site. Another option is to burn the plastics, along with other forms of waste, using incinerators. However, this process converts many synthetics into hazardous chemicals that are then released into the air (Hoag, 2006).

Compared to citizens of the developed world, citizens of developing countries use few resources and recycle the resources they do use. This is more out of necessity than out of environmental consciousness. Unfortunately, city authorities in the developing world seem set on duplicating the solid waste management systems of developed countries without considering the people who make their living from picking through waste (Pacione, 2001). It is possible that when these cities begin to develop economically, they will be less environmentally friendly than the average North American city is today because of the lack of environmental consciousness.

Non-renewable Resources

All industrial societies use massive amounts of energy because energy—derived from resources such as petroleum, coal, natural gas, nuclear, hydroelectricity—powers technology. The first three of these cannot be renewed once we have exhausted the planet's supplies.

The United States Energy Information Administration (2001) has estimated that the world's energy consumption will have increased from 382 quadrillion British thermal units (382×10^{15} BTUs) in 1999 to 607 quintillion (607×10^{18}) BTUs in 2020. As US president George W. Bush noted in his State of the Union address in early 2006, "America is addicted to oil." The same could be said of most Western industrial nations, including Canada. Supporting evidence is found in the steady increase of global energy consumption from 2010 to 2011, with 71 per cent of the growth contributed by China (BP Global, 2012). Commodity HQ (2014) reports,

> [A]ccording to the EIA, America uses approximately 18.9 million barrels of crude per day; that nets out to nearly 7 billion barrels per year, an astonishing figure. What's more is that the next nearest consumer is China, who utilizes 9.8 million barrels each day. Each day, the U.S. spends exorbitant amounts of money on this fossil fuel. Assuming a price of $95/barrel, $1.795 billion is spent each day on crude oil in America; that is over $655 billion annually.

Peak oil The peak in global oil production, when the maximum rate of global petroleum extraction is reached, after which the rate of production goes into permanent decline.

We are already beginning to suffer the economic consequences of the world's declining fossil fuel reserves, with gas prices in Canada and elsewhere increasing significantly since the early 1980s. The issue of **peak oil** has emerged as a major topic of concern within the global geopolitical debate (Balaban and Tsatskin, 2010). Crude oil reserves are limited, and once oil is taken from the ground, the supply cannot be replenished. In addition, what remains in the ground is deeper down and more difficult and expensive to remove (Curtis, 2009).

As supplies slowly dwindle, control over the remaining petroleum reserves—mainly located in the Middle East, with the Alberta oil sands accounting for a significant secondary source—will become the focus of political, military, and economic interests, much more than it already has. The term "peak oil" refers to the theoretical point at which world oil production reaches its maximum level and then begins to decline (Eriksson, 2009). According to most expert projections, the global peak period has either already occurred or will occur within the next decade (Klare, 2004).

Other non-renewable resources are no better for the environment than oil. The burning of coal contributes substantially to the carbon dioxide and sulphur dioxide production that increases global warming and acid rain. However, since first becoming aware of the potential energy crisis, some people have given thought to renewable energy sources, such as hydroelectric, solar, wind, and geothermal energy (Elena and Velazquez, 2010;

Verbruggen et al., 2010). Of these alternative options, the least expensive and therefore most widely used is hydroelectric power. Even so, hydroelectricity is not without its drawbacks, mainly in the form of environmental damage caused to the local wildlife, waterways, and ecosystems by the massive dams constructed to harness the water's energy (Cizek, 2004).

Health Consequences of Environmental Problems

Environmental problems have harmful health consequences. This is especially striking in the poorer regions of the developing world. The World Health Organization (WHO, 1999) estimates, for instance, that "poor environmental quality is directly responsible for 25 per cent of all preventable ill-health in the world today, with diarrheal diseases and respiratory infections heading the list." In 2013, WHO stated that 23 per cent of the global disease burden is due to the environment, that 2 million deaths occur each year owing to exposure to household air pollution, and that 88 per cent of diarrheal deaths are due to poor water and sanitation (WHO, 2013a).

Health consequences are also influenced by social factors. Children account for the majority of victims of poor environmental conditions. Further, children and adults living in rural and semi-urban areas are more affected than people in urban areas (WHO, 1997; see also Aronowitz and Cutler, 1998; Helfgott, 1988). According to the WHO's database, the PM10 level, used to measure air pollution, averages 71 $\mu g/m^3$ for the entire globe, a level considerably greater than the appropriate level of 50 $\mu g/m^3$. Some areas in the Eastern Mediterranean, Southeast Asia, and the Western Pacific have double the average pollution rate (WHO, 2013). Developed nations are not safe from health problems caused by pollutants, chemicals, and other environmental hazards either. Some of the world's greatest cities are beset by extremely high levels of air pollution, as we see in Figure 15.3.

A major Canadian example occurred during the summer of 2000, when an outbreak of E. coli bacteria in the water supply of Walkerton, Ontario, killed seven people and infected thousands more. Although a board of inquiry looking into the deaths eventually blamed insufficient government regulation and human error, this event proved that water supplies in even the most technologically advanced regions are not safe from contamination. Likewise, Lake Athabasca's close proximity to Alberta's huge oil sands projects and the radioactive tailings from uranium mining in northern Saskatchewan are seen as a contributors to the unusually high cancer rates, among other health issues, experienced by the Native community of Fort Chipewyan on the shores of Lake Athabasca.

The list of health consequences is too long to present here, but consider just a few more examples. The number of asthma cases treated in hospital emergency departments increases after a period of severe air pollution (Li et al., 2010; Yogev-Baggio et al., 2010). Noise pollution, most apparent in dense urban environments and a result of our industrialized lifestyle, has been shown to contribute to hearing loss (Neitzel et al., 2009). The thinning of the ozone layer has meant an increase in the amount of harmful UV rays that penetrate the atmosphere (Debrovner, 2002); this has resulted in a parallel increase in the number of skin cancer cases, especially melanomas, which have increased 15 times in prevalence in the past 60 years. This upsurge in UV-caused cancer accounts for 8 out of every 10 skin-cancer deaths.

The use and haphazard dumping of ecologically harmful chemicals into the local environment have allowed persistent organic pollutants (POPs), such as pesticides, to

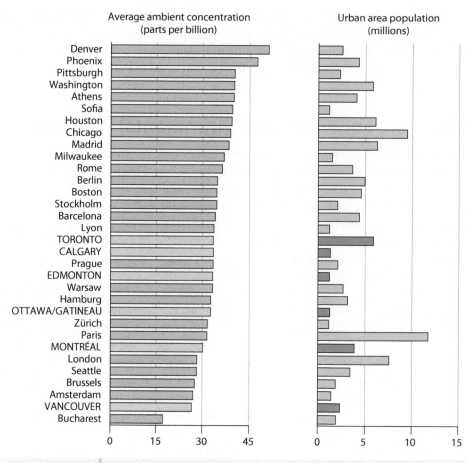

Average ambient concentration (parts per billion)	Urban area population (millions)
Denver	
Phoenix	
Pittsburgh	
Washington	
Athens	
Sofia	
Houston	
Chicago	
Madrid	
Milwaukee	
Rome	
Berlin	
Boston	
Stockholm	
Barcelona	
Lyon	
TORONTO	
CALGARY	
Prague	
EDMONTON	
Warsaw	
Hamburg	
OTTAWA/GATINEAU	
Zürich	
Paris	
MONTRÉAL	
London	
Seattle	
Brussels	
Amsterdam	
VANCOUVER	
Bucharest	

FIGURE 15.3 | Annual Average Concentrations of Fine Particulate Matter for Selected Canadian and International Cities, 2011

Source: Environment Canada, at: <www.ec.gc.ca/indicateurs-indicators/default.asp?lang=en&n=FDBB2779-1>. © Her Majesty The Queen in Right of Canada, Environment Canada, 2014. Reproduced with the permission of the Minister of Public Works and Government Services Canada.

Body burden A buildup of harmful synthetic chemicals and heavy metals in our bodies.

accumulate in the food chain and, eventually, in human food supplies. Chronic exposure to POPs in our food and air has resulted in an alarming buildup of harmful synthetic chemicals and heavy metals in our bodies, a phenomenon that has been termed **body burden** (Coming Clean, 2006).

However, not everyone is affected to the same degree. Children in both developed and developing nations are especially vulnerable to chemical, physical, and biological pollutants in the environment, since their immune systems are only partly developed. Indoor air pollution caused by fossil-fuel combustion (for cooking and heating) is responsible for respiratory infections that cause 20 per cent of the deaths among children less than five years of age. Diarrheal diseases claim another 2 million children a year, mainly because of unclean drinking water and poor hygiene. Ailing and elderly members of society are also at a higher than average risk because of their declining health.

Environmental contamination events continue to raise public concern about health. The public has become much less tolerant of unintended environmental consequences

The Canadian Press/Jason Franson

University of Alberta professor David Schindler holds a deformed white fish caught in Lake Athabasca, near Fort Chipewyan, during a press conference in Edmonton, Alberta. Dozens of top scientists from around the world have criticized the Canadian government's decision not to provide laboratories with funding to study the environmental impacts of the oil sands development.

associated with technology and industrial development. Many Canadians are aware of infamous global environmental catastrophes, such as the nuclear meltdowns in Chernobyl and Fukushima. These incidents have raised public awareness regarding people's health and safety worldwide.

Populations in Canada, too, have suffered health consequences because of environmental contamination. In Cape Breton, Nova Scotia, the Sydney tar ponds have been referred to as "the most contaminated industrial site in the country" and arguably the worst in North America (Burra et al., 2006). Over 100 years of improper waste disposal practices—associated with steel production and coke-oven operations—have severely contaminated soil and surface groundwater. This site contains over 700,000 tonnes of contaminated sediments, including PAHs, hydrocarbon (HC) compounds, coal tar, PCBs, coal dust, and municipal sewage (Haalboom et al., 2006).

Numerous health studies have been conducted as a result of community concerns, specifically regarding cancer and reproductive outcomes. According to Burra et al. (2006), "[r]esidents of Sydney have been shown to experience higher mortality rates as well as a higher incidence of particular cancers than elsewhere in the province." In fact, stomach, breast, and lung cancers occur at a rate more than double the national averages—in 19 per cent of men and 14 per cent of women (ibid.).

As well, it should be noted that people with disabilities or other chronic health problems experience environmental issues in especially marked ways, as is evident in Box 15.3. This is especially true of their experience of the "built environment."

CANADIAN researchers

BOX 15.2 | Raymond Murphy, University of Ottawa

Normally, social activists—including environmental activists—are idealistic in their goals and their expectations of success. But so are people who choose to ignore the prospects of environmental disaster; they are faith-driven to the point of near blindness. So, what would be a realistic approach to environmental problems that need our attention? That's the question troubling Raymond Murphy, Professor Emeritus at the University of Ottawa.

In his 2006 paper "Environmental Realism: From Apologetics to Substance," Murphy reminds us that what is wrong with common present-day thinking about the environment is a "cornucopian view" that complacently supposes that economic rationality and technological mastery will prevent or overcome unexpected natural emergencies. We need to be realistic, not blind, to the risk of natural disasters and societal collapse. Disaster research and studies of collapsed societies can teach us about the failure of foresight we must avoid, the dreadful consequences of such disasters, the uncertainties involved in foreseeing natural dynamics, and the social barriers that keep us from learning from past mistakes. We cannot afford to let ignorance about environmental issues, fed by economic greed, blind us to the potential disasters on the horizon. But how can we motivate attentiveness?

In a 2004 paper, "Disaster or Sustainability: The Dance of Human Agents with Nature's Actants," Murphy calls

attention to the complex and delicate interaction between uncontrollable nature—as exemplified in the remarkable ice storm of January 1998—and human attempts to construct meaning around such events. One issue that concerns Murphy is the tendency of people in authority to replace openness with secrecy in the face of a disaster and to use disasters for other purposes: for example, to justify extraordinary (but irrelevant) spending or legislation.

Beyond that, environmental issues engage a long time frame and conflicting motivations. In a 2012 paper, "The Tragedy of the Atmospheric Commons: Discounting Future Costs and Risks in Pursuit of Immediate Fossil-Fuel Benefits," Murphy and his collaborator Maya Murphy note that climate change is slow and gradual, with long time lags, a global scale, and shifting locations. This complexity poses problems, because the mere chance of a distant disaster will fail to motivate action. Fear motivates people only if the threat is immediate, visible, and dangerous. Climate change does not satisfy the first two of these conditions. Therefore, many are inclined to shift to a strategy of hope and the promise of benefits in the event of environmental change. However, as we seek to make good on this promise, we encounter new difficulties, especially given the costs associated with the foregoing opportunities. People tend to discount costs and harm in the distant future—likewise costs and harm to distant poor countries.

The Risk Society

Risk society A society in which risk is increased by technological and economic developments, raising the need for more cautious awareness, but also in which active risk-taking is considered a core element of economic and social progress.

The Sydney, Nova Scotia, case represents what Beck (1992) and Giddens (1990) have called a **risk society**—a technology- and science-driven society that embraces both the benefits and drawbacks of progress. Contemporary risks, in this view, are chronic disease, environmental destruction, pollution, and so on, which are pervasive, non-class-specific problems that span nations, populations, and cultures, without pinpointing the industrial sources of those risks. In 2009, Benn, Brown and North-Samardzic provided evidence for continuing to support the notion of a "risk society"; this was in the case study of excessive hexachlorobenzene (HCB) waste in Sydney, where they found a growing movement against scientific evidence of toxic risk.

The technologies devised to improve our material conditions and advance our collective quality of life can also have adverse health implications. These technologies include X-rays, food preservatives, breast implants, and pesticides. As we suggested above,

Public Issues *and* Public Policy

BOX 15.3 | **Disability and Environmental Issues**

The urban environment poses many challenges and risks to disabled people who rely on wheelchair use. Since the urban environment is a built environment, it can be manipulated to fit the requirements of those with accessibility needs.

Nevertheless, analyses of urban environments around the world reveal that public spaces in cities are not completely compatible with wheelchair use, thus making it difficult or sometimes impossible for wheelchair users to access them. In Al Ain, United Arab Emirates, architectural barriers were assessed for 17 public buildings (e.g., shopping malls or banks) with regard to parking accessibility, ramps, entrance accessibility, internal accessible routes, appropriate toilets, elevators, public telephones, and water fountains (Rivano-Fischer, 2004). None of these buildings met the appropriate standards for wheelchair accessibility 100 per cent (ibid.). While good efforts were made to increase accessibility, only 5 of the 17 sites had handicapped parking spaces (and none of those spaces were the appropriate width), only 3 of the 17 had designated accessible toilets, and only 10

of the 17 had an elevator that was accessible from the entrance (ibid.).

Another study assessed the accessibility of public buildings in the central business district of Istanbul, Turkey (Evcil, 2009). Similarly, many aspects of the layout of public buildings decreased their accessibility to wheelchair users (ibid.). The problems included all 26 buildings not being accessible by public transport; narrow sidewalks and paving issues in front of the buildings that obstructed proper wheelchair navigation; narrow bathroom doors and high sinks; and a limited number of places with accessible parking areas (ibid.). While 297 businesses assessed for parking, entrance, and interior wheelchair accessibility in Montana, USA, reveal much higher accessibility rates, 10 per cent of buildings (financial institutions, retail businesses, entertainment facilities, and consumer service locations) were nonetheless inaccessible to wheelchair users (Seekins et al., 2012).

Not being able to enter banks, get into certain stores, go to some university classes, or work in certain office buildings is the everyday reality for many people in wheelchairs.

industrialized societies are experiencing more and more technological emergencies, including accidents involving hazardous materials or nuclear power or mass transportation.

In a highly technological society like ours, technological problems—even disasters—are predictable and inevitable. In that sense, we are sure to experience what sociologist Charles Perrow (1999) has called **normal accidents**—those that are likely to take place in complex systems of people and machines and that result from the unanticipated interaction of multiple failures—that is, normal accidents. To prove this point, Perrow examined a variety of technological disasters—including the nuclear accidents at Three Mile Island in Pennsylvania and at Chernobyl in Ukraine—and concluded that nuclear power was a high-risk system for producing energy. He also examined detailed records on aircraft accidents, marine accidents, and accidents at dams, mines, and petrochemical plants. For Perrow, the "villains" in all these cases of catastrophe were system complexities, on the one hand, and subsystem couplings, on the other.

Conventional engineering tries to ensure safety by building in extra warnings and safeguards. However, this approach fails because it increases system complexity. Complexity not only makes systems more likely to fail, it creates new and unexpected kinds of accidents. In other words, highly complex systems have more chances of failing and more ways to fail. The more tightly connected (or coupled) a system's parts are, the higher the likelihood of a chain reaction of errors occurring. Thus, simplicity and loose

Normal accidents Likely accidents in complex systems of people and machines, resulting from the unanticipated interaction of multiple failures.

coupling are preferable from a safety standpoint, but complexity and tight coupling are increasingly the norm.

Technological catastrophes are often blamed on human error, but invariably such error is the social side of a built-in technological risk. Another, more controversial example of technology having potentially negative health consequences is the implementation of agricultural biotechnology, molecular biology research, and applied engineering to farming (Madeley, 2009). For millennia, farmers have experimented with natural cross-pollination and selective breeding techniques to improve the genetic stock of crops and livestock. However, the long-term health effects of this new technology, which involves the introduction of genetic material from other species to create fast-growing, disease-resistant "super" plants and livestock, may lead to the creation of new allergies and other, more serious forms of technology-induced disease (Wolfenbarger, 2002).

Environmental concerns have also been raised over the agribusiness industry's practice of monoculture, where entire fields are planted over multiple growth cycles with a single genetically modified (GM) crop; this practice destroys diversity and soil health, contaminates the genetic pool of non-GM crops, and may create harmful complications in the developmental cycle of other species.

Concerns over the unknown medium- and long-term effects of GM foods on human and environmental health led the European Union (EU) to impose in 1998 a six-year moratorium on new GM crops. When the ban was lifted, the EU implemented a series of strict regulations, requiring that food-packaging labels identify the presence of GM ingredients and that these GM ingredients be traced through the production process. Powerful agribusiness lobbyists in the US, Canada, and Brazil oppose these regulations, claiming that they violate international free trade agreements. It remains to be seen whether the artificial manipulation of other species will create more nutritious and healthier products to the benefit of human kind or whether it will introduce new health problems and cause irreversible harm to ecosystems.

Social Responses and Solutions to Environmental Problems

The ways we think, work, create, and purchase have significantly changed because of increased concern for our natural environment. As we have suggested, however, this does not mean that all of our problems with environmental degradation are by any means solved. These concerns and emerging changes only represent an important step in the right direction.

Today, concern for the environment has become embedded within popular culture (Curran, 2006). Many would propose that there is now widespread agreement that we face pervasive environmental challenges and that social, economic, and political change must occur if we are to meet to these challenges successfully. In other words, unless human beings around the world change their behaviours in a meaningful way, the quality of life on earth—or life itself—will be threatened. For example, it is now widely regarded that if climate change continues at the current rate, we will be faced with extremely negative consequences (Norgaard, 2002). In the following section, we outline several initiatives and changes that have emerged as a result of this threat.

Environmental Social Movements

Various environmental movements and pressure groups emerged during the 1970s, and environmental problems became significant areas of discussion within national political arenas. Even in countries resistant to discussions of climate change, such as the United States, people started to take the problem seriously.

Gallup poll data from the US show a marked change in people's views about climate change, in the direction of greater concern. People who identify themselves politically as Democrats or Independents showed increasing environmental concern between 2000 and 2010, while those identifying as Republicans showed a mild backlash, with an increased number saying they were unsympathetic to the environmental movement.

Environmental social movements have emerged as the most "vibrant, diverse, and powerful social movements occurring today, across all corners of the globe" (Doyle, 2005). At the beginning of this century, for example, the United States "boast[ed] at least 150 national environmental organizations, 12,000 grassroots groups, and an estimated 14 million members" (Carter, 2001).

Most pressure group activity involves conventional political activities, such as lobbying and educational initiatives. During the 1980s, the rapid growth of this movement provided a wealth of resources to help groups to "become highly professional organizations and to win regular access to policy elites" (ibid.). Undoubtedly, these groups have become largely responsible for the progressive environmental change that has occurred in Canada and the United States.

Two notable waves of pressure-group mobilization can be identified. The first, emerging during the late nineteenth century, was the *conservationist* movement. This focused on wildlife protection as well as on the preservation of natural resources. The second wave of pressure-group mobilization emerged during the 1960s, resulting in increased group size and greater involvement. As Carter explains, "[r]eflecting the international nature of modern environmentalism, new groups such as Friends of the Earth and Greenpeace rapidly became international organizations with national affiliates in many countries"

TABLE 15.2	Orientation toward Environmental Movement, by Party ID		
	DEMOCRAT %	INDEPENDENT %	REPUBLICAN %
2010			
An active participant	24	19	15
Sympathetic, but not active	50	40	36
Neutral	22	31	30
Unsympathetic	3	10	18
2000			
An active participant	14	19	14
Sympathetic, but not active	63	51	50
Neutral	20	22	27-
Unsympathetic	2	4	8-

Source: Gallup poll, at: <www.gallup.com/poll/127487/environmental-movement-endures-less-consensus.aspx>.

(ibid.). Industrial pollution, nuclear power, and the increased magnitude of global problems became prominent issues within these groups during this time.

Environmental pressure groups (EPGs) are varied in target and purpose. As a result, some observers suggest that we should not identify the environmental movement as a single movement "because the differences between the groups are more significant than the similarities" (ibid.). However, Dalton (1994) proposes the "green rainbow" as an all-inclusive term: "Differences between groups reflect tendencies along a continuum between a conservative orientation and an ecological orientation." This approach, as Roots (1999) remarks, illustrates a "broad network of people and organizations engaged in collective action in the pursuit of environmental benefits."

Still, regardless of how we classify or conceptualize EPGs as a social movement, it is clear that a considerable amount of environmental change has occurred as a result of their activities. Binder and Neumayer (2005) conducted an empirical study testing the effects of EPGs. They found that the stronger the force of the group, the greater impact they have on air pollution levels. EPGs achieve effectiveness through eliciting the help of foundations, donors, international organizations, and stakeholders who are also seeking to reduce the air pollution in their environment.

Population Control

As discussed in the previous chapter, a growing global population is not in itself a social problem. However, overpopulation in the developing world and underpopulation in the developed world are problems because they reveal flaws in the organization and migration of human populations.

Industrialization, urbanization, education, mass literacy, and the emancipation of women were all key parts of the voluntary reduction in child-bearing over the past century and a half. Invariably, birth rates have fallen wherever women have received more education, have delayed marriage, and have enjoyed more social, economic, and political equality with men (Couchman, 1986). An example is provided by the desegregation of American schools in 1970. Yan Liu et al. (2012) point to the 3.2 per cent decrease in the number of black adolescents attending school from 1970 to 1980, marking the negative correlation between access to education and birth rate.

Several developing societies—among them Costa Rica, Sri Lanka, and Kerala State in India—have had notable success in lowering birth rates. In these societies, low mortality and fertility rates are the result of a long process that began with fairer income distribution, better nutrition, more education and autonomy (especially for women), higher rates of political awareness and participation, and universal access to health services. In addition, income and land redistribution have given people an increased sense of involvement in their own lives—hence, they feel they have more to gain from changing their fertility decisions. This is especially true of women, who with more education and autonomy are no longer as reliant on children for income security or for the maintenance of their social roles in the larger social fabric.

Today's Canada is underpopulated by any definition of the word. Yet some people view high rates of immigration as a population problem and a social problem. Immigration has become an explosive political issue. Many people who have immigrated want the chance to bring their relatives to Canada, and many outside the country want a chance to get in. However, whenever the economy weakens, many Canadians resist the push for more immigrants. Some even want the immigration rate cut back.

Classic **STUDIES**

BOX 15.4 | The Limits to Growth

As the world population rapidly approached 4 billion people around the third quarter of the twentieth century—it currently exceeds 7 billion—researchers Donella H. Meadows, Dennis L. Meadows, Jørgen Randers, and William W. Behrens III published *The Limits to Growth* (1972), a book that examines the consequences of human population growth for human survival.

These four authors, international experts who assembled at the MIT Sloan School of Management, had been commissioned to write this book by the Club of Rome. The "Club" had been founded a few years earlier as a global think tank (or policy institute) focusing on pressing international issues. To carry out their commission, the authors created the "World3 model," a computerized method for studying the future of the world by simulating interlinked changes over a 100-year-long imaginary history. The goal of this computer simulation was to track how complex human systems have changed, and will change, over time. The authors built the model to investigate five major trends of global concern: accelerating industrialization, rapid population growth, widespread malnutrition, depletion of non-renewable resources, and a deteriorating environment.

The researchers assumed that each of these variables increases exponentially while the capability of technology to increase the availability of resources grows linearly—an assumption as old as the first demographer, Thomas Malthus. The results of the simulation shocked the world and provoked debate about "global overshoot." Most of all, the research has focused our attention on humanity's tendency to demand too much of nature—much more than the biosphere can readily supply or replace.

The Limits to Growth was intended not so much to make specific predictions about the future as to examine how exponential growth affects finite resources. The book analyzed 12 different scenarios, all of which showed that should the then-current economic growth and population trends continue, within 100 years the world's natural resources would be either exhausted or too expensive to buy. Hugely influential at the time, the report was translated into dozens of languages and read by millions. It came to two key conclusions. The first was that if population, industrialization, pollution, food production, and resource depletion continue to grow at the current rate, humanity will reach "the limit to growth" on this planet at some time in the next 100 years. The result will be an immediate and uncorrectable decline in both world population and industrial capacity.

The second conclusion, however, was that the rate of growth could be curbed. Slowing growth to zero would ideally mean achieving a state of global equilibrium in which all basic material needs are fulfilled and every person can reach his or her human potential. However, it might not be possible to achieve this equilibrium at the highest current levels of human consumption. Cutbacks in spending, buying, and consuming would be necessary. Said another way, while it would be impossible to achieve world equilibrium at North American standards of living, it would be possible to achieve equilibrium at standards far higher than those currently enjoyed by most of humanity.

The authors concluded that the sooner people begin to strive for global equilibrium, the sooner it will be attained, and doing this would eliminate the dire risks of the world-wide system collapse spelled out in their computer model. These conclusions were widely criticized and, in the end, ignored. Yet, nothing in the past 40 years has invalidated the book's central warning—that humanity is in trouble, that it is living beyond its means. If anything, that fact is even clearer today than it was when our population was a third smaller and before we understood the dangers of climate change.

Continuing interest in the topic gave rise, in 2004, to an update of the classic work, now titled *Limits to Growth: The 30-Year Update*, by Meadows, Meadows, and Randers. Here, the authors try again to gain public attention with their message. They stress that humanity is coming seriously close to "global overshoot." The new book asserts that in the next 70 years or so, the system collapse will no longer be preventable, as environmental decline is inevitable. Instead, the challenge will be to contain and limit damage to the earth and to humanity (Meadows et al., 2004). The authors conclude that it is too late for sustainable development. Now we must choose between unrestrained collapse and what we might call "harm reduction"—a conscious reduction (to supportable levels) of the energy and materials we consume. In this updated version, World3 is used to provide 10 new scenarios in which the gap between the rich and poor expands, the industrial production in developed nations declines, and essential non-renewable resources become harder to obtain and more expensive to use.

Still, the book remains largely unread, the message largely ignored.

Because population is not the sole cause of urban problems or environmental damage, population control alone cannot solve these problems. However, social organization is harder to improve and social problems are harder to solve when a population is large and growing rapidly. So much effort and money have to be diverted to maintaining and providing for the population—for example, the care and education of the young or the creation and maintenance of housing and roads—that money is unavailable for new initiatives like job creation or research and development.

Science as an Environmental Claims-Making Activity

Think for a moment about a pressing environmental problem—global warming, ozone depletion, or water and air pollution, to name a few. All of these are examples of problems that have been uncovered through scientific observation. In fact, it is rare to find an environmental problem that is not strongly associated with a body of scientific research. Scientific researchers act as "gatekeepers," screening potential claims for credibility (Hannigan, 1995). The support and focus of the scientific community lift environmental problems into the mainstream, often above most other social problems and inequalities that are dependent on moral claims alone (ibid.).

Yet, here lies the crux of the problematic relationship between science and the environment. Far too often, the self-appointed, government-appointed, and industry-appointed and -refereed gatekeepers and experts do not have the practical knowledge base to carry out their functions efficiently and accurately. The collapse of the North Atlantic cod fishery might have been averted if federal Fisheries and Oceans scientists, who are responsible for setting quotas and estimating stock biomass, had listened to inshore fishers and learned from their local ecological knowledge in the years and decades preceding the collapse in the early 1990s, rather than relying on theoretical models and the biased observations of the fish processors who, equipped with technology capable of mass-trawling, urged for ever-higher quotas (Coward et al., 2000).

What happened after the massive oil spill in the Gulf of Mexico would have been averted if economics, greed, and science had not trumped the essential tenet of the environment and development issue—the precautionary principle. Economics and science can create an unholy alliance where cost/benefit analysis determines what can or might be done, and most people would be appalled and alarmed to know what, in these scientific models, is considered a bearable "cost" (even in a "polluter pays" scenario) in terms of environmental degradation and of human and other life.

However, science has become the focus of environmental claims-making. Consider, for example, the debate surrounding genetic engineering and its harmful effects on the natural environment. In this case, claims-makers reject science for traditional, cultural rationality, ultimately arguing that science is interfering with the natural order of our environment.

Environmental Policies

Environmental problems, because of their broad, snowballing nature, are difficult and expensive to solve. Still, all levels of society must seek remedies because of the seriousness of the problems and their costs to humanity and the planet.

Precautionary principle A tenet of environmentalism as it interfaces with economic development; it insists that when serious or irreversible damage could result from development, the wise and necessary decision is to not go ahead with that course of action, regardless of assumptions that technology could or will resolve any future problems or damage.

DARWIN'S NIGHTMARE
This important 2004 film shows how poverty and the remnants of colonialism cause horrible environmental damage in modern-day Tanzania.

At the highest levels, national and international policies are needed to ensure that we follow a common, co-operative path. Under this approach, governments should try to establish policies that will make it profitable for industries to clean up the environment and exercise ecologically friendly practices. We must also demand greater readiness on the part of emergency response organizations—local government, fire and police departments, and special response teams—to respond to crises caused by insufficiently regulated industries.

Government policy should encourage people to reduce their impact on the environment. Borek and Bohon (2008) examined the effect of the national environmental policies of EU countries on people's decisions to drive an automobile. They determined that people living in nations that adopt strong pro-environmental policies report a greater likelihood of their driving less for environmental reasons. Ultimately, this suggests that national policies that focus on environmental sustainability are associated with people's pro-environmental behaviour and attitudes. While this research looked specifically at member countries of the EU, it also logically aligns with evidence from North America. As such, the United States' (Vogel, 2003; Zito, 2005) and Canada's (CBC News, 2007) refusal to meet Kyoto requirements is understandable: Americans and Canadians are among the greatest global consumers of energy and water, and they produce some of the highest rates of pollution in the world.

Despite actions to reduce greenhouse gases in Canada, businesses, voluntary groups, and various political leaders have made only weak efforts. Greater international co-operation and strengthened domestic policy on environmental issues are necessary if the behaviour of individuals is to improve.

Post-materialist Values

A theory proposed by Ronald Inglehart, a political scientist at the University of Michigan, suggests that there is widespread public support for solving the problems of technology and environment we have discussed here. He attributes this new environmental activism to a culture shift that originated in a generation accustomed to prosperity. Inglehart (1990; see also Tepperman, 2001) proposes that people who grow up in prosperous and secure conditions develop high personal and social goals. These include the goals of belonging, having self-esteem, and achieving self-actualization.

Over time, the post-war generation replaced earlier generations as voters and in elite positions of influence. In the West, according to Inglehart, the result is a new political culture. The new generation's goals have increasingly come to define the political agenda of Western democracies. It is post-materialist in the sense that it places less importance than earlier generations on personal wealth, economic development, and economic determinants of social life. In this respect, the new outlook is also post-Marxist. The new **post-materialist culture** contains political attitudes favouring action and the potential for action. It encourages more political involvement, and more protest, than the materialist culture did. However, much of this activity occurs outside the framework of elections and traditional political parties.

Inglehart's research examines anti-establishment grassroots politics and skepticism about material progress. One major part of this post-materialist shift is the growing support for environmentalism and for movements that seek solutions to these problems. Linked as they are to specific political issues and parties, these "new" needs produce

Post-materialist culture A new cultural orientation that puts less emphasis on material consumption and class issues and more on non-material (quality of collective life) benefits, such as environmental improvement.

"new" political behaviours, including shifts in goals and partisanship. Post-materialists, who also report higher levels of material satisfaction, are more politically active than materialists (Inglehart, 1977). This shift is most marked in the prosperous Western nations, among the most-educated and youngest people.

If Inglehart's theory is valid, the problems we have discussed in this chapter are already on the way to being solved. New environmentalist movements and political parties will gain ever more support, form governments, and ban environmentally unsound practices. Human life will become healthier and happier. Yet, the evidence does not support the theory's predictions (Tepperman, 2001). Some say that Inglehart's approach is surprisingly simple or naive—a one-dimensional view of political culture that pits materialism against post-materialism. Some say that we cannot assume that a shift in cultural values towards environmentalism will translate into political action. We need only look at the negative North American political response to the Kyoto agreement to know that strong feelings about the environment do not necessarily equate with committed political action when elected officials must also contend with competing economic and political interests in a highly complex world.

We may not be able to rely on a new political culture of post-materialism to bring about environmental or technological change, to improve our health and well-being. People will have to mobilize to consider, discuss, protest, and enact new policies. Furthermore, several factors, including global capitalism, stand in the way. So long as "the commons" is not understood to include the entire planet, "the tragedy" will continue to play itself out as those with power and influence seek personal short-term gain over longer-term equity.

Resource Management

Part of the social nature of environmental problems comes in the form of resource management. More specifically, the social process of deciding who should get what amount of resources can lead to intergroup strife, political tension, and, at times, violence. As resources dwindle, competition for what remains will become increasingly fierce (Homer-Dixon, 1994).

Ryabov and Blasius (2011) report influences of social interaction in the competition for environmental resources. Their research on a phytoplankton model shows that access to resources varies depending on the other species' co-existence and position in the resource supply. However, they also note that co-existence between species with differing goals for their resources also contribute to a stable and beneficial environment for both existing species.

Therefore, conflict over resources is not inevitable. Further evidence is provided by a case from northern British Columbia involving the formation of an alliance between the Cheslatta T'en, a First Nations tribe, and non-Native local residents (Larsen, 2003). Beginning in the 1980s, the Cheslatta leaders sought to expand their social networks to increase their political power and gain control over land they saw as rightfully theirs. Through grassroots efforts, a coalition was formed that helped all locals, Native and non-Native, to legally bypass the (often lengthy) treaty settlement process. In addition to bringing together disparate groups, this inter-ethnic alliance fought effectively to protect the environment.

According to Larsen (ibid., 74), "Cheslatta leaders used cultural exchanges and social networks generated by the alliance to fashion territorial initiatives that, when taken together, channel popular environmentalism, provincial forestry policies, and ancestral ethnoecology into collective identity, action, and authority. As a result, the band has attained political influence over its traditional lands without participating in the province's treaty settlement process." In short, this strategy of serving the environment through social and political mobilization is an important example in simultaneously improving our social and natural worlds.

Effective resource management is not only the result of grassroots activists; consumers and business owners can help combat negative environmental trends as well, as evidenced by the Clayoquot Sound protests of the 1990s. The Pacific coast of British Columbia contains some of the last areas of temperate rainforest in the world (Suzuki and Dressel, 2002). During the 1990s, logging companies successfully lobbied for the permission to cut down a portion of this forest. Despite the loggers' having consent from the government, a boycott of wood taken from the BC forests forced all parties involved to agree to a moratorium on logging in the most vulnerable areas of this temperate rainforest ecosystem (ibid.).

Further discussion of individual strategies will highlight how you can hope to make a difference.

Voluntary Simplicity

The term "voluntary simplicity" refers to people choosing to reduce spending on goods and services, replacing these behaviours with non-materialistic sources of satisfaction

Stephen Lovekin/Getty Images

Graham Hill, an entrepreneur from Sutton, Quebec, at eBay's Future of Shopping event. Hill is the CEO of LifeEdited.com, a project devoted to living well with less.

and meaning (Etzioni, 2004). Voluntary simplicity movements have emerged as a criticism of consumerism as well as in an overall discomfort with the overarching goal of the capitalist economy.

Originally, support for this movement was slight, occurring mainly among the followers of various countercultures. However, in recent years, a significant number of people in Western societies have embraced these values. As Inglehart (1977: 3) suggests, "the values of Western publics have been shifting from an overwhelming emphasis on material well-being and physical security toward greater emphasis on the quality of life." When people engage in voluntary simplicity, they autonomously decide to reduce—if not erase—conspicuous consumption and pursue activities and experiences that have greater intangible rewards.

Levels of voluntary simplicity are wide-ranging and occur along a scale of least to most consumption reduction: (1) downshifters—consumption is only moderately reduced; (2) strong simplification—a significant reduction in consumerism occurs; and (3) holistic simplification—people change (and simplify) their entire lifestyle to ensure a smaller global footprint.

Downshifters are typically affluent, well-off members of society who reduce consumption while maintaining a rich and consumption-oriented lifestyle. They may decide to "dress down," "wearing jeans and inexpensive loafers, t-shirts, and driving beat-up cars" (Etzioni, 2004), taking pride in their moderate tastes and modest lifestyles.

Strong simplifiers take this process one step further by giving up high-paying and prestigious jobs to work fewer hours and earn less income. This group chooses less income and lower pension payouts for a more leisurely, family-oriented lifestyle.

The final group, the *holistic simplifiers*, adjust their entire life pattern according to voluntary simplicity ideologies. According to Etzioni, "[t]hey often move from affluent suburbs or gentrified parts of major cities to smaller towns, the countryside, farms and less affluent or less urbanized parts of the country with the explicit goal of leading a 'simpler' life" (ibid., 409). As a result, a social movement with a plainly anti-consumerist philosophy—sometimes called "the simple living movement"—has emerged.

Chapter Summary

In this chapter, we have discussed the causes and consequences of environmental problems and environmental degradation. Ironically, both the causes and solutions are a result of human ingenuity. The problems discussed in this chapter include some of the greatest challenges faced today because many of the problems hold wide-ranging and potentially irreversible effects. For this reason, the actions that we take today—either "problem-solving" or "problem-creating"—will be long-lasting. Environmental social movements have been important, both historically and today, in seeking solutions.

Environmental destruction is a problem that occurs on a global level. This destruction will increase as a function of population growth, urban concentration, and technologies associated with industrial production. Disposing of solid and toxic waste is a major problem, as it demands new landfills and can disrupt the ecosystem. Depleting non-renewable resources is also a serious problem. Developed countries are most to blame here, as they are far more wasteful than developing countries. Since industry is profit-oriented, it is not likely to take responsibility for pollution; more government regulation will be needed.

We have shown that environmental problems have harmful health outcomes. Those affected most are the poor living in rural areas. Environmental harm accounts for 3 million premature deaths from exposure to air pollution alone, and 90 per cent of these deaths occur in developing countries. Climate change resulting from global warming has led to a rise in droughts and famines, especially in Africa and in other regions along the equator; it has also led to more frequent natural disasters, such as floods and violent storms.

As we have seen, the reckless use of technology is an increasing concern. Humanity's tendency to focus on short-term gain and practise wilful ignorance about environmental consequences has had devastating results. Even today, many are still prepared to sacrifice the environment for short-term gains in comfort and wealth. This will continue without large-scale change in attitudes and legislation to protect the environment.

Questions for Critical Thought

1. In your view, does technology lead human beings to destruction or to progress? Give examples and explain. Also, do you agree with the "normal accidents" theory of Charles Perrow, which holds that technological problems are predictable and unavoidable?

2. Do you think that the reputation of scientific evidence is suffering as a result of claims for and/or against environmental conditions? What do you think environmental researchers can do to justify their results? What strategies might they employ to appropriately inform the public of their findings?

3. Can you name a few organizations that represent an environment pressure group (EPG)? Do you think EPGs truly have an impact on reducing environmental damage? If so, could this provide a way for all companies to change their strategies and become more environmentally friendly?

4. Do you think it is possible for our society to reach a stable rate of environmental consumption? Given what we know about the potential advantages and disadvantages in resource management, what are some alternative ways to manage resources effectively?

5. Why do you think societies continue their practices that harm the environment even when they know that poor environmental conditions lead to poorer health?

6. If an individualistic mindset in Western culture leads to a "tragedy of the commons," what do you think the benefits and consequences would be for a collectivist mindset such as seen in Eastern cultures?

Recommended Readings

Fox, Jonathan A., and Brown, David L. 1998. *Global Environmental Accord: Strategies for Sustainability and Institutional Innovation*. Cambridge, MA: MIT Press.

Kheel, Marti. 2007. *Nature Ethics: An Ecofeminist Perspective*. Lanham, MD: Rowman and Littlefield Publishers.

Rawcliffe, Peter. 1998. *Environmental Pressure Groups in Transition (Issues in Environmental Politics)*. Manchester, UK: Manchester University Press.

Zehner, Ozzie. 2012. *Green Illusions*. Lincoln: University of Nebraska Press.

Part 5

The Future

MarioGuti/Thinkstock

16

What Problems Are on the Way?

Nipitphand/Thinkstock

LEARNING OBJECTIVES

- To discover and understand what is meant by "future studies."
- To examine what past theorists have predicted for our future.
- To acknowledge the constantly changing definition of "social problems."
- To discuss potential social problems that may persist into or arise in the future.
- To examine the emergence, current uses, and future implications of technological innovations.
- To understand the implications of the future of cyberspace.

Introduction

Unlike the topics previously discussed in this book—poverty, crime, addiction, and so on—which are only partly socially constructed, "the future" is entirely constructed (Fuller and Loogma, 2009). It does not exist yet; we have to imagine it, based on current trends, hopes, wishes, fears, and calculations.

Thinking about the Future

A recurring theme in this book is the interconnected nature of social problems—they do not stand in isolation; rather, they are all related to one another. Such complexity suggests that a change in one realm of social life will have an impact in other areas. Another important aspect of social problems is their historical basis. Most problems today are the result of long-standing neglect and simmering conflict.

At the same time, definitions and perceptions of social problems constantly change. As we saw in the chapter on alcohol and drug abuse, for example, what is thought of as an unlawful substance and therefore a social problem when used or abused can shift markedly over time (Herzog et al., 2009; Lopez, 2013). Cocaine and opiates were once considered appropriate medicinal and recreational drugs but now are strictly banned by the criminal justice system (Katz and Mazer, 2009). Recently, Human Growth Hormone (HGH) has become one of the most stigmatized and persecuted doping drugs owing to widespread media attention regarding its alleged health consequences. Despite the lack of empirical evidence to substantiate these claims, campaigns urging the eradication of HGH continue to grow (Lopez, 2013). Then there's the case of marijuana, first considered legal by public officials, then illegal. Today, we have legal access to marijuana strictly for therapeutic purposes, and there is the prospect that marijuana use will eventually be effectively decriminalized (Hyshka, 2009). Not all social problems have long histories, and it is evident that people and societies, for various reasons, will continue to create and influence new problems.

The dynamic nature of social problems poses problems not only for people actively working to improve social conditions, but also for researchers trying to foresee the social problems of the future. While improvements can be made, the haphazardness of sociological research makes precise forecasting difficult (Aligica, 2009). Our goal as sociologists in thinking about the future is to formulate possible solutions to the social problems that we predict are likely to occur or recur.

What Is Futures Studies?

People have been discussing the possibilities and problems of studying and predicting the future for centuries. Writing about "utopias"—places where everything works in perfect harmony—started with ancient peoples imagining the origins of humanity and the afterlife. Since Sir Thomas More's novel *Utopia* (1516), authors have repeatedly invented societies to illustrate important principles of social organization. One invention includes "dystopias," which depict negative principles of social organization—things to avoid. Of these books, one of the most well-known is George Orwell's *1984*, which demonstrates the dangers of the Soviet totalitarian regime.

The history of the debate about the value of utopia parallels the history of utopian thinking. Over 50 years ago, American social theorist Andrew Hacker (1955) identified three categories of utopian-thinking critics: Democrats, Dialecticians, and Devil-Hunters. The Democrats believe that a utopia may invoke dictatorial tendencies. Historically, many idealized societies, starting with Plato's *Republic*, have imagined unequal and unfree, although humane, societies. The Dialecticians believe in the value of discovering historical laws. For them, utopian thought is perceived as idle speculation or dreaming. Finally, the Devil-Hunters are concerned with the importance of overcoming original sin or, at least, the notion that humans are *unable* to change their ways significantly.

Futures studies The area of research concerned with forecasting possible scenarios—technological, economic, political, social, environmental—in order to prepare for and shape what may come.

Utopian thinking is valuable if it is rooted in empirical knowledge about human beings and their behaviour. This means that **futures studies** seek to make use of our understanding of both the past and present. Humans will not inevitably repeat the past, but it is improbable that they will completely depart from past behaviour. Humans are unlikely—suddenly and en masse—to become saints or devils. What some define as "human nature" is not going to change, for the most part. Our best guess about the future is that people will continue to respond positively to new opportunities that will likely be supported and enhanced by new technology (Sandars, 2012).

Therefore, "technology can offer some aid in predicting the future—as science moves through networks of implication, and each discovery suggests a set of later steps. From these data, scenarios of possible alternative futures are created, which are then used as choices within strategic planning initiatives" (University of Houston–Clear Lake, 2001). This is the reason most futurology and futures research focuses on technological change. Almost as often—for example, in market and political research—it focuses on demographic change. In the following discussion, we will consider both of these foci. What they have in common is an attempt to predict or "forecast" the future on the basis of knowledge from the past (Pourezzat et al., 2008).

Alternative Forecasting Methods

Forecasting methods fall into several main categories, many of which were identified by David Walonick (1993). One such method is *genius forecasting*, which relies mainly on intuition and insight; a prime example would be the forecasts provided by H.G. Wells (1902), some of which are discussed below. Many genius forecasts turn out to be wrong, but others turn out to be right. As Malcolm Gladwell (2009) has argued, individuals make very rapid intuitive judgements, decisions, and predictions that often turn out to be correct. Some people produce consistently accurate forecasts by this method, and their forecasts are useful because they are reliably accurate, even if we do not understand how these individuals achieve their accuracy. Likely, the reason genius forecasting works as well as it does is because it builds on our own experiences. In this respect, it is a personal form of "trend extrapolation."

Trend extrapolation involves examining historical trends and cycles; it uses mathematical techniques to predict the future based on the past; for example, it uses the birth rate patterns between 1950 and 2006 to predict the birth rate in 2050 in Canada. The strength of this method is that it roots the future in historical experience. The weakness is that the further into the future we try to forecast, the less certain the forecast becomes;

conditions change, and some processes change quickly and repeatedly. The stability of the environment is central in determining whether trend extrapolation will be a suitable forecasting model.

Data-smoothing methods separate historical data into trends: seasonal and random segments. Mathematical models based on the observed trends use smoothing constants, coefficients, and other features that must be chosen carefully by the forecaster. The choice of these features largely determines the outcome of the forecast. So, once again, the quality of the forecast depends on the expertise, experience, and intuition of the forecaster.

Forecasting complex systems often involves seeking expert opinions from more than one person. This is called the *consensus method* of forecasting. The best known "consensus method" is the Delphi method (Jones and Hunter, 1995). In a series of iterations, experts offer judgements on the likelihood of certain outcomes and then evaluate the answers given by their peers. This approach is intended to produce a rapid narrowing of opinions among experts. It provides more accurate forecasting than group discussions, is more reliable than judgements by individual geniuses, and makes better use of expert knowledge than mathematical trend extrapolation. However, since this method demands the co-operation of many experts over an extended period, its implementation is often impractical.

Simulation methods employ analogs to model complex systems. Game analogs may be used to model the interactions of players in imagined social interactions (Walonick, 1993)—for example, in studying negotiation and bargaining. Mathematical analogs have been successful in forecasting outcomes, especially in the physical sciences (Segall et al., 2002). Many of these use advanced statistical techniques to model complex systems involving relationships between two or more variables (known as "multivariate analyses"). "Multiple regression analysis" is the mathematical analog of a systems approach, and it has become the primary forecasting tool of economists and qualitative sociologists.

Conversely, strong correlations between predictor variables create unstable forecasts; a slight change in one variable can have a large effect on another variable (Walonick, 1993). In a multiple regression (and systems) approach, as the relationships between the parts of the system become stronger and more numerous, our ability to predict any given part decreases. This was one of the criticisms levelled at what was perhaps the most famous future simulation in social science history, the "limits to growth" exercise developed under the auspices of the Club of Rome (Meadows et al., 1972). This exercise showed a variety of ways the world could come to an end, destroying humanity; all prospects were cataclysmic, none were entirely believable.

The *scenario method* is a narrative-based forecast that describes a potential course of events. This method recognizes the interrelationships of system components while considering events such as new technology, population shifts, and changing consumer preferences. Scenarios, written as long-term predictions of the future, force decision-makers to ask: (1) Can we survive the *worst possible* scenario? (2) Will we be happy with the *most likely* scenario? (3) Are we able to take advantage of the *best possible* scenario? (Walonick, 1993, 2004).

Scenario modelling directly prompts the need to make choices and decisions; this, in turn, leads to models of decision-making. *Decision trees* provide a graphic illustration of the relationships between choices. Computer technology has made it possible to create complex decision trees, with many subsystems and feedback loops.

Every decision can be expected to produce a variety of outcomes, some desired and some undesired, and each of these outcomes will have an assignable value for us. *Decision theory*, using decision trees, is based on the notion that the expected value of an outcome variable can be calculated as the average value for that variable. In other words, the value of a decision is the "value" of the outcome it produces, calculated as the total of all estimated positive and negative outcomes in the decision tree (Raiffa and Schaifer, 1961).

The goal of forecasting is to be as accurate as possible and to enable social scientists, policy-makers, and the wider society to efficiently and effectively plan the use of resources. However, the utility of a forecast is not always associated with its accuracy. The value of a forecast depends on various factors, including the type of information being forecast, our confidence in the accuracy of the forecast, the magnitude of our dissatisfaction with the forecast, and the variety of ways we can adapt to or modify the forecast. We predict the future on the basis of knowledge, intuition, and logic. A forecast may or may not become part of the creative process. If two people make mutually exclusive forecasts, both of them cannot be true—at least one of the predictions must be wrong. Does one person's forecast create the future while the other person's forecast does not? The mechanisms involved in the construction of the future are not well understood on an individual or societal level. Because of the potential for a forecast to influence the future, forecasting itself may be part of a self-interested quest for power.

If the future is a social construct, are predictions of the future a form of propaganda designed to evoke particular behaviours? Some believe that a desire for control is hidden in all forecasts (Dublin, 1989). Since decisions made today are based on forecasts, forecasts may be attempts, whether knowingly or unknowingly, to control today's decisions. One can see this in the global warming "debate," which has been maintained by some political and business interests long after overwhelming scientific evidence of climate change suggested there was nothing to debate. In this respect, forecasting is a type of agenda-setting, a way of forcing everyone to think about the future and to make decisions in particular ways.

Since forecasts can and often do take on a creative role, is it necessary to discuss the ethics of making forecasts that involve other people's future? Each person has the right to create his or her own future. On the other hand, forecasting can alter the course of an entire society.

Ideally, we use forecasting to create socially desirable futures. For example, sociologists might favour peaceful coexistence, ecological sustainability, and a fairer distribution of the world's assets. However, the idea of a *desirable future* is subjective. If a goal of forecasting is to create desirable futures, then the forecaster must ask the ethical question "Desirable for whom?" Forecasters should at least try to engage as many people as possible in the forecasting process to increase their understanding of the issue and the accuracy of their forecasts. This would empower the people affected by the forecast, as they would become co-creators of their own future. In principle, according to Alexis de Tocqueville and Adam Smith, among others, such widespread engagement will yield collective well-being through the pursuit of informed personal well-being.

Theoretical Perspectives on Future Studies

TABLE 16.1	Theoretical Perspectives
THEORY	**MAIN POINTS**
Structural Functionalism	• Futures studies look into alternative futures and identify the most probable social trends. • Forecasting contributes to today's decision-making and planning by aiding politicians in devising social policies. • Looking to the future encourages people to reflect on current patterns of events and to make adjustments in preparation for the future.
Conflict Theory	• Different forecasting and simulation methods produce varying insights into the nature and probability of the occurrence of certain events that may favour one population subgroup over another. • Various interest groups compete for government support by raising and perhaps exaggerating the acuity of particular concerns.
Symbolic Interactionism	• Gossip and rumour may spread misinformation and create moral panics or fear. • The rise of cyberspace and virtual communities hides social factors (e.g., gender, race, and class) that often prevent similar people from interacting with one another.
Feminist Theory	• Despite ongoing efforts made by women to overcome gender discrimination, inequalities in wage and job opportunities will continue to persist. • Modern mothers must learn to negotiate a fine balance between work and family responsibilities as their participation in the labour force increases.
Social Constructionism	• The future is a social construct, a form of propaganda designed to evoke a particular set of behaviours. • Media portrayals of social problems and trends can exert a strong influence on people's perspectives of society, spark social movements, and contribute to policy-making.

Feminist contributions to the field of futures studies have been quite limited. Male dominance in this field is partially attributed to social and political activism that was geared towards conditions that overshadow the work of many feminist and women's groups (Milojevic et al., 2008).

The lack of female presence in futures studies is also linked to such specific limitations as "the hyper-technological and scientific orientation of professional 'mainstream' futurism, the focus on 'expert' opinion in the Delphi method, quantifiable trend analysis, and techno-utopianism and social dystopianism, which are supposedly beyond the comfort level of knowledge for many feminists" (ibid.). Furthermore, much of feminist efforts is deemed as "special" or optional issues within the field (ibid.).

When predictions of alternative futures are addressed, the forecasts of feminists tend to go either way. In the more positive scenarios, women are becoming more aware of their capabilities and acquiring a stronger presence in public life, while the negative scenarios depict a growing a divide and breakdown in communication between women of different classes (Hurley et al., 2008).

There are no clear rules regarding the ethics of forecasting. For this reason, forecasting must address specific relevant physical, cultural, and societal values. In addition, forecasters must examine their own biases, which are likely to influence the forecasting process. As previously mentioned, even the most rigorous forecasting techniques build on assumptions that can dramatically alter the forecast.

Changes in What the Public Sees as Social Problems

What people at one point in time consider to be serious social problems sometimes change in response to shifts in social, political, and economic conditions. A social problems textbook from 1898, for instance, listed "Dumping Garbage," "Over-Production," "Public Debts and Indirect Taxation," and "Slavery" among its chapter headings (George, 1898). Another text, published only 18 years later, already showed concern for some of the harmful social conditions that continue to affect the world today, including "Unemployment," "Crime and Punishment," "The Liquor Problem," "Poverty," and "The Conservation of Natural Resources" (Towne, 1916).

After the Russian Revolution in 1917, Western capitalist societies worried about Soviet communism and the dangers of subversion and war, while Soviet Communists worried about Western capitalism and the dangers of subversion and war. Between 1917 and 1967, through two world wars and two minor wars (Korea and Vietnam), a global depression, and hunts for traitors in the Soviet Union (in the 1930s) and the United States (in the 1950s), people on both sides waited for the worst to happen—a final war between Communist and capitalist nations (Mueller, 2005).

It didn't happen, and as the risk diminished and the two political bodies entered agreements to reduce and dismantle their stockpile of nuclear weapons, national concerns over military conflict declined. With the economic and political decline of the USSR, the Western nations' fear of war with Soviet Russia was replaced with concerns over the domestic economy and unemployment. North America rode a technology-driven, record-breaking boom in the marketplace during the 1990s, and crime and other social issues became the main social problems in the public eye.

Trends in Social Problems Projected to the Near Future

In years to come, many predictions by today's leading futures researchers will prove to be wrong. Others will come close to the reality of life in 2100, and a few may even hit the bull's eye (Cole, 2008). Figure 16.1 demonstrates a projection of the 15 most pressing challenges of the twenty-first century.

Noted thinker Noam Chomsky is pessimistic about the prospects of futures research: "The record of prediction in human affairs has not been inspiring, even short-range. The most plausible prediction is that any prediction about serious matters is likely to be off the mark, except by accident" (Chomsky, 1999: 30). However, the goal of futures studies is only partly to illustrate life for future generations. Its task is also to imagine a desirable alternative future for people to work towards, a future that is actively shaped by the decisions of people living today. With this in mind, let us consider the likely future of several different categories of social problems.

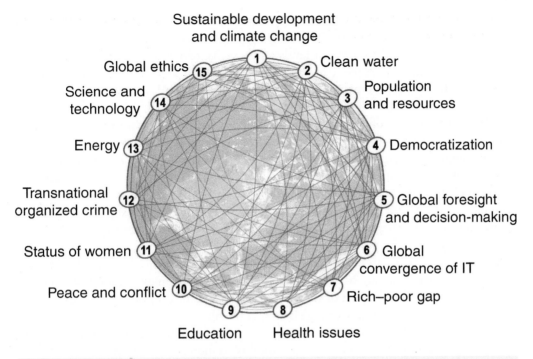

Sustainable development
and climate change

Global ethics (15)   (1)   (2) Clean water

Science and (14)   (3) Population
technology   and resources

Energy (13)   (4) Democratization

Transnational (12)   (5) Global foresight
organized crime   and decision-making

Status of women (11)   (6) Global
                                convergence of IT

Peace and conflict (10)   (7) Rich–poor gap

(9)   (8)

Education   Health issues

FIGURE 16.1 | A Projection of the 15 Most Pressing Global Challenges Facing Humanity during the Twenty-First Century

Source: 2010 State of the Future by Jerome C. Glenn, Theodore J. Gordon, and Elizabeth Florescu, The Millennium Project, at: <www.millennium-project.org/millennium/challenges.html>. © 2009 The Millennium Project.

Environmental Damage

The degradation of the environment is a growing social problem. Many scientists and theorists believe that even if changes are made immediately, environmental problems will become more severe and their effects more intense in the future. We need only to consider the ongoing oil-spill disaster in the Gulf of Mexico to realize this.

F. Sherwood Rowland, whose early warnings of the effects of chlorofluorocarbons (CFCs) on ozone depletion in 1974 earned him a Nobel Prize in chemistry, hypothesizes that

> the global prevalence of smog will rise in the next century because more and more people will use cars. The twenty-first century will therefore begin with three major atmospheric problems firmly entrenched globally: stratospheric ozone depletion, the greenhouse effect from increasing carbon dioxide and other trace gases with accompanying global warming and urban and regional smog. My expectation in the coming decades is that the climatic consequences from continued greenhouse gas emissions will be more and more noticeable, and much more ominous. (Rowland, 1999: 209–10)

Already, the world's temperature has increased, especially since the 1990s. This has led to more frequent droughts and famines, higher rates of skin cancer, and more extreme weather conditions throughout the year (Larsen and Gunnarsson-Ostling, 2009). In Canada, a predicted increase of 2.5–5.4°C by 2080 would result in a 10–25 per cent loss of agriculture yields; increased levels and severity of flooding, which would affect 775,000 to 5.5 million people (compared to the 36,000 in 1995); a rise in the mortality rate by 60,000 to 165,000 people, owing to excessive heat and massive economic losses (Ciscar et al., 2011).

The consequences of environmental damage are especially common in Northern Canada, particularly Nunavut. Warmer weather has had a severe impact on the inhabitants through the contamination of food and water, the melting of the permafrost, increased isolation thanks to restricted mobility (thanks to loss of snow cover), and the loss of their way of life and livelihood (Allardyce, 2011). According to members of the community, they have to travel farther in dangerous conditions, using new modes of transportation, and they miss favourite activities such as snowmobiling, hunting, and camping (ibid.).

Furthermore, with an estimated increase of 75 million people worldwide who will go hungry in 2017 (Sarkar, 2012) and a 70 per cent increase in global food demands by 2050 (Anya, 2012), the impact of climate change on agriculture could greatly exacerbate issues of food security. Climate change is among the numerous factors responsible for the growing food crisis owing to its impact on food production and availability, the stability of food supplies, and the wide-spread accessibility to food for nutrition.

Increasing levels of tropsepheric, or surface level, ozone (O_3) as well as rising temperature rates have been recognized as major contributors to declining plant growth and

The Canadian Press/AP Photo/Ted S. Warren

More than on any other people, global warming may be having a greater effect on the estimated 155,000 Inuit in Canada, Greenland, Russia, and the United States, as the ice provides them with animals to feed and clothe their families and hunting seasons and territories have been reduced by earlier and earlier melting times each year.

crop yield (Sarkar et al., 2012). According to Hertel and Rosch (2010), a 2°C increase in global temperatures would result in a decrease of 15 per cent of spring wheat, 22 per cent of soybean and 27 per cent of maize yield production. Furthermore, an estimated 600 million additional people are at risk of hunger if the temperature increases by 3°C (Anya, 2012). In order to combat or reduce the detrimental impacts of climate change on food production, farmers and scientists must work together to formulate new technologies to make agriculture more resilient and/or increase agriculture yields in a more efficient manner.

Financial Crisis/Indebtedness

Numerous periods of world history have encountered financial crises and recessions. The nineteenth-century financial situation was characterized by a lack of central-bank, commodity-based currencies and a fragmented banking system. These distinctive features led to the crises of 1820 (the result of a decline in European demand for agriculture), the 1857 bank failures, the 1873 stock market crash, and the railroad and bank bankruptcies of 1893. The twentieth century witnessed a major stock market crash, which led to a severe recession known as the Great Depression (Shachmurove, 2010).

More recently, the 2008 financial meltdown was primarily triggered by a dramatic decline in housing prices and has been identified as the worst financial crisis since the Great Depression. Fifty-five million of the 80 million houses in the United States had mortgages, and 4 million of these were behind on their payments, leading to an unprecedented rate of foreclosures. Furthermore, the large trade deficit of the United States meant high levels of foreign investment, which translated into a global economic downturn (ibid.).

This financial crisis is likely to prompt changes in financial management in the future. In particular, most predictions envision increased government regulation and supervision, greater focus on asset price inflation, improved insurance and protection of deposits, improvements in governance (especially regarding oversight and risk management), development of better remuneration policies, increased participation by market participants and policy-makers, and, finally, international co-operation (Davis, 2010).

Similarly, the recent Greek/Eurozone debt crisis has prompted discussions and debate over policy changes and the effectiveness of the current system. This crisis was triggered by improper economic policies that created a situation characterized by high government spending, weak revenues, structural rigidities, and inadequate fiscal monitoring, resulting in massive deficits and debt (Abdel and Rady, 2012). Some of the stakeholders are now likely questioning the efficiency and practicality of a common monetary policy. Future developments may involve a variety of changes, including an emphasis on export-led growth, wage moderation (to keep cost of products low), conservative fiscal policies, high savings levels, and increasing privatization (ibid.). However, it is difficult to implement some of these changes because of the economic recession in Europe.

The Problem of Aging

We mentioned earlier that two kinds of forecasting are particularly common: forecasting based on changes in technology and forecasting based on changes in demography, or population structure. Changes in demography—say, in the age composition of a

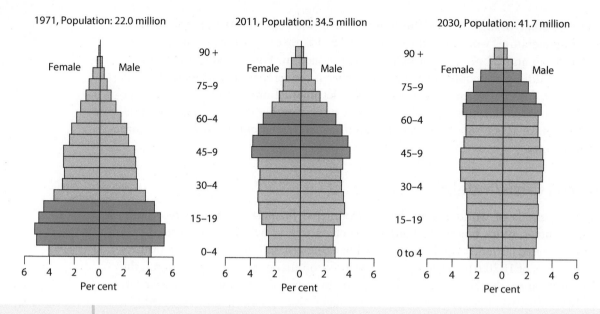

society—are important because behaviour differs according to one's age. People of different ages buy different kinds of products, have different lifestyles, and vote for different political candidates. Age—along with sex and education—is one of the most reliable predictors of behaviour.

Declining fertility rates, increased longevity, and earlier retirement have resulted in an aging population in Canada. Figure 16.2 shows the projected demographic changes in Canada based on age. These changes will make it increasingly unlikely that Canadians' income and standard of living will continue to improve; as projected in Figure 16.3, the proportion of the population of working age (15 to 64) will shrink

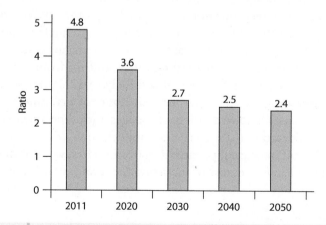

by nearly half in the near future. This will inevitably lead to a decline in employment rates (Department of Finance Canada, 2012). It is unknown whether younger generations will be able to support the aging population or whether the health-care system will be able cope with increasing demands (Raphael, 2009). How society deals with an aging population will determine what social problems will be associated with ageism in Canada in the future.

Several possibilities present themselves. In the face of an aging population, the first initiative could be to boost the productivity of Canadian workers through innovation, human capital, and business investment. Improvements in technology, workplace organization, and government policy initiatives could greatly aid in productivity. Another possibility is to increase the skills required for effective participation in the workforce through the inclusion of Aboriginal peoples, recent skilled immigrants, young people, and persons with disabilities (Department of Finance Canada, 2012). It is unlikely that such a policy would win support from Canadian workers, who would perceive it as a means to increase the competition for jobs. Finally, a larger proportion of the national budget could be invested in health care.

Issues Related to International Migration

International migration is now occurring at an unprecedented rate, with an estimated 200 million people living outside their countries of birth (Kasinitz, 2012). Growing disparities in development, demography, and demographic processes, as well as the increasing ease of migration due to aid from individuals and agents (e.g., labour recruits, immigration lawyers, brokers, and so on) have contributed to the growing number of migrants recently (Koser, 2010).

Despite the increasing prevalence of migrants, there are no United Nations or international migration organizations that focus on international migration; states remain the principal actors, which leads to a wide range of laws, agreements, and policies among them (ibid.). This, in turn, results in high vulnerability: migrants often die while trying to cross land and sea borders without being detected by authorities (averaging 2,000 deaths a year); they are at a higher risk of exploitation by employers; they are more likely to be victims of human trafficking; they make less use of public services; they are the group most sensitive to job loss; and they have less human rights protection (ibid).

Furthermore, the number of international migrants is likely to grow in the future owing to an increasing demand for migrant workers in the developed world (partly in response to the aging population previously mentioned) and to climate change (which would compel many to leave their less fertile and arable lands, damaged by temperature fluctuations) (ibid.).

The level of international migration can no longer be managed effectively by national governments. This fact has prompted discussions about greater international co-operation in the future (ibid.). The idea of exercising global governance has emerged as a solution to this issue and as a method to tackle common objectives, including fewer deaths during transit, reduction of criminal networks, minimization of tension between migrants and host communities, greater safety for migrations, increased national security, and so on. However, states continue to be reluctant to relinquish their power and control to an international authority (Newland, 2010).

Issues of Security and Surveillance

The 9/11 attacks prompted widespread government surveillance and increased monitoring that simultaneously fostered problems of privacy and security that will likely persist into the future, particularly in the United States. The Communication to Assistance Law Enforcement Act (CALEA) was passed in 1994, granting telephone companies the right to monitor court targets immediately after obtaining a warrant (Hibbard, 2012). Conversely, President Obama expressed the desire to extend CALEA to include all services that enable communication cellphones, game consoles that enable conversation, word-processing software, social networking websites, and peer-to-peer messaging software, allowing them to be legally wiretapped with a court order (ibid). Similarly, in Canada, the surveillance powers of the Criminal Code have been amended since 2001, making it easier to use electronic surveillance against terrorist groups (Xhelili and Crowne, 2012). It is now easier than ever to wiretap dated information without the consent of the user (ibid.).

Currently, all cellular devices have a global position system embedded within them, which allows both the local and national government access to real-time and historical information regarding the owner's location; this can be done without a warrant (Hibbard, 2012). In the United States, for example, a warrant is only necessary to gain access to Facebook inbox messages less than 181 days old; everything else can be obtained without a court order (ibid). This information is increasingly used in court: for example, in divorce proceedings, 81 per cent of attorneys reported using or facing evidence derived from a social network (Semitsu, 2011); and courts made 4,287 requests for user information on Google between January 2010 and June 2010 (Fisher, 2013).

These new technologies have great implications for the future of privacy and the associated risks. With the increased capacity to wiretap, there is a growing risk of unauthorized third parties retrieving unauthorized personal information. Slight impediments to the freedom of speech may occur because of the potential fear of speaking candidly associated with increased monitoring. Finally, national and foreign technological innovation and production may stall or slow down owing to the need to comply with additional laws and measures related to security.

Technology: Making and Solving Problems

Technology The manifestation of human knowledge and ingenuity applied to the solution of a problem or need; applied science.

The key to social life of the future is clearly connected to the future of technology. In a sense, sociology itself emerged as part of the same knowledge revolution that gave us science and technology. Some say that it evolved alongside the new social problems arising from industrialization, urbanization, and political revolutions in France and other parts of Europe. Others place more importance on the changes associated with the Enlightenment: the rise of science, increasing skepticism about religious belief, and a general questioning of tradition (Goldman, 2007).

Social science, particularly sociology, arose out of a desire to explain differences and to find patterns in social relations, living arrangements, and ways of doing things among individuals. The founders of sociology (as well as many current sociologists) saw their project as identifying and then providing solutions to problems in society. Some dreamed of becoming the professional managers of society just as physicians organized to become the professional arbiters of the human body. In that sense, sociology has always been orientated towards problem-solving: to finding better ways of living together given the visible

INTERNATIONAL **COMPARISONS**

BOX 16.1 | **The Millennium Project's "Rich Get Richer" Scenario**

Throughout the twentieth century, the rising inequality of incomes within and between nations had been a matter of increasing concern. In 1997, the most prosperous group of workers in the world—the skilled workers of the industrial countries—earned on average 60 times more than the poorest group—the farmers of sub-Saharan Africa. Even on a national basis, taking account of all income and workers, the gap was huge. In terms of GDP per capita, by 2050 the expected difference between the richest country (the US) and the poorest region (Africa) will be almost 50 to 1.

As one looks back from the vantage point of the mid-century [i.e., 2050], it's clear that there were two separate and distinct periods. At the beginning of the century, economic and social conditions in many of the poorer countries deteriorated—increasing the gap between rich and poor countries. In the last two decades, however, conditions in even the poorest countries have been improving, exceeding those 50 years ago. In other words, through the last 50 years, the rich got richer, and recently—in the last two decades—conditions in even the poorest countries have improved.

It was the pace of change and the challenges of the early twenty-first century that caused some nations to stumble while others surged ahead. Regions of South Asia—Bangladesh and Sri Lanka; sub-Saharan Africa—Nigeria, Senegal and Rwanda; and Central and East Europe—Moldova, Romania, and the Russian Republic, fell behind due to their limited ability to effectively manage transition economies, integrate into the world economy, initiate institutional reform, and invest in human capital, human development, and quality education. Take these burdens and add overspending on military preparedness, soaring health-care costs, relief aid due to outbreaks of infectious disease, environmental emergencies, and high unemployment. Corruption and organized crime made their unholy contributions to the chaos.

Inevitably, some of these lagging nations lost credit worthiness, and foreign investment waned.

Relatively high population growth early in the century compounded their problems. Economic growth often promotes diminished birth rates, so the stagnation of economic growth tended to increase birth rates. With high birth rates, labour forces grow—if the economy does not grow in parallel to population, jobs become precious, and political turmoil follows. Though birth rates were falling everywhere, even in Africa, the poorer countries dropped at a slower rate than their richer cousins.

While the poorer countries in Africa and Asia ran into this plethora of problems, the richer countries experienced a period of robust GNP growth. Advancements in science led to improvements in productivity, advances in biotechnology and genetics improved agriculture, health, and longevity, information technology revolutionized education and almost every industry, and new industries emerged to fuel the economic momentum. Forces for globalization worked to their benefit; their use of cheaper labour in poorer countries was welcomed by those countries because it provided needed jobs. With a few notable exceptions, their foreign investments were generally shrewd, taking advantage of local conditions and need. So, while many of the poorer countries were trapped by their own ineptitude and external circumstances, many of the richer countries achieved impressive growth.

Communications technologies put the differences in living standards in bold relief and also offered tempting but elusive solutions (e.g., video-education). Nevertheless these solutions remained largely unimplemented because of low profit potential and small markets. Thus, the differences in income and living standards remained sharp: in the first two decades of the new century, the conditions in the rich countries improved while those in the poor countries deteriorated.

Source: Glenn, Jerome C., Gordon, Theodore J., and Florescu, Elizabeth (2009).

difficulties associated with industrialization, urbanization, poverty, political upheaval, and so on. In periods of dramatic change, such questions are motivated by a sense of urgency as well as fascination. During the nineteenth and twentieth centuries, thinkers struggled to develop a language that could effectively describe these new problems. As in every science, precise language, theories, and methods of research advanced as sociology matured. This development has always corresponded with technological innovation.

Urban Technology

Technological development resulting from urbanization and industrialization greatly benefited sociology. For centuries, cities have relied on sophisticated technology because they are built environments—humanly constructed ways of separating people from the natural environment. In the effort to improve and enlarge our built environments, innovations in various realms are essential. Consider the components necessary to build and occupy a tall condominium, apartment, or office building—the kinds of buildings most prevalent in societies today. The construction of these structures is based on a combination of strong, durable, relatively lightweight, readily available materials and a knowledge of building techniques that will allow these materials to be used in easy, cheap, and reliably engineered ways.

Second, all tall buildings demand elevators, stairs, reliable heating and cooling, complex electrical wiring, and developed communication technology (to enable people on the upper and lower floors to communicate with one another). There is a created need for telephones, computers, cellphones, fax machines, and so on. Today, we view traditional methods of communicating, such as "snail mail" and rotary telephones, as insufficient and inadequate; however, prior to the arrival of cellphones and the Internet, large cities like New York functioned perfectly—some would even argue that they operated far better than today.

Technology and Toolmaking

Where did these tools and technologies come from? When and how did they make their first human appearance? Why are humans more skilled at making tools than our animal relatives? Likely, our first tools were sticks and stones: sticks aided us in walking, reaching high objects, or fending off wild animals; stones enabled us to stun edible animals or kill enemies (Plummer, 2004). Eventually, sticks and stones gained practicality: a flattened stick, used with a stone as a fulcrum, can form a lever that greatly extends the strength of the user. With the appropriate materials in hand, our earliest forebears could have certainty invented the lever, which has emerged as an incredibly important tool in today's society. Similarly, the later invention of the wheel was far-reaching. Most of human technology prior to the twentieth century (that is, pre-electronic) was based on the use of wheels—to move heavy objects or to function as toothed gears in machines or clocks (Basalla, 1988). Even today, our automobiles and many other forms of transportation rely on wheels. Yet, the concept of a wheel is seemingly cognitively simple—a discovery that involves little prior technology; all you need do to make a wheel is to cut a slice from a tree trunk.

In practice, however, that task is far more complex, requiring other developments. Slicing a tree trunk requires a saw, which involves metallurgy—a strategy for finding, refining, and crafting minerals. How do you convert underground minerals into a sheet of metal that is harder than the tree trunk you are trying to cut? How do you then shape that piece of metal to give it handles and sharp teeth? These were questions our earliest ancestors must have solved prior to the construction of wheels and the undertaking of major construction or transport projects.

Of course, some would argue that the greatest turning point has been the shift from mechanical to electronic devices. Transistors, for instance, are critical because they're more compact than tubes, making electronic devices more portable and convenient. However, the importance of the wheel is undeniable—especially if you ride a bicycle to work, as hundreds of millions do. Early knowledge about metal craft and other activities like wheel-making was likely passed along across lifespans and between communities.

In this gradual, unheralded, and painstaking manner, man the toolmaker (*homo faber*) invented his world and laid the foundations for a built environment. As anthropologist V. Gordon Childe (1936) says, "Man made himself" through the invention of tools and technologies and, in that way, created what Marx and Engels (1978 [1848]) termed "the means of production." Each new tool further separated humanity from its animal forebears and from the natural environment, giving us a greater advantage.

We can speculate that humanity enjoys a few natural advantages over our animal counterparts. One is the opposable thumb, which allows humans to grasp and manipulate tools more precisely. Another is erect posture, which provides humanity with a different, less-grounded perspective on the environment and more rapid mobility. While a number of animals can outrun humans for short bursts, "with the help of our upright stance . . . and our profuse sweating, we can outrun just about any other animal on the planet if the race extends over hours in searing midday heat" (Epstein, 2010: 56). Conversely, humanity also suffers disadvantages that have necessitated the presence of tools. Because of their relative physical weakness, comparatively slow mobility over short distances, and lack of sharp teeth and claws, humans had no choice but to capitalize on their toolmaking abilities in order to flourish.

Weapons Technology

The development of technology gave humans control over other animals, and it also gave them control over other humans. Much of history has been characterized by organized warfare, ongoing arms races involving deadly weapons, and strategies that use new weapons more effectively. The history of imperial conquest is the history of more technologically advanced nations conquering less technologically advanced nations.

Even religious history has a military, and therefore technological, aspect: ideas have often spread on the ends of swords. Islam and Christianity did not spread around the world merely because of their spiritual merit: they also circulated through the efforts of armed zealots (e.g., during the Crusades). Military concerns have been instrumental in the development of tools and technology with uses in civilian life, and they have also contributed significantly to improvements in medicine and health (Ponteva, 2002). For instance, the shell shock experienced by troops during World War I is often noted as critical in the development of modern psychological medicine (Loughran, 2009), while the development of trauma practices in intensive-care units owes much to skills learned during certain historical armed conflicts (Murray, 2011).

Advances in weaponry have come at an ever-faster rate in the last two centuries. In part, this is due to the increased importance of technology for warfare, industry, and global commerce. Everywhere, machines have come to supplement and even replace human labour. The rapidly increasing importance of technology has also been the result of significant social and cultural change. First, it reflects capitalism's central concern with profit-making, which is often maximized by improving the combination of human labour, capital, and technology. Second, the growth of technology reflects society's concerns with material improvement.

© Nano Calvo/Alamy

This photo depicts a new Phantom drone, a remote-controlled helicopter mounted with a digital video camera, in flight. These drones are used by the military to survey areas that are too dangerous for piloted aircraft to fly over.

Technology and the Institutionalization of Science

Advances in technology—for cities, weaponry, and other purposes—are extensions of the scientific revolution that began in Europe 500 years ago. These advances rest on empirical, often experimental, research that obeys the "norms of science," termed "CUDOS" by Robert Merton (1973 [1942]). This acronym outlines the important processes that have moved science forward: **C**ommunalism (the results of science are public and free for anyone to use); **U**niversalism (the evaluation of scientific claims is based on universal criteria not specific to the researchers themselves); **D**isinterest (scientific knowledge is pursued and presented without the expectation of personal reward or advancement); and **O**rganized **S**kepticism (active and critical evaluation of claims; postponement of judgement until sufficient reasons for or against a claim have been presented).

The "invention" of science represented a huge break with traditional religious thinking; specifically, it represented a new way to carry out inquiries. Science is culturally and socially orientated towards the search for knowledge: at its forefront is a combination of empirical observation and mathematical reasoning.

Science—and therefore, technology—advances largely through independent disinterested research, public reviews of findings, and the application of universal judgement criteria. Most important of all, science demands organized skepticism. Scientific claims are critically evaluated and conclusions are considered "tentative," awaiting disproof. In Canada, many complain of a lack of technological advancement because of a relative absence of research and development work here; however, compared to pre-industrial societies, Canada has always valued technology as a force in the country's development.

CANADIAN researchers

BOX 16.2 | **Satoshi Ikeda, Concordia University**

Satoshi Ikeda holds a Tier II Canada Research Chair in Political Sociology of Global Futures in the Department of Sociology and Anthropology at Concordia University. In his work, he examines the failure of the corporate economy and the consequences of neo-liberalism. Ikeda seeks just alternatives to the corporate economy in light of the pervasive inequalities that have emerged alongside neoliberal globalization. In a 2004 article, "Imperial Subjects, National Citizenship, and Corporate Subjects: Cycles of Political Participation/Exclusion in the Modern World-System," Ikeda notes that income inequality has drastically risen in most modern societies, and argues that this is the result of capitalism and neo-liberal globalization. As he suggests, "the contemporary system of accumulation has dismantled the nation state as the vehicle of economic development and diluted citizenship through neoliberal policies" (2004: 333). For Ikeda, transnational corporations have eroded local economies, especially in developing countries. Local economies become subordinate to multinational corporations in terms of employment, consumption, investment, and culture.

Satoshi Ikeda suggests that *sustainable community development* is a necessary alternative to the current corporate-dominated system. This type of economic system would promote small-scale environmentally and socially sustainable communities that would be free from multinational corporations. In doing so, it would grant communities the economic autonomy they require to preserve their distinct social and cultural identities. Ikeda notes that some sustainable communities already exist in the global South. Their continued prosperity in the future remains to be seen, however. Nonetheless, Ikeda's work is an example of the *forward thinking* we discuss in this chapter.

Source: Ikeda (2004).

Besides the rise of science and cities, no other social change has so transformed modern life as the development of industry and industrial working classes, a consequence of *industrial technology*. "Classes" in sociological thinking are groups of people who share a common economic condition, interest, or, as Marx and Engels described it, relationship to the means of production. In turn, the means of production are, precisely, the combination of technology and capital. It is technology's potential to increase profitability, to strengthen control over labour, and even to permit the low-cost replacement of human labour that makes it both a friend and enemy of modern humanity.

The relationship of people to the means of production separates those who must sell their work, their time, or their labour to earn wages so they can survive from those who buy this work and gain profits from the goods and services that workers produce. The profit gained by the second group depends mainly on the price of the manufactured product minus the cost of labour. As a result, profit-making depends on keeping prices high and wages (and other costs of production) low.

Some have argued that this transformation—the increased significance of technology plus capital in the productive process and the refinement of computerized production—has created a "knowledge society" or "information society" (Webster, 2002). This thinking, in turn, has largely transformed the ways we try to educate people for labour force participation. However, because of the greater significance of technology, many people today may be over-educated for the work they are doing (Dolton and Vignoles, 2000). Some might say that our society values conformity and consumerism above all else. Capital and technology are still important; the rest of learning and production is window dressing.

The Social Effects of Technology

With the aid of technology, we have separated ourselves from nature and, most of the time, we view nature through the windows of our home, office, or car. We live inside the most luxurious homes we can afford and technology can provide. Occasionally, we spend time at a cottage or camping "in the wild," but we always return to the material comforts our ancestors gradually and painstakingly developed for us. After all, it is only within this secure environment that we can carry out the tasks that set humanity apart from raccoons, squirrels, skunks, and other animal species—activities that include reading or writing sociology textbooks, listening to the music of Beethoven, watching television, and pondering current events.

In what sense are these uniquely human activities "higher"? That is a difficult question to answer. However, two facts are apparent. First, technology has set humanity socially and culturally apart from the rest of the natural world. On the other hand, it has given humanity a huge capacity for good and evil. Consider an example of a new aspect of technology: the adoption of cellphones and social media as the primary medium of communication. Social media, as well as cellphones, are now indispensible in our social life; they aid in developing, maintaining, and even terminating social and personal relationships. While cellphones enable citizens to satisfy their communicative needs anywhere and anytime with ease, they may play a detrimental role in the development of social skills.

Those who have adopted cellphones as their primary means of communication tend to have less involvement in face-to-face communication. This in turn negatively impacts the development of communication skills, the lack of which is significantly associated with higher rates of loneliness and social isolation (Jin and Park, 2012).

The Internet has profoundly shaped how we communicate with others. Without a doubt, it has made the world a much smaller place in terms of global interaction. Yet, spending too much time on the Internet—or on other various technologies—may affect our personal relationships, in particular relationships with family members. For example, Mesch and Talmud (2007) show that the frequency of Internet use does not change the time that adolescents spend with their peers, but it significantly decreases the time they spend with their parents. This has led others to claim that families may no longer have the same intimacy that they once did.

Consider another example of technological evil. Cultural parochialism has for centuries allowed "developed societies" to use highly developed technology—especially, weaponry—to overwhelm less powerful, "less advanced" societies. Modern warfare relies on unemotional killing and advanced technology. Because of advances in military technology, the modern weapons used in combat are exponentially more deadly than ever before. A single precision-guided missile released by a B-52 bomber many thousands of feet above a war zone can kill hundreds of enemy soldiers and civilians. The atomic bomb dropped on Hiroshima more than 65 years ago in the last days of World War II is estimated to have killed 80,000 people instantly. The potential for mass destruction has grown exponentially since then.

Technology, Families, and Communities

Researchers disagree about the overall effect of information technology (IT) on family and community life. On the one hand, increased connectedness makes it easier to contact

Increased Internet usage may be affecting teens' relationships with their parents far more than their relationships with their peers.

friends, neighbours, acquaintances, spouses, children, parents, and siblings. Relations can be maintained even from a distance. On the other hand, the new connectedness may intrude on traditional family life, disturbing rituals and cohesion. Computers and other IT (for example, PSP) can isolate families, individuate family members across generations, separate them from one another in individual activities, and lead to addictive behaviour. Some researchers argue that extensive Internet use increases the risk of depression and loneliness by isolating the user from sources of support and sociability (Morrison and Gore, 2010). It seems clear that communication technologies will have unpredictable effects, at least for a while.

The effects of technology on intimacy seem to depend on the *type* of close relationship (Baym et al., 2004). Among strongly tied (that is, closely related) people, easy and relatively cheap technologies such as email do not replace traditional communication media like face-to-face meetings or telephone calls. Closely related communicators use new as well as old technologies and communicate frequently. More communication (and more varied communication) strengthens a relationship. By contrast, weakly tied communicators rely on one medium and are less motivated to explore new technologies. Their relationships remain distant as a result.

Over the last 150 years, changes in communications and transport technologies have made contact among kin and friends, whether they live near to one another or great distances apart, less expensive, faster, and easier. As email and Internet use increases, geographic constraints on social relationships decrease. Changes in technology that simplify contact among family and friends are likely to contribute to the quality and cohesion of relationships. The spread of easy communication shrinks distances, and we can expect this shrinking of distance to continue. Yet despite the constant changes in the technological context of social relationships, most social theory continues to assume that people will form and preserve close relationships mainly through face-to-face interaction.

One strategy for studying cross-national and cross-regional relations is to examine how technology has affected close relations in the past. New technologies rapidly traverse traditional social barriers and achieve wide adoption. Consider the history of two important communication technologies: the telephone and email.

In the beginning, telephones were used mainly for long-distance calling. Commercial interests advertised the telephone as a means to link family and friends; women were shown in advertisements using it for "kin-keeping." The telephone improved communication: people expressed their views in their own voices, it was simple to use, and (once the private line replaced the party line) was as private as face-to-face communication. As a result, the telephone was widely adopted and used to preserve close relations, even at a distance. People quickly became dependent on this new communication instrument.

Surprisingly, the effects of the telephone on social life have been modest. There is no systematic evidence that the telephone has changed close relations. At most, the telephone helped them by keeping people in touch between face-to-face meetings.

Some of the advantages of email are similar to those of the telephone. However, email is not as disruptive as the telephone, nor is it dependent on both parties being available at the same time. Because email is written and involves computer technology and some literacy, it is not quite as simple or inexpensive to use as the telephone. Beyond that, email carries a variety of dangers of its own. Faceless anonymity poses the risk of indiscretion, misunderstanding, misquoting, wide dissemination of material intended to be private, and invasion of privacy. The shield of visual and vocal anonymity may encourage blunt disclosure and misrepresentation. As well, people are more likely to express themselves intemperately and thoughtlessly through email and text-messaging.

Still, the lack of temporal and spatial boundaries associated with the telephone and email frees relationships and makes new ones possible. It also makes relationships with online communicators possible for people formerly prevented from socializing—for example, people housebound by illness or child care. The proven effects of email on social life have been modest so far. However, the telephone and email certainly have made cross-regional, cross-national, and cross-empire communication easier than ever before.

Technology and Mass Communication

Today, business success depends on finding and persuading as many consumers as possible. Likewise, political success depends on finding and persuading as many voters as possible. Finding and *rapidly* persuading large numbers of people relies on technology that simply wasn't available not that long ago. The radio, invented just over a century ago, really only came into widespread popular use 80 or 90 years ago. Modern mass communication—television, movie DVDs, and the Internet, for example—are much more recent than that. So, we have to realize that the modern mass media have changed human life dramatically since the birth of our great-grandparents.

Mass communication is the communication of a message from a single source to multiple recipients who receive the message at the same time. This kind of all-at-once communication is only possible using the technology that we call "mass media," a collection of tools that includes the printing press, the radio, television, the photocopier, and

The Canadian Press/AP Photo/Lee Jin-man

During a special session on Internet addiction prevention at a school in Seoul, South Korea, a consultant, left, asks students to record how many hours they use the Internet a day.

the camera. All of these, individually or working together, can reproduce and disseminate thousands, even millions, of copies of one original message.

The age of mass media began with the invention of the printing press around 1447 by German goldsmith and inventor Johannes Gutenberg (1398–1468). With his use of movable type, Gutenberg changed the world. By 1500, his printing technology had spread throughout Europe; within a very short time, ordinary people were reading the first widely distributed reading matter—the Holy Bible. The effects within the Church were revolutionary; then, within society, more widespread. Since then, we have come to associate civilization with literacy, and modernity with the media. Today, communications technology is central to our culture, politics, and society.

Because of their capacity to reach millions, nothing in society is so integrative, *in principle*, as the media and the information that they carry. If anything can help us live together well, surely it is the mass media. After all, television, radio, movies, newspapers, magazines, CDs, DVDs—all are dedicated to serving society at large. However, in practice, the media can also be disintegrative. The messages that the media convey do not always serve society well. In the end, the media are only neutral vehicles that are used in as many ethical and evil ways as humans can conceive.

Communications technology has been influenced by increasingly sophisticated marketing research in recent decades. People spend their money differently, although certain commonalities are visible. Items that were once considered to be luxuries are now necessities. The mass media have played a key role in the promotion of consumerism and "neediness." In the influence they wield over consumers, market researchers—manipulating the mass media like orchestra conductors waving batons—are "captains of consciousness." In the words of social historian Stuart Ewen (1976: 70), "They mold the desires, needs, and intentions of the spending public."

Market research has become ever more sophisticated with repeated surveys of purchasing behaviour and the development of demographic and psychographic models. The focus is on consumer spending patterns by age, income, education, and gender across multiple market sectors. The purpose is to guess who will buy suvs, frozen meat pies, Asian-style cooking sauces, vacations in the South Pacific, and Viagra—and with what inducements.

The Internet

Information Age A historical time—the present—in which information of all forms is quickly and easily accessible via the Internet and computers. At the same time, there is far more information than existed only a few years or decades ago, and information drives work processes to a far greater extent than in the past.

We are living today in what some have called the **Information Age**, meaning we have more information and more ideas than ever before in history (Webster, 2002). We also make more use of this information, exchanging it and transforming it into commodities. Information is a good to be bought and sold. What's more, the increasing spread of access to information has the potential to integrate society—to help us live together better—more than ever before.

Information truly has exploded. Five centuries ago, scholars could agree on what made up the sum total of knowledge in a literate society, whether in China or in Western Europe. It was possible for someone to imagine becoming an expert in *everything*. The Renaissance scholar Erasmus has been thought of in these terms, as a "universal" scholar; many would see Leonardo da Vinci in the same way. Even 50 years ago, scholars could still demarcate the boundaries of knowledge, that is, the boundaries of what was known and knowable. But by then the demarcated body of knowledge was far beyond the reach of a single person, and so specialization was needed even within fields (e.g., within chemistry, anthropology, or literature).

This idea of a body of knowledge, of what educated people should or could know, was limited by the technology of the day and by definitions of what constituted "knowledge." For a long time, most knowledge was spread orally and by example and preserved by human memory. Most knowledge or information (such as how to grow food, weave fibres, or work with metal) was transferred from person to person. Until the invention of the printing press, there was no concept of "authorship" as we know it today. Earlier authors participated in and extended the traditional culture, taking their own ideas from older ideas and their legitimacy from older traditions. They did not seek to reject the traditional culture in expressing their individual insight.

The act of writing underwent a transformation. In medieval Europe, monks copied manuscripts, believed to be the word of God. The printing press changed all this by making fast, accurate copies of what had previously taken months or years to produce by hand. Knowledge became an item that could be spread among strangers. Printers sought out new material. Even so, it took several centuries for authorship to gain its modern form. The idea that knowledge could be owned as a form of property was followed by a concept of "standards." Eventually, in the popular mind, standard information became associated with what had been printed. Printing endowed a halo of authority or credibility.

Today, we still distinguish between knowledge producers and knowledge consumers. *Producers* are people who are seen as "experts" and who can get their works into print. *Consumers*, by contrast, are people who use the knowledge produced in these ways. They buy "how-to" books. They go to school and college to gain knowledge, and from there to the world of work. In the workplace, at least in theory, they use this knowledge. Often they may find that they need more knowledge and information. However, the Internet has been altering this link between consumers, producers, and knowledge. Indeed, the Internet has changed the way we produce information and understand the concept of knowledge; in short, it has changed the relations of its production.

At the same time, a wide **digital divide** exists between wealthy and poor countries, as well as between the rich and poor within countries. By 2008, an estimated 84 per cent of Canadians were using the Internet. Internetworldstats.com provides comparisons: 73 per cent of Americans and 19 per cent of the rest of the world. The growth of Internet use has increased in Canada by 121 per cent since the year 2000. Most important, many of these Internet users are both information consumers *and* information producers.

Many would argue for a distinction between the great knowledge producers of the past—for example, philosophers, writers, and scientists—and the casual, often misguided bloggers of today. Certainly much of what passes for "information" on the Internet is dither, bluster, hot air, false, and misinformation; moreover, for those who produce all this to be considered producers of information (or knowledge) certainly signals a shift from the understandings of past generations as to what constitutes information (knowledge). On the other hand, much of what passes for information on the Internet is valuable and true, though sometimes lacking a formal pedigree. And much of what passes for information in the commercial press or halls of academe is without much merit. So, perhaps our notions of knowledge are in a process of change, and we will need to develop new ways of assessing and controlling quality.

The revolutionary potential of the Internet is that it recreates information as something that is commonly shared and exchanged, not as a commodity to be owned. The Internet was described by Howard Rheingold (2000) as the *agora*, after the ancient Greek word for "marketplace," the social space in which people walked and talked. In our contemporary terms, this information marketplace is huge; some see it as spinning out of control, impossible to map accurately, and used far beyond its original aims. The size and chaos of the Internet is indeed worrisome from some standpoints. Without quality checks and quality controls, we are at risk of something that we may call "mind pollution" whenever we set foot in **cyberspace**.

However, the upside of cyberspace is that it gives ordinary people the chance to return to being producers or creators, rather than remaining only consumers. Indeed, of today's Internet users, nearly half are estimated to contribute actively to *content* rather than to simply read. Some of the material contributed in this way is ill-informed and ridiculous, but much of it is no worse than the material supplied by professional journalists and spin doctors and some is contributed by educated people and by academics.

Another important aspect of the electronic agora is that it is made up of people who have probably never met one another face to face, yet share beliefs and ideologies, give one another support, and regularly exchange ideas. The result is a creation of worldwide virtual communities: communities of interest and shared viewpoint, unhampered by distance and many of the social factors (age, race, gender, class) that often keep otherwise similar people from meeting or interacting with one another.

Problems of Information Anarchy

The Internet is somewhat anarchic. There is no centralized control, including quality control, but many believe this decentralization is both good and healthy. If access to the

Digital divide The separation between those who have access to electronic technology and the Internet ("haves") and those who do not ("have-nots").

Cyberspace The abstract concept of "where" computer-stored information is exchanged.

Internet is free and open, anyone can post what he or she wants. Freedom leaves scope for new ideas to surface. But it also leaves scope for hate literature, obscenity, and pornography, plus an immense amount of sludge. Many wonder how the Internet community can control the latter without limiting free speech.

Some Internet providers have tried voluntary controls, asking that people not post offensive material on their sites. This does seem to work, to an extent. However, there have also been campaigns to censor whole categories of material, and some countries have even gone beyond this. China, for example, completely controls Internet access in and out of the country through gateways with the complicit involvement of international conglomerates. The US has tried several methods of state censorship, some of which have been struck down. There have been challenges and counterchallenges related to spam and to free access for legal minors. It seems clear that any censorship of the Internet has the potential to prevent important ideas from being openly debated. In an **information economy**, this amounts to societal suicide.

And too much control also poses political dangers. Without vigilance by users, the Internet could be transformed from an anarchic network of information providers and communicators to a means of political surveillance. Already authorities have the ability to track the messages and website addresses of individual users, and in some countries, they are already doing so. The threat here is that the Internet could become a **panopticon**, an all-seeing eye that allows those in authority to oversee people's actions, thoughts, and communications. Some Internet users are campaigning on issues of privacy and security of information, including the information they pass on when they connect to any site.

Internet communication is changing society, and it is also changing the mass media. There is no room for the traditional media to be complacent when not-for-profit information producers are making available material that is (sometimes) more entertaining, informative, honest, and insightful—for free. True, a lot of the material in cyberspace is illiterate rubbish, but at least it is (usually) honest rubbish. Will the Internet remain a free marketplace? Or will it become a forum that is ultimately controlled by a larger power and from which startling or sensitive material is excluded to protect vulnerable members of society?

Internet issues throw into clear relief the abstract issues of rights to intellectual property, liberty versus authority, geographic community versus virtual community, and technology-in-theory versus technology-in-social-use. We are faced with having to resolve—democratically—issues that, before the rise of the Internet, were mainly of theoretical interest.

Of all the changes bearing on the future of societies and on the future of social problems, none is likely to have more impact than cyberspace and the information that resides there. In that sense, as social problems emerge in the twenty-first century, nothing will be more real in its effect than virtual reality. An information economy such as ours invests in information as a major source of wealth and power, and more and more information is coming to reside in cyberspace at little cost to the consumer.

Information economy An economy in which information is treated like any other commodity; it can be bought, sold, traded, and so on.

Panopticon An all-seeing eye of authority, as proposed architecturally for maximum prison surveillance by the English utilitarian social philosopher Jeremy Bentham (1748–1832). A century and a half later the French social theorist Michel Foucault used Bentham's concept of the Panopticon as a metaphor for the modern-day surveillance society embodied in contemporary institutions.

Chapter Summary

Knowledge is, to an important extent, empowering. Wrong information, in the form of stereotypes and rumours, can produce a great deal of social harm. Good information, in the form of science and technology, can transform society for the better.

As educated people, we must differentiate between fact and fantasy. It is our job as sociologists to understand and, if possible, to control the formation of fantasy, with the conviction that it is better to understand public issues than not to understand them. Armed with a greater comprehension of the social problems we face, we are more capable of pursuing solutions through individual and collective actions. While individual solutions are easier to achieve, collective solutions result in long-lasting changes.

As this book has shown, there are a few central problems in the forefront—in particular, inequality and exclusion, ignorance and misinformation—and they play out in numerous combinations and historical variations. Our future, as a species, will depend on our ability to understand and mitigate the more harmful versions of these problems. Cyberspace, in particular, offers us various exciting, challenging, and dangerous opportunities: to create communities that have no visible location, to participate in events almost instantaneously, to observe human life in every part of the world. Cyberspace reduces some constraints of space and time sharply; in doing so, it plunges us into a larger, more crowded pond than we have ever known. Can we face the challenge?

As with all technological advancements in the last two centuries, the development of cyberspace enables the creation of both more egalitarian and more totalitarian aspects of society; we can cure our deadly diseases and create new ones; we can tell each other more truths and more lies—more quickly (and persuasively) than ever before. How we will survive this ordeal by information remains to be seen.

Nothing shows more clearly than cyberspace the opportunities and dangers that will face humanity when new information technology produces "new societies" without tradition or regulation. Nothing shows more clearly than futures studies the desire of humanity to imagine and, through imagination, to shape the future. Like our colleagues in the past, we must continue to imagine and struggle to create a new society.

Questions for Critical Thought

1. Can you think of a social problem (one not listed in the text) that will likely persist into the near future? Can you think of one that will not be an issue in the near future? Explain why.
2. Future predictions are often used to determine several possible alternative futures. What are some alternative futures regarding the social issues surrounding environmental damage? Or cyberspace?
3. What are some current and future problems associated with the widespread adoption of cyberspace?
4. The rate at which information spreads is related to its content. Consider the daily newspaper versus tabloids. Compare the number of people, for example, who know the reasons for the conflict in the Middle East with the number who are up to date on who is dating whom in Hollywood. Discuss possible explanations for this.

Recommended Readings

Bell, Wendell. 2010. *Foundations of Futures Studies: Human Science for a New Era: History, Purposes, and Knowledge.* Piscataway, NJ: Transaction Publishers.

Blinder, Alan. 2013. *After the Music Stopped: The Financial Crisis, the Response, and the Work Ahead.* New York: Penguin Press.

Cook, Ian, and Jamie Halsall. 2012. *Aging in Comparative Perspective: Processes and Policies (International Perspectives on Aging).* New York: Springer.

Gore, Al. *The Future: Six Drivers of Global Change.* 2013. New York: Random House.

Goudie, Andrew. 2013. *The Human Impact on the Natural Environment: Past, Present, and Future.* Hoboken, NJ: John Wiley and Sons.

Saad, Maida Bne. 2013. *The Global Hunger Crisis: Tackling Food Insecurity in Developing Countries.* London: Pluto Press.

Swire, Peter, and Kenesa Ahmad. 2012. *Privacy and Surveillance with New Technologies.* New York: International Debate Education Association.

Teich, Albert. 2013. *Technology and the Future.* Stamford, CT: Cengage Learning.

Glossary

Absolute poverty Lack of the basic necessities (food, shelter, medicine) for basic survival. Starvation is an example of absolute poverty.

Achieved statuses Social statuses (or positions) that are not inborn but are the result of effort and accomplishment, such as educational or occupational attainment.

Addiction Socially disapproved behaviour that is uncontrollable, repetitive, and possibly harmful.

Ageism Prejudice or discrimination, mostly against seniors, but by implication against any member of society, based on their age.

Age pyramid A graphic depiction of the age composition of a population, broken down by age and sex; pyramid-shaped if the birth rate is high but otherwise more rectangular.

Alienation This experience involves feelings of powerlessness, meaninglessness, normlessness, estrangement, and social isolation in the workplace.

Ascribed statuses Statuses assigned to people because of certain traits beyond their control.

Aversive racists Those who sympathize with the victims of past injustice and support public policies that promote racial equality but who nonetheless hold prejudicial views towards other races.

Biological determinism An attempt to interpret all human and social behaviour from a biological perspective; based on the assumption that human behaviour is controlled by a person's genes.

Biomedical view of medicine A medical perspective that emphasizes Western scientific principles, defines health as the absence of illness, views the human body as a machine that sometimes requires repair, and promotes the use of therapeutic intervention (e.g., drugs, surgery) to "cure" disease and injury.

Biopsychosocial view of health and illness A medical perspective that considers health and disease as products of the interaction between body, mind, and environment.

Body burden A buildup of harmful synthetic chemicals and heavy metals in our bodies.

Body mass index (BMI) Weight in kilograms divided by the square of height in metres (kg/m^2); "overweight" is defined as $25 \ kg/m^2$ and "obesity" as $30 \ kg/m^2$.

Bullying Any form of repeated aggression marked by an observable power differential between individuals.

Bureaucracy A large, complex organization employing highly specialized workers who work within the context of what Max Weber called a legal-rational authority structure.

Capitalism The economic system in which private individuals or corporate groups own the means of production and distribution. Capitalists invest capital to produce goods and services, which they sell for profit in a competitive free market.

Chain migration The successful migration of one family member creates a chain for the kin and community network. Migration is not random but is increasingly about networks, rational choices, and kinship relations.

Claims-making The promotion of a particular moral vision of social life and, thus, anything people do to propagate a view of who or what is a problem and what should be done about it.

Climate change A departure from expected patterns of temperature and other climatic properties resulting mainly from an accumulation of greenhouse gases in the atmosphere, trapping the heat reflected off the earth's surface.

Collective violence Often organized by a group of individuals or a social movement, this type of violence is used to promote an agenda or to resist an oppressive other.

Co-morbidity The predisposition of an individual with an illness to additional health problems.

Conflict theory A theoretical paradigm, derived from the writings of Marx and Engels, that emphasizes conflict and change as the regular and permanent features of society; a macrosociological research approach that focuses on processes within the whole society.

Conventional crimes The traditionally illegal behaviours that most people think of as "crime." For example, homicide and sexual assault are given the most media coverage but account for only 12 per cent of all crimes.

Cornucopian view of nature Nature is seen as an almost endless storehouse of resources that exist only for use by humans, especially by those currently living.

Credential inflation The tendency of schools to provide and employers to demand ever-more schooling and ever-higher credentials for work that has not become more demanding or complex.

Credentialism A process of social selection that gives class advantage and social status to people who possess academic advantage.

Crime Any behaviour that, in a given time and place, is prohibited by applicable statutory law. When a law is violated, a crime is said to have been committed.

Culture The way of life of a society that includes dress, language, norms of behaviour, foods, tools, beliefs, and folklore. This framework of values and practices adapts to the changing socio-historical context.

Culture of poverty Theory developed by Oscar Lewis characterizing the urban poor as having a distinct set of values and norms, including short-sightedness, impulsiveness, and a tendency to accept their marginalized status in society, and as remaining poor because they pass on these values to future generations.

Cyberbullying A technological extension of physical bullying occurring when an individual uses information technology (IT) to embarrass, harass, intimidate, or threaten others.

Cyberspace The abstract concept of "where" computer-stored information is exchanged.

Cyberterrorism A technological and electronic attack on the enemy's technology and communications infrastructure, e.g., targeted "virus" and "worm" programs that collapse normal computer programming.

Demographic transition Shift in a population or society through a series of stages from high birth and death rates to low birth and death rates.

Deterrence A justice system based on deterrence assumes that crimes are rational acts in which the offender weighs the perceived benefits of committing the crime against the probability of being caught and the severity of the punishment. It assumes that the probability of being punished is high and that law enforcement agencies are competent and efficient in apprehending offenders.

Diaspora The dispersal of any group of people throughout the world; originally applied to the tribes of Israel. Almost any migrant community with some degree of international heritage is referred to as "diasporic."

Differential socialization The processes whereby people learn to behave in accordance with prevailing standards of culture or gender. For example, boys and men learn to be less inhibited in using aggressive and violent actions, and this may account for the disproportionate number of males involved in criminal activity.

Digital divide The separation between those who have access to electronic technology and the Internet ("haves") and those who do not ("have-nots").

Discouraged workers People who are not actively seeking employment. Specifically, they are thought to have turned their backs on the traditional work system and to have abandoned any desire to be gainfully employed.

Discriminatory unemployment Unemployment resulting from discrimination against particular groups, such as ethnic minorities and women.

Disengagement theory The theory that as people age, they voluntarily and normally remove themselves from activities and social contacts to ease their passage into a less active lifestyle.

Double shift Modern women's dual roles as breadwinner and homemaker.

Drug Any substance that causes a biochemical reaction in the body.

Drug abuse This concept begins with the notion of excessive or inappropriate drug use resulting in social, psychological, and/or physiological impairments. It stems from a chronic physical and psychological compulsion to continue taking a drug in order to avoid unpleasant withdrawal symptoms.

Drug dependency The routine need for a drug for physiological and/or psychological reasons.

Drug subculture A group of people who share common attitudes, beliefs, and behaviours surrounding drug use. These attitudes and beliefs differ significantly from those of most people in the wider society.

Economic inequality Large differences in income and wealth across individuals and groups within a society; differences in the economic power of nations.

Entrance status The status granted to an individual upon official entry into Canada. Statuses may be temporary (visitor visa, student authorization, live-in caregiver) or permanent (independent, professional, or skilled worker class).

Environmental racism A type of discrimination that results in the concentration of poor racial minorities in densely packed, poorly served urban neighbourhoods, often with higher levels of pollution and located near waste dumps and heavy industry.

Epidemiology An applied science that examines the causes, distribution, and control of disease in a population.

Extended family More than two generations of relatives living together in a household. The arrangement often includes grandparents, aunts, uncles, and dependent nephews and nieces.

Extrinsic rewards When work rewards the worker with money, prestige, respect, and social recognition.

Family A group of people related by kinship or similar close ties in which the adults assume responsibility for the care and upbringing of their natural or adopted children. Members of a family support one another financially, materially, and emotionally.

Femininity A socially constructed idea of how girls and women should act, or the various qualities that people expect to find in a typical female.

Feminization of poverty Women are over-represented among the impoverished people of the world. In the West, economic liberalization and the dominance of the market have meant that those with the least earning power—single mothers with children—have suffered most.

Filial responsibility Adult children's sense that they have a personal obligation or duty to protect, care for, and support their aging parents; filial piety.

Futures studies The area of research concerned with forecasting possible scenarios—technological, economic, political, social, environmental—in order to prepare for and shape what may come.

Gemeinschaft Social situations in which those involved treat one another as ends rather than as means; primary relationships based on sentiment, found most often in rural life.

Gender A social division referring to the social and psycho-social attributes by which humans are categorized as "male" or "female." Biology is deemed somewhat irrelevant to an understanding of the social distinctions between males and females. Gender encompasses the shared understandings of how women and men, girls and boys, should look and act. It is a label that subsumes a large assortment of traits, beliefs, values, and mannerisms, and defines how we should practise social interactions.

Gender inequality The differential success of men and women in gaining access to valued rewards. This tends to stem from structural arrangements, interpersonal discrimination, and cultural beliefs.

Gender roles The patterns of behaviour that a society expects of males and females and that all members of the society learn, to a greater or lesser extent, as part of the socialization process.

Gender socialization The process by which people learn their gender-based behaviour. This socialization process links gender to personal identity in the form of gender identity and to distinctive activities in the form of gender roles. The major agents of socialization all serve to reinforce cultural definitions of masculinity and femininity.

Genocide The deliberate, systematic, and planned killing of an entire national, ethnic, racial, or political group.

Gentrification The restoration and upgrading of deteriorated urban property by middle-class or affluent people, often resulting in displacement of lower-income people.

Gesellschaft Social situations in which those involved treat one another as means rather than as ends; secondary relations based primarily on calculation and individual interest, found most often in city life.

Glass ceiling Women can have considerable success, but can rarely reach and enter the topmost positions.

Globalization The integration on a world scale of economic activities and peoples by units of private capital and improved communications technology and transportation. In other words, globalization is the trend of increasing interdependence among the economies and societies of the world.

Greenwashing The process of promoting false ideas about the environmental friendliness of certain commercial products.

Growth ethic A cultural or subcultural commitment to the idea that economic growth is good in itself, whatever its social effects.

Heterosexism Discrimination against homosexuals in favour of heterosexuals.

Homicide The killing of a human being by another, directly or indirectly, by any means, including murder—that is, the unlawful killing of another human being with malicious intent—and manslaughter, the unlawful killing of another person without sufficient intent to constitute murder.

Homophobia Fear or hatred of homosexuals, or behaviour that suggests such fear or hatred.

Homosexuality Sexual attraction to people of the same sex.

Human Development Index (HDI) A combined measure of achievement in three basic areas of human development—life expectancy at birth; literacy; and GDP per capita—used by the United Nations Development Program to monitor social and economic progress across countries.

Ideology A system of beliefs that explains how society is, or should be; any system of ideas underlying and informing political action. In a Marxist sense, ideological ideas justify and legitimate subordination of one group to another.

Imperialism The exercise of political and economic control by one state over another, often by military means. Developing countries are often the focus of imperialistic and exploitive activities that stifle their own development and concentrate their resources and labour for the profit of advanced capitalist countries.

Individualism Belief in the primary importance of the individual and the need to protect individual liberty and choice against collective social or governmental restriction.

Individual racism "Classic" form of prejudice in which a person makes unfounded assumptions about the motives and abilities of others based on a stereotypical understanding of the person's racial or ethnic group characteristics.

Infant mortality rate Number of deaths of children under one year of age per 1,000 live births.

Information Age A historical time—the present—in which information of all forms is quickly and easily accessible via the Internet and computers. At the same time, there is far more information than existed only a few years or decades ago, and information drives work processes to a far greater extent than in the past.

Information economy An economy in which information is treated like any other commodity; it can be bought, sold, traded, and so on.

Institutional completeness A measure of the degree to which an immigrant ethnic group gives its own members the services they need through its own institutions.

Institutional (structural) racism Any form of racism that occurs specifically from within an institution, such as public government bodies and private business corporations. This form of racism is considered to be "built into" these prominent structures.

Intergenerational income elasticity The correlation between a parent's and a child's income.

Internalized racism When members of an ethnic or racial group accept and behave according to imposed stereotypes.

Interpersonal violence Violent interactions occurring between individuals, such as murder, rape, and domestic and child abuse.

Intrinsic rewards When work rewards the worker with the feeling of a "job well done."

Labelling The process of defining and treating others as deviant. Labelling theory explores the effects of negative labels on individuals' self-conceptions and is interested in the development of a "deviant identity." Social reactions of condemnation and criminalization can lead actors to alter their individual characteristics and to adopt the values of their labelled identity.

Latent functions Hidden, unstated, and sometimes unintended consequences of activities in an organization or institution.

Laws Rules of conduct that may provide for the punishment of violators—in other words, the formal rules about what a society's members can and cannot do.

LGBT Acronym for lesbian, gay, bisexual, transgendered—often used to speak of the LGBT community.

Life expectancy The average number of years remaining to a person at a particular age, given current age-specific mortality rates.

Low-income cut-offs (LICOs) A formal definition used by Statistics Canada for measuring relative poverty on the basis of the percentage of income devoted to daily necessities (food, shelter, clothing) and determined both regionally and by population (size of city or rural).

Low-income measures (LIMs) A set of figures representing 50 per cent of the median "adjusted family income." Actual incomes are compared with LIMs to determine whether or not a family can be considered "low-income."

Manifest functions The visible and intended goals or effects of social structures and institutions.

Market-basket measure (MBM) A way of measuring income and poverty in absolute, non-relative terms that was added in 2003 to Statistics Canada's methods of measuring income and poverty. It is based on an imaginary basket of market-priced goods and services and on the income needed to purchase the items in the basket. The determination of what goes into this imaginary basket, however, is subjective and tends to exclude all but the absolute essentials of bare survival.

Masculinity A socially constructed idea of how boys and men should act; qualities that people in our society expect to find in a typical man.

Maternal mortality rate The number of deaths of women due to complications during pregnancy, childbirth, or abortion, typically measured as deaths per year per 1,000 live births.

Mechanical solidarity Durkheim's term for the kind of tight, homogeneous social order typical of a pre-industrial, primarily rural society.

Medicalization The process through which behaviours are reconceived as instances of illness and are deemed no longer sinful, since they are outside personal control; also, the process whereby the medical profession comes to be viewed as being relevant to an ever-widening range of traditionally non-medical aspects of life.

Medical sociology The field of sociology that examines the social context of health, illness, and health care.

Mental disorder A condition "characterized by alterations in thinking, mood, or behaviour (or some combination thereof) associated with significant distress and impaired functioning over an extended period of time" (Health Canada, 2006).

Mental health The capacity for people to feel, think, and act in ways that enhance the quality of daily functioning, the range and depth of social relationships, and the ability to adapt to both positive and negative life changes.

Mental illness Clinical diagnosis of mental disorder requiring medical and/or psychotherapeutic treatment.

Meritocracy The holding of power or authority by people selected because of their ability.

Moral entrepreneurs Term coined to describe people who "discover" and try to publicize deviant behaviours. Moral entrepreneurs are crusading reformers who are disturbed by particular types of evil they see in the world and who will not rest until something is done to correct the problem.

Moral panic The process of arousing social concern over an issue—usually the work of moral entrepreneurs and the mass media.

Morbidity rate The extent of disease in a population, reported by incidence (the number of new cases in a given population during a given period) and/or its prevalence (the total number of cases of a disease in the population at a particular time).

Mortality rate The death rate of a given disease or population, typically measured as deaths per year per 1,000 people.

Neighbourhood effects Influences on people's lives that result from living in one type of neighbourhood (e.g., rich versus poor, or dangerous versus safe) rather than another.

Normal accidents Likely accidents in complex systems of people and machines, resulting from the unanticipated interaction of multiple failures.

Norms The rules and expectations of the society pertaining to appropriate behaviours under various social circumstances. Norms regulate behaviour in different situations, and large-scale norm violation is often viewed as a social problem; a problem occurs when traditionally normative behaviour is violated.

Nuclear family A family unit comprising one or two parents and any dependent children who live together in one household separate from relatives.

Objective elements The measurable features of a negative social condition. Such a condition might include crime, poverty, or alcohol abuse and can be considered an objective reality.

Organic solidarity Durkheim's term for the new social order of industrial society, which was based on interdependent, though not necessarily intimate, relationships.

Organized crime A group or system of professional criminals who practise illegal activities as a way of life and whose criminal activities are co-ordinated and controlled through a hierarchical system of bosses.

Over-education Having more education than is actually needed to perform employment roles and functions successfully.

Panopticon An all-seeing eye of authority, as proposed architecturally for maximum prison surveillance by the English utilitarian social philosopher Jeremy Bentham (1748–1832). A century and a half later the French social theorist Michel Foucault used Bentham's concept of the Panopticon as a metaphor for the modern-day surveillance society embodied in contemporary institutions.

Patriarchy Male dominance that is justified in a society's system of values. This dominance is tied to the ideology of gender and can be found in practically every society.

Peak oil The peak in global oil production, when the maximum rate of global petroleum extraction is reached, after which the rate of production goes into permanent decline.

Population density The number of people who live within a geographic area, usually expressed as people per square mile or square kilometre.

Population health perspective An approach to health that focuses on social determinants of health and, therefore, on preventive societal strategies and societal responses to health problems.

Positive checks Part of Malthusian theory, these prevent overpopulation by increasing the death rate. They include war, famine, pestilence, and disease.

Post-materialist culture A new cultural orientation that puts less emphasis on material consumption and class issues and more on non-material (quality of collective life) benefits, such as environmental improvement.

Post-traumatic stress disorder (PTSD) A form of psychological distress produced by a traumatic experience such as crime victimization, sexual assault, or military combat. Symptoms include nervousness, sleep disturbances, disruption of concentration, anxiety, depression, irrational fear, and flashbacks triggered by loud noises such as thunder or a car's backfiring.

Poverty line Also called the human poverty index. It represents a usual standard of living and differs across countries. The definition of poverty varies by society, within societies, and also over time.

Precautionary principle A tenet of environmentalism as it interfaces with economic development; it insists that when serious or irreversible damage could result from development, the wise and necessary decision is to not go ahead with that course of action, regardless of assumptions that technology could or will resolve any future problems or damage.

Prejudice A hostile or aversive attitude towards a person who belongs to a particular group just because of that person's membership in the group.

Preventive checks In Malthusian theory, these prevent overpopulation by limiting the number or survivals of live births. They include abortion, infanticide, sexual abstinence, delayed marriage, and contraceptive technologies.

Primary labour market High-paying jobs that provide good chances to "get ahead" and that offer job security.

Primary prevention Proactive steps taken to prevent a disease from occurring.

Primogeniture A system of inheritance in which only one child, the oldest son, inherits all of the family property on the death of his parents.

Professionalization The process by which an occupation raises its standing by limiting the number of entrants and regulating their behaviour. When used to refer to the medical industry, it is the gradual process whereby physicians establish autonomous control over the institution of health care and elevate their collective status in society to become authoritative judges of disease definitions and gatekeepers of medical services.

Queer An umbrella term for anyone who does not identify as heterosexual.

Quid pro quo sexual harassment The blatant demand by employers for sexual favours in exchange for promotion opportunities, salary increases, and preferential treatment.

Racial discrimination "Any distinction, exclusion, restriction, or preference based on race, colour, descent, or national or ethnic origin that has the purpose or effect of nullifying or impairing the recognition, enjoyment of exercise . . . of human rights and fundamental freedoms" (Office of the High Commissioner for Human Rights, 1969).

Racialization The tendency in a community to introduce racial distinctions into situations that can be understood and managed without such distinctions—in other words, the way social institutions impose racial identities on minorities.

Relative deprivation The feelings and judgements of an individual or members of a group when they compare themselves to others who are better off materially. People make judgements relative to standards or frames of reference. The feelings generated contribute to the formation of social movements.

Relative income hypothesis The proposal that income inequality alone (as opposed to absolute deprivation) is enough to bring on various health problems, including premature mortality, within a population.

Relative poverty Survival, but far below the general living standards of the society or social group in which they live; affects people's lives in dramatic ways.

Reporting relationships Official hierarchical relationships established within a bureaucracy. These relationships are characterized by a power dynamic in which subordinate members adhere to a set of predetermined roles, processes, and functions.

Risk society A society in which risk is increased by technological and economic developments, raising the need for more cautious awareness, but also in which active risk-taking is considered a core element of economic and social progress.

Roles The specific duties and obligations expected of those who occupy a specific social status.

Rumours Information diffusion in which the content is not pure misinformation but is conceived for a purpose with limited reliability. As information provided to solve an ill-defined problem, rumours based on stereotypes or ideal images are more likely than other rumours to gain media and popular currency and to resist denial.

Secondary (marginal) labour market High-turnover, lower-paying, and generally unstable or insecure employment. These jobs offer little chance to get ahead and little job security.

Secondary victimization Additional pain and suffering caused to a victim of crime by the negative responses of the justice system (e.g., police) and significant individuals (e.g., family members) following his or her original victimization.

Self-reporting The victim reports to authorities that a crime has occurred. This is the most direct method of measuring crime rates. However, it is not the most accurate, as changes in the crime rate reflect changes in victims' willingness to report.

Senescence The biological aging of an organism as it lives beyond its maturity, usually accompanied by chemical and organic changes.

Sex A biological concept that differentiates female and male. Most people are (mainly) male or (mainly) female from the moment of conception, with biological differences between the sexes that are anatomic, genetic, and hormonal.

Sexism Discrimination and derogatory attitudes and beliefs that promote stereotyping of people because of their gender. Sexism and gender stereotyping are problems for both men and women, and they are most often experienced in institutions and social relationships.

Sexual harassment Any unwanted physical or verbal conduct directed towards a person that is sexually offensive or humiliating.

Sexual identity How a person self-identifies—whether as straight, gay, lesbian, or transgendered.

Sexual orientation One's sexual attraction to people of a specific sex.

Social bond theory A type of control theory. A strong social bond prevents most people from succumbing to the temptation to engage in criminal activities.

Social capital Sociologists call having larger, more varied, and more powerful interpersonal networks "having greater social capital."

Social causation Common social factors that produce widespread health problems. Prime examples might include the effects of epidemics and other infectious diseases and the effects of poverty, access to health care, and work-related health problems; related to social determinants of health.

Social constructionism A sociological research approach that examines the ways people interact to create a shared social reality.

Social determinants of health The complex causal relationships between various social, economic, and political factors and population health outcomes.

Social disorder The uncertain and unpredictable condition in which rules are not obeyed. The environment is generally unsafe, and the boundaries of acceptable behaviour have broken down.

Social distance Feelings of aloofness and unapproachability often felt between members of different social strata or of different ethnic or "racial" origins.

Social group A set of people, defined by formal or informal criteria of membership, who feel unified or are bound together in stable patterns of interaction.

Socialism An alternative economic and political ideology that flourished in the nineteenth and twentieth centuries. It favours the public ownership of the means of production and distribution and the investment of public capital in producing goods and services.

Socialization The process by which people internalize and learn their culture, much of which occurs during childhood.

Social mobility The movement—usually of individuals but sometimes of whole groups—between different positions within the system of social stratification in any society. Most sociological attention has focused on intergenerational mobility by comparing parents and their children.

Social movements Broad social alliances of people who seek to affect or block an aspect of social change within a society. They may be informally organized at first, but in time they often turn into formal organizations such as political parties and labour unions. Examples of social movements include political movements, labour movements, the women's movement, environmental movements, and peace movements.

Social order The prevalence of harmonious relationships; used synonymously with "social organization." This condition exists when rules are obeyed and social situations are controlled and predictable. Rules serve not only to indicate which behaviours are acceptable, but also to allow participants to anticipate the behaviour of others.

Social problem A social condition or pattern of behaviour that is believed to warrant public concern and collective action.

Social selection A correlation suggesting but not proving causation, because a third, unmeasured factor is involved; also known as "adverse selectivity."

Sociological imagination A term used by sociologist C. Wright Mills in his 1959 book *The Sociological Imagination*, which describes the sociologist's ability to connect seemingly impersonal and remote historical forces to the most basic incidents of an individual's life. The sociological imagination enables people to distinguish between personal troubles and public issues.

Strain (anomie) theory Merton holds that strain is produced when social structure prevents people from achieving culturally defined goals through legitimate means, and according to Durkheim, anomie is a condition characterized by a breakdown of norms and personal disorganization, which may lead to crime. Merton outlines various adaptive strategies: conformity, ritualism, retreatism, rebellion, and innovation. Innovation is most commonly associated with criminal activities, which include theft, robbery, tax fraud, embezzlement, and organized crime.

Structural functionalism A theoretical paradigm emphasizing the way each part of society functions to fulfill the needs of the society as a whole; also called "functionalism"; a macrosociological approach that focuses on the societal, as opposed to the individual, level.

Structural unemployment Unemployment caused by social and economic factors that affect workers equally across all groups, such as corporate downsizing, capital flight (caused by corporate mergers and the move of operations to another geographic region—"runaway plants"), and the automation of work processes.

Subculture theory This approach to the study of deviance investigates the norms that set a group apart from mainstream society. Specifically, it gives special insight into the subculture of the criminal, looking into the values and belief systems that may be conducive to delinquent and criminal action.

Subjective elements People's evaluations of objective conditions and the processes that influence their evaluations. They include the moral labels that people apply to particular acts or situations and the accounts they give for these acts and situations.

Suburbanization The process by which housing spreads almost unhindered into once-rural regions surrounding the city core. This greatly expands the geographic size of cities and takes out of production valuable agricultural land, and there is a noticeable shift of the affluent from the urban centre to these surrounding areas.

Suffrage movement The central aim of many in the "first wave" of the women's movement in the late nineteenth and early twentieth centuries was the right for women to vote in elections. With women's suffrage (i.e., voting rights), other goals—social reform, legal rights—would then be more readily attainable.

Symbolic interactionism A theoretical paradigm that studies the process by which individuals interpret and respond to the actions of others and that conceives of society as the product of this continuous face-to-face interaction; a microsociological approach that focuses on individuals and small groups.

Symbols Gestures, artifacts, and words that represent something else.

Technology The manifestation of human knowledge and ingenuity applied to the solution of a problem or need; applied science.

Telehealth The use of computer and communication technologies to facilitate health-care delivery across geographic space.

Tolerance A symptom of repeated and frequent drug use. It refers to the decreased effectiveness of any given drug.

Tragedy of the commons A market system based on the capitalist belief that economies work best when left alone. With each self-interested actor seeking what is personally best, it may work against the common good by polluting, destroying, and exhausting common goods that are not owned by a single individual but are shared by all of us—goods such as bodies of water, the air, the land, ecosystems, and, especially, renewable resources such as fish and forests.

Under-five mortality rate (U5MR) Number of deaths of children under five years of age per 1,000 live births.

Urbanization The growth in the proportion of the population living in urbanized areas. There is also an increasing appearance in rural and small-town areas of behaviour patterns and cultural values associated with big-city life.

Vertical mosaic Coined by John Porter, a socio-economic hierarchy in which French and English Canadians live at the top and other ethnic groups are positioned below.

Vice crimes Deviant behaviour that may be defined as immoral (e.g., gambling, prostitution, drug trafficking). These crimes provide the greatest opportunity for organized crime.

Victimization surveys Samples of people are asked how many times within a given time period they have been the victim of particular crimes.

War A state of armed conflict between different nations or states or different groups within a nation or state.

Well-being A positive state of existence characterized by happiness, prosperity, and the satisfaction of basic human needs, and not simply by the absence of negative conditions, such as illness or injury.

Whistle-blowers Employees in a bureaucratic organization who bring forward valid information about wrongdoing or illegal conduct by their organization and who are often punished for doing so.

White-collar crimes The crimes committed by white-collar workers and management in the course of their occupations. They are always distinguished from conventional criminal offences such as robbery or murder. White-collar crimes are performed in the course of normal work and usually occur in reputable organizations.

World system theory Provides an account of the transnational development of capitalism and a theory of the global structure of inequality among nations. Along with dependency theory, it challenged the prevailing modernization theories of the 1960s.

References

Chapter 1

Ajdukovic, Marina. 2008. "Social Problems, Social Risks and Modern Social Work," *Revija Za Socijalnu Politiku* 15, 3: 395–414.

Alvarez, Rodolfo. 2001. "The Social Problem as an Enterprise: Values as a Defining Factor," *Social Problems* 48: 3–10.

Becker, Howard. 1963. *Outsiders: Studies in the Sociology of Deviance*. New York: Free Press.

Berger, Peter L., and Thomas Luckmann. 1966. *The Social Construction of Reality: Treatise in the Sociology of Knowledge*. Garden City, NY: Anchor.

Blumer, Herbert. 1971. "Social Problems as Collective Behavior," *Social Problems* 8, 3: 298–396.

Bockman, S. 1991. "Interest, Ideology, and Claims-Making Activity," *Sociological Inquiry* 61, 4: 452–70.

Bodner, Ehud, and Aryeh Lazar. 2008. "Ageism among Israeli Students: Structure and Demographic Influences," *International Psychogeriatrics* 20, 5: 1046–58.

Boguslaw, Robert. 1965. *The New Utopians: A Study of System Design and Social Change*. Englewood Cliffs, NJ: Prentice-Hall.

Burr, Vivienne. 1995. "What Is Social Constructionism?," in Burr, *An Introduction to Social Constructionism*. London: Routledge, 1–16.

Butler-Jones, David. 2009. *The Chief Public Health Officer's Report on the State of Public Health in Canada*. Ottawa: Public Health Agency of Canada, Publication no. HP2–10/2009E, 20 Oct. At: <www.phac-aspc.gc.ca/publicat/2009/cphorsphc-respcacsp/index-eng.php>.

Caan, Woody. 2009. "Unemployment and Suicide: Is Alcohol the Missing Link?," *Lancet* 374, 9697: 1241–2.

Calabresi, Guido, and Philip Bobbitt. 1981. *Tragic Choices*. New York: W.W. Norton and Company.

Cohen, Stanley. 1972. *Folk Devils and Moral Panics*. London: MacGibbon and Kee.

Ding, Huiling. 2009. "Rhetorics of Alternative Media in an Emerging Epidemic: SARS, Censorship, and Extra-Institutional Risk Communication," *Technical Communication Quarterly* 18, 4: 327–50.

Domenico, Desirae M., and Karen H. Jones. 2007. "Adolescent Pregnancy in America: Causes and Responses," *Journal for Vocational Special Needs Education* 30, 1: 4–12.

Durkheim, Émile. 1951 [1897]. *Suicide*, trans. John A. Spaulding and George Simpson. New York: Free Press.

———. 1964 [1893]. *The Division of Labor in Society*, trans. George Simpson. New York: Free Press.

———. 1965 [1912]. *The Elementary Forms of Religious Life*, trans. Joseph Ward Swain. New York: Free Press.

Edwards, Craig. 2009. "Changing Functions, Moral Responsibility, and Mental Illness," *Philosophy, Psychiatry & Psychology* 16, 1: 105.

Fine, Gary, and Corey Fields. 2008. "Culture and Microsociology: The Anthill and the Veldt," *Annals, American Academy of Political and Social Science* 619, 1: 130–48.

Frank, J.W. 1995. "Why 'Population Health'?," *Canadian Journal of Public Health* 86, 3: 162–4.

Goffman, Erving. 1959. *The Presentation of Self in Everyday Life*. Garden City, NY: Doubleday-Anchor.

Hagan, John, and Bill McCarthy. 1998. *Mean Streets: Youth, Crime and Homelessness*. Cambridge: Cambridge University Press.

HRSDC (Human Resources and Skills Development Canada). 2010. "Health—Self-Rated Health." At: <www4.hrsdc.gc.ca/.3ndic.1t.4r@-eng.jsp?iif=10>.

Krejci, Jaroslav. 1994. "What Is Macrosociology About?," *Sociologicky Casopis* 30, 3: 317–28.

Krinsky, John. 2008. *Free Labor: Workfare and the Contested Language of Neoliberalism*. Chicago: University of Chicago Press.

McConatha, Jasmin Tahmaseb, et al. 2004. "Turkish and US Attitudes toward Aging," *Educational Gerontology* 30, 3: 169–83.

McMullin, Julie. 2004. *Understanding Social Inequality: Intersections of Class, Age, Gender, Ethnicity, and Race in Canada*. Toronto: Oxford University Press.

Marx, Karl. 1990 [1862–3]. *Capital, Volume I*, trans. Ben Fowkes. London: Penguin.

Marx, Karl, and Friedrich Engels. 1998 [1848]. *The Communist Manifesto*, introduction by Martin Malia. New York: Penguin.

Mead, George Herbert. 1934. *Mind, Self, and Society from the Standpoint of a Social Behaviorist*. Chicago: University of Chicago Press.

Merton, Robert K. 1968. *Social Theory and Social Structure*. New York: Free Press.

Mills, C. Wright. 1959. *The Sociological Imagination*. New York: Oxford University Press.

Moore, Michael, Ho Ming Yuen, Nick Dunn, Mark A. Mullee, Joe Maskell, and Tony Kendrick. 2009. "Explaining the Rise in Antidepressant Prescribing: A Descriptive Study Using the General Practice Research Database," *British Medical Journal* 339, 7727: 956–7.

Morgan, Stephen, David B. Grusky, and Gary S. Fields. 2006. *Mobility and Inequality*. Stanford, CA: Stanford University Press.

Öberg, Peter, and Lars Tornstam. 2003. "Attitudes toward Embodied Old Age among Swedes," *International Journal of Aging and Human Development* 56, 2: 133–53.

Raphael, Dennis. 2004. *Social Determinants of Health: Canadian Perspectives*. Toronto: Canadian Scholars' Press.

Ryan, Ellen Bouchard, Young-Sun Jin, and Ann P. Anas. 2009. "Cross-Cultural Beliefs about Memory and Aging for Self and Others: South Korea and Canada," *International Journal of Aging and Human Development* 68, 3: 185–94.

Searle, John R. 2006. "Reality and Social Construction: Reply to Friedman," *Anthropological Theory* 6, 1: 81–8.

Simmel, Georg. 1976. "The Stranger," in *The Sociology of Georg Simmel*. New York: Free Press.

Staeheli, L.A. 2008. "Political Geography: Difference, Recognition and the Contested Terrains of Political Claims-Making," *Progress in Human Geography* 32, 4: 561–70.

Taft, Jessica K. 2009. "Growing Up and Rising Up: Teenage Girl Activists and Social Movements in the Americas," *Dissertation Abstracts International, A: The Humanities and Social Sciences* 69, 09: 3747.

Tanner, Julian. 2009. "Making Schools Safer: The Unintended Consequences of Good Intentions," *Education Canada* 49, 3: 12–25.

Tippelt, Hynek. 2009. "Globalization, War and the Death Drive," *Mezinarodni Vztahy* 44, 2: 65–72.

Weir-Hughes, Dickon. 2009. "President's Report," *International Journal of Nursing Terminologies and Classifications* 20, 3: 155–6.

Westcott, Emma. 2005. "Equality of Opportunity and Inclusion," *Journal of Education for Teaching: International Research and Pedagogy* 31, 4: 273–4.

Wilkinson, Richard G., and Kate E. Pickett. 2007. "The Problems of Relative Deprivation: Why Some Societies Do Better Than Others," *Social Science and Medicine* 65, 9: 1965–78.

Zazar, Kresimir. 2008. "What Is Sociology?," *Revija Za Sociologiju* 39, 3: 205–9.

Chapter 2

Addison, Tony, David Hulme, and Ravi Kanbur, eds. 2009. *Poverty Dynamics: Interdisciplinary Perspectives*. New York: Oxford University Press.

Andersen, Robert, and Josh Curtis, 2012. "The Polarizing Effect of Economic Inequality on Class Identification: Evidence from 44 Countries," *Research in Social Stratification and Mobility* 30, 1: 129–41.

Andersen, Robert, and Mitch McIvor. 2013. *Growing Inequality and Its Impacts in Canada*. Report to the European Commission, Brussels, Jan. 2013. GINI (Growing Inequalities' Impacts international research project),

7th Framework Programme. At <www.gini-researc.org/CR-Canada>.

Aratani, Yumiko. 2009. *Homeless Children and Youth: Causes and Consequences*. New York: National Center for Children in Poverty, Mailman School of Public Health, Columbia University.

Baron, Stephen W. 2006. "Street Youth, Strain Theory, and Crime," *Journal of Criminal Justice* 34, 2: 209–23.

Barraclough, Geoffrey. 1967. *An Introduction to Contemporary History*. Harmondsworth, UK: Penguin.

Bosma, Hans, Michael G. Marmot, Harry Hemingway, Amanda G. Nicholson, Eric Brunner, and Stephen A. Stansfield. 1997. "Low Job Control and Risk of Coronary Heart Disease in Whitehall II (Prospective Cohort) Study," *British Medical Journal* 314: 558–65.

Bradley, Christopher, and Dennis J. Cole. 2002. "Causal Attributions and the Significance of Self-Efficacy in Predicting Solutions to Poverty," *Sociological Focus* 35, 4: 381–96.

Braun, Denny. 1995. "Negative Consequences to the Rise of Income Inequality," *Research in Politics and Society* 5: 3–31.

Breau, Sébastien. 2007. "Income Inequality across Canadian Provinces in an Era of Globalization: Explaining Recent Trends," *Canadian Geographer* 51, 1: 72–90.

Breen, R., and J.O. Jonsson. 2007. "Explaining Change in Social Fluidity: Educational Equalization and Educational Expansion in the Twentieth-Century Sweden," *American Journal of Sociology* 112: 1775–810.

Calvano, Lisa. 2008. "Multinational Corporations and Local Communities: A Critical Analysis of Conflict," *Journal of Business Ethics* 82, 4: 793–805.

CBC News. 2007. "Homelessness 'Chronic' in Canada: Study," 26 June. At: <www.cbc.ca/canada/story/2007/06/26/shelter.html>.

CCSD (Canadian Council on Social Development). 2001. *Defining and Re-defining Poverty: A CCSD Perspective*. At: <www.ccsd.ca/index.php/policy-initiatives/policy-statements-briefs-submissions/112-defining-and-re-defining-poverty-a-ccsd-perspective>.

Chitrakar, Roshan. 2009. *Overcoming Barriers to Girls' Education in South Asia: Deepening the Analysis*. Kathmandu,

Nepal: United Nations Children's Fund.

Corak, Miles. 2013. "Income Inequality, Equality, Equality of Opportunity, and Intergenerational Mobility," *Journal of Economic Perspectives* (American Economic Association) 27, 3: 79–102.

Currie, C.L., T.C. Wild, D.P. Schopflocher, L. Laing, and P. Veugelers. 2011. "Illicit and Prescription Drug Problems among Urban Aboriginal Adults in Canada: The Role of Traditional Culture in Protection and Resilience," *Social Science and Medicine* 88: 1–9.

Curry-Stevens, Ann. 2004. "Income Security and Employment in Canada," in Dennis Raphael, ed., *Social Determinants of Health: Canadian Perspectives*. Toronto: Canadian Scholars' Press, 21–38.

Curtis, Josh. 2013. "Middle Class Identity in the Modern World: How Politics and Economics Matter," *Canadian Review of Sociology* 50, 2: 203–26.

Daniels, Norman, Bruce Kennedy, and Ichiro Kawachi. 2000. "Justice Is Good for Our Health," in Daniels, Kennedy, and Kawachi, eds, *Is Inequality Bad for Our Health?* Boston: Beacon Press, 3–33.

Davis, Catherine. 2008. "Book Review: J.M. Grimshaw, *Family Homelessness—Causes, Consequences and the Policy Response in England*," *Housing Studies* 23, 6: 943–5.

Davis, K., and W.E. Moore. 1945. "Some Principles of Stratification," *American Sociological Review* 10: 242–9.

Defina, Robert H., and Kishor Thanawala. 2009. "The Impact of Unemployment and Inequality in Canada," *Indian Journal of Economics and Business* 4: 17–26.

De Looper, Michael, ed. 2009. *Health Update*. Publication no. 7. Geneva: OECD, Jan. At: <www.oecd.org/dataoecd/63/18/43305158.pdf>.

Diekmeyer, Peter. 2001. "Measuring Poverty," *CMA Management* 75, 9: 52–3.

Edwards, Richard. 1979. *Contested Terrain: The Transformation of the Workplace in the Twentieth Century*. New York: Basic Books.

Esping-Andersen, Gosta. 1990. *The Three Worlds of Welfare Capitalism*. Princeton, NJ: Princeton University Press.

Fauth, R.C., T. Leventhal, and J. Brooks-Gunn. 2007. "Welcome to the Neighbourhood? Long-Term Impacts of Moving to Low-Poverty Neighbourhoods on Poor Children's and Adolescents' Outcomes," *Journal of Research on Adolescence* 17, 2: 249–84.

Fisher, Gordon M. 1998. "Using a Little-Known Body of Historical Knowledge: What Can the History of U.S. Poverty Lines Contribute to Present-Day Comparative Poverty Research?," paper presented at the annual meeting of the International Sociological Association.

Gallupe, Owen, and Stephen W. Baron. 2009. "Street Youth, Relational Strain, and Drug Use," *Journal of Drug Issues* 39, 3: 523–45.

Garnett, Bruce, Neil Guppy, and Gerry Veenstra. 2008. "Careers Open to Talent: Educational Credentials, Cultural Talent, and Skilled Employment," *Sociological Forum* 23, 1: 144–64.

Gravelle, Hugh, and Matt Sutton. 2009. "Income, Relative Income, and Self-reported Health in Britain 1979–2000," *Health Economics* 18, 2: 125–45.

Guppy, N., P.D. Mikicich, and R. Pendakur. 1984. "Changing Patterns of Educational Inequality in Canada," *Canadian Journal of Sociology* 9, 3: 319–31.

Hagan, John. 1994. *Crime and Disrepute.* Thousand Oaks, CA: Pine Forge Press.

Heflin, C.M., and J. Iceland. 2009. "Poverty, Material Hardship, and Depression," *Social Science Quarterly* 90, 5: 1051–71.

Hills, John, Tom Sefton, and Kitty Stewart, eds. 2009. *Towards a More Equal Society? Poverty, Inequality and Public Policy since 1997.* Bristol, UK: Policy Press.

Hobsbawm, E.J. 1959. *Primitive Rebels: Studies in Archaic Forms of Social Movement in the 19th and 20th Centuries.* New York: Norton.

ILO (International Labour Organization). 2008. *ILO Action against Trafficking in Human Beings.* Rep. no. 978–92–2–121008–5. At: <www2.ilo.org/wcmsp5/groups/public/ed_norm/declaration/documents/publication/wcms_090356.pdf>.

Jones-Webb, Rhonda, Lonnie Snowden, Denise Herd, Brian Short, and Peter Hannan. 1997. "Alcohol-Related Problems among Black, Hispanic and White Men: The Contribution of Neighborhood Poverty," *Journal of Studies on Alcohol* 58: 539–45.

Kanter, R.M. 1972. *Commitment and Community: Communes and Utopias in Sociological Perspective.* Cambridge, MA: Harvard University Press.

———. 1977. *Men and Women of the Corporation.* New York: Basic Books.

Kennedy, Bruce P., Ichiro Kawachi, Deborah Prothrow-Stith, Kimberly Lochner, and Vanita Gupta. 1998. "Social Capital, Income Inequality, and Firearm Violent Crime," *Social Science and Medicine* 47, 1: 7–17.

Kirkpatrick, Sharon, and Valerie Tarasuk. 2003. "The Relationship between Low Income and Household Food Expenditure in Canada," *Public Health and Nutrition* 6, 6: 589–97.

Lipset, S.M., and H.L. Zetterberg. 1959. "Social Mobility in Industrial Societies," in S.M. Lipset and R. Bendix, eds, *Social Mobility in Industrial Society.* Berkeley: University of California Press.

Lipset, Seymour Martin, James S. Coleman, and Martin A. Trow. 1963. *Union Democracy: The Internal Politics of the International Typographical Union.* New York: Simon & Schuster.

McMullin, Julie. 2004. *Understanding Social Inequality: Intersections of Class, Age, Gender, Ethnicity, and Race in Canada.* Toronto: Oxford University Press.

Marmot, M.G., M. Kogevinas, and M.A. Elston. 1987. "Social/Economic Status and Disease," *Annual Review of Public Health* 8: 111–35.

Marmot, M.G., M.J. Shipley, and G. Rose. 1984. "Inequalities in Death—Specific Explanations of a General Pattern?," *Lancet*, no. 1: 1003–6.

Marmot, M.G., G. Davey Smith, S. Stansfield et al. 1991. "Health Inequalities among British Civil Servants: The Whitehall II Study," *Lancet* 337 (8754): 1387–93.

Marx, Karl, and Friedrich Engels. 1955 [1848]. *The Communist Manifesto*, trans. Samuel Moore. New York: Appleton Century Crofts.

Marzuk, Peter M., Kenneth Tardiff, Andrew C. Leon, Charles S. Hirsch, Marina Stajic, Laura Portera, and Nancy Hartwell. 1997. "Poverty and Fatal Accidental Drug Overdoses of Cocaine and Opiates in New York City: An Ecological Study," *American Journal of Drug and Alcohol Abuse* 23: 221–8.

Merton, Robert K. 1957. *Social Theory and Social Structure*, rev. edn. New York: Free Press.

Michels, Robert. 1962 [1916]. *Political Parties: A Sociological Study of the Oligarchical Tendencies of Modern Democracy*, trans. Eden Paul and Cedar Paul. New York: Free Press.

Mills, C. Wright. 1959. *The Sociological Imagination.* Oxford: Oxford University Press.

Mooney, Linda A., David Knox, Caroline Schacht, and Adie Nelson. 2001. *Understanding Social Problems*, 1st Can. edn. Scarborough, ON: Nelson Thompson.

Morgan, Stephen, David B. Grusky, and Gary S. Fields. 2006. *Mobility and Inequality.* Stanford, CA: Stanford University Press.

Myers, Cindy L. 2005. "Talking Poverty: Power Arrangements in Poverty Discourse," *Dissertation Abstracts International, A: The Humanities and Social Sciences* 66, 3: 1186-A.

Myles, John. 1998. "How to Design a 'Liberal' Welfare State: A Comparison of Canada and the United States," *Social Policy and Administration* 32, 4: 341–64.

Nation, The. 2009. "Ten Things You Need to Know to Live on the Streets," 289, 4: 8–9.

National Advisory Council on Aging. 2005. *Aging in Poverty in Canada.* At: <dsp-psd.pwgsc.gc.ca/collection/H88-5-3-2005E.pdf>.

Obinger, Hebert, Stephan Leibfried, and Francis Castles. 2005. *Federalism and the Welfare State: New World and European Experiences.* Cambridge: Cambridge University Press.

Poliakova, S.V., and A.G. Reut. 2008. "Evaluating the Impact of Social Protection Programs on Poverty in Ukraine," *Problems of Economic Transition* 51, 8: 21–6.

Porter, John. 1965. *The Vertical Mosaic.* Toronto: University of Toronto Press.

Prus, Steven G. 2007. "Age, SES, and Health: A Population Level Analysis of Health Inequalities over the Lifecourse," *Sociology of Health and Illness* 29, 2: 275–96.

Putnam, Robert D. 2000. *Bowling Alone: The Collapse and Revival of American*

Community. New York: Simon & Schuster.

Raphael, Dennis. 2004. *Social Determinants of Health: Canadian Perspectives*. Toronto: Canadian Scholars' Press.

Raza, M., R. Beaujot, and G. Woldemicael. 2013. "Social Capital and Economic Integration of Visible Minority Immigrants in Canada," *Journal of International Migration and Integration* 14, 2: 263–85.

Reese, Ellen. 2009. "The Failed Welfare Revolution: America's Struggle over Guaranteed Income Policy," *Contemporary Sociology* 38, 3: 260–1.

Reitz, G. Jeffrey. 2007a. "Immigrant Employment Success in Canada, Part I: Individual and Contextual Causes," *Journal of International Migration and Integration* 8, 1: 11–36.

———. 2007b. "Immigrant Employment Success in Canada, Part II: Understanding the Decline," *Journal of International Migration and Integration* 8, 1: 37–62.

Sanmartin, Claudia. 2009. *Health Services Research at Statistics Canada: It Really Does Exist!* Ottawa: Statistics Canada.

Sarlo, Chris. 2006. "Comparing Measures of Poverty," *Fraser Forum* 1: 3–4.

———. 2007. "Measuring Poverty—What Happened to Copenhagen?," *Economic Affairs* 27, 3: 6–14.

Sauvy, Alfred. 1969. *Conjoncture et prévision économiques*. France: Presses Universitaires de France.

Schieman, Scott. 2002. "Socioeconomic Status, Job Conditions, and Well-Being: Self-Concept Explanations for Gender-Contingent Effects," *Sociological Quarterly* 43, 4: 627–46.

Smith, George Davey, Danny Dorling, David Gordon, and Mary Shaw. 1999. "The Widening Health Gap: What Are the Solutions?," *Critical Public Health* 9, 2: 151–70.

Statistics Canada. 2006. At: <www.statcan.gc.ca/pub/75f0002m/2012002/lico-sfr-eng.htm>.

———. 2009. "Income of Canadians," *The Daily*, 3 June. At: <www.statcan.gc.ca/daily-quotidien/090603/dq090603a-eng.htm>.

———. 2012a. At: <www.statcan.gc.ca/pub/75f0002m/2012002/lico-sfr-eng.htm>.

———. 2012b. At: <www.statcan.gc.ca/tables-tableaux/sum-som/l01/cst01/labor02b-eng.htm>.

———. 2013a. At: <www.esdc.gc.ca/eng/jobs/aboriginal/bulletins/spring2013.shtml>.

———. 2013b. At: <www.statcan.gc.ca/pub/75f0002m/2013002/mbm-mpc-eng.htm>.

Trovato, Frank. 2001. "Aboriginal Mortality in Canada, the United States and New Zealand," *Journal of Biosocial Science* 33, 1: 67–86.

Trypuc, B., and J. Robinson. 2009. *Homeless in Canada: A Funder's Primer in Understanding the Tragedy on Canada's Streets*. Toronto: Charity Intelligence Canada.

UNDP (United Nations Development Program). 2005. *Human Development Report 2005: International Cooperation at a Crossroads—Aid, Trade, and Security in an Unequal World*. New York: UNDP.

———. 2013. "The Rise of the South: Human Progress in a Diverse World." UNDP-HDRO Human Development Reports, 2013. At SSRN: <ssrn.com/abstract=2294673>.

UNICEF. 2013. "Children Are Everyone's Business: Workbook 2.0," *United Nations Children's Fund*. Geneva: UNICEF.

Watson, Pat. 2003. "Poverty Measure Shows Nothing New," *Share* 26, 9: 8.

Wellesley Institute. 2011. At: <www.wellesleyinstitute.com/housing/latest-cmhc-numbers-confirm-federal-housing-cuts-will-grow-deeper-as-housing-needs-grow>.

Wilkinson, Richard G. 1994. "Income Distribution and Life Expectancy," *British Medical Journal* 304: 165–8.

———. 1996. *Unhealthy Societies: The Afflictions of Inequality*. London: Routledge.

Wratten, Ellen. 2010. "Conceptualizing Urban Poverty (1995)," in Howard Lune, Enrique S. Pumar, and Ross Koppel, eds, *Perspectives in Social Research Methods and Analysis: A Reader for Sociology*. Thousand Oaks, CA: Sage, 85–110.

Chapter 3

Abu-Laban, Yasmeen, and Abigail B. Bakan. 2008. "The Racial Contract: Israel/Palestine and Canada," *Social Identities* 14, 5: 637–60.

Abu-Laban, Yasmeen, and Christina Gabriel. 2004. "Selling Diversity: Immigration, Multiculturalism, Employment Equity, and Globalization," *British Journal of Canadian Studies* 17, 1: 128–30.

Adams, Michael. 2007. *Unlikely Utopia: The Surprising Triumph of Canadian Pluralism*. Toronto: Viking Canada.

Adler, N.E., and Ostrove, J.M. 2006. "Socioeconomic Status and Health: What We Know and What We Don't," *Annals of the New York Academy of Sciences* 896: 3–15.

Allport, Gordon. 1954. *The Nature of Prejudice*. Reading, MA: Addison-Wesley.

Aranda, Elizabeth M., and Guillermo Rebollo-Gil. 2004. "Ethnoracism and the 'Sandwiched' Minorities," *American Behavioral Scientist* 47, 7: 910–27.

Attewell, P., P. Kasinitz, and K. Dunn. 2010. "Black Canadians and Black Americans: Racial Income Inequality in Comparative Perspective," *Ethnic and Racial Studies* 33, 3: 473–95.

Austin, Christopher, and David Este. 2001. "The Working Experiences of Underemployed Immigrant and Refugee Men," *Canadian Social Work Review* 18, 2: 213–29.

Bailie et al. 2006. *Canadian Issues*, Spring. Published by ACS, Montreal. At: <canada.metropolis.net/pdfs/CITC_Spring06_Families_FINAL-FullVersion.pdf>.

Banks, R.R., J.L. Eberhardt, and L. Ross. 2006. *California Law Review* 94, 4: 1169–90.

Baran, Michael D. 2008. "Race, Color and Culture: Questioning Categories and Concepts in Southern Bahia, Brazil," *Dissertation Abstracts International, A: The Humanities and Social Sciences* 68, 10: 4357.

Bauder, Harald, and Bob Sharpe. 2002. "Residential Segregation of Visible Minorities in Canada's Gateway Cities," *Canadian Geographer* 46, 3: 204–22.

Beck, J. Helen, Jeffrey G. Reitz, and Nan Weiner. 2002. "Addressing Systemic Racial Discrimination in Employment: The Health Canada Case and Implications of Legislative Change," *Canadian Public Policy* 28, 3: 373–94.

Bertrand, M., and S. Mullainathan. 2004. "Are Emily and Greg More Employable Than Lakisha and Jamal? A Field Experiment on Labor Market Discrimination," *American Economic Review* 94, 4: 991–1013.

Best, Joel. 1989. "Social Progress and Social Problems: Toward a Sociology of Gloom," *Sociological Quarterly* 42, 1: 1–12.

Blatz, Craig W., and Michael Ross. 2009. "Principled Ideology or Racism: Why Do Modern Racists Oppose Race-Based Social Justice Programs?," *Journal of Experimental Social Psychology* 45, 1: 258–61.

Bogardus, Emory S. 1933. "A Social Distance Scale," *Sociology and Social Research* 17: 265–71.

Boyd, Monica. 2002. "Educational Attainments of Immigrant Offspring: Success or Segmented Assimilation?," *International Migration Review* 36 (Winter): 1037–60.

———. 2009. "Social Origins and the Educational and Occupational Achievements of the 1.5 and Second Generations," *Canadian Review of Sociology* 46, 4: 339–69.

Boyd, Monica, and Grant Schellenberg. 2007. "Re-accreditation and the Occupations of Immigrant Doctors and Engineers," *Canadian Social Trends*. Statistics Canada Catalogue no. 11-008. At: <www.statcan.gc.ca/pub/11-008-x/2007004/pdf/10312-eng.pdf>.

Breton, Raymond. 1964. "Institutional Completeness of Ethnic Communities and Personal Relations to Immigrants," *American Journal of Sociology* 70: 193–205.

———. 1978. "Stratification and Conflict between Ethnolinguistic Communities with Different Social Structures," *Canadian Review of Sociology and Anthropology* 15: 138–57.

Breton, Raymond, Jeffrey G. Reitz, and Victor Valentine. 1980. *Cultural Boundaries and the Cohesion of Canada*. Montreal: Institute for Research on Public Policy.

Bryant, Wesley W. 2009. "African American Male Youth Violence and Internalized Racism." ProQuest Information & Learning, US.

Burns, Thomas J. 2002. "How Claims Spread: Cross-National Diffusion of Social Problems," *Social Forces* 81, 1:376–8.

Cea D'Ancona, Ma A. 2009. "The Complex Detection of Racism and Xenophobia through Survey Methods: A Step Forward in Their Measurement," *Revista Espanola De Investigaciones Sociologicas* 125: 13–45.

Chandra, K., ed. 2012. "Constructivist Theories of Ethnic Politics," unpublished manuscript, Department of Political Science, New York University.

Citizenship and Immigration Canada. 2011. "Permanent Residents by Category, 1987 to 2011" (graph), *Facts and Figures 2011—Immigration Overview: Permanent and Temporary Residents*. At: <www.cic.gc.ca/english/resources/statistics/facts2011/permanent/01.asp#figure3>.

Cort, Malcolm A., Eugene S. Tull, Keratiloe Gwebu, Priscilla Dlamini, Erica Pinkney, Eundene Gramby, Shanitria Cuthbertson, Ashley Daniels, Shay Luu, and Ephraim T. Gwebu. 2009. "Education and Internalized Racism in Socio-Political Context: Zimbabwe and Swaziland," *Social Science Journal* 46, 4: 644–55.

Coser, Lewis A. 1965. *The Functions of Social Conflict*. London: Routledge & Kegan Paul.

Costigan, Catherine, Tina F. Su, and Josephine M. Hua. 2009. "Ethnic Identity among Chinese Canadian Youth: A Review of the Canadian Literature," *Canadian Psychology/Psychologie Canadienne* 50, 4: 261–72.

D'Arcy, Carl. 1998. "Social Distribution of Health among Canadians," in David Coburn, Carl D'Arcy, and George M. Torrance, eds, *Health and Canadian Society: Sociological Perspectives*, 3rd edn. Toronto: University of Toronto Press, 73–101.

Demakakos, P., J. Nazroo, E. Breeze, and M. Marmot. 2008. "Socioeconomic Status and Health: The Role of Subjective Social Status," *Social and Science Medicine* 67, 2: 330–40.

Demuth, S. 2003. "Racial and Ethnic Differences in Pretrial Release Decisions and Outcomes: A Comparison of Hispanic, Black, and White Felony Arrestees," *Criminology* 41: 873–907.

Derluyn, I., C. Mels, and E. Broekaert. 2009. "Mental Health Problems in Separated Refugee Adolescents," *Journal of Adolescent Health* 44, 3: 291–7.

Dharmapala, D., and S.L. Ross. 2004. "Racial Bias in Motor Vehicle Searches: Additional Theory and Evidence," *B.E. Journal of Economic Analysis & Policy* 3, 1: 1–23.

Elhaik, E. 2012. "Empiral Distributions of FST from Large-Scale Human Polymorphism Data," *PLoS One* 7, 11: e49837. PMCID: PMC3504095.

Ezeonu, Celestine I. 2006. "The Social Construction of 'Black-on-Black' Violence in Toronto (Ontario)," *Dissertation Abstracts International, A: The Humanities and Social Sciences* 66, 10: 3815.

Fenlon, Brodie. 2008. "Canada Apologizes," *Globe and Mail*, 11 June, A2–3.

Fleras, Augie, and Jean Elliott. 2009. *Unequal Relations: An Introduction to Race, Ethnicity and Aboriginal Dynamics in Canada*. Scarborough, ON: Prentice-Hall.

Forgues, Éric. 2007. "The Canadian State and the Empowerment of the Francophone Minority Communities Regarding Their Economic Development," *International Journal of the Sociology of Language* 185, 1: 163–86.

Fujiwara, Aya. 2008. "From Anglo-Conformity to Multiculturalism: The Role of Scottish, Ukrainian, and Japanese Ethnicity in the Transformation of Canadian Identity, 1919–1971." ProQuest Information & Learning, US.

Gabbidon, Shaun L. 2010. *Race, Ethnicity, Crime, and Justice: An International Dilemma*. Thousand Oaks, CA: Sage.

Gaertner, Samuel L., and John F. Dovidio. 2000. "The Aversive Form of Racism," in Charles Stangor, ed., *Stereotypes and Prejudice: Essential Readings*. Philadelphia: Psychology Press, 289–304.

Galabuzi, G.E. 2006. *Canada's Economic Apartheid: The Social Exclusion of Racialized Groups in the New Century*. Toronto: Canadian Scholars' Press.

Gee, Ellen M., and Steven G. Prus. 2000. "Income Inequality in Canada: A Racial Divide," in Madeline A. Kalbach and Warren E. Kalbach, eds, *Perspectives on Ethnicity in Canada: A Reader*. Toronto: Harcourt Canada, 238–56.

Gee, G.C., M.S. Spencer, J. Chen, and D. Takeuchi. 2007. "A Nationwide Study of Discrimination and Chronic Health Conditions among Asian Americans," *American Journal of Public Health* 97, 7: 1275–82.

Gerrish K., R. Chau, A. Sobowale, and E. Birks. "Bridging the Language Barrier: The Use of Interpreters in Primary Care Nursing," *Health & Social Care in the Community* 12, 5: 407–13.

Godwyn, Mary. 2009. "'This Place Makes Me Proud to Be a Woman': Theoretical

Explanations for Success in Entrepreneurship Education for Low-Income Women," *Research in Social Stratification and Mobility* 27, 1: 50–64.

Green, Joyce. 2001. "Canaries in the Mines of Citizenship: Indian Women in Canada," *Canadian Journal of Political Science* 34, 4: 715–38.

Greenwald, A.G., T. Poehlman, A. Uhlmann, E. Luis, and M.R. Banaji. 2009. "Understanding and Using the Implicit Association Test: III: Meta-analysis of Predictive Validity," *Journal of Personality and Social Psychology* 97, 1: 17–41.

Haque, Eve. 2007. "Multiculturalism within a Bilingual Framework: Language and the Racial Ordering of Difference and Belonging in Canada," *Dissertation Abstracts International, A: The Humanities and Social Sciences* 68, 01: 0054.

Harper, S., D. Rushani, and J.S. Kaufman. 2012. "Trends in the Black-White Life Expectancy Gap, 2003–2008," *Journal of the American Medical Association* 307, 21: 2257–9.

Harrell, Shelly P. 2000. "A Multidimensional Conceptualization of Racism-Related Stress: Implications for the Well-Being of People of Color," *American Journal of Orthopsychiatry* 70, 1: 42–57.

Hayward, Mark D., and Melanie Heron. 1999. "Racial Inequality in Active Life among Adult Americans," *Demography* 36: 77–91.

Heaton, T.B., and C.K. Jacobson. 2008. "Comparative Patterns of Interracial Marriage: Structural Opportunities, Third-Party Factors, and Temporal Change in Immigrant Societies," *Journal of Comparative Family Studies* 39, 15: 129.

Henry, Frances. 1999. "Two Studies of Racial Discrimination in Employment," in Curtis et al. (1999: 226–35).

Henry, Frances, and Effie Ginzberg. 1985. *Who Gets the Work: A Test of Racial Discrimination in Employment*. Toronto: Urban Alliance on Race Relations in Employment and Social Planning Council of Metropolitan Toronto.

Hong, Young-Hwa. 2008. "Engendering Migration in the Transnational World: Highly Skilled Korean Immigrant Women in the Canadian Labour Market." ProQuest Information & Learning, US.

Hou, Feng, and T.R. Balakrishnan. 1996. "The Integration of Visible Minorities in Contemporary Society," *Canadian Journal of Sociology* 21: 307–16.

Hou, Feng, and Garnett Picot. 2004. "Visible Minority Neighbourhoods in Toronto, Montréal, and Vancouver," *Canadian Social Trends* (Spring): 8–13.

Kashefi, Mahmoud. 2004. "Racial Differences on Organizational Attachment? Structural Explanation of Attitude Differences between White and African American Employees," *Journal of Black Studies* 34, 5: 702–18.

Kent, Mike. 2009. "Excellence Is Colour Neutral," *Times Educational Supplement* 4867: 44.

Lamarche, Lucie, Rachel Chagnon, Francine Tougas, and Martine Lagacé. 2006. "Conflict Management and the Employment Equity Act: Visible Minorities in Canada," *Canadian Public Policy* 32, 3: 243–58.

Landrine, Hope, and Elizabeth A. Klonoff. 1996. "The Schedule of Racist Events: A Measure of Racial Discrimination and a Study of Its Negative Physical and Mental Health Consequences," *Journal of Black Psychology* 22: 144–68.

Landry, Rodrigue, Real Allard, and Kenneth Deveau. 2007. "Bilingual Schooling of the Canadian Francophone Minority: A Cultural Autonomy Model," *International Journal of the Sociology of Language* 185 (May): 133–62.

Laroche, Mireille. 2000. "Health Status and Health Services Utilization of Canada's Immigrant and Non-immigrant Populations," *Canadian Public Policy* 26: 51–73.

Lavalle, James B., with Stacy Lundin Yale. 2004. *Cracking the Metabolic Code*. North Bergen, NJ: Basic Health Publications.

Lee, Sharon, and Monica Boyd. 2008. "Marrying Out: The Marital Blending and Integration of Asians in North America," *Social Science Research* 37: 311–29.

McConahay, J.B. 1981. "Has Racism Declined in America? It Depends on Who Is Asking and What Is Asked," *Journal of Conflict Resolution* 25, 4: 563–79.

———. 1986. "Modern Racism, Ambivalence, and the Modern Racism Scale," in J.F. Dovidio and S.L. Gaertner, eds, *Prejudice, Discrimination, and Racism*. New York: Academic Press, 91–125.

McKown, Clark, and Michael J. Strambler. 2009. "Developmental Antecedents and Social and Academic Consequences of Stereotype-Consciousness in Middle Childhood," *Child Development* 80, 6: 1643.

Malin, Merridy. 2000. "A 'Whole of Life' View of Aboriginal Education for Health: Emerging Models," keynote address at the Australian Medical Association, Northern Territory, Conference 2000, "Learning Lessons: Approaching Indigenous Health Through Education." At: <www.atsis.uq.edu.au/ajie/docs/20033285100.pdf>.

Mays, V.M., S.D. Cochran, and N.W. Barnes. 2007. "Race, Race-Based Discrimination, and Health Outcomes among African Americans," *Annual Review of Psychology* 58: 201–25.

Milan, A., H. Maheux, and T. Chui. 2010. "A Portrait Of Couples In Mixed Unions," *Statistics Canada*. At: <www.statcan.gc.ca/pub/11-008-x/2010001/article/11143-eng.htm>.

Moghissi, Haideh, Saeed Rahnema, and Mark J. Goodman. 2009. *Diaspora by Design: Muslim Immigrants in Canada and Beyond*. Toronto: University of Toronto Press.

Moreau, Sylvie, Cecile Rousseau, and Abdelwahed Mekki Berrada. 1999. "Immigration Policies and the Mental Health of Refugees: The Profile and Impact of Family Separations," *Nouvelles Pratiques Sociales* 11, 1: 177–96.

Morris, Theresa. 2008. "Branch Banking and Institutional Racism in the U.S. Banking Industry," *Humanity and Society* 32, 2: 144–67.

Office of the High Commissioner for Human Rights. 1969. *International Convention on the Elimination of All Forms of Racial Discrimination*. At: <www.unhchr.ch/html/menu3/b/d_icerd.htm>.

Okin, Susan Moller. 1998. *Is Multiculturalism Bad for Women?* Princeton, NJ: Princeton University Press.

Omi, Michael, and Howland Winant. 2009. *Racial Formation in the United States: From the 1960s to the 1990s*, 2nd edn. New York: Routledge.

Oreopoulos, P. 2009. "Why Do Skilled Immigrants Struggle in the Labor Market? A Field Experiment with Six Thousand Resumes." Metropolis British Columbia, Working Paper series, 9 (3).

At: <mbc.metropolis.net/assets/uploads/files/wp/2009/WP09-03.pdf>.

Pager, D. 2007. "Studies of Employment Discrimination: Contributions, Critiques, and Directions for the Future," *Annals of the American Academy, American Academy of Political and Social Science* 609.

Park, J., E. Malachi, O. Sternin, and R. Tevet. 2009. "Subtle Bias against Muslim Job Applicants in Personnel Decisions," *Journal of Applied Social Psychology* 39, 9: 2174–90.

Parmar, Alpa. 2007. "Racial Profiling in Canada: Challenging the Myth of 'a Few Bad Apples,'" *Ethnic and Racial Studies* 30, 6: 1171–4.

Penner, L.A, J.F. Dovidio, T.V. West, S.L. Gaertner, T.L. Albrecht, R.K. Dailey, and T. Markova. 2010. "Aversive Racism and Medical Interactions with Black Patients: A Field Study," *Journal of Experimental Social Psychology* 46, 2: 436–40.

Pettit, B., and B. Western. 2004. "Mass Imprisonment and the Life Course: Race and Class Inequality in U.S. Incarceration," *American Sociological Review* 69: 151–69.

Porter, John. 1965. *The Vertical Mosaic.* Toronto: University of Toronto Press.

Pruitt, D.G., J.Z. Rubin, and S.H. Kim. 2003. *Social Conflict: Escalation, Stalemate, and Settlement.* McGraw-Hill Professional.

Quan, H., A. Fong, C. De Coster, J. Wang, R. Musto, T.W. Noseworthy, and W.A. Ghali. 2006. "Variation in Health Services Utilization among Ethnic Populations," *Canadian Medical Association Journal* 174, 6: 787–91.

Quillian, L. 2008. "Does Unconscious Racism Exist?," *Social Psychology Quarterly* 71, 1: 6–11.

Ramirez, D., K.G. Engel, and T.S. Tang. 2008. "Language Interpreter Utilization in the Emergency Department Setting: A Clinical Review," *Journal of Health Care for the Poor and Underserved* 19, 2: 352–62.

Reitman, O. 2005. "Multiculturalism and Feminism," *Ethnicities* 5, 2: 216–47.

Reitz, J.G., and R. Banerjee. 2007. "Racial Inequality, Social Cohesion, and Policy Issues in Canada," in T.J. Courchene, K. Banting, and W. Wuttunee, eds, *Belonging? Diversity, Recognition and Shared Citizenship in Canada.*

Montreal: Institute for Research on Public Policy, 489–545.

Reitz, Jeffrey G. 2001. "Immigrant Success in the Knowledge Economy: Institutional Change and the Immigrant Experience in Canada, 1970–1995," *Journal of Social Issues* 57, 3: 579–613.

———. 2007a. "Immigrant Employment Success in Canada, Part I: Individual and Contextual Causes," *Journal of International Migration and Integration* 8, 1: 11–36.

———. 2007b. "Immigrant Employment Success in Canada, Part II: Understanding the Decline," *Journal of International Migration and Integration* 8, 1: 37–62.

Reitz, Jeffrey G., Rupa Banerjee, Mai Phan, and Jordan Thompson. 2009. "Race, Religion, and the Social Integration of New Immigrant Minorities in Canada," *International Migration Review* 43, 4: 695–726.

Reitz, Jeffrey G., and Raymond Breton. 1999. "Prejudice and Discrimination toward Minorities in Canada and the United States," in James Curtis, Edward Grabb, and Neil Guppy, eds, *Social Inequality in Canada: Patterns, Problems, Policies,* 3rd edn. Scarborough, ON: Prentice-Hall, 357–70.

Roberts, Julian V., and Anthony N. Doob. 1997. "Race, Ethnicity, and Criminal Justice in Canada," in Michael Tonry, ed., *Ethnicity, Crime and Immigration: Comparative and Cross-national Perspectives.* Chicago: University of Chicago Press, 469–522.

Robertson, Lawrence. 1997. "The Constructed Nature of Ethnopolitics," *International Politics* 34: 267–83.

Rodlandt, Theo J.A. 1996. "Ethnic Stratification: The Emergence of a New Social and Economic Issue?," *Netherlands Journal of Social Sciences* 32, 1: 39–50.

Rodney, Patricia, and Esker Copeland. 2009. "The Health Status of Black Canadians: Do Aggregated Racial and Ethnic Variables Hide Health Disparities?," *Journal of Health Care for the Poor and Underserved* 20, 3: 817–23.

Rollock, David, and Edmund W. Gordon. 2000. "Racism and Mental Health into the 21st Century: Perspectives and Parameters," *American Journal of Orthopsychiatry* 70, 1: 5–13.

Rooth, Dan-Olof. 2010. "Automatic Associations and Discrimination in

Hiring: Real World Evidence," *Labour Economics* 17, 3: 523–34.

Ruffin, Betsy. 2009. "How Are We the Same and Different?/We Are the Earth/What Is Culture?/What Is Religion?," *Library Media Connection* 28, 2: 98.

Scottham, Krista M., and Ciara P. Smalls. 2009. "Unpacking Racial Socialization: Considering Female African American Primary Caregivers' Racial Identity," *Journal of Marriage and Family* 71, 4: 807–19.

Segura Escobar, Nora. 2000. "Colombia: A New Century, an Old War, and More Internal Displacement," *International Journal of Politics, Culture, and Society* 14: 107–27.

Seren, E., and S. Seren. 2009. "Morphological Adaptation of the Nasal Valve Area to Climate," *Medical Hypotheses* 72, 4: 471–2.

Smith, C.C. 2007. *Conflict, Crisis and Accountability: Racial Profiling and Law Enforcement in Canada.* Ottawa: Canadian Centre for Policy Alternatives.

Spencer, N. 1996. "Race and Ethnicity as Determinants of Child Health: A Personal View," *Child: Care, Health and Development* 22: 327–45.

Spinner-Halev, Jeff. 2001. "Feminism, Multiculturalism, Oppression, and the State," *Ethics* 112 (Oct.): 84–113.

Statistics Canada, 2011a. "Foreign-Born Population, as a Proportion of the Total Population, G8 Countries and Australia" (graph), *National Household Survey.* Statistics Canada Catalogue no. 99-010-X2011001. At: <www12.statcan.gc.ca/nhs-enm/2011/as-sa/99-010-x/2011001/c-g/c-g01-eng.cfm>.

———. 2011b. "Visible Minority Population and Top Three Visible Minority Groups, Selected Census Metropolitan Areas, Canada, 2011" (table), *National Household Survey.* Catalogue no. 99-010-X2011001. At: <www12.statcan.gc.ca/nhs-enm/2011/as-sa/99-010-x/2011001/tbl/tbl2-eng.cfm>.

———. 2012a. "Police-Reported Hate Crimes by Crime Category and Type of Motivation, Canada, 2010," *Juristat.* Catalogue no. 85-002-x2012001. At: <www.statcan.gc.ca/pub/85-002-x/2012001/article/11635/tbl/tbl04-eng.htm>.

———. 2012b. "Rate of Employment among Immigrants and Canadian Born Aged 25–54, by Province or Region, 2011" (graph). *Study:*

Canada's Immigrant Labour Market, 2008 to 2011. The Daily. At: <www.statcan.gc.ca/daily-quotidien/121214/dq121214b-eng.htm>.

———. 2013a. "Labour Force Characteristics by Immigrant Status, by Detailed Age Group" (table), *Summary Tables.* CANSIM table 282-0104. At: <www.statcan.gc.ca/tables-tableaux/sum-som/l01/cst01/labor91a-eng.htm>.

———. 2013b. "Labour Force Characteristics by Immigrant Status of Population Aged 25 to 54, and by Educational Attainment." At: <www.statcan.gc.ca/tables-tableaux/sum-som/l01/cst01/labor90a-eng.htm>.

Swainson, Gail. 2010. "Housing Subsidy Blasted," *Toronto Star*, 19 Feb. At: <www.thestar.com/news/gta/2010/02/19/housing_subsidy_blasted.html>.

Tang, S.Y. 1999. "Interpreter Services in Healthcare: Policy Recommendations for Healthcare Agencies," *Journal of Nursing Administration* 29, 6: 23–9.

Teelucksingh, C., and G.-E. Galabuzi. 2005. "Working Precariously: The Impact of Race and Immigrants Status on Employment Opportunities and Outcomes in Canada," published by Canadian Race Relations Foundation. At: <www.socialjustice.org/uploads/pubs/WorkingPrecariously.pdf>.

Thomas, Derrick. 2001. "Evolving Family Living Arrangements of Canada's Immigrants," *Canadian Social Trends* (Summer), 16–22. At: <www.statcan.gc.ca/pub/11-008-x/2001001/article/5704-eng.pdf>.

Thomas, W.I., and Florien Znaniecki. 1971 [1919]. *The Polish Peasant in America*. New York: Octagon Books.

Thompson, Venetia. 2008. "The Masters of the Universe Have Turned to Drink," *Spectator*, 4 Oct.

Waldram, James P., Ann D. Herring, and T. Kue Young. 1996. *Aboriginal Health in Canada: Historical, Cultural, and Epidemiological Perspectives*. Toronto: University of Toronto.

Wardman, D., K. Clement, and D. Quantz. 2005. "Access and Utilization of Health Services by British Columbia's Rural Aboriginal Population," *International Journal of Health Care Quality Assurance* 18, 2 and 3: xxvi–xxxi.

Wen, S.W., V. Goel, and J.I. Williams. 1996. "Utilization of Health Care Services by Immigrants and Other Ethnic/Cultural Groups in Ontario," *Ethnicity and Health* 1, 1: 99–109.

Williams, D.R., and P.B. Jackson. 2005. "Social Sources of Racial Disparities in Health," *Health Affairs* 24, 2: 325–34.

Williams, D.R., and S.A. Mohammed. 2009. "Discrimination and Racial Disparities in Health: Evidence and Needed Research," *Journal of Behavioral Medicine* 32, 1: 20–47.

Williams, David R., Yan Yu, James S. Jackson, and Norman B. Anderson. 1997. "Racial Differences in Physical and Mental Health: Socio-economic Status, Stress, and Discrimination," *Journal of Health Psychology* 2: 335–51.

Wu, Z., M.J. Penning, and C.M. Schimmele. 2005. "Immigrant Status and Unmet Health Care Needs," *Canadian Journal of Public Health* 96, 5: 369–73.

Yamamoto, Satomi. 2009. "Intermediaries and Migration in the United States." ProQuest Information & Learning, US.

Zhang, Yuanting, and Jennifer Van Hook. 2009. "Marital Dissolution among Interracial Couples," *Journal of Marriage and Family* 71, 1: 95–107.

Zietsma, Danielle. 2010. *Aboriginal People Living Off-Reserve and the Labour Market: Estimates from the Labour Force Survey, 2008–2009.* The Aboriginal Labour Force Analysis series, Labour Statistics Division, Statistics Canada Catalogue no. 71-588-X, no. 2.

Chapter 4

Abbasi-Shavazi, Mohammad J., S.P. Morgan, Meimanat Hossein-Chavoshi, and Peter McDonald. 2009. "Family Change and Continuity in Iran: Birth Control Use before First Pregnancy," *Journal of Marriage and Family* 71, 5: 1309–24.

Abott, J.Y. 2007. "The Positive Functions of 'Negative' Rhetoric: Feminists' Expository Campaign against the Promise Keepers," *Women's Studies in Communication* 30, 1: 1–33.

Adams, M., and S. Coltrane. 2006. "Framing Divorce Reform: Media, Morality, and the Politics of Family," *Family Process* 46, 1: 17–34.

Angeles, Leonora C. 2009. "Rethinking the 'Feminisation of Poverty' Thesis," *Sex Roles* 61, 3 and 4: 293–6.

Antecol, H., and D. Cobb-Clark. 2006. "The Sexual Harassment of Female Active-Duty Personel: Effects on Job Satisfaction and Intentions to Remain in the Military," *Journal of Economic Behaviour and Organization* 61, 1: 55–80.

Auld, A., and S. Bailey. "Sex Assault Complaints against Former Petty Officer Probed." At: <www.theglobeandmail.com/news/national/sex-assault-complaints-against-former-petty-officer-probed/article11448906>.

Bacchi, Carol Lee. 1999. *Women, Policy and Politics: The Construction of Policy Problems*. London: Sage.

Baker, M. 2012. "Gendered Families, Academic Work, and the 'Motherhood Penalty,'" *Women's Studies Journal* 26, 1: 11–24.

Baker, M., J. Gruber, and K. Milligan. 2008. "Universal Child Care, Maternal Labor Supply, and Family Well-Being," *Journal of Political Economy* 116, 4: 709–45.

Barreto, Manuela, Michelle K. Ryan, and Michael T. Schmitt, eds. 2009. *The Glass Ceiling in the 21st Century: Understanding Barriers to Gender Equality*, 2nd edn. Washington: American Psychological Association.

Baxter, J., B. Hewitt, and M. Haynes. 2010. "Pathways into Marriage: Cohabitation and the Domestic Division of Labour," *Journal of Family Issues* 31, 11: 1507–29.

Benokraitis, Nijole V. 2008. *Marriages and Families: Changes, Choices, and Constraints*, 6th edn. Upper Saddle River, NJ: Prentice-Hall/Pearson.

Biehle, S.N., and K.D. Mickelson. 2012. "First-Time Parents' Expectations about the Division of Childcare and Play," *Journal of Family Psychology* 26, 1: 36–45.

Bloom, Adi. 2009. "Are We Going Back to This?," *Times Educational Supplement* 4869: 18.

Canadian Institute for Health Information. 2011. "Induced Abortions Reported in Canada in 2011." At: <www.cihi.ca/cihi-ext-portal/internet/en/document/types+of+care/hospital+care/acute+care/announce_21feb13>.

Carlson, M.J., N.V. Pilkauskas, S.S. McLanahan, and J. Brooks-Gunn. 2011. "Couples as Partners and Parents over Children's Early Years," *Journal of Family and Marriage* 73, 2: 317–34.

Chodorow, Nancy. 1978. *The Reproduction of Mothering: Psychoanalysis and the Sociology of Gender*. Berkeley: University of California Press.

Coltrane, Scott, and Michele Adams. 2003. "The Social Construction of the Divorce 'Problem': Morality, Child Victims, and the Politics of Gender," *Family Relations* 52: 363–72.

Coltrane, Scott, and Masako Ishii-Kuntz. 1990. "Men's Housework and Child Care: A Life Course Perspective," paper presented at the annual meeting of the American Sociological Association.

Cowan, Carolyn Pape, and Philip A. Cowan. 1995. "Interventions to Ease the Transition to Parenthood: Why They Are Needed and What They Can Do," *Family Relations* 44: 412–23.

Crespo, Stephane. 2007. "Changes in Labor Market Participation over the Life Course of Men and Women in Canada," *Cahiers Québécois de Démographie* 36, 1: 49–83.

Crocker, J., and L.E. Park. 2003. "Seeking Self-Esteem: Construction, Maintenance, and Protection of Self-Worth," in M. Leary and J. Tangney, eds, *Handbook of Self and Identity*. New York: Guilford, 291–313.

Das, Hari, and Mallika Das. 2009. "Gender Stereotyping in Contemporary Indian Magazine Fiction," *Asian Studies Review* 33, 1: 63–82.

Estrich, Susan. 2007. "Real Rape," in Barbara A. Arrighi, ed., *Understanding Inequality*. Lanham, MD: Rowman & Littlefield, 309–25.

Evans, J., B. Frank, J.L. Oliffe, and D. Gregory. 2011. "Health, Illness, Men and Masculinties (HIMM): A Theoretical Framework for Understanding Men and Their Health," *Journal of Men's Health* 8, 1: 7–15.

Foster, Mindi. 2009. "The Dynamic Nature of Coping with Gender Discrimination: Appraisals, Strategies and Well-Being over Time," *Sex Roles* 60, 9 and 10: 694–707.

Fox, Bonnie. 2001. "The Formative Years: How Parenthood Creates Gender," *Canadian Review of Sociology and Anthropology* 38: 373–90.

Gordon, L. 2012. "Citizenship and the Right to Birth Control," *Dissent* 54, 4: 60–4.

Gough, Brendan, and Paul Peace. 2000. "Reconstructing Gender at University: Men as Victims," *Gender and Education* 12, 3: 385–98.

Gregson, Nicky, and Michelle Lowe. 1994. "Waged Domestic Labor and the Renegotiation of the Domestic Division of Labor within Dual-Career Households," *Sociology* 28: 55–79.

Heath, Melanie. 2003. "Soft-Boiled Masculinity," *Gender and Society* 17, 3: 423–44.

Hovmand, P.S., D.N. Ford, I. Flom, and S. Kyriakakis. 2009. "Victims Arrested for Domestic Violence: Unintended Consequences of Arrest Policies," *System Dynamics Review* 25, 3: 161–81.

Humphreys, Terry P., and Ed Herold. 1996. "Date Rape: A Comparative Analysis and Integration of Theory," *Canadian Journal of Human Sexuality* 5, 2: 69–82.

Ishii-Kuntz, Masako, and Scott Coltrane. 1992. "Remarriage, Stepparenting, and Household Labor," *Journal of Family Issues* 13: 215–33.

Jung, Jaehee, and Michael Peterson. 2007. "Body Dissatisfaction and Patterns of Media Use among Preadolescent Children," *Family and Consumer Sciences Research Journal* 36, 1: 40–54.

Knudson-Martin, Carmen, and Anne Rankin Mahoney. 2009. *Couples, Gender, and Power: Creating Change in Intimate Relationships*. New York: Springer.

LaChance-Grzela M., and G. Bouchard. 2010. "Why Do Women Do the Lion's Share of Housework? A Decade of Research," *Feminist Forum Review Article* 63, 11: 767–80.

Lauritsen, J., and K. Carbone-Lopez. 2011. "Gender Differences in Risk Factors for Violent Victimization: An Examination of Individual-, Family-, and Community-Level Predictors," *Journal of Research in Crime and Delinquency* 48, 4: 538–65.

Leisenring, A. 2006. "Confronting 'Victim' Discourses: The Identity Work of Battered Women," *Symbolic Interaction* 29, 3: 307–30.

Lillian, D.L. 2007. "A Thorn by Any Other Name: Sexist Discourse as Hate Speech," *Discourse and Society* 18, 6: 719–40.

Mane. R. 2012. "Transmuting Grammars of Whiteness in Third-Wave Feminism: Interrogating Postrace Histories,

Postmodern Abstraction, and the Proliferation of Difference in Third-Wave Texts," *Signs, 38, 1: 71–98.*

Mason, Karen Oppenheim, and Karen Kuhlthau. 1989. "Determinants of Child Care Ideals among Mothers of Preschool-Aged Children," *Journal of Marriage and the Family* 51: 593–603.

Minto, C.L., L.M. Liao, C.R. Woodhouse, P.G Ransley, and S.M Creighton. 2003. "The Effect of Clitoral Surgery on Sexual Outcome in Individuals Who Have Intersex Conditions with Ambiguous Genitalia: A Cross-Sectional Study," *Lancet* 361: 1252–7.

Mitchell, A.B. 2010. "Midlife Marital Happiness and Ethnic Culture: A Life Course Perspective," *Journal of Comparative Family Studies* 41, 1: 167–83.

Mohr, J.J., R.M. Chopp, and S.J. Wong. 2013. "Psychotherapists' Stereotypes of Heterosexual, Gay and Bisexual Men," *Journal of Gay & Lesbian Social Services* 25, 1: 37–55.

Monk, Timothy H., Marilyn J. Essex, Nancy A. Snider, Marjorie H. Klein, et al. 1996. "The Impact of the Birth of a Baby on the Time Structure and Social Mixture of a Couple's Daily Life and Its Consequences for Well-Being," *Journal of Applied Social Psychology* 26: 1237–58.

Nagoshi J., S. Brzuzy, and H. Terrell. 2012. "Deconstructing the Complex Perceptions of Gender Roles, Gender Identity, and Sexual Orientation among Transgender Individuals," *Feminism and Psychology* 22, 4: 405–22.

Oakley, Ann. 1974. *The Sociology of Housework*. London: Martin Robertson.

Obeid, N., D.F. Chang, and J. Ginges. 2010. "Beliefs about Wife Beating: An Exploratory Study with Lebanese Students," *Violence against Women* 16, 6: 691–712.

Olso, T.M, C.B. Gudde, E. Wullum, and O.M. Linaker. 2011. "Gender-Specific Correlates of Substance Use in Patients with Serious Mental Illness," *Mental Health and Substance Use* 5, 1: 31–41.

Parliament of Canada. 2010. "Women in the Canadian House of Commons since 1984." At: <www.parl.gc.ca/content/lop/researchpublications/prb0562-e.htm>.

Parsons, Talcott. 1951. *The Social System*. Glencoe, IL: Free Press.

Piercy, K. 2012. "Late-Life Transitions and Interventions," in P. Noller and

G.C. Karantzas, *The Wiley-Blackwell Handbook of Couples and Family Relationships*. At: <onlinelibrary.wiley.com/doi/10.1002/9781444354119.ch7/summary>.

Powell, A., B. Bagilhole, and A. Dainty. 2009. "How Women Engineers Do and Undo Gender: Consequences for Gender Equality," *Gender, Work and Organization* 16, 4: 411–28.

Public Health Agency. 2006. Chapter 7: "Eating Disorders," *Public Health Canada.* At: <www.phac-aspc.gc.ca/publicat/human-humain06/10-eng.php>.

Raley, S., S.M. Bianchi, and W. Wang. 2012. "When Do Fathers Care? Mothers' Economic Contribution and Fathers' Involvement in Child Care," *American Journal of Sociology* 5, 1: 1422–59.

Rammohan, A., and P.E. Robertson. 2011. "Human Capital, Kinship, and Gender Inequality," *Oxford Economic Papers* 64, 3: 417–38.

Rodriguez-Dominguez, Luis, Isabel Gallego-Alvarez, and Isabel Maria Garcia-Sanchez. 2009. "Corporate Governance and Codes of Ethics," *Journal of Business Ethics* 90, 2: 187–202.

Royo Vela y Otros, Marcelo. 2005. "Gender Role and Sexism in Spanish Magazine Advertisements: An Analysis of the Twentieth Century's Last Three Decades," *Comunicacion y Sociedad* 18, 1: 113–52.

Sachs, Jeffrey D. 2005. *The End of Poverty: Economic Possibilities for Our Time.* New York: Penguin Books.

Schiller, Bill. 2010. "China's Happy Two-Child Experiment," *Toronto Star*, 23 Apr. At: <www.thestar.com/.../799721--china-s-happy-two-child-experiment>.

Smith, M.E. 2009. *Poverty Is Hazardous to Women's Health.* Retrieved from UVic-Space: <hdl.handle.net/1828/4159>.

Sokoloff, N.J., and I. Dupont. 2005. "Domestic Violence at the Intersection of Race, Class, and Gender: Challenges and Contributions to Understanding Violence against Marginalized Women in Diverse Communities," *Violence against Women* 11, 1: 38–64.

Srinath, K. 2008. "Gender and Coastal Zone Biodiversity," *Gender, Technology and Development* 12, 2: 209–27.

Statistics Canada. 2009. *Family Violence in Canada: A Statistical Profile.* At: <www.statcan.gc.ca/pub/85-224-x/85-224-x2010000-eng.pdf>.

———. 2010. *Victim Services Survey, One-Day Snapshot of Number of Clients Served, by Type of Victimization.* At: <www5.statcan.gc.ca/cansim/a26?lang=eng&retrLang=eng&id=2560021&paSer=&pattern=&stByVal=1&p1=1&p2=-1&tabMode=dataTable&csid=>.

———. 2011a. *Violence against Women.* At: <www.statcan.gc.ca/daily-quotidien/130225/dq130225a-eng.htm>.

———. 2011b. "Mood Disorders, by Age Group and Sex." At: <www.statcan.gc.ca/tables-tableaux/sum-som/l01/cst01/health113a-eng.html>.

———. 2012. "Income of Canadians, 2010." At: <www.statcan.gc.ca/daily-quotidien/120618/dq120618b-eng.htm>.

———. 2013a. At: <www.statcan.gc.ca/pub/89-503-x/2010001/article/11416/c-g/c-g004-eng.htm>.

———. 2013b. "Paid Work." At: <www.statcan.gc.ca/pub/89-503-x/2010001/article/11387-eng.htm>.

Staudt, K. 2009. "Gendering the World Bank: Neoliberalism and the Gendered Foundations of Global Governance," *Choice* 47, 4: 763.

Thien, D., and V. Del Casino Jr. 2012. "Unhealthy Men, Masculinities, and the Geographies of Health," *Annals Association of American Geographers* 102, 5: 1146–56.

Tichy, Lauren L., Judith V. Becker, and Melissa M. Sisco. 2009. "The Downside of Patriarchal Benevolence: Ambivalence in Addressing Domestic Violence and Socio-Economic Considerations for Women of Tamil Nadu, India," *Journal of Family Violence* 24, 8: 547–58.

Tilly, Louise A., and Joan W. Scott. 1987. *Women, Work, and Family.* New York: Routledge.

Tomczak, L.M. 2012. "Childfree or Voluntarily Childless? The Lived Experiences of Women Choosing Non-motherhood." ProQuest Digital Dissertations.

Tyyska, Vappu Kaarina. 1994. "The Women's Movement and the Welfare State: Child Care Policy in Canada and Finland, 1960–1990," PhD diss., University of Toronto.

Vallee, Marie-Helene. 2002. "Unaccompanied Women Immigrating to Canada during the 1920s: Laying Down a Policy Founded on 'Gender,'" *Recherches Feministes* 15, 2: 65–85.

Van Hooff, J.H. 2011. "Rationalising Inequality: Heterosexual Couples' Explanations and Justifications for the Division of Housework along Traditionally Gendered Lines," *Journal of Gender Studies* 20, 1: 19–30.

van Steenbergen, E.F., E.S. Kluwer, and B.R. Karney. 2011. "Workload and the Trajectory of Marital Satisfaction in Newlyweds: Job Satisfaction, Gender, and Parental Status as Moderators," *Journal of Family Psychology* 25, 3: 345–55.

Weizmann-Henelius, Ghitta, Hanna Putkonen, Hannu Naukkarinen, and Markku Eronen. 2009. "Intoxication and Violent Women," *Archives of Women's Mental Health* 12, 1: 15–25.

Willen, Helena, and Henry Montgomery. 1996. "The Impact of Wishing for Children and Having Children on Attainment and Importance of Life Values," *Journal of Comparative Family Studies* 27: 499–518.

World Health Organization (WHO). 2012. *World Health Statistics.* At: <www.who.int/gho/publications/world_health_statistics/EN_WHS2012_Full.pdf>.

Chapter 5

Allport, Gordon. 1979 [1954]. *The Nature of Prejudice.* Reading, MA: Addison-Wesley.

Alpaslan, Assim, Theresa Johnston, and Veonna Goliath. 2009. "Parents' Experiences Regarding the Coming-Out Process of a Gay or Lesbian Child," *Maatskaplike Werk/Social Work* 45, 1: 27–46.

Anapol, Deborah. 2012. *Polyamory in the 21st Century: Love and Intimacy with Multiple Partners.* Lanham, MD: Rowman & Littlefield.

Anderlinin-D'onfrio, Serena. 2009. *Gaia and the New Politics of Love: Notes for a Poly Planet.* Berkeley, CA: North Atlantic Books.

Bahreini, Raha. 2008. "From Perversion to Pathology: Discourses and Practices of Gender Policing in the Islamic Republic of Iran," *Muslim World Journal of Human Rights* 5, 1 (article 2, electronic publication).

Balkin, Richard S., Lewis Z. Schlosser, and Dana H. Levitt. 2009. "Religious Identity and Cultural Diversity: Exploring the Relationships between Religious Identity, Sexism, Homophobia, and

Multicultural Competence," *Journal of Counseling & Development* 87, 4: 420–7.

Berbrier, Mitch, and Elaine Pruett. 2006. "When Is Inequality a Problem? Victim Contests, Injustice Frames, and the Case of the Office of Gay, Lesbian, and Bisexual Student Support Services at Indiana University," *Journal of Contemporary Ethnography* 35, 3: 257–84.

Biblarz, T.J., and J. Stacey. 2010. "How Does the Gender of Parents Matter?," *Journal of Marriage and the Family* 72, 1: 3–22.

Blashill, Aaron J., and Kimberly K. Powlishta. 2009. "Gay Stereotypes: The Use of Sexual Orientation as a Cue for Gender-Related Attributes," *Sex Roles* 61, 11 and 12: 783–93.

Bogaert, Anthony F., and Carolyn L. Hafer. 2009. "Predicting the Timing of Coming Out in Gay and Bisexual Men from World Beliefs, Physical Attractiveness, and Childhood Gender Identity/Role," *Journal of Applied Social Psychology* 39, 8: 1991–2019.

Bonds-Raacke, J.M., E.T. Cady, R. Schlegel, R.J. Harris, and L. Firebaugh. 2007. "Remembering Gay and Lesbian Media Characters: Can Ellen and Will Improve Attitudes toward Homosexuals?," *Journal of Homosexuality* 53: 19–34.

Bos, Henry, and Theo Sandfort. 2010. "Children's Gender Identity in Lesbian and Heterosexual Two-Parent Families," *Sex Roles* 62, 1–2: 114–26.

Boysen, Guy A., and David L. Vogel. 2007. "Biased Assimilation and Attitude Polarization in Response to Learning about Biological Explanations of Homosexuality," *Sex Roles* 57, 9–10: 755–62.

Brubaker, Michael D., Michael T. Garrett, and Brian J. Dew. 2009. "Examining the Relationship between Internalized Heterosexism and Substance Abuse among Lesbian, Gay, and Bisexual Individuals: A Critical Review," *Journal of LGBT Issues in Counseling* 3, 1: 62–89.

Bryld, M. 2001. "The Infertility Clinic and the Birth of the Lesbian: The Political Debate in Assisted Reproduction in Denmark," *European Journal of Women's Studies* 8, 3: 299–312.

Chaitman, Steven. 2013. "Asexuals Make Presence Known, Seek LGBTQ Allies," *Windy City Times*, n.p., 2 Jan. Web, 4 Jan.

Chesir-Teran, Daniel, and Diane Hughes. 2009. "Heterosexism in High School and Victimization among Lesbian, Gay, Bisexual, and Questioning Students," *Journal of Youth and Adolescence* 38, 7: 963–75.

Chow, Pizza K., and Sheung-Tak Cheng. 2010. "Shame, Internalized Heterosexism, Lesbian Identity, and Coming Out to Others: A Comparative Study of Lesbians in Mainland China and Hong Kong," *Journal of Counseling Psychology* 57, 1: 92–104.

Cohen, Taya R., Deborah L. Hall, and Jennifer Tuttle. 2009. "Attitudes toward Stereotypical versus Counter-stereotypical Gay Men and Lesbians," *Journal of Sex Research* 46, 4: 274–81.

Conlon, Deirdre. 2004. "Productive Bodies, Performative Spaces: Everyday Life in Christopher Park," *Sexualities* 7, 4: 462–79.

Corrigan, Patrick W., Jonathon E. Larson, Julie Hautamaki, Alicia Mathews, Sachi Kuwabara, Jennifer Rafacz, Jessica Walton, Abigail Wassel, and John O'Shaughnessy. 2009. "What Lessons Do Coming Out as Gay Men or Lesbians Have for People Stigmatized by Mental Illness?," *Community Mental Health Journal* 45, 5: 366–74.

Crawley, S., and K.L. Broad. 2008. "The Construction of Sex and Sexualities," in J. Holstein and J. Gubrium, eds, *Handbook of Constructionist Research*. New York: Guilford Press, 545–66.

Crowl, Alicia, Soyeon Ahn, and Jean Baker. 2008. "A Meta-Analysis of Developmental Outcomes for Children of Same-Sex and Heterosexual Parents," *Journal of GLBT Family Studies* 4, 3: 385–407.

Day, Nancy E., and Patricia G. Greene. 2008. "A Case for Sexual Orientation Diversity Management in Small and Large Organizations," *Human Resource Management* 47, 3: 637–54.

DeJordy, R. 2008. "Just Passing Through—Stigma, Passing, and Identity Decoupling in the Work Place," *Group & Organization Management* 33, 5: 504–31.

Denike, Margaret Ann. 2007. "Religion, Rights, and Relationships: The Dream of Relational Equality," *Hypatia* 22, 1: 71–91.

DePalma, Renee, and Elizabeth Atkinson. 2009. "'No Outsiders': Moving Beyond a Discourse of Tolerance to Challenge Heteronormativity in Primary Schools," *British Educational Research Journal* 35, 6: 837–55.

Dermer, Shannon B., Shannon D. Smith, and Korenna K. Barto. 2010. "Identifying and Correctly Labeling Sexual Prejudice, Discrimination, and Oppression," *Journal of Counseling and Development* 88, 3: 325–31.

Diaz, N., I. Serrano-Garcia, and J. Toro-Alfonso. 2005. "AIDS-Related Stigma and Social Interaction: Puerto Ricans Living with HIV/AIDS," *Qualitative Health Research* 15, 2: 169–87.

Emens, E.F. 2004. "Monogamy's Law: Compulsory Monogamy and Polyamorous Existence," University of Chicago Public Law Working Paper, No. 58. *New York University Review of Law & Social Change* 29: 277–329.

Engle, M.J., J.A. McFalls Jr, B.J. Gallagher III, and K. Curtis. 2006. "The Attitudes of American Sociologists toward Causal Theories of Male Homosexuality," *American Sociologist* 37, 1: 68–76.

Esmail, S., K. Darry, W. Ashlea, and H. Knupp. 2010. "Attitudes and Perceptions towards Disability and Sexuality," *Disability & Rehabilitation* 32, 14: 1148–55.

Findlay, James F., Jr. 2006. "Glimpses of Recent History: The National Council of Churches, 1974–2004," *Journal of Presbyterian History* 84, 2: 152–69.

Frost, David M., and Linda M. Bastone. 2008. "The Role of Stigma Concealment in the Retrospective High School Experiences of Gay, Lesbian, and Bisexual Individuals," *Journal of LGBT Youth* 5, 1: 27–36.

Garland-Thomson, Rosemarie. 2002. "Integrating Disability, Transforming Feminist Theory," *NWSA Journal* 14, 3: 1–32.

Gates, G.J. 2011. "How Many People Are Lesbian, Gay, Bisexual and Transgender?," *The Williams Institute*. At: <williamsinstitute.law.ucla.edu/wp-content/uploads/Gates-How-Many-People-LGBT-Apr-2011.pdf>.

Gauthier, DeAnn K., and Nancy K. Chaudoir. 2004. "Tranny Boyz: Cyber Community Support in Negotiating Sex and Gender Mobility among Female to Male Transsexuals," *Deviant Behavior* 25, 4: 375–98.

Gebhard, Paul H., and Michael Reece. 2008. "Kinsey and Beyond: Past, Present, and Future Considerations for

Research on Male Bisexuality," *Journal of Bisexuality* 8, 3 and 4: 175–89.

Geller, Pamela L. 2009. "Bodyscapes, Biology, and Heteronormativity," *American Anthropologist* 111, 4: 504–16.

Gillespie, Wayne. 2008. "Thirty-Five Years after Stonewall: An Exploratory Study of Satisfaction with Police among Gay, Lesbian, and Bisexual Persons at the 34th Annual Atlanta Pride Festival," *Journal of Homosexuality* 55, 4: 619–47.

Gillespie, Wayne, and Roger L. Blackwell. 2009. "Substance Use Patterns and Consequences among Lesbians, Gays, and Bisexuals," *Journal of Gay & Lesbian Social Services: Issues in Practice, Policy & Research* 21, 1: 90–108.

Greenlee, Timothy B. 2005. "Queer Eye for a Gay Guy: Using Market-Specific Symbols in Advertising to Attract Gay Consumers without Alienating the Mainstream," *Psychology & Marketing* 22, 5: 421–39.

Gross, Robert, and Gregory P. Bisson. 2009. "Evaluating the President's Emergency Plan for AIDS Relief: Time to Scale It Up," *Annals of Internal Medicine* 150, 10: 727.

Haider-Markel, Donald P., Mark R. Joslyn. 2008. "Beliefs about the Origins of Homosexuality and Support for Gay Rights: An Empirical Test of Attribution Theory," *Public Opinion Quarterly* 72, 2: 291–310.

Halperin, David M. 1990. *One Hundred Years of Homosexuality and Other Essays on Greek Love*. London and New York: Routledge.

Hammers, Corie. 2009. "Space, Agency, and the Transfiguring of Lesbian/Queer Desire," *Journal of Homosexuality* 56, 6: 757–85.

Harding, Rosie. 2007. "Sir Mark Potter and the Protection of the Traditional Family: Why Same-Sex Marriage Is (Still) a Feminist Issue," *Feminist Legal Studies* 15, 2: 223–34.

Harris, Angelique C. 2009. "Marginalization by the Marginalized: Race, Homophobia, Heterosexism, and 'the Problem of the 21st Century,'" *Journal of Gay & Lesbian Social Services* 21, 4: 430–48.

Haslam, Nick, and Sheri R. Levy. 2006. "Essentialist Beliefs about Homosexuality: Structure and Implications for Prejudice," *Personality and Social Psychology Bulletin* 32, 4: 471–85.

Heiss, Sarah. 2011. "Locating the Bodies of Women and Disability in Definitions of Beauty: An Analysis of Dove's Campaign for Real Beauty," *Disability Studies Quarterly* 31, 1.

Herek, Gregory M. 2004. "Beyond 'Homophobia': Thinking about Sexual Prejudice and Stigma in the Twenty-First Century," *Sexuality Research and Social Policy* 1, 2: 6–24.

Kim, Saeromi. 2007. "Gatekeeping and Homophobia: From Bouncers in Bars to the Macro-Social, Interpersonal, and Intrapsychological Practices of Homophobia," *Integrative Psychological & Behavioral Science* (special Issue: "Relating to Gender—A New Look at Gender Identity") 41, 3 and 4: 303–7.

King, E.B., C. Reilly, and M. Hebl. 2008. "The Best of Times, the Worst of Times—Exploring Dual Perspectives of 'Coming Out' in the Workplace," *Group & Organization Management* 33, 5: 566–601.

Lax, Jeffrey R., and Justin H. Phillips. 2009. "Gay Rights in the States: Public Opinion and Policy Responsiveness," *American Political Science Review* 103, 3: 367–86.

Lee, I-Ching, and Mary Crawford. 2007. "Lesbians and Bisexual Women in the Eyes of Scientific Psychology," *Feminism and Psychology* 17, 1: 109–27.

Liu, Ting. 2009. "Conflicting Discourses on Boys' Love and Subcultural Tactics in Mainland China and Hong Kong," *Intersections: Gender and Sexuality in Asia and the Pacific*, No. 20. At: <intersections.anu.edu.au/issue20/liu.htm>.

McCabe M.P., R.A. Cummins, and A.A. Deeks. 2000. "Sexuality and Quality of Life among People with Physical Disability," *Sexuality and Disability* 18: 115–23.

McCabe, Sean Esteban, Tonda L. Hughes, Wendy B. Bostwick, Brady T. West, and Carol J. Boyd. 2009. "Sexual Orientation, Substance Use Behaviors and Substance Dependence in the United States," *Addiction* 104, 8: 1333–45.

McQueeney, Krista B. 2003. "The New Religious Rite: A Symbolic Interactionist Case Study of Lesbian Commitment Rituals," *Journal of Lesbian Studies* 7, 2: 49–70.

Madureira, Ana Flávia do Amaral. 2007. "The Psychological Basis of Homophobia: Cultural Construction of a

Barrier," *Integrative Psychological & Behavioral Science* 41, 3 and 4: 225–47.

Mamo, Laura. 2007. *Queering Reproduction: Achieving Pregnancy in the Age of Technoscience*. Durham, NC: Duke University Press.

Marinos, V., D. Griffiths, L. Gosse, J. Robinson, G. Olley, and W. Lindsay. 2008. "Legal Rights and Persons with Intellectual Disabilities," in F. Owen and D. Griffiths, eds, *Challenges to the Human Rights of People with Intellectual Disabilities*. Cambridge, MA: Athenaeum Press.

Mattingly, Marybeth J., and Robert N. Bozick. 2001. "Children Raised by Same-Sex Couples: Much Ado about Nothing," paper presented to Southern Sociological Society conference.

Mayers, K.S., D.K. Heller, and J.A. Heller. 2003. "Damaged Sexual Self-Esteem: A Kind of Disability," *Sexuality and Disability* 21: 269–82.

Meyer-Cook, Fiona, and Diane Labelle. 2004. "Namaji: Two-Spirit Organizing in Montreal, Canada," *Journal of Gay & Lesbian Social Services* 16, 1: 29–51.

Miall, C., and K. March. 2005. "Open Adoption as a Family Form: Community Assessments and Social Support," *Journal of Family Issues* 26, 3: 380–410.

Moin, Victor, Ilana Duvdevany, and Daniela Mazor. 2009. "Sexual Identity, Body Image and Life Satisfaction among Women with and without Physical Disability," *Sexuality and Disability* 27, 2: 83–95.

Moore, M.R. 2009. "New Choices, New Families: How Lesbians Decide about Motherhood," *Journal of Marriage and the Family* 71, 5: 1350–2.

Nell, Patricia. 2005. "'Traditional' Marriage: A Secular Affair," *Gay & Lesbian Review Worldwide* 12, 3: 10.

Neufeld, J.A., F. Klingbeil, D.N. Bryen, B. Silverman, and A. Thomas. 2002. "Adolescent Sexuality and Disability," *Physical Medicine & Rehabilitation Clinics of North America* 13, 4 (Nov.): 857–73.

O'Higgins-Norman, James. 2009. "Straight Talking: Explorations on Homosexuality and Homophobia in Secondary Schools in Ireland," *Sex Education: Sexuality, Society and Learning* 9, 4: 381–93.

Oakenfull, Gillian K., Michael S. McCarthy, and Timothy B. Greenlee. 2008. "Targeting a Minority without

Alienating the Majority: Advertising to Gays and Lesbians in Mainstream Media," *Journal of Advertising Research* 48, 2: 191–8.

O'Ryan, Leslie W., and William P. McFarland. 2010. "A Phenomenological Exploration of the Experiences of Dual-Career Lesbian and Gay Couples," *Journal of Counseling & Development* 88, 1: 71–9.

Osterlund, Katherine. 2009. "Love, Freedom and Governance: Same-Sex Marriage in Canada," *Social & Legal Studies* 18, 1: 93–109.

Ottosson, Daniel. 2009. *State-Sponsored Homophobia: A World Survey of Laws Prohibiting Same Sex Activity between Consenting Adults.* International Lesbian, Gay Bisexual, Trans and Intersex Association (ILGA) report.

Pallotta-Chiarolli, Maria. 2010. "To Pass, Border or Pollute," in Meg Barker and Darren Langdridge, eds, *Understanding Non-monogamies.* New York: Routledge, 182–7.

Pallotta-Chiarolli, M., P. Haydon, A. Hunter. 2013. "'These Are *Our* Children': Polyamorous Parenting," in Katherine Allen and Abbie Goldberg, eds, *LGBT-Parent Families: Possibilities for New Research and Implications for Practice.* London: Springer, 117–31.

Patterson, Charlotte J. 2006. "Children of Lesbian and Gay Parents," *Current Directions in Psychological Science* 15, 5: 241–4.

Peel, Elizabeth. 2008. "De-heterosexualising Health: Exploring Lesbian, Gay, Bisexual and Trans Health Issues and Policy in Britain," *Sex Roles* 59, 7 and 8: 609–10.

Plummer, David C. 2001. "The Quest for Modern Manhood: Masculine Stereotypes, Peer Culture, and the Social Significance of Homophobia," *Journal of Adolescence* 24, 1: 15–23.

Popenoe, David. 1993. "American Family Decline, 1960–1990: A Review and Appraisal," *Journal of Marriage and Family* 55: 527–42.

Potoczniak, Daniel, Margaret Crosbie-Burnett, and Nikki Saltzburg. 2009. "Experiences Regarding Coming Out to Parents among African American, Hispanic, and White Gay, Lesbian, Bisexual, Transgender, and Questioning Adolescents," *Journal of Gay & Lesbian Social Services: Issues in Practice, Policy & Research* 21, 2 and 3: 189–205.

Próspero, M. 2008. "The Effect of Coercion on Aggression and Mental Health among Reciprocally Violent Couples," *Journal of Family Violence* 23, 3: 195–202.

Ragins, Belle Rose, John M. Cornwell, and Janice S. Miller. 2003. "Heterosexism in the Workplace: Do Race and Gender Matter?," *Group and Organization Management* 28, 1: 45–74.

Ramsey, E.M., and Gladys Santiago. 2004. "The Conflation of Male Homosexuality and Femininity in Queer Eye for the Straight Guy," *Feminist Media Studies* 4, 3: 353–5.

Richlin, Amy. 2005. "Eros Underground: Greece and Rome in Gay Print Culture, 1953–65," *Journal of Homosexuality* 49, 3 and 4: 421–61.

Ristock, Janice. 2001. *No More Secrets: Violence in Lesbian Relationships.* London: Routledge.

Röndahl, Gerd, Elisabeth Bruhner, and Jenny Lindhe. 2009. "Heteronormative Communication with Lesbian Families in Antenatal Care, Childbirth and Postnatal Care," *Journal of Advanced Nursing* 65, 11: 2337–44.

Rosker, Jana S. 2009. "The Golden Orchid Relationships: Female Marriages and Same-Sex Families in the Chinese Province of Guangdong during the 19th Century," *Socialno delo* 48, 1–3: 99–110.

Rutledge, Scott E., Neil Abell, Jacqueline Padmore, and Theresa J. McCann. 2009. "AIDS Stigma in Health Services in the Eastern Caribbean," *Sociology of Health and Illness* 31, 1: 17–34.

Savell, K. 2004. "Sex and the Sacred: Sterilization and Bodily Integrity in English and Canadian Law," *McGill Law Journal* 49: 1093.

Savin-Williams, R.C., and K.G. Esterberg. 2000. "Lesbian, Gay, and Bisexual Families," in D.H. Demo, K.R. Allen, and M.A. Fine, eds, *Handbook of Family Diversity.* New York: Oxford University Press.

Seidman, Steven. 2002. *Beyond the Closet: The Transformation of Gay and Lesbian Life.* New York: Routledge.

Sheff, Elisabeth. 2005. "Polyamorous Women, Sexual Subjectivity, and Power," *Journal of Contemporary Ethnography* 20, 10: 1–34.

Smith, Tom W. 1998. *American Sexual Behavior: Trends, Socio-Demographic Differences, and Risk Behavior.* Chicago:

National Opinion Research Center, University of Chicago, GSS Topical Report No. 25.

Speziale, B., and C. Ring. 2006. "Intimate Violence among Lesbian Couples: Emerging Data and Critical Needs," *Journal of Feminist Family Therapy* 18, 1 and 2: 85–96.

Stacey, J., and T. Meadow. 2009. "New Slants on the Slippery Slope: The Politics of Polygamy and Gay Family Rights in South Africa and the United States," *Politics & Society* 37, 2: 167–202.

Statistics Canada. 2010. "Canadian Community Health Survey," *The Daily,* 15 June. At: <www.statcan.gc.ca/daily-quotidien/100615/dq100615b-eng.htm>.

Stimson, Adrian A. 2006 "Two Spirited for You: The Absence of 'Two Spirit' People in Western Culture and Media," *West Coast Line* 40, 1: 78

Tasker, Fiona. 2005. "Lesbian Mothers, Gay Fathers, and Their Children: A Review," *Journal of Developmental Behavioral Pediatrics* 26, 3: 224–40.

Tomsen, Stephen. 2006. "Homophobic Violence, Cultural Essentialism and Shifting Sexual Attitudes," *Social & Legal Studies* 15, 3: 389–407.

Towle, Evan B., and Lynn Marie Morgan. 2002. "Romancing the Transgender Native: Rethinking the Use of the 'Third Gender' Concept," *GLQ: A Journal of Lesbian and Gay Studies* 8, 4: 469–97.

Turner, William B. 2009. "Gay Rights and Moral Panic: The Origins of America's Debate on Homosexuality," *Journal of American History* 96, 3: 928–9.

Uzzell, David, and Nathalie Horne. 2006. "The Influence of Biological Sex, Sexuality and Gender Role on Interpersonal Distance," *British Journal of Social Psychology* 45, 3: 579–97.

Valentine, G., and L. Waite. 2012. "Negotiating Difference through Everyday Encounters: The Case of Sexual Orientation and Religion and Belief," *Antipode* 44, 2 (Mar.): 474–92.

Valverde, Mariana, and Miomir Cirak. 2003. "Governing Bodies, Creating Gay Spaces: Policing and Security Issues in 'Gay' Downtown Toronto," *British Journal of Criminology* 43, 1: 102–21.

VanderLaan, D.P., and P.L. Vasey. 2008. "Born Gay: The Psychobiology of Sex Orientation," *Archives of Sexual Behavior* 37, 4: 673–4.

Volpp, Serenayuan, and Jack Drescher. "What Has the Lesbian Family Structure Taught Us about Child Rearing by Gay Adults?," *Clinical Psychiatry News* 39, 3: 7.

Walcott, Rinaldo. 2009. "David Rayside, Queer Inclusions, Continental Divisions: Public Recognition of Sexual Diversity in Canada and the United States," *Labour/Le Travail* 64: 227–30.

Waldner, L.K., H. Martin, and L. Capeder. 2006. "Ideology of Gay Racialist Skinheads and Stigma Management Techniques," *Journal of Political & Military Sociology* 34, 1: 165–84.

Walters, K.L., T. Evans-Campbell, J. Simoni, T. Ronquillo, and R. Bhuyan. 2006. "'My Spirit in My Heart': Identity Experiences and Challenges among American Indian Two-Spirit Women," *Journal of Lesbian Studies* 10, 1 and 2: 125–49.

Wang, Frank, Herng-Dar Bih, and David Brennan. 2009. "'Have They Really Come Out?' Gay Men and Their Parents in Taiwan," *Culture, Health and Sexuality* 11, 3: 285–96.

Weinberg, George. 1983 [1972]. *Society and the Healthy Homosexual*. New York: St Martin's Press.

Whitehead, A.L. 2010. "Sacred Rites and Civil Rights: Religion's Effect on Attitudes toward Same-Sex Unions and the Perceived Cause of Homosexuality," *Social Science Quarterly* 91, 1: 63–79.

Wiegerink, Diana, et al. 2011. "Sexuality of Young Adults with Cerebral Palsy: Experienced Limitations and Needs," *Sexuality and Disability* 29, 2: 119–28.

Chapter 6

Addington, Lynn. 2013. "Who You Calling Old? Measuring 'Elderly' and What It Means for Homicide Research," *Homicide Studies* 17, 2: 134–53.

Alzheimer's Association. 2014. "2014 Alzheimer's Disease Facts and Figures," *Alzheimer's and Dementia* 10, 2: 1–75.

Angus, Jocelyn, and Patricia Reeve. 2006. "Ageism: A Threat to 'Aging Well' in the 21st Century," *Journal of Applied Gerontology* 25, 2: 137–52.

Antonucci, Toni C., Jennifer E. Lansford, and Lynne Schaberg. 2001. "Widowhood and Illness: A Comparison of Social Network Characteristics in France, Germany, Japan, and the United States," *Psychology and Aging* 16, 4: 655–65.

Ayalon, L., S. Shiovitz-Ezra, and Y. Palgi. 2013. "Associations of Loneliness in Older Married Men and Women," *Aging and Mental Health* 17, 1: 33–9.

Bengtson, Vern L., Glen H. Elder Jr, and Norella M. Putney. 2012. "The Life Course Perspective on Aging: Linked Lives, Timing, and History," in Jeanne Katz, Sheila Peace, and Sue Spurr, eds, *Adult Lives: A Life Course Perspective*. Bristol, UK: Policy Press.

Ben-Moshe, Liat. 2004. "Juxtaposing Disability and Old Age as Constructed Identities," paper presented at meeting of the Society for the Study of Social Problems, San Francisco.

Bezerra, Jani Cleria Pereira, Alessandro Carrielo, Estelio Henrique Martin Dantas, Andre Dias de Oliveira Fernandes, Carlos Soares Pernambuco, and Bernardo Minelli Rodrigues. 2012. "Quality of Life, Elderly and Physical Activity," *Health* 4, 2 (Feb.): 88.

Blit-Cohen, E., and H. Litwin. 2004. "Elder Participation in Cyberspace: A Qualitative Analysis of Israeli Retirees," *Journal of Aging Studies* 18, 4: 385–98.

Bonnet, Carole, and Jean-Michel Hourriez. 2009. "Widowhood, the Survivor's Pension and Maintaining a Standard of Living after the Death of a Spouse: An Analysis of Type Cases," *Retraite et Société* 56: 71–103.

Brooke, Libby. 2009. "Prolonging the Careers of Older Information Technology Workers: Continuity, Exit or Retirement Transitions?," *Ageing and Society* 29, pt 2: 237–56.

CARP (Canadian Association of Retired People). 2001. "What Is CARP?" At: <www.fiftyplus.net/CARP/about/main.cfm>.

Chatterjee, Pranab, Darlyne Bailey, and Nina Aronoff. 2002. "Adolescence and Old Age in Twelve Communities," *Journal of Sociology and Social Welfare* 28, 4: 121–59.

Clarke, Laura H., and Meridith Griffin. 2008. "Visible and Invisible Ageing: Beauty Work as a Response to Ageism," *Ageing and Society* 28, pt 5: 653–74.

Coppin, A.K., L. Ferrucci, F. Lauretani, C. Phillips, M. Chang, and J.M. Guralnik. 2006. "Low Socioeconomic Status and Disability in Old Age: Evidence from the InChianti study for the Mediating Role of Physiological Impairments," *Journals of Gerontology Series A: Biological Sciences and Medical Sciences* 6, 1: 86–91.

Cornwell, Benjamin. 2009. "Network Bridging Potential in Later Life: Life-Course Experiences and Social Network Position," *Journal of Aging and Health* 21, 1: 129–54.

Cullen, Jennifer C., Leslie B. Hammer, and Margaret B. Neal. 2009. "Development of a Typology of Dual-Earner Couples Caring for Children and Aging Parents," *Journal of Family Issues* 30, 4: 458–83.

Cumming, E., and W.E. Henry. 1961. *Growing Old: The Process of Disengagement*. New York: Basic Books.

Degnen, Cathrine. 2007. "Minding the Gap: The Construction of Old Age and Oldness amongst Peers," *Journal of Aging Studies* 21, 1: 69–80.

Dobbs, Debra, J.K. Eckert, Bob Rubinstein, Lynn Keimig, Leanne Clark, Ann C. Frankowski, and Sheryl Zimmerman. 2008. "An Ethnographic Study of Stigma and Ageism in Residential Care or Assisted Living," *The Gerontologist* 48, 4: 517–26.

Dosman, Donna, and Norah Keating. 2009. "Social Capital and the Care Networks of Frail Seniors," *Canadian Review of Sociology* 46, 4: 301–18.

Dupuis, Sara B. 2009. "An Ecological Examination of Older Remarried Couples," *Journal of Divorce and Remarriage* 50, 6: 369–87.

Elder, Glen H., Jr. 1999. "The Life Course and Aging: Some Reflections," Distinguished Scholar lecture given at the annual meeting of the American Sociological Association. At: <www.unc.edu/~elder/asa/asacharts.pdf>.

Esping-Andersen, Gosta. 2003. "A Model for Pension Reform in 21st Century Europe." At: <www.socialdialogue.net/en/en_cha_key_003.jsp>.

FitzGerald, Brian A.P. 2008. "Everything Old Is New Again: A Reflection on the State of the Defined-Benefit Pension Plan," *Canadian Public Policy* (Nov.): 23–8.

Foner, Anne. 2000. "Age Integration or Age Conflict as Society Ages?," *The Gerontologist* 40, 3: 272–6.

Gadalla. 2009. "Sense of Mastery, Social Support, and Health in Elderly Canadians," *Journal of Aging and Health* 21, 4: 581–95.

Gagliardi, Cristina, Fiorella Marcellini, Roberta Papa, Cinzia Giuli, and Heidrun Mollenkopf. 2010. "Associations of Personal and Mobility Resources with Subjective Well-Being among Older Adults in Italy and Germany," *Archives of Gerontology and Geriatrics* 50, 1: 42–7.

Gans, Daphna, and Merril Silverstein. 2006. "Norms of Filial Responsibility for Aging Parents across Time and Generations," *Journal of Marriage and Family* 68, 4: 961–76.

Garber, Carol E., Jenifer E. Allsworth, and Bess H. Marcus. 2008. "Correlates of the Stages of Change for Physical Activity in a Population Survey," *American Journal of Public Health* 98, 5: 897–904.

Giblin, Joanne C. 2011. "Successful Aging," *Journal of Psychosocial Nursing & Mental Health Services* 49, 3: 23–6.

Gillen, Martie, and Hyungsoo Kim. 2009. "Older Women and Poverty Transition: Consequences of Income Source Changes from Widowhood," *Journal of Applied Gerontology* 28, 3: 320–41.

Gottlieb, Beatrice. 1993. *The Family in the Western World: From the Black Death to the Industrial Age*. New York: Oxford University Press.

Guerra, Ricardo O., Beatriz Eugenia Alvarado, and Maria Victoria Zunzunegui. 2008. "Life Course, Gender and Ethnic Inequalities in Functional Disability in a Brazilian Urban Elderly Population," *Aging Clinical and Experimental Research* 20, 1: 53–61.

Hanlon, Neil, and Greg Halseth. 2005. "The Greying of Resource Communities in Northern British Columbia: Implications for Health Care Delivery in Already-Underserviced Communities," *Canadian Geographer* 49, 1: 1–24.

Hardwicke, Shannon, and Margaret Sproule. 2010. "Physical Education for the Elderly," *Vahperd Journal* 31, 1: 25–6.

Harkins, S., T. Elliott, and T. Wan. 2006. "Emotional Distress and Urinary Incontinence among Older Women," *Rehabilitation Psychology* 51: 346–55.

Havighurst, Robert, and Ruth Albrecht. 1953. *Older People*. New York: Longman, Green.

Helliwell, J.F., and S. Wang. 2011. "Trust and Wellbeing," *International Journal of Wellbeing* 1, 1: 42–78.

Hicks, Jennifer, and Eric R. Kingston. 2009. "The Economic Crisis: How Fare Older Americans?," *Generations* 33, 3: 6–11.

Ho, Jeong-Hwa, and James M. Raymo. 2009. "Expectations and Realization of Joint Retirement among Dual-Worker Couples," *Research on Aging* 31, 2: 153–79.

Jaggera, Carol, and Nicola A. Spiersa. 2005. "Socioeconomic Factors Associated with the Onset of Disability in Older Age: A Longitudinal Study of People Aged 75 Years and Over," *Social Science & Medicine* 61: 1567–75.

Johnson, Wendy, Ian J. Deary, Matt McGue, and Kaare Christensen. 2009. "Genetic and Environmental Links between Cognitive and Physical Functions in Old Age," *Journals of Gerontology, Series B: Psychological Sciences and Social Sciences* 64B, 1: 65–72.

Jonson, Hakan, and Annika T. Larsson. 2009. "The Exclusion of Older People in Disability Activism and Policies—A Case of Inadvertent Ageism?," *Journal of Aging Studies* 23, 1: 69–77.

Kaestner, Robert, Jay A. Pearson, Danya Keene, and Arline T. Geronimus. 2009. "Stress, Allostatic Load, and Health of Mexican Immigrants," *Social Science Quarterly* 90, 5: 1089–111.

Kehl Wiebel, Susana, and J. Manuel Fernandez Fernandez. 2001. "The Social Construction of Old Age," *Cuadernos de Trabajo Social*, no. 14: 125–61.

Kemmerling, A., and M. Neugart. 2009. "Financial Market Lobbies and Pension Reform," *European Journal of Political Economy* 25, 2: 163–73.

Kim, Jeungkun. 2009. "Early Retirement in Three Types of Welfare States," *Research on Aging* 31, 5: 520–48.

Lasch, Christopher. 1977. *Haven in a Heartless World: The Family Besieged*. New York: Basic Books.

Lau, Denys T., and James B. Kirby. 2009. "The Relationship between Living Arrangement and Preventive Care Use among Community-Dwelling Elderly Persons," *American Journal of Public Health* 99, 7: 1315–21.

Lewis, D.C., K. Medvedev, and D.M. Seponski. 2011. "Awakening to the Desires of Older Women: Deconstructing Ageism within Fashion Magazines," *Journal of Aging Studies* 25, 2: 101–9.

Lin, Ju-Ping, and Chin-Chun Yi. 2009. "Types of Relations between Adult Children and Elderly Parents in Taiwan: Mechanisms Accounting for Various Relational Types," *Journal of Comparative Family Studies* 40, 2 (Spring): 305.

Lindström, Martin. 2009. "Marital Status, Social Capital, Material Conditions and Self-Rated Health: A Population-Based Study," *Health Policy* 93, 2 and 3: 172–9.

Lundberg, Michael. 2009. "Our Parents' Keepers: The Current Status of American Filial Responsibility Laws," *Journal of Law & Family Studies* 11, 2: 533–4.

Lysaght, Patricia. 2002. Book Review of Arensberg and Kimball, *Family and Community in Ireland*, 3rd edn (2001), *Bealoideas: Journal of the Folklore of Ireland*. Clare Local Studies Project. At: <www.clarelibrary.ie/eolas/library/local-studies/clasp/publications/reviews/bealoideas_family_community_review.htm>.

McDaniel, Susan A., Amber Gazso, and Seongge Um. 2013. "Generationing Relations in Challenging Times: Americans and Canadians in Midlife in the Great Recession," *Current Sociology* 61, 3: 301–21.

McGarry, J., and C. Simpson. 2008. "Identifying, Reporting and Preventing Elder Abuse in the Practice Setting," *Nursing Standard* 22: 49–56, 60.

McGuinness, S., and M. Wooden. 2009. "Overskilling, Job Insecurity and Career Mobility," *Industrial Relations* 48, 2.

McMunn, Anne, James Nazroo, Morten Wahrendorf, Elizabeth Breeze, and Paola Zaninotto. 2009. "Participation in Socially-Productive Activities, Reciprocity and Wellbeing in Later Life: Baseline Results in England," *Ageing & Society* 29, 5: 765–82.

McMurtrey, Mark, James P. Downey, Steven M. Zeltmann, and Ronald E. McGaughey. 2011. "Seniors and Technology: Results from a Field Study," *Journal of Computer Information Systems* 51, 4 (Summer): 22–30.

Magnusson, Lennart, Elizabeth Hanson, and Mike Nolan. 2005. "The Impact of Information and Communication Technology on Family Carers of Older People and Professionals in Sweden," *Ageing and Society* 25, pt 5: 693–714.

Marshall, Barbara L. 2007. "Climacteric Redux? (Re)medicalizing the Male Menopause," *Men and Masculinities* 9, 4 (Apr.): 509–29.

Matthews, Anne Martin. 2011. "Revisiting Widowhood in Later Life: Changes in Patterns and Profiles, Advances in Research and Understanding," *Canadian Journal on Aging/La Revue canadienne du vieillissement* 30, 3 (Oct.): 339–54.

Mendenhall, Ruby, Ariel Kalil, Laurel J. Spindel, and Cassandra M.D. Hart. 2008. "Job Loss at Mid-life: Managers and Executives Face the 'New Risk Economy,'" *Social Forces* 87, 1: 187–209.

Merz, Eva-Maria, Carlo Schuengel, and Hans-Joachim Schulze. 2007. "Intergenerational Solidarity: An Attachment Perspective," *Journal of Aging Studies* 21, 2: 175–86.

Muehlbauer, M., and P.A. Crane. 2006. "Elder Abuse and Neglect," *Journal of Psychosocial Nursing and Mental Health Services* 44, 11: 43–8.

Myles, John. 1984. *Old Age in the Welfare State: The Political Economy of Public Pensions*, rev. edn. Lawrence: University Press of Kansas.

National Advisory Council on Aging. 2006. *Newsletter on Aging* 9, 2 (June). At: <www.naca.ca/expression/9-2/exp_9-2_e.html>.

O'Rand, Angela M., and Kim M. Shuey. 2007. "Gender and the Devolution of Pension Risks in the US," *Current Sociology* 55, 2: 287–304.

Payling, S.J. 2001. "The Economics of Marriage in Late Medieval England: The Marriage of Heiresses," *Economic History Review* 54, 3: 413–29.

Pew, R.W., and S.B. Van Hemel, eds. 2004. *Technology for Adaptive Aging*. Washington: National Academies Press.

Poon, Cecilia Y.M., and Bob G. Knight. 2009. "Influence of Sad Mood and Old Age Schema on Older Adults' Attention to Physical Symptoms," *Journals of Gerontology, Series B: Psychological Sciences and Social Sciences* 64B, 1: 41–4.

Public Health Agency of Canada. 2012. *Elder Abuse in Canada: A Gender Based Analysis*. At: <publications.gc.ca/collections/collection_2012/aspc-phac/HP10-21-2012-eng.pdf>.

Pyper, W. 2006. "Aging, Health, and Work," *Perspectives on Labour and Income* 7, 2: 5–15.

Ramsay, Sheena E., P.H. Whincup, L. Lennon, and S.G. Wannamethee.

2008. "Extent of Social Inequalities in Disability in the Elderly: Results from a Population-Based Study of British Men," *Annals of Epidemiology* 18, 12: 896–903.

Rosenthal, Carolyn J. 1997. "The Changing Contexts of Family Care in Canada," *Ageing International* 24, 1: 13–31.

Ross-Sheriff, Fariyal. 2008. "Aging and Gender, Feminist Theory, and Social Work Practice Concerns," *Affilia* 23, 4 (Nov.): 309–11.

Rubin, Rose M., and Shelley I. White-Means. 2009. "Informal Caregiving: Dilemmas of Sandwiched Caregivers," *Alternative Lifestyles* 30, 3: 252–67.

Russell, Cherry. 2007. "What Do Older Women and Men Want? Gender Differences in the 'Lived Experience' of Ageing," *Current Sociology* 55, 2 (Mar.): 173–92.

Saini, Sarita, and Sushma Jaswal. 2009. "A Comparative Appraisal of Quality of Life (QOL) of Aged Living with Sons and Living with Daughters," *The Anthropologist* 11, 2: 139–46.

Savard, Jacinthe, et al. 2006. "Caregiver Satisfaction with Support Services: Influence of Different Types of Services," *Journal of Aging and Health* 18, 1 (Feb.): 3–27.

Schellenberg, G., and Y. Ostrovsky. 2008. "The Retirement Plans and Expectations of Older Workers," *Canadian Social Trends*, Statistics Canada Catalogue no. 11-008.

Sev'er, Aysan. 2009. "More Than Wife Abuse That Has Gone Old: A Conceptual Model for Violence against the Aged in Canada and the US," *Journal of Comparative Family Studies* 40, 2 (Spring): 279–92.

Shugrue, Noreen, and Julie Robison. 2009. "Intensifying Individual, Family, and Caregiver Stress: Health and Social Effects of Economic Crisis," *Generations* 33, 3: 34–9.

Smith, Hilda L. 2001. "'Aging': A Problematic Concept for Women," *Journal of Women's History* 12, 4: 77–86.

Statistics Canada. n.d. "Complete Life Table, Canada, 2000 to 2002, Females." At: <www.statcan.ca/english/freepub/84-537-XIE/tables/pdftables/caf.pdf>.

———. 2011a. At: <www12.statcan.gc.ca/census-recensement/2011/as-sa/98-312-x/2011003/fig/desc/desc3_4-4-eng.cfm>.

———. 2011b. At: <www12.statcan.gc.ca/census-recensement/2011/as-sa/98-312-x/2011003/tbl/tbl3_4-1-eng.cfm>.

———. 2011c. At: <www12.statcan.gc.ca/census-recensement/2011/dp-pd/pyramid-pyramide/his/index-eng.cfm>.

———. 2012. At: <www.statcan.gc.ca/pub/85-002-x/2012001/article/11643-eng.htm>.

Ugiagbe, Ernest O., Kokunre Agbontaen-Eghafona, and Tracy B.E. Omorogiuwa. 2007. "An Evaluation of the Principles of Primogeniture and Inheritance Laws among the Benin People of Nigeria," *Journal of Family History* 32, 1: 90–101.

Uhlenberg, Peter, Jenny de Jong Gierveld. 2004. "Age-Segregation in Later Life: An Examination of Personal Networks," *Ageing and Society* 24, 1: 5–28.

Vares, T. 2009. "Reading the 'Sexy Oldie': Gender, Age(ing) and Embodiment," *Sexualities* 12, 4: 503–24.

Vincent, John. 1996. "Who's Afraid of an Ageing Population? Nationalism, the Free Market, and the Construction of Old Age as an Issue," *Critical Social Policy* 16 (May): 3–26.

Waldron, I., C. McCloskey, and I. Earle. 2005. "Trends in Gender Differences in Accident Mortality: Relationships to Changing Gender Roles and Other Societal Trends," *Demographic Research* 13: 415–54.

Wassel J.I. 2006. "Financial Planning and the 'Senior Sandwich' Generation," *Journal of Financial Service Professionals* 60 (Mar.).

Wilhelmson, K., C. Andersson, M. Waern, and P. Allebeck. 2005. "Elderly People's Perspectives on Quality of Life," *Aging and Society* 25, 4: 585–600.

Williams, Cara. 2004. "The Sandwich Generation," *Perspectives on Labour and Income*. Ottawa: Statistics Canada Catalogue no. 75-001-XIE (vol. 5, no. 9). At: <www.statcan.ca:8096/bsolc/english/bsolc?catno=75-001-X20041097033>.

Windsor, Tim. 2009. "Persistence in Goal Striving and Positive Reappraisal as Psychosocial Resources for Ageing Well: A Dyadic Analysis," *Aging and Mental Health* 13, 6: 874–84.

Wong, Rebeca, and Deborah S. DeGraff. 2009. "Old-Age Wealth in Mexico: The Role of Reproductive, Human

Capital, and Employment Decisions," *Research on Aging* 31, 4: 413–39.

Xie, Li-Qin, Jing-Ping Zhang, Fang Peng, and Na-Na Jiao. 2010. "Prevalence and Related Influencing Factors of Depressive Symptoms for Empty-Nest Elderly Living in the Rural Area of YongZhou, China," *Archives of Gerontology and Geriatrics* 50, 1: 24–9.

Yang, Keming, and Christina R. Victor. 2008. "The Prevalence of and Risk Factors for Loneliness among Older People in China," *Ageing & Society* 28, 3: 305–27.

Young, Claire. 2011. "Pensions, Privatization, and Poverty: The Gendered Impact." *Canadian Journal of Women and the Law* 23, 2: 661–85. *Project MUSE*. Web. 25 Jan. 2013. At: <muse .jhu.edu>.

Chapter 7

Aizer, A. 2010. "The Gender Wage Gap and Domestic Violence," *American Economic Review* 100, 4: 1847–59.

Alaggia, Ramona, Cheryl Regehr, and Giselle Rishchynski. 2009. "Intimate Partner Violence and Immigration Laws in Canada: How Far Have We Come?," *International Journal of Law and Psychiatry* 32, 6: 335–41.

Almén, D., and M. Nordin. 2011. "Long Term Unemployment and Violent Crimes—Using Post-2000 Data to Reinvestigate the Relationship between Unemployment and Crime," Lund University, Department of Economics Working Papers.

Aradau, Claudia, and Rens Van Munster. 2009. "Exceptionalism and the 'War on Terror': Criminology Meets International Relations," *British Journal of Criminology* 49, 5: 686–717.

Arnold, Robert, Carl Keane, and Stephen Baron. 2005. "Assessing Risk of Victimization through Epidemiological Concepts: An Alternative Analytic Strategy Applied to Routine Activities Theory," *Canadian Review of Sociology and Anthropology* 42, 3: 345–64.

AuCoin, Kathy. 2005. "Stalking-Criminal Harassment," *Family Violence in Canada: A Statistical Profile, 2005.* Statistics Canada Catalogue no. 85-224-XIE. At: <www.statcan.gc.ca/pub/85-224-x/ 85-224-x2005000-eng.pdf>.

Baum, K. 2005. "Juvenile Victimization and Offending, 1993–2003" (p. 10).

US Department of Justice, Office of Justice Programs, Bureau of Justice Statistics.

Bourns, W.F. 2000. "Police Gerontology Services for the Elderly: A Policy Guide," *Criminal Justice Studies* 13, 2: 179–92.

Braithwaite, John. 1993. "Crime and the Average American," *Law and Society Review* 27: 215–32.

Brennan, Shannon. 2012. "Police-Reported Crime Statistics in Canada, 2011," *Juristat*. Statistics Canada Catalogue no. 85-002-X. At: <www .statcan.gc.ca/pub/85-002-x/2012001/ article/11692-eng.pdf>.

Brennan, Shannon, and Mia Dauvergne. 2011. "Police-Reported Crime Statistics in Canada, 2010." Statistics Canada. At: <www.statcan.gc.ca/pub/85-002-x/ 2011001/article/11523-eng.htm>.

Britt, Chester L. 2001. "Health Consequences of Criminal Victimization," *International Review of Victimology* 8, 1: 63–73.

Burrow, J.D., and R. Apel. 2008. "Youth Behavior, School Structure, and Student Risk of Victimization," *Justice Quarterly* 25, 2: 349–80.

Bush, Vanessa. 2010. Review of *I Don't Wish Nobody to Have a Life Like Mine: Tales of Kids in Adult Lockup* by David Chura. *Booklist* 106, 11: 8.

Byrne, J.M., and F.S. Taxman. 2006. "Crime Control Strategies and Community Change-Reframing the Surveillance vs. Treatment Debate," *Federal Probation* 70, 3.

Canadian Resource Centre for Victims of Crime. 2005. "Impact of Victimization." At: <www.crcvc.ca/en>.

———. 2006. "Victims' Rights in Canada." At: <www.crcvc.ca/en>.

Chandler, R.K., B.W. Fletcher, and N.D. Volkow. 2009. "Treating Drug Abuse and Addiction in the Criminal Justice System," *Journal of the American Medical Association* 301, 2: 183–90.

Cheloukhine, S. 2008. "The Roots of Russian Organized Crime: From Old-Fashioned Professionals to the Organized Criminal Groups of Today," *Crime Law and Social Change* 50, 4 and 5: 353–74.

Chen, M. Keith, and Jesse M. Shapiro. 2007. "Do Harsher Prison Conditions Reduce Recidivism? A Discontinuity-Based Approach," *American Law and Economics Review* 9, 1: 1–29.

Chiodo, D., D.A. Wolfe, C. Crooks, R. Hughes, and P. Jaffe. 2009. "Impact of Sexual Harassment Victimization by Peers on Subsequent Adolescent Victimization and Adjustment: A Longitudinal Study," *Journal of Adolescent Health* 45, 3: 246–52.

Chubaty, Donna. 2001. "Victimization, Fear, and Coping in Prison," PhD diss., University of Manitoba.

Church, Wesley T. II, Tracy Wharton, and Julie K. Taylor. 2009. "An Examination of Differential Association and Social Control Theory: Family Systems and Delinquency," *Youth Violence and Juvenile Justice* 7, 1: 3–15.

Cole, J.H., and A.M. Gramajo. 2009. "Homicide Rates in a Cross-Section of Countries: Evidence and Interpretations," *Population and Development Review* 35, 4: 749–76.

Dauvergne, Mia. 2012. *Adult Correctional Statistics in Canada, 2010/2011.* Statistics Canada. At: <www.statcan.gc.ca/ pub/85-002-x/2012001/article/11715-eng.htm>.

Davies, P. 2008. "Looking Out a Broken Old Window: Community Safety, Gendered Crimes and Victimizations," *Crime Prevention & Community Safety* 10, 4: 207–25.

Dawson, Jenna. 2009. "The Impact of Organized Crime on the Canadian Economy," *Police Chief* 76, 1: 64.

Department of Justice. 2012. "The Role of the Victim in the Criminal Process: A Literature Review—1989 to 1999." At: <www.justice.gc.ca/eng/pi/rs/ rep-rap/2000/rr00_vic20/p3221 .html>.

Doepke, Matthias, and Michele Tertilt. 2009. "Women's Liberation: What's in It for Men?," *Quarterly Journal of Economics* 124, 4: 1541–91.

Dolan, P., and T. Peasgood. 2006, "Estimating the Economic and Social Costs of the Fear of Crime," *British Journal of Criminology* 47, 1: 121–32.

Durkheim, Émile. 1951 [1897]. *Suicide*, trans. John A. Spaulding and George Simpson. New York: Free Press.

Dutcher, J.S. 2005. "From the Boardroom to the Cellblock: The Justifications for Harsher Punishment of White-Collar and Corporate Crime," *Arizona State Law Journal* 37: 1295–319.

Ericson, Richard. 1982. *Reproducing Order: A Study of Police Patrol Work.* Toronto: University of Toronto Press.

Farrell, G. 2010. "Situational Crime Prevention and Its Discontents: Rational Choice and Harm Reduction versus 'Cultural Criminology,'" *Social Policy and Administration* 44, 1: 40–66.

Friedrichs, D.O. 2009. *Trusted Criminals: White Collar Crime in Contemporary Society*. California: Wadsworth Publishing Company.

Gartner, Rosemary. 1997. "Crime: Variations across Cultures and Nations," in C. Ember and M. Ember, eds, *Cross-Cultural Research for Social Science*. Englewood Cliffs, NJ: Prentice-Hall, 101–19.

Gibson, J., and B. Kim. 2006. "Measurement Error and the Effect of Inequality on Experienced versus Reported Crime," Department of Economics, Working Paper in Economics. Hamilton, NZ: University of Waikato.

Global Research. 2012. At: <www .globalresearch.ca/turnover-of-global-organized-crime-870-billion-a-year/ 31995>.

Green, D.L., and D. Pomeroy. 2007. "Crime Victimization: Assessing Differences between Violent and Nonviolent Experiences," *Victims and Offenders* 2: 63–76.

Griffin, Timothy, and Monica Miller. 2008. "Child Abduction, AMBER Alert, and Crime Control Theater," *Criminal Justice Review* (June): 159–76.

Hayman, Stephanie. 2011. "Older People in Canada: Their Victimization and Fear of Crime," *Canadian Journal on Aging/La Revue Canadienne du Vieillissement* 30, 3: 423–36.

Hirschi, Travis. 1969. *Causes of Delinquency*. Berkeley: University of California Press.

Holcomb, J., and A. Pizam. 2006. "Do Incidents of Theft at Tourist Destinations Have a Negative Effect on Tourists' Decisions to Travel to Affected Destinations?," in Yoel Mansfeld and Abraham Pizam, eds, *Tourism, Security & Safety: From Theory to Practice*. Oxford, UK: Butterworth-Heinemann, 105–24.

Jackson, Jonathan, and Ben Bradford. 2009. "Crime, Policing and Social Order: On the Expressive Nature of Public Confidence in Policing," *British Journal of Sociology* 60, 3: 493–521.

Jenness, Valerie. 1995. "Hate Crimes in the United States: The Transformation of Injured Persons into Victims and the Extension of Victim Status to Multiple Constituencies," in Joel Best, ed., *Images and Issues: Typifying Contemporary Social Problems*. New York: Aldine de Gruyter, 213–37.

Joffee, S. 2009. "Validating Victims: Enforcing Victims' Rights through Mandatory Mandamus," *Utah Law Review* 241: 242–5.

Jones, Jeffrey S., Carmen Alexander, Barbara N. Wynn, Linda Rossman, and Chris Dunnuck. 2009. "Why Women Don't Report Sexual Assault to the Police: The Influence of Psychosocial Variables and Traumatic Injury," *Journal of Emergency Medicine* 36, 4: 417–24.

Kissner, Jason, and David C. Pyrooz. 2009. "Self-Control, Differential Association, and Gang Membership: A Theoretical and Empirical Extension of the Literature," *Journal of Criminal Justice* 37, 5: 478–87.

Kitchen, Peter, and Allison Williams. 2010. "Quality of Life and Perceptions of Crime in Saskatoon, Canada," *Social Indicators Research* 95, 1: 33–61.

Knight, W. Andy, and Tom Keating. 2010. *Global Politics: Emerging Networks, Trends, and Challenges*. Toronto: Oxford University Press.

Kupers, Terry A. 1996. "Trauma and Its Sequelae in Male Prisons: Effects of Confinement, Overcrowding and Diminished Services," *American Journal of Orthopsychiatry* 66: 189–96.

Lauritsen, Janet L., and Karen Heimer. 2008. "The Gender Gap in Violent Victimization, 1973–2004," *Journal of Quantitative Criminology* 24, 2: 125–47.

Leddy, J., and M. O'Connell. 2002. "The Prevalence, Nature and Psychological Correlates of Bullying in Irish Prisons," *Legal and Criminological Psychology* 7, 2: 131–40.

Lee, Matthew R. 2000. "Community Cohesion and Violent Predatory Victimization: A Theoretical Extension and Cross-National Test of Opportunity Theory," *Social Forces* 79: 683–706.

Liem, M., and D.W. Roberts. 2009. "Intimate Partner Homicide by Presence or Absence of a Self-Destructive Act," *Homicide Studies* 13, 4: 339–54.

Lovell, Jarret. 2009. *Crimes of Dissent*. New York: New York University Press.

Lyons, Christopher J. 2008. "Defending Turf: Racial Demographics and Hate Crime against Blacks and Whites," *Social Forces* 87, 1: 357–85.

McKee, Kevin J., and Caroline Milner. 2000. "Health, Fear of Crime and Psychosocial Functioning in Older People," *Journal of Health Psychology* 5, 4: 473–86.

McMullin, D., and J.W. White. 2006. "Long-Term Effects of Labeling a Rape Experience," *Psychology of Women Quarterly* 30: 96–105.

Massoglia, Michael. 2008. "Incarceration as Exposure: The Prison, Infectious Disease, and Other Stress-Related Illnesses," *Journal of Health and Social Behavior* 49, 1: 56–71.

Mechanic, Mindy B., Mary H. Uhlmansiek, Terri L. Weaver, and Patricia A. Resick. 2000. "The Impact of Severe Stalking Experienced by Acutely Battered Women: An Examination of Violence, Psychological Symptoms and Strategic Responding," *Violence and Victims* 15: 443–58.

Merton, Robert K. 1938. "Social Structure and Anomie," *American Sociological Review* 3, 5: 672–82.

Mertus, J. 2007. "The Rejection of Human Rights Framings: The Case of LGBT Advocacy in the US," *Human Rights Quarterly* 29, 4: 1036–64.

Mishra, S., and M. Lalumière. 2009. "Is the Crime Drop of the 1990s in Canada and the USA Associated with a General Decline in Risky and Health-Related Behavior?," *Social Science & Medicine* 68, 1: 39–48.

Moore, Elizabeth, and Michael Mills. 2001. "The Neglected Victims and Unexamined Costs of White-Collar Crime," in Neal Shover and John P. Wright, eds, *Crimes of Privilege: Readings in White-Collar Crime*. New York: Oxford University Press, 51–7.

OECD Better Life Index. 2011. "Safety." At: <www.oecdbetterlifeindex.org/ topics/safety>.

OHRC (Ontario Human Rights Commission)., n.d. At: <www.ohrc.on.ca/en/ what-racial-profiling-fact-sheet>.

Palmer, Emma J., Clive R. Hollin, and Laura S. Caulfield. 2005. "Surveying Fear: Crime, Buses and New Paint," *Crime Prevention and Community Safety* 7, 4: 47–58.

Pepinsky, Harold E., and Paul Jesilow. 1984. *Myths That Cause Crime*. Cabin John, MD: Seven Locks Press.

Perreault, Samuel. 2009. "The Incarceration of Aboriginal People Adult Correctional Services," *Juristat*. Statistics

Canada Catalogue no. 85-002-X. At: <www.statcan.gc.ca/pub/85-002-x/2009003/article/10903-eng.htm>.

Pottinger, Audrey M., and Angela G. Stair. 2009. "Bullying of Students by Teachers and Peers and Its Effect on the Psychological Well-Being of Students in Jamaican Schools," *Journal of School Violence* 8, 4: 312–27.

Rosenfeld, Richard. 2009. "Crime Is the Problem: Homicide, Acquisitive Crime, and Economic Conditions," *Journal of Quantitative Criminology* 25, 3: 287–306.

Ruback, R. Barry, and Martie P. Thompson. 2001. *Social and Psychological Consequences of Violent Victimization.* Thousand Oaks, CA: Sage.

Sanborn, Joseph B., Jr. 2001. "Victims' Rights in Juvenile Court: Has the Pendulum Swung Too Far?," *Judicature* 85, 3: 140–6.

Schnittker, Jason, and Andrea John. 2007. "Enduring Stigma: The Long-Term Effects of Incarceration on Health," *Journal of Health and Social Behavior* 48, 2: 115–30.

Shapland, J., and M. Hall. 2007. "What Do We Know about the Effects of Crime on Victims?," *International Review of Victimology* 14, 2: 175–217.

Sheridan, Lorraine, and Karl Roberts. 2011. "Key Questions to Consider in Stalking Cases," *Behavioural Sciences and the Law* 29: 255–70.

Shichor, D. 2012. "The Late Trading and Market-Timing Scandal of Mutual Funds," *Crime, Law and Social Change* 57, 1: 15–32.

Silvestri, A., M. Oldfield, P. Squires, and R. Grimshaw. 2009. *Young People, Knives and Guns: A Comprehensive Review, Analysis and Critique of Gun and Knife Crime Strategies.* London: Centre for Crime and Justice Studies.

Statistics Canada. 2005. "Adult Correctional Services in Canada, 2003/04," *Juristat* 25, 8: 14. At: <www.statcan.gc.ca/pub/85-002-x/85-002-x2005008-eng.pdf>.

———. 2008. *Police Resources in Canada, 2008*, 12 Dec. At: <dsp-psd.pwgsc.gc.ca/collection_2008/statcan/85-225-X/85-225-x2008000-eng.pdf>.

———. 2011a. "Police-Reported Crime Statistics in Canada, 2011." At: <www.statcan.gc.ca/pub/85-002-x/2012001/article/11692-eng.htm#a6>.

———. 2011b. *Police Resources in Canada, 2011*. At: <www.statcan.gc.ca/pub/85-225-x/2011000/part-partie1-eng.htm>.

Stogner, J., and C.L Gibson. 2010. "Healthy, Wealthy, and Wise: Incorporating Health Issues as a Source of Strain in Agnew's General Strain Theory," *Journal of Criminal Justice* 38, 6: 1150–9.

Straus, M.A. 2011. "Gender Symmetry and Mutuality in Perpetration of Clinical-Level Partner Violence: Empirical Evidence and Implications for Prevention and Treatment," *Aggression and Violent Behavior* 16, 4: 279–88.

Sung, H.E. 2006. "Police Effectiveness and Democracy: Shape and Direction of the Relationship," *Policing: An International Journal of Police Strategies and Management* 29, 2: 347–67.

Sutherland, Edwin H. 1949. *White Collar Crime.* New York: Dryden Press.

Tiby, E. 2001. "Victimization and Fear among Lesbians and Gay Men in Stockholm," *International Review of Victimology* 8, 2: 217–43.

Turner, Heather A., David Finkelhor, and Richard Ormrod. 2010. "The Effects of Adolescent Victimization on Self-Concept and Depressive Symptoms," *Child Maltreatment* 15, 1: 76–90.

US National Research Council. 1994. *Violence in Urban America: Mobilizing a Response.* Washington: National Academy Press.

Vaughn, Michael S., and Linda G. Smith. 1999. "Practicing Penal Harm Medicine in the United States: Prisoners' Voices from Jail," *Justice Quarterly* 16, 1: 175–231.

Vollaard, B., and P. Koning. 2009. "The Effect of Police on Crime, Disorder and Victim Precaution: Evidence from a Dutch Victimization Survey," *International Review of Law and Economics* 29, 4: 336–48.

Whaley, R.B., and S. Messner. 2002. "Gender Equality and Gendered Homicide," *Homicide Studies* 6, 3: 188–210.

White, Jacqueline, Robin M. Kowalski, Amy Lyndon, and Sherri Valentine. 2000. "An Integrative Contextual Developmental Model of Male Stalking," *Violence and Victims* 15: 373–88.

Whyte, William Foote. 1981 [1943]. *Street Corner Society: Social Structure of an Italian Slum*, 3rd edn. Chicago: University of Chicago Press.

Wilkinson, R.G., I. Kawachi, and B.P. Kennedy. 2008. "Mortality, the Social Environment, Crime and Violence," *Sociology of Health & Illness* 20, 5: 578–97.

Wortley, Scot, and Akwasi Owusu-Bempah. 2011. "The Usual Suspects: Police Stop and Search Practices," in *Canada, Policing and Society* 21, 4: 395–407.

Wortley, Scot, and Julian Tanner. n.d. "Discrimination or 'Good' Policing: The Racial Profiling Debate in Canada," in *Our Diverse Cities*. York University, p. 200. At: <www.yorku.ca/lfoster/2013-14/RESP%204052/lectures/Discrimination%20or%20Good%20Policing_WortleyTanner.pdf>.

———. 2004. "Racial Profiling in Canada: Survey Evidence from Toronto," *Canadian Review of Policing Research* 1, 1: 24–36.

Wu, D., and Z. Wu. 2012. "Crime, Inequality and Unemployment in England and Wales," *Applied Economics* 44, 29: 3765–75.

Xu, J. 2010. "Motorcycle Taxi Drivers and Motorcycle Ban Policy in the Pearl River Delta," PhD diss., University of Hong Kong.

Chapter 8

Adlaf, Edward M., Patricia Begin, and Ed Sawka, eds. 2005a. *Canadian Addiction Survey (CAS): A National Survey of Canadians' Use of Alcohol and Other Drugs: Prevalence of Use and Related Harms: Detailed Report.* Ottawa: Canadian Centre on Substance Abuse.

Adlaf, Edward M., Andrée Demers, and Louis Gliksman, eds. 2005b. *Canadian Campus Survey 2004.* Toronto: Centre for Addiction and Mental Health.

Afifi, T.O., B.J. Cox, P.J. Martens, J. Sareen, and M.W. Enns. 2010. "The Relation between Types and Frequency of Gambling Activities and Problem Gambling among Women in Canada," *Canadian Journal of Psychiatry* 55, 1: 21–8.

Arnaud, Sophie, André Jeannin, and Françoise Dubois-Arber. 2011. "Estimating National-Level Syringe Availability to Injecting Drug Users and Injection Coverage: Switzerland," *International Journal of Drug Policy* 22, 3: 226–32.

Baer, J.S. 2005. "Student Factors: Understanding Individual Variation in College Drinking," *College Drinking—Changing the Culture*. At: <www.collegedrinkingprevention.gov/supportingresearch/journal/baer.aspx>.

Bailey, Sue. 2013. "Innu Kids as Young as Seven Sniff Gas: RCMP," The Canadian Press, last modified 20 Sept. At: <news.ca.msn.com/canada/cp-article.aspx?cp-documentid=253846812>.

Becker, Howard. 1963. *Outsiders: Studies in the Sociology of Deviance*. New York: Free Press.

Becker, J.B., and M. Hu. 2008. "Sex Differences in Drug Abuse," *Neuroendocrinology* 29: 36–47. At: <journals1.scholarsportal.info.myaccess.library.utoronto.ca/tmp/6135628597542678714.pdf>.

Beeby, Dean. 2013. At: <www.marijuanalaws.ca/canada-industry-business.html>.

Bener, Abdulbari, and Dinesh Bhugra. 2013. "Lifestyle and Depressive Risk Factors Associated with Problematic Internet Use in Adolescents in an Arabian Gulf Culture," *Journal of Addiction Medicine* 7, 4: 236–42.

Bensley, L.S., S.J. Spieker, J. Van Eenwyk, and J. Schoder. 1999. "Self-Reported Abuse History and Adolescent Problem Behaviours. II. Alcohol and Drug Use," *Journal of Adolescent Health* 24, 3: 174–80.

Borras, Laurence, Khazaal Yasser, Riaz Khan, Sylvia Mohr, Yves-Alexandre Kaufmann, Daniele Zullino, Philippe Huguelet, Allaman Allamani, Manuella Adrian, Theodore Godlaski, Bourgois Phillippe, Laurie Kain Hart, Stephen Magura, Michael Montagne, and Zili Sloboda. 2010. "The Relationship between Addiction and Religion and Its Possible Implication for Care," *Substance Use and Misuse* 45, 14: 2357–410.

Canadian Press, The. 2012. "RCMP Warn of Violence, Injury as Gas-Sniffing Escalates in Natuashish," *CTV News*. Last modified 20 Sept. At: <www.ctvnews.ca/canada/rcmp-warn-of-violence-injury-as-gas-sniffing-escalates-in-natuashish-1.965020>.

Carey, K.B., and K.S. DeMartini. 2010. "The Motivational Context for Mandated Alcohol Interventions for College Students by Gender and Family History," *Addictive Behaviors* 35, 3: 218–23.

Carruthers, Cynthia. 1993. "Leisure and Alcohol Expectancies," *Journal of Leisure Research* 25, 3: 229–44.

Chan, K.Y., M.A. Stoove, and D.D. Reidpath. 2008. "Stigma, Social Reciprocity and Exclusion of HIV/AIDS Patients with Illicit Drug Histories: A Study of Thai Nurses' Attitudes," *Harm Reduction Journal* 5, 28. At: <www.harmreductionjournal.com/content/5/1/28>.

Cheung, J.T.W., et al. 2010. "Anxiety and Mood Disorders and Cannabis Use," *American Journal of Drug and Alcohol Abuse* 36: 118–22.

Clancy, N. 2004 "Sheshatshiu: An Innu Community's Battle with Addiction," *CBC News*. At: <www.cbc.ca/news2/background/aboriginals/sheshatshiu.html>.

Coker, Donna. 2003. "Foreword: Addressing the Real World of Racial Injustice in the Criminal Justice System," *Journal of Criminal Law and Criminology* 93, 4: 827–79.

Criminal Intelligence Service Canada. 2006. *CISC Annual Report on Organized Crime in Canada*. At: <www.cisc.gc.ca>.

Currie, Cheryl, Cameron Wild, Donald Schopflocher, Lory Laing, and Paul Veugelers. 2013. "Illicit and Prescription Drug Problems among Urban Aboriginal Adults in Canada: The Role of Traditional Culture in Protection and Resilience," *Social Science & Medicine* 88: 1–9.

Dauvergne, M. 2009. "Trends in Police-Reported Drug Offences in Canada," *Juristat: Canadian Centre for Justice Statistics* 29, 2. At: <www.statcan.gc.ca/pub/85-002-x/2009002/article/10847-eng.pdf>.

DeBeck, K., Thomas Kerr, Kathy Li, Benedikt Fischer, Jane Buxton, Julio Montaner, and Evan Wood. 2009. "Smoking of Crack Cocaine as a Risk Factor for HIV Infection among People Who Use Injection Drugs," *CMAJ: Canadian Medical Association Journal* 181, 9: 585–90.

DeBeck, K., W. Small, E. Wood, K. Li, J. Montaner, and T. Kerr. 2009. "Public Injecting among a Cohort of Injecting Drug Users in Vancouver, Canada," *Journal of Epidemiology and Community Health* 63, 1: 81–6.

Delfabbro, Paul. 2012. "Australian Gambling Review (1992–2011)," *Independent Gambling of South Australia*. At: <www.iga.sa.gov.au/pdf/agr-2011-5.pdf>.

Derevensky, Jeffrey L., and Rina Gupta. 2004. *Gambling Problems in Youths: Theoretical and Applied Perspectives*. New York: Kluwer Academic/Plenum.

Di Nicola, Marco, Daniela Tedeschi, Marianna Mazza, Giovanni Martinotti, Desiree Harnic, Valeria Catalano, Angelo Bruschi, Gino Pozzi, Pietro Bria, and Luigi Janiri. 2010. "Behavioural Addictions in Bipolar Disorder Patients: Role of Impulsivity and Personality Dimensions," *Journal of Affective Disorders* 125, 1–3: 82–8.

Duster, Troy. 1997. "Pattern, Purpose, and Race in the Drug War: The Crisis of Credibility in Criminal Justice," in Reinarman and Levine (1997: 260–87).

Ellickson, Phyllis L., Rebecca L. Collins, and Robert M. Bell. 1999. "Adolescent Use of Illicit Drugs Other Than Marijuana: How Important Is Social Bonding and for Which Ethnic Groups?," *Substance Use and Misuse* 34: 317–46.

Erceg-Hurn, David M. 2008. "Drugs, Money, and Graphic Ads: A Critical Analysis of the Montana Meth Project," *Prevention Science* 9, 4: 256–63.

Erickson, Patricia G. 1998. "Neglected and Rejected: A Case Study of the Impact of Social Research on Canadian Drug Policy," *Canadian Journal of Sociology* 23: 263–80.

Escobar-Chaves, Soledad Liliana, and Craig A. Anderson. 2008. "Media and Risky Behaviors," *Future of Children* 18, 1: 147–80.

Evans, Elizabeth, Suzanne E. Spear, Yu-Chang Huang, and Yih-Ing Hser. 2006. "Outcomes of Drug and Alcohol Treatment Programs among American Indians in California," *American Journal of Public Health* 96, 5: 889–96.

French, L.A. 2008. "Psychoactive Agents and Native American Spirituality: Past and Present," *Contemporary Justice Review* 11, 2: 155–63.

Galvani, S., and N. Hughes. 2010. "Working with Alcohol and Drug Use: Exploring the Knowledge and Attitudes of Social Work Students," *British Journal of Social Work* 40: 946–62. At: <journals1.scholarsportal.info.myaccess.library.utoronto.ca/tmp/15810142923303949939.pdf>.

Gordon, T. 2006. "Neoliberalism, Racism, and the War on Drugs in Canada," *Social Justice* 33, 1: 59–78. At: <www.jstor.org.myaccess.library.utoronto.ca/stable/29768352>.

Government of Canada. 2013. "National Anti-Drug Strategy." Last modified 30 May 30. At: <www.nationalantidrugstrategy.gc.ca/nads-sna.html>.

Griesbach, Dawn, Amanda Amos, and Candace Currie. 2003. "Adolescent Smoking and Family Structure in Europe," *Social Science and Medicine* 56: 41–52.

Griffiths, Mark. 2009. *Gambling: An Addiction?* At: <www.bps.org.uk/downloadfile.cfm?file_uuid=C2B84867-E9C0-9B94-26FE-A6A958F4AF4F&ext=pdf>.

Grinman, M.N., S. Chiu, D.A. Redelmeier, W. Levinson, A. Kiss, G. Tolomiczenko, L. Cowan, and S.W. Hwang. 2010. "Drug Problems among Homeless Individuals in Toronto, Canada: Prevalence, Drugs of Choice, and Relation to Health Status," *BMC Public Health* 10, 94. At: <www.biomedcentral.com.myaccess.library.utoronto.ca/1471-2458/10/94>.

Haans, Dave. N.d. "The Effects of Decriminalization of Marijuana." At: <www.chass.utoronto.ca/~haans/misc/mjdcrim.html>.

Hall, W., and R.L. Pacula. 2003. *Cannabis Use and Dependence: Public Health and Public Policy.* Cambridge: Cambridge University Press.

Hathaway, A.D., R.C. Callaghan, S. MacDonald, and P.G. Erickson. 2009. "Cannabis Dependence as a Primary Drug Use–Related Problem: The Case for Harm Reduction-Oriented Treatment Options," *Substance Use and Misuse* 44, 7: 990–1008.

Hathaway, Andrew, and Patricia Erickson. 2003. "Drug Reform Principles and Policy Debates: Harm Reduction Prospects for Cannabis in Canada," *Journal of Drug Issues* 33, 2: 465.

Health Canada. 2008. "Chapter 6: Changes in the Use of Alcohol, Cannabis and Other Illicit Drugs Over Time (continued)," *Health Canada.* Last modified 3 July. At: <www.hc-sc.gc.ca/hc-ps/pubs/adp-apd/cas_gender-etc_sexe/chap6_tbl1-eng.php>.

———. 2012a. "Canadian and Drug Use Monitoring Survey: Summary Results for 2011," *Health Canada.*

Last modified 3 July. At: <www.hc-sc.gc.ca/hc-ps/drugs-drogues/stat/_2011/summary-sommaire-eng.php#a5>.

———. 2012b. "Fetal Alcohol/Fetal Alcohol Effects," *Health Canada.* At:<www.hc-sc.gc.ca/fniah-spnia/famil/preg-gros/intro-eng.php>.

Heinz, Adrienne, Johnny Wu, Katie Witkiewitz, David Epstein, and Kenzie Preston. 2009. "Marriage and Relationship Closeness as Predictors of Cocaine and Heroin Use," *Addictive Behaviours* 34, 3: 258–63.

Herd, Denise. "Prohibition, Racism and Class Politics in the Post-reconstruction South," *Journal of Drug Issues* 13 (1984): 77–94.

Herzog, Benno, Esperanza Gomez-Guardeno, Rafael Aleixandre-Benavent, and Juan C. Valderrama-Zurian. 2009. "Discourses on Drugs and Immigration: The Social Construction of a Problem," *Forum Qualitative Sozialforschung/Forum: Qualitative Social Research* 10, 1.

Hodgins, David C., JianLi Wang, Nady el-Guebaly, Harold Wynne, and Natalie V. Miller. 2008. "Replication of Low-Risk Gambling Limits Using Canadian Provincial Gambling Prevalence Data," *Journal of Gambling Studies* 24, 3: 321–35.

Hogan, Sean R. 2009. "The Social Construction of Drug Policy and Its Impact on Substance Abuse Treatment Philosophies in the United States," in A. Browne-Miller, ed., *The Praeger International Collection on Addictions,* vol. 3: *Characteristics and Treatment Perspectives.* Santa Barbara, CA: Praeger/ABC-CLIO, 3–21.

Hughes, C.E., and A. Stevens. 2010. "What Can We Learn from the Portuguese Decriminalization of Illicit Drugs?," *British Journal of Criminology* 50, 6: 999–1022. At: <bjc.oxfordjournals.org/content/50/6/999.short>.

Janz, T. 2012. "Percentage of Current and Daily Smokers," *Statistics Canada.* At: <www.statcan.gc.ca/pub/82-624-x/2012001/article/11676-eng.htm>.

Johnston, M., A. Shrivastava, and M. Tsuang. 2011. "Cannabis Use and Cognitive Dysfunction," *Indian Journal of Psychiatry* 53, 3: 187. At: <go.galegroup.com.myaccess.library.utoronto.ca/ps/i.do?action=interpret&id=GALE%7CA272571184&v=2.1&u=

utoronto_main&it=r&p=HRCA&sw=w&authCount=1>.

Johnston, M., T. Williamson, E. Wheaton, V. Wittrock, H. Nelson, L. Vandamme, H. Hesseln, J. Pittman, and M. Lebel. 2008. *Climate Change Adaptive Capacity of Forestry Stakeholders in the Boreal Plains Ecozone.* Final Report submitted to Natural Resources Canada Climate Change Impacts and Adaptations Program. Ottawa: Natural Resources Canada.

Kanato, M. 2008. "Drug Use and Health among Prison Inmates," *Current Opinion in Psychiatry* 21, 3: 252–4.

Karp, Igor, Jennifer O'Loughlin, Gilles Paradis, James Hanley, and Joseph Difranza. 2005. "Smoking Trajectories of Adolescent Novice Smokers in a Longitudinal Study of Tobacco Use," *Annals of Epidemiology* 15, 6: 445–52.

Kunitz, Stephen J. 2008. "Risk Factors for Polydrug Use in a Native American Population," *Substance Use and Misuse* 43, 3 and 4: 331–9.

Kuntsche, Emmanuel, Ronald Knibbe, Rutger Engels, and Gerhard Gmel. 2010. "Being Drunk to Have Fun or to Forget Problems? Identifying Enhancement and Coping Drinkers among Risky Drinking Adolescents," *European Journal of Psychological Assessment* 26, 1: 46–54.

Kuo, Feng-Yang, Chiung-Wen Hsu, and Rong-Fuh Day. 2009. "An Exploratory Study of Cognitive Effort Involved in Decision under Framing—An Application of the Eye-Tracking Technology," *Decision Support Systems* 48, 1: 81.

Kuss, Daria J., Antonius J. van Rooij, Gillian W. Shorter, Mark D. Griffiths, and Dike van de Mheen. 2013. "Internet Addiction in Adolescents: Prevalence and Risk Factors," *Computers in Human Behavior* 29, 5: 1987–96.

Leatherdale, S.T., P.W. McDonald, R. Cameron, and K.S. Brown. 2005. "A Multilevel Analysis Examining the Relationship between Social Influences for Smoking and Smoking Onset," *American Journal of Health Behavior* 29, 6: 520–30.

Leonard, K.E., and G.G. Homish. 2005. "Changes in Marijuana Use over the Transition into Marriage," *Journal of Drug Issues* 35, 2: 409–29.

Liu, X., and H.B. Kaplan. 1999. "Explaining the Gender Difference in Adolescent Delinquent Behavior: A

Longitudinal Test of Mediating Mechanisms," *Criminology* 37, 1: 195–216.

Livingston, M. 2008. "Alcohol Outlet Density and Assault: A Spatial Analysis," *Addiction* 103, 4: 619–28.

Livosa, Ekaterina. 2010. "Adolescent Drug Addiction: The Essence of the Problem and How It Is Manifested," *Anthropology & Archeology of Eurasia* 48, 3: 91–7.

Lozgacheva, Evgeniia A. 2008. "Gambling Dependency: Features and Social Consequences," *Monitoring Obshchestvennogo Mneniia* 3, 87: 126–32.

McBride, Andrew J., Richard Pates, and Morfydd Keen. 1998. "Drug Trends in Wales," *Journal of Drug Issues* 28, 1: 107–25.

McClure, A.C., S. Dal Cin, and J.D. Sargent. 2006. "Ownership of Alcohol-Branded Merchandise and Initiation of Teen Drinking," *American Journal of Preventive Medicine* 30, 4: 277–83.

McComb, Jennifer L., Bonnie K. Lee, and Douglas H. Sprenkle. 2009. "Conceptualizing and Treating Problem Gambling as a Family Issue," *Journal of Marital and Family Therapy* 35, 4: 415–31.

McComb, Jennifer, and Catherine Sabiston. 2010. "Family Influences on Adolescent Gambling Behaviour: A Review of Literature," *Journal of Gambling Studies* 26, 4: 503–20.

McCormick, R.M. 2000. "Aboriginal Traditions in the Treatment of Substance Abuse," *Canadian Journal of Counselling* 34, 1: 25–32.

Markowitz, S. 2005. "Alcohol, Drugs and Violent Crime," *International Review of Law and Economics* 25: 20–44.

Martin, K.J., N. McCarthy, R.D. Conger, F.X. Gibbons, R.L. Simons, C.E. Cutrona, and G.H. Brody. 2011. "The Enduring Significance of Racism: Discrimination and Delinquency among Black American Youth," *Authors Journal of Research on Adolescence* 21, 3: 662–76.

Mateu-Gelabert, P., C. Maslow, P.L. Flom, M. Sandoval, M. Bolyard, and S.R. Friedman. 2005. "Keeping It Together: Stigma, Response, and Perception of Risk in Relationships between Drug Injectors and Crack Smokers, and Other Community Residents," *AIDS Care* 17, 7: 802–13.

Mehrabadi, Azar, K.J.P. Craib, K. Patterson, W. Adam, A. Moniruzzaman, B. Ward-Burkitte, M. T. Schechter, and P.M. Spittal. 2008. "The Cedar Project: A Comparison of HIV-Related Vulnerabilities amongst Young Aboriginal Women Surviving Drug Use and Sex Work in Two Canadian Cities," *International Journal of Drug Policy* 19, 2: 159–69.

Merton, Robert K. 1957. "Social Structure and Anomie," in Merton, *Social Theory and Social Structure*, rev. edn. New York: Free Press.

Moodie, Crawford, and Gerard Hastings. 2009. "Social Marketing and Problem Gambling: A Critical Perspective," *Addiction* 104, 5: 692–3.

Moon, Dreama G., Michael L. Hecht, Kristina M. Jackson, and Regina E. Spellers. 1999. "Ethnic and Gender Differences and Similarities in Adolescent Drug Use and Refusals of Drug Offers," *Substance Use and Misuse* 34: 1059–183.

Moreno, Amira Y., and Kim D. Janda. 2009. "Immunopharmacotherapy: Vaccination Strategies as a Treatment for Drug Abuse and Dependence," *Pharmacology, Biochemistry and Behavior* 92, 2: 199–205.

Mulia, Nina, Yu Ye, Sarah E. Zemore, and Thomas K. Greenfield. 2008. "Social Disadvantage, Stress, and Alcohol Use among Black, Hispanic, and White Americans: Findings from the 2005 U.S. National Alcohol Survey," *Journal of Studies on Alcohol and Drugs* 69, 6: 824–33.

Munro, Alice, and Julain Allan. 2011. "Can Family-Focused Interventions Improve Problematic Substance Use in Aboriginal Communities? A Role for Social Work," *Australian Social Work* 64, 2: 169–82.

Murphy, Jennifer. 2009. "Therapy and Punishment: Negotiating Authority in the Management of Drug Addiction." ProQuest Information & Learning, US.

Murray, Robert P., Suzanne L. Tyas, Wanda Snow, Okechukwu Ekuma, Ruth Bond, and Gordon E. Barnes. 2010. "Exploring the Boundary between Health Protective and Hazardous Drinking in a Community Cohort," *Addictive Behaviors* 35, 3: 278–81.

National Institute on Alcohol Abuse and Alcoholism. 2004. *Alcohol Alert: Alcohol's Damaging Effects on the Brain*. NIAA.

At: <pubs.niaaa.nih.gov/publications/aa63/aa63.htm>.

Oldham, G.R., and B.I. Gordon. 1999. "Job Complexity and Employee Substance Use: The Moderating Effects of Cognitive Ability," *Journal of Health Society Behavior* 40: 290–306.

OSDUHS. 2011. "Drug Use among Ontario Students, 1977–2011." CAMH Research Document Series, no. 32.

Park, Soo Kyung, Jin-Yeong Kim, and Choon Bum Cho. 2008. "Prevalence of Internet Addiction and Correlations with Family Factors among South Korean Adolescents," *Adolescence* 43, 172: 895–909.

Pascual-Leone, Antonio, Kevin Gomes, Emily Orr, Kristen Kaploun, and Christopher Abeare. 2011. "Affective and Cognitive Correlates of Gambling Behaviour in University Students," *Journal of Gambling Studies* 27, 3: 401–8.

Provine, Doris. 2011. "Race and Inequality in the War on Drugs," *Annual Review of Law and Social Science* 7: 41–60.

Public Health Agency of Canada. 2012. "Summary: Estimates of HIV Prevalence and Incidence in Canada, 2011," *Public Health Agency of Canada*.

Reinarman, Craig. 2005. "Addiction as Accomplishment: The Discursive Construction of Disease" 13, 4: 307–20.

Reinarman, Craig, and Harry G. Levine, eds. 1997. *Crack in America: Demon Drugs and Social Justice*. Berkeley: University of California Press.

SAMHSA. 2010. "2010 National Survey on Drug Use & Health—Full Report," *SAMHSA*.

Schieman, Scott, Melissa Milkie, and Paul Glavin. 2009. "When Work Interferes with Life: Work-Nonwork Interference and the Influence of Work Related Demands and Resources," *American Sociological Review* 74, 6: 966–88.

Schierenbeck, I. 2010. "Medicalization of Sickness Absence," *Work* 37, 3: 241–50.

Senate Special Committee on Illegal Drugs. 2002. *Report*. At: <www.parl.gc.ca/common/committee_senrep.asp?language= e&parl=37&Ses=1&comm_id=85>.

Shaw, Martha, and Donald W. Black. "Internet addiction," *CNS Drugs* 22, 5: 353–65.

Shield, K., M. Rylett, Gs Gmel, G. Gmel, T. Kehoe-Chan, and J. Rehm. 2013. "Global Alcohol Exposure Estimates by Country, Territory and Region for 2005: A Contribution to the Comparative Risk Assessment for the 2010 Global Burden of Disease Study," *Addiction*, published online 4 March 2013. At: <www.ncbi.nlm.nih.gov/pubmed/23347092>.

Spillane, Nichea S. 2008. "A Test of an Integrative Theory of Reservation-Dwelling American Indian Alcohol Use Risk." ProQuest Information & Learning, US.

Statistics Canada. 2006. "Canadian Cancer Statistics 2006. At: <publications.gc.ca/site/archivee-archived.html?url=http://publications.gc.ca/collections/Collection/CS2-37-2006E.pdf>.

———. 2012. "Canadian Community Health Survey, 2011." Last modified 19 June. <www.statcan.gc.ca/daily-quotidien/120619/dq120619b-eng.htm>.

Stavropoulos, Vasilis, Kiriaki Alexandraki, and Frosso Motti-Stefanidi. 2013. "Recognizing Internet Addiction: Prevalence and Relationship to Academic Achievement in Adolescents Enrolled in Urban and Rural Greek High Schools," *Journal of Adolescence* 36, 3: 565–76.

Suissa, Amnon J. 2007. "Addiction and Medicalization: Signs and Psychosocial Issues," *Nouvelles Pratiques Sociales* 19, 2: 92–110.

Svetlana, P., R. Jurgen, and P. Jayadeep. 2006. "Illegal Drug-Attributable Mortality and Potential Years of Life Lost in Canada 2002: Implications for Prevention and Policy," *Contemporary Drug Problems* 33, 3: 343–66.

Tamburri, R. 2012. "Heavy Drinking a Problem at Most Canadian Campuses: Report," *University Affairs: Affaires universitaires*. At: <www.universityaffairs.ca/heavy-drinking-a-problem-at-most-canadian-campuses-report.aspx>.

Valentine, Leanne. 2009. "Exposure to Gambling-Related Media and Its Relation to Gambling Expectancies and Behaviors." ProQuest Information & Learning, US.

Valverde, Mariana. 1998. *Diseases of the Will: Alcohol and the Dilemmas of Freedom*. Cambridge: Cambridge University Press.

Vaughan, Ellen L., William R. Corbin, and Kim Fromme. 2009. "Academic and Social Motives and Drinking Behavior," *Psychology of Addictive Behaviors* 23, 4: 564–76.

Wagner, David. 1995. "Historicizing Social Constructionist Perspectives: The Example of Temperance Movements," paper presented at the annual meeting of the Society for the Study of Social Problems.

Warden, Narelle L., James G. Phillips, and James R.P. Ogloff. 2004. "Internet Addiction," *Psychiatry, Psychology and Law* 11, 2: 280–95.

Warner, Jessica, Robin Room, and Edward M. Adlaf. 1999. "Rules and Limits in the Use of Marijuana among High-School Students: The Results of a Qualitative Study in Ontario," *Journal of Youth Studies* 2: 59–76.

Warner, Jessica, Timothy R. Weber, and Ricardo Albanes. 1999. "'Girls Are Retarded When They're Stoned': Marijuana and the Construction of Gender Roles among Adolescent Females," *Sex Roles* 40: 25–43.

Westphal, James. 2007. "Emerging Conceptual Models of Excessive Behaviors," *International Journal of Mental Health and Addiction* 5, 2: 107–16.

White, H.R., and E.W. Labouvie. 1994. "Generality vs. Specificity of Problem Behavior: Psychological and Functional Differences," *Journal of Drug Issues* 24, 1: 55–74.

Williams, Robert, Rachel Volberg, and Rhys Stevens. 2012. "The Population Prevalence of Problem Gambling: Methodological Influences, Standardized Rates, Jurisdictional Differences, and Worldwide Trends," *Ontario Problem Gambling Research Center & The Ontario Ministry of Health and Long Term Care*. Last modified 8 May. At: <www.uleth.ca/dspace/bitstream/handle/10133/3068/2012-PREVALENCE-OPGRC%20(2).pdf?sequence=3>.

Witters, Weldon, Peter Venturelli, and Glen Hanson. 1992. *Drugs and Society*, 3rd edn. Boston: Jones and Bartlett.

Yarnold, Barbara. 1999. "Cocaine Use among Miami's Public School Students, 1992: Religion versus Peers and Availability," *Journal of Health and Social Policy* 11, 2: 69–84.

Zhang, Lixuan, Clinton Amos, and William C. McDowell. 2008. "A Comparative Study of Internet Addiction between the United States and China," *CyberPsychology and Behavior* 11, 6: 727–9.

Chapter 9

Alborz, A., R. McNally, and C. Glendinning. 2005. "Access to Healthcare for People with Learning Disabilities: Mapping the Issues and Reviewing the Evidence," *Journal of Health Services Research Policy* 10, 3: 173–82.

Altman, Lawrence. 1981. "Rare Cancer Seen in 41 Homosexuals," *New York Times*, 3 July.

American Psychiatric Association. 1994. *Diagnostic and Statistical Manual of Mental Disorders*, 4th edn. Washington: American Psychiatric Association.

Aronowitz, Robert. 2008. "Framing Disease: An Underappreciated Mechanism for the Social Patterning of Health," *Social Science and Medicine* 67, 1: 1–9.

Avery, A.M., R.E. Hellman, and L.K. Sudderth. 2001. "Satisfaction with Mental Health Services among Sexual Minorities with Major Mental Illness," *American Journal of Public Health* 91: 990–2.

Barlow, G.L. 2002. "Auditing Hospital Queuing," *Managerial Auditing Journal* 17: 397–403.

Bartholomew, Sharon, and Rob Liston. 2006. "Maternal Mortality: An Important Priority," *Canadian Medical Association Journal* 174, 10: 1447. At: <www.ncbi.nlm.nih.gov/pmc/articles/PMC1455436>.

Bauer, G.R., R. Hammond, R. Travers, M. Kaay, K.M. Hohenadel, and M. Boyce. 2009. "'I don't think this is theoretical; this is our lives': How Erasure Impacts Health Care for Transgender People," *Journal of the Association of Nurses in AIDS Care* 20: 348–61.

Becker, Howard. *Outsiders: Studies in the Sociology of Deviance*. New York: The Free Press, 1963.

Begum, Rashida, and O. Desai. 2010. "A Comparative Study to Evaluate Psychological Status of Mothers of Children with Cerebral Palsy and Mothers of Normal Children," *Indian Journal of Occupational Therapy* 42, 2: 3–9.

Bercovitz, K.L. 2000. "A Critical Analysis of Canada's 'Active Living': Science or Politics?," *Critical Public Health* 10, 1: 19–39.

Bern-Klug, Mercedes. 2009. "A Framework for Categorizing Social Interactions Related to End-of-Life Care in Nursing Homes," *The Gerontologist* 49, 4: 495–507.

Bockting, W., G. Knudson, and J. Goldberg. 2006. *Counselling and Mental Health Care of Transgender Adults and Loved Ones*. Vancouver: Vancouver Coastal Health—Transgender Health Program.

Caballero, Benjamin. 2001. "Symposium: Obesity in Developing Countries: Biological and Ecological Factors (Introduction)," *Journal of Nutrition* 131 (suppl.): 866S–70S.

Cameron, Adrian J., Timothy A. Welborn, Paul Z. Zimmet, David W. Dunstan, Neville Owen, et al. 2003. "Overweight and Obesity in Australia: The 1999–2000 Australian Diabetes, Obesity and Lifestyle Study (AusDiab)," *Medical Journal of Australia* 187, 9: 427–32.

Canadian Centre on Substance abuse. 2009. *Substance Abuse in Canada: Concurrent Disorders*. Ottawa: Canadian Centre on Substance Abuse.

Canadian Encyclopedia, The. 2013. At: <www.thecanadianencyclopedia.ca/en/article/foreign-aid>.

Canadian Institute for Health Information. See CIHI.

Center for Disease Control (CDC). 2012. "Monitoring Selected National HIV Prevention and Care Objectives by Using HIV Surveillance Data—United States and 6 U.S. Dependent Areas—2010," *HIV Surveillance Supplemental Report* 17, 3.

CIA (Central Intelligence Agency). 2012. "Country Comparison: Life Expectancy at Birth." At: <www.cia.gov/library/publications/the-world-factbook/rankorder/2102rank.html>, n.d. 20 Dec. 2012.

CIHI (Canadian Institute for Health Information). 2010. "Canada's Health Care Spending Growth Slows: Provincial and Territorial Government Health Expenditure Expected to Grow 3.1%, Lowest Since 1997." At: <www.cihi.ca/cihi-ext-portal/internet/en/document/spending+and+health+workforce/spending/release_30oct12>.

CIHI and PHAC. 2011. *Obesity in Canada: A Joint Report from the Public Health Agency of Canada and the Canadian Institute for Health Information*. Ottawa.

Clarke, Alan. 2001. *The Sociology of Healthcare*. Essex, UK: Prentice-Hall.

Conference Board of Canada. 2003. *The Economic Impact of SARS*. Ottawa: Canadian Tourism Research Institute, Conference Board of Canada. At: <www.conferenceboard.ca/e-library/abstract.aspx?did=539>.

Conner-Spady, B., A. Estey, G. Arnett, K. Ness, J. McGurran, R. Bear, T. Noseworthy, and Steering Committee of the Western Canada Waiting List Project. 2005. "Determinants of Patient and Surgeon Perspectives on Maximum Acceptable Waiting Times for Hip and Knee Arthroplasty," *Journal of Health Services Research and Policy* 10, 2: 84–90.

Contandriopoulos, Damien, and Henriette Bilodeau. 2009. "The Political Use of Poll Results about Public Support for a Privatized Healthcare System in Canada," *Health Policy* 90, 1: 104–12.

Currie, Janet, and Mark Stabile. 2003. "Socioeconomic Status and Child Health: Why Is the Relationship Stronger for Older Children?," *American Economic Review* 93, 5.

Cutcliffe, J.R. 2003. "Research Endeavors into Suicide: A Need to Shift the Emphasis," *British Journal of Nursing* 12, 2: 92–9.

De Santis, J.P. 2009. "HIV Infection Risk Factors among Male-to-Female Transgender Persons: A Review of the Literature, *Journal of the Association of Nurses in AIDS Care* 20: 362–72.

Durkheim, Émile. 1951 [1897]. *Suicide*. New York: Free Press.

Eckes, Thomas B., and Hanns M. Trautner. 2000. *The Developmental Social Psychology of Gender*. Hillsdale, NJ: Lawrence Erlbaum Associates.

Emerson, E., and S. Baines. 2010. *Health Inequalities and People with Learning Disabilities in the UK: 2010*. Lancaster, UK: Learning Disabilities Observatory.

Engel, George L. 1977. "The Need for a New Medical Model: A Challenge for Biomedicine," *Science* 196: 129–36.

Engels, Friedrich. 1987 [1844]. *The Condition of the Working Class in England*. New York: Penguin.

Fitzsimons, D., K. Parahoo, S.G. Richardson, and M. Stringer. 2003. "Patient Anxiety While on a Waiting List for Coronary Artery Bypass Surgery: A Qualitative and Quantitative Analysis," *Heart & Lung: Journal of Acute and Critical Care* 32, 1: 23–31.

Flegel, K.M. 1999. "The Obesity Epidemic in Children and Adults: Current Evidence and Research Issues," *Medicine and Science in Sports and Exercise* 31 (suppl. 11): S509–14.

Food Banks Canada. 2012. *HungerCount 2012*. At: <foodbankscanada.ca/getmedia/3b946e67-fbe2-490e-90dc-4a313dfb97e5/HungerCount2012.pdf.aspx>.

Fox, Ashley M., and Benjamin Mason Meier. 2009. "Health as Freedom: Addressing Social Determinants of Global Health Inequities through the Human Right to Development," *Bioethics* 23, 2: 112–22.

Frank, Lawrence D., Martin A. Andresen, and Thomas L. Schmid. 2004. "Obesity Relationships with Community Design, Physical Activity, and Time Spent in Cars," *American Journal of Preventative Medicine* 27, 2: 87–96.

Gasher, M., M. Hayes, R. Hackett, D. Gutstein, I. Ross, and J. Dunn. 2007. "Spreading the News: Social Determinants of Health Reportage in Canadian Daily Newspapers," *Canadian Journal of Communication* 32, 3: 557–74.

Gilmore, Linda, and Monica Cuskelly. 2012. "Parenting Satisfaction and Self-Efficacy: A Longitudinal Study of Mothers of Children with Down Syndrome," *Journal of Family Studies* 18, 1: 28–35.

Goldsmith, L., H. Skirton, and C. Webb. 2008. "Informed Consent to Healthcare Interventions in People with Learning Disabilities—an Integrative Review, *Journal of Advanced Nursing* 64, 6: 549–63.

Green, Sara Eleanor. 2007. "'We're tired, not sad': Benefits and Burdens of Mothering a Child with a Disability," *Social Science and Medicine* 64, 1: 150–63.

Health Canada. 2006. "A Report on Mental Illnesses in Canada. Ottawa, Canada 2002." At: <www.phac-aspc.gc.ca/publicat/miic-mmac/pdf/men_ill_e.pdf>.

Hecht, Robert, Lori Bollinger, John Stover, William McGreevey, Farzana Muhib, Callisto Emas Madavo, and David de Ferranti. 2009. "Critical Choices in Financing the Response to the Global HIV/AIDS Pandemic," *Health Affairs* 28, 6: 1591–605.

Hibbard, Roberta, Jane Barlow, Harriet MacMillan, and the Committee on Child Abuse and Neglect and American Academy of Child and Adolescent Psychiatry, Child Maltreatment and Violence Committee. 2012. "Psychological Maltreatment," *Pediatrics* 130: 372.

Hudson, Christopher G. 2005. "Socioeconomic Status and Mental Illness: Tests of the Social Causation and Selection Hypotheses," *American Journal of Orthopsychiatry* 75, 1: 3–18.

Hung, Jen-Wen, et al. 2010. "Mental Health of Parents Having Children with Physical Disabilities," *Chang Gung Medical Journal* 33, 1: 82–91.

Joint Working Group on the Voluntary Sector. 1999. *Building the Relationship between National Voluntary Organizations Working in Health and Health Canada: A Framework for Action.* Ottawa: Health Canada.

Jorgensen, M. 2005. "A Disability Paradox," *Canadian Family Physician* 51: 1474–6.

Kenagy, G.P. 2005. "Transgender Health: Findings from Two Needs Assessment Studies in Philadelphia," *Health & Social Work* 30: 19–26.

Kessler, Ronald C., Wai Tat Chiu, Olga Demler, and Ellen E. Walters. 2005. "Prevalence, Severity, and Comorbidity of 12-Month DSM-IV Disorders in the National Comorbidity Survey Replication," *Archives of General Psychiatry* 62, 6: 617–27.

Kirmayer, L.J., G.M. Brass, T. Holton, K. Paul, C. Simpson, and C. Tait. 2007. *Suicide among Aboriginal People in Canada.* Ottawa: Aboriginal Healing Foundation.

Krahn, G.L., L. Hammond, and A. Turner. 2006. "A Cascade of Disparities: Health and Health Care Access for People with Intellectual Disabilities," *Mental Retardation and Developmental Disabilities Research Reviews* 12, 1: 70–82

Kroll-Smith, Steven. 2000. "The Social Construction of the Drowsy Person," *Perspectives on Social Problems* 12: 89–109.

Langlois, K.A., A.V. Samokhvalov, J. Rehm, S.T. Spence, S.K. Connor Gorber. 2011. *Health State Descriptions for Canadians: Mental Illnesses.*

Ottawa: Statistics Canada Catalogue no. 82-619-MIE2005002.

Le Petit, Christel, and Jean-Marie Berthelot. 2005. *Obesity: A Growing Issue.* Ottawa: Statistics Canada Catalogue no. 82–618–MWE2005003. At: <www.statcan.ca/bsolc/english/bsolc?catno=82-618-M2005003>.

Lombardi E. 2007. "Substance Use Treatment Experiences of Transgender/Transsexual Men and Women," *Journal of LGBT Health Resources* 3: 37–47.

Lopez-Pacheco, Alexandra. 2013. *Financial Post,* 5 Feb. At: <business.financialpost.com/2013/02/05/the-economic-cost-of-mental-illness>.

Louria, Donald B. 2000. "Emerging and Re-emerging Infections: The Societal Determinants," *Futures* 32, 6: 581–94.

Mackenbach, Johan P., and Martijntje J. Bakker. 2003. "Tackling Socioeconomic Inequalities in Health: Analysis of European Experiences," *Lancet* 362: 1409–14.

McPherson, S., and D. Armstrong. 2009. "Negotiating 'Depression' in Primary Care: A Qualitative Study," *Social Science and Medicine* 69, 8: 1137–43.

Malone, R.E., E. Boyd, and L.A. Bero. 2000. "Science in the News: Journalists' Constructions of Passive Smoking as a Social Problem," *Social Studies of Science* 30, 5: 713–35.

Marmot, Michael. 2004. *The Status Syndrome: How Social Standing Affects Our Health and Longevity.* New York: Henry Holt.

———. 2005. "Social Determinants of Health Inequalities," *Lancet* 365: 1099–104.

Mathers, Colin D., Christina Bernard, Kim M. Iburg, Mie Inoue, Doris Ma Fat, et al. 2003. *Global Burden of Disease in 2002: Data Sources, Methods and Results.* Geneva: WHO.

Matsushita, Y., N. Yoshiike, F. Kaneda, K. Yoshita, and H. Takimoto. 2004. "Trends in Childhood Obesity in Japan over the Last 25 Years from the National Nutrition Survey," *Obesity Research* 12, 2: 205–14.

Melchiorre, Maria Gabriella, Carlos Chiatti, Giovanni Lamura, Francisco Torres-Gonzales, Mindaugas Stankunas, Jutta Lindert, Elisabeth Ioannidi-Kapolou, Henrique Barros, Gloria Macassa, and Joaquim F.J. Soares. 2013. "Social Support, Socio-economic Status, Health and Abuse among Older

People in Seven European Countries," *PLoS ONE* 8, 1: e54856.

Mikkonen, J., and D. Raphael. 2010. *Social Determinants of Health: The Canadian Facts.* Toronto: York University School of Health Policy and Management.

NARTH (National Association for Research and Therapy of Homosexuality). 2007. "Gender Identity Disorders in Childhood and Adolescence: A Critical Inquiry and Review of the Kenneth Zucker Research," paper prepared by the NARTH Scientific Advisory Committee.

Norman, W.V. 2012. "Induced Abortion in Canada 1974–2005: Trends over the First Generation with Legal Access," *Contraception* 85, 2: 185–91.

Nosek, M., and H.P. Kennedy. 2010. "Silence, Stigma and Shame: A Postmodern Analysis of Distress during Menopause," *Advances in Nursing Science* 33, 3: E24–E36.

Parry, Monica J.E. 2004. "Physiologic and Psychological Responses of Men and Women Waiting for Coronary Artery Bypass Graft Surgery," MA thesis, Queen's University.

Parsons, Talcott. 1951. *The Social System.* Glencoe, IL: Free Press.

Pescosolido, Bernice, A. Tait, R. Medina, Jack K. Martin, and J. Scott Long. 2013. "The 'Backbone' of Stigma: Identifying the Global Core of Public Prejudice Associated with Mental Illness," *American Journal of Public Health* 103, 5 (May): 853–60.

Pieterman, Roel. 2007. "The Social Construction of Fat: Care and Control in the Public Concern for Healthy Behaviour," *Sociology Compass* 1, 1: 309–21.

Plakun, E.M. 2009. "Series Epilogue: A View from Riggs: Treatment Resistance and Patient Authority," *Journal of the American Academy of Psychoanalysis* 37: 699–700.

Potter, W.J. 2003. *The 11 Myths of Media Violence.* Thousand Oaks, CA: Sage.

Public Health Agency of Canada. 2006. *HIV and AIDS in Canada: Surveillance Report to June 30, 2005.* Ottawa: Surveillance and Risk Assessment Division, Centre for Infectious Disease Prevention and Control, Public Health Agency of Canada.

Rachlin, K., J. Green, and E. Lombardi. 2008. "Utilization of Health Care among Female-to-Male Transgender

Individuals in the United States," *Journal of Homosexuality* 54: 243–58.

Raphael, Dennis. 2002. *Social Justice Is Good for Our Hearts: Why Societal Factors—Not Lifestyles—Are Major Causes of Heart Disease in Canada and Elsewhere*. Toronto: Canadian Centre for Social Justice Foundation for Research and Education.

———, ed. 2004, 2008. *The Social Determinants of Health: A Canadian Perspective*. Toronto: Canadian Scholars' Press.

———. 2009. "Poverty, Human Development and Health in Canada: Research, Practice, and Advocacy Dilemmas," *Canadian Journal of Nursing Research* 41, 2: 7–18.

Rather, L.J., ed. 1985. *Rudolf Virchow: Collected Essays on Public Health and Epidemiology*. Canton, MA: Science History Publications.

Rennie, K.L., and S.A. Jebb. 2005. "Prevalence of Obesity in Great Britain," *Obesity Reviews* 6, 1: 11–12.

Ritsatakis, Anna. 2009. "Equity and Social Determinants of Health at a City Level," *Health Promotion International* 24 (suppl. 1): 181–90.

Romanow, Roy J. 2002. *Building on Values: The Future of Health Care in Canada*. Final Report of the Royal Commission on the Future of Health Care in Canada. At: <www.hc-sc.gc.ca/english/care/romanow/hcc0086.html>.

Rothman, K.J. 2012. *Epidemiology: An Introduction*. New York: Oxford University Press.

Sanmartin, C., and N. Ross. 2006. "Experiencing Difficulties Accessing First-Contact Health Services in Canada," *Healthcare Policy* 1, 2: 103–19.

Sevean, P., S. Dampier, et al. 2009. "Patients' and Families' Experiences with Video Telehealth in Rural/Remote Communities in Northern Canada," *Journal of Clinical Nursing* 18: 2573–9.

Siciliani, Luigi, and Rossella Verzulli. 2009. "Waiting Times and Socioeconomic Status among Elderly Europeans: Evidence from SHARE," *Health Economics* 18, 11: 1295–306.

Snelgrove, J., A.M. Jasudavisius, B.W. Rowe, E.M. Head, and G.R. Bauer. 2012. "'Completely Out-at-Sea' with 'Two-Gender Medicine': A Qualitative Analysis of Physician-Side Barriers to Providing Healthcare for Transgender Patients," *BMC Health Services Research*

12: 110. At: <www.biomedcentral.com/1472-6963/12/110>.

So, Alvin Y., and Ngai Pun. 2004. "Introduction: Globalization and Anti-globalization of SARS in Chinese Societies," *Asian Perspective* 28, 1: 5–17.

Soremekun, O.A., J.K. Takeyesu, and S.J. Bohan. 2011. "Framework for Analyzing Wait Times and Other Factors That Impact Patient Satisfaction in an Emergency Department," *Journal of Emergency Medicine* 41, 6.

Statistics Canada. 2008. Canadian Community Health Survey, *The Daily*, 18 June.

———. 2010. Canadian Community Health Survey, *The Daily*, 15 June.

Stephens, Thomas, and Natacha Joubert. 2001. "The Economic Burden of Mental Health Problems in Canada," *Chronic Diseases in Canada* 22, 1: 18–23.

Szasz, Thomas. 2011. "The Myth of Mental Illness: 50 Years Later," *The Psychiatrist* 35, 5 (May): 179–82.

Tracey, Peter, Randy Goossen, Susan Chipperfield, Marion Cooper, Annette Alix-Roussin, Anne-Marie Brown, Diana Clarke, Barry Fogg, Bev Pageau, and Liping Zhang. 2009. *Manitoba Adult Suicide Mortality Review: Risk Factors Associated with Mental Health & Substance Use Disorders*. Winnipeg: Winnipeg Regional Health Authority.

Trute, Barry, et al. 2010. "Accentuate the Positive to Mitigate the Negative: Mother Psychological Coping Resources and Family Adjustment in Childhood Disability," *Journal of Intellectual and Developmental Disability* 35, 1: 36–43.

UN (United Nations). 2005. *The Millennium Development Goals Report 2005*. New York: UN.

———. 2008. *The Millennium Development Goals Report*. At: <www.un.org/millenniumgoals/2008highlevel/pdf/newsroom/mdg%20reports/MDG_Report_2008_ENGLISH.pdf>.

UNAIDS (*Joint United Nations Programme on HIV/AIDS*). 2012. Report on the Global AIDS Epidemic. At: <www.unaids.org/en/resources/publications/2012/name,76121,en.asp>.

UNICEF. 2005. *The State of the World's Children 2006: Excluded and Invisible*. New York: UNICEF.

Veltman, A., D.E. Stewart, G.S. Tardif, and M. Branigan. 2001. "Perceptions

of Primary Healthcare Services among People with Physical Disabilities. Part 1: Access Issues," *Medscape General Medicine* 3: 18.

Vermeulen, Karin M., Otto H. Bosma, Wim van der Bij, Gerard H. Koëter, and Elizabeth M. Tenvergert. 2005. "Stress, Psychological Distress, and Coping in Patients on the Waiting List for Lung Transplantation: An Exploratory Study," *Transplant International* 18, 8: 954–9.

White, Peter, ed. 2005. *Biopsychosocial Medicine: An Integrated Approach to Understanding Illness*. Oxford: Oxford University Press.

WHO (World Health Organization). 1946. Preamble to the *Constitution of the World Health Organization* as adopted by the International Health Conference, New York, 19–22 June; signed 22 July 1946 by the representatives of 61 states (Official Records of WHO, no. 2, p. 100) and entered into force 7 Apr. 1948.

———. 1970. Twenty-Third World Health Assembly, Geneva, 5–22 May, Plenary Meetings, Summary Records and Reports, Geneva, Dec. At: <extranet.who.int/iris/restricted/bitstream/10665/85825/1/Official_record185_eng.pdf>.

———. 2004. "Global Burden of Disease Estimates." At: <www.who.int/healthinfo/bodestimates/en/index.html>.

———. 2011. Mental Health Atlas. At: <www.who.int/mental_health/publications/mental_health_atlas_2011/en>.

———. 2012. At: <apps.who.int/gho/data/view.main-amro.700?lang=en>.

———. 2013. "Global Health Observatory." At: <www.who.int/gho/child_health/mortality/mortality_under_five_text/en/index.html>.

———. 2014. "Maternal Mortality: Fact Sheet." At <www.who.int/mediacentre/factsheets/fs348/en>.

Wilkinson, R., and M. Marmot. 2003. *Social Determinants of Health: The Solid Facts*, 2nd edn. Geneva: WHO.

World Bank. 2010. "HIV/AIDS in India." June. At: <www.worldbank.org/en/news/2012/07/10/hiv-aids-india>.

World Tourism Organization. 2013. At: <tourlib.net/wto/UNWTO_Barometer_2013_01.pdf>.

Wright, S.M., and L.J. Aronne. 2012. "Causes of Obesity," *Abdom Imaging* 37, 5 (Oct.): 730–2.

Chapter 10

Babic, Dragutin. 2002. "The Croatian Government and Programs Regarding the Return of War Migrants: Between Plans and Realizations—The Experience of the Brod-Posavina County," *Migracijske i etnicke teme* 18, 1: 63–83.

Bass, Gary Jonathan. 2002. "Stay the Hand of Vengeance: The Politics of War Crimes Tribunals," *International Studies Review* 4, 1: 129–39.

Beah, Ishmael. 2007. *A Long Way Gone: Memoirs of a Boy Soldier*. Vancouver: Douglas & McIntyre.

Besley, Timothy, and Torsten Persson. 2011. "The Logic of Political Violence," *Quarterly Journal of Economics*, no. 3: 1411–45.

Blanchard, Eric M. 2003. "Gender, International Relations, and the Development of Feminist Security Theory," *Signs* 28, 2: 1289–312.

Brands, Hal. 2011. "Inside the Iraqi State Records: Saddam Hussein, 'Irangate,' and the United States," *Journal of Strategic Studies*, no. 1: 95–118.

Calhoun, Martin L. 1996. "Cleaning Up the Military's Toxic Legacy," *USA Today Magazine* 124: 60–4.

Clausewitz, Carl von. 1993 [1833]. *On War*, trans. Michael Howard and Peter Paret. New York: Knopf.

Clement, Dominique. 2008. "The October Crisis of 1970: Human Rights Abuses under the War Measures Act," *Journal of Canadian Studies* 42, 2: 160–87.

Coalition to Stop the Use of Child Soldiers. 2009. *Child Soldiers Global Report 2008*. London: Coalition to Stop the Use of Child Soldiers.

Coates, Colin M. 1997. "The Culture of Rural Quebec," *Journal of Canadian Studies* 32, 1: 167–71.

Cooper, Sandi E. 2002. "Peace as a Human Right: The Invasion of Women into the World of High International Politics," *Journal of Women's History* 14, 2: 9–25.

Cromer, Gerald. 2005. "The Rhetoric of Victimization: An Analysis of the Coverage of Intifada El-Aqsa in the Israeli Press," *International Review of Victimology* 12, 3: 235–45.

Dahl, Edgar. 2010. "Gendercide? A Commentary on the Economist's report about the Worldwide War on Baby Girls," *Journal of Evolution & Technology* 21, 2: 20–2.

Dhamoon, Rita, and Yasmeen Abu-Laban. 2009. "Dangerous (Internal) Foreigners and Nation-Building: The Case of Canada," *International Political Science Review* 30, 2: 163–83.

Dinstein, Yoram. 2011. *War, Aggression and Self-Defence*. Cambridge: Cambridge University Press.

Engle, Karen. 2005. "Feminism and Its (Dis)contents: Criminalizing Wartime Rape in Bosnia and Herzegovina," *American Journal of International Law* 99, 4: 778–816.

Enloe, C.M. 1987. "Feminists Thinking about War, Militarism, and Peace," in B.B Hess and M. M. Ferree, eds, *Analyzing Gender. A Handbook of Social Science Research*. Beverley Hills, CA: Sage, 526–47.

Fanon, Frantz. 1968. *The Wretched of the Earth*. New York: Grove Weidenfeld.

Friedman, George, and Meredith Friedman. 1998. *The Future of War: Power, Technology and American World Dominance in the Twenty-First Century*. New York: Macmillan.

Gatti, Antonietta M., and Stefano Montanari. 2008. "Nanopollution: The Invisible Fog of Future Wars," *The Futurist* 4, 3: 32–4.

Girvan, Susan, ed. 2000. *Canadian Global Almanac 2000*. Toronto: Macmillan Canada.

Global Firepower. 2013. "Comparisons of World Military Strengths Results: Military Strength Comparison Results." Last modified 1 Mar. At: <www.google.ca/url?sa=t&rct=j&q=&esrc=s&sourc e=web&cd=1&ved=0CBwQFjAA&url =http%3A%2F%2Ficebergfinanza .finanza.com%2Ffiles%2F2014%2F04 %2FUcraine%2520Military%2520Str ength%2520Comparison.pdf&ei=K0- 0U83hGufz8AG3poCIBg&usg=AFQj CNHknV0Szc_khU-aM1v0bPUl-aDt 3w&sig2=u7pLwQEYycEQZ0jVnhp7 3w&bvm=bv.70138588,d.b2U>.

Greenfeld, Karl Taro. 2006. "The Long Way Home," *Sports Illustrated*, 15 May.

Haig, Jane, Anas Karzai, Guy Kirby Letts, Merminia Meireles Teixeira, and Marianne Vardalos. 2009. *Engaging Terror: A Critical and Interdisciplinary Approach*. Boca Raton, FL: Brown Walker Press, 2009.

Holbrook, Troy Lisa, Michael R. Galarneau, Judy L. Dye, Kimberly Quinn, and Amber L. Dougherty. 2010. "Morphine Use after Combat Injury in Iraq and Post-Traumatic Stress Disorder," *New England Journal of Medicine* 362, 2: 110–17.

Human Rights Watch. n.d. "Stop the Use of Child Soldiers!" At: <www.hrw.org/ campaigns/crp/index.htm>.

Johnson, Chalmers. 2006. *Nemesis: The Last Days of the American Republic*. New York: Metropolitan Books.

Kage, Tatsuo. 2002. "War Measures Act: Japanese Canadian Experience," workshop held at a meeting on Immigration and Security, Our Voices, Our Strategies: Asian Canadians against Racism, 7–9 June, University of British Columbia, Vancouver.

Knight, W. Andy, and Tom Keating. 2010. *Global Politics: Emerging Networks, Trends, and Challenges*. Toronto: Oxford University Press.

LePoire, David J., and Jerome C. Glenn. 2007. "Technology and the Hydra of Terrorism?," *Technological Forecasting and Social Change* 74, 2: 139–47.

Loza, Wagdy, 2007. "The Psychology of Extremism and Terrorism: A Middle-Eastern Perspective," *Aggression and Violent Behaviour* 12: 141–55.

McDonald, Marci. 2010. *The Armageddon Factor: The Rise of Christian Nationalism in Canada*. Toronto: Random House.

Meyer, David S. 2009. "Constructing Threats and Opportunities after 9/11," *American Behavioral Scientist* 53, 1: 10–26.

Miller, Kenneth E., and Andrew Rasmussen. 2010. "War Exposure, Daily Stressors, and Mental Health in Conflict and Post-Conflict Settings: Bridging the Divide between Trauma-Focused and Psychosocial Frameworks," *Social Science & Medicine* 70, 1: 7.

Mills, C. Wright. 1956. *The Power Elite*. New York: Oxford University Press.

Moore, Barrington. 1967. *Social Origins of Dictatorship and Democracy: Lord and Peasant in the Making of the Modern World*. Boston: Beacon Press.

Moore, Colin D. 2009. "Institutions of Empire: Information, Delegation, and the Political Control of American Imperialism, 1890–1913." ProQuest, Ann Arbor, MI.

Moore, George, and Berwyn Moore. 2009. "Threats to Our Nation, 1957– 1959: A Public Health Retrospective," *Public Health Reports* 124, 2: 323–7.

Mowat, Farley. 1984. *Sea of Slaughter*. Toronto: McClelland & Stewart.

Navarro, Joe. 2009. "Unmasking Terrorists—Two Critical Characteristics! Key Signs Which Point to Potential Terrorist Activity," *Psychology Today*, 31 Dec. At: <www.psychologytoday.com/blog/spycatcher/200912/unmasking-terrorists-two-critical-characteristics>.

Petrosian, D., and N. Fatkina. 2009. "'Economic Imperialism' and Macro Theory of Management of Human Behavior," *Obshchestvennye Nauki i Sovremennost* 1: 166–70.

Porter, Bruce D. 1994. *War and the Rise of the State: The Military Foundations of Modern Politics*. New York: Free Press.

Ross, Carne. 2011. *The Leaderless Revolution: How Ordinary People Will Take Power and Change Politics in the 21st Century*. New York: Blue Rider Press.

SIPRI (Stockholm International Peace Research Institute). 2008. *TIV of Arms Exports from the Top 10 Largest Exporters*. At: <www.sipri.org/contents/armstrad/output_types_TIV.html>.

———. 2011. "Defence Expenditures, 2010." At: <www.rickety.us/2011/06/2010-defense-spending-by-country>.

———. 2013. "Recent Trends in Military Expenditure." At: <www.globalissues.org/article/75/world-military-spending#WorldMilitarySpending>.

Skocpol, Theda. 1979. *States and Social Revolutions: A Comparative Analysis of France, Russia, and China*. Cambridge: Cambridge University Press.

Summerfield, P. 2000. "'It did me good in lots of ways': British Women in Transition from War to Peace," in C. Duchen and I. Bandhauer-Schoffmann, eds, *When the War Was Over: Women, War and Peace in Europe, 1940–1956*. Leicester, UK: Leicester University Press, 13–28.

Thomas, Emma F., Craig McGarty, and Kenneth I. Mavor. 2009. "Aligning Identities, Emotions, and Beliefs to Create Commitment to Sustainable Social and Political Action," *Personality and Social Psychology Review* 13, 3: 194–218.

Tucker, Robert C. 1978. "Introduction," in Karl Marx and Friedrich Engels, *The Marx-Engels Reader*. New York: Norton.

US Department of State. 2010. "State Sponsors of Terrorism." At: <www.state.gov/s/ct/c14151.htm>.

Vision of Humanity. 2009. "Global Peace Index." At: <www.visionofhumanity.org/gpi-data//2009/scor>.

Wallerstein, Immanuel. 1976. *The Modern World-System: Capitalist Agriculture and the Origins of the European World-Economy in the Sixteenth Century*. New York: Academic Press.

———. 2004. *World-Systems Analysis: An Introduction*. Durham, NC: Duke University Press.

Weber, Max. 1946. *Max Weber: Essays in Sociology*, trans. and ed. H.H. Gerth and C.W. Mills. New York: Oxford University Press.

Weimann, Gabriel. 2004. "Cyberterrorism: How Real Is the Threat?" United States Institute of Peace. Special Report 119.

Chapter 11

Al-Krenawi, Alean, John R. Graham, and Fakir Al Gharaibeh. 2011. "A Comparison Study of Psychological, Family Function Marital and Life Satisfactions of Polygamous and Monogamous Women in Jordan," *Community Mental Health Journal* 47, 5: 594–602.

Ambert, A.M. 2005. *Divorce: Facts, Causes, and Consequences*. Ottawa: Vanier Institute of the Family.

Ambert, Anne-Marie. 2009. *Divorce: Facts, Causes, and Consequences*, 3rd edn. Ottawa: Vanier Institute of the Family.

Aune, Kristin. 2008. "Evangelical Christianity and Women's Changing Lives," *European Journal of Women's Studies* 15, 3: 277–94.

Baklinski, Thaddeus M. 2009. "Divorce Rates Down for All of Canada Except Quebec: Study," 25 Nov. At: <www.lifesitenews.com/ldn/2009/nov/09112508.html>.

Balestrino, Alessandro, and Cinzia Ciardi. 2008. "Social Norms, Cognitive Dissonance and the Timing of Marriage," *Journal of Socio-economics* 37, 6: 2399–410.

Balram, Indira K. 2005. "The Evolving, Yet Still Inadequate, Legal Protections Afforded Battered Immigrant Women," *University of Maryland Law Journal of Race, Religion, Gender and Class* 5: 387–410.

Barber, Nigel. 2008. "Explaining Cross-National Differences in Polygyny Intensity Resource-Defense, Sex Ratio, and Infectious Diseases," *Cross-Cultural Research* 42, 2: 103–17.

Begum, Rashida, and O. Desai. 2010. "A Comparative Study to Evaluate Psychological Status of Mothers of Children with Cerebral Palsy and Mothers of Normal Children," *Indian Journal of Occupational Therapy* 42, 2: 3–9.

Benzies, Karen, Suzanne Tough, Karen Tofflemire, Corine Frick, Alexandra Faber, and Christine Newburn-Cook. 2006. "Factors Influencing Women's Decisions about Timing of Motherhood," *Journal of Obstetric, Gynecologic, and Neonatal Nursing* 35, 5: 625–33.

Bianchi, Suzanne M., Lekha Subaiya, and Joan R. Kahn. 1999. "The Gender Gap in the Economic Well-Being of Nonresident Fathers and Custodial Mothers," *Demography (pre-2011)* 36, 2: 195–203.

Blosnich, John R., and Robert M. Bossarte. 2009. "Comparisons of Intimate Partner Violence among Partners in Same-Sex and Opposite-Sex Relationships in the United States," *American Journal of Public Health* 99, 12: 2182–5.

Bould, Sally, Gunther Schmaus, and Claire Gavray. 2008. "Welfare Regimes and the Economic Situation of Men and Women after Separation," paper presented at the International Sociological Association meeting, Barcelona.

Brabant, Sarah. 2006. "Metaphors as Tools in Clinical Sociology: Bereavement Education and Counseling," *Journal of Applied Sociology* 23, 2: 78–91.

Brower, T. 2009. "It's Not Just Shopping Urban Lofts, and the Lesbian Gay-By Boom: How Sexual Orientation Demographics Can Inform Family Courts," *American University Journal of Gender, Social Policy & the Law* 17: 1.

Bryson, Valerie. 2003. *Feminist Political Theory: An Introduction*, 2nd edn. New York: Palgrave Macmillan.

Chambers, Deborah. 2000. "Representations of Familism in the British Popular Media," *European Journal of Cultural Studies* 3: 195–214.

Cheah, Charissa S.L., and V. Chirkov. 2008. "Parents' Personal and Cultural Beliefs Regarding Young Children: A Cross-Cultural Study of Aboriginal and Euro-Canadian Mothers," *Journal of Cross-Cultural Psychology* 39: 402–23.

CIA (Central Intelligence Agency). 2005. *The World Fact Book 2005*. Washington: CIA. At: <www.cia.gov/cia/publications/factbook/geos/ch.html>.

Clark, Warren. 2007. "Delayed Transitions of Young Adults," *Canadian Social Trends*. At: <www.statcan.gc.ca/pub/11-008-x/2007004/10311-eng.htm>.

Demerouti, E., and S. Geurts. 2004. "Towards a Typology of Work–Home Interaction," *Community, Work & Family* 7, 3: 285–309.

Dixon, Kathrine. 2007. "Working with Mixed Commons/Anticommons Property: Mobilizing Customary Land in Papua New Guinea the Melanesian Way," *Harvard Environmental Law Review* 31, 1: 219–77.

Dronkers, Jaap. 1996. "The Effects of Parental Conflicts and Divorce on the Average Well-Being of Pupils in Secondary Education," American Sociological Association, conference paper.

Gilmore, Linda, and Monica Cuskelly. 2012. "Parenting Satisfaction and Self-Efficacy: A Longitudinal Study of Mothers of Children with Down Syndrome," *Journal of Family Studies* 18, 1: 28–35.

Goode, William J. 1963. *World Revolution and Family Patterns*. New York: Free Press.

Green, Sara Eleanor. 2007. "'We're tired, not sad': Benefits and Burdens of Mothering a Child with a Disability," *Social Science and Medicine* 64, 1: 150–63.

Grutzmacher, Stephanie K. 2007. "Family Structure and Income Redistribution Policies: Comparing Child Poverty Outcomes in Canada, the United Kingdom, and the United States," *Dissertation Abstracts International, A: The Humanities and Social Sciences* 68, 4: 1683.

Grych, J.H. 2005. "Interparental Conflict as a Risk Factor for Child Maladjustment: Implications for the Development of Prevention Programs," *Family Court Review* 43, 1: 97–108.

Han, E.L. 2003. "Mandatory Arrest and No-Drop Policies: Victim Empowerment in Domestic Violence Cases," *Boston College Third World Law Journal* 23: 159.

Hawkins, Daniel, and Alan Booth. 2005. "Unhappily Ever After: Effects of Long-Term, Low-Quality Marriages on Well-Being," *Social Forces* 84, 1: 451–71.

Heathcote, J., K. Cauch-Dudek, and D. Rhyne. 1997. "The Professional Lives of Women in Gastroenterology: A Canadian Comparison Study with Men," *Gastroenterology* 113, 2: 669–74.

Hesketh, Therese, Li Lu, and Zhu Wei Xing. 2005. "The Effect of China's One-Child Family Policy after 25 Years," *New England Journal of Medicine* 353, 11: 1171–6.

Hochschild, Arlie Russell. 1997. *The Time Bind: When Work Becomes Home and Home Becomes Work*. New York: Henry Holt.

Holt-Lunstad, Julianne, Wendy Birmingham, and Brandon Q. Jones. 2008. "Is There Something Unique about Marriage? The Relative Impact of Marital Status, Relationship Quality, and Network Social Support on Ambulatory Blood Pressure and Mental Health," *Annals of Behavioral Medicine* 35, 2: 239–44.

Houseknecht, Sharon K., Suzanne Vaughan, and Anne Statham. 1987. "The Impact of Singlehood on the Career Patterns of Professional Women," *Journal of Marriage and the Family* 49, 2: 353–66.

Hung, Jen-Wen, Jen-Wen Hung, Yee-Hwa Wu, Yi-Chien Chiang, Wen-Chi Wu, and Chao-Hsing Yeh. 2010. "Mental Health of Parents Having Children with Physical Disabilities," *Chang Gung Medical Journal* 33, 1: 82–91.

Immerman, Ronald S., and Wade C. Mackey. 1999. "The Societal Dilemma of Multiple Sexual Partners: The Costs of the Loss of Pair-Bonding," *Marriage and Family Review* 29, 1: 3–19.

Kaplan, S.J. 2000. "Family Violence," *New Directions for Mental Health Services* 86: 49–62.

Kim, Hyun Sik. 2011. "Consequences of Parental Divorce for Child Development," *American Sociological Review* 76, 3: 487–511.

King, Michael. 2007. "The Sociology of Childhood as Scientific Communication: Observations from a Social Systems Perspective," *Childhood* 14, 2: 193–213.

Ledoux, S., P. Miller, M. Choquet, and M. Plant. 2002. "Family Structure, Parent–Child Relationships, and Alcohol and Other Drug Use among Teenagers in France and the United Kingdom," *Alcohol and Alcoholism* 37, 1: 52–60.

Lehmann, Jennifer M. 1994. *Durkheim and Women*. Lincoln: University of Nebraska Press.

Longman, Chia. 2008. "Sacrificing the Career or the Family? Orthodox Jewish Women between Secular Work and the Sacred Home," *European Journal of Women's Studies* 15, 3: 223–39.

Loveless, A. Scott, and Thomas B. Holman, eds. 2007. *The Family in the New Millennium: World Voices Supporting the 'Natural' Clan*, vol. 2: *Marriage and Human Dignity*. Westport, CN: Praeger/Greenwood.

Lutze, F.E., and J.G. van Wormer. 2007. "The Nexus between Drug and Alcohol Treatment Program Integrity and Drug Court Effectiveness," *Criminal Justice Policy Review* 18, 3: 226–45.

Luxton, Meg, and Bonnie Fox. 2009. "Conceptualizing 'Family,'" in B. Fox, ed., *Family Patterns, Gender Relations*, 3rd edn. Toronto: Oxford University Press.

McManus, P.A., and T.A. DiPrete. 2001. "Losers and Winners: The Financial Consequences of Separation and Divorce for Men," *American Sociological Review* 66, 2: 246–68.

McMullin, Julie. 2004. *Understanding Social Inequality: Intersections of Class, Age, Gender, Ethnicity, and Race in Canada*. Toronto: Oxford University Press.

Malo, Claire, Jacques Moreau, Claire Chamberland, Sophie Léveillé, and Catherine Roy. 2004. "Parental Cognition, Emotions, and Behaviors Associated with the Risk of Psychological Maltreatment of Preschoolers," *Journal of Emotional Abuse* 4, 2: 1–26.

Marshall, Katherine. 2009. "The Family Work Week," *Perspectives on Labour and Income* 21, 2: 21–9.

Martin, Steven P. 2000. "Diverging Fertility among US Women Who Delay Childbearing Past Age 30," *Demography* 37, 4: 523–33.

Mason, Mary Ann, and Marc Goulden. 2004. "Do Babies Matter (Part II)," *Academe* 90, 6: 11–15.

Maxwell, N.G., and R. Donner. 2006. "The Psychological Consequences of Judicially Imposed Closets in Child Custody and Visitation Disputes Involving Gay and Lesbian Parents," *William and Mary Journal of Women and the Law* 13: 305.

Maytal, A. 2008. "Specialized Domestic Violence Courts: Are They Worth the Trouble in Massachusetts," *Boston University Public Interest Law Journal* 18: 197.

Medeiros, Marcelo, Rafael G. Osorio, and Joana Costa. 2007. *Gender Inequalities in Allocating Time to Paid and Unpaid Work: Evidence from Bolivia.* Brasília: International Poverty Centre Working Paper 34.

Mitchell, Barbara A. 1998. "Too Close for Comfort? Parental Assessments of 'Boomerang Kid' Living Arrangements," *Canadian Journal of Sociology* 23: 21–46.

———. 2005. *The Boomerang Age: Transitions to Adulthood in Families.* New Brunswick, NJ: Transaction.

Mitchell, Barbara A., Andrew V. Wister, and Ellen M. Gee. 2000. "Culture and Co-residence: An Exploration of Variation in Home-Returning among Canadian Young Adults," *Canadian Review of Sociology and Anthropology* 37: 197–222.

Morton, D. 2000. "1900: A New Century Begins," *The Beaver* 79, 6: 23–9.

Murdock, George P. 1949. *Social Structure.* New York: Macmillan.

Naylor, M.D., C. Stephens, K.H. Bowles, and M.B. Bixby. 2005. "Cognitively Impaired Older Adults: From Hospital to Home: An Exploratory Study of These Patients and Their Caregivers," *American Journal of Nursing* 105, 2: 52–61.

Nguyen, Hung V., George P. Moschis, and Randall Shannon. 2009. "Effects of Family Structure and Socialization on Materialism: A Life Course Study in Thailand," *International Journal of Consumer Studies* 33, 4: 486–95.

Nofziger, S., and D. Kurtz. 2005. "Violent Lives: A Lifestyle Model Linking Exposure to Violence to Juvenile Violent Offending," *Journal of Research in Crime and Delinquency* 42, 1: 3–26.

Parsons, Talcott, and Robert F. Bales. 1955. *Family Socialization and Interaction Process.* New York: Free Press.

Petten, Cheryl. 2007. "Organizations Preparing for Impact of Compensation Money," *Saskatchewan Sage* 11, 12: 4–5.

Petts, Richard J. 2009. "Family and Religious Characteristics' Influence on Delinquency Trajectories from Adolescence to Young Adulthood," *American Sociological Review* 74, 3: 465–83.

Phillips, Richard. 2009. "Settler Colonialism and the Nuclear Family," *Canadian Geographer* 53, 2: 239–53.

Pollak, R.A. 2004. "An Intergenerational Model of Domestic Violence," *Journal of Population Economics* 17, 2: 311–29.

Rao, Nitya. 2005. "Kinship Matters: Women's Land Claims in the Santal Parganas, Jharkhand," *Journal of the Royal Anthropological Institute* 11, 4: 725–46.

Raphael, Dennis. 2009. *Social Determinants of Health: Canadian Perspectives.* Toronto: Canadian Scholars' Press.

Read, Dwight W. 2010. "The Algebraic Logic of Kinship Terminology Structures," *Behavioral and Brain Sciences* 33, 5: 399–401.

Sanders, Matthew R., Warren Cann, and Carol Markie-Dadds. 2003. "The Triple P-Positive Parenting Programme: A Universal Population-Level Approach to the Prevention of Child Abuse," *Child Abuse Review* 12, 3: 155–71.

Schulz, Richard, and Paula R. Sherwood. 2008. "Physical and Mental Health Effects of Family Caregiving," *Journal of Social Work Education* 44: 105–13.

Schwarz, B., G. Trommsdorff, I. Albert, and B. Mayer. 2005. "Adult Parent–Child Relationships: Relationship Quality, Support, and Reciprocity," *Applied Psychology* 54, 3: 396–417.

Shkedi, Nicole M. 2005. "When Harry Met Lawrence: Allowing Gays and Lesbians to Adopt," *Seton Hall Law Review* 35, 2: 873.

Skoda, Uwe. 2007. "The Kinship System of the Aghria: A Case Study of Peasants in Middle India," *Journal of the Royal Anthropological Institute* 13, 3: 679–701.

Statistics Canada. 2008. "Till Death Do Us Part? The Risk of First and Second Marriage Dissolution." At: <www.statcan.gc.ca/pub/11-008-x/2006001/9198-eng.htm>.

———. 2011a. *2011 Census of Population.* Statistics Canada Catalogue no. 98-312-XCB2011044.

———. 2011b. "Living Arrangements of Young Adults Aged 20 to 29," Census (2011). At: <www12.statcan.gc.ca/census-recensement/2011/as-sa/98-312-x/98-312-x2011003_3-eng.cfm#fn1>.

———. 2012a. "The Canadian Population in 2011: Age and Sex" (May). At: <www12.statcan.ca/census-recensement/2011/as-sa/98-311-x/98-311-x2011001-eng.cfm>.

———. 2012b. "Economic Family." At: <www.statcan.gc.ca/concepts/definitions/fam-econ-eng.htm>.

———. 2012c. *Fifty Years of Families in Canada: 1961 to 2011.* Ottawa: Statistics Canada Catalogue no. 98-312-X2011003.

———. 2012d. "Women in Canada at a Glance: Statistical Highlights," in Statistics Canada and Status of Women Canada, *Women in Canada: A Gender-Based Statistical Report*, 6th edn. At: <www.swc-cfc.gc.ca/rc-cr/stat/wic-fac-2012/glance-statistical-eng.pdf>.

Strohschein, Lisa, Peggy McDonough, Georges Monette, and Qing Shao. 2005. "Marital Transitions and Mental Health: Are There Gender Differences in the Short-Term Effects of Marital Status Change?," *Social Science and Medicine* 61, 11: 2293–303.

Trias, E.R. 2000. "Dealing with the Economic Consequences of Divorce for Wives: Alimony under the Spanish Civil Code," *International Journal of Law, Policy and the Family* 14, 1: 45–58.

Trute, Barry, Karen M. Benzies, Catherine Worthington, John R. Reddon, and Melanie Moore. 2010. "Accentuate the Positive to Mitigate the Negative: Mother Psychological Coping Resources and Family Adjustment in Childhood Disability," *Journal of Intellectual and Developmental Disability* 35, 1: 36–43.

Ungar, Michael, Leslie M. Tutty, Sheri McConnell, Ken Barter, and Judi Fairholm. 2009. "What Canadian Youth Tell Us about Disclosing Abuse," *Child Abuse & Neglect* 33, 10: 699–708.

Vanier Institute of the Family. 2010. *Families Count—Profiling Canada's Families IV.* Ottawa: Vanier Institute of the Family.

Waite, Linda J. 2000. "The Negative Effects of Cohabitation," *The Responsive Community* 10, 1: 31–8.

Wang, Feng, Yong Cai, and Baochang Gu. 2013. "Population, Policy, and Politics: How Will History Judge China's One-Child Policy?," *Population and Development Review* 38: 115–29.

Chapter 12

Abramovich, Evelyn. 2005. "Childhood Sexual Abuse as a Risk Factor for Subsequent Involvement in Sex Work," *Journal of Psychology and Human Sexuality* 17, 1–2: 131–46.

Abrams, Burton A., Jing Li, and James G. Mulligan. 2009. "The Steam Engine and U.S. Urban Growth during the Late Nineteenth Century," University of Delaware, Department of Economics, Working Papers.

Aiken, G.E. 2009. "Industrializing the Corn Belt: Agriculture, Technology, and Environment, 1945–1972," *Choice* 46, 10: 1961–2.

Angus Reid Public Opinion. 2010. "Half of Canadians Willing to Allow Adults to Engage in Prostitution." Angus Reid Global, at: <www.angusreidglobal.com/polls/43405/half-of-canadians-willing-to-allow-adults-to-engage-in-prostitution>.

Ariganello, Anthony. 2009. "Tackling Workplace Stress/s'attaquer au stress en milieu de travail," *CGA Magazine* 43, 3: 39.

Association of Workers' Compensation Boards of Canada. 2011. "Number of Workplace Fatalities, by Province 1998–2011," AWCBC. At: <www.awcbc.org/en/statistics.asp>.

Avison, William R. 2001. "Unemployment and Its Consequences for Mental Health," in Victor Marshal, Walter R. Heinz, Helga Kruger, and Anil Verma, eds, *Restructuring Work and the Life Course*. Toronto: University of Toronto Press, 177–200.

Bamgbose, Oluyemisi. 2002. "Teenage Prostitution and the Future of the Female Adolescent in Nigeria," *International Journal of Offender Therapy and Comparative Criminology* 46, 5: 569–85.

Bello, Deidre, Lauretta Claussen, Marvin V. Greene, and Kyle W. Morrison. 2009. "Congressional Committees Review OSHA Enforcement Issues," *Safety & Health* 179, 6: 12.

Bernstein, Elizabeth. 2002. *Economies of Desire: Sexual Commerce and Post-industrial Culture*." Berkeley: Department of Sociology, University of California.

Besen-Cassino, Yasemin. 2008. "The Cost of Being a Girl: Gender Earning Differentials in the Early Labor Markets," *NWSA Journal* 20, 1: 146–60.

Blanchflower, David G., and Alex Bryson. 2010. "The Wage Impact of Trade Unions in the UK Public and Private Sectors," *Economica* 77, 305: 18–110.

Blendon, Robert, and John Benson. 2009. "America's Response to a Deep Recession," *Challenge* 52, 4: 32–52.

Brumback, Gary B. 2007. "Review of *The Modern Firm: Organizational Design for Performance and Growth*," *Personnel Psychology* 60, 1: 260–4.

Burchardt, Tania. 2000. "The Dynamics of Being Disabled," *Journal of Social Policy* 29: 645–68.

Bureau of Labor Statistics. 2012. "National Census of Fatal Occupational Injuries in 2011." At: <www.bls.gov/iif/oshoiics.htm>.

Burke, Ronald J., and Lisa Fiksenbaum. 2009. "Work Motivations, Satisfactions, and Health among Managers: Passion versus Addiction," *Cross-Cultural Research* 43, 4: 349–65.

Burstrom, B., M. Whitehead, C. Lindholm, and F. Diderichsen. 2000. "Inequality in the Social Consequences of Illness: How Well Do People with Long-Term Illness Fare in the British and Swedish Labor Markets?," *International Journal of Health Services* 30: 435–51.

Caetano, R., S. Nelson, and C. Cunradi. 2001. "Intimate Partner Violence, Dependence Symptoms and Social Consequences from Drinking among White, Black and Hispanic Couples in the United States," *American Journal on Addictions* 10: 60–9.

Carlopio, Jim. 2010. *Strategy by Design: A Process of Strategy Innovation*. New York: Palgrave Macmillan.

CBC News. 2007. "Workplace Safety Inspections," 17 Jan. At: <www.cbc.ca/news/background/workplace-safety>.

Chen, Shu-Peng, Cheng-Hu Zhou, and Qiu-Xiao Chen. 2003. "Global Charm of the Changjiang River Delta," *Chinese Geographical Science* 13, 4: 289–99.

Chowdhury, Anis, Iyanatul Islam, and Donald Lee. 2013. "The Great Recession, Jobs and Social Crises: Policies Matter," *International Journal of Social Economics* 40, 3: 220– 45.

Comino, E.J., E. Harris, D. Silove, V. Manicavasagar, and M.F. Harris. 2000. "Prevalence, Detection and Management of Anxiety and Depressive Symptoms in Unemployed Patients Attending General Practitioners," *Australian and New Zealand Journal of Psychiatry* 34: 107–13.

Crisman, Kevin. 2009. "Horses at Work: Harnessing Power in Industrial America," *Journal of American History* 96, 3: 838–9.

Cullen, D.O. 2009. "They Are All Red out Here': Socialist Politics in the Pacific Northwest, 1895–1925," *Choice* 47, 4: 752–3.

Dean, Art. 2012. "Some Canadian Facts on Workplace Safety," University of Alberta, 29 Mar. At: <www.wln.ualberta.ca/en/~/media/wln/Documents/Events/Deane_Safety_Notes12.pdf>.

Decker, Michele R. 2013. "Sex Trafficking, Sex Work, and Violence: Evidence for a New Era," *International Journal of Gynaecology and Obstetrics: The Official Organ of the International Federation of Gynaecology and Obstetrics* 120, 2: 113–14.

de Goede, M., E. Spruijt, C. Maas, and V. Duindam. 2000. "Family Problems and Youth Unemployment," *Adolescence* 35: 587–601.

Desmarais, Danielle. 1991. "Linking Unemployment, Health and Employment in Women's Accounts of Unemployment: Understanding as a Prerequisite to Social Intervention," paper presented at the annual meeting of the Sociological Practice Association/ISA Working Group in Clinical Sociology.

Dorling, Danny. 2011. "Inequality Constitutes a Particular Place," *Social and Cultural Geography* 13, 1: 1–9.

Druss, B.G., S.C. Marcus, R.A. Rosenheck, M. Olfson, T. Talielian, and H.A. Pincus. 2000. "Understanding Disability in Mental and General Medical Conditions," *American Journal of Psychiatry* 157: 1485–91.

Durkheim, Émile. 1964 [1893]. *The Division of Labor in Society*, trans. George Simpson. New York: Free Press.

Edwards, Richard. 1979. *Contested Terrain: The Transformation of the Workplace in the Twentieth Century*. New York: Basic Books.

Eze, Mercy. 2009. "A Woman on a Mission," *New African*, no. 490: 26.

Farooq, Shujaat, and Usman Ahmed. 2007. "Underemployment, Education, and Job Satisfaction," *Pakistan Development Review* 46, 4: n.p.

Ferguson, James. 2006. *Global Shadows: Africa in the Neoliberal World Order*. Durham, NC: Duke University Press.

Fukuyama, Francis. 1992. *The End of History and the Last Man*. New York: Free Press.

Gien, L.T. 2000. "Land and Sea Connection: The East Coast Fishery

Closure, Unemployment, and Health," *Canadian Journal of Public Health* 91, 2: 121–4.

Godard, John. 2009. "The Exceptional Decline of the American Labor Movement," *Industrial and Labor Relations Review* 63, 1: 82–109.

Golden, Timothy D., and John F. Veiga. 2005. "The Impact of Extent of Telecommuting on Job Satisfaction: Resolving Inconsistent Findings," *Journal of Management* 31, 2: 301–18.

Gonzalez, Luque J.C., and Artalejo F. Rodriguez. 2000. "The Relationship of Different Socioeconomic Variables and Alcohol Consumption with Nighttime Fatal Traffic Crashes in Spain: 1978–1993," *European Journal of Epidemiology* 16: 955–61.

Grant, J.M., L.A. Mottet, and J. Tanis. 2011. "Injustice at Every Turn: A Report of the National Transgender Discrimination Survey." At: <www.thetaskforce.org/reports_and_research/ntds>.

Hanke, Steve H. 1996. "Class Warfare," *Forbes* 157, 11: 60–1.

Heaton, C., and Paul Oslington. 2010. "Micro vs Macro Explanations of Postwar US Unemployment Movements," *Economics Letters* 106, 2: 87–91.

Hecht, M. 2001. *Theme Paper for the Second World Congress against Commercial Sexual Exploitation of Children: The Role and Involvement of the Private Sector*. Human Rights Internet.

Heilbronner, Nancy. 2013. "The STEM Pathway for Women: What Has Changed?," *Gifted Child Quarterly* 57, 1: 39–55.

Heinrich, Erik. 2008. "Opportunity Play," *Global Finance* 22, 3: 28–30.

Hirsch, Barry T., and David A. Macpherson. 2004. "Wages, Sorting on Skill, and the Racial Composition of Jobs," *Journal of Labor Economics* 22, 1: 189–210.

Hoskyns, Catherine, and Shirin M. Rai. 2007. "Recasting the Global Political Economy: Counting Women's Unpaid Work," *New Political Economy* 12, 3: 297–317.

HRDC (Human Resources Development Canada). 2000. *Work Safely for a Healthy Future: Statistical Analysis Occupational Injuries and Fatalities Canada*. Occupational Safety and Health, Human Resources Development Canada.

———. 2013. *Work—Work Related Injuries*. At:<www4.hrsdc.gc.ca/.3ndic.1t.4r@-eng.jsp?iid=20>.

Hubbard, Phil, and Teela Sanders. 2003. "Making Space for Sex Work: Female Street Prostitution and the Production of Urban Space," *International Journal of Urban and Regional Research* 27, 1: 75–89.

Jacobs, Eva E. 2008. *Handbook of U.S. Labor Statistics 2008: Employment, Earning, Prices, Productivity, and Other Labor Data*. 11th edn. Lanham, MD: Bernan Press.

James, Jeffrey. 2002. "The Digital Divide between Nations as International Technological Dualism," *International Journal of Development Issues* 1, 2: 25–40.

———. 2003. *Bridging the Global Digital Divide*. Northampton, MA: Elgar.

Johnston, D.D., and D.H. Swanson. 2007. "Cognitive Acrobatics in the Construction of the Worker-Mother Identity," *Sex Roles: A Journal of Research* 57, 5–6: 447–59.

Kanter, Rosabeth M. 1977. *Men and Women of the Corporation*. New York: Basic Books.

Kelan, Elizabeth. 2007. "'I Don't Know Why'—Accounting for the Scarcity of Women in ICT Work," *Women's Studies International Forum* 30, 6: 499–511.

Kondilis, Elias, Stathis Giannakopoulos, Magda Gavana, Ioanna Ierodiakonou, and Howard Waitzkin. 2013. "Economic Crisis, Restrictive Policies, and the Population's Health and Health Care: The Greek Case," *American Journal of Public Health* 103, 6 (June): 973–80.

Korpi, W. 1983. *The Democratic Class Struggle*. London: Routledge & Keagan Paul.

Lambert, Eric G., Nancy L. Hogan, and Kasey A. Tucker. 2009. "Problems at Work: Exploring the Correlates of Role Stress among Correctional Staff," *Prison Journal* 89, 4: 460–81.

Langfred, C.W., and N.A. Moye. 2004. "Effects of Task Autonomy on Performance: An Extended Model Considering Motivational, Informational, and Structural Mechanisms," *Journal of Applied Psychology* 89, 6: 934–45.

Langman, Lauren. 2008. "Massive Change: The Exhibit as Apology for 'New Capitalism,'" *Rethinking Marxism* 20, 3: 464–71.

Li, Peter. 2003. "Initial Earnings and Catch-up Capacity of Immigrants," *Canadian Public Policy* 29, 3: 319–37.

Liira, J., and Arjas P. Leino. 1999. "Predictors and Consequences of Unemployment in Construction and Forest Work during a 5-Year Follow-up," *Scandinavian Journal of Work, Environment and Health* 25, 1: 42–9.

Lindsay, Colin. 2009. "In a Lonely Place? Social Networks, Job Seeking and the Experience of Long-Term Unemployment," *Social Policy and Society* 9, 1: 25.

Liu, Cathy Yang. 2011. "Employment Concentration and Job Quality for Low-Skilled Latino Immigrants," *Journal of Urban Affairs* 33, 2: 117–42.

Lundetræ, K., E. Gabrielsen, and R. Mykletun. 2010. "Do Basic Skills Predict Youth Unemployment (16- to 24-Year-Olds) Also When Controlled for Accomplished Upper-Secondary School? A Cross-Country Comparison," *Journal of Education and Work* 23, 3: 233–54.

McCarty, C.A., M. Burgess, and J.E. Keeffe. 1999. "Unemployment and Underemployment in Adults with Vision Impairment: The RVIB Employment Survey," *Australian and New Zealand Journal of Ophthalmology* 27, 3 and 4: 190–3.

MacDonald, Z., and S. Pudney. 2000. "Illicit Drug Use, Unemployment, and Occupational Attainment," *Journal of Health Economics* 19: 1089–15.

Magee, William, and Janani Umamaheswar. 2011. "Immigrant Group Differences in Job Satisfaction," *Immigrant Group Differences in Job Satisfaction*. Springer Science+Business Media (Sept.). At: <scienceindex.com/stories/1845471/Immigrant_Group_Differences_in_Job_Satisfaction.html>.

Maich, Steve. 2008. "Facts and Fairy Tales of Paulson's Bailout," *Maclean's* 121, 41: 47.

Manopaiboon, C., R.E. Bunnell, P.H. Kilmarx, S. Chaikummao, K. Limpakarnjanarat, S. Supawitkul, M.E. St Louis, and T.D. Mastro. 2003. "Leaving Sex Work: Barriers, Facilitating Factors and Consequences for Female Sex Workers in Northern Thailand," *AIDS Care* 15, 1: 39–52.

Marx, Karl. 1936 (1887). *Capital: A Critique of Political Economy*, trans. Samuel Moore and Edward Aveling, ed. Frederick Engels. Moscow: Progress Publishers.

Mathieu, Lilian. 2003. "The Emergence and Uncertain Outcomes of Prostitutes' Social Movements," *European Journal of Women's Studies* 10, 1: 29–50.

Meadows, Donella H., Dennis L. Meadows, Jorgen Randers, and William H. Behrens III. 1972. *The Limits to Growth.* New York: Universe Books.

Nixon, Kendra, Leslie Tutty, Pamela Downe, Kelly Gorkoff, and Jane Ursel. 2002. "The Everyday Occurrence: Violence in the Lives of Girls Exploited through Prostitution," *Violence against Women* 8, 9: 1016–43.

Ochsen, Carsten. 2011. "Subjective Well-Being and Aggregate Unemployment: Further Evidence," *Scottish Journal of Political Economy* 58, 5: 634–55.

Ooka, Emi, and Barry Wellman. 2006. "Does Social Capital Pay Off More within or between Ethnic Groups? Analysing Job Searches in Five Toronto Ethnic Groups," in Eric Fong, ed., *Inside the Mosaic.* Toronto: University of Toronto Press, 199–226.

Ostry, Aleck, Steve A. Marion, L. Green, Paul A. Demers, Kay Teshke, Ruth Hershler, Shona Kelly, and Clyde Hertzman. 2000. "The Relationship between Unemployment, Technological Change and Psychosocial Work Conditions in British Columbia Sawmills," *Critical Public Health* 10: 179–91.

Patrick, Megan E., and John E. Schulenberg. 2011. "How Trajectories of Reasons for Alcohol Use Relate to Trajectories of Binge Drinking: National Panel Data Spanning Late Adolescence to Early Adulthood," *Developmental Psychology* 47, 2: 311–17.

Paul, Karsten I., and Klaus Moser. 2009. "Unemployment Impairs Mental Health: Meta-Analyses," *Journal of Vocational Behavior* 74, 3: 264–82.

Popovici, Ioana, and Michael T. French. 2013. "Does Unemployment Lead to Greater Alcohol Consumption?," *Industrial Relations* 52, 2: 444–66.

Reitz, Jeffrey G., and Raymond Breton. 1998. "Prejudice and Discrimination in Canada and the United States: A Comparison," in V. Satzewich, ed., *Racism and Social Inequality in Canada.* Toronto: Thompson Educational Publishing, 47–68.

Renzetti, Claire M., and Daniel J Curran, eds. 2003. *Women, Men, and Society,* 5th edn. Boston: Pearson Education.

Rose, Nancy E. 2009. "Lessons from the New Deal Public Employment Programs," *Monthly Review* 61, 5: 21–32.

Rosenberg, Nathan, and Manuel Trajtenberg. 2004. "A General-Purpose Technology at Work: The Corliss Steam Engine in the Late 19th Century US," *Journal of Economic History* 64, 1: 61–99.

Ross-Smith, Anne, and Kate Huppatz. 2010. "Management, Women and Gender Capital," *Gender, Work & Organization* 17, 5: 547–66.

Sandy, Larissa. 2009. "'Behind Closed Doors': Debt-Bonded Sex Workers in Sihanoukville, Cambodia," *Asia Pacific Journal of Anthropology* 10, 3: 216–30.

Saurel Cubizolles, M.J., P. Romito, P.Y. Ancel, and N. Lelong. 2000. "Unemployment and Psychological Distress One Year after Childbirth in France," *Journal of Epidemiology and Community Health* 54: 185–91.

Schildt, Gerhard. 2006. "The Decline of the Volume of Labour in the Industrial Age," *Geschichte und Gesellschaft* 32, 1: 119–48.

Schmitt, E. 2001. "Significance of Employment and Unemployment in Middle and Advanced Adult Age for Subjective Perception of Aging and Realization of Potentials and Barriers of a Responsible Life," *Zeitschrift fur Gerontologie und Geriatrie* 34: 218–31.

Schuring, M., J. Mackenbach, T. Voorham, and A. Burdorf. 2011. "The Effect of Re-employment on Perceived Health," *Journal of Epidemiology and Community Health* 65, 7: 639–44.

Sikora, Patricia B. 2002. "Enlarging the View of Participation in Organizations: A Proposed Framework and Analysis via Structural Equation Modeling," PhD diss., University of Boulder.

Slebarska, Katarzyna, Klaus Moser, and George Gunnesch-Luca. 2009. "Unemployment, Social Support, Individual Resources, and Job Search Behavior," *Journal of Employment Counseling* 46, 4: 159–71.

Stanton, Jeffrey M., Peter D. Bachiochi, Chet Robie, Lisa M. Perez, and Patricia C. Smith. 2002. "Revising the JDI Work Satisfaction Subscale: Insights into Stress and Control," *Educational*

and Psychological Measurement 62, 5: 877–95.

Taylor, J. 2000. "Bureaucracy and Informal Practices in the Workplace," *Sociology Review* 9, 4: 17–20.

Tombs, Steve, and David Whyte. 2010. "A Deadly Consensus: Worker Safety and Regulatory Degradation under New Labour," *British Journal of Criminology* 50, 1: 46.

Torney, Colin, Zoltan Neufeld, and Iain D. Couzin. 2009. "Context-Dependent Interaction Leads to Emergent Search Behavior in Social Aggregates," *Proceedings of the National Academy of Sciences of the United States of America* 106, 52: 22055–60.

Turcotte, Martin. 2010. "Working at Home: An Update." Statistics Canada Catalogue no. 11-008-X.

Turcotte, Martin, and Grant Schellenberg. 2005. "Job Strain and Retirement," *Perspectives on Labour and Income* 17, 3: 35–9.

Twitty, Crystal Y. 2003. "Pretty Pennies for Pretty Faces: Trafficking of Women for the International Sex Trade," *Regent Journal of International Law* 2: 115.

UFCW (United Food and Commercial Workers). 2013. "By the Numbers: Workplace Fatalities and Time-Loss Injuries in Canada." *UFCW Canada.* At: <www.ufcw.ca/index .php?option=com_content>.

United Nations Population Fund. 2000. *State of World Population 2000: Lives Together, Worlds Apart: Men and Women in a Time of Change.* At: <www.unfpa .org/swp/2000/english/index.html>.

Vieira, J. 2005. "Skill Mismatches and Job Satisfaction," *Economics Letters* 89, 1: 39–47.

Virtanen, Pekka, Urban Janlert, and Anne Hammarström. 2011. "Exposure to Temporary Employment and Job Insecurity: A Longitudinal Study of the Health Effects," *Occupational and Environmental Medicine* 68, 8: 570–4.

Wallace, Jean E., and Fiona M. Kay. 2009. "Are Small Firms More Beautiful or Is Bigger Better? A Study of Compensating Differentials and Law Firm Internal Labor Markets," *Sociological Quarterly* 50, 3: 474–96.

Walsh, Brendan, and Dermot Walsh. 2011. "Suicide in Ireland: The Influence of Alcohol and Unemployment," *Economic and Social Review* 42, 1: 27–47.

Weber, Max. 1947. *The Theory of Social and Economic Organization*, trans. A.M. Henderson and Talcott Parsons. New York: Free Press.

Williamson, Celia, and Terry Cluse-Tolar. 2002. "Pimp-Controlled Prostitution: Still an Integral Part of Street Life," *Violence against Women* 8, 9: 1074–92.

Wray, Linda A. 2000. "Does Mental Health Affect Transitions out of the Labour Force in Older Workers?," paper presented at the annual meeting of the American Sociological Association.

Yap, Margaret, and Alison M. Konrad. 2009. "Gender and Racial Differentials in Promotions: Is There a Sticky Floor, a Mid-level Bottleneck, or a Glass Ceiling?," *Relations Industrielles* 64, 4: 593–619.

Yelin, E., J. Henke, P.P. Katz, M.D. Eisner, and P.D. Blanc. 1999. "Work Dynamics of Adults with Asthma," *American Journal of Industrial Medicine* 35: 472–80.

Yoon, Sang-Chul. 2001. "Essays on International Trade in Knowledge-Based Services." At: <gateway .proquest.com.myaccess.library .utoronto.ca/openurl?url_ver=Z39 .88-2004&rft_val_fmt=info:ofi/ fmt:kev:mtx:dissertation&res_dat=xri: pqdiss&rft_dat=xri:pqdiss:3010876>.

Ytterdahl, T., and P. Fugelli. 2000. "Health and Quality of Life among Long-Term Unemployed," *Tidsskrift for Den Norske Laegeforening* 120: 1308–11.

Zaleski, Marcos, Ilana Pinsky, Ronaldo Laranjeira, Suhasini Ramisetty-Mikler, and Raul Caetano. 2010. "Intimate Partner Violence and Contribution of Drinking and Sociodemographics: The Brazilian National Alcohol Survey," *Journal of Interpersonal Violence* 25, 4: 648–65.

Chapter 13

Aalsma, Matthew C., and James R. Brown. 2008. "What Is Bullying?," *Journal of Adolescent Health* 43, 2 (Aug.): 101–2.

Adams, R.B., and P. Funk, 2011. "Beyond the Glass Ceiling: Does Gender Matter?," *Management Science* 58, 2: 219–35. At: <mansci.journal.informs .org.myaccess.library.utoronto.ca/ content/58/2/219.full.pdf+html>.

Akiba, M., G.K. LeTendre, and J.P. Scribner. 2007. "Teacher Quality, Opportunity Gap, and National Achievement in 46 Countries," *Educational Researchers* 36, 7: 369–87.

Arnot, Madeleine, Miriam David, and Gaby Weiner. 1999. *Closing the Gender Gap: Postwar Education and Social Change*. Cambridge: Policy Press.

Bouie, J. 2012. "The Other Glass Ceiling," *American Prospect* 23, 3: 6–7, 9, 11. At: <search.proquest.com.myaccess.library .utoronto.ca/docview/1243385393>.

Bowlby, Geoff, and Kathryn McMullen. 2002. *At the Crossroads: First Results of the 18 to 20 Years Old Cohort of Youth in Transition Survey*. Ottawa: Human Resources and Development Canada, Catalogue no. H64–12/2002E.

Brank, E.M., L.A. Hoetger, and K.P. Hazen. 2012. "Bullying," *Annual Review of Law and Social Science* 8: 213–30. At: <www.annualreviews .org.myaccess.library.utoronto.ca/ doi/pdf/10.1146/annurev-lawsocsci-102811-173820>

Brown, Louise. 2009. "Africentric School Makes History," *Toronto Star*, 9 Sept. At: <www.thestar.com/ printArticle/692804>.

Canadian Council on Learning. 2009. "The State of Aboriginal Learning in Canada." At: <www.ccl-cca .ca/pdfs/StateAboriginalLearning/ SAL-FINALReport_EN.PDF>.

Canadian Internet Registration Authority. 2013. *CIRA Factbook 2013*. At: <www .cira.ca/factbook/2013/ca-and-the-world.html>.

Canadian Press, The. 2013. At: <www .huffingtonpost.ca/2013/04/10/unicef-child-well-being-canada_n_3050119 .html>.

Chiswick, Barry R., and Paul W. Miller. 2008. *The Economics of Language: International Analyses*. New York: Routledge.

Coleman, J.S., E.Q. Campbell, C.J. Hobson, F. McPartland, A.M. Mood, F.D. Weinfeld et al. 1966. *Equality of Educational Opportunity*. Washington, DC: US Government Printing Office.

Collins, Randall. 1979. *The Credential Society*. New York: Academic Press.

Colt, James P., Nancy B. Meyer, and Samuel C. McQuade. 2009. *Cyber Bullying: Protecting Kids and Adults from Bullies*. Westport, CN: Praeger.

CRTC (Canadian Radio-television and Telecommunications Commission). 2011.

Davies, Scott, and Neil Guppy. 2006. *The Schooled Society: An Introduction to the Sociology of Education*. Toronto: Oxford University Press.

Dillabough, J., and M. Arnot. 2002. "Feminist Perspectives in Sociology of Education: Continuity and Transformation in the Field," in D. Levinson, R. Sadovnik, and P. Cookson, eds, *Sociology of Education: An Encyclopedia*. New York: Taylor and Francis.

Donnelly, Rory. 2009. "Career Behaviour in the Knowledge Economy: Experiences and Perceptions of Career Mobility among Management and IT Consultants in the UK and the US," *Journal of Vocational Behaviour* 75, 3: 319–28.

Dorn, Richard, Gary Bowen, and Judith Blau. 2006. "The Impact of Community Diversity and Consolidated Inequality on Dropping Out of High School," *Family Relations* 55: 105–18.

Furlong, Andy. 2008. "The Japanese Hikikomori Phenomenon: Acute Social Withdrawal among Young People," *Sociological Review* 56, 2: 309–25.

Furniss, Elizabeth. 1992. *Victims of Benevolence: The Dark Side of the Williams Lake Residential School*. Vancouver: Arsenal Pulp Press.

Goldthorpe, John H. 1985. "On Economic Development and Social Mobility," *British Journal of Sociology* 36, 4: 549–73.

Gomme, I. 2004. "Education," in R.J. Brym, ed., *New Society: Sociology for the 21st Century*, 4th edn. Scarborough, ON: Nelson Thomson, 359–81.

Greening, Daniel W., and Daniel B. Turban. 2000. "Corporate Social Performance as a Competitive Advantage in Attracting a Quality Workforce," *Business and Society* 39, 3: 254–80.

Guerra, Carmen E., Megan Krumholz, and Judy A. Shea. 2005. "Literacy and Knowledge, Attitudes and Behavior about Mammography in Latinas," *Journal of Health Care for the Poor and Underserved* 16, 1: 152–66.

Guppy, Neil, and Scott Davies. 1998. *Education in Canada: Recent Trends and Future Challenges*. Ottawa: Statistics Canada Catalogue no. 96–321.

Gupta, P.C., and C.S. Ray. 2007. "Tobacco, Education & Health,"

Indian Journal of Medical Research 126, 4: 289–99.

Halperin, Keith M. 1990. "Helping Rising Stars Shine as Managers," *Training and Development Journal* 44, 7: 76.

Harkness, Suzan. 2001. "Women and Work: Dynamics of the Glass Ceiling and Public Policy Perspectives," PhD thesis, University of Hawaii.

Harmon, Amy. 2004. "Internet Gives Teenage Bullies Weapons to Wound from Afar," *New York Times*, 26 Aug. At: <www.nytimes.com./2004/08/26/education>.

Hiebert, Daniel. 2012. *A New Residential Order? The Social Geography of Visible Minority and Religious Groups in Montreal, Toronto, and Vancouver in 2031*. Ottawa: Citizenship and Immigration Canada, July.

Hinduja, S., and J.W. Patchin. 2010. "Bullying, Cyberbullying, and Suicide," *Archives of Suicide Research* 14: 206–21. At: <journals2.scholarsportal.info.myaccess.library.utoronto.ca/tmp/16338818849577392505.pdf>.

HRSDC (Human Resources and Skills Development Canada). 2013. "Learning—School Drop-Outs," *Human Resources and Skills Development Canada*. At: <www4.hrsdc.gc.ca/.3ndic.1t.4r@-eng.jsp?iid=32>.

Ishikawa, H., and T. Kiuchi. 2010. "Health Literacy and Health Communication," *BioPsychoSocial Medicine* 18, 4. At: <www.bpsmedicine.com/content/4/1/18>.

Johnson, David. 2009. "Ontario's Best Public Schools, 2005/06–2007/08: An Update to *Signposts of Success* (2005)." Toronto: C.D. Howe Institute. At: <www.cdhowe.org/pdf/ebrief_85.pdf>.

Lagerquist, J. 2012. "Student Debt: Average Payback Takes 14 Years," *Financial Post*. At: <business.financialpost.com/2012/09/04/student-debt-average-payback-takes-14-years>.

Livingstone, D., D. Hart, and L.E. Davie. 2003. *Public Attitudes towards Education in Ontario: The 14th OISE/UT Survey*. Toronto: Ontario Institute for Studies in Education.

Luong, M. 2010. "The Financial Impact of Student Loans," *Statistics Canada*. At: <users.encs.concordia.ca/~ecsga/Financial%20impact%20of%20student%20loans.pdf>.

McMullen, K. 2011. "Postsecondary Education Participation among Underrepresented and Minority Groups," *Statistics Canada*. At: <www.statcan.gc.ca/pub/81-004-x/2011004/article/11595-eng.htm#a>.

McMullin, Julie Ann. 2004. *Understanding Social Inequality: Intersections of Class, Age, Gender, Ethnicity, and Race in Canada*. Toronto: Oxford University Press.

Meerkerk, Elise van Nederveen. 2006. "Segmentation in the Pre-industrial Labour Market: Women's Work in the Dutch Textile Industry, 1581–1810," *International Review of Social History* 51, 2: 189–216.

Ministry of Aboriginal Affairs. 2012. "Aboriginal Education," *Ministry of Aboriginal Affairs*. At: <www.aboriginalaffairs.gov.on.ca/english/services/datasheets/education.asp>.

Murphy, Raymond. 1979. *Sociological Theories of Education*. Toronto: McGraw-Hill Ryerson.

Ng, Roxanna. 1993. "Racism, Sexism and Nation-Building in Canada," in Cameron McCarthy and Warren Crichlow, eds, *Race, Identity and Representation in Education*. New York: Routledge, 50–9.

Nicholas, Andrea Bear. 2001. "Canada's Colonial Mission: The Great White Bird," in K.P. Binda, ed., with Sharilyn Calliou, *Aboriginal Education in Canada: A Study in Decolonization*. Mississauga, ON: Canadian Educators' Press.

OECD (Organisation for Economic Co-operation and Development). 2005. *Teachers Matter: Attracting, Developing and Retaining Effective Teachers*. Paris: OECD.

————. 2013. *Education at a Glance 2013: OECD Indicators*. At: <www.oecd.org/education/eag.htm>.

Our Kids. 2012. "At Risk Teen Girls," *Our Kids*. At: <www.ourkids.net/at-risk-girls-teens.php>.

Pitts, J., and P. Smith. 1995. *Preventing School Bullying*. Police Research Group, Crime Detection and Prevention Series Paper 63. London: Home Office.

Quint, Janet, Saskia Levy Thompson, and Margaret Bald, with Julia Bernstein and Kaura Sztejnberg. 2008. *Relationships, Rigor, and Readiness: Strategies for Improving High Schools*. New York: MDRC, Oct.

Reitz, Jeffrey G. 2001. "Immigrant Skill Utilization in the Canadian Labour Market: Implications of Human Capital Research," *Journal of International Migration and Integration* 2, 3: 347–78.

Roach Anleu, Sharyn, and Kathy Mack. 2008. "The Professionalization of Australian Magistrates: Autonomy, Credentials and Prestige," *Journal of Sociology* 44, 2: 185–203.

Ronson, Barbara, and Irving Rootman. 2004. "Literacy: One of the Most Important Determinants of Health Today," in Dennis Raphael, ed., *Social Determinants of Health: Canadian Perspectives*. Toronto: Canadian Scholars' Press.

Rosenbaum, James E. 2001. *Beyond College for All Career Paths for the Forgotten Half*. New York: Russell Sage Foundation.

Sanders, William L., and June C. Rivers. 1996. *Cumulative and Residual Effects of Teachers on Future Student Academic Achievement*. Knoxville: University of Tennessee Value-Added Research and Assessment Center.

Santiago, Paulo. 2004. "The Labour Market for Teachers," in G. Johnes and J. Jones, eds, *International Handbook on the Economics of Education*. Cheltenham, UK: Edward Elgar.

Sasaki, Yosei. 2000. "Effects of Ascribed Status on Educational Attainment," *Shakaigaku Hyoron/Japanese Sociological Review* 51, 2: 33–48.

Schacter, John, and Yeow Meng Thum. 2004. "Paying for High and Low-Quality Teaching," *Economics of Education Review* 23: 411–30.

Shaker, E. 2012. "The High Cost of Learning: There's No Excuse for the Soaring Tuition Fees in Canada," *Canadian Centre for Policy Alternatives*. At: <www.policyalternatives.ca/publications/monitor/high-cost-learning>.

Shariff, Shaheen. 2005. "Cyber-Dilemmas in the New Millennium: School Obligations to Provide Student Safety in a Virtual School Environment," *McGill Journal of Education* 40, 3: 467–87.

Sianou-Kyrgiou, E. 2008. "Social Class and Access to Higher Education in Greece: Supportive Preparation Lessons and Success In National Exams," *International Studies in Sociology of Education* 18, 3–4: 173–83. At: <journals1.scholarsportal.info.myaccess.library.utoronto.ca/tmp/14378177066057083501.pdf>.

Statistics Canada. 2009a. "Quality of Employment for Immigrants to Canada." At: <www.statcan.gc.ca/pub/71-606-x/2009001/part-partie1-eng.htm>.

———. 2009b. "Self-Reported Internet Victimization in Canada," *Statistics Canada*. At: <www.statcan.gc.ca/daily-quotidien/110915/dq110915c-eng.htm>.

———. 2010a. "Intensity of Internet Use in Canada: Understanding Different Types of Users," *Statistics Canada*. At: <www.statcan.gc.ca/pub/88f0006x/2010002/part-partie1-eng.htm>.

———. 2010b. "University Enrolment," *Statistics Canada*. At: <www.statcan.gc.ca/daily-quotidien/100714/dq100714a-eng.htm>.

———. 2011. *Self-Reported Internet Victimization in Canada, 2009*, by Samuel Perreault. *Statistics Canada*. At <www.statcan.gc.ca/pub/85-002-x/2011001/article/11530-eng.htm>.

———. 2012. "Education Indicators in Canada: An International Perspective, 2010," *Statistics Canada*. At: <www.statcan.gc.ca/daily-quotidien/120911/dq120911b-eng.pdf>.

———. 2013a. "The Educational Attainment of Aboriginal Peoples in Canada." At: <www12.statcan.gc.ca/nhs-enm/2011/as-sa/99-012-x/99-012-x2011003_3-eng.cfm>.

———. 2013b. "2011 National Household Survey: Aboriginal Peoples in Canada: First Nations People, Métis and Inuit," *Statistics Canada*. At: <www12.statcan.gc.ca/nhs-enm/2011/as-sa/99-011-x/99-011-x2011001-eng.cfm>.

Stonefish, Brent. 2007. *Moving Beyond: Understanding the Impacts of Residential School*. Owen Sound, ON: Ningwakwe Learning Press.

Wollstonecraft, Mary. 1997 [1792]. *The Vindication of the Rights of Women*. London: Penguin.

Xue, L., and L. Xu. 2010. "Employment Outcomes of Postsecondary Educated Immigrants, 2006 Census," *Citizenship and Immigration Canada*. At: <www.cic.gc.ca/english/resources/research/employment.asp>.

Zhunio, M.C., S. Vishwasrao, and E.P. Chiang. 2012. "The Influence on Remittances on Education and Health Outcomes: A Cross Country Study,"
Applied Economics 44: 4605–16. At: <journals1.scholarsportal.info.myaccess.library.utoronto.ca/tmp/2396016502146325771.pdf>.

Chapter 14

Alasia, Alessandro, Alfons Weersink, Ray D. Bollman, and John Cranfield. 2009. "Off-Farm Labour Decision of Canadian Farm Operators: Urbanization Effects and Rural Labour Market Linkages," *Journal of Rural Studies* 25, 1: 12–24.

Ali, Abu Muhammad Shajaat. 2007. "Population Pressure, Agricultural Intensification and Changes in Rural Systems in Bangladesh," *Geoforum* 38, 4: 720–38.

Andersson, Roger. 2008. "Neighbourhood Effects and the Welfare State: Towards a European Research Agenda?," *Schmollers Jahrbuch* 128, 1: 49–63.

Atkinson, Rowland. 2003. "Introduction: Misunderstanding Saviour or Vengeful Wrecker? The Many Meanings and Problems of Gentrification," *Urban Studies* 40, 12: 2343–50.

Attane, Isabelle. 2006. "The Demographic Impact of a Female Deficit in China, 2000–2050," *Population and Development Review* 32, 4: 755–70.

Authier, Jean-Yves. 2008. "The Urban Dwellers and Their Neighborhood: Surveys of Residents from Inner-City Neighborhoods in France" [Les citadins et leur quartier. Enquetes aupres d'habitants de quartiers anciens centraux en France], *L'Annee sociologique* 58, 1: 21–46.

Baker, Rochelle. 2009. "Homeless in the City: Bruce Lived Here," *Abbotsford News*, 25 Sept. At: <www.bclocalnews.com/fraser_valley/abbynews/news/61562687.html>.

Bandy, Matthew S. 2005. "New World Settlement Evidence for a Two-Stage Neolithic Demographic Transition," *Current Anthropology* 46 (suppl.): S109–S115.

Brint, Steven. 2001. "Gemeinschaft Revisited: A Critique and Reconstruction of the Community Concept," *Sociological Theory* 19, 1: 1–23.

Browning, Christopher R., Lori A. Burrington, Tama Leventhal, and Jeanne Brooks-Gunn. 2008. "Neighborhood Structural Inequality, Collective Efficacy, and Sexual Risk Behavior
among Urban Youth," *Journal of Health and Social Behavior* 49, 3: 269–85.

Burdette, Amy M., and Terrence D. Hill. 2008. "An Examination of Processes Linking Perceived Neighborhood Disorder and Obesity," *Social Science and Medicine* 67, 1: 38–46.

Button, Deeanna M. 2008. "Social Disadvantage and Family Violence: Neighborhood Effects on Attitudes about Intimate Partner Violence and Corporal Punishment," *American Journal of Criminal Justice* 33, 1: 130–47.

Carpiano, Richard M. 2008. "Actual or Potential Neighborhood Resources and Access to Them: Testing Hypotheses of Social Capital for the Health of Female Caregivers," *Social Science and Medicine* 67, 4: 568–82.

Clark, Gregory, and Neil Cummins. 2009. "Urbanization, Mortality, and Fertility in Malthusian England," *American Economic Review* 99, 2: 242–7.

Cohen, Joel. 1995. "Population Growth and Earth's Human Carrying Capacity," *Science* 269 (5222): 341–6.

Crafts, N., and T.C. Mills. 2009. "From Malthus to Solow: How Did the Malthusian Economy Really Evolve?," *Journal of Macroeconomics* 31, 1: 68–93.

Daily Bread Food Bank. 2002, 2006. *Poorer People, Poorer Health: The Health of Food Bank Recipients, Spring Food Drive*. Toronto: Daily Bread Food Bank.

Dear, Michael. 2003. "The Los Angeles School of Urbanism: An Intellectual History," *Urban Geography* 24, 6: 493–509.

Dickason, Olive Patricia. 2002. *Canada's First Nations: A History of Founding Peoples from Earliest Times*, 3rd edn. Toronto: Oxford University Press.

Duke-Williams, Oliver, and Nicola Shelton. 2008. "Small Area Inequalities in Health: Are We Underestimating Them?," *Social Science and Medicine* 67, 6: 891–9.

Durkheim, Émile. 1964 [1893]. *Division of Labor in Society*, trans. George Simpson. Glencoe, IL: Free Press.

Ehrmann, Nicholas, and Douglas S. Massey. 2008. "Gender-Specific Effects of Ecological Conditions on College Achievement," *Social Science Research* 37, 1: 220–38.

Emerson, Michael O., George Yancey, and Karen J. Chai. 2001. "Does Race Matter in Residential Segregation?

Exploring the Preferences of White Americans," *American Sociological Review* 66: 922–35.

Fazal, Shahab. 2006. "Addressing Congestion and Transport-Related Air Pollution in Saharanpur, India," *Environment & Urbanization* 18, 1: 141–54.

Flowerdew, Robin, David J. Manley, and Clive E. Sabel. 2008. "Neighbourhood Effects on Health: Does It Matter Where You Draw the Boundaries?," *Social Science and Medicine* 66, 6: 1241–55.

Fong, Eric, and Kumiko Shibuya. 2000. "Spatial Separation of the Poor in Canadian Cities," *Demography* 37, 4: 449–59.

Fortin, Andrée, Marie-Helene Villeneuve, and Martin Rioux. 2008. "Never without My Car? Suburbanites in the Area Surrounding Quebec City," *Recherches Sociographiques* 49, 3: 447–73.

Gajdos, Peter. 2009. "Globalization Context of Urban Development and Its Socio-Spatial Particularities," *Sociologia—Slovak Sociological Review* 41, 4: 304–28.

Galster, George C. 2008. "Quantifying the Effect of Neighbourhood on Individuals: Challenges, Alternative Approaches, and Promising Directions," *Schmollers Jahrbuch* 128, 1: 7–48.

Gans, Herbert. 1982. *The Urban Villagers: Group and Class in the Life of Italian-Americans*, 2nd edn. New York: Free Press.

Ghitter, Geoff, and Alan Smart. 2009. "Mad Cows, Regional Governance, and Urban Sprawl: Path Dependence and Unintended Consequences in the Calgary Region," *Urban Affairs Review* 44, 5: 617–44.

Gilbert, J., and K. Wehr. 2003. "Dairy Industrialization in the First Place: Urbanization, Immigration, and Political Economy in Los Angeles County, 1920–1970," *Rural Sociology* 68, 4: 467–90.

Glaeser, Edward L., and Joshua D. Gottlieb. 2006. "Urban Resurgence and the Consumer City," *Urban Studies* 43, 8: 1275–99.

Goode, William. 1963. *World Revolution and Family Patterns*. New York: Free Press.

Haub, Carl. 2012. "Fact Sheet: World Population Trends 2012," in Population Reference Bureau. At: <www.prb .org/Publications/Datasheets/2012/ world-population-data-sheet/fact-sheet-world-population.aspx>.

Haussermann, Hartmut. 2005. "The End of the European City?," *European Review* 13, 2: 237–49.

Hoffmann, John P. 2004. "Social and Environmental Influences on Endangered Species: A Cross-National Study," *Sociological Perspectives* 47, 1: 79–107.

Huiban, Jean-Pierre. 2009. "Urban versus Rural Firms: Does Location Affect Labor Demand?," *Growth and Change* 40, 4: 649–72.

Johnson, Katherine M., and Charles G. Schmidt. 2009. "'Room to Grow': Urban Ambitions and the Limits to Growth in Weld County, Colorado," *Urban Affairs Review* 44, 4: 525–53.

Johnson-Hanks, Jennifer. 2008. "Demographic Transitions and Modernity," *Annual Review of Anthropology* 37: 301–15.

Jung, Changhoon, Chul-Young Roh, and Younguck Kang. 2009. "Longitudinal Effects of Impact Fees and Special Assessments on the Level of Capital Spending, Taxes, and Long-Term Debt in American Cities," *Public Finance Review* 37, 5: 613–36.

Kalkhoff, Will, Stanford W. Gregory Jr, and David Melamed. 2009. "Effects of Dichotically Enhanced Electronic Communication on Crash Risk and Performance during Simulated Driving," *Perceptual and Motor Skills* 108, 2: 449–64.

Kasman, Adnan, and Evrim Turgutlu. 2009. "Cost Efficiency and Scale Economies in the Turkish Insurance Industry," *Applied Economics* 41, 24: 3151.

Kellett, Livia, Lyla Peter, and Kelley Moore. 2008. "The City of Saskatoon's Local Area Planning Program: A Case Study," *Social Indicators Research* 85, 1: 159–67.

Kirk, David S. 2008. "The Neighborhood Context of Racial and Ethnic Disparities in Arrest," *Demography* 45, 1: 55–77.

Lehr, C.S. 2009. "Evidence on the Demographic Transition," *Review of Economics and Statistics* 91, 4: 871–87.

Lutz, Wolfgang, Warren Sanderson, and Sergei Scherbov. 2001. "The End of the World Population Growth," *Nature* 412: 543–5.

———. 2006. "The Coming Acceleration of Global Population Ageing," *Nature* 451, 1: 716–19.

Machum, Susan. 1992. "The Impact of Agribusiness on Women's Work in the Household, on-the-Farm and off-the-Farm: A New Brunswick Case Study." UMI Dissertations Publishing.

———. 2005. "The Persistence of Family Farming in the Wake of Agribusiness: A New Brunswick, Canada Case Study," *Journal of Comparative Family Studies* 36, 3: 337–90.

MacIntyre, Sally, Laura MacDonald, and Anne Ellaway. 2008. "Do Poorer People Have Poorer Access to Local Resources and Facilities? The Distribution of Local Resources by Area Deprivation in Glasgow, Scotland," *Social Science and Medicine* 67, 6: 900–14.

McKenzie, Kwame. 2008. "Urbanization, Social Capital and Mental Health," *Global Social Policy* 8, 3: 359–77.

Malmberg, Bo, and Tsegaye Tegenu. 2007. "Population Pressure and Dynamics of Household Livelihoods in an Ethiopian Village: An Elaboration of the Boserup-Chayanovian Framework," *Population and Environment* 29, 2: 39–67.

Malthus, Thomas R. 1959 [1798]. *Population: The First Essay*. Ann Arbor: University of Michigan Press.

Miller, Keva M., and Michael. H. Phillips. 2005. "Correlates of Urban Stress and Mental Health: The Impact of Social Context on Resilience," *Journal of Social Distress and the Homeless* 14, 1: 46–64.

Millward, Hugh. 2008. "Evolution of Population Densities: Five Canadian Cities, 1971–2001," *Urban Geography* 29, 7: 616–38.

Millward, Hugh, and Trudi Bunting. 2008. "Patterning in Urban Population Densities: A Spatiotemporal Model Compared with Toronto 1971–2001," *Environment and Planning A* 40, 2: 283–302.

Muhajarine, Nazeem, Ronald Labonte, Allison Williams, and James Randall. 2008. "Person, Perception, and Place: What Matters to Health and Quality of Life," *Social Indicators Research* 85, 1: 53–80.

Ng, Shu W., E.C. Norton, and B.M. Popkin. 2009. "Why Have Physical Activity Levels Declined among Chinese Adults? Findings from the 1991–2006 China Health and Nutrition Surveys," *Social Science and Medicine* 68, 7: 1305–14.

Nicolini, Esteban A. 2007. "Was Malthus Right? A VAR Analysis of Economic and Demographic Interactions in Pre-industrial England," *European Review of Economic History* 11, 1: 99–121.

Norton, William. 2010. *Human Geography*, 7th edn. Toronto: Oxford University Press.

Oreopoulos, Philip. 2008. "Neighbourhood Effects in Canada: A Critique," *Canadian Public Policy* 34, 2: 237–58.

Otte, Gunnar, and Nina Baur. 2008. "Urbanism as a Way of Life? Spatial Variations in Lifestyles in Germany," *Zeitschrift Für Soziologie* 37, 2: 93–116.

Pastor, Manuel, Jr, Rachel Morello Frosch, and James L. Sadd. 2005. "The Air Is Always Cleaner on the Other Side: Race, Space, and Ambient Air Toxics Exposures in California," *Journal of Urban Affairs* 27, 2: 127–48.

Pastor, Manuel, Jr, James L. Sadd, and Rachel Morello-Frosch. 2004. "Waiting to Inhale: The Demographics of Toxic Air Release Facilities in 21st-Century California," *Social Science Quarterly* 85, 2: 420–40.

Platt, Lucinda. 2009. "Social Activity, Social Isolation and Ethnicity," *Sociological Review* 57, 4: 670–702.

Poulton, Michael. 2007. "When America Became Suburban," *Canadian Journal of Urban Research* 16, 2: 182–4.

Powdthavee, Nattavudh. 2008. "Putting a Price Tag on Friends, Relatives, and Neighbours: Using Surveys of Life Satisfaction to Value Social Relationships," *Journal of Socio-economics* 37, 4: 1459–80.

Reading, Richard, Andrew Jones, Robin Haynes, Konstantinos Daras, and Alan Emond. 2008. "Individual Factors Explain Neighbourhood Variations in Accidents to Children under 5 Years of Age," *Social Science and Medicine* 67, 6: 915–27.

Sahoo, Pravakar, and Ranjan K. Dash. 2009. "Infrastructure Development and Economic Growth in India," *Journal of the Asia Pacific Economy* 14, 4: 351–65.

Sauvy, Alfred, and Paul Demeny. 1990. "Alfred Sauvy on the World Population Problem: A View in 1949," *Population and Development Review* 16: 759–74.

Schieman, Scott. 2009. "Residential Stability, Neighborhood Racial Composition, and the Subjective Assessment of Neighborhood Problems among Older Adults," *Sociological Quarterly* 50, 4: 608–32.

Shandra, John M., Bruce London, and John B. Williamson. 2003. "Environmental Degradation, Environmental Sustainability, and Overurbanization in the Developing World: A Quantitative, Cross-National Analysis," *Sociological Perspectives* 46, 3: 309–29.

Simkins, Charles. 2001. "Can South Africa Avoid a Malthusian Positive Check?," *Daedalus* 130, 1: 123–50.

Simmel, Georg. 1950 [1917]. *The Sociology of Georg Simmel*, trans. Kurt Wolff. New York: Free Press.

Simon, Julian L. 1996. *The Ultimate Resource 2*. Princeton, NJ: Princeton University Press.

Squires, Richard. 2008. "The Interstate Sprawl System," *Society* 45, 3: 277–82.

Tönnies, Ferdinand. 1957 [1887]. *Community and Society (Gemeinschaft und Gesellschaft)*. New York: Harper and Row.

United Nations Population Division (UNPD). 2006. *World Urbanization Prospects: The 2003 Revision Population Database*. At: <esa.un.org/unup>.

Urban, Susanne. 2009. "Is the Neighbourhood Effect an Economic or an Immigrant Issue? A Study of the Importance of the Childhood Neighbourhood for Future Integration into the Labour Market," *Urban Studies* 46, 3: 583–603.

van Alphen, Laura M., Anton J.M. Dijker, Arjan E.R. Bos, Bart H.W. van den Borne, and Leopold M.G. Curfs. 2011. "Explaining Not-in-My-Backyard Responses to Different Social Groups: The Role of Group Characteristics and Emotions," *Social Psychological and Personality Science* 2, 3: 245–52.

Vortkamp, Wolfgang. 1998. "Participation and Community: Louis Wirth's Sociology of Modernity in the Chicago School Tradition," *Soziale Welt* 49, 3: 275–94.

Wassmer, Robert W. 2008. "Causes of Urban Sprawl in the United States: Auto Reliance as Compared to Natural Evolution, Flight from Blight, and Local Revenue Reliance," *Journal of Policy Analysis and Management* 27, 3: 536–55.

Weber, Max. 1958 [1921]. *The City*, trans. Don Martindale and Gertrud Neuwirth. New York: Free Press.

———. 1981 [1924]. *General Economic History*. New Brunswick, NJ: Transaction Books.

Weil, David N., and Joshua Wilde. 2009. "How Relevant Is Malthus for the Economic Development Today?," *American Economic Review* 99, 2: 255–61.

Weir, L., D. Etelson, and D. Brand. 2006. "Parents' Perceptions of Neighborhood Safety and Children's Physical Activity," *Preventive Medicine* 43, 3: 212–17.

Westaway, M.S. 2007. "Life and Neighborhood Satisfaction of Black and White Residents in a Middle-Class Suburb of Johannesburg," *Psychological Reports* 100, 2: 489–94.

Williams, Allison M., Nazeem Muhajarine, James Randall, Ronald Labonte, and Peter Kitchen. 2008. "Volunteerism and Residential Longevity in Saskatoon, Saskatchewan, Canada," *Social Indicators Research* 85, 1: 97–110.

Wirth, Louis. 1996 [1938]. "Urbanism as a Way of Life," in Richard T. LeGates and Frederic Stout, eds, *The City Reader*. New York: Routledge, 97–105.

Wright, Judith, and Nazeem Muhajarine. 2008. "Respiratory Illness in Saskatoon Infants: The Impact of Housing and Neighbourhood Characteristics," *Social Indicators Research* 85, 1: 81–95.

Wrobel, David. 2008. "Paradise Pondered: Urban California, 1850–2000," *Journal of Urban History* 34, 6: 1029–43.

Xu, Z.L., and N. Zhu. 2009. "City Size Distribution in China: Are Large Cities Dominant?," *Urban Studies* 46, 10: 2159–85.

Yao, Li, and Stephanie A. Robert. 2008. "The Contributions of Race, Individual Socioeconomic Status, and Neighborhood Socioeconomic Context on the Self-Rated Health Trajectories and Mortality of Older Adults," *Research on Aging* 30, 2: 251–73.

Young, M.G. 2012. "Necessary but Insufficient: NIMBY and the Development of a Therapeutic Community for Homeless Persons with Co-morbid Disorders," *Local Environment* 17, 3: 281–93.

Yu, Wei-hsin. 2008. "The Psychological Cost of Market Transition: Mental Health Disparities in Reform-Era China," *Social Problems* 55, 3: 347–69.

Yuan, Anastasia S. Vogt. 2008. "Racial Composition of Neighborhood and Emotional Well-Being," *Sociological Spectrum* 28, 1: 105–29.

Chapter 15

Anonymous. 2008. "Nigeria: The Desert Is Fast Encroaching, but Why?," *Civil Engineering: Magazine of the South African Institution of Civil Engineering* 16, 5: 75.

Aronowitz, Stanley, and Jonathan Cutler, eds. 1998. *Post-work: The Wages of Cybernation*. New York: Routledge.

Balaban, Oded, and A. Tsatskin. 2010. "The Paradox of Oil Reserve Forecasts: The Political Implications of Predicting Oil Reserves and Oil Consumption," *Energy Policy* 38, 3: 1340–4.

Bandarage, Asoka. 2008. "Control Cash Not People," *The Ecologist* 38, 8: 58.

Beck, Ulrich. 1992. *Risk Society: Towards a New Modernity*. London: Sage.

Benn, S., P. Brown, and A. North-Samardzic. 2009. "A Commentary on Decision-Making and Organizational Legitimacy in the Risk Society," *Journal of Environmental Management* 90, 4: 1655–62.

Binder, Seth, and Eric Neumayer. 2005. "Environmental Pressure Group Strength and Air Pollution: An Empirical Analysis," *Ecological Economics* 55, 4: 527–38.

Borek, Erika, and A. Bohon Stephanie. 2008. "Policy Climates and Reductions in Automobile Use," *Social Science Quarterly* 89, 5: 1293–311.

Boyd, David. 2001. *Canada vs. the OECD: An Environment Comparison*. Victoria, BC: Eco-Research Chair, University of Victoria. At: <www.environmentalindicators.com/htdocs/PDF/CanadavsOECD.pdf>.

BP Global. 2012. "Statistical Review of World Energy 2012," *BP Global*. At: <www.bp.com/sectiongenericarticle800.do?categoryId=9037128&contentId=7068555>.

Burra, Tara A., Susan J. Elliott, John D. Eyles, Pavlos S. Kanaroglou, Bruce C. Wainman, and Henry Muggah. 2006. "Effects of Residential Exposure to Steel Mills and Coking Works on Birth Weight and Preterm Births among Residents of Sydney, Nova Scotia," *Canadian Geographer* 50, 2: 242–55. At: <www.accessmylibrary.com/article-1G1-149462231/effects-residential-exposure-steel.html>.

Canadian Press, The. 2010. "Canadians Waste Water Resources: Expert," *CBC News, Montreal*. At: <www.cbc.ca/news/canada/montreal/story/2010/04/21/mtl-millenium-summit-water.html>.

Carter, Neil. 2001. *The Politics of the Environment: Ideas, Activism, Policy*. Cambridge: Cambridge University Press.

CBC News. 2007. "Kyoto and Beyond: Kyoto FAQs," 14 Feb. At: <www.cbc.ca/news/background/kyoto>.

Cizek, Petr. 2004. "Hydro Hype, Dam Delusions: The Proposal to Dam the Deh Cho for Hydroelectricity Is a Classic Case of Short-Sighted Energy Planning," *Alternatives Journal* 30, 1: 28–9.

Comim, Flavio, Pushpam Kumar, and Nicolas Sirven. 2009. "Poverty and Environment Links: An Illustration from Africa," *Journal of International Development* 21, 3: 447–69.

Coming Clean. 2006. "Body Burden." At: <www.chemicalbodyburden.org>.

Commodity HQ. 2014. At: <commodityhq.com/what-you-can-buy-with-americas-daily-oil-consumption>.

Copeland, Brian R., and Scott Taylor. 2004. "Trade, Growth, and Environmental Quality," *American Economic Review* 16: 147–68.

Couchman, Robert. 1986. "The International Social Revolution: Its Impact on Canadian Family Life," *Canadian Home Economics Journal* 36, 1: 10–12.

Coward, Harold, Rosemary Ommer, and Tony Pitcher, eds. 2000. *Just Fish: Ethics and Canadian Marine Fisheries*. St John's: ISER Books.

Crawford, K. 2009. "Emergency Environmentalism on Fear, Lifestyle Politics and Subjectivity," *Angelaki Journal of the Theoretical Humanities* 14, 2: 29–35.

Curran, Giorel. 2006. "Whither Environmentalism? Environmental Politics in the 21st Century," *Social Alternatives* 25, 2: 48–53.

Curtis, F. 2009. "Peak Globalization: Climate Change, Oil Depletion and Global Trade," *Ecological Economics* 69, 2: 427–34.

Dalton, Russell. 1994. *The Green Rainbow: Environmental Groups in Western Europe*. New Haven, CT: Yale University Press.

Davis, R. 2012. "A Popular Environmentalism: Making the Connections between Nature, Place and People," *Soundings* 51 (May).

Debrovner, Diane. 2002. "Save Your Child from Skin Cancer," *Parents* 77, 5: 108–12.

Doyle, Timothy. 2005. *Environmental Movements in Minority and Majority Worlds: A Global Perspective*. New Brunswick, NJ: Rutgers University Press.

Elena, Galan-del-Castillo, and Esther Velazquez. 2010. "From Water to Energy: The Virtual Water Content and Water Footprint of Biofuel Consumption in Spain," *Energy Policy* 38, 3: 1345–52.

Environment Canada. 2011. "Wise Water Use," *Environment Canada*. At: <www.ec.gc.ca/eau-water/default.asp?lang=En&n=F25C70EC-1>.

———. 2012. "Impacts of Air Pollution," *Environment Canada*. At: <www.ec.gc.ca/indicateurs-indicators/default.asp?lang=en&n=D189C09D-1>.

Eriksson, Sonja. 2009. "The Transition Initiative Comes to Cohousing," *Communities* 144: 51–3.

Etzioni, Amitai. 2004. "The Post-affluent Society," *Review of Social Economy* 62, 3: 407–20.

Evcil, A. Nilay. 2009. "Wheelchair Accessibility to Public Buildings in Istanbul," *Disability and Rehabilitation: Assistive Technology* 4, 2: 76–85.

Gaard, Greta, ed. 1993. *Ecofeminism: Women, Animals, Nature*. Philadelphia: Temple University Press.

Giddens, Anthony. 1990. *The Consequences of Modernity*. Cambridge, UK: Polity Press.

Gilbertson, Michael, and Andrew E. Watterson. 2007. "Diversionary Reframing of the Great Lakes Water Quality Agreement," *Journal of Public Health Policy* 28, 2: 201–15.

Greenberg, Michael R. 2009. "How Much Do People Who Live Near Major Nuclear Facilities Worry about Those Facilities? Analysis of National and Site-Specific Data," *Journal of Environmental Planning and Management* 52, 7: 919–37.

Greenpeace. 2001. "Pacific in Peril." At: <www.greenpeace.org>.

Haalboom, Bethany, Susan J. Elliott, John Eyles, and Henry Muggah. 2006. "The Risk Society at Work in the Sydney

'Tar Ponds,'" *Canadian Geographer* 50, 2: 227, 241.

Hannigan, John A. 1995. *Environmental Sociology: A Social Constructionist Perspective*. London: Routledge.

———. 2008. "Environmental Sociology: A Social Constructionist Perspective," *Organization and Environment* 21, 4: 503–5.

Helfgott, Roy B. 1988. *Computerized Manufacturing and Human Resources: Innovation through Employee Involvement*. Lexington, MA: Lexington Books.

Hoag, Hannah. 2006. "Burn, Baby, Burn?," *Canadian Wildlife* 12, 5: 30–3.

Homer-Dixon, Thomas. 1994. "Environmental Scarcities and Violent Conflict: Evidence from Cases," *International Security* 19, 1: 5–40.

Humphrey, Craig, Tammy L. Lewis, and Fredrick H. Buttel. 2002. *Environment, Energy, and Society: A New Synthesis*. Belmont, CA: Wadsworth.

Inglehart, Ronald. 1977. *The Silent Revolution: Changing Values and Political Styles among Western Publics*. Princeton, NJ: Princeton University Press.

———. 1990. *Culture Shift in Advanced Industrial Society*. Princeton, NJ: Princeton University Press.

Klare, Michael T. 2004. "Crude Awakening," *The Nation* 279, 15: 35–8, 40–1.

Lamal, Peter. 2009. "The Varied Concepts of 'Epidemic' and Our Varied Reactions," *The Skeptical Inquirer* 33, 5: 58.

Larsen, Soren. 2003. "Promoting Aboriginal Territoriality through Interethnic Alliances: The Case of the Cheslatta T'en in Northern British Columbia," *Human Organization* 62, 1: 74–84.

Li, Yi, Wen Wang, Haidong Kan, Bingheng Chen, and Xiaohui Xu. 2010. "Air Quality and Outpatient Visits for Asthma in Adults during the 2008 Summer Olympic Games in Beijing," *Science of the Total Environment* 408, 5: 1226–7.

Liu, S.Y, C.D. Linkletter, E.B. Loucks, M.M. Glymour, and S.L. Buka. 2012. "Decreased Births among Black Female Adolescents Following School Desegregation," *Social Science & Medicine* 74, 7: 982–8.

Madeley, John. 2009. "GM Contamination, Technology and Control," *Appropriate Technology* 36, 4: 16.

Martell, Luke. 2008. "Beck's Cosmopolitan Politics," *Contemporary Politics* 14, 2: 129–43.

Meadows, Donella, Jorgen Randers, and Dennis Meadows. 2004. *Limits to Growth: The 30-Year Update*. White River Jct., VT: Chelsea Green Publishing.

Murphy, Raymond. 2004. "Disaster or Sustainability: The Dance of Human Agents with Nature's Actants," *Canadian Review of Sociology and Anthropology* 41, 3: 249–67.

NASA (National Aeronautics and Space Administration). 2006. "2005 Warmest Year in over a Century." At: <www.nasa.gov/vision/earth/environment/2005_warmest.html>.

———. 2014. *Global Climate Change: Vital Signs of the Planet*. At: <climate.nasa.gov/key_indicators>.

Natural Resources Canada. 2012. *The State of Canada's Forests, Annual Report 2012*. Ottawa: Natural Resources Canada, Canadian Forest Service.

Nature.com. At: <blogs.nature.com/news/2012/02/world%E2%80%99s-water-footprint-linked-to-free-trade.html>.

Neitzel, Richard, Robyn R.M. Gershon, Marina Zeltser, Allison Canton, and Muhammad Akram. 2009. "Noise Levels Associated with New York City's Mass Transit Systems," *American Journal of Public Health* 99, 8: 1393–9.

Norgaard, Kari M. 2002. "Experiencing Global Warming: The Social Organization of Awareness, Denial and Innocence," paper presented at the World Congress of the International Sociological Association, Brisbane, Australia, 7–13 July.

Pacione, Michael. 2001. *Urban Geography: A Global Perspective*. New York: Routledge.

Perrow, Charles. 1999. *Normal Accidents: Living with High Risk Technologies*, 2nd edn. Princeton, NJ: Princeton University Press.

Phillips, Kate. 2006. "Report Cites Concerns over Fragrances in Lake Sediments," *Chemical Week* 168, 29: 45.

Plant, Judith. 1990. "The Place of Women in Polluted Places," in I. Diamond and G. Orenstein, eds, *Reweaving the World: The Emergence of Feminism*. San Francisco: Sierra Club Books, 173–88.

Population Reference Bureau. 2008. *Population Bulletin* 63, 3 (Sept.). At: <www.prb.org/pdf08/63.3highlights.pdf>.

Rivano-Fischer, D. 2004. "Wheelchair Accessibility of Public Buildings in Al-Ain, United Arab Emirates (UAE)," *Disability and Rehabilitation* 26, 19: 1150–7.

Roots, Chris. 1999. "Environmental Movements: From the Local to the Global," *Environmental Politics* 8, 1: 1–12.

Ryabov, A.B., and B. Blasius. 2011. "A Graphical Theory of Competition on Spatial Resource Gradients," *Ecology Letters* 14: 220–8.

Rynbrandt, Linda J., and Mary Jo Deegan. 2002. "The Ecofeminist Pragmatism of Caroline Bartlett Crane, 1896–1935," *American Sociologist* 33, 3: 58–69.

Scheelhaase, Janina, Wolfgang Grimme, and Martin Schaefer. 2010. "The Inclusion of Aviation into the EU Emission Trading Scheme—Impacts on Competition between European and Non-European Network Airlines," *Transportation Research: Part D: Transport and Environment* 15, 1: 14–25.

Scoffield, Heather. 2012. "Rio 20: Canada Exits Environmental Summit 'Very Happy' with Lack of Firm Commitments for Change," *Huffingtonpost.ca*, The Canadian Press, 22 June. At: <www.huffingtonpost.ca/2012/06/22/rio20-canada-peter-kent-environment-climate_n_1619612.html>.

Seekins, Tom, Nancy Arnold, and Catherine Ipsen. 2012. "Developing Methods for Grading the Accessibility of a Communality's Infrastructure," *Journal of Urban Planning and Development* 138, 3: 270–6.

Smith, Keith. 2001. *Environmental Hazards: Assessing Risk and Reducing Disaster*, 3rd edn. New York: Routledge.

Suzuki, David, and Holly Dressel. 2002. *Good News for a Change: How Everyday People Are Helping the Planet*. Vancouver: Greystone.

Tepperman, Lorne. 2001. "The Postmaterialist Thesis: Has There Been a Shift in Political Cultures?," in Douglas Baer, ed., *Political Sociology: Canadian Perspectives*. Toronto: Oxford University Press, 15–36.

United Nations Statistics Division. 2010. "Environmental Indicators: Natural Disasters." At: <unstats.un.org/unsd/environment/Hydro_disasters.htm>.

United States Energy Information Administration. 2001. "World Primary Energy Consumption (Btu) 1990–1999, Table E1." At: <www.eia.doe.gov/emeu/iea/tablee1.html>.

Verbruggen, A., M. Fischedick, W. Moomaw, T. Weir, A. Nadai, L.J. Nilsson, J. Nyboer, and J. Sathaye. 2010. "Renewable Energy Costs, Potentials, Barriers: Conceptual Issues," *Energy Policy* 38, 2: 850–61.

Vogel, David. 2003. "The Hare and the Tortoise Revisited: The New Politics of Consumer and Environmental Regulation in Europe," *British Journal of Political Science* 33: 557–80.

Waldie, Paul. 2012. "Environmental Summits Lose Value as Past Pledges Go Unmet," *Theglobeandmail.com*. 19 June. At: <www.theglobeandmail.com/news/politics/environmental-summits-lose-value-as-past-pledges-go-unmet/article4353692>.

Walkom, Thomas. "Walkom: At Rio 20, Canada Furiously Backpedals on Environment," *Thestar.com*. At: <www.thestar.com/news/canada/politics/article/1215710--walkom-at-rio-20-canada-furiously-backpedals-on-environment>.

WHO (World Health Organization). 1997. *Health and Environment in Sustainable Development: Five Years after the Earth Summit.* Geneva: WHO.

———. 1999. *Report on Infectious Diseases.* Geneva: WHO. At: <www.who.int/infectious-disease-report/index-rpt99.html>.

———. 2013a. "Database: Outdoor Air Pollution in Cities," *World Health Organization.* At: <www.who.int/phe/health_topics/outdoorair/databases/en/index.html>.

———. 2013b. "Global Health Observatory (WHO)," *World Health Organization.* At: <www.who.int/gho/phe/en/index.html>.

Windsor, J.E., and J.A. McVey. 2004. "The Annihilation of Both Place and Sense of Place: The Experience of the Cheslatta T'En Canadian First Nation within the Context of Large-Scale Environmental Projects," *Geographical Journal* 171, 2: 146–65.

Wolfenbarger, L.L. 2002. "Genetically Engineered Organisms: Assessing Environmental and Human Health Effects," *American Journal of Alternative Agriculture* 17, 4: 203–4.

World Meteorological Organization (WMO). 2000. "WMO Statement on the Status of the Global Climate in 1999," WMO, no. 913. At: <www.wmo.ch/web/wcp/wcdmp/statement/html/913-1999.html>.

Yogev-Baggio, T., H. Bibi, J. Dubnov, K. Or-Hen, R. Carel, and Boris A. Portnov. 2010. "Who Is Affected More by Air Pollution? Sick or Healthy? Some Evidence from a Health Survey of Schoolchildren Living in the Vicinity of a Coal-Fired Power Plant in Northern Israel," *Health and Place* 16, 2: 399–408.

Zito, Anthony R. 2005. "The European Union an Environmental Leader in a Global Environment," *Globalizations* 2, 3: 363–75.

Chapter 16

Abdel, Dina, and Moneim Rady. 2012. "Greece Debt Crisis: Causes, Implications and Policy Options," *Academy of Accounting and Financial Studies Journal* 16: 87.

Aligica, Paul D. 2009. "Social Predictions, Institutional Design and Prestige Loops: Richard Henshel's Contribution to Futures Studies," *Futures* 41, 3: 147–55.

Allardyce, L., A. Aningmiuq, G.K. Healey, B. Issaluk, R. Kamookak, and R. Mackenzie. 2011. "Community Perspectives on the Impact of Climate Change on Health in Nunavut, Canada," *Arctic* 64, 1: 89–97.

Anya, M.I., N.I. Ofem, W.B. Binang, and E.P. Umoren. 2012. "Climate Change and Food Security in Africa," *Asian Journal of Agricultural Research* 6, 2: 52–9.

Basalla, George. 1988. *The Evolution of Technology.* Cambridge: Cambridge University Press.

Baym, Nancy K., Yan Bing Zhang, and Mei-Chen Lin. 2004. "Social Interactions across Media," *New Media and Society* 6, 3: 299–318.

Childe, V. Gordon. 1936. *Man Makes Himself.* London: Watts and Co.

Chomsky, Noam. 1999. "Language Design," in Griffiths (1999).

Ciscar, Juan-Carlos, Ana Iglesias, Luc Feyen, Laszlo Szabo, Denise Van Regemorter, Bas Amelung, Robert Nicholls, Paul Watkiss, Ole Christensen, Rutger Dankers, Luis Garrote, Clare Goodess, Alistair Hunt, Alvaro Moreno, Julie Richards, and Antonio Soria. 2011. "Physical and Economic Consequences of Climate Change in Europe," *Proceedings of the National Academy of Sciences of the United States of America* 108, 7: 2678–83.

Cole, S. 2008. "The Zeitgeist of Futures?," *Futures* 40, 10: 894–902.

Davis, Kevin. 2010. "Regulatory Responses to the Financial Sector Crisis," *Griffith Law Review* 19, 1: 117–37.

Department of Finance Canada. 2012. "Economic and Fiscal Implications of Canada's Aging Population," *Government of Canada.* At: <www.fin.gc.ca/pub/eficap-rebvpc/report-rapport-eng.asp>.

Dolton, P., and A. Vignoles. 2000. "The Incidence and Effects of Over-Education in the UK Graduate Labour Market," *Economics of Education Review* 19, 2: 179–98.

Dublin, M. 1989. *Futurehype: The Tyranny of Prophecy.* New York: Plume.

Epstein, David. 2010. "Sports Genes," *Sports Illustrated*, 17 May, 53–65.

Ewen, Stuart. 1976. *Captains of Consciousness: Advertising and the Social Roots of the Consumer Culture.* New York: McGraw-Hill.

Fisher, Dennis. 2013. "U.S. Government Requests for Google User Data Doubled since 2010," *Threat Post.* At: <threatpost.com/u-s-government-requests-for-google-user-data-doubled-since-2010/102929>.

Fuller, Ted, and Krista Loogma. 2009. "Constructing Futures: A Social Constructionist Perspective on Foresight Methodology," *Futures* 41, 2: 71–9.

George, Henry. 1898. *Social Problems.* New York: Doubleday and McClure.

Gladwell, Malcolm. 2009. *What the Dog Saw and Other Adventures.* New York: Little, Brown.

Glenn, Jerome C., Gordon, Theodore J., and Florescu, Elizabeth, "2010 State of the Future," The Millennium Project © 2009, at: www.millennium-project.org/millennium/scenarios/explor-s.html

Goldman, Lawrence. 2007. "Foundations of British Sociology 1880–1930: Contexts and Biographies," *Sociological Review* 55, 3: 431–40.

Griffiths, Sian, ed. 1999. *Predictions.* New York: Oxford University Press.

Hacker, Andrew. 1955. "In Defense of Utopia," *Ethics* 65: 135–8.

Hertel, Thomas, and Stephanie Rosch. 2010. "Climate Change, Agriculture, and Poverty," *Applied Economic Perspectives and Policy* 32, 3: 355–85.

Herzog, Benno, Esperanza Gómez-Guardeño, Victor Agulló, Rafael Aleixandre-Benavent, and Juan Carlos

Valderrama-Zurian. 2009. "Discourses on Drugs and Immigration: The Social Construction of a Problem," *Forum Qualitative Sozialforschung/Forum: Qualitative Social Research* 10, 1.

Hibbard, Christa. 2012. "Wiretapping the Internet: The Expansion of the Communications Assistance to Law Enforcement Act to Extend Government Surveillance," *Federal Communications Law Journal* 64, 2: 371–99.

Hurley, K., E. Masini, W. Boulding, R. Eisler, S. Premchander, P. McCorduck, et al. 2008. "Futures Studies and Feminism," *Futures* 40, 4: 388–407.

Hyshka, Elaine. 2009. "The Saga Continues: Canadian Legislative Attempts to Reform Cannabis Law in the Twenty-First Century," *Canadian Journal of Criminology and Criminal Justice* 51, 1: 73–91.

Ikeda, Satoshi. 2004. "Imperial Subjects, National Citizenship, and Corporate Subjects: Cycles of Political Participation/Exclusion in the Modern World-System," *Citizenship Studies* 8, 4: 333–47.

Jin, Boraw, and Namkee Park. 2012. "Mobile Voice Communication and Loneliness: Cell Phone Use and the Social Skills Deficit Hypothesis," *New Media and Society* 15, 7: 1094–111.

Jones, Jeremy, and Duncan Hunter. 1995. "Consensus Methods for Medical and Health Services Research," *British Medical Journal* 311, 7001: 376–80.

Kasinitz, Philip. 2012. "The Sociology of International Migration: Where We Have Been; Where Do We Go from Here?," *Sociological Forum* 27, 3: 579–90.

Katz, Nathaniel, and Norman A. Mazer. 2009. "The Impact of Opioids on the Endocrine System," *Clinical Journal of Pain* 25, 2: 170–5.

Koser, Khalid. 2010. "Introduction: International Migration and Global Governance," *Global Governance* 16, 3: 301–15.

Larsen, K., and U. Gunnarsson-Ostling. 2009. "Climate Change Scenarios and Citizen-Participation: Mitigation and Adaptation Perspectives in Constructing Sustainable Futures," *Habitat International* 33, 3: 260–6.

Lopez, Bernat. 2013 "The Social Construction of Human Growth Hormone as a Dangerous Doping Drug," *International Review for the Sociology of Sport* 48, 2: 220–37.

Loughran, Tracey. 2009. "Shell-Shock and Psychological Medicine in First World War Britain," *Social History of Medicine* 22, 1: 79–95.

Marx, Karl, and Friedrich Engels. 1978 [1848]. *Manifesto of the Communist Party*. Moscow: Foreign Language Publishing House.

Meadows, Donella H., Dennis L. Meadows, Jorgen Randers, and William W. Behrens III. 1972. *Limits to Growth*. New York: Universe Books.

Merton, Robert K. 1973 [1942]. "The Normative Structure of Science," in Merton, *The Sociology of Science: Theoretical and Empirical Investigations*. Chicago: University of Chicago Press.

Mesch, Gustavo S., and Ilan Talmud. 2007. Similarity and the Quality of Online and Offline Social Relationships among Adolescents in Israel, *Journal of Research in Adolescence* 17, 2: 455–66.

Milojevic, I., K. Hurley, and A. Jenkins. 2008. "Futures of Feminism," *Futures* 40, 4: 313–18.

More, Sir Thomas. 1992. *Utopia*. Ed. Robert M. Adams. New York: Norton and Company.

Morrison, Catriona M., and Helen Gore. 2010. "The Relationship between Excessive Internet Use and Depression: A Questionnaire-Based Study of 1,319 Young People and Adults," *Psychopathology* 43, 2: 121–6.

Mueller, John. 2005. "Simplicity and Spook: Terrorism and the Dynamics of Threat Exaggeration," *International Studies Perspectives* 6: 208–34.

Murray, Michael. 2011. "Review: The Influence of Armed Conflict on the Development of Critical Care Medicine," *Military Medicine* 176, 6: 674–8.

Newland, Kathleen. 2010. "Governance of International Migration: Mechanisms, Processes, and Institutions," *Global Governance* 16, 3: 331–43.

Plummer, Thomas. 2004. "Flaked Stones and Old Bones: Biological and Cultural Evolution at the Dawn of Technology," *American Journal of Physical Anthropology* 125, S39: 118–64.

Ponteva, M. 2002. "The Impact of Warfare on Medicine," in I. Taipale et al., eds, *War or Health? A Reader*. London/New York: Zed Books, 36–41.

Pourezzat, Ali A., Abdolazim Mollaee, and Morteza Firouzabadi. 2008. "Building the Future: Undertaking Proactive Strategy for National Outlook," *Futures* 40, 10: 887–92.

Raphael, Dennis. 2009. *Social Determinants of Health: Canadian Perspectives*. Toronto: Canadian Scholars' Press.

Rheingold, Howard. 2000. *The Virtual Community: Homesteading on the Electronic Frontier*. Cambridge, MA: MIT Press.

Rowland, F. Sherwood. 1999. "Sequestration," in Griffiths (1999: 208–11).

Sandars, John. 2012. "Technology and the Delivery of the Curriculum of the Future: Opportunities and Challenges," *Medical Teacher* 34, 7: 534–8.

Sarkar, Abhijit, S.B Agrawal, Randeep Rakwal, Junko Shibato, and Ganesh Agrawal. 2012. "Toward Sustainable Agriculture through Integrated 'OMICS' Technologies: A Quest for Future Global Food Security," *Journal of Developments in Sustainable Agriculture* 7, 1: 103–10.

Segall, M.D., P.J.D. Lindan, M.J. Probert, C.J. Picard, P.J. Hasnip, et al. 2002. "First-Principles Simulation: Ideas, Illustrations and the CASTEP Code," *Journal of Physics: Condensed Matter* 14, 11: 2717–44.

Semitsu, Junichi. 2011. "From Facebook to Mug Shot: How the Death of Social Networking Privacy Rights Revolutionized Online Government Surveillance," *Pace Review* 13, 1: 291–381.

Shachmurove, Yochanan. 2010. "Economic Crises: Past, Present and Future," *International Journal of Business* 15, 4: 363–75.

Towne, Ezra Thayer. 1916. *Social Problems: A Study of Present Day Social Conditions*. New York: Macmillan.

University of Houston–Clear Lake. 2001. "What Is Futures Studies?" At: <www.cl.uh.edu/futureweb/futdef.html>.

Walonick, David S. 1993. "An Overview of Forecasting Methodology," At: <www.statpac.com/research-papers/forecasting.htm>.

———. 2004. *Survival Statistics*. Bloomington, MN: StatPac.

Webster, Frank. 2002. *Theories of the Information Society*. London: Routledge.

Wells, H.G. 1902. *Anticipations of the Reaction of Mechanical and Scientific Progress upon Human Life and Thought*. New York: Harper.

Xhelili, Besar, and Emir Crowne. 2012. "Privacy and Terrorism Review—Where Have We Come in 10 Years?," *Journal of International Commercial Law and Technology* 7, 2: 121–35.

Credits

Grateful acknowledgement is made for permission to reprint the following:

Block quote, page 37: http://www.cbc.ca/news/canada/homelessness-chronic-in-canada-study-1.674356

Book review in Box 6.1, page 148: Used with the permission of Patricia Lysaght.

Box 6.2, page 151: Used with the permission of Sandi Hirst.

Box 6.3, page 158: Used with the permission of Gøsta Esping-Andersen.

Block quote, pages 189–90: Public Interest Alberta. Used with permission.

Box 12.2, page 318: From AOL Jobs, 14 May 2013 © 2013 AOL Inc.. All rights reserved. Used by permission and protected by the Copyright Laws of the United States. The printing, copying, redistribution, or retransmission of this Content without express written permission is prohibited.

Box 13.3, page 341: Reprinted with permission—Torstar Syndication Services

Box 16.1, page 437: Jerome C. Glenn, Theodore J. Gordon, and Elizabeth Florescu, "2010 State of the Future," The Millennium Project © 2009, at: www.millennium-project.org/millennium/scenarios/explor-s.html

Index